Inland Waterways of Great Britain

Jane Cumberlidge

Imray Laurie Norie & Wilson Ltd
St Ives Cambridgeshire England

Published by
Imray, Laurie, Norie & Wilson Ltd
Wych House, St Ives, Huntingdon,
Cambridgeshire PE17 4BT, England
☎ +44 (0)1480 462114 *Fax* +44 (0)1480 496109
E-mail ilnw@imray.com
1998

First edition	1939
Second edition	1947
Third revised and enlarged edition	1950
Fourth edition	1962
Fifth revised and reset edition	1972
Sixth revised and enlarged edition	1985
Reprinted	1988
Seventh fully revised and reset edition	1998

© Jane Cumberlidge 1998

ISBN 0 85288 355 2

British Library Cataloguing in Publication Data.
A catalogue record for this book is available from the
British Library.

CAUTION
While every care has been taken to ensure accuracy,
neither the Publishers nor the Author will hold
themselves responsible for errors, omissions or
alterations in this publication. They will at all times
be grateful to receive information which tends to the
improvement of the work.

Printed in Great Britain by Butler & Tanner Ltd,
Frome, Somerset.

Contents

Preface

As author and editor of the seventh edition of this long-running book, I feel that my role is that of custodian of a venerable tradition. Indeed the *Inland Waterways of Great Britain* has had so many contributors and architects over the years that it now, in a very real sense, enjoys a life and spirit of its own. My task with this new edition has been, first and foremost, to try and ensure that all the information, facts and figures are as up-to-date as possible, and to help steer the book in the right direction for the new century, so that it remains relevant to all users of our splendid waterways, whatever their particular interests.

The original work from which this edition is descended, *Bradshaw's Canals and Navigable Rivers of England and Wales*, was first published in 1904, nearly a century ago. The requirements of readers at the end of the twentieth century are very different to those who leafed through the pages of *Bradshaw*, but the essential style and coverage of the book remains much the same, based around a comprehensive list of navigable waterways in Britain that gives accurate distances along each waterway and the dimensions of craft that can use them.

Compiled by Henry Rodolph de Salis, the original book was sub-titled 'A Handbook of Inland Navigation for Manufacturers, Merchants, Traders and Others'. Over a period of eleven years, Henry de Salis, a director of the carrying company Fellows, Morton and Clayton Ltd, covered over 14,000 miles in his own boats to carry out a personal survey of each waterway, documenting the distances between locks, bridges, manufacturers, wharves and other information of use to carrying companies.

In his preface to the 1904 book, de Salis recognised that many canal companies were partly instrumental in hastening their own demise, because they ' . . forced the railways to purchase or lease their undertakings at substantial prices before constructing their lines'. There was a serious lack of coordination between canal companies, both in the physical structure of the canals and in their administration. At a time of acute competition from the railways, the organisational problems on the canals made life very difficult for canal carriers; a carrier would have to deal with each canal company individually if his boat was travelling across several navigations. From the point-of-view of manufacturers and carriers, there was a lack of comprehensive, practical information about the whole waterways network.

It was in response to these problems that Henry de Salis embarked on his massive project of compiling *Bradshaw's Canals and Navigable Rivers of England and Wales*, which included a folded map of the waterways in a pocket in the back of the book. A second edition of the book was published in 1918, a third edition in 1928 and a facsimile of the first edition, by then a historic tome, was reprinted by David and Charles in 1969.

In June 1939, the first edition of *Inland Waterways of Great Britain* was published by Imray, Laurie, Norie and Wilson Ltd at 8s 6d. Based on *Bradshaw's,* W Eric Wilson himself compiled the new volume, whose sub-title was given as 'A handbook giving the more important particulars of the Principal Canals and Rivers of England and Scotland, arranged in a concise form for Yachtsmen'.

Each waterway was numbered and the numbers related to a coloured map which was tucked into the back of the book. The number of waterways covered was greatly reduced from the original 1904 edition and the distance tables for each waterway were omitted. The essential information was all presented in a simple and accessible form, including the navigation authority for each waterway, what permission was required for navigation, the navigable length of the waterway and where it went from and to, maximum craft dimensions, the number of locks, speed limits and charges. The four Scottish canals were brought into the book and a selection of routes of interest to yachtsmen was included as an appendix. The term 'yachtsman' was used to mean anyone who went boating on the waterways for pleasure as opposed to commerce.

After the Second World War, with growing interest in the inland waterways and the prospect of nationalisation for many of them, a new edition of the book was published by Imray, Laurie, Norie and Wilson Ltd in June 1947, again compiled by W Eric Wilson. In 1950, a greatly extended edition was published, edited by Lewis A (Teddy) Edwards, who was at that time the Hon. Secretary of the Inland Waterways Association. The foreword to this edition was written by Robert Aickman, then Chairman of the IWA.

The layout of this 1950 edition followed the pattern of the previous two, but the distance tables from *Bradshaw's* were reinstated and the number of waterways was increased to 138, including eight in Scotland and seven in Northern Ireland. For the first time there was a black-and-white photograph as a frontispiece, showing a working narrowboat transporting goods near Watford; another photograph was included at the beginning of the appendix. In this edition L A Edwards included, in the appendix, a section on the history of the canals,

'Navigation Hints For Pleasure Craft', a list of derelict waterways and information for canoeists. He retained the original navigable routes first suggested by W E Wilson and brought back Henry de Salis' glossary and also much of his introductory material on canal structures such as locks and lifts, tunnels, aqueducts and bridges.

This is essentially how the book has remained into the 1980s, with the gradual addition of more photographs, the introduction in the sixth edition of charts for each waterway and the brief appearance in the fourth edition of the Irish waterways. During this time the *Inland Waterways of Great Britain* has become a standard reference for all kinds of people interested in the canals and navigable rivers, whether they were planning cruises or busy restoring and improving the network.

The most recent edition was published in 1985 and has gradually fallen out-of-date as improvements and changes to the network have taken place. In this new edition, several waterways which have been returned to navigation in the last fifteen years have been reinstated. I have also included various waterways currently under restoration for which the day of reopening is coming soon. The charts have all been redrawn and the map of the national network is included again in the back of the book.

I have also tried to widen the appeal of the book to encompass all those diverse groups of people now interested in the waterways, be they boat owners, hirers, walkers, fishermen, bird-watchers, canoeists, cyclists or indeed anyone with a sympathy for the extensive and varied network of Britain's waterways which is so much a part of our industrial history and landscape.

As we approach the 21st century, perhaps the best way to help ensure a rosy future for our waterways network is to use and enjoy them regularly, albeit with due consideration for the great age of many of the canal structures. We must also encourage others to discover the magic and endless fascination of the waterways, which are now seen as a major environmental asset rather than as a crumbling relic of the past. I hope that this completely revised edition will help play a part in that process.

Acknowledgements

As with any work of this extent, numerous people have been generous with their time and knowledge. I would like to thank all those individuals and organisations that so kindly responded to requests for information which were printed in various waterways and boating magazines. To list everyone individually would take so much space that I must ask all of you to accept this thank you on behalf of myself, the publishers, and all those who will make use of the new edition. This grateful thanks includes all the IWA local branches who sent up-to-date information on work in their local areas, numerous canal societies and trusts around the country and individuals who had information on particular parts of the waterways they know well.

The British Waterways staff at offices around the country have all been unfailingly helpful and courteous, even when I have phoned two or three times on the same afternoon to check a detail. The staff of the National Rivers Authority and their successors, the Environment Agency, have also given willingly of their time to answer numerous questions. I must particularly thank Mike Woodhead from the Inland Waterways Amenity Advisory Council, who gave me a list of up-to-date contacts for various waterways bodies.

Mark Wakelin, Chief Navigation Officer of the Broads Authority, very kindly revised the section on the Broads; Geoff Cave, for the Middle Level Commissioners, corrected the Middle Level entry. Mike Webb gave me valuable advice on the Manchester Ship Canal and the Bridgewater Canal, and Kathryn Beardmore supplied me with the latest information on navigation matters within the Lake District National Park. Sir John Knill and members of the Commercial Narrowboat Operators Association have contributed a great deal to the section in the book dealing with commercial use of the waterways and Ian Sinclair gave advice on the complex question of the Public Right of Navigation.

Several harbourmasters around the coast have helped with information for boats navigating coastal waters, port authorities provided me with information relevant to private vessels visiting their ports and local authority officers have filled in countless details of waterways within their jurisdiction. Blakes Holidays were helpful with information on the Broads, holiday hiring and chartering. Carol Quaif, of the British Canoe Union, advised on recommendations for canoeists and Stuart Robertson also kept me up to date with canoeing information.

Guthrie Hutton has provided much current information on the Scottish canals and John and Margaret Fletcher carefully vetted the entries for their area and also obtained some up-to-date details for canals with which they are not personally involved. David Morris and Richard Sandland have let me use photographs from their canal cruises and Anne Stevenson kept me up-to-date with all manner of on-the-spot information gleaned around the country.

My thanks must go to Willie Wilson, for giving me the opportunity to help carry on the tradition of this book, to the drawing staff at Imray for making such a clear job of the new plans, Clare Hughes for helping to check the copy, Julia Knight for the new layout of the book and all the other staff who found references, maps and generally kept me on the right road.

My apologies to anyone I have missed specifically, but please accept my sincere thanks for all your contributions to *The Inland Waterways of Great Britain*.

Jane Cumberlidge
April 1998

Introduction

Canals today

From the busy heart of London to the dramatic natural grandeur of the Great Glen in the Highlands, from the industry of the Black Country Potteries to the rural peace of the Brecon Beacons, from the summit of the Pennines to well below sea level in the Middle Level canals; some part of our waterways network is said to be less than 5 miles from nearly half of Britain's population. The slower pace of 'life on the cut' is now appreciated by thousands of people every year as an ideal way to spend at least part of their free time. Canals and rivers are used for recreation in narrow boats and canoes, by walkers, by fishermen and by cyclists. Two hundred years after the height of 'canal mania', the canals and navigable rivers of Britain are probably used now more widely than at any other time in their history.

There has certainly been a decline in the commercial use of the waterways, a decline which started almost before construction of the network was completed. This was caused by the competition from the new railways. Rail transport was faster and more flexible than canal transport and, in a similar way, our railways have been progressively overtaken by fast developing road transport since the end of the Second World War.

Of course, the change from commercial to predominantly leisure use of the canals has brought its own problems. The use of locks is now concentrated into a much shorter period of the year, which can put enormous strain on water supply on some routes. Yet, this increasing emphasis on canals for leisure has ensured a future for this fascinating part of our landscape into its third century.

Historic canal architecture, such as aqueducts, bridges, toll houses, canalside buildings and wharves, all contribute to our diverse landscape and help tell the story of Britain's industrial development. It isn't even necessary to get afloat to appreciate the tranquillity and beauty of the canals and to marvel at the ingenuity, hard work and sheer persistence required for the cutting of a new

The use of iron in canal structures provided the opportunity for quite decorative bridges to be produced. *David Morris*

waterway from scratch. At the time, canal construction certainly made a major impact on the British economy and the pace and extent of the Industrial Revolution. The development of the British canals accelerated our industrialisation by providing a reliable means of transporting large tonnages of raw materials to factories and finished products to customers. Today, most of this traffic has been taken off the waterways and it is thanks to the foresight, energy and vigilance of a small group of people just after the Second World War that we still have a waterways network to enjoy for pleasure in a way which would have been inconceivable to the boatmen of the 19th century.

The Inland Waterways Association

The publication in 1944 of Tom Rolt's book *Narrow Boat* struck a chord with a number of other people who were concerned about the steady deterioration of Britain's inland waterways. Two of these people were Charles Hadfield and Robert Aickman. In 1945, Robert Aickman visited Tom Rolt aboard his boat *Cressy* at Tardebigge on the Worcester and Birmingham Canal. Later, in May 1946, they met again in London with Charles Hadfield and four others who together founded the Inland Waterways Association.

The aim of the Inland Waterways Association (IWA) is the same today as it was in 1946 '. . . to campaign for the retention, conservation, restoration and development of the Inland Waterways for the fullest possible commercial and recreational use.'

Within a short time of its inception, the IWA had generated considerable public interest and membership increased quickly, including a number of influential MPs. Press reports started to show how many of Britain's canals and rivers were becoming derelict and threatened with plans for abandonment. Priorities had to be set, and the most urgent cases were identified as the Kennet and Avon Canal, the River Stour in Suffolk, the Stratford-on-Avon Canal and the River Derwent in Yorkshire.

Under the Labour Government in the late 1940s, the nationalisation of transport brought the waterways into the remit of the Ministry of Transport and within the specific responsibility of the Docks and Inland Waterways Executive. Throughout Britain, this was a time of hope and renewal, and enthusiasm for restoration of the waterways became widespread as awareness of the threat to their future grew. The idea of promoting the use of canals for recreation was even helped in 1948 by an article in *The Times* entitled 'Holidays Afloat'.

At about the same time, the IWA was appreciating the value of having local groups to concentrate campaigns for particular waterways, and a group

was started in Newbury for the Kennet and Avon Canal. Other waterways coming under threat were the Huddersfield Narrow Canal and the Llangollen Canal. The campaigning for waterways took many forms. Lobbying of MPs was important, as were regular meetings with the Docks and Inland Waterways Executive (DIWE), but actually cruising along threatened waterways was a very effective way of bringing the problems to the attention of local people who were often unaware of the value, and sometimes the existence, of their local waterway.

On one of these pioneering cruises, Tom Rolt took *Cressy* along the Stratford-on-Avon Canal and a bridge had to be physically lifted for her to pass. Another such cruise was the last passage of a boat through the Standedge Tunnel on the Huddersfield Narrow Canal. Robert Aickman undertook this trip as part of a six-week cruise and Tom Rolt was also on the boat when they went through the tunnel.

In 1950, a waterways festival was held at Market Harborough which was attended by 100 craft and over 50,000 people. This was a visual display of how the waterways could be of value to all kinds of people, and extensive press coverage brought the message home to many others who could not visit the event. These festivals have become regular IWA activities and provide wonderful opportunities for people outside the organisation to see what the IWA is doing and how the association is continuing to protect the waterways of Britain.

By 1960, 25 conservation schemes were underway around the country and the IWA had several branches in different areas. At the same time, the government was looking at the canal network and a report classified canals into three groups: canals to be developed; canals to be retained; and canals to be disposed of.

Among the last group were some of the waterways which the IWA had been working so hard to preserve, and so the campaigning fervour was increased. One of the earliest campaigns had been to preserve the Lower Avon Navigation, and in 1962 this was the first waterway to be re-opened. Although this was encouraging news, the overall battle was by no means won as more waterways were threatened with closure.

In addition to creating awareness of the problems, IWA members were always keen to get their hands dirty and become actively involved in the physical restoration work, clearing blocked canals, rebuilding bridges and locks, restoring towpaths and planting new hedges. By 1970, the Waterway Recovery Group (WRG) was formed. Today, throughout the waterways of Britain, you can see brick, concrete and living reminders of all the hard work and energy that has been put in by the WRG, whose work still continues somewhere around the network during most weekends.

Of the early waterways under threat of closure, some were restored relatively quickly and many users today may take their existence for granted. The Stratford-on-Avon Canal, for example, is now one of the most popular holiday routes. Other canals took rather longer to restore. The Kennet and Avon was re-opened to through traffic in 1990, over 40 years after the start of the campaign. Others are still waiting for that magic day – the Dearne and Dove, the Derby and Sandiacre, the Huddersfield Narrow have yet to come back into the waterways network, but work continues steadily.

In 1996, the IWA celebrated its Golden Jubilee, an appropriate time not only to take stock of what has been achieved but also to plan for the future. Maintenance of large canal structures, which have stood for over 200 years, is costly and funds must be found for major engineering projects, such as the repairs on the Dundas Aqueduct on the Kennet and Avon Canal. Substantial works are underway on the Caledonian Canal, which will take a number of years to complete. There are still many canals in the network which are not navigable and could be restored when the money and manpower are available.

The advent of the National Lottery has offered many canal restoration projects the prospect of some much-needed additional finance. The Kennet and Avon, the Huddersfield Narrow, the Forth and Clyde and the Union canals have all been successful in their bids for substantial funds for restoration and improvements. But conflicts of interest continue, and the IWA has to be ever vigilant when, for example, proposals for new road schemes could blight the prospect of canal restorations. The lengthy work on the Thames and Severn Canal could have been severely affected by the Department of Transport's initial refusal to include

a navigable culvert in the Latton bypass, despite Department of the Environment support for the restoration programme. A similar battle is being waged in Derbyshire over the South Derby ring road, where it crosses the route of the Derby and Sandiacre Canal.

Government attitudes towards the funding of the waterways seem little different now to those of 50 years ago when the Inland Waterways Association was started. The role of the association is therefore as vital as ever to the continuing existence of a healthy waterway system.

Twenty-five years of canal digging

by Mike Palmer, Chairman of the Waterway Recovery Group

The Waterway Recovery Group has, for over 25 years, been using voluntary labour to restore Britain's historic canal and river navigations. These represent a unique combination of nature and industrial archaeology constituting a national asset. The waterways are a living record of Britain's industrial heritage, as well as being the fastest route from the city to nature and the best way to get nature back into our cities. Where else can a short walk from a city centre take you past colourful boats, industrial wharves, kingfishers, waterside pubs and lockside cottages all set in beautiful scenery?

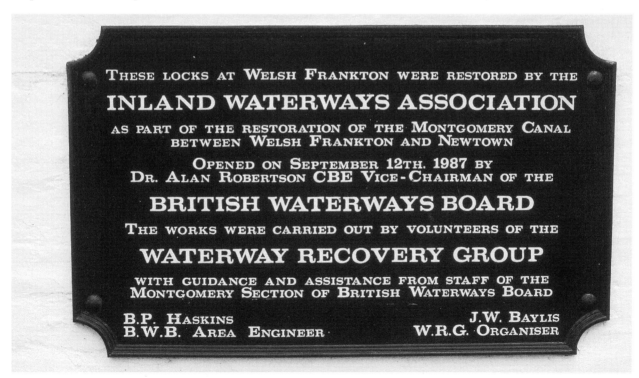

The Waterway Recovery Group have worked untiringly for over twenty five years on numerous restoration projects around the country. *David Morris*

However, in the years following their decline in use for carrying cargo and before their historic value and leisure potential were generally appreciated, many canals ceased to earn enough money to pay for their maintenance. Their owners either legally abandoned them and sold off the land that they were built on, or simply ceased to maintain them and allowed them to fall derelict. These are the waterways which the Waterway Recovery Group is helping to restore.

Founded in 1970 by volunteers who had been active in some of the early efforts to restore canals, the Waterway Recovery Group, or WRG (usually pronounced 'WERG') is a national co-ordinating body for volunteer canal restoration throughout Britain. All over the country, local canal societies and branches of the Inland Waterways Association are actively working to restore abandoned canals and bring them back into use. WRG can provide these societies with a pool of labour, expertise and machinery to help them to achieve their aims.

WRG has six regional groups, who hold regular weekend working-parties throughout the year. They are not attached to any particular canal restoration project, but work on any waterway that wants their help. This provides a huge variety in the work required of us and, of course, ever changing scenery.

For those who fancy a whole week's work, WRG runs canal camps on such varied sites as the Bude Canal in Cornwall, the Stowmarket Navigation in Suffolk and the Ulster Canal in Ireland. Canal camps are a unique type of holiday offering a superb way of getting back to nature, enjoying yourselves and making new friends.

Finally, there are the 'big digs'. Back in the 1960s and 1970s, a series of major working-parties brought several hundred volunteers to work on various canals, including the Ashton, Basingstoke, Droitwich and Montgomery. In each case, a phenomenal amount was achieved in a single weekend, both in terms of practical work and also in generating publicity for the restoration, at a time when local authorities regarded canals more as a nuisance than an asset. In the 1990s, 'big digs' have been revived; a large working-party every autumn acts as a canal camps reunion weekend as well as furthering the restoration of the canal concerned.

Over the past 25 years, the nature of our work has changed dramatically. In the early days, we really did dig canals – volunteers stood knee-deep in slime at the bottom of a derelict lock chamber, shovelling all kinds of unmentionable substances into barrows to be taken away. These days, when our volunteers clear a lock chamber, they do it mechanically. Many of our volunteers are trained to use excavators, dumpers, cranes and other types of machinery, and the tasks we perform manually are more likely to be skilful ones such as bricklaying or stonework. But for real mud enthusiasts, we can still provide opportunities to get seriously muddy.

The canals that we work on have changed too. Many of the early restoration schemes – the Ashton,

Peak Forest, Kennet and Avon, Basingstoke and Stourbridge canals, for example – have been completed and the canals are once again open to boats. In their place have come restoration projects that would have been written-off as impossible by many in the early days: the Wey and Arun, the Wiltshire and Berkshire, the Lichfield and Hatherton canals among others. They may not have seemed so at the time, but most of the restoration schemes that the early volunteers worked on were the 'easy' ones: canals that had never officially been abandoned, their navigation structures were largely intact, and they had not been ploughed up, built on or obliterated by road improvements. Some of them had had boats on them within the previous 20 years. Nowadays, 20-years closure seems more like an extended stoppage than a genuinely derelict canal. The waterways that volunteers work on in the 1990s have mostly not seen a boat for 50 or 100 years. Before we can restore a lock we may well have to find it, then completely rebuild it. On some canals, there is as much new construction as restoration. On the Wey and Arun, for example, all the remaining original canal bridges have now been restored; the rest have been demolished and will need to be replaced.

Some things, however, have not changed. Despite our increasingly professional approach, with organised training in such areas as bricklaying, operation of machinery and first aid, WRG is, always has been and will continue to be an entirely voluntary organisation, run by dedicated (if not certifiable) waterways enthusiasts coming from all walks of life and all ages. Everything we do, be it actual restoration work, site services support for IWA festivals, maintenance of the catering and the tool kits used on canal camps, or the production of publications dealing with various aspects of canal restoration, we do it for the satisfaction and the fun of it. And WRG volunteers will continue to have fun, whether they are out restoring canals or enjoying their busy social life.

So how will we occupy ourselves for our second quarter century? Will we run out of canals to restore? This seems unlikely. Even though on a number of waterways the initial volunteer effort has had a 'pump-priming' effect and brought in money from outside bodies to pay contractors to complete them, there will still be plenty of volunteer work needed elsewhere. Already we have held camps in Ireland and we have been approached with a view to holding one in France. If we ever run out of canal restoration schemes to work on, we can always start building some new canals or completing some of the ones that the original builders never finished. And if you think that sounds a bit far-fetched, think again. In 1996 the first WRG Canal Camp was held on the Ribble Link, a new navigation being built to join the isolated Lancaster Canal with the River Ribble and thence the national network.

Recreation on the waterways

'Simply messing about in boats' is probably the first occupation which comes to mind when thinking of recreational uses of the waterways. There is nothing quite like it, as Ratty once opined, and this is certainly an increasingly popular way to spend time on Britain's canals and rivers. There are now many hire companies offering everything from a weekend or short-break to two- or three-weeks rental of a boat for a wide-ranging cruise around the network. In many places, you can also hire a small motorboat for a day, or a rowing boat for an hour or two. Canoeists and rowers are seen paddling on rivers and canals throughout the country and, for the less energetic, there are trip boats and hotel boats that allow you to watch the waterway world go by while someone else does the work.

Probably more people visit the canals along the towpaths than ever actually get afloat. In towns, cities and the countryside, towpaths are popular places to walk the dog or get involved in bird-watching, photography or landscape painting. There are now a number of well-organised long-distance walks along towpaths which are becoming increasingly well used. The Thames Path is 213 miles from the source of the Thames in the Cotswolds to the Thames Barrier at Woolwich. The Grand Union Canal Walk was opened in 1993 to commemorate the 200th anniversary of this famous canal; this was the first National Waterway Walk and it extends for 147 miles from Little Venice in London to Gas Street Basin, Birmingham.

Angling is said to be the most popular participation sport in Britain. Throughout the country, there are thousands of angling clubs and many of them have the fishing rights along lengths of the canals. The little green fisherman's igloos are a common sight along the far side of Limehouse Basin at the end of the Regent's Canal, and indeed along most other canals. Anyone wishing to fish must have a licence, and you should check if an angling club has rights on the stretch of water you would like to fish. While fishing, you should always have due consideration for moored craft and residential boats and never obstruct the towpath. Don't fish at locks or beside bridges and be careful of overhead power cables.

Cycling is allowed on some towpaths, but a towpath is principally for walking so all cyclists must give way to other towpath users. In some areas, towpaths are being upgraded to cycleways, but on many the surface is unsuitable even for mountain bikes. All cyclists must have a bell and warn walkers of their approach. A British Waterways cycle permit is required before you use any of the towpaths. These are issued free and will be sent to you with a list of 'towpaths open to cyclists'. Anyone interested in long distance touring by bike should contact Customer Services at British Waterways Head Office at Watford, who will send full information sheets for the whole network for a minimal charge. Cyclists should always dismount to pass under bridges and near locks. On the Kennet and Avon Canal, a scheme to charge cyclists for a permit came into force in July 1997, and the revenue will be used to help improve the management and maintenance of the towpath.

Commercial carrying by canal

Britain's canals and waterways were created to improve the transport of large quantities of heavy goods. In the middle of the 18th century, road transport was very limited and precarious, with most roads becoming little more than mud tracks during wet weather and hard, rutted ones in dry weather. A horse might pull a load of up to two tons on a flat road, but loaded pack animals could only carry a fraction of that weight. Breakages of fragile goods, such as china and glass would be frequent and so carriage costs were high.

With over 2500 miles of interlinking waterways, the possibilities of increasing the movement of goods in greater safety and at reduced cost offered the opportunity to develop trade throughout the country. Narrowboats could carry 20 to 30 tons of cargo which one horse could pull, while passenger traffic was often twice as fast as by road. The principal cargoes for canal boats were raw materials, such as coal or china clay, into the manufacturing areas and finished products out, pottery from the Wedgwood works at Etruria, for example. Agricultural produce was also moved into the rapidly expanding towns and cities.

Railway competition through the second half of the 19th century reduced commercial activity on the remoter and less profitable waterways, but it was not until after the First World War that this process began to accelerate seriously. Throughout the Second World War, the canals played an important role in moving coal, components and spare parts for factories and other goods. Teams of young women were trained to work canal boats when the men were called up. At the end of the war, road haulage became the most serious competitor with cheaper rates and door-to-door delivery which reduced handling.

Since the Second World War, the revival in interest in the inland waterways has prevented the closure of some canals and caused others to be re-opened, so that over 2000 miles are navigable today. The level of commercial use of the waterways has dropped, and yet as a quiet, efficient and environmentally friendly means of transport, a canal boat has many advantages which may become increasingly significant. Over recent years, lorries have become larger, heavier and more noisy. As we become increasingly and forcibly aware of the impact of roads on the environment, many of the serious disadvantages and hidden, unpaid costs of road transport are being recognised. It is quite possible that certain waterway routes may come into their own once again, and it is not inconceivable, even in Britain, that new, more efficient canals might be cut in the future in place of certain roads, when the true, full costs of new roads begin to be taken into account by decision-makers.

Coal has always been one of the most common cargoes on inland waterways and special compartment boats called 'Tom Puddings' were towed or pushed in trains on the Aire and Calder Navigation. Grain is still moved by narrow boat in some areas and other canal cargoes include timber, salt, chemicals and waste material. After the recent fire at Windsor Castle, the heavy stone for the rebuilding was transported by canal from Bath. Many exceptionally large or heavy loads can be transported by water when to move them by road would cause enormous disruption, particularly if the load has to be dismantled or divided before transportation.

It is still possible to travel from the River Thames to the Mersey, the Severn or the Humber by boat, and there are companies offering waterway carriage. It takes about 4½ days to travel from Brentford to Birmingham or 10 days from Warwickshire to Bath, and the regular passage of well loaded boats helps to keep waterways open and reduce silting. Of course, transit times increase during the summer along popular holiday routes, with congestion at locks when lots of boats are waiting to pass through. Speed is also reduced when travelling through stretches of canal which have large numbers of moorings.

Increased use of the waterways to move freight could help to reduce road congestion and pollution, but this would require both a positive approach to water transport and a fully costed appraisal of roads. In the mid-1990s, the Department of Transport figures showed a slight rise in the amount of freight moved by water at just over 7 million tonnes on inland routes.

The Commercial Narrowboat Operators Association represents the owners of a total of around 40 boats still regularly carrying freight by canal, but there is no comparable organisation for other working boats. The Inland Waterways Association Inland Shipping Group is active in promoting greater use of the waterways for freight and frequently lobbies Parliament on these issues. Commercial carrying by canal is by no means dead and could well play a greater part in Britain's transport system in the future. At Stoke Bruerne, you can often see commercial narrowboats being loaded and unloaded, and they are also loaded at Hawkesbury. Commercial boats also regularly attend narrowboat shows and festivals, such as the National Festival held each August Bank Holiday or the popular Braunston Boat Show in May.

Conservation and wildlife of the waterways

Britain's 3000 miles of canals and navigable rivers offer a vast diversity of wildlife habitats which are actively promoted and preserved by the various authorities. Within its own jurisdiction, British Waterways has 64 Sites of Special Scientific Interest (SSSI's). The Broads Authority has responsibility for many stretches of waterway which fall into the category of Environmentally Sensitive Areas, while the Environment Agency has taken on the National River Authority's conservation strategy for all the navigations within its remit.

Over the past 20 years or so, developing legislation allied to the growing public awareness of wildlife and environmental issues has spurred on these organisations to improve the water quality in canals and rivers, and with this improvement many species have re-established habitats around the country. Some unrestored waterways have provided unique habitats which did not exist before, and this has the potential to cause conflict when a campaign to restore a route to navigation would destroy a valuable habitat that has become established since the abandonment of the canal. This problem has arisen in Greywell Tunnel on the Basingstoke Canal, where a colony of bats is now firmly in residence. A similar situation arose on the Pocklington Canal where there are three Sites of Special Scientific Interest. A Management Agreement between British Waterways and English Nature now contains wording that could limit any future return to full navigation on the canal, and requires there to be careful consultation and discussion to arrive at a workable restoration that will satisfy all interested parties.

Plants, birds, insects or animals do not need to be rare or endangered to enhance the pleasure of using the canals. Swans frequently nest along canal banks, and herons can be seen standing motionless, waiting to spot a tasty fish. A sudden flash of blue can make you realise that you have just missed a kingfisher. Along the bankside you are likely see yellow flag iris and marsh marigolds in the spring, thriving under the many species of willow. Later in the season, hedgerows of may create a spectacular white cascade while dog roses and honeysuckle climb through them. In the canal itself, there are reeds and rushes with dab chicks darting in and out; yellow and white waterlilies flourish and you may catch the clear blue of dragon flies and damsel flies.

One of the greatest successes of the drive to improve water quality is the return of otters to many stretches of waterway. In some areas, artificial holts have been constructed to attract otters back to rivers and canals, and as long as the water quality is high these measures are successful. Another mammal you might see along the canal bank is the water vole, the inimitable Ratty from *The Wind in the Willows*. The water vole is now a threatened species and numbers have declined at an alarming rate. Campaigns are underway to record sightings of voles and work is being carried out by several wildlife organisations to protect the water vole and create an environment in which it can re-establish a successful breeding population.

Insect life on the waterways is probably the most diverse, with numerous water beetles and water boatmen skating around on the surface to provide tempting meals for swallows, house martins and sand martins. Below the surface of the water, life is a teeming soup for many species of fish and mammals. Frog and toad spawn can be seen in clumps or strings and these also offer a tasty snack. You may see common newts eggs, which are usually found singly stuck to the underside of a leaf.

It is always worth taking a comprehensive naturalists' identification book when you visit a canal, be it by foot, bike or boat. Nothing is more frustrating than thinking you have spotted some mammal, bird or fish, but not being able to remember the name. Binoculars are an asset as you often can't get close enough to identify small creatures before they vanish again at your approach. Some canals are particularly noted for their wildlife and these include the Montgomery Canal, part of the Shropshire Union network, the Basingstoke, the Grand Western Canal in Devon and the hidden interest in the Cromford Canal where nature is reasserting herself.

Fish have benefited enormously from the improvements in water quality and perch, roach and pike are all caught regularly by the thousands of anglers who use Britain's canals and rivers. You can also see sticklebacks and minnows darting around, desperately trying to avoid getting on the menu for a lurking pike.

Canal and waterway societies and organisations

Throughout Britain, there are now numerous trusts, societies and voluntary groups working to preserve and improve the waterways network. The Inland Waterways Association is a national body which campaigns for the network as a whole and is active in lobbying Parliament for better funding, to prevent the closure of waterways, for improvements to access, and to protect routes of abandoned canals with the long-term aim of re-opening them and numerous other areas for the benefit of all of us who use the waterways. Within the IWA, there are specialist groups such as the Waterway Recovery Group and the Inland Shipping Group. Around the country, the IWA has local branches which carry on their own restoration activities as well as participating in centrally organised events and campaigns.

Almost every waterway also has its own society. These societies are locally based and work to maintain, restore and improve their waterways. The waterways press regularly carry items about local societies and their activities, generally giving the name of the local secretary as a contact. *Waterways World* magazine brings out a supplement called *Canalmanac* early each year, which contains a comprehensive list of waterway societies and organisations with contact names and addresses for each; these now include, where appropriate, Internet sites and e-mail addresses.

The following addresses may be useful:

Association of Pleasure Craft Operators, Parkland House, Audley Avenue, Newport, Shropshire TF10 7AT ☎ 01952 813572 *Fax* 01952 820363

Association of Waterways Cruising Clubs, Valentine, Cat Street, East Hendred, Oxfordshire OX12 8JT. ☎/*Fax* 01235 833312

British Canoe Union, Adbolton Lane, West Bridgford, Nottingham NG2 5AS ☎ 0115 982 1100 *Fax* 0115 982 1797

Inland Waterways Amenity Advisory Council, City Road Lock, 38 Graham Street, Islington, London N1 8JX ☎ 0171 253 1745 *Fax* 0171 490 7656

Inland Waterways Association, 14 Regent's Park Road, London NW1 8UQ ☎ 0171 586 2556/2510 *Fax* 0171 722 7213

Railway and Canal Historical Society, 17 Clumber Crescent North, The Park, Nottingham NG7 1EY ☎/*Fax* 0115 941 4844

Royal Yachting Association, RYA House, Romsey Road, Eastleigh, Hampshire SO50 9YA ☎ 01703 627400 *Fax* 01703 629924

Scottish Inland Waterways Association, 139 Old Dalkeith Road, Little France, Edinburgh EH16 4SZ ☎ 0131 664 1070

History

A short history of the waterways of Britain

In the middle of the 18th century, industrialisation was developing quickly in Britain, with factories springing up throughout the Midlands and those areas where coal and iron ore were readily available. The main constraint to further development became the problem of transport, since most manufactured goods could only be sold within a relatively local area. Roads at that time were poor at best and dangerous at worst, as well as being expensive – tolls were charged by each authority along the route. During the winter, mud and frost caused travelling conditions to deteriorate even further.

Raw materials could easily be transported in bulk by sea, but the nearest coastal port might be 50 miles away from the manufacturer so that loads had to be split into smaller quantities and transported by cart or even pack-horse overland. Delivering the finished product to the customer was also a problem, especially considering the diversity of goods that needed to be moved, be they fragile products, such as a china dinner service for a wealthy family, or heavy and bulky materials such as the coal needed in large quantities by the rapidly growing urban population.

River transport has been known since trade began and in Roman Britain artificial waterways were cut for this purpose. The Fossdyke is still used for navigation today, joining the River Witham to the River Trent. During the Middle Ages, some significant river improvements were carried out as a result of laws and decrees made by the monarch, and river transport was used successfully on the Tyne, Ouse, Ure and Humber in the northeast; the Witham, Stour, Great Ouse, Lee and Thames in the east; the Itchen, Western Rother, Stour, Ouse, and Cuckmere on the south coast; and the Exe, Avon and Dart in the West Country. During this period, there was also mention of the 'New River' in Hampshire, which referred to an artificial cut to improve navigation on the Itchen near Winchester.

The navigable distances on some rivers could be extended by using weirs to maintain water levels in the higher reaches, and then flash locks would allow boats to pass up and down. Navigation works to improve transport on rivers were frequently opposed by mill owners, who perceived them as a threat to their water supply. Early weirs had often been built by the mill owners to keep a head of water to drive the mill wheel without any intention to aid navigation. Although the millers charged for boats to pass the flash lock, they frequently felt it was insufficient compensation for the interruption to the milling and so would hold boats in a queue until there were enough there to justify opening the lock – a sure way to cause irritation with the boat owners.

Boats usually sailed in the wider reaches and were bow-hauled by considerable teams of men when it wasn't possible to sail, if the current was too strong, over shallows and up through flash locks. This was an extremely slow and laborious job, with the towing path often quite a long way from the boat owing to the nature of the river bed. The earliest record of a horse towing path is in the 1760s.

Pound locks were known in China in the first century AD and Leonardo da Vinci is reputed to have designed a lock with mitred gates for the Duke of Milan in the late 1400s. The first pound lock and canal in Britain is usually accepted as the Exeter Canal, built in 1563 to enable ships to reach the city and avoid a shallow part of the River Exe. In France, a canal linking the Loire to the Seine had been built by 1642 and this was the first major canal scheme in Europe. The Canal du Midi was opened in 1681, connecting the Garonne at Toulouse through to the Étang de Thau, thereby providing a navigable route from the Mediterranean to Bordeaux and the Atlantic.

The pressures of commerce, and some say an unhappy love affair, provided the stimulus for the first totally man-made canal in Britain. The Third Duke of Bridgewater wanted a means of transporting coal cheaply from his mines at Worsley to the rapidly growing population of Manchester. It is probable that he had seen the Canal du Midi when on a tour of Europe and with his agent, John Gilbert, and James Brindley as the engineer, the Duke set about constructing a canal to Manchester. It had to pass over the River Irwell and so an aqueduct was built. This became a notable feature of the canal, with people coming to the area just to see boats pass along it. Smaller waterways were cut into the mines to transport coal away from the face and also to drain them, thus providing a source of water for the canal. Once the canal was in operation, the more efficient transport meant that the price of coal in Manchester was halved, as it was a few years later in Birmingham when the Birmingham Canal was finished in 1769. Then the price of coal fell from 13 shillings (65p) a ton when transported over land to 7 shillings (35p) a ton by canal.

The success of the Bridgewater Canal did not immediately spark off the construction of other canals. To build a canal required an Act of Parliament which authorised a company to raise finance, and to achieve such an Act could be a costly business. A survey of the proposed route had to be prepared and details provided of properties through which it would pass, stating whether the owners were in favour, against or neutral to the idea. Local landowners frequently opposed the idea of a canal passing through their estate and often had to be compensated in some way, as did existing river navigation companies and road transport businesses which feared a loss of trade. It was nearly 30 years before the confidence in the new transport system, coupled with a demand for better transport from industry, brought about what came to be known as 'canal mania'.

In 1765, James Brindley met Josiah Wedgwood who was interested in building a canal to serve his growing pottery business in Staffordshire. The Act to construct the Trent and Mersey Canal was passed in 1766 and the first part of what became known as Brindley's Grand Cross was underway. The idea was to link the Thames, the Severn, the Trent and the Mersey by a cross of waterways to facilitate trade. By 1790, the Humber was connected to the Mersey via the River Trent and then the Trent and Mersey Canal; the Staffordshire and Worcestershire Canal ran from the Severn at Stourport to join the Trent and Mersey Canal at Great Hayward and from Birmingham goods could reach London via the Coventry and Oxford canals and the River Thames. In the same period, the Thames and Severn Canal was opened offering a more direct route from London to the Severn and Bristol.

This was a period of steady development of canal transport and gradually the benefits of canals were appreciated around the country. Newspapers carried reports about some of the more spectacular canal meetings, thousands of pounds being subscribed to canal projects in single meetings, and the fervour for canal building gathered momentum. In 1792 the first book about British canals was published, *General History of Inland Navigation* by John Phillips, further encouraging confidence in the new transport system.

Between 1792 and 1794, the height of 'canal mania', Acts of Parliament authorising the construction of 39 canals were passed. Some of these were not completed until well into the 19th century, but this activity demonstrates the interest and enthusiasm for canals at the time. The earliest promoters were usually those involved in the industries which would benefit from the cutting of a canal, but as the potential profits from canals became more widely known, more speculators were keen to buy canal shares. One newspaper of the time reported the sale of a £140 share in the Birmingham Navigation for £1150, a considerable sum of money at the end of the 18th century.

Outside events also affected canal projects. Problems with the colonies in America, eventually leading to the American War of Independence in the late 1770s and 1780s, had a pronounced effect on the British economy. Once the situation in America had been settled, the economy at home revived and investment in new ideas flourished once again. At the other end of the main canal building era, the French wars in the early 1800s served as a spur to some canals for specific military and supply purposes, but they were also a major drain on the country's finances and on the manpower available to build the canals. Another effect of the war was to raise the cost of food which, after some delay and a few riots, necessitated a rise in wages, and coupled with increases in the cost of raw materials, the cost of building a canal rose steeply.

With the exception of the Royal Military Canal and the Caledonian Canal, canals in Britain were privately funded. This may have led indirectly to their commercial demise. To contain construction costs as far as possible, the canals were built to what were considered minimum specifications, with locks 72ft long by 7ft wide; thus the British narrowboat (sometimes called a monkey boat) was born, with a carrying capacity of 20–35 tons. This became the standard size through much of the Midlands, but some other canals, such as the Kennet and Avon, the Rochdale and the Leeds and Liverpool, were built to a broad size with 14ft wide locks. The Scottish canals were built to ship dimensions, but were not linked into the main network of English canals. By the time the narrowboat was considered to carry too small a load, the cost of enlarging the canal system and creating ship-sized locks was prohibitive and railways had already arrived.

Another problem of privately owned canals was the rivalry and lack of co-operation between canal companies. Water supply was a frequent cause of dispute and elaborate systems were devised to prevent water being taken by one canal from another. Where two canals met but were owned by different companies, there was usually a 'stop lock' preventing water from being drained out of one canal by the other. At Gas Street Basin in Birmingham, you can still see the Worcester Bar which was a solid barrier to prevent traffic coming up the Worcester and Birmingham Canal from proceeding on through the Birmingham Canal. All goods had to be transhipped across the Bar, but a lock was built into the Bar in 1815 not long after the canal was completed.

Early canals were mostly built along a contour with as few major structures as possible. This tended to make them very long and winding, which slowed down transportation, although we now find these twists and turns the most picturesque for leisure cruising. As competition from railways developed and engineering skills improved, straighter canals could be built using tunnels, massive embankments, aqueducts and long flights of locks to make the canal as direct as possible and speed up traffic.

Through the 1830s and 1840s, railways were being built all over the country. At first the railways tended to carry mostly passenger traffic, but very soon bulk cargoes were being transported and competition with canal carrying developed. Despite some government intervention on the question of tolls and rates of carriage to try to help canals remain competitive, canal companies started to lease their canals or sell out to railway companies. By the middle of the 19th century, the railways owned many miles of British waterways.

An Act of 1854 was intended to ensure fair competition for the waterways, whether railway owned or independent, but by 1873 a further Railway and Canal Traffic Act was passed appointing commissioners to deal with complaints. Railway companies were already allowing some canals to fall into disrepair through neglect, little dredging was carried out, and railway tolls were making it more difficult for the canal companies to offer a dividend to their shareholders. Some attempts were made by canal companies to present a concerted front, but co-operation had come too late and by the end of the 19th century the railways had a stronghold over transport in Britain.

For 11 years, around the turn of the century, Henry de Salis, a director of one of the principal canal carrying companies – Fellows, Morton and Clayton Ltd – toured the canals and rivers of Britain compiling a list of distance tables for each waterway, thereby providing transport companies with precise information as to the location of wharves, docks and junctions. Henry de Salis's work was published in 1904 as *Bradshaw's Canals and Navigable Rivers of England and Wales*, which was the original edition of this present book. This detailed publication was one further attempt to improve co-operation between canal companies and stem the decline in cargo-carrying by water.

One very positive event at this time was the opening of the Manchester Ship Canal in 1894. This project gave a considerable boost to waterway interests and demonstrated how a waterway could be a positive benefit to a large urban industrial community. The local councils and city committees competed to lend money to the undertaking, which turned Manchester into a major shipping port despite its distance from the sea.

In 1906, a Royal Commission was set up to look at inland navigations in Britain. The Commission took five years to consider various possibilities, looking at some European systems during that time, and its final recommendations were to improve Brindley's original cross of canals linking the Thames, Severn, Humber and Mersey to take 100-ton barges, though some said a 300-ton standard would be preferable. These recommendations were never implemented, although some improvements to the southern end of the Grand Union Canal were carried out in the 1930s. Traffic continued to decline on the waterways up to the Second World War, with many smaller canals falling into disrepair, some being legally abandoned and others just gently silting up.

From 1939 to 1945, the railway-owned canals became the responsibility of the Ministry of Transport and in many cases their role was enhanced. Teams of young women were taken on to run the boats and replace the men who had been called up, and the canal routes from the Thames to the Midlands were busy throughout the war. Under the 1947 Transport Act, railway-owned canals were nationalised and subsequently administered by the Docks and Inland Waterways Executive. The British Waterways Board took over these duties in 1963.

In 1953 and 1956, two more committees looked in detail at the inland waterways and made proposals for their future. In both reports, the canals were divided into three groups: those to be developed, those to be maintained, and those to be closed or handed over to private interests. In 1959, the Inland Waterways Redevelopment Advisory Committee was appointed which had, as part of its remit, the opportunity of commenting on any proposals for the closure of canals. In several cases, their refusal to allow canals to be abandoned saved some which have since become popular holiday routes or vital parts of a 'ring'.

The formation of the Inland Waterways Association in 1946, by a group of people who had the foresight to envisage a future recreational role for the waterways, can undoubtedly be thanked for the fact that we still have an inland waterway network today. The enormous amount of time and energy put in by the early IWA members and committee to prevent waterways from being abandoned has ensured that Britain's historic and unique canal system will enter its third century.

There are now numerous fascinating books on the history of the canals. For a very entertaining introduction, covering all aspects of the story of canals in Britain, it would be hard to beat *The Great Days of the Canals* by Anthony Burton.

The men behind the canals

Probably the most famous of the canal engineers were James Brindley, William Jessop, John Rennie, Thomas Telford and Robert Whitworth. However, during the 18th century, when most of the canals were built, there were many more unsung engineers working on canals around the country. Canal engineering was often a family affair with many fathers and sons being involved. The Thomas Dadfords were responsible for many canals in South Wales and the Midlands, John Rennie's two sons, George and John, also became engineers, though they were less involved in canals than their father. William Crosley, father and son, were involved with the Rochdale Canal and William Jessop's son, Josias, was also a canal engineer. In the middle of the 19th century, Edward Leader Williams became engineer to the Weaver Navigation and later he was responsible for the Manchester Ship Canal, including the famous Barton Swing Aqueduct.

When canal construction started in Britain, the role of engineer was only just developing. James Brindley was apprenticed to a mill-wright and set up as a mill-wright himself in Staffordshire. Thomas Telford was a stone mason from southeast Scotland before starting his career in London as an architect. John Rennie, also from southeast Scotland, was another mill-wright. Engineering developed with these men, although William Jessop trained formally as an engineer with John Smeaton, who was responsible for the Eddystone Lighthouse. The principle engineers on later canals often worked as assistants to the famous early engineers. Samuel Simcock and Robert Whitworth were pupils of James Brindley; Thomas Telford worked under Jessop on the Ellesmere Canal, while Telford himself had several engineers who worked under him. A role developed for assistants who would act as resident engineers on the construction of particular canals, while the more famous men were overseeing several projects.

Many of the early engineers toured the country continually, inspecting progress on the various projects in which they were involved. These journeys were frequently undertaken on horseback at a time when travel was hard and often dangerous. James Brindley, who was middle-aged when he took on the Bridgewater Canal, was the engineer for numerous projects and incurred criticism from Josiah Wedgwood for taking on too much – the implication being that Brindley wasn't giving sufficient time to the Trent and Mersey Canal. Brindley died as a result of a chill he caught while surveying the Caldon Canal in 1772. Thomas Telford covered hundreds of miles a year to visit all the sites for which he was responsible, and he was also consulted by Count Baltzar von Platen on the Göta Canal which entailed visiting Sweden twice and maintaining a regular correspondence with the Count.

Some contractors gained sufficient experience from working with engineers on canal projects to become engineers in their own right. They would then branch out into surveying and designing canals themselves. One such was Josiah Clowes, who was originally a contractor on the Trent and Mersey Canal under Brindley and later became the resident engineer on the Thames and Severn Canal. The Pinkerton brothers, John and James, were associated with many of William Jessop's projects. It was really the canal age which developed the system of using contractors for major engineering projects, with many of the contractors travelling from job to job with the principal engineer.

The Third Duke of Bridgewater, Francis Egerton, and his brother-in-law Earl Gower, were two of the prime players in the start of the canal movement. Businessmen such as Josiah Wedgwood, the potteries owner, were also keen to promote canals and were prepared to put substantial amounts of personal capital into waterways projects; one of his partners in the Trent and Mersey Canal was Dr Erasmus Darwin, grandfather of Charles Darwin. In South Wales, many of the ironmasters and colliery owners financed canals as they did in the Midlands and northern England. Substantial sums of money were required to build the canals. Most projects regularly ran out of money and had to borrow more as work progressed. Many wealthy landowners followed the Duke of Bridgewater in investing in canals as did hundreds of professionals, tradesmen and local businessmen as they saw canal companies offering good dividends. Towards the end of the canal building era, many people lost money heavily as canal projects failed or were overtaken by railway developments.

Many intriguing biographies have been written about individuals involved in the British canals, and for an introduction to some of the main engineers, promoters and canal personalities, Edward Paget-Tomlinson includes a fascinating chapter in his book *The Illustrated History of Canal and River Navigations*.

One essential group of men who should not be forgotten are those who did the actual work, the thousands of 'navvies' who worked long hours in all weathers for little money to cut the canals from scratch. Very early canals were usually built by local farm-workers between peaks in labour on the land, so that when hay-making or the corn harvest came around the men would go back to the farm. Soon canal cutting was gaining such momentum that more workers were needed and this was when gangs of men started moving around the country from site to site. They became known as 'navigators', the men who built navigations, and this is where the term 'navvy' originated. As the demand for canal labour increased, more men came over from Ireland looking for work and gangs of Irish navvies working on canals became common.

Early canals were fairly simply constructed channels which followed the contour of the land, but as engineering techniques developed so did the skills of the navvies and their work became harder. Almost every ton of earth in the canals was moved by man-power, later with horse assistance and later still using steam-engines. The huge scale of some cuttings and embankments meant that the mud and rock frequently had to be moved twice to relocate it from where it had been cut out to where it would be used to build up the level. The muddy earth used to line the canals and make them watertight had to be found as near as possible to the canals, dug out, barrowed to the canal beds and spread along them. This mud had to contain high levels of clay and with added water it was 'puddled' until it became the right consistency to line the canals. Several layers of clay might be needed to provide a good base and each one had to be trodden and trampled in – an exhausting occupation.

Specialist craftsmen, such as carpenters, blacksmiths and masons, were also employed on the canals. Locks had to be built with their accurately fitting gates and sluices. In canal tunnels, miners were used first to do the excavating, carpenters followed on to put up timber shuttering and then bricklayers finally lined the tunnels to form a solid roof and walls. Aqueducts had to be built on pillars which stood in the river bed, so carpenters first had to construct coffer dams to keep the water out while the foundations were built. When iron troughs were used for building aqueducts, the sections would be made at the factory and put together on site by the blacksmith.

Anthony Burton has written extensively on the history of the canals in Britain. His absorbing book, *The Canal Builders* provides a wonderful insight into the men who created the waterways network we enjoy so much today.

Canal engineering

Using locks on canals and rivers

British Waterways' guide *The Waterways Code for Boaters* explains the correct procedure for using a lock with short descriptions of the most common types of gear you may find around the waterways. Many traditional rack and pinion gate paddles are being replaced by hydraulic mechanisms. As most of the canals were constructed by separate companies, this list cannot be exhaustive and so always check if there are special instructions at the lock and if in doubt about how something works *ASK*.

All hire companies will provide a short period of instruction on how to use a lock and, for those going on the canals for the first time, someone will demonstrate how to take your boat through a lock. In some places there are side ponds between locks which halves the amount of water used each time a boat passes through the locks – make sure you use these correctly.

Always try to conserve water. Before you empty or fill a lock of water, check if there is a boat travelling in the opposite direction which could make use of it. Emptying a full lock of water can waste up to 60,000 gallons. Whenever possible lock through with another boat; this is more likely to apply in broad locks but a small boat may be able to share a narrow lock with another boat.

A flight of locks is a series of locks running together to take a boat up or down a steep incline. Each lock is separate with a short pound between two locks. Boats going up and down can usually pass in these pounds. A staircase comprises from two to five locks together where the bottom gates of one lock serve as the top gates of the lock below. These need a slightly modified locking technique

and two boats travelling in opposite directions cannot pass on a staircase.

General locking technique

- If there is a lock keeper, which is likely on river locks, always wait for his instructions before entering or leaving a lock.

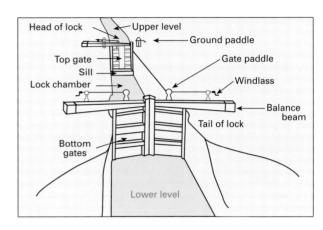

Fig. 1

- When entering a lock, keep the engine in forward gear until the boat is inside the gates or you will lose steerage way.
- Don't be in too much hurry; going through locks is a major part of the fun of being on the canals and rivers.
- The gate will open more easily when the water level each side has equalised and the turbulence has died away, so take your time.
- Never open the gates by pushing with the bow. This is very bad practice and can cause damage to gates and other lock gear.
- Always wind the paddles back down after use. Damage can be caused if they are just allowed to drop.

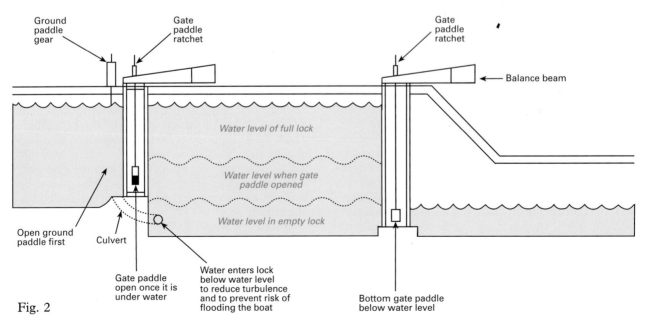

Fig. 2

- At the top of the lock there is a sill against which the top gate rests. This may protrude as far as 5ft into the lock so you must be sure the boat is well into the lock, at least 6ft from the gate, to avoid damage to the rudder or propeller.
- Always take notice of any special instructions posted next to a lock or a flight of locks.
- It is generally not necessary to tie up in a narrow lock but in a broad lock it is advisable to use a breast rope if there is another boat in the lock or ropes from the bow and stern. In a river lock, you should always secure the boat taking directions from the lock-keeper as to which side to go and which bollards to use.

Going uphill

1. Approach the lock steadily and slowly. Let a crew member off at the bank to check if the lock is full or empty.
2. If the lock is full, and no approaching downhill boat can use the water, check that the top gate(s) and all its paddles (both gate and ground paddles) are shut. Slowly raise the paddles on the bottom gates to empty the lock. Keep the boat well clear of the gates as the water comes out.
3. Open the bottom gates and enter the lock slowly but steadily.

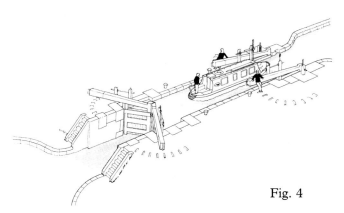

Fig. 4

Going downhill

1. Approach the lock steadily and slowly. Let a crew member off at the bank to check if the lock is full or empty.
2. If the lock is empty, and there is no approaching uphill boat, check that the bottom gates and paddles are shut. Slowly open the paddles at the top gates to fill the lock.
3. Open the top gates and enter the lock slowly.

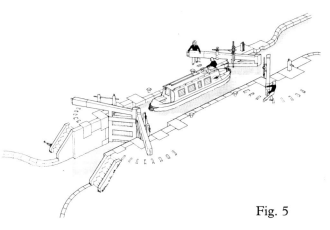

Fig. 5

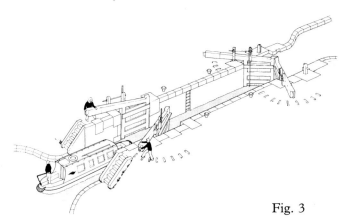

Fig. 3

4. Position the boat carefully to keep clear of both gates.
5. Close the bottom gates and lower the paddles.
6. If there are ground paddles by the top gates, open these part-way first to let the water come in, and as the rate slows down open them fully. In a broad lock, open the ground paddle the same side as the boat first to prevent the water turbulence pushing the boat across the lock.
7. Open the top gate paddles. While the boat rises, keep checking its position to ensure it doesn't get caught under timbers on the gates either end.
8. When the lock is full, open the top gate or gates.
9. Leave the lock steadily and not too fast.
10. Close the top gate and all the paddles.
11. Remember to take your windlass with you.

4. Position the stern of the boat at least 6ft from the top gate to prevent the risk of the rudder and propeller being caught on the sill.
5. Close the top gate and lower the paddles. Close the ground paddles if there are any.
6. Open the bottom gate paddles to empty the lock.
7. When the lock is empty, open the bottom gates and leave the lock slowly.
8. Close the bottom gates and the gate paddles behind you.
9. Don't forget your windlass.

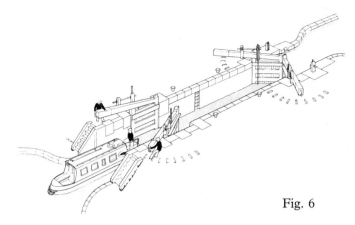

Fig. 6

Staircases

Prepare all the locks in a staircase by checking that gates and paddles are shut before you enter the first lock. If you are unsure how to work a staircase of locks *ASK* someone before you start.

Going uphill – see diagram of locks – Fig 7
1. Before you enter a staircase the bottom lock must be empty and all other locks full.
2. Follow the same procedure as for a single lock, carefully checking all paddles as you go.
3. Always check that all gates and paddles have been left closed.

Going downhill – see diagram of locks – Fig 8
1. Before you enter the staircase, the top lock must be full and all other locks empty.
2. Follow the same procedure as for descending a single lock. Always check that the lock below is empty before you release water from a lock.
3. Always check that all gates and paddles have been left closed.

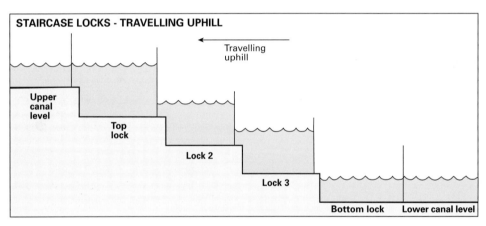

Fig. 7

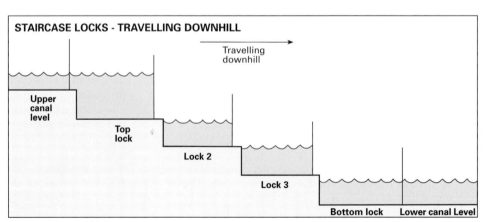

Fig. 8

Waterways structures

As we travel around Britain, historic aqueducts, bridges, locks, tunnels and canalside buildings are all reminders of the canal age. Canals often seem so much part of the landscape that it is easy to forget that they are totally man-made structures. At the time they were built, canals caused as much controversy and had as great an impact on the landscape as new motorways do today, but the use of local materials has helped them blend into the countryside with the passing of time. Many canal structures in the Midlands were made of brick, pale sandstone was used on the Kennet and Avon, or dark granite on many of the northern canals. Today, we appreciate these materials as enhancing the landscape, and it's doubtful whether the same will be said of the M1 or the M5 in 100 years time.

Aqueducts

The Romans built aqueducts for water supply, but the first aqueduct of the English Canal Age was across the River Irwell to carry the Bridgewater Canal and it was opened in 1761. This fine structure was the work of the Duke of Bridgewater, John Gilbert his agent and James Brindley the engineer. There is some debate about who should really take the final credit for the aqueduct, but in any event it was a magnificent engineering and aesthetic achievement, attracting much ridicule in the planning and much amazement and admiration when completed.

Aqueducts were frequently built to carry a canal over a river valley, a road or later a railway line. The high cost of building an aqueduct was generally offset by the fact that locks were not needed to take the canal down to a river valley and up the other side again, and there was also a substantial saving in water by maintaining the canal on a level. On economic grounds, aqueducts were invariably constructed to the minimum width and depth for a single boat to pass over and this parsimony could cause hold-ups when the canals were busy. The towpath was always an integral part of the aqueduct, a feature seen to good effect on the Brynich Aqueduct which takes the Brecon and Abergavenny Canal across the River Usk. Sometimes the towpath was constructed on a slightly lower or higher level than the canal trough, as on the Pontcysyllte Aqueduct on the Llangollen Canal.

Many of Brindley's early aqueducts were quite modest, low level structures, such as that over the River Dove on the Trent and Mersey, but as the Canal Age progressed better engineering techniques were developed and aqueducts became more ambitious and dramatic. Robert Whitworth built the beautiful stone aqueduct over the River Kelvin on the Forth and Clyde Canal, which should see passing boats again once the restoration project for the canal is completed. This aqueduct was probably the inspiration for John Rennie when he was designing the Dundas Aqueduct on the Kennet and Avon. Both the Dundas and Avoncliff aqueducts seem to set the scene for the architecture of Bath, as distinctive Georgian influences can be seen in their construction. Possibly one of the finest stone aqueducts is another Rennie design carrying the Lancaster Canal across the River Lune.

The cast-iron aqueduct at Longton-on-Tern was Thomas Telford's first experiment with the new material and was the precursor to the Pontcysyllte aqueduct. *Robin Smithett*

Early aqueducts were usually made of stone with a puddled clay lining. This made them very heavy structures and the supports had to be enormous. In some cases, the river being crossed was widened in order to reduce the flow and therefore the water force pushing against the pillars. A few aqueducts were constructed of brick, such as the Rugeley on the Trent and Mersey, but this much softer material was not commonly used.

With the development of iron working, the opportunity to construct lighter structures offered canal engineers a new dimension in their designs. Aqueducts could cross valleys at much higher levels as the piers holding the trough could be of lighter construction and therefore taller. The magnificent sweeping Pontcysyllte Aqueduct carries the Llangollen Canal over the River Dee and is surely the ultimate example of this type. Designed by William Jessop and Thomas Telford, the aqueduct is 1007ft long and 126ft high – not recommended for helmsmen who suffer from vertigo. It was opened in 1805 and the piers were solid at the base but hollow from 70ft up to the trough. The cast iron trough required no clay puddle to make it water tight, thus greatly reducing the weight of the structure.

The Barton Swing Aqueduct now carries the Bridgewater Canal across the Manchester Ship Canal. Built in 1893, it replaced Brindley's original aqueduct over the River Irwell. This aqueduct is essentially a trough, 235ft long, 18ft wide and 6ft deep, which can be closed off from the canal at either end. Then the whole structure, weighing 1400 tons, pivots and swings at right angles to lie in line with the Manchester Ship Canal and allow large ships to pass up to the docks in the heart of the city. Traffic has tailed off substantially on the Manchester Ship Canal, but if you are lucky you may still see the Barton Aqueduct swing open for an ocean-going ship.

Aqueducts have continued to be built through the 20th century, though with rather less style and using more prosaic materials – mostly reinforced concrete – to carry canals over roads and motorways. One popular aqueduct carries the Grand Union Canal over the North Circular Road in Greater London, and two of the newest aqueducts in the network are on the Basingstoke Canal, opened in 1995, to carry the canal over the new bypass just east of Aldershot, and the River Perry Aqueduct on the Montgomery Canal.

Bridges

Long before canals were thought of, bridges were built in Britain for crossing rivers, often at the site of a ford. Many remain today, reminders of a slower age when it seemed such structures could be both functional and beautiful. The Church was frequently involved in the construction of bridges where they provided access to abbeys, monasteries or were sited along routes of pilgrimage. The 15th century bridge at St Ives on the Great Ouse is one of the four remaining bridges which has a chapel built on it. Early bridges in major towns and cities often had houses and shops built along them, and today many visitors to Bath stroll across Pulteney Bridge completely unaware that the River Avon is flowing underneath.

Canal bridge construction can sometimes offer clues to the engineer who designed the canal itself and the actual contractor who built the bridge. Neighbouring bridges, for example, could look quite different when two contractors were involved on one length of canal. Brindley was not keen on the skew bridge, so he ensured that roads crossed canals at right angles, whereas Brunel's wonderful angled railway bridge at Moulsford across the Thames has twisted piers to allow them to sit in line with the stream and present the minimum resistance to the current. Early canal engineers were developing new technology as they went along, and the skills and materials available progressed rapidly during the main period of English canal construction from 1760 to 1840. This progression is reflected in bridge design as well as aqueducts and tunnels.

Where a canal was planned to run through a great park or the grounds of a wealthy landowner, a much more ornate bridge might be constructed to enhance the view from the house. Many landowners were far from happy at the prospect of a working canal running through their estates and the engineer often had lengthy negotiations to conduct before arriving at an arrangement agreeable to both parties. In such discussions, an elegant bridge might well be a useful bargaining point.

On the land of less powerful farmers, an accommodation bridge would be the familiar hump-back type or possibly just a wooden bridge which swung or lifted to allow the horse and boat through. The canal companies preferred the latter type of bridge as it kept the cost down and finance was always a problem. Today, opening the lifting bridges along the Llangollen or South Oxford canals is often one of the highlights of a waterways holiday, but for working boatmen this was but one more aspect of a hard life. Nowadays, the swing bridges on the Caledonian and Crinan canals and on the River Weaver are all operated by bridge-keepers.

Various ingenious methods were developed to accommodate a towpath changing sides, and to prevent the towing line from having to be unhitched from the horse in the process. In some cases, the two halves of the bridge did not quite meet and the line could be passed through the narrow gap in the centre; good examples of this can be seen on the Stratford-on-Avon Canal. Where the horse had to cross the canal to a towpath on the opposite bank, a turnover or roving bridge might be constructed, which had two sweeping curves to allow the horse to plod slowly over the bridge while the boat gently drifted towards it; the Macclesfield Canal is well known for its fascinating turnover bridges.

Frequently, a bridge would be built at the tail of a lock, as this could then be level with the land on either side and avoid the need for constructing ramps to allow headroom for the boat. These bridges often provided access to the lock cottages. Towpath bridges were usually constructed at canal junctions or where a canal climbed past a river weir. These structures were sometimes quite complicated to ensure that both towpaths were continuous and the horses did not have to be unhitched.

Canalside architecture

Today, as we cruise in a leisurely fashion along the waterways, the welcoming canalside pub with an attractive garden appears to have been put there for no other reason than to provide us with a cool drink and a pleasant lunch in the warm days of summer, but the history of such pubs shows that they were a vital part of working life for canal families. The pubs might have been owned privately or by the canal company, many of them no more than one room in a cottage with a brew house and stables outside. Few boatmen could read or write, so word of mouth was how they kept up with both business and social events. Messages could be left with the publican or his wife for a boat following on, and events from off the cut would be passed on in the pub. Canals were worked predominantly for freight, with little passenger traffic, so the later development of large

hotels for railway passengers did not happen to any great extent on the canals.

On certain canals, water supply was a recurring problem and in some cases water had to be pumped back up to the summit level from lower down in the canal, or topped up from a river or reservoir. Pumping stations, therefore, are a striking feature of many canals. On the Kennet and Avon, the Claverton Pumping Station used large lift-pumps driven by waterwheel to pump water from the River Avon up to the canal. Further east at Crofton, two steam-driven engines were used for the same purpose. Many smaller pumps were wind-powered because they were cheaper to build and run. However, lack of wind during summer months often meant that these pumps were of little use at the time when they were most needed. The pumping stations varied from simple structures built in local stone to more grandiose designs built by the Victorians when they were replacing older, more functional buildings. One such is the Leawood Pumping Station on the Cromford Canal, which has recently been restored to working order.

Lock cottages and bridge-keepers' houses vary enormously in size and style throughout the canal system. Along the Gloucester and Sharpness Canal, the bridge houses have very distinctive white-painted porticos with Doric columns, which lend an elegance and gracious charm to a trip along the canal. On the Stratford-on-Avon Canal it is common to see barrel shaped roofs on lock cottages,

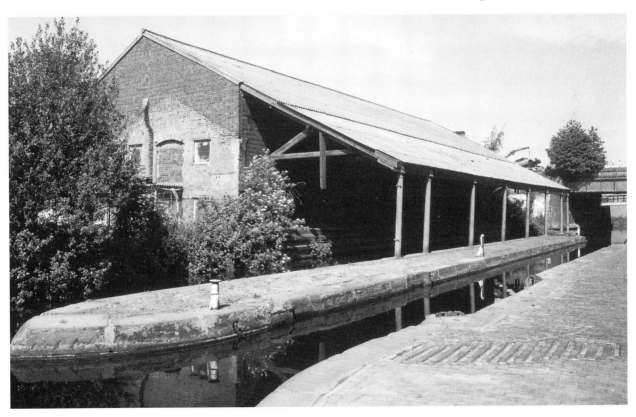

A covered loading bay at one of the numerous canalside businesses on the Birmingham Canal Navigations.
Jane Cumberlidge

Audlem Mill has found a new role as a canal shop. *Roy Westlake*

while the cottage at Grindley Brook on the Llangollen Canal looks more like a roadside toll-house than a lock cottage.

Other buildings to look out for as you travel the English canals are those small, rather ordinary huts which were built simply to offer some shelter to lengthsmen, leggers or other workers on the canal. These huts may not even have had a window, but there would always be a fireplace and you would find a great variety of design and materials used in the construction of these simple buildings.

The toll clerk's hut can usually be found at a canal junction where the clerk would inspect a boat's cargo, measure the freeboard and then charge for the use of the canal. More impressive canalside houses can still be seen which would have been used by canal managers or senior officials of the canal company. Some of these were quite substantial, elegant properties. The canal companies often built themselves impressive administrative offices, and one particularly fine example is at Sydney Gardens in Bath, the office of the Kennet and Avon Canal Company.

At Shardlow in Derbyshire or Stourport in Worcestershire, you can still see a complete inland port with wharves and warehouses around large basins almost as they would have been in the 19th century. Many of the original buildings have now been converted to other uses, but in both these cases the façades have remained virtually unaffected. In Stourport, the white clocktower over the central warehouse is still there, although now it overlooks motorboats moored alongside rather than commercial narrowboats. One of the warehouses at Shardlow has been converted into a pub and restaurant, but retains the archway over the water which offered the sheltered, inside loading of goods. The massive warehouses at Llanthony Wharf still overlook the elegant Gloucester Docks and have also been tastefully converted. Part of these buildings are now used to house the National Waterways Museum.

Travelling the canals by boat, you will also see maintenance yards and workshops strategically placed to serve many miles of canal in the area. New lock gates would have been made in these workshops, as virtually every gate on the system had to be measured and built individually – there was no such thing as standard gates or mass production. Most of the maintenance yards would have had stores and stables, a dry dock for boat repairs and probably a forge. Many of the yards in use today would have been built in the 19th century when canal companies felt the need to do the work themselves, whereas earlier maintenance work would often have been carried out by local contractors. In some parts of the Midlands, you may come across transfer sheds, where the canal ran alongside a railway station and goods were transferred between them. Unfortunately, many of these sheds have been demolished in various operations to tidy up the railways, but some are now listed buildings and a few can be seen around the Birmingham Canal Navigations.

Lifts and inclined planes

Despite our rather moist climate, water supply has always been a problem on British canals. Each boat which passed through a lock system, from the summit level to the base level, would use 25,000–30,000 gallons in a narrow lock and 55,000–60,000 gallons in a broad lock. This was quite an expensive way of moving a boat a few feet between different levels and so various other methods of moving boats up and down significant inclines were tried around the country. The object was to try and find faster ways of moving boats and to use less water in the process.

For tub boats and other smaller boats, inclined planes were used successfully on the Shropshire Canal at The Hay and Ketley. This sytem was a kind of boat-ramp, a sophisticated method of portage, which usually carried the boat dry up a set of tracks. There were six sets of inclined planes on the Bude Canal, for example, most of which were worked by the laden boat descending and counterbalancing the empty boat which was hauled up. On the Tavistock Canal, a plane was used to descend 237ft to the River Tamar at Morwellham Quay.

Probably the best example of an inclined plane was at Foxton, where a system was devised to improve passage along the Leicester line of the Grand Junction Canal. Two *caissons* could each take two narrow or one wide boat up a rise of 75ft. The *caissons* were moved by a steam-engine and from 1900 to 1910 boats could be lifted through this significant height in only 12 minutes, with a considerable saving of water over using the locks. Unfortunately, the proposed inclined plane at Watford was never built and so passage reverted to the famous staircase locks at Foxton, which took over an hour and a quarter to work. Restoration of the Foxton Inclined Plane is now underway and so another part of our unique canal heritage will be preserved for posterity.

Vertical lifts were another possible means of moving boats between levels. Several systems were tried during the 19th century, but only the Anderton Boat Lift, between the River Weaver and the Trent and Mersey Canal, was really successful. The original lift was opened in 1875. Designed by Edwin Clark, it worked on the principle of hydraulic rams, powered by steam, which supported two counterbalanced *caissons* which could hold one wide or two narrowboats each. The system worked well until 1905, when it was discovered that acid in the water of the River Weaver was corroding the hydraulic rams. It was decided to convert the lift to electric power, so that each *caisson* could work independently, balanced by 250-ton weights. The lift worked until 1982 and is now undergoing a full restoration programme. If all goes well, the Anderton Boat Lift should be back in working order by the year 2000.

Locks

The earliest documented attempts to improve navigation on rivers were carried out by the Romans, who were the first to cut practical artificial waterways. The Foss Dyke is still used as part of the Fossdyke and Witham Navigation. The first developments on rivers included weirs to maintain water levels and then flash locks which allowed boats to pass from one level to another. Flash locks varied in design around the country. Guillotine gates were common in East Anglia, where these locks were called staunches. Many of the staunches on the River Nene were only replaced with pound locks shortly before the Second World War and the guillotine gate at the lower end still remains.

Today, when we refer to a lock, we mean a 'pound lock'. This simple yet rather clever device was used in China in the 1st century AD and could be seen in Europe in the 15th century. The first recorded pound lock in Britain was on the Exeter Canal in the 1560s. Early pound locks were turf-sided, but even on rivers the loss of water from turf-sided locks caused them to be replaced by stone or brick chambers during the 17th and 18th centuries. Water

was always crucial for canals and so it wasn't long before all canal locks were built of brick or stone. A lock is usually a rectangular chamber, though other shapes can sometimes be seen on different waterways. Broad locks usually have a pair of gates at each end while narrow locks often have a single top gate and two gates at the tail of the lock. The gates are generally mitred and the pressure of water works to keep the gates shut, so the mitre points towards the head of water, or the upper pound.

Paddles (or sluices) in the gate are raised and lowered to allow water in and out of the chamber, thus raising or lowering the boat. In some locks there are also ground paddles which let water into the lock from the upper pound through a culvert. With ground paddles, water enters the lock below the water surface, reducing turbulence and cutting out the risk of flooding a boat when a gate paddle, higher than the bow of the boat, is opened too quickly. The paddle designs, together with the means of raising and lowering them, have evolved slowly over the years. With many locks, the paddles have been replaced many times, starting with the old system of 'peg and pull' and ending up with the now common ratchet with a windlass. Because of the considerable water pressures involved, windlasses are essential for opening paddles. Special keys or handles are needed to turn the mechanisms, whose shape and design varies throughout the country.

In steep terrain, locks were joined into flights, with short pounds between them, or into complete 'staircases', where the bottom gates of one lock act as the top gates of the lock below. Because there are no passing places, boats have to travel up the complete staircase before another boat can work down, so long staircases could cause serious delays in the days of working barges. The Banavie Staircase of eight locks, at the west end of the Caledonian Canal, is a particularly spectacular site and the view from the top lock out towards Loch Linnhe is breathtaking. At the other end of Britain, the 29 lock flight at Caen Hill on the Kennet and Avon Canal is equally impressive in a distinctively English way.

As a means of saving water, some lock flights are provided with side ponds. Using this sytem, half a lockful of water is emptied into the side pond until the lock and pond are level and then the second half is emptied in the usual way. When the next boat is climbing up the flight, the water from the side pond is emptied into the lock before water is released from above. This system effectively halves the quantity of water used by a boat passing through the flight. On some busy canals, locks were 'doubled up' and so one lock would act as a side pond for its partner alongside. Pumping stations were also built on canals which suffered severely from water shortages, and more recently modern back-pumping systems have been installed on a number of canals to return water to the head of a flight of locks.

Tunnels

As well as aqueducts, other means were employed to maintain a constant level on a canal across difficult terrain. Embankments, for example, would be used to raise the level of low ground or cuttings would be dug through high ground. Where the depth was too great for a cutting, it would be necessary to build a tunnel. Tunnel construction has always been difficult, expensive and frequently dangerous, but many impressive tunnels were completed using meagre resources and are still used through the canal system today.

Tunnel construction techniques developed rapidly with experience, and sometimes dramatic trial and error. The earliest canal tunnels were the minimum size to allow a boat passage, with no spare height and no tow path. Later tunnels were built on a more generous scale, sometimes with two towpaths. However the engineering was achieved, the process of cutting and reinforcing a tunnel was always laborious and dangerous.

Initially, the proposed line of a tunnel would be marked out on the surface with pegs and then shafts would be sunk to the level of the canal. These shafts would be brick or timber lined and the miners would descend them and start excavating the tunnel in each direction. Once the miners started enlarging the hole, the spoil would be removed up the shaft and bricklayers would follow on behind the miners to line the tunnel. Flooding, fire and roof falls were all common hazards for the workers involved.

The first long canal tunnel to be built in England was the Harecastle Tunnel on the Trent and Mersey Canal. Designed by James Brindley, it was 2,880 yards long and took nine years to complete. The tunnel was extremely narrow and boats had to be 'legged' through. This laborious process entailed two men lying sideways on planks or 'wings' at the bow of the boat and walking along the walls of the tunnel, thus propelling the boat forwards. Legging required steady co-ordination between the two leggers and a long tunnel would take a considerable time to negotiate. The tunnel therefore became a serious bottleneck on the Trent and Mersey Canal, and in 1824 a second tunnel was built alongside, with Telford as the engineer. This tunnel, which is still used today, is 3,000 yards long and took only three years to build as construction techniques had developed so much during the intervening years. The New Harecastle Tunnel was much larger than the original, with a generous towpath.

The longest tunnel on a British canal is the Standedge Tunnel on the Huddersfield Narrow Canal. Standedge has been closed for many years now but, with the restoration project now well underway on the canal it should be possible to take a boat through the tunnel again by the year 2000. Another tunnel which hopefully will re-open one day is the famous Sapperton Tunnel on the Thames and Severn Canal. This is one of the few tunnels which has quite ornate portals at either end, which are well worth going to see even before you can cruise under them.

As few tunnels were provided with tow paths, special horse-paths were created to take the horse from one end of the tunnel to meet the boat again at the other end. In many areas, these old horse-paths are now fascinating walks over hills, where you come across occasional intriguing reminders of the presence of the tunnel deep below you. At Braunston, for example, the horse-path passes the rather mysterious ventilation shafts for the tunnel. At Shrewley Tunnel on the Grand Union Canal, the horse-path itself went through a shorter tunnel at a higher level than the canal.

The theory and practice of surveying were in their infancy early in the canal building period and sometimes the tunnels were not as straight as later ones. The first Harecastle Tunnel was rather wiggly and most tunnels in the network require concentration by the helmsman as few are without bends. Modern boats have the advantage of good electric lights, but working through a meandering tunnel by feeble flickering candlelight would not be an enviable task. Many myths and stories became associated with canal tunnels and there are various reported encounters with strange waterways ghosts.

Canal tunnels of Great Britain
(over 50 yards long)

Name	Waterway	Yards
Standedge	Huddersfield Narrow Canal (open for ventilation only)	5698
Strood	Gravesend and Rochester Canal (now used as a railway tunnel)	3946
Dudley	Birmingham Canal Navigations (not continuous)	3154
Blisworth	Grand Union Canal	3076
Netherton[1]	Birmingham Canal Navigations	3027
Harecastle	Trent and Mersey Canal	2919
West Hill (or Wast)	Worcester and Birmingham Canal	2726
Braunston	Grand Union Canal	2048
Foulridge	Leeds and Liverpool Canal	1640
Crick	Grand Union Canal	1528
Preston Brook	Trent and Mersey Canal	1239
Husband's Bosworth	Grand Union Canal	1166
Islington	Grand Union Canal	960
Saddington	Grand Union Canal	880
Shortwood	Worcester and Birmingham Canal	613
Tardebigge	Worcester and Birmingham Canal	613
Barnton	Trent and Mersey Canal	572
Gannow	Leeds and Liverpool Canal	559
Gosty Hill	Birmingham Canal Navigation	557
Savernake	Kennet and Avon Canal	502
Chirk[1]	Shropshire Union Canal	433
Shrewley	Grand Union Canal	433
Saltersford	Trent and Mersey Canal	424
Ashford	Brecon and Abergavenny Canal	375
Coseley[1]	Birmingham Canal Navigation	360
King's Norton	Stratford-on-Avon Canal (Brandwood)	352
Hyde Bank	Peak Forest Canal	308
Maida Hill	Grand Union Canal	272

Name	Waterway	Yards
Newbold[1]	Oxford Canal (two towpaths)	250
Snarestone	Ashby Canal	250
Dunhampstead	Worcester and Birmingham Canal	236
Whitehouses[1]	Shropshire Union Canal	191
Woodley[1]	Peak Forest Canal	167
Drakeholes	Chesterfield Canal	154
Armitage[1]	Trent and Mersey Canal (opened out 1971)	130
Leek	Trent and Mersey Canal (Leek Branch)	130
Galton	Birmingham Canal Navigation (opened 1974)	122
Edgbaston[1]	Worcester and Birmingham Canal	105
Ashted[1]	Birmingham Canal Navigation	103
Summit Tunnel	Birmingham Canal Navigation	103
Ellesmere[1]	Shropshire Union Canal	87
Cwmbran	Monmouthshire Canal	87
Cowley[1]	Shropshire Union Canal	81
Knott Mill[1]	Rochdale Canal	78
Froghall	Trent and Mersey Canal (Caldon Branch)	76
Cookley[1]	Staffordshire and Worcester	65
Bath[1]	Kennet and Avon Canal	59
Curdworth[1]	Birmingham Canal Navigation	57
Bath[1]	Kennet and Avon Canal	55

The following canal tunnels (over 50 yards long) are no longer in use being derelict or abandoned. Some may be restored and re-opened.

Name	Waterway	Yards
Pensax	Kington, Leominster and Stourport Canal (uncompleted)	3850
Sapperton	Thames and Severn Canal	3808
Lappal	Birmingham Canal	3795
Norwood	Chesterfield Canal	3102
Butterley	Cromford Canal	3063
Old Harecastle	Trent and Mersey Canal	2897
(Now replaced by New Harecastle Tunnel)		
Morwelldown	Tavistock Canal	2540
Oxenhall	Hereford & Gloucester Canal	2192
Crimson Hill	Chard Canal	1800
Southnet	Kington, Leominster and Stourport Canal (completed but never used)	1250
Greywell	Basingstoke Canal	1200
Berwick	Shropshire Union Canal	970
Southampton	Southampton and Salisbury Canal (never completed)	880
Falkirk	Union Canal	696
Manchester	Manchester and Salford Junction Canal	499
Aylestone	Herefordshire and Gloucestershire Canal	440
Wellow	Somerset Coal Canal (Radstock Arm)	405
Ashperton	Herefordshire and Gloucestershire Canal	400
Hincaster	Lancaster Canal	377
Hardham	Arun Navigation	375
Scout	Huddersfield Narrow Canal	220
Coombe Hay	Somerset Coal Canal	195
Bury	Manchester Bolton and Bury Canal	141
Cardiff	Glamorganshire Canal	115
Cricklade	North Wiltshire Canal	100
Hag[1]	Cromford Canal	93
Cwmbran	Monmouthshire Canal	87
Knott Mill	Rochdale Canal (Manchester)	78
Gregory[1]	Cromford Canal	76

Name	Waterway	Yards
Salford	Manchester, Bolton and Bury Canal (two short lengths)	50
Buckland Hollow[1]	Cromford Canal	50
Sowerby Long Bridge	Rochdale Canal	50
Little Tunnel	Basingstoke Canal	50

1. These tunnels have a tow path

For anyone interested in more engineering detail on canal structures and associated works, Nigel Crowe's book *Canals* or Edward Paget-Tomlinson's *The Illustrated History of Canal and River Navigations* are good starting points.

Navigation

Narrowboats and other waterway craft

Traditional inland waterway craft divide broadly into three groups:

- Narrowboats of standard 7ft beam, up to 70ft long with a capacity of 20–30 tons, designed for use on the narrow canals.
- Wide boats of 14ft beam, varying in length from about 52ft to 72ft.
- River craft which often used sails and had keels. River craft were very varied and often a particular type of boat would be used in a very limited location with draught and capacity reflecting the local conditions. In addition there were many boats designed for a particular job which would only be found in a specific area.

Narrow boats

When James Brindley was planning the Trent and Mersey Canal, he designed the locks 72ft long by 7ft wide to take boats capable of carrying 20 tons of coal. Early narrowboats were made of wood, but iron knees were often used later as metalwork techniques improved. Later boats were mostly made of steel, although some builders continued to use wood. The basic structure of narrowboats was similar but each yard had its own particular style and way of working. Enthusiasts can still tell a boat's builder or which company owned her by tell-tale details in the shape of a bow or the lines of the hull or cabin.

It was soon discovered that, with bulkier cargoes, the capacity of the traditional narrowboat was rather limited and the first major adaptation was to provide a cratch and top planks running back to the cabin. Bulky light cargoes could be loaded onto the boat and piled up quite high, and then a system of side cloths and tarpaulins was used to cover the cargo and protect it from the weather. Considerable agility was needed to work along the boat pulling up and tying the cloths as there was virtually no side deck and the top planks were very narrow.

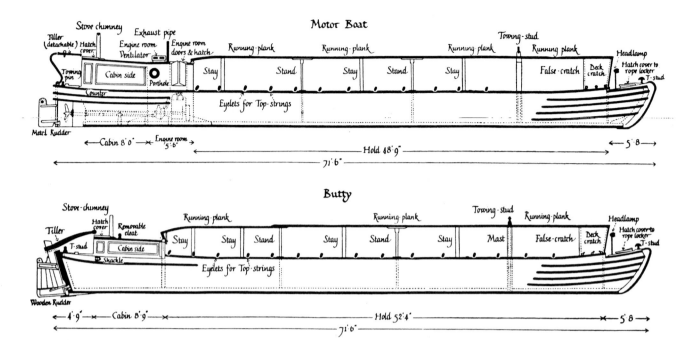

A PAIR OF NARROW BOATS

Traditional narrowboats

As the distances travelled by boats increased, the cabin developed into a moving home and the boatman's wife and family moved around the canals with him, living in the cabin which was usually 10ft by 6ft with only 5ft headroom. Enormous ingenuity was used to stow all the necessities for a family in such a small space. In very unusual circumstances, an even smaller cabin might be constructed right in the bow, but as this took precious cargo space a forecabin was quite a rare event.

One horse usually pulled a single boat, but as motors were put into the boats a more common combination was for a motorboat to pull a 'butty'. This was a boat without an engine but it still had a cabin which provided additional space for the family. The cargo space in the motorboat was reduced by the space required for the engine, but with a pair of boats working together a cargo of 50–55 tons could be transported.

Many working narrowboats have been converted into cruising boats and new boats are generally built on traditional lines. One of the most popular features of the narrowboat is the tradition of painted decoration. The distinctive colourful motifs on doors and cabin sides are usually a combination of geometric patterns and pictures of roses and castles. The origin of the roses and castles as the most common design is unclear, but the sight of a line of brightly painted narrowboats along a towpath or in a canal basin is always a delight.

Wide boats

As can be surmised from the name, wide boats were used on the broad canals which had locks of 14ft 6in actual width. In the southern section of the Grand Union Canal, full length wide beam boats were used, but some of the northern canals had shorter locks and boats of 58 or 62ft were the norm. The Kennet and Avon was also built as a broad canal and wide boats were used on the Wey Navigation and the Basingstoke Canal. In the north of England, wide boats would have been seen on the Bridgewater, Leeds and Liverpool and Rochdale canals. The arrangements and construction were similar to that of narrowboats, although many of them had open holds. The extra beam offered a considerably greater carrying capacity.

Other canal boats

In addition to the narrow and wide boats which carried cargo over long distances, there were many specialised boats built for working a particular area. On the River Don, for example, and on the Aire and Calder Navigation, 'compartment boats' were used to move coal down to Goole. These were towed in trains and became familiarly known as Tom Puddings. Each boat was lifted on a hoist to unload its 35 tons of coal into a ship – an early example of containerisation.

In other parts of the country 'tub boats' were used. Those on the Bude Canal had wheels so that they could be hauled up the inclined planes within the system. Tub boat canals were also built in East Shropshire. Special boats were built for the Chelmer and Blackwater Navigation. These were 60ft long by 16ft beam, but had a draught of only 2ft as this navigation is the shallowest in the country.

The fast 'fly-boats' or express-boats had precedent over other canal craft and often travelled through the night. Teams of horses were needed as they were changed frequently, but the speed of delivery of high-value goods justified the cost of the service. The boats were generally flat bottomed but with a sleek stem and stern. They rarely carried their full tonnage as speed was the most important factor, with schedules frequently being run to meet up with sailing ships at a coastal port. There was a twice weekly fly-boat service from Birmingham to Ellesmere Port and a regular service from Leeds to Goole or Hull. On the Lancaster Canal, a fast passenger service ran from Kendal to Preston and on the Forth and Clyde and Union Canals a passenger service was run between Glasgow and Edinburgh. Passenger boats usually had separate cabins for different classes of passenger and refreshments were available.

The Scottish canals were built to ship size and, with the advent of steam, the famous 'puffers' were used through the canals and serving the islands on the west coast. One of the remaining Admiralty-built puffers, *VIC 32*, can still be seen on the Caledonian and Crinan canals operating weekly hotel cruises along these spectacular waterways.

Sailing barges, keels and wherries

Not so very long ago, it was common to see sailing barges on the many estuaries and river navigations around the British coasts. On the wide Thames Estuary, the sprit-sail barge was a common sight, carrying cargoes between the various working ports of Suffolk, Essex and Kent. The barges were shallow-draughted and flat-bottomed to be able to work safely amongst the tricky sandbanks of the Thames Estuary and sail right up into the upper reaches of the rivers. Many Thames barges have now been restored and are used for sailing holidays and day trips. There is no finer sight than a Thames sprit-sail barge under full canvas in a fresh breeze, slipping effortlessly through the short steep chop of the estuary.

On the Norfolk Broads the 'wherry' was the traditional cargo boat, with its single sail on a tall mast which could be easily lowered for passing under bridges. Wherries were very shallow draughted to enable them to penetrate right up into the Broads to serve the inland towns and villages. Towards the end of the 19th century, the developing railways started to bring tourists into the Broads and wherry owners saw the opportunity to convert their boats for charter. Today, it is still possible to take a holiday on a traditional wherry sailing around the Broads.

The Severn trow was another shallow-draught cargo boat which developed on a particularly tricky estuary with its shifting sandbanks and considerable tides. Trows were built so that they could take the

ground safely on a sandbank and wait for the next tide. In the middle reaches of the Severn, 'Wich barges traded on the Droitwich Canal, mostly transporting salt. On the east coast at about the same time, you would find Humber sloops and keels, the sloops mostly doing estuary work and the keels trading up the Ouse, the Trent, the Fossdyke and other smaller navigations.

Many books have been written about individual types of waterways craft, but an excellent introduction for anyone keen to find out more about different designs is Edward Paget-Tomlinson's *The Illustrated History of Canal and River Navigations*. This excellent book includes an informative chapter on the various local craft once commonly seen on English rivers and canals. The well-known *Shell Book of Inland Waterways* by Hugh McKnight also has a fascinating chapter on the varied types of local boat found around the country. There are now several preservation trusts for different types of craft, and boats can be seen at a number of museums. Unfortunately, the once thriving Exeter Maritime Museum has closed and the exhibits have been sold and moved to other locations.

Navigation notes

Speed

Always be aware of other waterway users, both on the water and along the bank, and make sure your activities do not inconvenience or endanger them. Boat speed on canals should be no more than 4mph and usually 6mph or 8mph on rivers depending on whether you are travelling up or downstream. In many instances, it will not be possible to go as fast as these speeds and the golden rule is that your boat should make no wash. A breaking wash can easily damage the banks of the canal or river, disturbs and endangers wildlife, can cause damage to moored craft and there is even a risk of swamping small craft such as canoeists and rowing boats. Check behind you regularly to be certain your wash is acceptable. You should always slow down to pass moored craft, fishermen, small boats and when approaching bridges, locks, weirs, canal junctions and blind bends

Commercial craft

Although there is now less freight carried by waterways, there are still many commercial vessels regularly using rivers and canals and, working in a different way, craft such as trip boats, ferries and hotel boats. You can meet some quite large vessels in estuaries and on the wide canals in the northeast. Always give way to commercial craft. They may have a schedule to keep or they may be restricted in their manoeuvrability by draught. Courtesy on the water costs nothing but makes life much safer and more pleasant for everyone.

Steering

The rule of the road for boats is that you keep to the right. Boats should always pass port to port and, when overtaking another boat you do so on the left. Keeping to the right does not mean you must stay close into the bank as there is likely to be more silting there and a risk of grounding, but ensure that you are to the right of centre and are able to move towards the right when another boat approaches. Slow down gradually as the boat approaches and steer gently to starboard as it gets closer. Trying to swerve at the last minute to avoid an oncoming boat is likely to put you aground in the mud at the side of the canal, often with the stern of the boat sticking well out into the channel and thus impeding the oncoming boat more dramatically.

There are still some horse-drawn boats on the canals and these must always be given the freedom of the towpath side, whether you then pass port to port or starboard to starboard. You are generally likely to find deeper water round the outside of bends, especially in rivers where the current has an effect on the shape of the bed. There will also be the probability of a shallower patch extending into the channel from the more slow-moving inside of a bend. The helmsman must weigh up these factors and take the most appropriate route through a bend depending on the conditions.

Overtaking

When overtaking, the responsibility lies with the overtaking boat to do so safely and without hindering other waterway users. Never overtake when approaching a bend, lock, bridge or weir. Slow down until a safe, straight length of canal is clear ahead and then you should only pass when the helmsman of the boat in front indicates that it is safe for you to do so. Overtaking in a boat is a surprisingly slow process and, unlike in a car, trying to accelerate to pass can actually slow you down because of the suction effect caused between the two boats.

When you are being overtaken, it is courteous to slow down and pull over a little towards the bank, without putting yourself at risk of grounding. If you see a boat coming up behind you which is likely to overtake, be prepared to beckon him on when you see the way clear ahead.

Turning

Turning a narrowboat requires practice and the longer the boat the more careful you have to be. Most canals are too narrow to be able to turn a boat, and so special 'lay-bys' called winding holes are provided at marked locations along the canal. Alternatively, you may be close to a junction, boatyard or marina where there is reasonable turning room. At slow speeds, the steering ability of the boat falls off markedly and a careful balance must be reached between speed and manoeuvrability.

Mooring

There are many designated mooring places along canals, where you will find bollards to tie-up to. When mooring in remote places, you will need to use pegs driven into the bank. Never take a mooring line across a towpath, as pedestrians, cyclists or even animals could injure themselves in the dark. Always be careful when driving pegs into the bank so as not to puncture the impervious lining of the canal, as this could start a serious breach.

Sound signals

There are officially recognised sound signals used by all boats on waterways and these should be known and understood by all the crew, both for indicating your own boat's intentions and for understanding what other boats are about to do. The signals are:

One short blast   I am altering course to starboard
Two short blasts   I am altering course to port
Three short blasts I am going astern
Four short blasts   I am unable to manoeuvre

Tidal information

Handling a boat in tidal waters can be very different to non-tidal conditions and should not be attempted by a novice. The boat itself must be suitable for tidal waters and its equipment must include at least one anchor, ropes long enough to adjust for tidal movement and an engine powerful enough to make headway against a current. The crew need to be familiar with tidal information and how to calculate changes in water level with the phases of the tide.

Tidal information is provided in almanacs and locally produced tide tables. Before making any trip which will involve a section of tideway, it's important to consult the tide tables and time your trip to take account of the predicted tidal conditions on that day. The significant aspects of the tide are the depth of water at any given time and the direction and speed of the tidal current. These factors are important for river and estuary navigation.

Remember that the local harbourmaster, boat and yacht clubs in the area are always happy to give advice and local information. Always make contact in advance of a visit to ensure you have the most up-to-date information. Many estuaries have sandbanks which shift as a result of severe weather and river flows, so that a published chart can sometimes be out of date before you buy it. The local harbour office will be able to provide the most current information on navigating in their area.

Tides are determined by the phases of the moon, but the timing and height of tides are also influenced by local weather conditions such as wind and air pressure. On rivers, the amount of freshwater coming downstream will also affect the level of tide and strength of the current. As a general rule, ebb tides usually flow faster and for slightly longer than flood tides. In some estuaries which have a large tidal range and a rapidly narrowing mouth, the flood tide can create a standing wave called a bore or eagre – for example, the famous tidal wave on the Severn Estuary and the River Parrett is known as a bore, while on the Trent the same phenomenon is called an eagre. Bores and eagres only occur at certain tides and a list of dates and predicted levels of the Severn Bore is available from the Environment Agency each year. A large tidal bore is a fascinating and slightly eerie spectacle, popular with the experienced surfboarders and canoeists who try to ride the tidal wave for miles inland.

A good practical introduction for the newcomer to canals and boating is *Canal and River Cruising* by Sheila Davenport. This is an IWA book which covers all aspects of general boating from a short history of the canals to boat handling, engines, rules of the road, hiring or looking for a boat of your own. For those considering buying a boat for the inland waterways, a valuable first investment would be *The Inland Waterways Manual* by Emrhys Barrell, which covers choosing a boat, boat handling and maintenance and repair. The RYA now have an Inland Waterways Helmsman's Certificate which can be gained by attending a course at a training establishment recognised by the RYA. Courses are advertised in the waterways magazines and a list of recognised teaching establishments can be obtained from the RYA.

The public right of navigation

Public right of navigation is a rather complex legal issue about which several books and numerous articles have been written. Practically, it is not necessary for every canal user to understand the legal niceties in detail, but it's important to be aware of the general principles governing one's rights, or otherwise, to navigate the waterways.

Waterways can be broadly divided into natural watercourses, such as rivers and streams, and artificial waterways such as canals. Many rivers, of course, have undergone alteration and improvement by man to aid navigation, and such work may have changed their status as a natural watercourse. This status is significant because an important starting point for 'right-of-navigation' law is the common right to navigate craft on the open sea. This right is presumed to extend up rivers as far as the discernible influence of the tide – the tidal limit, as it is usually called. On artificial waterways and above the tidal limit of natural watercourses, any right of navigation has had to be conferred by some explicit permission or statute.

Probably the earliest documented right-of-navigation of this type was passed in 1065 by Edward the Confessor to make the rivers Thames, Trent, Severn and Yorkshire Ouse navigable by the general public and restricting the previously asserted rights of mill and fisheries owners on those rivers. Other statutory rights of navigation have been in existence since *Magna Carta*, which was signed by King John in 1215. During the Middle Ages, navigation rights were sometimes conferred arbitrarily by the Monarch using 'Letters Patent', but after the 17th century an Act of Parliament was required to establish navigation rights.

From the middle of the 18th century, navigation rights were formally and explicitly established on the new artificial waterways that were being constructed. These rights were usually incorporated in the Act enabling a company to raise money to build and operate a new canal. During his research for a previous edition of this book, L A (Teddy) Edwards discovered that the only canal Act which did not confer a statutory right of navigation was that for the Derby Canal. This is one of the factors which will have to be resolved as part of the present restoration project for the canal.

During the later part of the nineteenth century, with the development of the railways and a general decline in canal traffic, proposals were put forward to extinguish various navigation rights and to close certain canals. As with the creation of a new navigation, it was necessary to pass an Act of Parliament for the abandonment of a canal. In some circumstances, later investigation has shown that certain canals have disappeared as a result of physical neglect and that, over a period of years, the navigation has ceased to exist and the canal company has vanished, although no Act has authorised an abandonment of the waterway. In such cases, the navigation right may still be held to exist. With the increased activity of restoration groups working on derelict canals around the country, the question of whether or not a navigation right has been legally extinguished becomes increasingly important.

The right of navigation on a waterway is either conferred by statute or may exist as a prescriptive right, which means the waterway has been used by the public 'for time immemorial'. This criterion is similar, although not identical to, the test for establishing a public right of way over land. In practice, prescriptive rights are not easy to prove and in recent years two important cases have been hotly debated – the right of navigation on the River Derwent in Yorkshire, and that on the River Wye on the Welsh Borders.

In the case of the River Derwent, the public right of navigation now only applies as far as the historic tidal limit, about 15½ miles above the new tidal barrier. The Law Lords have ruled that there is no public right of navigation on the Upper River Derwent. In the case of the River Wye, the Environment Agency have applied to become the navigation authority, where previously the river was an open navigation. The ruling on this case is likely to be announced at the end of 1997 after the deliberations of a Public Enquiry.

The right to navigate a waterway does not automatically confer a right to moor to the bank or to land. Particularly in the case of rivers, setting foot on the bank may constitute trespass as the banks are likely to be the property of the riparian owner. The right to navigate should also not be confused with the subject of regulations which may be imposed by the navigation authority for a particular waterway. Information on local byelaws, licences and other regulations which apply to individual waterways can be obtained from the relevant navigation authority, details of which are provided in the main text of this book under each waterway entry.

For anyone wishing to study the legal aspects of this subject, the following publications would be a good starting point:

Water Law – Principles and Practice, by Professor Richard Macrory, published 1985 by Longmans. Chapter 7 deals with Navigation Rights.

Inland Waterways: Legal aspects of public access and enjoyment, by Sheila Smith, Journal of Planning and Environmental Law 44 (1985).

The Public Right of Navigation, by Arthur Telling and Rosemary Smith, Study 27, published by The Sports Council, July 1985

Waterway authorities

There are three major bodies with responsibility for Britain's waterways. British Waterways manages over 2,000 miles of inland waterways, mostly the canals but they also have responsibility for some rivers. The Broads Authority is responsible for the Norfolk and Suffolk Broads including all the water associated activities. The Environment Agency came into being in April 1996 in England and Wales and is responsible for water quality, flood prevention and, on certain rivers, navigation. These responsibilities fall to the Scottish Environmental Protection Agency in Scotland.

In addition to these principle bodies there are many local authorities and private companies or individuals who are the navigation authorities and owners for certain waterways or parts of waterways, for example, the Manchester Ship Canal Company is the authority for both the Ship Canal and the Bridgewater Canal, and the National Trust is the owner and navigation authority for the River Wey and Godalming Navigation. On newly restored waterways canal societies and trusts are increasingly taking the role of navigation authority as with the Rochdale Canal. Port authorities, such as the Port of London Authority, have responsibility for estuaries, harbours and river mouths around the country.

Very good co-operation exists between the various agencies and, where boats are registered and licensed with one authority but travel along waterways administered by another, there may be reciprocal arrangements to cover licences, but it is the responsibility of the boat owner to verify the situation. Rivers, especially in Scotland, do not necessarily have a public right of navigation or of access and anyone intending to use a waterway must ensure that they have the requisite permissions. This applies particularly to canoeists.

British Waterways
British Waterways (BW) took over the management and running of about 2,000 miles of canal and river navigations in 1963. Five years later, after a lengthy review, the Transport Act 1968, classified waterways into three groups which are still used today. Commercial Waterways are principally for the carriage of freight; Cruising Waterways are to be available for cruising, fishing and other recreational purposes; and Remainder Waterways are to be maintained as economically as possible but with due consideration for health and safety. Improvements can be made to the last group provided the cost is not covered directly be BW but can be found from other interested parties, such as local authorities, local trusts and private business or individuals.

In the late 1970s the towpaths were opened to the public; prior to that access had been by permit only. There is no public right of way along towpaths but since that time BW has encouraged a greater use of the extensive network of towpaths for walking, fishing, cycling in some areas, and for educational purposes for parties of school children.

BW comes under the control of the Department of the Environment and is financed in part by Grant-in-Aid from the Government. Users now contribute substantially to BW through licences, mooring fees etc. and BW's other business activities also contribute to its funding. For full details about the extensive role BW plays in maintaining the waterways environment contact the Customer Services Department at BW's Head Office which is always ready to help.

In addition to the canals and rivers, BW are responsible for numerous structures from bridges, tunnels and aqueducts to canalside cottages, factories and pumping stations. All these are living reminders of a period of British history more than 200 years-old. Many of the locks and reservoirs date from the early days of canal construction and maintaining them in good working order is a continual process.

Wildlife and environmental issues are also high on BW's priorities with over 60 Sites of Special Scientific Interest (SSSIs) in its care. Water quality has improved dramatically over recent years and the variety of plants, fish, birds and animals that can be seen along the waterways increases all the time.

For detailed information about individual waterways contact either Customer Services in Watford or the local Waterways Manager, whose telephone number will be in the local telephone directory, or the regional office. Leaflets are available about each waterway managed or owned by BW with information on mooring sites, sanitary stations, local wildlife and other facilities and amenities.

Head Office Willow Grange, Church Road, Watford, Hertfordshire WD1 3QA ☎ 01923 226422 *Fax* 01923 226081

Regional Offices Scottish Region, Canal House, Applecross Street, Glasgow G4 9SP ☎ 0141 332 6936 *Fax* 0141 331 1688

North West Region, Navigation Road, Northwich, Cheshire CW8 1BH ☎ 01606 74321 *Fax* 01606 871471

North East Region, 1 Dock Street, Leeds LS1 1HH ☎ 0113 281 6800 *Fax* 0113 281 6886

Midlands/South West Region, Peel's Wharf, Lichfield Street, Fazeley, Tamworth, Staffordshire B78 3QZ ☎ 01827 252000 *Fax* 01827 288071

Southern Region, Brindley House, Corner Hall, Lawn Lane, Hemel Hempstead, Hertfordshire HP3 9YT ☎ 01442 235400 *Fax* 01442 234932

In England and Wales, British Waterways Pleasure Boat Licences are valid on Commercial and Cruising Waterways. Some Remainder Waterways may also be used for pleasure cruising but restrictions to draught and headroom may be necessary. Unpowered or small open boats powered by an outboard motor are restricted on Commercial Waterways for safety reasons.

Every boat on BW waterways must have a valid BW licence or certificate which should be clearly visible at all times from outside the boat. Full details of licences and restrictions are available from Customer Services at the BW headquarters at Watford.

Commercial waterways

(Transport Act 1968 and 1983)

The main navigable channels of the following waterways are designated as commercial waterways:

The Aire and Calder Navigation from the tail of River Lock, Leeds, and from the Calder and Hebble Navigation at Wakefield, to its entrance to Goole Docks and to its junction with the River Ouse at Selby.

The Calder and Hebble Navigation from the tail of Greenwood Lock to its junction with the Aire and Calder Navigation at Wakefield.

The Caledonian Canal.

The Crinan Canal.

The Sheffield and South Yorkshire Navigation from the tail of the bottom lock at Tinsley to its junction with the River Trent at Keadby.

The New Junction Canal connecting the Sheffield and South Yorkshire Navigation with the Aire and Calder Navigation.

The Trent Navigation from the tail of Meadow Lane Lock, Nottingham, to Gainsborough Bridge.

The Weaver Navigation and the Weston Canal from Winsford Bridge to the junctions with the Manchester Ship Canal at Marsh Lock and at Delamere Dock.

The River Severn from Stourport to its junction with the Gloucester and Sharpness Canal at Gloucester.

The Gloucester and Sharpness Canal.

The River Lee Navigation from Hertford to the River Thames at Limehouse and to the tail of Bow Locks.

Cruising waterways

The main navigable channels of the following waterways:

The Ashby Canal from its junction with the Coventry Canal to Snarestone.

The Ashton Canal from its junction with the Rochdale Canal at Ducie Street to its junction with the lower Peak Forest Canal at Dukinfield.

The Birmingham Canal from its junction with the Birmingham and Fazeley Canal at Farmer's Bridge and from its junction with the Worcester and Birmingham Canal at Worcester Bar to its junction with the Staffordshire and Worcestershire Canal at Aldersley by way of the Birmingham level as far as the head of Factory Locks, Tipton, and then by way of the Wolverhampton Level, including the branch leading to its junction with the Stourbridge Canal at Black Delph by way of the Netherton Tunnel.

The Birmingham and Fazeley Canal from its junction with the Birmingham Canal at Farmer's Bridge to its junction with the Trent and Mersey Canal at Fradley, including the detached portion of the Coventry Canal between Huddlesford Junction and Fradley Junction and the Digbeth branch.

The Calder and Hebble Navigation from Sowerby Bridge to the tail of Greenwood Lock, including the Huddersfield Broad Canal to Apsley Basin.

The Caldon Branch of the Trent and Mersey Canal (otherwise known as the Caldon Canal) from its junction with the Trent and Mersey Canal at Etruria to its termination at Froghall Wharf.

The Caldon Canal (Leek Branch), the Leek Branch of the Trent and Mersey Canal from Hazelhurst Denford to Wall Grange.

The Chesterfield Canal from the tail of Morse Lock, Worksop, to its junction with the River Trent.

The Coventry Canal from its junction with the Birmingham and Fazeley Canal at Fazeley to Coventry.

The Erewash Canal from Tamworth Road Bridge to its junction with the River Trent.

The Erewash Canal from Langley Mill to Tamworth Road Bridge, Long Eaton.

The Fossdyke Navigation.

The Grand Union Canal (Slough Arm) from its junction with the Grand Union Canal at Cowley Peachey to its termination at Slough Basin.

The Grand Union Canal from its junctions with the Birmingham and Fazeley Canal at Digbeth and Salford to its junctions with the River Thames at Brentford and at Regent's Canal Dock, including the branches to Northampton and Aylesbury and the Hertford Union Canal leading to the River Lee at Old Ford.

The Grand Union Canal from Leicester to Norton Junction, including the branch to Market Harborough and to Welford.

The Kennet and Avon Canal from High Bridge, Reading, to the tail of Tyle Mill Lock, and from the head of Bull's Lock to the tail of Hamstead Lock, and from the tail of Hanham Lock to the tail of the bottom lock at Bath.

The Lancaster Canal from Preston to Tewitfield, including the branch to Glasson Dock.

The Leeds and Liverpool Canal from Old Roan Bridge, Aintree, to Leeds, including the branches to Tarleton and Leigh, Springs and Walton Summit Branches.

The Macclesfield Canal.

The Monmouthshire and Brecon Canal from Crown Bridge, Sebastopol, Cwmbran to a point 450yds west of the bridge known as Gas Works Bridge, Brecon.

The Oxford Canal from its junction with the Grand Union Canal at Braunston to its junction with the Coventry Canal at Hawkesbury and from its junction with the Grand Union Canal from Napton to Oxford, including the branch to the River Thames.

The Peak Forest Canal from the top of Marple Locks to Whaley Bridge.

The Lower Peak Forest Canal from its junction with the Ashton Canal at Dukinfield to the top of Number 1 Lock at Marple.

The Ripon Canal from its junction with the River Ure to the tail of Littlethorpe Lock.

The River Ouse Navigation between the River Ure Navigation and the Humber Estuary with access to the Selby Canal.

The Sheffield and Tinsley Canal between Sheffield Basin and the base of the Tinsley Flight of locks.

The Shropshire Union Canal from its junction with the Manchester Ship Canal at Ellesmere Port to its junction with the Staffordshire and Worcestershire Canal at Autherley, including the branches to the River Dee at Chester, to Llantisilio and to Middlewich.

The River Soar Navigation from its junction with the River Trent to Leicester.

The Staffordshire and Worcestershire Canal.

The River Stort Navigation.

The Stourbridge Canal from its junction with the Birmingham Canal at Black Delph to its junction with the Staffordshire and Worcestershire Canal at Stourton.

The Stratford-on-Avon Canal from its junction with the Worcester and Birmingham Canal at King's Norton to its junction with the Grand Union Canal at Kingswood.

The Trent and Mersey Canal, including the branch to Hall Green.

The Trent Navigation from Shardlow to the tail of Meadow Lane Lock, Nottingham, by way of the Beeston Canal and part of the Nottingham Canal and including the branch to the River Soar and the length of the River Trent from its junction with the Nottingham Canal to Beeston Weir.

The River Ure Navigation from its junction with the Ripon Canal to Swale Nab.

The Witham Navigation from Lincoln to Boston.

The Worcester and Birmingham Canal from Gas Street Basin to its junction with the River Severn at Diglis.

Remainder waterways
On special terms, subject to restricted headroom and depth of water and interrupted navigability.

The Birmingham Canal including:

Old Main Line from Smethwick Junction to Factory Junction, including Spon Lane Locks and Gower Branch.

Titford Canal from junction with Old Main Line to Titford Pools.

Old Loops: Soho, Icknield Port, Oozell Street.

Dudley Tunnel Branch from junction with Old Main Line, Tipton, to junction with Birmingham level at Park Head.

Dudley No 2 Canal from junction with Birmingham level at Windmill End to Hawne Basin.

Wendesbury Oak Canal from junction with Birmingham level at Pudding Green Junction to Swan Village.

Walsall Canal from junction with Wendesbury Oak Canal at Ryders Green to junction with Wyrley and Essington Canal at Birchills Junction.

Tame Valley Canal from junction with Walsall Canal at Doe Bank to junction with Birmingham and Fazeley Canal at Salford Bridge.

Rushall Canal from junction with Tame Valley Canal to junction with Wyrley and Essington Canal at Catshill Junction.

Anglesey Branch.

Cannock Extension.

Wyrley and Essington Canal from Catshill Junction to Chasewater and from Pelsall to Norton.

Bridgwater and Taunton Canal from a point 100 metres below French Weir on the River Tone in Taunton to Newton Lock in Bridgwater.

Calder and Hebble, Dewsbury Arm and Halifax Arm.

Chesterfield Canal from the tail of Morse Lock, Worksop to Norwood Tunnel.

Grand Union Canal, Wendover Branch from Bulbourne Junction to limit of navigation near Tringford Pumping Station.

Grantham Canal.

Kennet and Avon Canal, those remainder lengths on which navigation is permitted by the Board from time to time.

Lancaster Canal from Tewitfield to Stainton.

Leeds and Liverpool Canal from Old Roan Bridge, Aintree, to Stanley Docks.

Peak Forest Canal, Buxworth Arm.

Pocklington Canal between Cottingwith Lock at the junction of the River Derwent to Melbourne.

Shropshire Union Canal, Montgomery Branch: those lengths on which the Board shall by notice permit navigation from time to time.

Stourbridge Canal, Branch to The Fens.

Stratford Canal from Kingswood Junction to its junction with the River Avon at Bancroft Basin.

Scotland

Pleasure Boat Licences are not valid in Scotland and different charges are made for the use of Scottish Waterways. Full information is available from the following offices:

Caledonian Canal Canal Office, Seaport Marina, Muirtown Wharf, Inverness IV3 5LS ☎ 01463 233140

Crinan Canal Canal House, Pier Square, Ardrishaig, Argyll PA30 8DZ ☎ 01546 603210/603797

Lowland Canals Canal House, Applecross Street, Glasgow G4 9SP ☎ 0141 332 6936

The above list is taken from a British Waterways document and corrected to October 1997. Local notices indicating actual limits, temporary stoppages or hazards which will vary according to circumstances should always be observed. Detailed and up-to-date information can always be obtained from British Waterways local offices.

Canalphone

Up-to-date information on waterway stoppages and engineering work is available on a 24-hour recorded message on the following telephone numbers:

North ☎ 01923 201401 for Scotland, North West, North East and Midlands/South West regions

South ☎ 01923 201402 for Midlands/South West and Southern regions

Maintenance stoppages

Stoppages for engineering work have to be carried out regularly if a 200-year-old system is to be kept in a safe and useable condition. The local office in the area you wish to travel will be able to give warnings of programmed stoppages. Waterway magazines also list stoppages and clubs and societies regularly receive a stoppage list from British Waterways. For emergency stoppages use the Canalphone telephone number.

Environment Agency

The Environment Agency was formed in April 1996 taking in the National Rivers Authority and assuming its responsibilities for water quality and in certain cases navigation rights. The Agency is responsible for improving facilities for visiting boat owners and is continuing the NRA's programme of providing new facilities on many rivers.

Head Office Rivers House, Waterside Drive, Aztec West, Almondsbury, Bristol BS12 4UD ☎ 01454 624400 *Fax* 01454 624409

Eastbury House, 30–34 Albert Embankment, London SE1 7TL ☎ 0171 820 0101 *Fax* 0171 820 1603

Regional Offices North East Region, Rivers House, 21 Park Square South, Leeds LS1 2QG ☎ 0113 244 0191 *Fax* 0113 246 1889

Anglian Region, Kingfisher House, Goldhay Way, Orton Goldhay, Peterborough PE2 5ZR ☎ 01733 37181 *Fax* 01733 231840

Thames Region, Kings Meadow House, Kings Meadow Road, Reading RG1 8DQ ☎ 0118 953 5000 *Fax* 0118 950 0388

Southern Region, Guildbourne House, Chatsworth Road, Worthing BN11 1LD ☎ 01903 820692 *Fax* 01903 821832

South West Region, Manley House, Kestrel Way, Exeter EX2 7LQ ☎ 01392 444000 *Fax* 01392 444238

Midlands Region, Sapphire East, 550 Streetsbrook Road, Solihull B91 1QT ☎ 0121 711 2324 *Fax* 0121 711 5824

Welsh Region, Rivers House/Plas-yr-Afon, St Mellons Business Park, St Mellons, Cardiff CF3 0LT ☎ 01222 770088 *Fax* 01222 798555

North West Region, Richard Fairclough House, Knutsford Road, Warrington WA4 1HG ☎ 01925 653999 *Fax* 01925 415961

A number of rivers, as will be noted from the text, are controlled by British Waterways as navigation authority. In such cases, the local office of the Environment Agency will have drainage, sewage and other functions under its control, but not navigation.

The Broads Authority

The Broads Authority is the Statutory Navigation Authority for its own 'Navigation Area' as defined in the Norfolk and Suffolk Broads Act 1988.

Head Office Thomas Harvey House, 18 Colegate, Norwich, Norfolk NR3 1BQ ☎ 01603 610734 *Fax* 01603 765710

The authority administers the area to conserve and enhance the natural beauty of the Broads, promote their enjoyment and protect the interests of navigation. It publishes and enforces bye-laws covering all aspects of boat use in the area.

Regulations on the inland waterways

The International Regulations for Preventing Collisions at Sea also apply to Britain's inland waterways, modified by local byelaws and regulations as appropriate. Specific regulations for any waterway will be available from the local office of the navigation authority for that waterway. The exception to this general rule is the Norfolk and Suffolk Broads, where the Broads Authority's Navigation Byelaws 1995 replace the International Rules for vessels navigating in the Broads Authority's navigation area.

On all waterways within the jurisdiction of British Waterways, a Boat Safety Certificate will be a requirement for all boats applying for a licence after 1 January 1998. The Environment Agency is phasing in the requirement for a certificate, with boats built before 1980 having to comply by 1 January 1998, boats built between 1981 and 1990 by 1 January 1999 and boats built after 1991 by 1 January 2000. This scheme is run jointly by British Waterways and the Environment Agency and boats will be required to undergo a test every four years. Many of the smaller navigation authorities are also implementing the Boat Safety Scheme. If in doubt, you should contact the relevant authority, which you will find named in each section of this book that refers to a particular waterway.

The Broads Authority has not joined the Boat Safety Scheme operated by British Waterways and the Environment Agency, but is evolving a Boat Safety Scheme of its own. This will be very similar to the other scheme but with certain exemptions or relaxations appropriate to the Broads navigation. The Broads Boat Safety Scheme is likely to apply on a voluntary basis for two years from 1 April 1998. It will then become compulsory, but on the basis of self-certification by the boat-owner for at least five years from 1 April 2000.

Boats visiting British Waterways or Environment Agency canals and rivers will be allowed access under any existing safety arrangements of their home waters. A visitor is allowed on inland waterways for a maximum of one month – 28 days in the case of the Broads – after which time they are required to apply for an annual licence, which would only be granted if the boat conformed to the Boat Safety Scheme for its year of manufacture. When a visiting boat reaches its first lock on an Environment Agency waterway, the owner will be asked to complete a declaration covering the safety of the boat. Any boat intending to transfer permanently to a British Waterways or Environment Agency location would, of course, have to comply with the Boat Safety Scheme in the usual way.

Insurance to cover third-party liability is required for boats within British Waterways jurisdiction. At present this is not a legal requirement on Environment Agency waterways, but third party insurance is strongly recommended for all boats. Responsible boat-owners on any waterway should take out third-party cover, at the very minimum, for their own protection.

One legal requirement most likely to present a problem for boats from coastal moorings visiting inland waterways is that for a sewage holding tank to be installed. No effluent may be discharged into the Broads, Environment Agency rivers or British Waterway canals and rivers. Pump-out stations and sanitary stations are increasingly widely provided on inland waterways for the disposal of sewage from boats. Coastal cruising boats passing through inland waterways will not be allowed to operate their sea toilets and must use, instead, the facilities provided ashore.

Cruising

Exploring Britain by water

Seen from the waterways Britain offers a different face to the traveller. Not only can you look at familiar places from an unfamiliar angle but the gentle pace of travel allows you to consider, contemplate and appreciate what you see which is rarely possible by car or even on a train. Nor is it necessary to be wealthy or a great navigator as the canals and rivers of Britain can be explored by boat, canoe, bicycle, on foot or by 'floating hotel'.

Many companies offer self-drive boat hire for short or long periods. You can book direct or through agencies which have companies all over the country and their brochures give you a good idea of the enormous scope of canal holidays. Four of the principal agencies are listed below followed by individual self-drive hire companies grouped by area of the country and canal. For initial boating forays on the canals, hiring a boat for the day is a good idea and companies offering this service are included in

Many pubs around the country had links with canals, The Navigation at Gilwern is alongside the Monmouthshire and Brecon Canal. *Roy Westlake*

Above The Anderton Boat Lift, now undergoing a full restoration.
Jane Cumberlidge

Opposite The lock flight at Gauxholme on the Rochdale Canal.
Robin Smithett

Below Approaching the Astwood locks, on the Worcester and Birmingham
Canal, the working pair *Roach* and *Bidford* are still busy on Christmas Eve.
Sian Barron

Woodwalton Fen, in the Middle Level, is one of the few remaining fragments of undrained fenland. *Sian Barron*

Below Marple Aqueduct on the Lower Peak Forest Canal. *Robin Smithett*

The Almond Aqueduct near Ratho on the Edinburgh Union Canal. *Guthrie Hutton*

the list. The periods of hire offered are denoted by D for daily or hourly hire, W for hire by the week or S/B for short breaks and weekends. For those who would like a little more luxury and less work there is a list of hotel boat companies at the end.

Safety on the water is vitally important. All hire companies provide instruction in boat handling at the time you take over your boat but this is inevitably quite limited. For details of courses in boat handling contact the Royal Yachting Association, RYA House, Romsey Road, Eastleigh, Hampshire SO50 9YA ☎ 01703 627400 *Fax* 01703 629924. Always ensure young children and non-swimmers wear buoyancy aids while on the boat and near the water's edge.

The Association of Pleasure Craft Operators (APCO) has members with all types of hire boat as well as passenger boats, restaurant and party boats, boat surveyors, chandlers, engineers, marina owners and many other activities associated with inland waterways. A booklet listing members' services and their names and addresses can be obtained from The Administrator, APCO, Parkland House, Audley Avenue, Newport, Shropshire TF10 7AT.

HOLIDAY HIRE AGENCIES

Anglo–Welsh Group plc, 5 Pritchard Street, Bristol BS2 8RH ☎ 0117 924 1200 *Fax* 0117 924 0202

Blakes Holidays Ltd, Wroxham, Norwich, Norfolk NR12 8DH ☎ 01603 782911(bookings), 01603 782141 (administration) *Fax* 01603 782871

Drifters, Drifters Leisure Ltd, PO Box 232, Worcester WR1 1BR ☎ 0345 626252

Hoseasons Holidays Ltd, Sunway House, Lowestoft, Suffolk NR32 2LW ☎ 01502 501010 (bookings), 01502 500505 (administration) *Fax* 01502 586781

Self-drive boat hire
NORTH OF ENGLAND
Bridgewater Canal
Brinks Boats, Worsley Dry Dock, Worsley Green, Worsley, Manchester M28 4WN ☎ 0161 728 1184 *W, S/B*

Claymoore Navigation, The Wharf, Preston Brook, Warrington, Cheshire WA4 4BA ☎ 01928 717273 *Fax* 01928 718888 *D, W*

Egerton Narrowboats, Arches Boatyard, Potato Wharf, Liverpool Road, Manchester M3 4NB ☎ 0161 833 9878 *D*

Calder and Hebble Navigation
Shire Cruisers, The Wharf, Sowerby Bridge, West Yorkshire HX6 2AG ☎ 01422 832712 *Fax* 01422 839565 (also Rochdale Canal) *W*

Lancaster Canal
Adventure Cruisers, The Boathouse, Canal Wharf, Catforth, Preston, Lancs PR4 0HE ☎ 01772 690232 *D*

Arlen Hire Boats, Ashton Basin, Tulketh Brow, Preston, Lancs PR2 2SD ☎ 01772 769183 *D, W*

Marina Park, Canal Wharf, Galgate, Lancashire LA2 0LQ ☎ 01524 751368 *D, W*

Nu-Way Acorn, Lundsfield, Carnforth, Lancashire LA5 9ND ☎ 01524 734457 *D, W, S/B*

Preston Hire Cruisers, Moons Bridge Wharf, Hollowforth Lane, Woodplumpton, Near Preston Lancashire PR4 0BD ☎ 01772 690627 *W, S/B*

Leeds and Liverpool Canal
Banks Hire Boats, 17 Ingleton Drive, Easingwold, York YO6 3JQ ☎ 01347 821772 *W* (also Aire and Calder Navigation and Selby Canal)

L & L Cruisers, Rawlinson Lane, Heath Charnock, Chorley, Lancashire PR7 4DE ☎ 01257 480825 *D, W*

Pennine Marine Ltd, The Boat Shop, 19 Coach Street, Skipton, Yorkshire BD23 1LH ☎ 01756 795478 *Fax* 01756 700213 *D, W, S/B*

Rodley Boat Centre, Canal Wharf, Canal Road, Rodley, Leeds LS13 1LP ☎/*Fax* 0113 257 6132 *D, W*

Silsden Boats, Canal Wharf, Silsden, Keighley, West Yorkshire BD20 0DE ☎/*Fax* 01535 653675 *W*

Snaygill Boats of Skipton, Skipton Road, Bradley, Skipton, Yorkshire BD20 9HA ☎ 01756 795150 *W*

River Ouse
York Marine Services, Kings Staith, York YO2 1SB ☎ 01904 704442 *D, W*

CENTRAL ENGLAND
Various Bases
Alvechurch Boat Centres, Scarfield Wharf, Alvechurch, Nr Birmingham B48 7SQ ☎ 0121 445 2909 *W, S/B*

Black Prince Holidays, Stoke Prior, Bromsgrove, Worcestershire B60 4LA ☎ 01527 575115 *Fax* 01527 575116 *W, S/B*

Viking Afloat Ltd, Lowesmoor Wharf, Lowesmoor, Worcester WR1 2RS ☎ 01905 610660 *Fax* 01905 616715 *W, S/B*

Ashby Canal
Ashby Boat Company, Canal Wharf, Stoke Golding, Nuneaton, Warwickshire CV13 6EY ☎ 01455 212671 *D, W*

River Avon
Bidford Boats, Riverside House, Bidford-on-Avon, Warwickshire B50 4BB ☎ 01789 773205 *W, S/B*

Evesham Marina Ltd, Kings Road, Evesham, Worcestershire WR11 5BU ☎ 01386 48906 *Fax* 01386 442827 *W*

Stratford Marina Ltd, The Boatyard, Clopton Bridge, Stratford-upon-Avon CV37 6YY ☎ 01789 269669 *Fax* 01789 204483 *W, S/B*

Telstar Cruisers Ltd, Riverside Walk, Back of Avon, Tewkesbury, Gloucestershire GL20 5UR ☎ 01684 294088 *D, W, S/B*

Birmingham Canal Navigations
Sherbourne Wharf, Sherbourne Street, Birmingham, B16 8DE ☎ 0121 455 6163 *D*

Coventry Canal
Club Line Cruisers, Swan Lane Wharf, Stoke Heath, Coventry CV2 4QN ☎ 01203 258864 *W, S/B*

Streethay Wharf, Streethay, Lichfield, Staffordshire WS13 8RJ ☎/*Fax* 01543 414808 *D*

Valley Cruises, Slacks Avenue, Atherstone, Warwickshire CV9 2AR ☎/*Fax* 01827 712602 *W, S/B*

Droitwich Canal
William and Ann Walton, Lock Cottage, Ladywood, Nr Worcester WR9 0AJ ☎ 01905 458352 *D*

Grand Union Canal
Blisworth Tunnel Boats, Unit 2C, Mill Wharf, Gayton Road, Blisworth, Northamptonshire NN7 3BN ☎ 01604 858868 *D, W*

Braunston Boats (Hire) Ltd, Bottom Lock, Braunston,
Northamptonshire NN11 7HL ☎ 01788 891079
Fax 01788 891934 (and Oxford Canal) *W*

Bridgewater Boats, Castle Wharf, Berkhampstead,
Hertfordshire HP4 2EB ☎ 01442 863615 *Fax* 01442
863619 *W*

Calcutt Boats, Stockton, Rugby, Warwickshire CV23
8HX ☎ 01926 813757 *W, S/B*

Canalboat Holidays Ltd, The Boatyard, High Street,
Weedon, Northamptonshire NN7 4QD ☎ 01327
340739 *W*

Foxton Boat Services, Bottom Lock, Foxton, Nr Market
Harborough, Leicestershire LE16 7RA ☎ 0116 279
2285 *Fax* 0116 279 3847 *D, W, S/B*

Grebe Canal Cruises, Pitstone Wharf, Pitstone,
Nr Leighton Buzzard, Bedfordshire LU7 9AD
☎ 01296 661920 *D, W*

Ian Goode Narrowboats, Debdale Wharfe, Kibworth,
Market Harborough LE8 0QD ☎ 0116 279 3034
D, W

Kate Boats Warwick, The Boatyard, Nelson Lane,
Warwick CV34 5JB ☎ 01926 492968 *W*

Millar Marine, Stowe Hill Wharf, Watling St, Weedon,
Northamptonshire NN7 4RZ ☎ 01327 349188 *D, W*

North Kilworth Narrowboats, Kilworth Marina, North
Kilworth, Lutterworth, Leicestershire LE17 6JB
☎ 01858 880484 *D, W*

Saisons, Tilbury House, Tilbury Road, East Haddon,
Northamptonshire NN6 8BX ☎ 01604 770424 *W*

Stoke Bruerne Boat Co, adjacent to Canal Museum,
Stoke Bruerne, Nr Towcester, Northamptonshire
NN12 7SF ☎/*Fax* 01604 862107 *D*

Union Canal Carriers Ltd, The Pump House, Bottom
Lock, Braunston, Daventry, Northamptonshire NN11
7HJ ☎ 01788 890784 *Fax* 01788 891950 *W*

Weltonfield Narrowboats Ltd, Welton Hythe, Daventry,
Northamptonshire NN11 5LG ☎ 01327 842282
Fax 01327 843754 *W*

The Wyvern Shipping Co Ltd, Rothschild Road,
Linslade, Leighton Buzzard, Bedfordshire LU7 7TF
☎ 01525 372355 *Fax* 01525 852308 *W*

River Great Ouse

Annesdale Marina, Riverside Boat Yard, Annesdale
Dock, Ely, Cambridgeshire CB7 4BN ☎ 01353
665420 *D, W* (and Middle Level)

Frojo Fleet, 4 Spruce Road, Clackclose Park, Downham
Market, Norfolk PE38 9PJ ☎ 01366 383618 *D, W*

Huntingdon Marine, Bridge Boatyard, Bridge Place,
Godmanchester, Cambridgeshire. PE18 8AD
☎ 01480 413517 *D*

Purvis Marine, Hartford Road, Huntingdon,
Cambridgeshire PE18 6RP ☎ 01480 453628 *D*

Macclesfield Canal

Heritage Narrowboats, The Marina, Kent Green,
Scholar Green, Kidsgrove, Cheshire ST7 3JZ
☎ 01782 785700 *D, W*

Peak Forest Cruisers, The Wharf, Buxton Road,
Macclesfield, Cheshire SK10 1LZ ☎ 01625 424172
W

Swettenham Wharf, Brook Street, Macclesfield,
Cheshire SK11 7AW ☎ 01625 420042 *D*

Middle Level Navigations

Fox Boats, 10 Marina Drive, March, Cambridgeshire
PE15 0AU ☎ 01354 652770 *Fax* 01354 650369 *W*

Norfolk Broads

There are numerous companies operating in the Broads
and a brochure is available from the Norwich Tourist
Information Centre ☎ 01603 666071

Oxford Canal

Clifton Cruisers, Vicarage Hill, Clifton-on-Dunsmore,
Nr Rugby, Warwickshire CV23 0DG ☎ 01788
543570 *W, S/B*

College Cruisers, Combe Road Wharf, Oxford OX10
0NB ☎ 01865 54343 *D, W*

Napton Narrowboats, Napton Marina, Stockton, Rugby,
Warwickshire CV23 8HX ☎ 01926 813644 *W, S/B*

Oxfordshire Narrowboats Ltd, Canal Wharf, Station
Road, Lower Heyford, Bicester Oxfordshire OX6 3PD
☎ 01869 340348 *W, S/B*

Rose Narrowboats, Fosse Way, Stretton-under-Fosse,
Nr Rugby, Warwickshire CV23 0PU ☎ 01788
832449 *Fax* 01788 832545 *D, W*

South Shore Narrowboats, Aynho Wharf, Station Road,
Aynho, Banbury, Oxfordshire OX17 3BP ☎ 01869
338483 *D*

Sovereign Narrowboats, Sovereign Wharf, Compton
Road, Banbury, Oxfordshire OX16 8PP ☎/*Fax* 01295
275657 *W*

Willow Wren Cruising Holidays, Rugby Wharf, Consul
Road, Rugby, Warkwickshire CV21 1PB ☎ 01788
562183 *Fax* 01788 540540 *W, S/B*

Peak Forest Canal

Furness Vale Marina, The Moorings, Station Road,
Furness Vale, Stockport, Cheshire SK12 7QA
☎ 01663 742971 *D, S/B*

R.D. Leisure Ltd, New Mills Wharf, Hibbert Street,
New Mills, Stockport, Cheshire SK12 3JJ ☎ 01663
745000 *Fax* 01663 741310 *D, W, S/B*

Top Lock Marine, 5 Lime Kiln Lane, Marple,
Stockport, Cheshire SK6 6BX ☎ 0161 427 5712
Fax 0161 449 7062 *D* (also Macclesfield Canal)

River Severn

Gullivers Cruisers, Upton Marina, Upton-on-Severn,
Worcestershire WR8 0PB ☎ /*Fax* 01684 593400
W, S/B

Handy Boat Hire, Upton Marina, Upton-on-Severn,
Worcestershire WR8 0PB ☎ 01684 593594
D, W, S/B

Pitchcroft Boating Station, Waterworks Road, Worcester
WR1 3EZ ☎ 01905 27949 *D*

Shropshire Union Canal

Chas Hardern and Co, Beeston Castle Wharf, Beeston,
Tarporley, Cheshire CW6 9NH ☎/*Fax* 01829 732595
W

Countrywide Cruisers (Brewood) Ltd, The Wharf, Off
Kiddemore Green Road, Brewood, Staffordshire ST19
9BG ☎ 01902 850166 *Fax* 01902 851662 *W, S/B*

Simolda, Basin End, Nantwich, Cheshire CW5 8LA
☎ 01270 624075 *D, W, S/B*

Water Travel Ltd, Autherley Junction, Oxley Moor
Road, Wolverhampton WV9 5HW ☎ 01902 782371
Fax 01902 787374 *W*

River Soar

Kegworth Marine, Kingston Lane, Kegworth, Near
Derby DE74 2FS ☎ 01509 672300 *D*

Leisure Hire, Proctors Park, Bridge Street, Barrow-
upon-Soar, Loughborough, Leicestershire LE12 7NF
☎ 01509 415001 *D*

Sileby Mill Boatyard, Mill Lane, Sileby, Loughborough,
Leicestershire LE12 7NF ☎ 01509 813583
Fax 01509 813404 *D, W*

Staffordshire and Worcestershire
Gailey Marine Ltd, The Wharf, Watling Street, Stafford, Staffordshire ST19 5PR ☎ 01902 790612 *Fax* 01902 791446 *W, S/B*

Severn Valley Cruisers Ltd, Boat Shop, Mart Lane, Stourport-on-Severn, Worcestershire DY13 9ER ☎ 01299 871165 *Fax* 01299 827211 *D, W* (also River Severn)

Stroudwater Cruisers, Engine Lane, Stourport-on-Severn, Worcestershire DY13 9EP ☎ 01299 877222 *W, S/B* (also River Severn)

Teddesley Boat Company, Park Gate Lock, Teddesley Road, Penkridge, Stafford ST19 5RH ☎ 01785 714692 *Fax* 01785 714894 *W, S/B*

Stratford-on-Avon Canal
Swallow Cruisers, Wharf Lane, Hockley Heath, Warwickshire B94 5NR ☎/*Fax* 01564 783442 *D*

Trent and Mersey Canal
Canal Cruising Co Ltd, Crown Street, Stone, Staffordshire ST15 8QN ☎ 01785 813982 *Fax* 01785 819041 *W, S/B*

Jannel Cruisers Ltd, Shobnall Marina, Shobnall Road, Burton-on-Trent, Staffordshire DE14 2AU ☎ 01283 542718 *Fax* 01283 545369 *W*

Midland Canal Centre, Stenson Marina, Stenson, Derby DE73 1HL ☎ 01283 701933 *Fax* 01283 702818 *D, W, S/B*

Middlewich Narrowboats, Canal Terrace, Middlewich, Cheshire CW10 9BD ☎ 01606 832460 *Fax* 01606 737912 *W* (also Shropshire Union Canal)

Staffordshire Narrowboats Ltd, The Wharf, Newcastle Road, Stone, Staffordshire ST15 8JW ☎ 01785 816871 *Fax* 01923 773891 *W, S/B*

Stenson Holiday Hire, Stenson Marina, Stenson, Derby DE73 1HL ☎ 01283 701933 *Fax* 01283 702818 *D, W, S/B*

Swan Line Cruisers, Fradely Junction, Alrewas, Burton-on-Trent, Staffordshire DE13 7DN ☎/*Fax* 01283 790332 *W, S/B*

River Witham
Adventure Afloat, The Sluice, Boston Lock, Lincolnshire PE22 9JF ☎ 01205 871439 *Fax* 01205 870335 *D*

Worcester and Birmingham Canal
Anglo Welsh Group plc, Alvechurch Boat Centres, Black Prince Holidays and Viking Afloat all operate here.

SOUTH OF ENGLAND
Basingstoke Canal
Daydream, Basingstoke Canal Centre, Mychett, Surrey GU16 6DD ☎ 01252 370073 *D*

Galleon Marine, Colt Hill, Old London Road, Odiham, Hampshire RG29 1AL ☎ 01256 703691 *D, W, S/B*

Chelmer and Blackwater Canal
Blackwater Boats, Bumblebee Cottage, Boxted Road, Colchester, Essex CO4 5HF ☎ 01206 853282 *D, W, S/B*

Kennet and Avon Canal
Bath and Dundas Canal Co, Brass Knocker Bottom, Monkton Combe, Bath BA2 7JD ☎ 01225 722292 *D*

Kennet Cruises, Burghfield, Nr Reading, Berkshire RG30 3SR ☎ 0118 987 1115 *Fax* 0118 987 5461 *D, W, S/B*

Norton Narrow Boats, Sydney Wharf, Bathwick Hill Bath BA2 4EL ☎ 01225 447276 *W*

Reading Marine Company, Aldermaston Wharf, Padworth, Reading, Berkshire RG7 4JS ☎ 0118 971 3666 *Fax* 0118 971 4271 *W, S/B*

Sally Boats, Bradford on Avon Marina, Trowbridge Road, Bradford-on-Avon BA15 1UD ☎ 01225 864923 *W, S/B*

Tranquil Boats, Lock House, Semington, Trowbridge, Wiltshire BA14 6JT ☎ 01380 870654 *D*

Wessex Narrowboats, Wessex Wharf, Hilperton Marina, Trowbridge, Wiltshire BA14 8RS ☎ 01225 769847 *Fax* 01225 769847 *W, S/B*

White Horse Boats, Bridge Inn, Horton Bridge, Nr Devizes, Wiltshire SN10 5AQ ☎/*Fax* 01380 728504 *D, W, S/B*

River Lee
Lee Valley Boat Centre, Old Nazeing Road, Broxbourne, Hertfordshire EN10 7AX ☎ 01992 462085 *D, W, S/B*

River Medway
Tovil Bridge Boatyard, Tovil Bridge, Maidstone, Kent ME15 6RU ☎ 01622 686341 *D, W, S/B*

River Thames
Bensons Pleasure Craft, Benson, Near Wallingford, Oxfordshire OX10 6SJ ☎ 01491 838304 *D, W*

Bray Boats, Lockbridge Boathouse, Ray Mead Road, Maidenhead, Berkshire SL6 8NJ ☎/*Fax* 01628 37880 *D*

Bridge Boats Ltd, Frys Island, De Montford Road, Reading RG1 5DG ☎ 0118 959 0346 *W, S/B*

Caversham Boat Services, The Boat House, Frys Island, Reading, Berkshire RG1 8DG ☎/*Fax* 0118 957 4323 *D, W*

Chertsey Meads Marine, The Meads, Chertsey, Surrey KT16 8LN ☎/*Fax* 01932 564699 *D, W*

D.B.H. Marine, Anglers Wharf, Manor Road, Walton, Surrey KT12 2PF ☎ 01932 228019 *D, S/B*

Geo. Wilson and Sons, Thames Street, Sunbury, Surrey TW16 6AQ ☎ 01932 782067 *D*

Harris Boatbuilders, Laleham Reach, Chertsey, Surrey KT16 8RP ☎ 01932 563111 *D*

King Craft, The Bridge, Abingdon, Oxfordshire OX14 3HX ☎/*Fax* 01235 521125 *D*

Kris Cruisers, The Waterfront, Datchet, Slough, Berkshire SL3 9BU ☎ 01753 543930 *Fax* 01753 584866 *D, W*

Nicholes Boatyard, Yard Mead, Windsor Road, Egham, Staines, Surrey TW20 0AA ☎ 01784 432342 *Fax* 01784 472770 *D*

R.J. Turk and Son, by Hampton Court Palace ☎ 0181 977 1567 *D*

Riverside Lechlade, Park End Wharf, Lechlade, Near Swindon, Wiltshire GL7 3AQ ☎ 01367 252229 *D*

Swancraft, George and Dragon Boathouse, Henley Road, Wargrave, Berkshire RG10 8HY ☎ 0118 940 2577 *D*

River Wey
Francombe Boat House, Catteshall Lock, Godalming, Surrey GU7 1NH ☎ 01483 421306 *D, S/B*

WALES
Llangollen Canal
Chirk Marina, Whitehouses, Wrexham, Clwyd L14 5AD ☎/*Fax* 01691 774558 *D, W*

English County Cruises, Wrenbury Mill, Wrenbury, Nantwich, Cheshire CW5 8HG ☎ 01270 780544 *Fax* 01270 780146 *W, S/B*

Maestermyn Marine, Ellesmere Road, Whittington, Oswestry, Shropshire SY11 4NU ☎/*Fax* 01691 662424 *W, S/B*

Trevor Wharf Services, Canal Wharf, Trevor,
   Llangollen, Clwyd LL20 7TY ☎ 01978 821749
   Fax 01978 824605 *D, W*
Viking Afloat, Wrexham Road, Whitchurch, Shropshire
   SY13 3AA ☎ 01905 28667 *W, S/B*

Monmouthshire and Brecon Canal
Beacon Park Boats, The Boathouse, Church Lane,
   Llanfoist, Abergavenny, Monmouthshire NP7 9NG
   ☎ 01873 858277 *W, S/B*
Brecon Boats, Travellers Rest, Talybont-on-Usk,
   Brecon, Powys LD3 7YP ☎ 01874 676401 *D*
Cambrian Cruisers, Ty Newydd, Pencelli, Brecon,
   Powys LD3 7LJ ☎/*Fax* 01874 665315 *D, W, S/B*
Castle Narrowboats, Church Road Wharf, Gilwern,
   Abergavenny, Monmouthshire NP7 0EP
   ☎/*Fax* 01873 830001 *W*
Country Craft Narrowboat Holidays, Cwm Crawnon
   Warehouse, Llangynidr, Crickhowell, Powys NP8 1LS
   ☎ 01874 730850 *W, S/B*
Red Line Boats, Goytre Wharf, Llanover, Abergavenny,
   Monmouthshire NP7 9EW ☎ 01873 880516
   Fax 01873 880522 *D, W*
Road House Narrowboats, 50 Main Road, Gilwern,
   Abergavenny, Monmouthshire NP7 0AS ☎ 01873
   830240 *W*

Montgomery Canal
Maesbury Wharf Cruisers, Maesbury Marsh, Maesbury,
   Nr Oswestry, Shropshire SY10 8JB ☎ 01691 670826
   or 670849 *D*
Montgomery Canal Cruisers, Severn Street Wharf,
   Welshpool, Powys SY21 9PQ ☎ 01938 553271
   D, S/B

SCOTLAND
Caledonian Canal
Caley Cruisers, Canal Road, Muirtown, Inverness IV3
   6NF ☎ 01463 236328 *Fax* 01463 714879 *W*
Loch Ness Boat Charter, Dochgarroch, Inverness IV3
   6JY ☎ 01463 861303 *Fax* 01463 861353 *W*
West Highland Sailing, Laggan Locks, Spean Bridge,
   Fort William PH34 4EB ☎/*Fax* 01809 501234
   W, S/B

HOTEL BOATS
Bath Hotel Boat Company, 2 Sydney Wharf, Bath, Avon
   BA2 4EF ☎/*Fax* 01225 448846
Country Hotel Narrowboats, 19 Church Street,
   Bingham, Nottinghamshire NG13 8AL ☎/*Fax* 01949
   83715
English Waterway Cruises, Wharf Cottage, 102 Clinton
   Road, Shirley, Solihull B90 4RQ ☎ 0121 745 8180 or
   0831 103522
Grand Union Canal Cruising Company, Canal Cottage,
   105, Simpson Road, Simpson Village, Milton Keynes,
   Buckinghamshire MK6 3AN ☎ 01908 667657
Heart of England Hotel Narrowboats, Basingstoke Canal
   Centre, Mytchett Place Road, Mytchett, Surrey GU16
   6DD ☎ 0831 566373 *Fax* 01252 371758
Highland Mini-Cruises, Muirtown Top Lock,
   Caledonian Canal, Canal Road, Inverness IV3 6NF
   ☎ 01463 711913
Highland Steamboat Holidays, The Change House,
   Crinan Ferry, Lochgilphead, Argyll PA31 8QH
   ☎ 01546 510232
Hotel Boat Voyages, 44 Riplingham Road, Kirkella, Hull
   HU10 7TD ☎/*Fax* 01482 653757
Inland Cruising Company Ltd, Swinford, Leicestershire
   LE17 6AY ☎ 01788 860372

Inland Waterway Holiday Cruises, Greenham Lock
   Cottage, London Road, Newbury, Berkshire RG14
   5SN ☎ 0831 110811 *Fax* 01635 42884
Narrowboat Hotel Co, Cross Lane House, Astley
   Abbots, Bridgnorth, Shropshire WV16 4SJ
   ☎ (Mobile) 0836 600029 *Fax* 01746 768667
Rushbrooke Narrow Boats, 10 Battle Court, Kineton,
   Warwickshire CV35 0LX ☎ 0836 636167 Mobile
   0836 636167
Willow Wren Cruising Holidays, Rugby Wharf, Consul
   Road, Rugby, Warwickshire CV21 1NR ☎ 01788
   569153 *Fax* 01788 540540 Mobile 0831 530412

Planning your route

For holiday planning purposes, there are now
numerous publications which give very detailed
information about particular waterways and there is
a comprehensive bibliography at the back of this
book. When hiring craft for a waterways holiday, the
hire company will usually provide information
which will help you to plan your route. But try not
to be over ambitious as it will spoil the holiday if you
find you have to push on all the time during the
second half if you are to get back to the hire base on
time. In some cases, where a company has bases at
different locations, it may be possible to arrange a
one-way cruise, for example, if you wanted to cross
the Pennines on the Leeds and Liverpool canal or
travel along the Kennet and Avon.

   To work out practical routes, it is best to use lock-
miles. This is a handy way of including the time
needed to pass through locks on your route as
working a lock can be roughly equated to travelling
a mile along the canal. With more crew, who can
prepare locks ahead and close them behind, it is
possible to increase daily mileage but why rush
when there is so much to see along the way. An
average of 4 lock-mph is a reasonable guide so a
stretch of 10 miles with 14 locks would be a good
day's cruising, 6 hours underway, for those who
don't want to start at the crack of dawn and like to
allow time to visit places en route.

   The enormous amount of restoration work
completed during the past 15 years has opened up
many more 'rings' so it is now possible to plan a
circular route for your cruise, particularly in the
Midlands area. Pearson's Guides cover groups of
canals and are a great help in planning circular
routes. Lockmaster maps cover areas and canal rings
and are also very useful when working out where
you want to start and finish and they give a shape to
your route. Other good planners, for both
experienced and novice crews, are the Waterway's
World Guides and Nicholson's Guides. A very
useful and practical book for getting afloat is *Canal
and River Cruising* by Sheila Davenport published by
the Inland Waterways Association.

   With nearly 3,000 miles of navigable waterways to
choose from where do you start? Here are just a few
ideas for cruising routes with an approximate
mileage and the number of locks.

SHORT CRUISES

See London by boat Few people realise how many miles of waterway there are in London in addition to the Thames. From a narrow boat on the canals you can spend a few days seeing the capital from a completely different perspective.

The Bridgewater Canal from Runcorn to Wigan Pier. 45 miles (72km) each way with three locks. Discover the truth about Wigan Pier and float across the Barton Swing Aqueduct. If you're very lucky you may see a ship coming up the Manchester Ship Canal and watch the aqueduct being opened.

Into the heart of Kent up the Medway 42 miles (67km) with ten locks. From Sheerness, on the River Thames, up to Tonbridge the historic River Medway winds through some of the loveliest countryside but it is only a short distance from London. One of the first people to write about his experiences on inland waterways, Frederic Doerflinger, called it 'The Little Med' because 'it offers such a variety of pleasures'.

ONE WEEK CRUISES

The Llangollen Canal 46 miles (74km) with 21 locks. Rightly famous for the Pontcysyllte Aqueduct it also has the Chirk Aqueduct and the Chirk Tunnel. This is a good introduction to the joys of canal travel and very soon it should be possible to explore the Montgomery Canal as well.

The Cheshire Ring 97 miles (155km) with 92 locks. This includes the Marple Aqueduct, passes the Anderton Boat Lift and takes you through Manchester. The eastern side along the Peak Forest Canal offers a possible diversion up to Whaley Bridge, waterway cruisers soon fall under the spell of exploring branch canals.

The Monmouthshire and Brecon Canal 35 miles (56km) with six locks. It is hard to imagine a more peaceful place to spend a week. Most of the route is within the Brecon Beacons National Park with wonderful views across the valley of the River Usk. Not recommended for those who crave exciting nightlife.

The Lancaster Canal 41 miles (67km) with no locks unless you venture down to Glasson Basin. This is a very underused canal but it travels through some lovely countryside so it would be a shame if too many people discovered its delights. From the present northern head of navigation, there is a further 15½ miles which can be explored on foot. The southern end is the site of a new canal to be built for the Millennium to link the Lancaster to the rest of the network via the River Ribble.

TWO WEEK CRUISES

The Four Counties Ring 110 miles (176km) with 94 locks. Some highly energetic crews do this ring in a week but if you prefer a gentler pace there is plenty to enjoy for a fortnight. This also allows time to visit the Anderton Boat Lift or take an excursion up the Macclesfield Canal.

The Avon Ring 112 miles (179km) with 132 locks. This route is a mixture of river and canal and includes the Tardebigge flight of locks, where Tom Rolt and Robert Aickman first met, and passes through Stratford-upon-Avon for those who enjoy a little culture. A short detour from King's Norton Junction takes you into Birmingham and the redeveloped Gas Street Basin.

From Oxford by the Thames to London then back up the Grand Union and down to Oxford again. 242 miles (387km) with 175 locks. Another route on both river and canal this takes you from the spires of the Oxford colleges, through rural reaches down to Henley and Reading before reaching the capital. Turning north again up the Grand Union Canal you will cover the waters travelled by the girls who took over from the boatmen during the war. Passing not far from Heathrow and under the M25 the pleasure of travelling at 4mph is immeasurable. You can call at the waterways museum at Stoke Bruerne before going through the Blisworth Tunnel then via Norton and Napton and back onto the Oxford Canal again. This route is not for the faint hearted.

The Norfolk Broads The Broads have been a popular area for holidays afloat since the late 1800s and, with 200 miles (320km) of waterways and lakes, the possibilities are endless. Unlike the canals there are no locks and the waterways are often quite wide with the possibility of sailing as well as motor boats. There is always something new to explore so however long you planned your holiday to be the chances are you will come back again because you didn't quite have enough time to visit some of the places you wanted to.

LONGER TRIPS

Across the Pennines on the Leeds and Liverpool Canal and the Aire and Calder Navigation from Wigan to Sowerby Bridge. 131 miles (210km) with 127 locks (each way). This is generally considered to be a hard route so it can take a long time if you want to take things steadily or much less time with a strong crew who are all gluttons for punishment. It travels through an amazing combination of breath taking countryside and intense industry with a mixture of river and canal and a chance to sample one of the few remaining commercial waterways. In due course, it may be possible to do a ring in the Pennines when the Huddersfield Narrow and Rochdale Canals are restored.

From the Severn to the Humber through Birmingham, along the Trent and Mersey Canal and down the River Trent. 207 miles (331km) with 127 locks (each way). One of the main objectives of the early canal builders was to enable goods to be carried across England between the four main rivers, the Severn, the Thames, the Mersey and the Humber. This route takes you diagonally across the industrial heartland of England to prove that 200 years later it can still be done.

These suggestions are to get you started but there are numerous other possibilities to suit your crew and your timetable. The Fenlands of East Anglia with the Nene, Middle Level and Great Ouse offer vast skies and reminders of the effect of efficient drainage, the Caledonian Canal traces the Great Glen with its dramatic mountains and deep lochs, and the Birmingham Canals are deep in the heart of an industrial city. Once you start exploring Britain by boat you may find yourself coming back for more.

Maximum craft dimensions

Maximum craft dimensions – these are not necessarily the absolute maximum that can be achieved but are safe working dimensions. Metric equivalents are always rounded down to allow a margin.

For waterways presently undergoing restoration the dimensions quoted are those which applied when the waterway was last in use and may change when restoration is completed.

After considerable deliberation it was decided to use miles and tenths of miles for the distance tables rather than the more traditional miles and furlongs. For practical purposes when travelling along canals locks and bridges are more readily used references than mileage which was originally put in place for the purpose of charging tolls. The new generation of canal user has grown up with metric units and with a modern edition of the work it is more appropriate to use modern terminology. Serious historians would no doubt consult original source material for reference purposes.

Lock gates are invariably individual and made for one particular lock. *Jane Cumberlidge*

Inland Waterways of
Great Britain
England

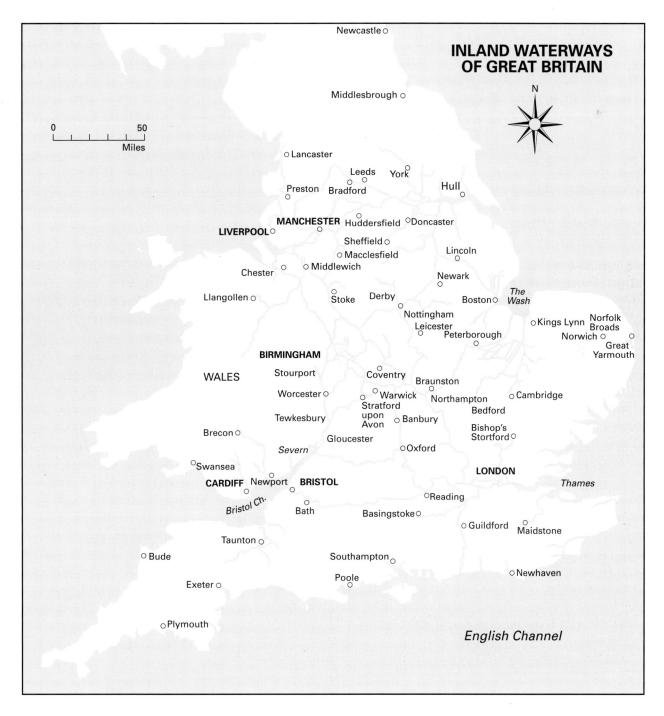

INLAND WATERWAYS
OF GREAT BRITAIN

N

0   50
Miles

Newcastle o

Middlesbrough o

o Lancaster

Leeds   York
Preston Bradford

MANCHESTER Huddersfield o Doncaster
LIVERPOOL o

Sheffield o
o Macclesfield

Chester o o Middlewich

Llangollen o

Lincoln

Newark

Stoke   Derby   Boston o   *The Wash*

Nottingham
Leicester   o Kings Lynn   Norfolk
        Peterborough   Broads
                              Norwich o   o
                                          Great
                                          Yarmouth

BIRMINGHAM
WALES   Stourport   Coventry
                                Braunston
        Worcester o   Warwick Northampton   o Cambridge
                    Stratford
                    upon   Bedford
        Tewkesbury Avon o Banbury
Brecon o   Bishop's
                    Gloucester   Stortford o
        Severn   o Oxford

o Swansea
CARDIFF Newport BRISTOL   LONDON
        o   *Thames*
Bristol Ch.   Bath   o Reading
                    Basingstoke o
                                    o Guildford o
Taunton o   Maidstone

o Bude   Southampton o
                    Poole   o Newhaven
Exeter o

o Plymouth
                              English Channel

37

River Adur

In the mid-1800s the River Adur was navigable to Baybridge but now it is a pleasant rural river for small boats as far as Shermanbury. The river joins the English Channel at the Port of Shoreham, a busy working port which should be entered by pleasure craft only after contact with the port control. Marina developments are under consideration in the canal, the eastern part of the port.

Authority *From the entrance to Old Shoreham Bridge and Southwick Canal* Shoreham Port Authority, Harbour Offices, Albion Street, Southwick, Brighton, Sussex BN42 4ED ☎ 01273 592613 *Fax* 01273 592492 Port Control ☎ 01273 592366.

Old Shoreham to Bines Bridge Environment Agency Southern Region, Guildbourne House, Chatsworth Road, Worthing, West Sussex, BN11 1LD ☎ 01903 205252 *Fax* 01903 821832.

Towpath From Bines Bridge to Old Shoreham Bridge.

Locks None. The two locks on the upper reaches of the river at West Grinstead and Lock Farm are derelict. At one time there were also three flash locks.

Connections The old River Adur forms a branch canal, from the eastern arm of the harbour to Portslade and Aldrington, a distance of 1¾ miles. The entrance locks to this canal are the Prince Philip Lock for commercial vessels and the Prince George Lock for yachts and fishing vessels.

Dimensions for the Prince George Lock
Length   170'6" (52m)
Beam   18' (5.50m)
Draught   18' (5.50m), depending on the tide

No overhead obstructions in the canal or port.

River Adur, Eastern Branch, is navigable to Mock Bridge (2 miles). (The dimensions of craft for the canal section also apply to the river to Tarmac Wharf.)

Speed limit 4mph

Navigation The tide ebbs very quickly, and this leaves only a narrow channel in between the banks. Craft should, if possible, leave Shoreham at 4 hours flood, so as to go upstream with the tide. A guide to Shoreham Harbour is available and gives directions for craft entering from the sea. There is a common law right of navigation to Shermanbury. High water at Beeding Bridge is approximately 1 hour after HW Shoreham. HW Shoreham is about 10 minutes after HW Dover.

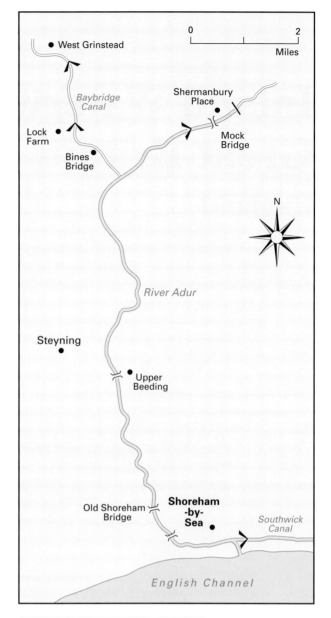

RIVER ADUR Maximum vessel dimension

From and to	Distance	Length	Beam	Draught	Headroom	Locks
Bines Bridge to river mouth	11.1 miles (17.8km)	Unlimited	Unlimited			None
To Upper Beeding Bridge				8' 6" (2.6m)	6 '9" (2.0m)	
To Bines Bridge				3' 10" (1.1m)	5' 6" (1.6m)	

Charts Imray C9, Admiralty 1656, 2044.

Facilities Mooring facilities are available at the Sussex Yacht Club just below Shoreham Bridge and in the Lady Bee Marina or the Aldrington Marina in the Southwick Canal.

Distance table	Miles
Bines Bridge (Road Bridge, B2135) to:	
Junction with River Adur (Eastern Branch)	0.9
Footbridge – opening	1.8
Upper Beeding Bridge	5.1
Old Shoreham Bridge	8.6
Railway Bridge	9.3
Norfolk Bridge	9.5
Kingston-by-Sea Wharf	10.6
Junction with Southwick Canal	11.0
Mouth of river	11.1

Aire and Calder Navigation and River Aire

Since the beginning of the 18th century the Aire and Calder network of waterways has been a commercial carrying route. The navigation has steadily improved as competition from railways and demands for larger tonnages have threatened its profitability and 300 years on it is still an active commercial waterway. It may lack some of the scenic beauty of its more rural neighbours but, through its connection with the Leeds and Liverpool

canal in Leeds, it is part of the North Sea to Irish Sea route from the Humber to the Mersey.

Coal and cloth were the principal cargoes in the late 1600s and in the late 1900s they are coal, oil, gravel and sand. When the navigation was first opened ships of 30 tons capacity were used but now tankers ply the route carrying 650–700 tons of cargo. Over 2.5 million tons of freight are now moved on the waterway every year.

The size of the Aire and Calder Navigation is similar to some of the smaller canals and waterways on the continent, although it seems very large compared to other British waterways. For pleasure boats it is exciting to travel along a commercial route and meet large working vessels, but extra care must be taken and users must be aware of the effect of the wash from a 500-ton ship in confined waters compared to passing a narrow boat in a small canal. Pleasure boats must always give way to commercial vessels, take note of all the traffic signals on the waterway and always follow instructions given by lock-keepers and other waterways staff.

In addition to being one of the oldest navigations the Aire and Calder is also one of the newest. After a dramatic breach of the River Aire into a mine in 1988 a new 1.9 mile (3km) bypass has been constructed between Lemonroyd and Kippax. This includes a lock, cottages, a weir, three bridges and a basin for 60 boats. The new Lemonroyd Lock replaces the old Lemonroyd and Kippax Locks making one less lock on the navigation. Another new development is the Royal Armouries Museum which has moved from the Tower of London to Leeds and is now a major attraction on the Leeds waterfront.

The Selby Canal was built in the 1770s when the Aire and Calder Canal Company became aware of rumours that a canal was to be constructed between Leeds and Selby which would have taken the traffic from the Aire and Calder. The lower reaches of the River Aire were difficult to navigate so a canal was cut from Haddesley to Selby, 5½ miles, which was the cheapest option. Unfortunately, the speed of construction of the canal (it was opened in 1778) was achieved at the expense of the depth which was

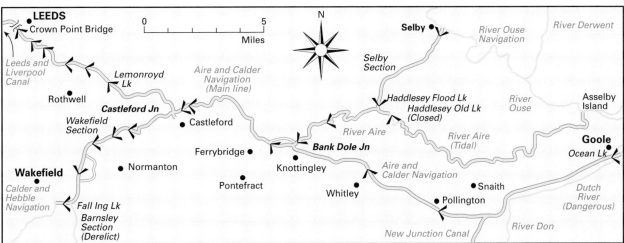

only 3ft 6in. As cargoes increased the canal became too shallow for the larger barges. By 1826, the new cut from Knottingley to Goole had taken much of the traffic from the Selby Canal. The lower part of the River Aire was always difficult to navigate and is no longer navigable.

Authority British Waterways, Lock Lane, Castleford, West Yorkshire WF10 2LH ☎ 01977 554351.

Port Manager, Associated British Ports, East Parade, Goole, DN14 5RB ☎ 01405 762691.

Lock keepers can be contacted on VHF Ch 16 or 74.

Bridges Numerous.

Towpath Throughout navigation although it is rather poorly maintained in parts.

Aqueducts Stanley Ferry across the River Calder, a fine cast iron trough opened in 1839 was designed by George Leather. A new concrete trough was opened in 1981 alongside the original which is still in water.

Speed limit 6mph on the Aire and Calder Navigation and 4mph on the Selby Canal.

Connections Leeds and Liverpool Canal at Leeds, Calder and Hebble Navigation at Wakefield, Barnsley Canal at Wakefield, New Junction Canal near Pollington and the tidal River Ouse at Goole and Selby.

Navigation This waterway is a combination of a river and a canal. The River Aire floods regularly and there are flood locks along the course of the navigation which will be closed by BW staff when conditions dictate. In certain circumstances no boat movements may be allowed on the waterway and boat crews should wait until they are advised by BW staff before proceeding.

Each lock has traffic lights upstream and downstream which denote the following:

Red light	Stop and moor up, the lock is in use
Amber light	No lock-keeper on duty, self-operate
Green light	Proceed into lock
Red and green lights together	The lock is available for use and the lock-keeper will operate it
Flashing red light	Flood conditions, unsafe for navigation

Facilities There are plenty of pubs and restaurants available and several mooring sites. Boatyards offering full facilities including pump-out are harder to find, there is one in Leeds, Stanley Ferry and Selby. Goole and Wakefield boatyards offer most facilities including slipways.

Distance table   *Miles*

Main Line
Junction with Leeds and Liverpool Canal at River Lock to:

Crown Point Bridge	0.5
Leeds Lock No 1	0.6
Clarence Dock, Royal Armouries Museum	0.7
Knostrop Flood Lock No 2	1.8
Knostrop Fall Lock No 3	1.9
Thwaite Mills Industrial Museum	2.2
Fishpond Lock No 4	4.0
Woodlesford Lock No 5	5.3
Swillington Bridge	5.5
Fleet Bridge	6.3
Lemonroyd Lock No 6	6.7
Shan House Bridge	7.3
Caroline Bridge	8.1
Allerton Bywater	9.0
Castleford – junction with Wakefield section	10.0
(Take care to avoid the branch to the weir)	
Castleford Flood Lock No 8	10.0
Short Branch: Castleford Dam and Mills through Castleford Middle Lock	
(a side lock 70' 8"wide)	10.3
Bulholme Lock No 9	10.8
Fairburn Ings Nature Reserve	13.3
Ferrybridge Lock No 10 (Flood Lock)	15.3
Mill Bridge	15.8
(Take care to avoid the branch to the weir)	
Cow Lane Bridge	16.8
Shepherds Bridge	16.9
Bank Dole Junction, junction with Selby Branch	17.0
Skew Bridge	17.1
Stubbs Bridge	18.4
Low Eggborough	20.2
Whitley Lock No 11	21.0
Heck Basin – South Yorkshire Boat Club	22.5
Pollington Lock No 12	24.1
Crowcroft Bridge	24.7
Junction with New Junction Canal	26.5
Beever's Bridge	27.5
South Dock Bridge	33.5
Entrance to Goole Docks, junction with River Ouse,	34.0

Wakefield Section
Fall Ing, junction with Calder and Hebble Navigation to:

Junction with Barnsley Canal (derelict)	0.4
Broadreach Lock No 1	1.1

AIRE AND CALDER NAVIGATION & RIVER AIRE Maximum vessel dimensions

From and to	Distance	Length	Beam	Draught	Headroom	Locks
Goole to Leeds Lock	34 miles (54.4km)	185' (56.5m)	18' 9" (5.7m)	8' (2.4m)	12' 3" (3.7m)	12
Castleford junc to Wakefield	7.5 miles (12km)	142' (43m)	17' 6" (5.3m)	7' (2.1m)	12' 3" (3.7m)	3
Selby Canal	11.75 miles (18.8km)	78' 6" (24.0m)	16' 6" (5.0m)	4' (1.2m)	8' (2.4m)	4
River Aire	11.75 miles (28km)	78 6" (24.0m)	16' 6" (5.0m)	5' 6" (1.7m)	11' (3.4m)	1

	Miles
Newland	13.5
Airmyn	15.8
Asselby Island, junction with River Ouse	16.8

River Alde and River Ore

From Shingle Street to Randalls Point, just above Orford, the river is called the Ore then it becomes the Alde past Aldeburgh and up to Snape, famous for the Maltings and Benjamin Britten. The entrance to the river shifts and changes frequently and anyone intending to enter should get hold of a copy of the sketch chart produced each year by the Aldeburgh Yacht Club. For all the rivers in this area a copy of *The East Coast* by Derek Bowskill, is strongly recommended.

Authority None, an open navigation.

Towpath None.

Navigation Mean rise and fall of tide at Aldeburgh is 8ft 6ins and the tidal stream runs at about 4 knots in the river, at the entrance it may run at up to 6 knots. It is high water at the bar 15 minutes before HW Walton-on-the-Naze and at Slaughden Quay about 1 hour 40 minutes after HW at the bar. There are anchorages in the river and it is possible to dry out alongside the quay at Snape.

Charts Imray C28, Y15, Admiralty 2693.

The new Royal Armouries museum next to the Aire and Calder Canal in the centre of Leeds. *Robin Smithett*

	Miles
Ramsdens Swing Bridge	2.1
Stanley Ferry Aqueduct	2.3
Birkwood Lock No 2	3.0
King's Road Lock No 3	4.0
Woodnook Lock No 4	5.5
Methley Bridge	6.5
Castleford Junction, junction with Main Line	7.5

Selby Section
Bank Dole Junction, Knottingley, to:

Bank Dole Lock No 1	0.5
Beal Bridge	2.5
Beal Lock No 2	2.8
Birkin Wharf	3.8
Commencement of Selby Canal and Haddesley	
Flood Lock No 3, junction with River Aire	6.5
Paper House Bridge	7.3
Gateforth Landing	7.8
Burton Hall Bridge	8.5
Burn Bridge	9.3
Brayton Railway Bridge	10.6
Bawtry Road Bridge	11.1
Selby Swing Bridge	11.5
Selby Lock No 4, junction with River Ouse	11.8

River Aire section (not navigable)
Junction with Selby Branch to:

Haddesley Old Lock (closed)	0.8
Temple Farm	2.3
Temple Hirst	4.0
Weeland	4.8
Snaith	8.3
Rawcliffe	12.0

Distance table

Snape Bridge to:

	Miles
Iken Cliff	1.3
Barber's Point	3.5
Cob Island	5.1
Slaughden Quay	7.0
Orford	11.6
Cuckold's Point	12.4
Dove Point	14.5
North Weir Point	17.0

RIVER ALDE AND RIVER ORE *Maximum vessel dimensions*

From and to	Distance	Length	Beam	Draught	Headroom	Locks
Snape Bridge to Shingle Street	21 miles (33.8km)	Unlimited	Unlimited	Slaughden Quay 10' (3.0m)	Unlimited	None
				Iken 4' 2" (1.2m)		
				Snape Bridge 5' (1.5m)		

River Ancholme

This is a very old navigation with records of river improvements as far back as 1287. Further Acts were passed in 1767 and early in the 1800s when John Rennie was involved with the work. During the second half of the 19th century a passenger packet ran from Brigg to South Ferriby where it connected with a steamer to Hull.

Facilities for boats and leisure use of the river have been improved over the years and many private boats now use the Ancholme. It is a river and this must be borne in mind after heavy rain when the navigation may be closed to craft as its use as a drainage channel for surrounding land is important. Water levels and flow rates may change very quickly.

Authority Environment Agency, Anglian Region (Northern Area), Harvey Street, Lincoln LN1 1TF ☎ 01522 513100 *Fax* 01522 512927.

Lock keeper at South Ferriby ☎ 01652 635219.

Bridges 13.

Speed limit 7mph South Ferriby to Brigg, 4mph on the rest of the river.

Towpath Throughout navigation.

Connections Not connected to the inland waterway network.

Navigation High water Ferriby Sluice is 18 minutes after HW Hull. South Ferriby Lock is normally manned 4 hours either side of HW. The lock-keeper listens on VHF Ch 74 but it is recommended to warn him on the telephone (number above) if you intend to enter the river.

Restoration Harlam Hill Lock has been restored by the Lincoln and South Humberside Branch of the IWA. Dimensions for this lock are 60ft long by 16ft wide by 3ft draught.

Facilities Full facilities are available at South Ferriby and mooring and local services are available at Brigg and Brandy Wharf.

Distance table	Miles
Bishopbridge to:	
Owersby Landing	1.5
Atterby Landing	2.0
Harlam Hill Lock No 1	2.5
Snitterby Bridge	2.8
Brandy Wharf	4.0
Redbourne Old River	6.3
North Kelsey Landing	6.5
Hibaldstow Bridge	6.8
Cadney Bridge	7.8
Southern junction with navigable loop line of Old River Ancholme through Brigg, 1.8 miles long	9.5
Brigg, town and new bridge	10.3
Northern junction with navigable loop line of Old River Ancholme through Brigg	10.8
Castlethorpe Bridge	11.5
Broughton Bridge	12.5
Worlaby Landing	13.5
Bonby Landing	14.8
Appleby Landing	16.0
Saxby Bridge	16.3

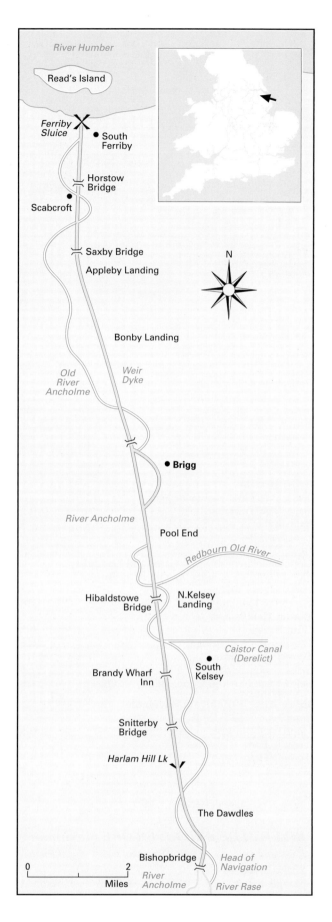

RIVER ANCHOLME Maximum vessel dimensions

From and to	Distance	Length	Beam	Draught	Headroom	Locks
South Ferriby Lock		68' (20.7m)	19' (5.8m)	10' (3.0m)	Unlimited	1
South Ferriby to						
Harlam Hill Lock	16.5 miles (26.5km)	40' (12.2m)	12' (3.6m)	6' 6" (2m)	15' (4.6m)	1

	Miles
Scabcroft	17.3
Horkstowe Bridge	17.8
South Ferriby Sluice, Lock No 2, junction with River Humber	19.0

River Arun

By leaving just before high water at Littlehampton it is possible to take a small craft up the River Arun on the tide as far as Pulborough. Although fairly workman-like in its lower reaches, the river above Arundel is very attractive and tranquil. The old Portsmouth and Arundel Canal joined the river near Ford but is no longer navigable.

Along the route there are a number of interesting places to visit and pleasant riverside pubs to stop at. The Arundel Wildlife and Wetland Centre is just north of the town on the east bank, beautiful Arundel Park stretches away to the west by Offham Loop, there is an Industrial Heritage Museum at Amberley and, of course, there are the attractions of Arundel itself with the castle on the hill above the river.

Authority *From the entrance to Arundel Bridge* The Littlehampton Harbour Board, Paines Wharf, Pier Road, Littlehampton, Sussex ☎ 01903 721215.

Above Arundel Bridge Environment Agency, Southern Region, Guildbourne House, Chatsworth Road, Worthing, Sussex BN11 1LD ☎ 01903 832000 *Fax* 01903 821832.

Bridges There are nine bridges, Littlehampton, Ford, Arundel by-pass, Offham and South Stoke Bridges have a clearance of 8ft at HW springs and

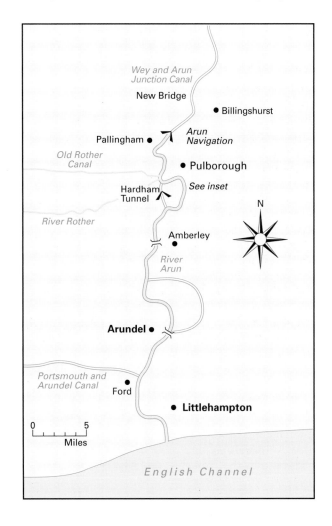

RIVER ARUN Maximum vessel dimensions

From and to	Distance	Length	Beam	Draught	Headroom	Locks
Pallingham Lock to Pulborough	3.5 miles (5.6km)		Small craft only			None
Pulborough to Arundel	15.3 miles (24.6km)		Small craft only			None
Arundel to Littlehampton	6.7 miles (10.8km)	95' (28.9m)	10' (3.0m)	3' (0.9m) LW	Min 5' (1.5m) HWS	None

Arundel Town Bridge, Houghton, Pulborough and Swan Bridges 5ft. Swan Bridge is impassable at LW.

Towpath In parts only.

Speed limit Littlehampton to Arundel Bridge 6.5 knots (7.5mph), Arundel Bridge to Palham Lock 5.5 knots (6.3mph).

Charges These apply only within the jurisdiction of the Littlehampton Harbour Board.

Navigation The river is tidal and is one of the fastest flowing in the country, streams run from 4 to 6 knots. The flood tide at Arundel Bridge and Ford Railway Bridge can be particularly strong. High water Littlehampton is 15 minutes after HW Dover with a tidal range of 5.2m at springs and 2.7m at neaps. HW Ford is 25 minutes after HW Littlehampton, HW Arundel 50 minutes, HW Houghton Bridge 1 hour 30 minutes and HW Pulborough 4 hours after. Amberley Pies are mud islands which lie between Timberley Bridge and Coldwaltham and must be navigated with extreme care. Upstream of Timberley Bridge, the river is only suitable for small craft. Depth of water varies considerably depending on tide and freshwater run-off.

Charts Imray C9, Admiralty 1652, 1991.

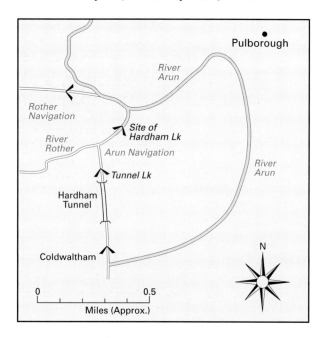

Facilities Moorings are available at County Wharf near the Harbour Office and also at Littlehampton Marina above the movable footbridge.

Distance table *Miles*
Pallingham Lock (derelict) to:

Stopham Bridge	2.3
Junction with River Rother (western)	2.5
Water's Edge Inn (mooring)	3.4
Pulborough Bridge (Swan Inn)	3.5
Greatham	5.8
Coldwaltham Bridge	6.6
Old Arun Canal junction (derelict)	7.4
Bury Wharf and Ferry	8.9
Houghton Bridge and Amberley Station	10.0
South Stoke	13.3
Offham Bridge	16.8
Black Rabbit Inn, Wildfowl Centre	17.8
Arundel Bridge	18.8
Ford Railway Bridge	21.8
Junction of Old Portsmouth and Arundel Canal	22.5
Littlehampton Ferry	24.8
Littlehampton Harbour mouth	25.5

Ashby Canal

Although this is sometimes called the Ashby-de-la-Zouch Canal it never reached that town. The original proposal was for a broad canal which would link the Coventry Canal to the River Trent at Burton-on-Trent. The broad, sweeping bridges built to take barges can be seen as reminders of the plan. The canal was to transport coal to the lime works near Ashby-de-la-Zouch and it also served the coal fields around Moira and Measham. The quality of the coal from Moira found a ready market in the Home Counties and coal was carried on the canal until 1981. The very mines which it had served caused the closure of the northern 9 miles of canal due to problems with subsidence.

This is a delightful rural canal, especially appealing to those not keen on too much locking as there are no locks along the 22 miles. The canal passes close to the site of the Battle of Bosworth Field and for railway enthusiasts the Battlefield Line runs parallel with the canal between Shackerstone and Shenton. Measham was well-known for its Meashamware or bargeware which many barge families would have had on board.

Authority British Waterways, Fradley Junction, Alrewas, Burton-on-Trent, Staffordshire DE13 7DN ☎ 01283 790236.

Bridges Numerous.

Towpath Throughout navigation, except Snarestone Tunnel.

Tunnels Snarestone, 250 yards. No towpath.

Connections Coventry Canal at Marston Junction.

ASHBY CANAL Maximum vessel dimensions

From and to	Distance	Length	Beam	Draught	Headroom	Locks
Marston Junction to Snarestone	22 miles (35.4km)	72' (21.9m)	7' (2.1m)	3' 6" (1.1m)	6' 6" (2.0m)	None

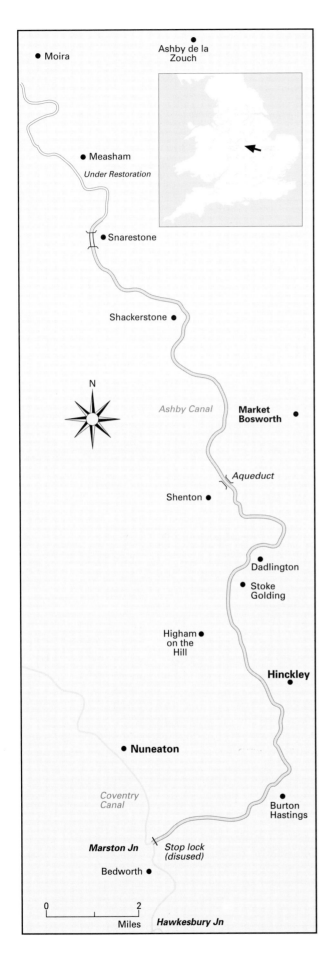

Restoration The Moira Furnace has been restored and work is underway to restore the 8 miles of canal from Snarestone to end in a centre at Bath Yard, Moira.

Facilities There are several pubs along the canal. There are three boatyards at Nuneaton but only the Ashby Boat Company offers pump-out facilities.

Distance table	*Miles*
Marston Junction (Coventry Canal) to:	
Railway Bridge	0.8
Burton Hastings	3.0
Watling Street Bridge No 15	5.0
Hinckley	5.6
Higham-on-the-Hill	7.5
Stoke Golding Wharf	8.8
Shenton Station (site of Bosworth Battle)	13.0
Bosworth Wharf Bridge	14.9
Carlton Bridge	15.8
Congerstone	17.1
Shackerstone	18.3
Snarestone tunnel	21.0
Head of Navigation (just above Bridge 61)	22.0

Ashton, Peak Forest and Macclesfield Canals

The Cheshire Ring has become a popular route for holiday cruising as so many of us prefer to travel a circle rather than to go 'there and back'. The Ashton, the Peak Forest and the Macclesfield Canals make up the eastern half of the ring with a little foray up the Upper Peak Forest Canal making a pleasant extra excursion to Whaley Bridge and Buxworth Basin.

The Macclesfield and Peak Forest canals are two of the highest navigable waterways in the country at over 500ft above sea level. A journey round the ring passes through a fascinating mix of urban and rural scenery, industrial heritage and modern developments, peaceful vistas and bustling activities.

Ashton Canal

Despite its relatively short length the Ashton Canal played an important part in the canal restoration story. After an initial threat of closure in 1961 volunteers acted decisively to maintain it as a navigable waterway. A further setback occurred in 1964 when a leak meant the canal had to be emptied and so became impassable. In late 1971, an agreement was reached between BW, the IWA and local authorities to restore the Ashton and Peak Forest Canals. The following spring the Waterways Recovery Group started to clear the canal with over 1,000 volunteers. Without this successful campaign to prevent the closure of the Ashton Canal the 100 miles of the Cheshire Ring would not be available to users today.

The canal runs through a heavily built up area for its whole length and care has to be taken when

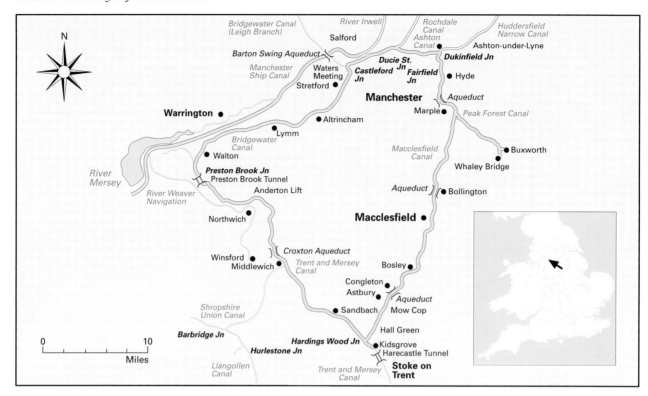

ASHTON CANAL Maximum vessel dimensions

From and to	Distance	Length	Beam	Draught	Headroom	Locks
Ducie Street to Ashton under Lyne	6.75 miles (10.9km)	70' (21.3m)	7' (2.1m)	2' 9" (0.8m)	5' 4" (1.6m)	18

choosing a mooring. Improvements have been made in recent years, but it is generally better not to leave the boat unattended and certainly don't leave anything handy lying about on the roof or on deck.

Authority British Waterways, Top Lock, Church Lane, Marple, Cheshire SK6 6BN ☎ 0161 427 1079.

Bridges Numerous including moveable bridges which need BW keys to unlock them.

Towpath Throughout canal.

Branches Fairbottom, Hollinwood, Islington and Stockport Branches are all closed.

Connections The Rochdale Canal at Ducie Street in Manchester, the Peak Forest Canal at Portland Basin and the Huddersfield Narrow Canal both in Ashton-under-Lyne.

Facilities Several pubs, BW toilet and moorings at Fairfield Junction but do not leave the boat unattended.

Distance table

Ducie Street to:	Miles
Ancoats Locks Nos 1–3	0.4
Beswick Locks Nos 4–7	1.3
Clayton Locks Nos 8–10	2.0
Clayton Junction	2.4
Clayton Locks Nos 11–16 (Top Lock)	3.0
Bridge 15	3.3

	Miles
Fairfield Locks Nos 17 and 18	3.6
Fairfield Junction,	3.8
Guide Bridge Railway Station	5.4
Ashton-under-Lyne, Walk Mill Bridge	6.0
Portland Basin, Dukinfield Junction	6.3
Ashton-under-Lyne, junction with Huddersfield Narrow Canal	6.7

Peak Forest Canal

The Peak Forest canal has two distinct parts, the lower and upper sections, the lower part running along the valley of the River Tame and the upper along the River Goyt. Between the two is Marple with its stone aqueduct carrying the canal 100ft above the River Goyt, the junction with the Macclesfield Canal and a rise of 214ft through 16 locks. These are the only locks on the canal and are grouped over about 1 mile with a railway aqueduct between locks 4 and 5.

Completed in 1800, the canal was intended to bring limestone down 1000ft from the high Derbyshire quarries. The stone came down to Buxworth and Whaley Bridge by tramroad and later railway where it was transhipped to narrow boats to continue on to Manchester. At Whaley Bridge, the under-cover transhippment shed can still be seen. The original terminus of the main line was at

PEAK FOREST CANAL Maximum vessel dimensions

From and to	Distance	Length	Beam	Draught	Headroom	Locks
Dukinfield to Buxworth Basin	14.75 miles (23.7km)	70' (21.3m)	7' (2.1m)	3' (0.9m)	6' (1.8m)	16

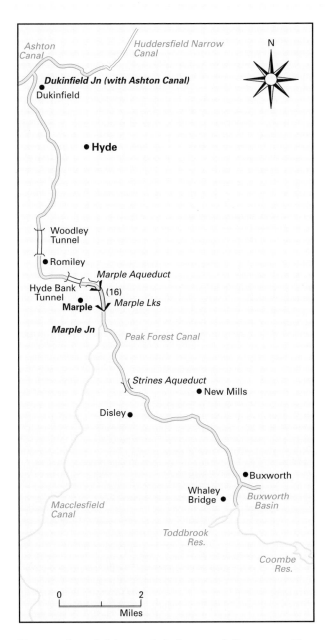

Buxworth and this area is being carefully restored by the Inland Waterways Preservation Society.

Authority British Waterways, Top Lock, Church Lane, Marple, Cheshire SK6 6BN ☎ 0161 427 1079.

Bridges Numerous including eight swing bridges.

Towpath Throughout canal and branch, except Hyde Bank Tunnel.

Tunnels Two. Woodley, 167yds long with 7ft 6in headroom, towpath through tunnel. Hyde Bank, 308yds long with 7ft headroom, no towpath.

Connections The Ashton Canal at Dukinfield Junction and the Macclesfield Canal at Marple.

Facilities Plenty of pubs and several boatyards. A slipway is available at New Mills Wharf on the Upper Peak Forest Canal.

Distance table	Miles
Dukinfield Junction to:	
River Tame Aqueduct	0.1
M67	2.3
Hyde	2.5
Apethorne Aqueduct over road	3.1
Windlehurst bridge	3.6
Woodley Tunnel	4.5
Leach Bridge	4.8
Hatherlow Aqueduct	5.5
Hyde Bank Tunnel	6.3
Marple Aqueduct	6.8
Marple Bottom Lock No 1	7.0
Marple Top Lock No 16, junction with Macclesfield Canal	8.0
Strines Aqueduct	9.7
Dryhurst Bridge	10.9
Bank End Bridge	12.0
Furness Vale	12.9
Greensdeep Bridge	13.6
Junction with Whaley Bridge Branch (½ mile long)	14.0
Aqueduct over River Goyt	14.1
Buxworth, termination of canal	14.7

Macclesfield Canal

The Macclesfield Canal was promoted by an Act in 1826 and is second only to the Welsh Canal in scenic beauty. It runs on a high contour from Marple to Bosley giving unrivalled views over the countryside. There are fine views of Mow Cop with its folly, 1000ft up. As one proceeds north on the Trent and Mersey Canal it should be remembered that the entrance to the Macclesfield Canal is on the left, as the canal crosses over the Trent and Mersey to run north to Marple. Summit level is 521ft above ordnance datum.

MACCLESFIELD CANAL Maximum vessel dimensions

From and to	Distance	Length	Beam	Draught	Headroom	Locks
Marple to Hall Green	26.3 miles (42.3km)	70' (21.3m)	7' (2.1m)	3' (0.9m)	6' (1.8m)	13

At Hall Green the canal joins the Trent and Mersey and here the stop lock has a rise of one foot to preserve the Trent and Mersey's water. The canal is famous for its beautiful turn-over bridges which were constructed in such a way that there was no need to unhitch the horse when the towpath changed sides across the canal.

Authority British Waterways, Top Lock, Church Lane, Marple, Cheshire SK6 6BN ☎ 0161 427 1079.

Bridges Numerous including swing bridges.

Towpath Throughout the canal and branch.

Branches High Lane Branch.

Connections The Peak Forest Canal at Marple and the Trent and Mersey Canal at Hardings Wood.

Facilities With its popularity as a holiday route the Macclesfield Canal can offer plenty of facilities. There are boatyards and hostelries to suit all tastes. Slipways are available in Macclesfield, Stockport and Stoke-on-Trent.

Distance table   *Miles*

Marple Junction to:

BW Yard	0.2
Clough Bridge	1.2
Windlehurst Bridge	1.8
Junction with High Lane Branch	2.3
Aqueduct over railway	2.6
Bullock's Bridge	2.9
Red Acre Aqueduct	4.5
Hibbert's Brow Bridge	6.1
Whiteley Green Bridge	7.0
Bollington Aqueduct	7.8
Clarke's Change Bridge	8.9
Chapel-en-le-Frith Road Bridge	10.3
Buxton Road Wharf, Macclesfield	10.9
Holland's Bridge	11.3
Sutton Aqueduct	12.3
Leek New Road Bridge	12.8
Fool's Nook	14.3
Crow Holt Bridge	15.5
Bosley, Locks Nos 1-10 commence	16.1
Bosley, Locks Nos 11 and 12	17.1

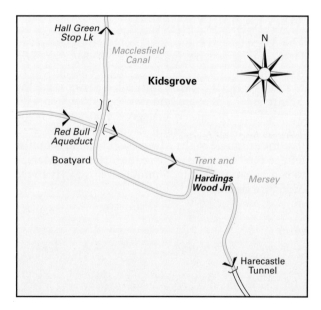

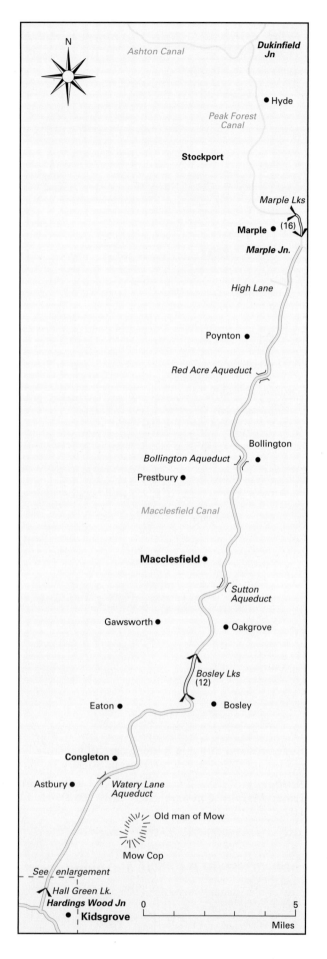

	Miles
Aqueduct over River Dane	17.4
Crossley Hall	18.4
Buglawton Road Bridge	18.9
Main Line Railway Bridge	20.4
Biddulph Valley Railway Aqueduct	20.9
Dog Lane Aqueduct	21.6
Congleton Wharf	21.8
Henshalls Bridge	22.9
Watery Lane Aqueduct	23.3
Mow Cop	24.8
Hall Green, junction with Trent and Mersey Canal, Hall Green Branch and Hall Green Stop Lock No 13	26.1

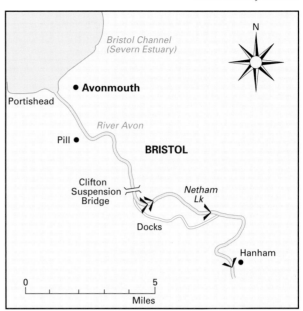

River Avon, Bristol

Despite being over 6 miles from the sea, Bristol has always been a port with the River Avon providing access. Ship owners learned to use the huge tidal range to advantage and all the associated trades and businesses developed in the city to support the ships. Acts of Parliament during the 18th century enabled improvements to be made to the navigation and, with the coming of the Kennet and Avon Canal, a through route from Bristol to London was created.

The famous Floating Harbour in Bristol city centre was created in 1810 allowing sea-going ships to come right into the centre where cargoes were unloaded and loaded. Work was carried out on the ships using local artisans, stores were provided by local merchants and Bristol was a port whose activity rivalled that of London. About 50 years later, docks were developed at Avonmouth and Portishead to accommodate the larger ships which no longer wound their way up the spectacular Avon Gorge and under Brunel's amazing Clifton Suspension Bridge.

Now the City Docks are being redeveloped for pleasure boats with marina facilities, shops and restaurants and retaining the importance of boats in the heart of the city.

Authority City Docks Manager, City Docks, Harbourmaster's Office, Underfall Yard, Cumberland Road, Bristol BS1 6XG ☎ 0117 926 4797 or 0117 929 7608.

Dockmaster, City Docks, The Watch House, Cumberland Basin, Lock Entrance, Brunel Lock Road, Bristol BS1 6XG ☎ 0117 927 3633, VHF Ch 14.

Bridges Two opening, and 11 fixed.

Towpath There is a towpath from Hanham Lock to Marsh Bridge, Bristol.

Speed limit 4mph above Netham Weir, 6mph in the harbour and downstream.

Connections Cumberland Basin Lock to Bristol Floating Harbour. The Kennet and Avon Canal at Hanham Lock.

Navigation For the *Bristol Harbour Information for Boat Owners* booklet contact the City Docks Manager. This booklet is comprehensive in its coverage of all the information for visiting boats such as moorings, lock use, all facilities, bridge restrictions, lock times, tidal information, vessel dimensions and navigation information for both the harbour and the feeder canal.

RIVER AVON, BRISTOL Maximum vessel dimensions

From and to	Distance	Length	Beam	Draught	Headroom	Locks
Hanham Lock to Netham Lock and the Feeder Canal	8.5 miles (12.8km)	80' (24.4m)	17' 8" (5.4m)	6' 3" (1.9m)	10' 2" (3.1m)	1
Floating Harbour to Avonmouth	6.5 miles (10.5km)	324' 9" (99.0m)	48' 10" (14.9m)	18' (5.5m)	88' 7" (27.0m)	1

Charts Imray C59, Admiralty 1176, 1859.

Facilities The best facilities after Hanham Lock are at Bristol where all services are available.

Distance Table	Miles
Junction with the Kennet and Avon Canal to:	
Hanham Colliery Wharf	1.5
Conham	1.9
Netham Lock No 1	3.5
Bristol, Cumberland Basin Entrance Lock No 2	6.5
Clifton Suspension Bridge	6.9
Pill	11.1
M5	11.6
Avonmouth, junction with Avonmouth Docks and estuary of River Severn	13.1

River Avon, Warwick

The idea of the River Avon being navigable from the Severn at Tewkesbury to Warwick has been considered for over 550 years. It was not until William Sandys of Fladbury proposed a navigation in 1636 that significant work was carried out. Over a century later, George Perrott found the Lower Avon Navigation was in very poor condition and over £4000 was spent in 10 years to make repairs to weirs and locks. By this time the navigation had been divided into upper and lower sections and around 400 30-ton barges were using the waterway each year.

During the later part of the 19th century the quality of the navigation deteriorated and, with competition from the railways, revenue from the waterway declined. Schemes were put forward to improve the waterway and increase traffic but they came to nothing. By the First World War, there was very little traffic along the Avon and silting was becoming a problem as well as deterioration in locks and weirs.

In 1949 a conference discussed the possibility of restoration and in 1950 the Lower Avon was bought for £1500 by C D Barwell and later that year the Lower Avon Navigation Trust was incorporated. Over the next 14 years a huge amount of work by volunteers completely restored the Lower Avon and in July 1964 the navigation was re-opened by H.M. The Queen Mother. It took another 10 years before she performed the same ceremony for the re-opening of the Upper Avon Navigation. The

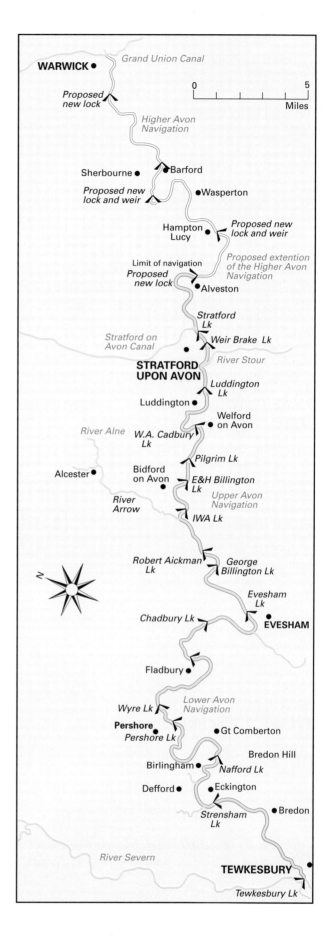

House over lock! River Avon. *Sian Barron*

reinstatement of navigation along the Avon opened up the possibility of doing a circular cruise and the Avon Ring is now one of the most popular routes for holiday cruising.

The Higher Avon Navigation Trust is looking at the possibility of restoring the distance from Alvestone Weir to Warwick with a connection to the Grand Union Canal at Warwick.

Authority *Upper Avon, Stratford-on-Avon to Evesham* The Upper Avon Navigation Trust Ltd, Bridge 63, Harvington, Evesham, Worcs WR11 5NR ☎ 01386 870526.

Lower Avon, Evesham to Tewkesbury Lower Avon Navigation Trust Ltd, Mill Wharf, Mill Lane, Wyre Piddle, Pershore, Worcestershire WR10 2JF ☎ 01386 552517.

Bridges 15. King John's Bridge in Tewkesbury is a fine stone structure but special care is needed when passing under it as visibility is restricted. There are also two ferries near Evesham.

Towpath There is no towpath as such but along much of the river there are public footpaths some of which are called the Avon Valley Footpath. Use a large scale OS map and make sure you are not trespassing on private land.

Speed limit 6mph travelling downstream, 4mph travelling upstream.

Navigation Always remember that this is a river and its character will change rapidly as water levels change. *Gateway to the Avon* published by the Lower Avon Navigation Trust Ltd and the *Upper Avon Navigation Guide* published by the Upper Avon Navigation Trust Ltd are invaluable to those wishing to take craft on the Avon. The guides have detailed charts, information about facilities, lock times and bridge heights. King John's Bridge in Tewkesbury is the gauge bridge for the navigation, but it must be remembered that if there is heavy rain while you are cruising on the river bridge clearances will reduce rapidly. Water levels and flow can change rapidly and this can affect how a boat handles under bridges, when passing weirs and entering or leaving locks.

Restoration The Higher Avon from Alveston Weir to Warwick is proposed but this would entail building up to seven new locks and two weirs.

Facilities Numerous pubs and restaurants along the river and in the many towns it passes through. There are several boatyards and marinas. When using river moorings extra care is required with warps in case of sudden changes in river level. Slipways are available at some of the marinas.

Distance table	*Miles*
Higher Avon Navigation	
Warwick Aqueduct to:	
Warwick Mill	1.0
Barford Mill	3.9
Wasperton	6.6
Hampton Lucy Mill	8.5
Charlecote	9.0
Upper Avon Navigation	
Alveston Weir to:	
Alveston Ferry	0.6
Clopton Bridge	3.2
Junction with Stratford-on-Avon Canal	3.3
Colin P Witter Lock	3.8
Weir Brake Lock	4.1
Luddington Lock	6.3
Binton Bridge	8.2
W.A. Cadbury Lock	9.2
Pilgrim Lock	10.9

RIVER AVON, WARWICK Maximum vessel dimensions

From and to	Distance	Length	Beam	Draught	Headroom	Locks
Lower Avon Navigation, Severn at Tewkesbury to Evesham	25.8 miles (41.5km)	70' (21.3m)	13' 6" (4.1m)	4' (1.2m)	10' max (3.0m)	8
Upper Avon Navigation, Evesham to Alveston	19.6 miles (31.6km)	70' (21.3m)	12' 6" (3.8m)	3' (0.9m)	10' (3.0m)	9
Higher Avon Navigation, Alveston Weir to Warwick	9 miles (14.5km)	Not navigable at present				

Pershore bridge on the Warwickshire Avon. *Roy Westlake*

	Miles
E. & H. Billington Lock (Barton)	11.8
Bidford Bridge (Bidford-upon-Avon)	12.5
IWA Lock	13.4
Robert Aickman Lock	16.2
George Billington Lock	16.8
Offenham	18.2

Lower Avon Navigation

Evesham Lock (UANT tolls apply)	19.6
Workman Bridge, Evesham	20.4
Chadbury Lock	21.6
Fladbury Lock	25.4
Wyre Lock	29.7
Pershore Lock	30.7
Nafford Lock	35.9
Eckington Bridge	37.4
Strensham Lock	39.4
Bredon Dock	41.2
Twyning Fleet (inn)	42.7
Tewkesbury (Avon Lock)	45.3
Tewkesbury, junction with River Severn	45.5

Barnsley Canal and Dearne and Dove Canal

The increasing demand for coal at the end of the 18th century encouraged more waterways to be built into coalfields. One such was the Barnsley Canal which ran from the Calder and Hebble Navigation at Heath near Wakefield to Barnsley and then up to Barnby Bridge. At Barnsley it met the Dearne and Dove Canal which entered the River Don at Swinton, 9½ miles long with two branches, one to Elsecar and one to Worsbrough.

The Barnsley Canal had an 11-mile pound from Barugh to Walton and, of its 20 locks, 15 were in the first 2.3 miles near the junction with the Calder and Hebble Navigation. In 1875, the canal was bought by the Aire and Calder Company which had leased it for the previous 21 years. The Dearne and Dove Canal was leased by the Don Company from 1846 and was purchased by the company 11 years later.

Water shortage and subsidence were problems on both the canals and needed costly repairs. By the middle of this century, subsidence was the main reason for the closure of the canals with the Barnsley being abandoned in 1953 and the Dearne and Dove in 1961.

BARNSLEY CANAL AND DEARNE & DOVE CANAL *Maximum vessel dimensions*

From and to	Distance	Length	Beam	Draught	Headroom	Locks
Barnsley Canal						
Heath to Barnsley	11 miles (17.7km)	84' (25.6m)	15' (4.6m)	6' 6" (2m)	9' (2.7m)	15
Barnsley to Barnby Bridge	15 miles (24.2km)	78' 6" (23.9m)	14' 6" (4.4m)	6' 6" (2m)	9' (2.7m)	5
Dearne and Dove Canal						
Swinton to Barnsley	9.5 miles (15.3km)	58' (17.7m)	14' 10" (4.5m)	5' 6" (1.6m)	9' 6" (2.8m)	19

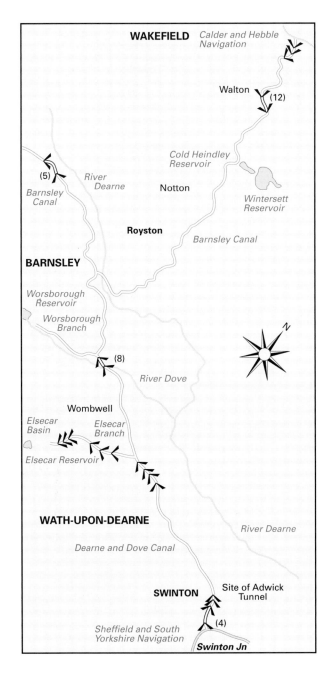

Towpath Parts of the Barnsley Canal are walkable, but only the 2½ miles of the Elsecar Branch of the Dearne and Dove.

Branches Elsecar 2.1 miles, Worsbrough 2½ miles, both on the Dearne and Dove Canal.

Restoration The Barnsley Canal Group is working towards full restoration of the two Barnsley canals. Work is progressing on the Elsecar Branch with clearance of the locks at Cobcar Bridge and Top Lock with the notrious Elsecar mud.

Basingstoke Canal

The Basingstoke Canal was opened in 1794 as a navigation to transport bulky agricultural products. The local nature of its business meant it was never a commercial success. Various proposals were put forward to link it with canals to Southampton or Portsmouth or via the Kennet and Avon to Bristol but these were never completed. It remained in private ownership, despite changing hands many times, and was bought by the Hampshire and Surrey County Councils in 1973 and 1976. The drive and energy of the Surrey and Hampshire Canal Society saw its restoration with a re-opening in 1991 for the 32 miles to Greywell. A new aqueduct was built and opened in 1995 along the Ash Embankment to accommodate a new road.

The canal has a wide range of flora and fauna and the management committee has drawn up a plan in conjunction with English Nature to ensure the use of the canal for amenity purposes does not endanger its conservation value to wildlife. Water supply continues to be a problem and many summers the canal is unavailable to boats owing to lack of water.

Authority The canal is owned by the Surrey and Hampshire County Councils and managed by the Basingstoke Canal Authority, Canal Centre, Mytchett Place Road, Mytchett, Surrey, GU16 6DD ☎ 01252 370073.

Bridges Numerous. Lifting bridge at North Warnborough and Crookhall swing bridge need a BW key.

Towpath Very good throughout the length of the navigation.

Tunnels Greywell, 1200 yards. This was originally closed owing to the collapse of the roof. It has now become a major habitat for bats and for ecological reasons will not be restored for navigation.

Restoration Discussions are continuing over the restoration of the last 5 miles to Basingstoke. Plans will be dependent on funding and the outcome of studies to consider the alternative routes proposed.

Facilities There are various pubs and restaurants along the canal as well as four boat hire companies: Galleon Marine, Odiham, Basingstoke Canal Cruises, Woking, Heart of England Hotel Narrowboats, Mytchett, and Surrey and Hants

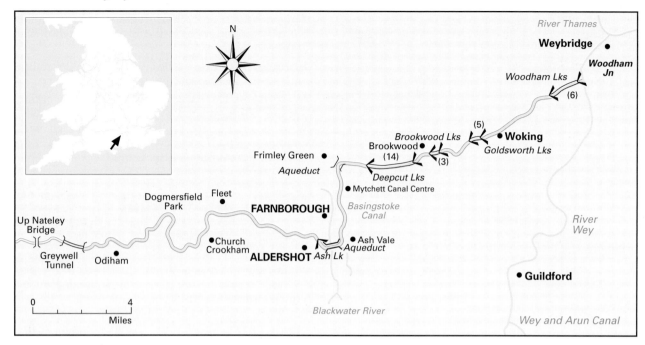

Canal Cruises Ltd. Slipways are available at Mytchett, Aldershot, Winchfield and Galleon Marine.

Distance table

Woodham, junction with River Wey to:

	Miles
Woodham Locks Nos 1–5	0.3
Woodham Top Lock No 6	1.5
Sheerwater	2.3
Maybury Hill	3.0
Woking, Wheatsheaf Bridge	3.9
Goldsworth Locks Nos 7–10	5.3
Goldsworth Top Lock No 11	5.6
Brookwood Locks Nos 12 and 13	7.4
Brookwood Top Lock No 14	7.5
Deepcut Locks Nos 15–27	8.6
Deepcut Top Lock No 28	10.5
Frimley Green	11.9
Mytchett Lake, Canal Centre	13.3
North Camp Railway Station	13.8
Ash Aqueduct	15.5
Ash Lock No 29 (slipway)	16.0
Aldershot, Main Road Bridge	17.8
Pondtail Bridge	20.6
Fleet	21.6
Crookham	23.6
Crondall Bridge	24.3
The Barley Mow (slipway)	25.5
Pilcot Bridge	26.8
Winchfield (slipway)	27.0
Odiham	29.0
North Warnborough	30.1
Greywell Lock No 30 (east end of Greywell Tunnel) (limit of navigation)	31.1
Up Nateley	32.6

Beaulieu River

The ownership of this river is almost unique in Britain in that the bed and foreshore are not Crown Property. In the 13th century King John gave the Beaulieu River to the monks who founded the abbey. In the early 18th century the rights passed to the second Duke of Montagu and it is still in the family. The Duke proposed a port at Buckler's Hard but in the event it became a major ship-building dock as the wars with France and Spain continued. The naval dock had the first call on oak from the New Forest and many of Nelson's warships were built there.

Today, the village is much as it was 250 years ago but the boats on the river are mostly yachts, although a few wooden mine sweepers were built

BASINGSTOKE CANAL *Maximum vessel dimensions*

From and to	Distance	Length	Beam	Draught	Headroom	Locks
Woodham, junction with River Wey to Greywell	32 miles (51.5km)	68' (20.7m)	13' (3.9m)	3' 6" (1.0m)	5' 10" (1.7m)	29

Everyone is free to enjoy Britain's waterways in their own way.
Jane Cumberlidge

Cruising under Worcester Cathedral on the River Severn. *Siân Barron*

Sharpness Marine provides moorings in the old spur down to the original locks joining the Gloucester and Sharpness Canal to the River Severn. *Jane Cumberlidge*

Below Vale Royal locks on the River Weaver. *Lester McCarthy - Motor Boat and Yachting*

BEAULIEU RIVER Maximum vessel dimensions

From and to	Distance	Length	Beam	Draught	Headroom	Locks
Stone Point to Beaulieu	8 miles (12.8km)	Unlimited	Unlimited	7' (2.1m) at HW	Unlimited	None

there during the First World War. There is now a Maritime Museum at Buckler's Hard and the famous Motor Museum at Beaulieu Abbey.

Authority The Montagu Estate. All enquiries should be made to The Harbourmaster, Harbourmaster's Office, Buckler's Hard, Beaulieu, Hampshire SO42 7XB ☎ 01590 616200/616234.

Bridges None.

Towpath None.

Navigation There is double high water in Beaulieu River, the first HW occurs about half an hour before HW Portsmouth, the second 2 hours after the first. Spring tides rise 10ft, neaps 9ft. Consult a good pilot book if you intend to cruise into the Beaulieu River, for example, *The Shell Channel Pilot* by Tom Cunliffe.

Charts Imray C15, Admiralty 2021, 2040, 1905.

Beverley Beck

This canal or creek was promoted under Acts of Parliament dated 1726 and 1744. It was used for many years before that date being kept in repair by the Corporation. Beverley is a very pleasant country town with its fine Minster and wealth of old domestic architecture dating back to the days when it was a wool town. Access is through Grovehill Lock which requires at least 36 hours notice to the lock-keeper.

Authority Beverley District Council, Lairgate Hall, Beverley HU17 8HL ☎ 01482 882255.

Towpath Throughout the canal.

Birmingham Canal Navigations

Birmingham is the heart of the English canal system. It is said that there are more miles of canal in Birmingham than in Venice and the enormous efforts made over the past ten years have put paid to the old idea that Birmingham's canals are an eyesore. With the increased awareness of the value of the canals British Waterways, Birmingham City Council, central government, local authorities and private enterprise are working together to improve the quality of the canals around Birmingham to encourage greater use for boating, walking, angling and cycling. The imaginative redevelopment of Gas Street Basin is just one of the projects which are turning the canals into a major attraction in Birmingham.

The BCN is an amalgamation of canals with branches, loops and private arms. You travel through tunnels and over aqueducts, past factories, through parks and under motorways, with an amazing mixture of industrial heritage and modern developments. The history of Britain's development as a manufacturing nation can be traced along the waterways of the second city.

In the middle of the 18th century, Birmingham had a population of just over 40,000 and covered an area between Gas Street Basin, Warwick Bar and Aston Junction. By the middle of the 19th century the city was four or five times as big with something of a population explosion. Much of this can be put down to the development of the canal system which put Birmingham at the centre of the cross to join the Thames, the Humber, the Severn and the Mersey. As traffic grew the number of cross canals, branches and arms increased providing waterside space for wharves and the development of industry.

The Birmingham Canal was to run from the Staffordshire and Worcestershire Canal outside Wolverhampton to Birmingham because neither the Staffordshire and Worcestershire nor the Trent and Mersey had a branch into Birmingham. The first section of canal was opened in 1769 bringing Wednesbury coal into the city. The canal was not completed to Aldersley until 1772. Designed by Brindley, this was a contour canal winding its way from the Staffordshire and Worcestershire to Gas Street Basin. This had the advantage of running close to many manufacturers but as trade grew the slow speed of travel became a disadvantage.

BEVERLEY BECK Maximum vessel dimensions

From and to	Distance	Length	Beam	Draught	Headroom	Locks
Beverley to River Hull at Grovehill	0.8 miles (1.3km)	65' (19.8m)	17' 6" (5.3m)	6' (1.8m)	Unlimited	1

And trade did grow rapidly with the canal company becoming very wealthy. This enabled the company to finance improvements and in 1783 an Act was passed to promote another canal from Birmingham to Fazeley. A rival company had been formed in the 1770s but by 1784 they were prepared to amalgamate with the Birmingham Canal Company, and in 1794 the Birmingham Canal Navigation came into being.

By the early 19th century, congestion was getting so bad on the canals that Thomas Telford was brought in to consider improvements. With greater confidence in the possibilities of engineering, he produced a much straighter canal, the New Main

Line, which was 7 miles shorter than the 22.6 miles of the Old Main Line. The Main Line, as we know it today, includes the Galton Valley Cutting and Bridge and runs at a lower level than the Old Main Line. The Worcester and Birmingham Canal Company also proposed a canal to Birmingham which would end in Gas Street Basin. Being jealous of both its trade and its water, the Birmingham Canal Company only agreed to this when an obstruction was created at Gas Street, the Worcester Bar, which can still be seen today although a stop lock was cut in it in 1815 allowing passage between the two canals. Prior to that all cargo had to be transhipped across the Bar.

Other canals had been proposed and built in the late 1700s. Some found favour with the BCN as they increased traffic while others were perceived as rivals. One such was the Dudley Canal which provided a link between the Stourbridge Canal, and ultimately the River Severn, through to the Worcester and Birmingham Canal at Selly Oak passing through the 3795-yard (3470m) Lapal Tunnel.

The BCN gradually evolved with waterways on three different levels, the Wolverhampton level at 473ft, Telford's Main Line at 453ft and the Walsall level at 408ft. The highest point in the system was 511ft at Oldbury, familiarly known as the 'Crow's Nest'. On the Wyrley and Essington Canal, the Essington Locks Branch rose to 527ft.

Many more cuts and branches were built and in 1844 the new Tame Valley Canal was opened to relieve congestion on the Farmer's Bridge flight of locks at the junction of the Birmingham Canal with the Birmingham and Fazeley Canal. Coal was still a very important commodity on the canals and new branches were built to tap into new colliery workings.

With the advent of the railways, there was fear that traffic would fall off but within the BCN the canals were so closely linked with industry that it was mostly only the longer distance traffic that was affected. It was not until after the Second World War that the enormous move towards road transport really hit the canal system in Birmingham. By the early 1970s, closures had reduced the BCN from its 160 miles of canal down to about 100 miles which are available today. Now there is the prospect of some of the abandoned waterways being restored and re-opened and the activities of local groups and the IWA is starting to encourage boats back into the heart of the canal system.

Authority British Waterways, Bradley Lane, Bilston, West Midlands WV14 8DW ☎ 01902 409010.

Bridges Numerous.

Towpath Extensive paths and cycleways throughout the navigation, for full details contact British Waterways.

Tunnels Summit tunnel, 102yds (31m) with towpath; Coseley, 360yds (109m) with towpath each side; Galton Tunnel, 123yds (37m) with towpath.

Speed limit 4mph.

Restoration There are a number of local societies undertaking and planning restoration projects on different parts of the BCN. The Lapal Canal Trust is working on the first section of the Dudley No 2 line in Leasowes Park and has proposals for the full restoration of the canal to Selly Oak and the

junction with the Worcester and Birmingham Canal, including Lapal Tunnel.

The Lichfield and Hatherton Canals Trust are working on both the Ogley to Huddlesford Section of the Wyrley and Essington Canal, also called the Lichfield Canal, and the Calf Heath end of the Hatherton Canal. This canal connected the Staffordshire and Worcestershire Canal with the Cannock Extension Canal in the BCN. The Trust has proposals for full restoration of both canals.

Facilities Within Birmingham all services and facilities are available. In some areas care must be taken when considering a suitable mooring if you wish to leave a boat unattended.

Distances of the main canals	*Miles*
Mainline	
Worcester Bar, junction with the Worcester and Birmingham Canal to Aldersley Junction with the Staffordshire and Worcestershire Canal	15.5
Birmingham and Fazeley Canal	
Farmer's Bridge Junction with the Worcester and Birmingham Canal to Fazeley Junction with the Coventry Canal	20.5
Wyrley and Essington Canal	
Horseley Fields Junction with the Main Line to Ogley Junction with the Anglesey Branch	23.5
Dudley Canal Line No 1	
Tipton Junction with the Mainline to Delph Bottom Lock and the Stourbridge Canal	4.5
Dudley Canal Line No 2	
Windmill End Junction with Dudley No 1 to Hawne Basin, from here through the Lapal Tunnel to the Worcester and Birmingham Canal is closed	5.8
Walsall Canal	
Ryders Green Junction with the Wednesbury Old Canal to Walsall	7.0
Tame Valley Canal	
Tame Valley Junction with Walsall Canal to Salford Junction with the Birmingham and Fazeley Canal	8.5
Branches	
Mainline	
Oozells Street Loop Line	0.3
Icknield Port Road Wharf Loop Line	0.8
Soho Branch Loop Line	1.3
Parker Branch (closed and filled in)	0.3
Dunkirk Branch (closed and filled in)	0.3
Dixons Branch (closed and filled in)	1.3
Wednesbury Oak Loop Line	
Ocker Hill Branch (closed)	0.4
Old Main Loop Line	
Engine Branch	0.6
Spon Lane Locks Branch	0.4
Titford Canal (short length only now open)	1.3
Oldbury Loop Line (closed)	1.0
Gower Branch Canal	0.5
Netherton Tunnel Branch	2.9
Dudley Canal Line No 1	
Withymoor Branch Canal (closed and filled in)	0.3
Bumble Hole Branch Canal (partly filled in)	0.5

BIRMINGHAM CANAL NAVIGATIONS Maximum vessel dimensions

From and to	Distance	Length	Beam	Draught	Headroom	Locks
Whole system	113.6 miles (182.9km)	70' (21.3m)	7' (2.1m)	2' 6" (0.8m)	6' 6" (2.0m)	113

	Miles
Bradley Locks Branch Canal	
(navigable to Bottom Lock only)	0.9
Tipton Green and Toll End Communication	
(closed)	1.5
Wednesbury Old Canal	
Ridgacre Branch Canal (restorable but weedy)	0.8
Dartmouth Branch Canal (closed)	0.6
Halford Branch Canal (closed)	0.5
Walsall Canal	
Haines Branch Canal (closed)	0.6
Danks Branch Canal (closed)	0.4
Lower Ocker Hill Branch Canal (closed)	0.1
Gospel Oak Branch Canal (closed)	0.5
Monway Branch Canal (closed)	0.3
Anson Branch Canal (navigable to M6 culvert)	0.5
Walsall Branch Canal	0.9
Bentley Canal (closed)	3.4
Nechells Branch Canal (closed)	0.5
Rushall Canal	2.8
Birmingham and Fazeley Canal	
Newhall Branch (completely filled in)	0.3
Digbeth Branch Canal	0.9
Wyrley and Essington Canal	
Sneyd Branch Canal	0.3
(The Wyrley Bank section of 3.3 miles to Wyrley Wharf is closed)	
Lord Hay's Branch Canal (closed)	0.9
Daw End Branch Canal	5.3
Anglesey Branch Canal	1.5
Cannock Extension Canal (closed except for 0.3 miles)	
Churchbridge Branch Canal (closed)	

Distance tables

Mainline
Worcester Bar, junction with Worcester and Birmingham Canal to:

	Miles
Farmer's Bridge, junction with Birmingham and Fazeley Canal (N) and junction with Oozells Street Loop (E)	0.3
Eastern junction with Icknield Port Loop	0.9
Western junction with Icknield Port Loop (left) and eastern junction with Soho Loop (right)	1.0
Western junction with Soho Loop	1.8
Smethwick Junction with Old Mainline from Tipton Factory Junction – Galton Canal Park	2.8
Bromford Junction with Spon Lane Locks Branch (right) and junction with Parker Branch (closed) (left)	5.0
Pudding Green Junction with Wednesbury Old Canal	5.8
Albion Junction with Gower Branch	6.3
Dunkirk Junction with Dunkirk Branch (closed)	6.4
Dudley Port Junction with Netherton Tunnel Branch Canal	7.0
Junction with Dixon's Branch (closed)	7.5
Watery Lane	8.0
Tipton Factory Junction with Old Mainline from Smethwick Junction – Tipton Factory Locks Nos 1–3	8.5
Bloomfield	8.8
Coseley Tunnel, south end	9.4
Deepfields Junction, northern junction with Wednesbury Oak Loop Line	10.1
Rough Hills	12.0
Horseley Fields, junction with Wyrley and Essington Canal	13.1

	Miles
Wolverhampton, Albion Wharf	13.3
Wolverhampton Lock No 4 (top)	13.8
Aldersley Junction with Staffordshire and Worcestershire Canal – Mainline and Wolverhampton Lock No 21 (bottom)	15.5

Soho Branch Loop Line
Eastern junction with Mainline to:

	Miles
Junction with Soho Branch, 0.5 mile to Soho Wharf	0.6
Winson Green Wharf	0.9
Western junction with Mainline	1.3

Wednesbury Oak Loop Line
British Waterways workshops to:

	Miles
Pothouse Bridge Wharf	0.6
Capponfield	1.0
Deepfields Junction, northern junction with Main Line	1.9
(The rest of the canal is closed.)	

Old Main Loop Line
From Smethwick Junction to Tipton Factory Smethwick Junction, junction with Mainline to:

	Miles
Junction with Engine Branch, Smethwick (Smethwick Lock Nos 1–3)	0.5
Spon Lane Wharf and Junction, junction with Spon Lane	
Locks Branch (Spon Lane, Lock Nos 1–3)	2.0
Oldbury Locks Junction, junction with Titford Canal	2.6
Junction with Houghton Branch Canal	2.8
Southern junction with Oldbury Loop Line	2.9
Northern junction with Oldbury Loop Line	3.3
(Oldbury Loop is closed.)	
Brades Hall Junction, junction with Gower Branch	3.9
Aqueduct over Netherton Tunnel Branch Canal	4.4
Tipton Junction, junction with Dudley Canal	5.5
Tipton Green Junction, junction with Tipton Green and Toll End Communication (closed)	5.8
Tipton Factory Junction, junction with Main Line	6.5

Titford Canal
Oldbury Locks Junction with Old Main Loop Line to:

	Miles
Oldbury Lock No 6	0.1
Top of Oldbury Locks, junction with Spon Lane Branch (5 furlongs)	
Oldbury Lock No 1 Spon Lane Branch can be navigated for about one furlong but there is no winding hole	0.3
Uncle Ben's Bridge	0.8
Junction with Portway Branch (100yards)	1.1
Causeway Green	1.2

Gower Branch Canal
Brades Hall Junction, junction with Old Mainline to:

	Miles
Brades Hall Lock No 1 (top)	0.1
Brades Hall Lock No 3 (bottom)	0.3
Albion Junction, junction with Mainline	0.5

Netherton Tunnel Branch Canal,
Dudley Port Junction, junction with Mainline to:

	Miles
North End of Netherton Tunnel	0.5
Windmill End Junction, junction with Dudley Canal	2.9

Dudley Canal Line No 1
Tipton Junction, junction with Old Main Loop Line to:

	Miles
North End of Dudley Tunnel	0.4
Junction with Pensnett Canal (closed) and Park Head Lock No 1	2.1

	Miles
Park Head Junction, junction with Dudley Canal (Line No 2) – Park Head Lock No 3 and top of Blowers Green Lock No 4	2.4
Woodside Junction, junction with Two Lock Line Canal (closed)	3.1
Brierley Hill, Delph Lock No 5 (top)	4.1
Black Delph Wharf, Delph Lock No 12 (bottom) and junction with Stourbridge Canal – Mainline	4.5

Dudley Canal Line No 2
Park Head Junction, junction with Dudley Canal Line No 1 to:

Blackbrook Junction, junction with Two Lock Line Canal (closed)	0.8
Primrose Hill Wharf	1.6
Southern junction with Bumble Hole Branch Canal	2.4
Windmill End Junction, junction with Netherton Tunnel Branch Canal and northern junction with Bumble Hole Branch canal (now closed)	2.6
Rowley Wharf	4.0
Old Hill and Northern end of Gosty Hill Tunnel	4.4
Coombeswood	5.0

(The canal is abandoned from this point to Selly Oak. Hawne Basin is owned by the Coombeswood Canal Trust)

Bradley Locks Branch Canal (derelict at present)

Bradley Branch Canal (derelict at present)
Bradley Locks Junction, junction with Wednesbury Oak Loop Line, and top of Bradley Locks to:

Moorcroft Junction, junction with Walsall Canal	0.9

(Bradley Lock Nos 1 to 9 are in this section)

Tipton Green and Toll End Communication
Tipton Green Locks are closed and it is no longer possible to reach the bottom of Tipton Locks from the Walsall Canal.

Wednesbury Old Canal
Pudding Green Junction, junction with Main Line to:

Riders Green Junction, junction with Walsall Canal	0.6
Junction with Ridgacre Branch Canal (the rest of the canal is closed)	1.2

Ridgacre Branch Canal (unnavigable but restorable)
Junction with Wednesbury Old Canal to:

Junction with Dartmouth Branch Canal (closed)	4.5
Junction with Halford Branch Canal (closed)	5.5
Termination of Canal	6.0

Walsall Canal
Ryders Green Junction, junction with Wednesbury Old Canal and top of Ryders Green Lock No 1 to:

Great Bridge, junction with Haines Branch, and bottom of Ryders Green Lock No 8	0.8
Junction with Danks Branch (closed)	1.0
Toll End	1.1
Junction with Lower Ocker Hill Branch (closed)	1.3
Junction with Tame Valley Canal	1.4
Junction with Gospel Oak Branch (closed)	2.1
Junction with Monway Branch (closed)	2.2
Moorcroft Junction, junction with Bradley Branch Canal	2.4
Moxley Stop	3.0
Junction with Bilston Branch (now closed)	3.3
Junction with Willenhall Branch (now closed)	3.5
Bug Hole Wharf	4.3
Darlaston Green Wharf	4.8
Junction with Anson Branch	5.1

	Miles
Walsall Junction, junction with Walsall Branch Canal	6.9
Walsall, Public Wharf	7.0

Anson Branch
Junction with Walsall Canal, junction with Bentley Canal to:

End of Branch (motorway culvert)	1.4

Walsall Branch Canal
Birchills Junction, junction with Wyrley and Essington Canal to:

Birchills Wharf, and top of Walsall Locks No 1	0.3
Walsall Junction, junction with Walsall Canal and bottom of Walsall Locks No 8	0.9

Bentley Canal (closed)

Tame Valley Canal
Junction with Walsall Canal to:

Golds Hill Bridge	0.4
Holloway Bank Bridge	1.0
Grand Junction Aqueduct	2.9
Rushall Junction, junction with Rushall Canal	3.5
Piercy Aqueduct	4.8
Perry Barr Top Lock	5.5
Perry Barr, 1st Flight, Lock No 7	6.0
Perry Barr, 2nd Flight, Lock Nos 8–11	6.3
Perry Barr Wharf	6.5
Perry Barr, 3rd Flight, Lock Nos 12 and 13	7.9
Salford Junction, junction with Birmingham and Fazeley Canal right and left, and junction with Birmingham and Warwick Section of the Grand Union Canal	8.5

Rushall Canal
Longwood Junction, junction with Daw End Branch of Wyrley and Essington Canal, and Rushall Lock No 1 (top) and No 2, to:

Bell Wharf and Rushall Lock Nos 3–9	1.5
Rushall Junction, junction with Tame Valley Canal	2.8

Birmingham and Fazeley Canal
Farmers Bridge, junction with Main Line to:

Junction with Newhall Branch Canal, and Farmers Bridge Lock No 1 (top)	0.1
Farmers Bridge Lock No 13	1.0
Aston Junction, junction with Digbeth Branch, and Aston Lock No 14 (top)	1.5
Aston Lock No 24 (bottom)	2.5
Salford Junction, junction with Grand Union – right, and junction with Tame Valley Canal – left	3.3
Erdington Wharf	5.1
Minworth Top Lock, No 25	6.3
Minworth 2nd Lock, No 26	6.6
Minworth Bottom Lock, No 27	7.1
Jeffrey's Dock Wharf	7.8
Dunton Wharf, Curdworth Lock, No 28	9.5
Curdworth Lock, No 29	9.9
Curdworth Lock, No 32	10.1
Curdworth Lock, No 33	10.3
Curdworth Lock, No 34	10.6
Curdworth Lock, No 35	11.1
Curdworth Lock, No 36	11.3
Curdworth Lock, No 37	11.7
Curdworth Bottom Lock, No 38	12.1
Fazeley Junction, junction with Coventry Canal	15.0
Hopwas	17.8

Whittington Brook, junction with Coventry Canal – detached portion	20.5

Digbeth Branch Canal
Aston Junction, junction with Birmingham and Fazeley Canal to:

Junction with Grand Union Canal	0.8
Bordesley Basin	0.9

Wyrley and Essington Canal
Horseley Fields Junction, junction with Main Line to:

Heath Town Wharf	0.9
Wednesfield Junction, junction with Bentley Canal	1.3
Sneyd Junction, junction with Sneyd and Wyrley Bank Branch Canal (closed)	6.3
Birchills Junction, junction with Walsall Branch Canal	8.0
Junction with Lord Hay's Branch Canal, near Little Bloxwich (now closed)	11.9
Pelsall Junction, junction with Cannock Extension Canal	12.9
Catshill Junction, junction with Daw End Branch Canal	15.4
Junction with Anglesey Branch and Ogley Lock No 1 (not usable)	16.4

(The canal from Ogley to Huddlesford is closed but under restoration.)

Daw End Branch Canal
Catshill Junction, junction with Wyrley and Essington Canal to:

Clayhanger Wharf	0.1
Black Cock Wharf	0.8
Aldridge Wharf	2.5
Daw End Wharf	4.0
Longwood Junction and Wharf, junction with Rushall Canal	5.3

Cannock Extension Canal
Pelsall Junction, junction with Wyrley and Essington Canal to:

Wyrley Grove Wharf	0.6
Norton Canes Docks	1.8

River Blyth

Until the 16th century Blythburgh was a busy port but gradually the river silted up. An Act of Parliament in 1757 made the river navigable again. By 1761, the river was open for 9 miles up to Halesworth with four locks. By the 1850s, trade was falling off and eventually the locks were closed in 1934.

Anyone wishing to visit the River Blyth is now likely to only go to Southwold Harbour at the entrance. Southwold is a reasonable walk to the north and a foot-ferry can take you across the river to Walberswick on the south shore.

Authority Waveney District Council, Southwold, Suffolk ☎ 01502 722366.

Drainage Authority Environment Agency, Kingfisher House, Goldhay Way, Orton Way, Peterborough PE2 5ZR ☎ 01733 37181 *Fax* 01733 231840.

Towpath None.

Navigation Once craft have entered the river, there is an average depth of 7ft at LWOS, the rise and fall being about 4ft 6in neaps and 6ft 6in springs. The river is navigable with decreasing depths to Blythburgh. High water at the entrance is about 35 minutes after HW Lowestoft. Contact the harbourmaster about the availability of moorings in Southwold, ☎ 01502 523003 or 0585 774689.

Charts Imray C28, Admiralty 1543.

Facilities Reasonable moorings on the north shore near the Harbourmaster's Office. The Harbour Inn is close by.

Bridgewater Canal

This is the canal which was the first of the canal age and its promoter, Francis Egerton, 3rd Duke of Bridgewater, is often called the 'Father of the Canals'. As a young man, he had done 'The Grand Tour' of Europe and while on the Continent saw a number of impressive canal projects, including what we now know as the Canal du Midi. In the 1730s, when he was considering ways to reduce the cost of transporting coal from his mines at Worsley to the rapidly growing town of Manchester, his agent, John Gilbert, rekindled this interest in canals and they looked at the idea of building a canal from Worsley to Manchester. James Brindley was also involved in the project as he had been working with the Duke of Bridgewater's brother-in-law, Earl Gower, on a plan to join the Trent and the Mersey by canal.

There is some difference of opinion as to which of the two engineers should take the credit for the Barton Aqueduct, which was built to cross the River Irwell, a stone structure 200yds long and 38ft above the river. This was opened in 1761 and then the

RIVER BLYTH Maximum vessel dimensions

From and to	Distance	Length	Beam	Draught	Headroom	Locks
Walberswick to Blythburgh	5.5 miles (8.8km)	Unlimited	Unlimited	4' (1.2m)	6' (1.8m)	None

BRIDGEWATER CANAL *Maximum vessel dimensions*

From and to	Distance	Length	Beam	Draught	Headroom	Locks
Bridgewater Canal						
Mainline: Rochdale Canal at Castlefield						
to Runcorn	28.1 miles (45.2km)	70' (21.3m)	14' 9" (4.5m)	4' (1.2m)	11' (3.3m)	None
Preston Brook Branch						
Preston Brook Junction on the Bridgewater Canal						
to Preston Brook	0.8 miles (1.3km)	70' (21.3m)	14' 9" (4.5m)	4' (1.2m)	11' (3.4m)	None
Stretford and Leigh Branch						
Stretford to junction with the Leeds and Liverpool						
Canal at Leigh	10.8 miles (17.4km)	70' (21.3m)	14' 9" (4.5m)	4' (1.2m)	8' 6" (2.6m)	None

canal was finished to Stretford. By 1765, it went through to Castlefield Wharf in Manchester and coal was delivered into Manchester for 4d per cwt. The Barton Aqueduct was demolished in 1893 during the construction of the Manchester Ship Canal and the Barton Swing Aqueduct, designed by Edward Leader Williams, was built to replace it and is still in use today.

At Worsley, there remains a network of underground canals into the coal mines, long disused and now closed as they are unsafe, though the entrance is still to be seen. The underground main line of the canal was 4 miles long, the upper canal 2 miles and the side branches totalled 40 miles. Inclined planes were used between the levels and a system was developed to use the flow of water to move strings of laden boats out of the mines and onto the canal. Proposals have now been put forward to re-open some of the mine canals as a tourist attraction.

The Bridgewater Canal was built as a contour canal, 83ft above sea level with no locks throughout its nearly 40 mile length. To enable it to join first the Mersey and then the Manchester Ship Canal at Runcorn, two flights of ten locks each were built but these have now been closed and the section from Preston Brook Branch to Runcorn is a dead end. The remains of the old locks have been uncovered and their future is being considered.

Although initially a great drain on the Duke's finances, the Bridgewater Canal went on to become a highly profitable undertaking. Commercial traffic started to decline after the First World War but did not stop on the canal until 1974. From the early 1950s, pleasure craft started using the canal and it is now a popular and busy cruising route. It forms most of the northern side of the Cheshire Ring and, with the improvements in Manchester, it is an interesting destination in its own right. In May 1995, Pomona Lock was opened offering access from the Bridgewater Canal to the upper reaches of the Manchester Ship Canal.

The Bridgewater Canal Trust was set up after a serious breach in 1971. It is made up of local authorities and is actively involved with the Manchester Ship Canal Company in funding and deciding policies for managing the amenity use of the canal.

Authority Manchester Ship Canal Company, Quay West, Trafford Wharf Road, Manchester M17 1PL ☎ 0161 872 2411 *Fax* 0161 877 0344.

Bridges Numerous.

Locks The new Pomona Lock joins the Bridgewater Canal to the Manchester Ship Canal. Its maximum dimensions are: length 71ft (21.6m), beam 15ft 6ins (4.7m) and draught 3ft 6ins (1.0m). Draught is the constraining measurement due to the height of the sill. Prior notification of 72 hours is essential for any craft wishing to use the Pomona Lock.

Towpath Throughout canal and branches.

Connections Besides having junctions with the Rochdale Canal and Manchester Ship Canal, this waterway has the following branches and junctions:

Stretford and Leigh Branch, joining the Leeds and Liverpool Canal at Leigh

The Preston Brook Branch from Waters Meeting, Main Canal to junction with the Trent and Mersey Canal at Preston Brook

Pomona Lock Branch to the Manchester Ship Canal and the Upper Reach.

Licences The Bridgewater Canal has its own licensing system. Under the reciprocal licensing arrangement BW licensed craft may transit the main canal but an additional charge is levied for the Pomona Lock into the Manchester Ship Canal. All information on charges, bye-laws, licences and navigation of the Bridgewater Canal can be obtained from the Manchester Ship Canal Company at the address above. A booklet describing the history of the canal is also available and this has a plan with details of mooring sites, shops, sanitary facilities, etc.

Facilities There are several boatyards with all facilities and plenty of pubs and restaurants available close to the canal.

Distance table   *Miles*
Mainline
Manchester, Castlefield, junction with Rochdale Canal – Mainline to:
Egerton Street Bridge, junction with former Hulme Locks Branch	0.3
Cornbrook Bridge	1.0
Pomona Dock, junction with the Pomona Lock Branch	1.2
Throstle Nest Footbridge	1.4

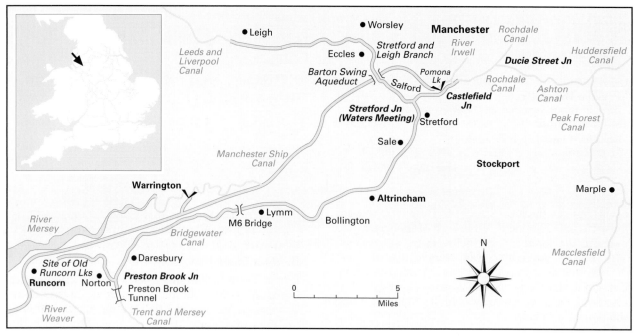

	Miles		*Miles*
Trafford Road Bridge	1.5	Hough's Bridge	19.4
Waters Meeting, junction with Stretford		Walton Lea Bridge	19.6
and Leigh Branch	2.8	Walton Bridge	19.9
Stretford Gas Works	3.0	Chester Road Underbridge	20.1
Longford Bridge	3.3	Thomason's Bridge	20.3
Stretford Boat club	3.5	Acton Grange Bridge	20.5
Edge Lane Bridge	3.8	Moore Bridge	21.0
Watch House Cruising Club	4.0	Moorefield Bridge	21.5
Barfoot Aqueduct, River Mersey	4.4	Keckwick Bridge	21.8
M63	4.6	Keckwick Hill Bridge	22.3
Dane Road Bridge	4.8	George Gleave's Bridge	22.4
Sale Bridge	5.3	Red Brow Underbridge	23.0
Marsland Bridge	5.9	Preston Brook, Waters Meeting, junction with Preston	
Timperley Bridge	6.9	Brook Branch	23.4
Railway Bridge (Stockport Line)	7.1	Cawley's Bridge	23.8
Railway Bridge	7.4	Borrow's Bridge	23.9
Broadheath Warehouse and Bridge	7.6	Railway Bridge	24.0
Seamon's Moss Bridge	8.5	Norton Town Bridge	24.3
Dunham School Bridge	9.4	Norton Bridge	24.6
Dunham Town Bridge	9.8	Norton Townfield Bridge	25.0
Dunham Underbridge	10.1	Greens Bridge	25.5
River Bollin Aqueduct	10.3	Astmoor Bridge	26.1
Bollington Underbridge	10.6	Bate's Bridge	26.8
Agden Bridge	11.4	Highfield Tannery	26.9
Burford Lane Underbridge	12.3	Delph Bridge	27.5
Grantham's Bridge	12.4	Sprinch Dockyard	27.6
Lloyd Bridge	12.8	Doctor's Bridge	28.0
Lymm Cruising Club	13.5	Runcorn, top of Locks, Waterloo Bridge	28.1
Lymm Bridge	13.6		
Whitborough Aqueduct	13.8	**Preston Brook Branch**	
Brookfield Bridge	13.9	*Preston Brook, junction with Main Line to:*	
Barsbank Aqueduct	14.3	Preston Brook. Bridge (Chester Road)	0.3
Ditchfield Bridge	14.6	Preston Brook junction with Trent and	
M6	15.0	Mersey Canal, Main Line	0.8
Thelwall Aqueduct	15.5		
Pickering's Bridge	15.8	**Stretford and Leigh Branch**	
Cliff Lane Underbridge	16.3	***Bridges** Numerous.*	
Grappenhall Bridge	16.6	*Stretford, Waters Meeting, junction with Main Line, to:*	
Stanny Lunt Bridge	17.0	Taylor's Bridge	0.1
Lumb Brook Underbridge	18.0	Barton Swing Aqueduct over Manchester	
Stockton Quay	18.5	Ship Canal	2.3
Red Lane Bridge	18.9	Worsley Cruising Club	2.6
		Patricroft Bridge	2.8

	Miles
Patricroft Railway Bridge	3.1
Monton Green Bridge	3.6
Worsley Bridge	4.8
M62	4.9
Boothshall Bridge	6.2
Boothstown Bridge	6.5
Vicar's Hall Bridge	7.0
Whitehead Hall Bridge	7.5
Astley Bridge	7.8
Lingard's Bridge	8.4
Morley's Bridge	8.5
Marsland Green Bridge	8.9
Great Fold Bridge	9.1
Hall House Bridge	9.4
Butt's Basin	9.8
Butt's Bridge	9.9
Mather's Lane Bridge	10.3
Junction with Leigh Branch of Leeds and Liverpool Canal	10.8

Hulme Lock Branch (this is no longer accessible)
Length from junction with Main Line to junction
with Irwell Upper Reach, Hulme Deep Lock 0.1

Bridgwater and Taunton Canal

Originally conceived as part of a scheme to join the Bristol and English Channels, the Bridgwater and Taunton Canal is one of the few sections that were actually built. Opened in 1827, the canal joined the River Parrett at Huntworth, then ten years later it was extended to Bridgwater.

Through the 19th century, Bridgwater was quite a substantial port with large wharves and warehouses around the docks. The main cargoes in were coal and iron from South Wales and agricultural produce would have been transported out. Commercial carrying continued until 1907 and after that the canal was mainly used for water supply.

Many of the swing bridges were fixed for defensive reasons during the Second World War and, although there was water in the canal, it was only navigable by canoes and small boats. BW and Somerset County Council restored the canal with the very active help of local inland waterway groups and it was fully re-opened in 1994.

It is an attractive, peaceful canal with slipway facilities at the YMCA in Bridgwater and at Taunton and a new slip planned for Bathpool. The dock at Bridgwater has been developed into a marina with shops, housing and restuarants around it. Unfortunately, it is not possible to gain access to the River Parrett from the Bridgwater and Taunton Canal.

Authority British Waterways, The Wharf, Govilon, Abergavenny, Gwent NP7 9NY ☎ 01873 830328 *Fax* 01873 831788.

Bridges Numerous.

Towpath Throughout navigation. Cycling is permitted but you must have a BW permit.

Connections River Tone at Firepool in Taunton, the River Parrett at Bridgwater (currently closed), the derelict Chard Canal near Creech St Michael.

Facilities These are mostly at each end of the canal though there is a useful shop at Maunsel Canal Centre, Lower Maunsel Lock.

Distance table *Miles*
Firepool Lock No 1, Taunton, junction with River Tone Navigation, to:
Bathpool 1.8

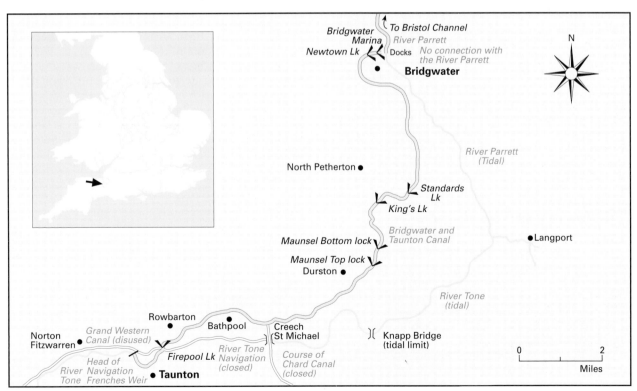

BRIDGWATER AND TAUNTON CANAL *Maximum vessel dimensions*

From and to	Distance	Length	Beam	Draught	Headroom	Locks
Taunton, junction with River Tone to Bridgwater	14.5 miles (23.3km)	50' (15.2m)	9' 10" (3.0m)	3' (0.9m)	6' 11" (2.1m)	6

	Miles
Creech St Michael	3.0
Charlton	4.2
A38 Roadbridge	5.6
Higher Maunsell Lock No 2	6.8
Lower Maunsell Lock No 3	7.0
North Newton	8.1
Kings Lock No 4	8.3
Standards Lock No 5	9.0
Fordgate	9.8
Huntworth	10.9
Mead	12.8
Lock No 6, Bridgwater Dock, end of canal	14.0
Junction with the River Parrett (no access)	14.2

The Broads

The Norfolk and Suffolk Broads have approximately 130 miles of navigable tidal rivers, together with many man-made side dykes and shallow lakes or broads. The combination of fen, marsh, woodland, farmland and open water represents Britain's largest and finest surviving wetland landscape, which is of international importance for conservation and recreational boating. The area was given special and nationally protected status similar to a national park by the passing of the Norfolk and Suffolk Broads Act 1988, which created the Broads Authority. The Authority seeks to achieve the integrated management of the area for the three equally prioritised purposes of conserving and enhancing the natural beauty of the Broads, promoting the enjoyment of the Broads by the public, and protecting the interests of navigation.

Since the late 19th century water-borne holidays have been a major attraction of the Broads and tourists in all types of craft are still a very important part of the Broads' life and economy. It is the task of the Broads Authority to maintain the fine balance between the use and enjoyment of the Broads and the wider needs of wildlife and the ecology of the area.

The history of The Broads

The history of the Broads is fascinating. It is often stated that the Broads are a result of peat cutting during the Middle Ages. In fact, the three principal rivers, Bure, Yare and Waveney, and their tributaries, the rivers Ant, Thurne, Wensum and Chet, are natural watercourses confined, in the lower reaches nearer Great Yarmouth, by man-made embankments. It is the shallow lakes or broads themselves which arguably are flooded peat diggings. Where these lay close to the natural rivers,

navigable links became established either naturally or by man's intervention for drainage and transport purposes, but in terms of the water area of the Broads navigation as a whole only a small part consists of flooded peat workings. There are about 40 small lakes or broads in all, but only about 12 of these are connected to the rivers and publicly navigable. A further handful, although connected to the rivers, are regarded as private water not available for public navigation. The remainder are not connected to the rivers systems, although on a few, small boating and fishing activity does take place.

In Roman times, a large part of the area we know today as Broadland consisted of a vast network of open tidal estuaries and salt marshes. During the Middle Ages and more recent centuries the wide low-lying grazing marshes we associate today with typical Broadland landscape were reclaimed by confining the rivers within man-made embankments. The rich grazing these low-lying marshes provided could only be sustained by careful management of water levels and hence the evolution of the large numbers of traditional Norfolk windmills, which in truth are not mills at all but wind driven pumps for lifting water out of the low marsh dykes back into the rivers. For a detailed history of the Broads, one of the most interesting starting points is *The Making of the Norfolk Broads* issued by the Royal Geographical Society 1960, much of which is based on work carried out by Dr Joyce Lambert. There are many other specialist books on the Broads for those who become thoroughly addicted to them.

For many centuries, river transport was the only way goods could be moved about and throughout the area each parish had a staithe where goods were off-loaded for the village. The word probably comes from the Anglo Saxon *staeth* meaning a landing place and some parish staithes have been in existence for 1,400 years or more. The legal status of many of these staithes is complex and during the 1960s the East Anglian Waterways Association started a study to look at the problem. In 1986, the Broads Authority commissioned a survey of staithes. Some of these are now owned or leased by the Broads Authority which operates them as overnight moorings for pleasure craft. Wherever possible, the authority tries to ensure that public access to staithes, and thus to the river, is maintained from landward and by boat.

The improvement of navigation on the rivers Yare, Bure and Waveney was proposed in Acts of Parliament passed in 1670, 1722, 1747 and 1772. In 1833, the Haddiscoe New Cut was opened. This connected the River Yare at Reedham to the River

Waveney at Haddiscoe and so to the Port of Lowestoft via Oulton Broad and Mutford Lock. This route bypasses the Port of Great Yarmouth through which the Broads rivers naturally discharge to the sea. The undertaking was promoted by the notable engineer, Sir Morton Peto, and the businesses of Norwich which sought an alternative route to the sea for their goods and had plans to make Norwich a major port. In the end, no major docks were ever built in Norwich and the New Cut was never a commercial success. Lowestoft tended to silt up and by 1842 the harbour had been sold to a railway contractor. River transport to Norwich reverted to the old route via Great Yarmouth and Norwich enjoyed significant sea-going coastal cargo trade until comparatively recent years. The last cargo ship to call at Norwich was in 1989. Nowadays, the only commercial cargo carrying vessel to operate in the Broads system is the tanker *Blackheath* which carries fuel oil to the sugar refinery at Cantley on the River Yare about half way between Great Yarmouth and Norwich.

Because the main rivers are natural channels through reed beds, marshes or woodlands, and where embanked there is usually a wide reed covered 'rond' between the river and the flood wall, towpaths are found nowhere in the Broads. From time immemorial, vessels have been moved either by poling along the river bed, known in Norfolk as 'quanting', using the tide for assistance, or by sail. Small open quanted lighters evolved first into the Norfolk keel, which had its simple square sailed rig mounted on a mast near the middle of the vessel, and later into the Norfolk wherry which we know as the traditional trading craft of the Broads.

The Norfolk wherry was a broad shallow, double-ended craft, clinker built. It had a massive single mast located right forward in the vessel, clear of the cargo hold. The mast had a forestay, but no other standing rigging, and was mounted in a tabernacle. It was counterbalanced with lead to allow easy and rapid lowering for the many Broads bridges. From it was set a single huge gaff sail with high peak to catch the winds above reed beds and trees. The sails were usually dressed and appeared black. Many wherries were fitted with a false, removable keel which could be unshipped to allow the wherry to operate in shallow dykes and reaches near the head of navigation.

The wherry, unlike the square sailed keel, had some ability to sail to windward and could, no doubt with the assistance of a great deal of quanting, make passages along the twisting Broads rivers against the general direction of the wind. It became therefore the main means of transport in the Broads until the railways and improved roads inexorably deprived the wherrymen of their livelihoods.

One advantage to the local economy of the coming of the railways was the ease with which visitors could reach the Broads. Sailing for pleasure had been well established in the Broads for many years and, in particular, there was a tradition of keen sailboat racing, albeit the province mainly of the well-to-do. With the coming of the railways, owners saw the possibilities of converting their wherries for leisure use, at first merely sweeping out their holds and providing rudimentary accommodation, but later with increasing sophistication. This led to the development of the 'wherry yacht', which retained the traditional rig of the trading wherry but which had more yacht-like hulls, carvel built and with graceful counter-stern. They were let out for hire with a paid hand who saw to the sailing of the vessel and cooking of meals for the holidaymakers.

The last wherry to trade under sail was the *Albion*, now preserved in sailing condition by the Norfolk Wherry Trust. Peter Bower and Barney Matthews of Wherry Yacht Charter offer the wherry yachts *Olive* and *Norada* and the traditional wherry *Hathor* for charter from Wroxham. Mike Barnes' Traditional Broads Yacht Company operates the wherry yacht *White Moth* from Horning. The wherry *Solace* is in private ownership and in 1996 the *Maud* was relaunched after a massive rebuilding project by Vincent Pargeter, which has taken well over a decade.

Sailing, and especially racing sail, is therefore a much more important part of the boating heritage in the Broads than in any other British inland waters. From the Broads, racing cutters of the late 19th and early 20th centuries and the wherry tradition has evolved a particular type of cabined cruising and racing yacht not found anywhere else in the world. The traditional Broads yacht has low freeboard and shallow draft, with wide side decks and usually a raising cabin roof to increase headroom. The mast is stepped in a tabernacle and is counter-balanced for rapid lowering. Like its modern off-shore racing and cruising counterparts, it has a short fin keel with a separate rudder, a configuration common in the Broads since before 1900, but discovered by sea-going yachtsmen only in the 1960s!

If the sailing heritage has been one principal characteristic of Broads boating, then the other must surely be the self-drive hire boat holiday. John Loynes first offered small yachts for hire in 1878. Other entrepreneurs were quick to follow suit. In 1908, Harry Blake started an agency in London to market holidays aboard yachts belonging to the well-known builder Ernest Collins of Wroxham. The business and the number of yards represented by Blakes grew progressively through the early years of the century with petrol-driven craft being introduced for hire in the period before the Second World War. After the war, Messrs Hoseasons agency was established and during the 1950s and 1960s there was tremendous and unchecked growth in the number of vessels being built and operated for self-drive hire, reaching a peak in the early 1980s when there were some 2,400 hire motor-cruisers operating in the Broads. Since that time, there has been a reduction in hire craft (about 1,600 hire motor-cruisers and 90 hire cabin-yachts in 1997), but the number of privately owned boats kept in the

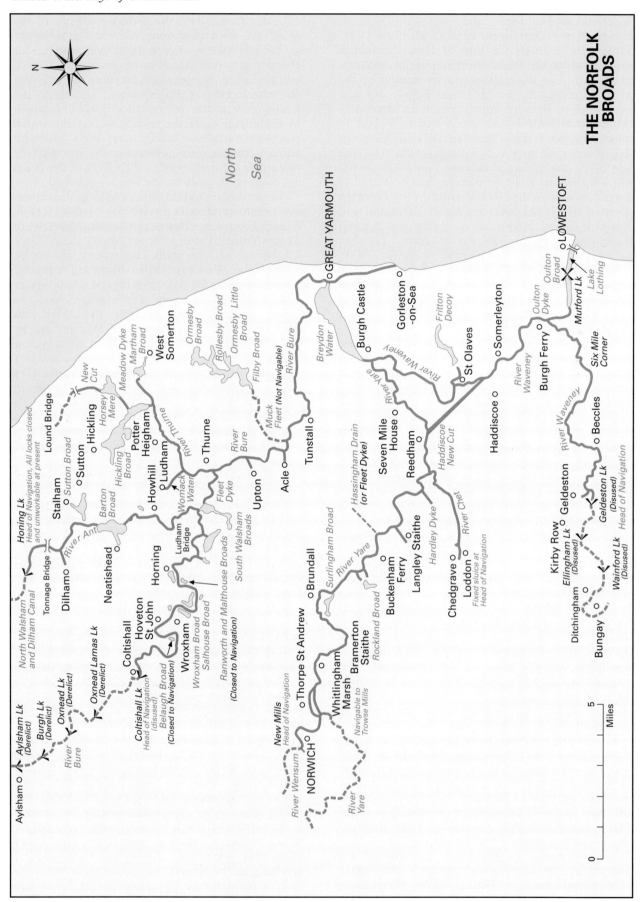

THE NORFOLK
BROADS

North
Sea

LOWESTOFT

GREAT YARMOUTH

Oulton
Broad

Lake
Lothing

Mutford Lk

Somerleyton

Oulton
Dyke

Burgh Ferry

Six Mile
Corner

River Waveney

Beccles

River Waveney

Kirby Row

Geldeston

Geldeston Lk
(Disused)
Head of Navigation

Wainford Lk
(Disused)

Ellingham Lk
(Disused)

Ditchingham

Bungay

Burgh Castle

Gorleston
-on-Sea

Fritton
Decoy

St Olaves

River Waveney

Haddiscoe

*Breydon
Water*

River Bure

Muck
Fleet *(Not Navigable)*

Filby Broad

*Ormesby
Little
Broad*

Rollesby Broad

Ormesby
Broad

Martham
Broad

Meadow Dyke

West
Somerton

*Horsey
Mere*

Hickling
Broad

Sutton Broad

Sutton

Hickling

*New
Cut*

Lound Bridge

Stalham

Barton
Broad

Dilham

Neatishead

Potter
Heigham

Howhill

Ludham

River Thurne

Womack
Water

Thurne

River Bure

Fleet
Dyke

Upton

Acle

Tunstall

River Yare

Hassingham Drain
(or Fleet Dyke)

Seven Mile
House

Reedham

Haddiscoe
New Cut

River Chet

Chedgrave

Loddon
*Fixed sluice at
Head of Navigation*

Langley Staithe

Buckenham
Ferry

Hardley Dyke

Surlingham Broad

River Yare

Brundall

Thorpe St Andrew

Bramerton
Staithe

Rockland Broad

Whitlingham
Marsh

*Navigable to
Trowse Mills*

New Mills
Head of Navigation

NORWICH

River Wensum

River Yare

River Ant

Honing Lk
*Head of Navigation. All locks closed
and unworkable at present*

North Walsham
and Dilham Canal

Tonnage Bridge

Oxnead Lamas Lk
(Derelict)

Oxnead Lk
(Derelict)

Burgh Lk
(Derelict)

Aylsham Lk
(Derelict)

Aylsham

*River
Bure*

Coltishall Lk
(disused)
Head of Navigation

Coltishall

Hoveton
St John

Belaugh Broad
(Closed to Navigation)

Wroxham

Wroxham Broad
(Closed to Navigation)

Salhouse Broad

Ludham
Bridge

Horning

Ranworth and Malthouse Broads
(Closed to Navigation)

South Walsham
Broads

Ludham

N

0   5
Miles

Broads has more than compensated for this. There are about 3,500 private motor-cruisers kept in the Broads and a similar number of private sailing craft. In all the Broads Authority registers over 13,000 boats for use in its navigation each year.

Conservation

Despite its long history as a holiday destination, it is still possible to find space, peace and quiet in the less frequented areas of the Broads where the illusion of wilderness remains. The Broads Authority actively promotes the use of the area for public relaxation and recreation, provided this is in keeping with its overall responsibilities to maintain water quality, preserve habitats and ecology and promote sound and sustainable development. The essence of the Broads Authority's message is that enjoyment should be of a nature and a scale which is appropriate to the area. The authority's policy is to promote sailing and to contain, within the limitations of its statutory powers, the growth in motor-boat numbers. There exists a public right of navigation over the great majority of the Broads system, and the authority does not therefore have the specific power to limit boat numbers. The authority promotes environmentally friendly and sustainable boating, including the development of low-wash hulls and the promotion of electric boating. Water skiing is allowed during certain hours on ten different stretches of the rivers Yare and Waveney (but nowhere in the northern part of the Broads), and the continuation of this activity is currently the subject of review by the authority.

Angling is an extremely popular activity, particularly in the middle and upper navigable reaches of the rivers and on the broads and fish stocks are good. Land-based activities, particularly those associated with wildlife and the environment, are also encouraged, again so long as numbers do no damage the habitats and creatures people are keen to see. The RSPB, Norfolk Wildlife Trust and Suffolk Wildlife Trust all offer bird-watching facilities, nature trails and guided walks, as well as interpretation centres.

During the 1960s and 1970s the Broads suffered a rapid and marked deterioration in water quality and it is one of the principal preoccupations of the Broads Authority to halt and reverse this decline. From clear water with thriving plant life, the Broads waters became in some parts a thick green algae-dominated soup. Whilst initially the increasing numbers and intensity of boating use was held to blame, subsequent research has shown the causes to be more complex. The root of the problem is one of eutrophication or excessive nutrient enrichment of the water, caused by run-off of nitrates from farm land and especially phosphates from sewage works discharges.

Boats do contribute to the problem in several ways: incessant passing and re-passing of craft through shallow waters leads to turbidity, further exacerbating the tendency of the dense algae to shut out light from water plants, and the wash of boats leads to increased erosion of the ronds and river banks which are losing their strengthening and protecting reed fringe, the reed dying back because of the excessive nutrient content in the waters. Erosion of the river banks leads to excessive siltation, which in turn leads to worsened turbidity and so on.

Seriously eroding banks threaten flood defences as well. Although the Broads Authority has undertaken much pioneering work on bank protection methods and soft engineering, which is sympathetic to wildlife and landscape, there is, in many situations, no alternative to traditional, unsightly and hugely expensive sheet piling.

Minimisation of erosion by boat wash is therefore a major element in the Broads Authority's strategy for restoring the organic health of the Broads' waters. Speed limits are marked throughout the Broads and are rigorously enforced by the authority's team of river inspectors, who operate eight patrol launches throughout the system (and who undertake speed checks on the banks as well!). The limits are 3, 4, 5 and 6mph and with fines of up to £1,000 for breaching them, it pays to obey them.

The Broads Authority has also championed the promotion of environmentally friendly boating, having undertaken research into the design of low-wash hulls for motor-cruisers and also encouraged the renaissance in electric boat propulsion.

The Broads Authority is required to publish periodically a strategic plan detailing its responsibilities and policies and explaining the problems and solutions on these and a much wider range of issues confronting the Broads. The current Broads Plan was published in March 1997 and for anyone interested in the area or in the wider challenges facing wetlands generally it is a fascinating read.

The Broads Navigation

The Broads system consists principally of tidal rivers over which there exists a presumption of public right of navigation. Over centuries, however, man-made dykes, channels and basins have been created adjoining the main rivers and broads and the legal status of some of these is unclear. The Broads Authority is the statutory navigation authority for its own 'navigation area' as defined in the Norfolk and Suffolk Broads Act 1988, but its statutory powers and bye-laws, the right to charge tolls and the obligation to dredge and so on do not apply in private waters out of the navigation area.

Because of the controversy and delay which would have resulted had they tried to define the navigation area precisely by maps or words, the draughtsmen of the Broads Act, rather understandably, 'fudged' the issue, and the Broads Authority's Navigation Area is defined by Section 8(i) of the Act as:

a. those stretches of the rivers Bure, Yare and Waveney and their tributaries, branches and embayments (including Oulton Broad) which at the passing of this Act were in use for navigation by virtue of any public right of navigation;
b. the banks of the waterways that make up those stretches; and
c. Haddiscoe New Cut and its banks.

It will be seen that this definition begs the question which waters were on the operative date (1 April 1989) 'in use for navigation by virtue of any public right of navigation'? How frequent or recent does the use have to be, and was the use by public right or by some other right or permission? These are questions which frequently exercise the minds of Broads boaters and Broads Authority officers!

Importantly, it must be noted that 'The Haven' is excluded from the Broads Authority's Navigation Area. By this is meant the waters which remained under the navigational jurisdiction of the Great Yarmouth Port Authority (previously known as Great Yarmouth Port and Haven Commissioners). The port authority remains in control of the commercial harbour of Great Yarmouth, all of Breydon Water and the lower reaches of the Lower Bure for a distance of about 1¼ miles up river from Bure Mouth. The Bure boundary corresponds approximately with the up-river end of the Port of Yarmouth Marina moorings. On the River Yare the boundary with the Broads Authority's Navigation Area is the root of Turntide Jetty (the wooden structure near Berney Arms where the two rivers divide). On the River Waveney, it is a line across the river about 229 metres up river of the entrance of Burgh Castle Marina. In these waters, the Broads Authority's powers and bye-laws do not operate. The port authority and the Broads Authority co-operate to maintain navigational posts and signage provided principally for the benefit of Broads' recreational craft in the port's waters. In carrying out its dredging and river maintenance duties, the Broads Authority has certain obligations to protect the Haven and, in managing traffic on the River Yare, there is an obligation to give precedence to commercial traffic although, sadly, only one vessel now operates to Cantley Sugar Refinery and there has been no cargo trade on the River Yare to Norwich since 1989.

Haddiscoe New Cut

It will be noted that Haddiscoe New Cut is also separately mentioned. This, being one of the very few entirely man-made stretches of principal navigation, has passed through the control of various organisations. Currently, the Environment Agency is responsible for the maintenance of its banks. The general duty on the Broads Authority to manage, dredge and maintain the navigation area, by Section 8 (vii), specifically does not apply to Haddiscoe Cut. The cut is in poor condition and, in recent years, has cost the National Rivers Authority and its successor, the Environment Agency,

substantial sums to keep open. It is usual in the Broads that, while the Broads Authority has the duty of dredging and maintaining the rivers for the purposes of navigation, the duty to maintain the banks, flood walls and defences falls on the Environment Agency. The Haddiscoe Cut has no significance for drainage or flood defence, and its only value now being as a 'short cut' for pleasure boat traffic. In strictly flood-defence terms, it would be far less costly for the Environment Agency simply to close off the ends of the cut and abandon it, and it is argued by some that the Broads Act would allow that.

The consequences of so doing would, however, be very serious. The cut allows craft of air draught up to 24ft to pass from the River Yare to the River Waveney beneath Haddiscoe flyover, whereas, if it were closed, they would have to go via St Olaves Bridge which has a clearance of only 8ft. For very many craft, the southern Broads would be effectively severed into two parts were the cut to be closed. The economic consequence for the hire trade, and especially for boatyards on the River Waveney and in the southern part of the system, which already trade at a significant disadvantage compared to those in the northern part of the Broads, would be dire. No final decision has been taken over the future of the Haddiscoe Cut, but it is a sad reflection on the narrow attitudes of modern administrators with their constant attention to 'cost/benefit analysis' that, with all of the technology and resources available to them approaching the year 2000, they should even be contemplating closure of an essential link such as this, dug by hand in 1833.

Heads of public navigation

Significant stretches of previously navigable water were lost with the demise in wherry trade in the years preceding the Second World War. Waterways previously navigable for trading craft, now officially closed to navigation, include the North Walsham and Dilham Canal (7¼ miles), the River Bure from Horstead Lock to Aylsham (9 miles) and the River Waveney from Geldeston to Bungay (4.2 miles). The currently recognised heads of public navigation for general traffic are as follows:

River Bure Horstead Lock, Coltishall (some use of rowing craft/canoes on reaches above the lock).

River Ant Dilham Staithe (no public right of navigation exists on the North Walsham and Dilham Canal. Dinghies/small craft can reach Tonnage Bridge on the canal over private water).

River Thurne Hickling Staithe.
Horsey Staithe (via Meadow Dyke).
Waxham Bridge (Waxham Cut).
West Somerton Staithe (Somerton Arm).

River Yare/Wensum Wensum – New Mills Bridge, Norwich. Yare – Trowse Mill
(Hire craft limits are Bishops Bridge on the Wensum in Norwich and, on the River Yare,

Trowse Eye which is the confluence of the two rivers on the eastern outskirts of the city).

River Chet Loddon Mill/Mooring Basin.

River Waveney Geldeston Locks (dinghies and canoes can reach Bungay Staithe, but must portage at Ellingham and Wainford Locks. The Broads Authority proposes to improve portages and to re-open navigation to Bungay for small unpowered craft. There is no current proposal to re-open the locks).

Navigational status of some of the principal broads

The navigational status of some of the principal broads is also controversial, particularly in the busiest area of the Upper Bure near Wroxham and Horning.

Wroxham Broad is considered to be a private broad, not within the navigation area. It is leased by the Norfolk Broads Yacht Club (whose impressive clubhouse stands on the western shore of the broad) from the Trafford Estate. The club does, however, allow general boating traffic on the broad.

Hoveton Great Broad, which is a very large but now much silted area of water on the north side of the river, is understood historically to have been open to navigation and to have been a short cut for wherries on the River Bure, but has been closed for many years and is currently a nature reserve which may be visited from moorings on the main river. Salhouse Broad is and always has been open for public navigation.

Hoveton Little Broad (Blackhorse Broad) is privately owned and regarded as outwith the navigation area although, following a celebrated mass trespass in 1947, led by Herbert Woods the then chairman of the Norfolk and Suffolk Broads Yacht Owners Association, an agreement was reached with the landowner that, without prejudice to the legal status of the navigation on the broad, it would be opened to the public for Easter Week and from the Whitsun (late May) Public Holiday to the end of October each year. That arrangement persists and has been re-executed in an agreement between the landowner and the Broads Authority. Mud weighting is permitted on the broad, but no landing or mooring to the shore. Pound End, the southern extremity of the broad, remains closed to boats and is managed by the Broads Authority for conservation purposes.

Decoy Broad, across the river and which is connected to the river only by a very narrow non-navigable dyke, is private and not open to boats.

Cockshoot Broad, down river of Horning, is closed off from the river and has been the subject of a major water quality restoration programme by the Broads Authority, involving pumping out of large quantities of nutrient-enriched mud. The river end of Cockshoot Dyke is a popular free mooring operated by the authority and boaters can access the restored broad by a boardwalk from the moorings. The difference in water quality and clarity in the broad, as compared to the water on the river side of the dam, is astonishing.

Ranworth Broad, the much larger twin of Malthouse Broad, is closed to navigation and is part of the Norfolk Wildlife Trust's nature reserve. The trust's floating field study centre is moored to the edge of the broad and moorings are provided for visitors to the centre. Visitors are carried on trips by electric reed lighter across the broad and into the network of marsh dykes beyond. An electric reed lighter operated by the Broads Authority also runs excursions across to the field centre from Ranworth Staithe.

Oulton Broad, Rockland Broad and Surlingham Broad (Bargate Water), in the southern part of the system (rivers Yare and Waveney) are the only three broads connected to the navigation. All three are open for public navigation.

Whitlingham Broad and Whitlingham Little Broad On the eastern fringe of the City of Norwich, close adjacent to the banks of the River Yare, two entirely new 'broads' are being created. These are at Whitlingham and are in fact major gravel workings which have been managed from conception to provide a country park and recreational opportunities when they are worked out. They will be known as Whitlingham Broad and Whitlingham Little Broad. The Little Broad is already complete. The main broad is about half completed. It will eventually offer international standard competitive rowing and facilities for sailing, canoeing, sail-boarding and fishing and with protected areas for nature conservation. Neither of these gravel-pit lakes will be connected to the main river so as to allow general navigation, but moorings will be provided on the main river so that boaters may visit and enjoy the lake and its surrounding country park.

Boat registration, river tolls, bye-laws

When the Broads Authority inherited navigational responsibility for the Broads from the Great Yarmouth Port and Haven Commissioners in 1989, it took on also the Commissioners' various bye-laws, some of which were somewhat antiquated. It was understood that the Broads Authority would bring in its own, new bye-laws to replace these and the old bye-laws have been kept in force by a series of extending orders from year to year since that time. The process of bringing in new bye-laws has been more complex and more challenging than could have been envisaged when the Broads Authority came into existence. The process of replacing the Port and Haven Commissioners' bye-laws is now, however, almost complete and it is anticipated that the job will be finished when the Broads Authority's new Registration Bye-laws come into effect, it is hoped on 1 April 1998.

There has been, since the 1930s, a scheme of compulsory boat registration in the Broads, although it has applied until now only to motor craft. With the passing of the new Registration Bye-laws, the registration requirement will be extended to sailing craft. Other than in this respect, the new Registration Bye-laws will not significantly change the Broads boat registration regime. All boats remaining in the Broads Navigation Area for more than 28 days will be (and all boats with engines presently are) required to be registered with the Broads Authority. There is no charge for registration. Each vessel is allocated a distinctive registration number consisting of a letter and three digits, which must be displayed in accordance with the requirements of the authority on both bows of the vessel and on the stern. The registered number stays with the vessel throughout its life in the Broads. This differs from the system operating in, for example, the River Thames, where vessels are not allocated a number but are required to have a unique name. There are obligations on the owner to inform the Authority when a vessel is sold and there are bye-law penalties for failure to register and failure to display the registration number.

The Broads Authority is empowered by the Harbours Act 1964 to make a charge to vessels kept in or using the navigation. In the Broads these are known as 'river tolls'. The Broads Authority's tolls year runs from 1 April to 31 March. Up to 28 days of 'short visit tolls' can be bought in any tolls year in multiples of seven days. The short-visit toll is based on the length of the vessel and whether it is a motor vessel (including all vessels with motors of any kind) or a sailing vessel. The charge for sailing vessels is approximately one half of that for motor craft. Vessels applying for a short-visit licence are issued with adhesive short-visit numbers which must be displayed on the vessel.

Vessels remaining in the system for more than 28 days must buy an annual licence which will run from date of application to the following 31 March. This is based on the square area (length x beam) of the vessel and there are three categories – motor craft, motorised sailing craft (which are sailing vessels having a small auxiliary motor of not more than 10bhp) and sailing craft. If a vessel is let out for hire or reward, the toll for it is exactly three times the equivalent private boat rate. Annually licensed vessels are issued with adhesive plaques which must be displayed on both bows of the vessel.

There are a number of special tolls, for example, the passage toll which allows a vessel to make a single one-way passage within one day through the Authority's Navigation Area at a charge (1997) of £3.40. There is also a race-craft toll of £1.35 per vessel per day for craft visiting the area to take part in an organised race, regatta or event. This is limited to a maximum of two consecutive days.

All tolls must be paid to the authority before the vessel is launched or used in the navigation area. Use of a vessel without the appropriate licence is an offence against the bye-laws which may result in prosecution and a substantial fine in addition to payment of the unpaid toll. Annual tolls must be paid to the Authority's Collector of Tolls at its head office at 18 Colegate, Norwich NR3 1BQ (☎ 01603 610734). Short-visit licences may be purchased from the authority's head office, from river inspectors or from a number of shops and boatyards around the Broads.

Navigation Bye-laws

The Broads Authority's Navigation Bye-laws 1995 came into effect on 1 January 1996. These bye-laws replace the International Regulations for Preventing Collisions at Sea for vessels navigating in the Broads Authority's Navigation Area. Note, however, that the International Collision Rules still apply in those parts of the system under the jurisdiction of the Great Yarmouth Port Authority. In addition to steering and sailing rules, which may differ in minor detail from the International Rules, the navigation bye-laws contain a number of offences concerning the nature of navigation. These include an obligation on a master of a vessel to navigate his vessel with care and caution and at a speed and in a manner which avoids injury to the occupants of other vessels, damage and the likelihood of damage to vessels, property, banks and so on, and which avoids giving reasonable grounds for annoyance to other persons using the navigation area. Navigators are also required to show reasonable consideration to persons fishing from boats or the banks. There are also bye-law restrictions on persons under the age of 14 years being at the helm of power driven vessels. Other bye-laws relate to navigating while under the influence of drink and drugs, and the making of noise and nuisance, and there are a number of bye-laws regulating the use of moorings. Copies of the bye-laws are available without charge from the Broads Authority.

Broads Authority speed limit Bye-laws 1992

These bye-laws came into operation on the 1 November 1992. All parts of the Broads Authority's Navigation Area are subject to a speed limit, which is 3, 4, 5 or 6mph depending on the location. Speed limits are clearly signed on the banks. Speed limits are measured over the ground. The speed limits apply to power-driven craft but not to sailing craft or manually propelled vessels. There are a number of exemptions: water skiing is presently permitted in ten areas of the rivers Yare and Waveney (but nowhere in the Northern Broads) during certain hours specified in the bye-laws. Water skiing may take place only with a permit issued by the Broads Authority and using a light sports vessel as defined by the bye-laws and registered with the authority as such. There are certain regulations governing water skiing. Water-ski vessels may exceed the speed limit only while towing a skier or in the immediate course of recovering a skier in the water. The authority is currently undertaking a review of the management and future of water skiing in the Broads.

Boatyard vessels, being vessels carrying a 'trade plate' registration mark under the bona fide control of a boatyard employee may exceed the speed limit in certain areas and during certain times for test purposes. Coaching vessels may exceed the speed limit whilst attending fast rowing craft. Sailing club and other rescue craft may exceed the speed limit in the case of genuine necessity in connection with a rescue and occasionally permission may be given for rescue-craft driver-training to take place in certain areas.

Broads Authority vessel dimension Bye-laws 1995

These bye-laws largely reproduce beam restrictions for vessels contained in earlier bye-laws but introduce a maximum length restriction in certain waters. A maximum beam of 3.8 metres (12ft 6ins) and maximum length of 14 metres (46ft) applies to vessels navigating in some of the narrower parts of the Broads, including the whole of the River Ant, the dykes connecting Hickling Broad and Horsey Mere to the River Thurne, all of the River Chet, Rockland and Surlingham Broads. Wider beam restrictions apply to vessels operating in other parts of the system. Vessels of length less than 14 metres (46ft) and beam less than 3.8 metres (12ft 6ins) are not affected by the bye-laws and those which are may make up to four passages each year on any stretch of water providing seven days prior notice has been given to the Broads Authority of the intended passage.

Boat Safety Bye-laws/Technical requirements

The Great Yarmouth Port and Haven Commissioners issued in 1982 a Code of Practice concerning the technical safety standards for boats operating in the Broads. This did not have legally enforceable status, but was adopted by the principal hire agencies as a condition of operating vessels for hire. The Broads Authority has not joined the Boat Safety Scheme now operating in British Waterways and Environment Agency waters, but is evolving a Boat Safety Scheme of its own which will be very closely based on that scheme with certain exemptions or relaxations reflecting the particular character of Broads navigation and of the craft in use on the Broads. It is expected that the Broads Boat Safety Scheme will apply on a voluntary and advisory basis for two years from 1 April 1998, to be followed by a period of at least five years from 1 April 2000 when the Broads Boat Safety Scheme will be compulsory, but on the basis of self-certification by the boat owner. During that period the Broads Authority may take powers to introduce random or incident based boat safety inspections. The Authority will consider the experience gained on this basis and will decide whether to introduce compulsory routine boat safety testing for all craft from a date not earlier than April 2005.

Discharge of effluent to the river

At present it is an offence against the bye-laws for a vessel which does not regularly proceed to sea to discharge effluent into the rivers. This does not strictly apply to sea-going yachts, although owners of such vessels are strongly discouraged from discharging lavatories to the river. The bye-law does not apply either to Broads sailing yachts. It is likely that more rigorous bye-laws controlling discharges will be introduced.

River inspectors

The Broads Authority maintains a force of 12 river inspectors operating eight patrol launches around the system, part of whose task is to ensure observance of the various bye-laws. The river inspectors are there to help and inform boaters but, in the event of a breach, a prosecution may be brought. The bye-laws carry varying fines up to £1,000. It is not uncommon for offenders against the speed-limit bye-laws to receive fines of several hundred pounds.

Parish staithes and public mooring

In earlier times when the rivers and dykes of the Broads were the principal arteries of trade and communication for remote villages, it was natural that each settlement should have a public mooring place or wharf at which keels and wherries could load or discharge cargo, reedcutters unload their lighters or wildfowlers go afloat in their punts. These were known as 'staithes' and that term is still used today to signify a public mooring place.

In those fortunate times, before the intense commercialisation of the waterways and before every square foot of waterside land acquired astronomical value, the indigenous population acknowledged the common public interest in the village staithe and found, in many cases, no need to protect that interest with legal deeds and formalities. Therein lies the unfortunate background to the vexed question of Broadland's lost and threatened staithes.

Various attempts have been made to record and regularise the status of Broads staithes. In the 1960s the East Anglian Waterways Association commenced a study of the problem. One of the first tasks of the Broads Authority, when it was merely a voluntary association of local authorities, before it was established as a statutory authority by the Norfolk and Suffolk Broads Act 1988, was to commission research which led to the publication of a Staithes Register which sought at least to list and record the existence of staithes. Much research was done, which it might now be impossible to repeat owing to the disastrous fire which destroyed the historic archives section of Norwich's City Library in 1995. It is clear, however, that for every staithe where title and status are clear, there is another, or may be several, the status of which is unclear or threatened. Some fortunate staithes have been the subject of an award under the Enclosures Acts. Others are vested in 'poors trusts' or staithe trustees. More recently, attempts have been made to register staithes as common land. Well-motivated parish councils have sought to register their title as freeholders, but have frequently come up against the difficulty that they cannot show the necessary history of 12 years uncontested 'acts consistent with ownership'. This means that there are today a number of small riverside areas which effectively have no owner. Where such a situation exists now, as in the past, there is often an acquisitive neighbouring landowner anxious to rescue the land from its ownerless state!

The Broads Authority has certain statutory powers to enter, maintain and assume management of staithes, but those powers only come into play once a public right to use the land has been established. Often it is that basic public entitlement which cannot be clearly shown and the authority's powers in this respect are therefore of limited value.

The authority has, however, done much to assist parish councils to clarify the status of their staithes and in some cases to prevent encroachment and return staithes to public ownership and use. Potter Heigham Staithe is an example.

In any event, changes in the nature and activities of the Broads population have rendered the true legal status of public mooring places less important. Since all cargo carrying trade within the Broads has long since ceased (Cantley Sugar Factory, for example, received its last load of sugar beet by wherry in 1965), it is now less critical whether a parishioner has the right to 'load and unload manure' at the staithe (as is found in some of the old Enclosure Awards). Again, while it was important and relevant to the small populations of Broadland villages to have a place to tie up boats which were essential to their livelihoods, it is less easy to see why someone who has perhaps recently moved into the area should by so doing acquire the right to moor his small pleasure craft for free or at a substantial discount on the commercial boatyard mooring rate. With the huge increase in ownership of small recreational craft, such arrangements, with their inevitable waiting lists, are difficult for parish councils and staithes trusts to operate, although in a few places such parish moorings do still exist (for example, Upton Dyke).

The pressure on mooring space throughout the Broads is so great that at any staithe or public mooring, there is a tension between the need to provide space for hire craft to moor short term and overnight (which brings customers for the village shop, post office and pub, but little or no income for the parish council or staithe trustees), and the provision of permanent or long-term moorings for private craft (which can generate important income for the parish council or staithe trust). In some cases, for example Ludham Womack Staithe, the parish council seeks to strike a balance with about half of the staithe given over to private moorings and

the rest available for overnight moorings. In other places, the parish council or trustees, seeking to avoid the complications of administering the moorings or concerned about the potential cost of maintaining and renewing quay headings, has leased the staithe to the Broads Authority to operate on a short-term/24-hour mooring basis with the authority taking on the repair liability.

The picture is further complicated by the fact that the Broads Authority, and before them the Great Yarmouth Port and Haven Commissioners, acknowledged the essential need to maintain adequate free short-term moorings to allow the practice of Broads cruising to continue. The Great Yarmouth Port and Haven Commissioners, in particular, did a good job by reaching arrangements with landowners in many locations to undertake essential bank maintenance and piling works in return for a long lease and permission to use the banks as free 24-hour moorings. By these and other means, including in some cases outright purchase, the authority now operates about 40 separate free overnight mooring areas, ranging in size to accommodate from two to several dozen boats.

The pressure on the Broads Authority to provide adequate public short-stay moorings is, however, increasingly difficult to sustain for several reasons. Firstly, the traditional reciprocal arrangement between hire boatyards to allow free overnight mooring for hire craft is threatened by the reduction in the number of boatyards involved in the hire trade (down from over 100 in the peak years to around 70 today). Secondly, many of the long leases negotiated by the Great Yarmouth Port and Haven Commissioners are now expiring and landlords are seeking to renew at much increased rents which the authority cannot sustain. Thirdly, the authority's necessary planning policies against allowing new mooring areas (a measure intended to curb growth in motor-boat numbers) make it difficult to provide new mooring areas, especially outside established village centres.

Broads staithes and public moorings
For the above reasons, the following is a list of moorings which are public in the sense that the public are welcome to tie up for short stays and overnight even though they may be charged a fee for doing so. It includes, for example, moorings at public houses where a charge may be made and in some cases this will be refundable against purchases. This list is arranged by river, the order running from head of navigation towards Great Yarmouth. The list includes some boatyard and marina moorings where overnight visitors, both hire and private, are encouraged and catered for, but not boatyard moorings which merely provide berths for hire craft on a reciprocal basis. In addition to these organised formal moorings, there are many locations around the system where informal mooring takes place, often to stretches of river bank piling installed for bank protection. One or two of these more established informal areas are included in the list.

List of public moorings by river

River Bure

Coltishall – The Rising Sun Pub mooring.

Coltishall – The Common Free 24 hour mooring operated by Broads Authority (leased from Coltishall Commons Trust) *Electric boat charging point.

Coltishall – Anchor Moorings Privately operated. Charge made.

Belaugh – Staithe Free 24 hour mooring operated by Broads Authority (leased from Trafford Estate).

Wroxham – Caen Meadow ('Castle Staithe') Free 24 hour mooring operated by Wroxham Parish Council (leased from Trafford Estate).

Wroxham – Hoveton Viaduct Free 24 hour mooring operated by Broads Authority (leased from Trafford Estate).

Wroxham – Hoveton Horseshoes Free 24 hour mooring owned/operated by Broads Authority (BA Information Centre).

Wroxham – Kings Head Pub mooring.

Wroxham – Hotel Wroxham Hotel mooring.

Wroxham Broad Island (main river side) Free 24 hour mooring owned/operated by Broads Authority.

Salhouse Broad Island (main river side) Free 24 hour mooring operated by Broads Authority (leased from Cator Estate).

Salhouse Broad, south side Free 24 hour mooring managed by Broads Authority (leased from Cator Estate).

Horning – The Swan Pub mooring.

Horning Village Staithe Free 24 hour mooring operated by Broads Authority (leased from Horning Parish Council).

Horning – Perci's Island Free 24 hour mooring owned/operated by Broads Authority (island across river from village staithe).

Horning – New Inn Pub mooring.

Horning – Ferry Inn Pub mooring.

Horning – Ferry Marina Marina and Leisure Centre. Charge made.

Horning – Woodbastwick Moorings Free 24 hour moorings operated by Broads Authority.

Horning – Cockshoot Dyke Free 24 hour moorings operated by Broads Authority (leased from Norfolk Wildlife Trust).

Ranworth Broad (entrance) Norfolk Wildlife Trust Field Centre. Moorings for Field Centre visitors. No overnight.

Malthouse Broad (north side) Messrs Mills' moorings (privately operated, charge made).

Malthouse Broad (Ranworth Staithe) Free 24 hour mooring operated by Blakes/Broads Authority (BA Information Centre).

Horning – St Benedicts Church Mooring for visitors to church. Donations.

Horning Waterworks Staithe Owned by Horning Parish Council. Mooring for dinghies/small craft only. No overnight.

St Benets Abbey Piled bank between Ant Mouth – St Benets. Informal mooring. No charge. Owned by Environment Agency. Leased to angling club. No mooring Saturday nights in fishing season.

South Walsham Fleet Dyke 2 areas informal mooring. Owned by Environment Agency. Leased to angling club.

South Walsham Parish Staithe Owned by South Walsham Parish Council. Mooring for small craft/dinghies only.

Upton Dyke/Upton Staithe Free 24 hour mooring at staithe. Owned/operated by Upton Parish Council. Parishioners moorings in dyke (very narrow).

Acle (true left bank upriver of bridge) Privately operated. Charge made.

Acle (true right bank upriver of bridge) Privately operated. Charge made.

Acle (true left bank downriver of bridge) Boatyard moorings. Charge made.

Acle – Bridge Inn Pub moorings.

Acle Boat Dyke/'Hermitage Dyke' Former public mooring/staithe now taken over by boatyard moorings.

Stokesby – Staithe Free 24 hour mooring operated by Broads Authority

Stokesby – Ferry Inn Pub mooring.

Stokesby – downriver of Ferry Inn Privately operated. Charge made.

Stracey Arms Pub mooring.

Stracey Mill Privately operated. Charge made (mill open to public and shop).

Great Yarmouth – Port of Yarmouth Marina Privately operated. Charge made. Commercial yacht station. Shop etc. (leased from Gt Yarmouth Borough Council).

Great Yarmouth Yacht Station Privately operated. Charge made (£10/night 1997). Poor facilities (leased from Gt Yarmouth Borough Council).

Great Yarmouth – Broads Authority Moorings Free 24 hour mooring operated by Broads Authority (leased from Gt Yarmouth Port Authority) (BA Information Centre).

River Ant

Dilham Staithe Free 24 hour mooring operated by Broads Authority leased from East Anglian Waterways Assoc).

Wayford Bridge – Woodfarm Inn Pub mooring.

Wayford Bridge (downriver of bridge) Free 24 hour mooring operated by Broads Authority.

Wayford Bridge (Smallburgh) Staithe Public staithe owned/operated by Smallburgh Parish Council. Small boat slipway. Private boat mooring. No public mooring.

Stalham Staithe Mooring for small craft. Stalham Parish Council.

Sutton Staithe Free 24 hour mooring owned/operated by Sutton Parish Council.

Sutton Staithe (Sutton Dyke) Free 24 hour mooring owned/operated by Sutton Parish Council.

Barton Turf Staithe (Pennygate Staithe) Part free 24 hour mooring operated by Broads Authority (leased from Barton Turf PC). Part parishioners moorings.

Barton Turf Paddy's Lane Free 24 hour mooring operated by Broads Authority (leased).

Neatishead – Gay's Staithe Free 24 hour mooring operated by Broads Authority (leased from Neatishead PC).

Neatishead Staithe Free 24 hour mooring operated by Broads Authority (leased from Neatishead PC).

Catfield Wood End Staithe Private mooring owned by Catfield Parish Council (?).

Irstead Staithe Free 24 hour mooring operated by Broads Authority. Part owned BA part owned Irstead PC.

How Hill Staithe Informal 24 hour mooring. No charge.

Ludham Bridge (upriver of bridge) Both banks informal 24 hour mooring. No charge (includes staithe on true left bank upriver of bridge).

Ludham Bridge (downriver of bridge) +/-60 metres downriver true right bank owned by Horning Parish Council used for private boat mooring. Remainder true right bank informal short term mooring. No charge. On true left bank downriver of boatyard bank owned by Environment Agency used for private boat mooring.

River Thurne

Hickling Staithe Part owned/operated by Hickling Parish Council for mooring of parishioners' small craft. Part owned/operated by Pleasure Boat Inn as public moorings. Charge made.

Catfield Common Staithe Part 24 hour free mooring operated by Broads Authority (leased from Catfield PC). Part parishioners' moorings.

Deep Dyke Moorings & Deep Go Dyke Moorings Both 24 hour free moorings operated by Broads Authority (leased from Norfolk Wildlife Trust).

Horsey Staithe Public short term mooring (+ private moorings) owned/operated by National Trust. Charge made.

West Somerton Parish Staithe Private small craft mooring. Somerton Parish Council.

West Somerton Dyke Moorings Public short term mooring. No charge.

Martham Ferry Dyke Public dyke and staithe. Private moorings. No public mooring. Martham Parish Council.

Martham Staithe Dyke Public short term moorings. Martham Parish Council.

Potter Heigham (true left bank upriver of bypass) 24 hour free mooring operated by Broads Authority (leased from Environment Agency).

Potter Heigham (true right bank upriver of bypass) Yacht masting mooring owned by Broads Authority (no motor craft).

Potter Heigham (true right bank between bridges) Short stay (2 hour) mooring owned by Broads Authority.

Potter Heigham Staithe (true right bank downriver of old bridge) Mooring for small craft only. Short stay. Potter Heigham Parish Council.

Repps Upper Staithe (true left bank downriver old bridge) Mooring for small craft only. Short stay. Repps Parish Council.

Potter Heigham (true left bank downriver of bridge) Free 24 hour mooring operated by Broads Authority (leased from Environment Agency).

Potter Heigham (true right bank downriver of boatyard entrance) Yacht masting mooring owned/operated by Broads Authority. No motor craft.

Repps Lower (Pug Street) Staithe Informal use for short term mooring. Repps Parish Council.

Ludham Womack Dyke Informal short stay mooring. No charge.

Ludham Womack Island (rear) Free 24 hour mooring owned/operated by Broads Authority.

Ludham Womack Staithe Part 24 hour mooring (charge) part private/parishioners moorings (Ludham Parish Council).

Thurne Dyke North Bank pub moorings, Thurne Lion. South bank privately operated (charge made).

Rivers Yare/Wensum/Chet

Norwich Yacht Station Public 24 hour moorings. Charge made. (£7 in 1997) (Norwich City Council).

Norwich Ferry Boat Inn Pub mooring.

Norwich Corporation Quay Private craft unable to pass Foundry Bridge only. (Norwich City Council).

Thorpe Green Free 24 hour mooring operated by Broads Authority (leased from Thorpe St Andrew Parish Council).

Thorpe Commissioners Cut Free 24 hour mooring owned/operated by Broads Authority.

Bramerton Woods End Inn Pub mooring.

Bramerton Common Free 24 hour mooring operated by Broads Authority (leased from Bramerton Parish Council).

Postwick Wharf Free 24 hour mooring owned/operated by Broads Authority.

Surlingham – Ferry House Inn Pub moorings.

Surlingham Staithe Accessible to canoes/rowing craft only. Ownership unclear.

Coldham Hall Inn Pub moorings.

Rockland St Mary Staithe Free 24 hour moorings operated by Broads Authority (leased from Rockland Staithe Trust).

Beauchamp Arms, Buckenham Ferry Pub moorings and informal bank moorings.

Langley Dyke Staithe disused. No record of public ownership. Privately operated short stay moorings in dyke (charge).

Cantley Red House Inn Pub moorings.

Cantley Parish Staithe Between Sugar Factory and Red House Inn. Cantley Parish Council. Mooring for dinghies/canoes only.

Hardley Dyke Staithe at head of dyke for small craft only. Dyke banks private moorings.

Hardley Cross Informal mooring to piling. No charge.

Loddon Mooring Basin Free 24 hour mooring owned/operated by South Norfolk District Council.

Loddon Pye's Mill Free 24 hour mooring owned/operated by South Norfolk District Council.

Loddon/Chedgrave Common Free 24 hour mooring operated by Broads Authority (leased).

Reedham Ferry Inn Pub moorings.

Reedham Quay Free 24 hour moorings operated by Broads Authority (leased from Broadland DC).

Reedham Lord Nelson Inn Pub moorings (part of quay).

Reedham Ship Inn Pub moorings.

Berney Arms – Berney Mill Owned by English Heritage. Charge made.

Berney Arms – RSPB RSPB owned/operated. Charge may be made.

Berney Arms – Berney Inn Pub moorings.

River Waveney/Oulton Broad

Geldeston Locks Free 24 hour mooring owned/operated by Broads Authority (adjacent Locks Inn Public House).

Geldeston Dyke Privately operated short stay moorings. Charge made.

Beccles Swimming Pool Public short stay mooring, pontoon. Charge made (Waveney District Council).

Beccles Yacht Station Public Yacht Station. Charge made (Waveney District Council).

Beccles Bypass Bridge Short stay mooring for vessels unable to transit bridge. Operated by Broads Authority.

Aldeby Moorings Free 24 hour moorings operated by Broads Authority (leased).

Worlingham Moorings Free 24 hour moorings owned/operated by Broads Authority.

Burgh St Peter – Waveney River Centre Private marina/leisure centre. Charge made. Old staithe and dyke taken over by marina.

Oulton Broad Free Quay Short stay quay adjacent Mutford Lock (Waveney District Council).

Oulton Broad Yacht Station Public Yacht Station. Charge made (Waveney District Council).

Oulton Broad Wherry Hotel Hotel moorings.

Somerleyton Staithe Free 24 hour moorings operated by Broads Authority (leased from Somerleyton Estate).

Herringfleet Moorings Free 24 hour moorings operated by Broads Authority (leased from Somerleyton Estate).

St Olaves Bell Inn Pub moorings.

St Olaves Moorings Free 24 hour moorings operated by Broads Authority.

Burgh Castle Moorings Free 24 hour mooring operated by Broads Authority (leased from Burgh C Marina).

Burgh Castle Fishermans Inn Pub moorings.

Mid-Broad mud weighting

In addition to the public moorings listed above vessels may lie to a mud weight in mid-broad in certain locations. Mud weighting in the rivers and dykes is not permitted otherwise than in emergency.

Broads where mud weighting is permitted are listed here:

Bridge Broad, Wroxham Off River Bure upriver of Wroxham.

Wroxham Broad Private broad leased to Norfolk Broads Yacht Club by Trafford Estate. Mud weighted vessels must keep clear of racing courses and must move if required.

Salhouse Broad Publicly navigable broad managed by Broads Authority, leased from Cator Estate.

Hoveton Little Broad (Blackhorse Broad) Private broad open to navigation Easter Week and from late May Holiday to end October. Mud weighting allowed in mid-broad but no landing or mooring to shore.

Malthouse Broad

South Walsham Outer/Main Broad No mud weighting in South Walsham Inner Broad.

Barton Broad Dredging work in progress 1996–1999. Keep clear of dredgers and pipelines.

Hickling Broad Keep clear of marked navigable channel.

Horsey Mere Closed on voluntary basis to powered craft November to March.

Womack Water Limited space for mud weighting

Rockland Broad Tidal and very shallow outside marked channel. Do not obstruct marked channel.

Oulton Broad Keep clear of private moorings and sailing and power-boat racing courses.

(The foregoing sections on the Norfolk and Suffolk Broads have been prepared with the close co-operation of Mark Wakelin, Chief Navigation Officer of the Broads Authority.)

Wildlife in The Broads

In 1926, the Norfolk Naturalists' Trust was founded. This was the first organisation in Britain to be set up whose sole aim was the protection and conservation of wildlife. It is a registered charity and was founded with the aim of acquiring properties in Norfolk as nature reserves. Over the years it has taken over responsibility for thousands of acres of countryside in the county which are managed for the benefit of wildlife. Within the Broads area, it manages over 2,600 acres in ten sites some of which are open to the public, with visitor centres at Ranworth Broad and Hickling Broad. The trust can be contacted at its headquarters at 72 Cathedral Close, Norwich NR1 4DF ☎ 01603 625540.

The Royal Society for the Protection of Birds and the Suffolk Wildlife Trust also have reserves and visitor centres in the Broads reflecting the national importance of the wildlife of the area. The Broads are home to many species which can be found nowhere else in Britain such as the swallowtail butterfly, the Norfolk hawker dragonfly, birds of prey and many plants.

Some of the Broads nature reserves are:

Barton Broad Nature Reserve run by the Norfolk Naturalists' Trust is on the River Ant near South Stalham.

Broadland Conservation Centre, Ranworth Broad This is a floating, reed-thatched building in the Bure Marshes. The Broad is closed to navigation for the benefit of wildlife.

Carlton Marshes Nature Reserve is run by Suffolk Wildlife Trust. There are many different habitats and, in the holidays, the trust runs activity days for children. The reserve lies to the southwest of Oulton Broad.

Hickling Broad National Nature Reserve This is the largest area of open water in the Broads. It lies to the north of the River Thurne above Potter Heigham. The reserve is run by the Norfolk Naturalists' Trust and a popular attraction is the boat trip around the reserve with experts pointing out the wildlife en route. The broad is quite close to the sea and so the water is slightly brackish.

How Hill This reserve is run by the Broads Authority. There is a Victorian eel-catcher's cottage showing what life would have been like in the 19th century. The reserve also demonstrates traditional fen management techniques.

Martham Broad Nature Reserve This is further along the River Thurne from Potter Heigham either side of the river near West Somerton. A navigable channel runs through the reserve which is run by the Norfolk Naturalists' Trust. The site is important for summer migrant birds.

Strumpshaw Fen and Surlingham Church Marsh are both owned by the RSPB. They are both next to the River Yare and many species of birds use the reserves as winter homes and breeding grounds. Numerous birds of prey have been seen at both locations.

Wheatfen was once part of the Yare Valley Swamp. It is now a nature reserve named after a Norfolk naturalist, Ted Ellis, who had studied the site since 1935.

Authority The Broads Authority, Thomas Harvey House, 18 Colegate, Norwich, Norfolk NR3 1BQ ☎ 01603 610734.

Great Yarmouth Harbour comes under the Port Superintendent, 21 South Quay, Great Yarmouth ☎ 01493 855151 and 663476 VHF Ch 12, 16. The port jurisdiction extends to the west end of Breydon Water and about 1 mile up the River Bure.

Lowestoft Harbour is run by Associated British Ports, Lowestoft ☎ 01502 572286. VHF Ch 14.

Lake Lothing comes within the jurisdiction of the Port of Lowestoft.

Speed limits Speed limits vary around the Broads. They are clearly marked and are 3, 4, 5 and 6mph. The limits are strictly enforced by patrol launches and electronic equipment with a maximum penalty for exceeding the limits of £1,000.

Registration All boats must pay Broads Authority tolls. A short-visit toll is payable for boats visiting the Broads for less than 28 days in the year. Over 28 days, boats must be registered, display their registration number and pay the annual fee.

Bridges There are numerous bridges around the Broads. The lowest bridges are Potter Heigham and Beccles Old Road with clearances of 6ft 8ins and 6ft 6ins respectively. Clearances may be affected by extreme tides. Many bridges have water level guages alongside. If in doubt tie up well before the bridge and check the clearance. Never approach a bridge with the tide unless you are absolutely certain there is sufficient clearance for your boat. Some bridges have sharply curving sides which may restrict the passage of beamier vessels.

Navigation The Broads are tidal. The greatest effect is felt nearest to Great Yarmouth and in the lower reaches of the rivers Yare and Waveney. The rise and fall ranges from 7ft at Great Yarmouth, 5ft at Reedham and St Olaves and up to 4ft at Beccles and Norwich. The flood continues for about 5 hours and the ebb for 7. The rate of tide varies between 0.5mph and 5mph with the ebb running up to 0.5mph faster than the flood. The tide at Yarmouth Bar is about 1 hour earlier than at Yarmouth Yacht Station. Always turn into the tide when mooring.

Facilities Throughout the Broads there are facilities to suit all types of boat crew. The principal yacht stations are at Oulton Broad, Great Yarmouth, Norwich and Beccles. Boat yards offer moorings for varying periods and there are 24-hour and temporary moorings in many villages and in more remote sections of rivers. Two useful guides for holiday planning are *What to do on the Norfolk Broads* published annually by Jarrold Publishing Ltd and the *GEOprojects Map of the Broads*.

Oulton Broad and Dyke

This waterway is one of the two routes into the Broads from the North Sea. It connects the River Waveney through Mutford Lock with Lake Lothing, Lowestoft Harbour and the sea. It is a very popular and active cruising area and covers about 130 acres.

Bridges All swing bridges. Proceeding through Lake Lothing from Lowestoft Harbour, care must be taken in navigating Lowestoft Swing Bridge. Its height is rather deceptive and numerous craft find trouble owing to this. Attention must also be given to the tides here.

Towpaths None.

Locks Mutford Lock is currently the only working lock on the Broads. Passage should be booked in advance ☎ 01502 531778 or 523003 VHF Ch 14. The bridge next to the lock has clearance of 2.1m MHWS and if this needs to be opened it should also be booked. There is a fee to pass through the lock.

Mutford Lock was fully refurbished in 1992 and at present discussions are under way for it to come fully under the jurisdiction of the Broads Authority. The lock is manned by staff of Waveney District Council on behalf of the Broads Authority.

Navigation High water at Lowestoft is about 40 minutes after HW Yarmouth Bar. Tidal range is springs 6ft 6in, neaps 5ft 3ins.

Distance table   *Miles*
Junction with River Waveney at north end of Oulton Dyke to:

Oulton Dyke South	1.3
West end of Oulton Broad	1.5
Oulton Broad Yacht Station	2.2
Mutford Bridge Lock and entrance to Lake Lothing	2.3
Lowestoft Bridge	4.1
Mouth of Lowestoft Harbour	4.5

River Waveney

The River Waveney forms the boundary between Norfolk and Suffolk from its rise in the Thetford Forest to St Olave's and then it meanders on through marshes until it meets the Yare and enters Breydon Water. The original head of navigation was at Bungay, a further 4.2 miles above the present limit at Geldeston Lock, but the public right of navigation is said to have been extinguished in 1934. Light craft which can be portaged can continue up to Bungay but the locks at Ellingham and Wainford have been replaced by sluices. The Broads Authority and Bungay Town Council are seeking to re-establish the navigation for unpowered craft and improve portaging facilities at the locks.

From Geldeston to Beccles the river is quiet as many boats cannot pass under the old town bridge with its 6ft 6ins headroom. This is a delightful excursion even if it does mean taking to the dinghy to experience it. An added incentive is the Locks Inn which is only accessible by water. Beccles was once a fishing port, which now seems hard to believe, but it has retained its charm without becoming quaint.

OULTON BROAD AND DYKE *Maximum vessel dimensions*

From and to	Distance	Length	Beam	Draught	Headroom	Locks
Lowestoft Harbour to						
River Waveney	4.5 miles (7.2km)	86' (26.2m)	20' (6.1m)	9' (2.7m)	Unlimited	1

RIVER WAVENEY Maximum vessel dimensions

From and to	Distance	Length	Beam	Draught	Headroom	Locks
Geldeston Lock to Beccles	3.2 miles (5.1km)	Unlimited	Unlimited	5' 6" (1.7m)	6' 6" (2.0m)	1
Beccles to the junction with the River Yare	18.4 miles (29.6km)	Unlimited	Unlimited	5' (1.7m)	8' 4" (2.5m)	None

HADDISCOE NEW CUT Maximum vessel dimensions

From and to	Distance	Length	Beam	Draught	Headroom	Locks
Links the Rivers Yare and Waveney	2.5 miles (4.0km)	Unlimited	Unlimited	5' (1.5m)	24' (7.3m)	None

Its associations with the sea are strong as it was in St Michael's Church, Beccles, that Lord Nelson's parents were married. Another attraction of the church is its detached bell tower.

The river continues through marshes with windmills and past carrs. Carr woodland is a type of mature woodland before oak or ash take over and the Broads Authority protect and carefully manage the 7,500 acres within their jurisdiction. Around Somerleyton and St Olave's there is plenty of activity before the river heads northeast towards Breydon Water and the Haddiscoe New Cut branches off northwestward to Reedham.

Towpath Footpaths along much of the route.

Bridges Beccles Old Bridge, Beccles New Bridge, Somerleyton Rail Bridge, swings, St Olaves Bridge.

Locks The lock at Geldeston is now disused. There were two further locks up to Bungay at Ellingham and Wainford.

Navigation High water St Olave's Bridge about 2½ hours after HW Yarmouth Bar and HW Beccles is about 4 hours after. The stream is very strong from the entrance to Somerleyton.

Connections Geldeston Dyke (½ mile long but very shallow), Oulton Dyke, Haddiscoe New Cut, River Yare and Breydon Water.

Distance table	Miles
Bungay Staithe to:	
Wainford Lock (disused)	0.6
Ellingham Lock (disused)	2.0
Geldeston Lock (disused) – present head of navigation	4.2
Beccles Town Bridge	7.4
Stanley Carrs	8.9
Aldeby Hall Staithe	10.1
Worlingham Staithe	10.5
Six Mile Corner Short Reach	11.8
Seven Mile Carr	12.6
Carlton Share Mill	14.1
Waveney River Centre	14.4
Junction with Oulton Dyke	15.3
Somerleyton Railway Bridge	18.2
Somerleyton Staithe	18.3
Junction with Haddiscoe New Cut	20.1
St Olave's Bridge and Staithes	20.4
Burgh Staithe	25.1
Burgh Castle	25.3
Junction with River Yare at west end of Breydon Water	25.8

Haddiscoe New Cut

The cut was dug in 1833 to connect the River Yare with the River Waveney and offer an alternative route to the North Sea via Lowestoft for vessels trading from Norwich. This route today greatly reduces the distance from Beccles to Norwich and avoids the tides around Breydon Water. The cut is completely straight and the railway runs alongside it. Mooring in the New Cut is prohibited.

Bridges A fixed bridge has replaced the old lift bridge.

Towpath None.

Navigation The cut is tidal with a rise of 2ft 6ins to 3ft. The tidal flow is to and from the River Yare. High Water is about 2½ hours after HW Yarmouth Bar.

Distance table	Miles
Reedham, junction with River Yare to:	
Road Bridge, Queens Head Inn	2.0
Haddiscoe, junction with River Waveney	2.5

River Yare

The River Wensum flows down from the Fens curving round the east side of Norwich city centre before heading off eastward to join the Yare for the rest of its journey to the sea at Great Yarmouth. Above Trowse Newton, the River Yare is narrow and shallow and continues well into Breckland to its source.

The Yare has been a major trading river for many centuries and coasters used to travel up to the wharves between Carrow Bridge and Foundary Bridge in Norwich. As recently as the late 1980s you could meet coasters in the narrow confines of the river which added certain spice for pleasure boat crews. If the railway bridge and Carrow Bridge were open it usually meant a coaster or commercial vessel was about to come through and pleasure boats had to keep well clear.

Over the centuries, Norwich developed into an important centre, much of its wealth being built on the wool trade. Today, it is still a delightful place to visit with the elegant spire of the cathedral providing a focal point in the city. The spire is 315ft high, second only to Salisbury, and it was rebuilt in 1480

RIVER YARE Maximum vessel dimensions

From and to	Distance	Length	Beam	Draught	Headroom	Locks
Norwich city to Trowse Newton	2.8 miles (4.5km)	Unlimited	Unlimited	10' 6" (3.2m)	9' 6" (2.8m)	None
Trowse Newton to Yarmouth Bar	28.8 miles (46.3km)	Unlimited	Unlimited	10' 6" (3.2m)	35' (10.6m)	None

having been blown down in a severe storm in 1362. Close to the cathedral is Bishop Bridge over the River Wensum. This is the oldest bridge in Norwich said to date back to 1340. The open market is rightly famous and the cobbled medieval streets and alleys can offer interesting possibilities for the most intrepid explorer. Among other things to see in Norwich is the castle which has a collection of paintings by artists of the Norwich School.

Below Norwich Thorpe Old River is a loop to the north which is available to pleasure craft and offers useful moorings from which to visit the city. There is a fixed rail bridge each end with about 6ft clearance. It was to avoid these two bridges that the new cutting was made in 1844. Continuing downstream is first Bramerton Wood's End and Bramerton Common and on the next bend is Surlingham Church Marsh Nature Reserve on the righthand side before Strumpshaw Fen Nature Reserve on the left.

After winding on past Rockland Broad and Cantley, the River Chet branches off on the right up towards Loddon and Chedgrave. Shortly after this you meet the Reedham Ferry which you must always pass behind leaving a safe distance for its chains to sink into the water. The ferry is the only passenger and car crossing between Norwich and Great Yarmouth. At Reedham, there is a swing railway bridge before the Haddiscoe New Cut branches off to the right and the river heads northeast again towards Breydon Water.

Bridges River Wensum has seven fixed, one lifting and one swing bridge up to the limit of navigation at New Mills. River Yare has three opening and one fixed bridge.

Navigation High Water Norwich is approx 4½ hours after HW Yarmouth Bar and HW Reedham is approximately 2½ hours after Yarmouth Bar. Tidal range is 1ft 6ins–2ft at Norwich and 2ft 6ins–3ft at Reedham. Tides run strongly through Breydon Water and Great Yarmouth. Only sea-going boats should proceed into Great Yarmouth under Haven Bridge. For advice on navigating in this area contact the Great Yarmouth Harbourmaster. Great Yarmouth is a busy commercial port and pleasure craft are not actively encouraged.

Towpath There is a riverside walk in Norwich city and footpaths in many places along the river.

Connections River Chet, Breydon Water, Haddiscoe New Cut, Hardley Dyke, Langley Dyke, Rockland Broad, Surlingham Broad, Thorpe Old River and the River Wensum.

Distance table

Norwich, New Mills, to:	Miles
Fye Bridge	0.6
Bishop Bridge	1.2
Foundry Bridge and Norwich Yacht Station	1.5
Carrow Bridge	2.1
Junction with Branch to Trowse Mills (River Yare)	2.8
West end of loop line of Thorpe Old River	3.1
East end of loop line of Thorpe Old River	3.8
Whitlingham	4.1
Postwick Hall	6.0
Bramerton Staithe	6.5
Surlingham Ferry and Staithe	8.3
Entrance to Surlingham Broad and Nature Reserve	9.4
Brundall Railway Station	9.8
Exit from Surlingham Broad	10.0
Coldham Hall	10.3
Strumpshaw Fen Nature Reserve	10.7
Junction with Rockland Dyke, leading to Rockland Broad	11.6
Buckenham Ferry Staithe	12.9
Junction with Hassingham Dyke (unnavigable)	13.6
Junction with Langley Dyke	14.8
Cantley Railway Station	15.8
Hardley Brickyard Staithe	17.1
Junction with Hardley Dyke	17.3
Hardley Cross, junction with River Chet	18.4
Norton Staithe	18.6
Reedham Ferry	18.9
Reedham Swing Railway Bridge	19.9
Reedham, junction with New Cut	20.3
Seven Mile House	21.9
Berney Arms Staithe and Railway Station	24.5
Junction with River Waveney and Breydon Water	24.8
Junction with River Bure and Great Yarmouth	28.6
Haven Bridge, Great Yarmouth	28.9
Gorleston Ferry	30.3
Gorleston, mouth of river	31.6

River Yare Broads and branches

River Chet

This shallow tributary of the Yare is worth exploring as it leads up to the charming market town of Loddon. At the river junction is the Hardley Cross which marks the boundary between the city of Norwich and Yarmouth. The only restriction on length of boats is the narrow channel and some tight bends. There is adequate space to turn at Loddon.

Navigation High Water is about 3 hours after HW Yarmouth Bar with an average rise of 2ft 6ins.

RIVER YARE BROADS AND BRANCHES Maximum vessel dimensions

From and to	Distance	Length	Beam	Draught	Headroom	Locks
Hardley Cross to Loddon	3.5 miles (5.6km)	32' 10" (10.0m)	16' (4.8m)	3' (0.9m)	Unlimited	None

Breydon Water

Lying to the west of Great Yarmouth, the River Yare runs through the wide, shallow lake known as Breydon Water. The evolution of this is from a sea estuary rather than peat diggings as with the broads further inland. Mudflats stretch right up to the marked channel and any deviation outside the stakes is very likely to put you aground; what may have looked like a short cut could turn into a long wait. The lake is about 4 miles long by a half mile wide and the flatness of the surrounding country means it is very exposed to the prevailing weather conditions.

At the eastern end the tides can run very swiftly, and throughout the area wind over tide can whip up quite steep seas. It is a wise precaution to have your anchor ready to be dropped in the event of engine trouble so that you are not swept out of the channel. But remember that coasters still pass along here so if you do need to anchor allow room for them to pass safely.

Anchoring is only permitted for emergencies and mooring is not allowed in Breydon Water. The closest moorings are at the Berney Arms on the River Yare and Burgh Castle Marina on the River Waveney. The channel is marked by green stakes to the north and red stakes to the south and these should be given a good 5 to 6 metres berth.

Rockland Broad

The Broad is reached via either Fleet Dyke or Short Dyke and once in Rockland Broad channels are marked by posts. The broad is quite shallow and boats should keep to the channels as they proceed to Rockland St Mary village and the staithe. The depth is about 3ft and the navigable distance is about a mile.

Surlingham Broad

Surlingham Broad is a nature reserve on the inside of a sweeping bend in the river. Access to Bargate Water is via Surlingham Fleet or Birds Dyke with a minimum depth of about 3ft and a navigable distance of about half a mile. The reserve is owned by the Norfolk Naturalists' Trust and covers just over 250 acres.

Hardley Dyke

This is a short spur of about ¼ mile on the south bank just upstream from Hardley Cross. There is a depth of about 3ft.

Langley Dyke

Another dyke of about a quarter of a mile on the south bank leading up to the ruins of Langley Abbey with Langley village about a quarter mile further inland. There is a depth of about 3ft.

Trowse Mills Cut (River Yare)

At the junction with the River Wensum, the River Yare branches off southwestward. This is navigable for about another mile up to a bridge with a depth of about 3ft.

River Bure

The River Bure is the most northerly of the three main Broads rivers. It rises in north Norfolk and flows into the North Sea at Great Yarmouth, meeting the River Yare at the eastern end of Breydon Water. Two tributaries of the Bure are the Ant and the Thurne which also offer interesting cruising. Wroxham, the home of Broads hiring history, and Horning lie on the Bure so it is probably the best known of the Broadland rivers.

Another of the Bure's claims to fame is that it is the link between the greatest number of broads. A few of these are private and others, such as Ranworth, are reserves and closed to navigation. Cockshoot Broad now supports a thriving habitat thanks to the work of the Broads Authority which has improved the water quality. The water had been seriously polluted by fertiliser run-off and sewage effluent and by pumping out mud the nutrient level has been reduced and wildlife has very quickly started to recolonise the broad.

Horning is reputedly the prettiest village on the Broads; Wroxham is famous for the largest 'village shop' in Roy's of Wroxham; and Acle has a well-known market on Thursdays when produce and furniture are sold. The Stracey Arms Windpump has been fully restored by the Norfolk Windmills' Trust and an exhibition inside tells the story of the drainage of the Broads by windpumps. With all these, and many other attractions, it is understandable that the River Bure is so popular with visitors.

The original Bure navigation continued for another 9 miles through Coltishall Lock and a further four locks to Aylsham. This is still possible

RIVER BURE Maximum vessel dimensions

From and to	Distance	Length	Beam	Draught	Headroom	Locks
Coltishall Lock to Wroxham	5.6 miles (9.0km)	75' (22.8m)	16' (4.8m)	5' (1.5m)	7' 3" (2.2m)	None
Wroxham to Yarmouth	25.7 miles (1.3km)	75' (22.8m)	16' (4.8m)	6' (1.8m)	7' (2.1m)	None

for light craft which can be portaged, but all the locks are now derelict.

Bridges Five fixed bridges.

Towpath There are footpaths along many stretches of the river.

Locks There were five locks on the old Aylsham Navigation above the present limit of navigation at Coltishall, these are now all closed.

Connections River Ant, River Thurne, River Yare and Breydon Water at Yarmouth.

Distance table	*Miles*
Coltishall Lock to:	
Coltishall Staithe	0.7
Anchor Wood	1.2
Belaugh Village	2.0
Wroxham Railway Bridge	5.4
Wroxham Bridge	4.7
North end of Wroxham Broad	6.7
Salhouse Little Broad	7.8
Salhouse Broad	8.0
Hoveton Great Broad Nature Reserve	8.7
Hoveton Little Broad	9.8
Lower Street, Horning, Swan Hotel	10.5
New Inn, Horning	10.6
Horning Foot Ferry and Ferry Inn	11.2
Cockshoot Dyke, leading to Cockshoot Broad	11.6
Junction with Ranworth Dam, leading to Malthouse Broad and Broadland Conservation Centre	13.0
Junction with River Ant	14.2
Junction with Fleet Dyke leading to South Walsham Broad	14.8
St Benedict's Abbey (ruins)	15.5
Thurne Mouth, junction with River Thurne	17.0
Junction with Upton Dyke	18.4
Acle Bridge	19.8
Junction with Acle Dyke	20.6
Muck Fleet Dyke (not navigable) leading to Lily, Filby, Rollesby and Ormesby Broads	21.1
Stokesby Staithe	21.7
Stracey Arms Staithe and Windpump	23.1
Six Mile House	25.0
Great Yarmouth Yacht Station	31.0
Acle Road Bridge	31.2
Yarmouth, junction with River Yare and Breydon Water	31.3

River Bure Broads and branches

South Walsham Broad

This broad is approached through Fleet Dyke which is about a mile long, the depth throughout is about 4ft with a rise and fall of about 3ft and the tide is 3½ hours after Yarmouth Bar. The outer broad is open to the public but the inner, or western, broad is private although sailing is permitted on it. From the quay, it is about a mile to South Walsham village and other attractions are several windpumps, St Benet's Abbey and the marshes.

Ranworth Broad

Ranworth Broad is a nature reserve run by the Norfolk Naturalists' Trust and it is not open to navigation. At the entrance is the Broadland Conservation Centre, while to the east is Malthouse Broad which is navigable and the village. The Malthouses were damaged by fire but have now been restored. From St Helen's Church tower it is possible to get spectacular views across the Broads. The approach channel, Ranworth Dam, is just under a mile long with a depth of about 5ft.

Cockshoot Broad and Dyke

Cockshoot Broad was dammed by the Broads Authority to allow it to be dredged to improve water quality. There is a walk and nature trail around the Broad but it is not open to navigation.

Salhouse Great Broad

This is a quiet broad about half way between Horning and Wroxham. The village is about half a mile away and there is a railway station. Water depth is 4 to 5ft.

Salhouse Little Broad

On the Wroxham side of Salhouse Great Broad with a depth of 4 to 5ft.

Wroxham Broad

Wroxham Broad is a well known sailing venue. It is about a mile away from Wroxham village and just off the river with two entrances offering about 80 acres of water. Although there are no moorings, you may anchor in the Broad for a small fee. Wroxham Broad is home to the Norfolk Broads Yacht Club which organises much of the yacht racing here.

Little Switzerland

This was an area of local canals connecting with the Bure. They are about half way between Wroxham and Coltishall. These canals were cut into the hillside to enable wherries to go up to the marl workings and load. One canal was over half a mile long.

Hoveton Great Broad

This is now a nature reserve and not open to navigation. Boats may moor at the quay on the river just by the broad to visit the reserve and follow the nature trail. The broad covers about 105 acres of marshes and there is a leaflet available from the warden to accompany the walk.

RIVER BURE BROADS & BRANCHES *Maximum vessel dimensions*

From and to	Distance	Length	Beam	Draught	Headroom	Locks
River Bure to North Walsham and Dilham Canal	8 miles (12.8km)	60' (18.2m)	17' (5.1m)	5' (1.5m)	8' 6" (2.5m)	None

Hoveton Little Broad
As its name suggests this is a fairly small broad but makes a pleasant anchorage and it is quite close to Horning. It can be shallow in places but mostly has 3 to 4ft of water.

Upton Dyke
The dyke is 700yds long and very narrow. There is a mooring from where it is a short walk to Upton Green village.

Acle Dyke
This dyke is about ¼ mile long leading to Acle village. It is narrow and there are no public moorings. Filby, Ormesby, Rollesby and Lily Broads are land locked but dinghies and rowing boats can be hired. Muck Fleet connects them to the River Bure but it is not navigable even for rowing boats.

River Ant

This is the narrowest and shallowest of the Broads rivers and offers the opportunity to explore some of the remoter and quieter places. The river twists through woodland and reedbeds with old windpumps alongside and the possibility of venturing into Barton and Sutton Broads.

The original navigation lead into the North Walsham and Dilham Canal and eventually up to Antingham, but this is no longer navigable and only light craft can continue as far as Honing. Just north of Wayford Bridge, Tyler's Cut, also called Dilham Dyke, branches off to the left towards Dilham village.

When crossing Barton Broad all craft proceeding towards the head of navigation should leave Pleasure Hill Island to port allowing it a good berth. Craft turning into Limekiln Dyke should leave the island to starboard.

Bridges Two fixed bridges.

Towpath None.

Tides There is little tidal effect beyond Ludham Bridge, tidal range is about 7ins.

Connections River Bure, Tyler's Cut, Sutton Broad, Lime Kiln Dyke and the North Walsham and Dilham Canal – now derelict.

Distance table	*Miles*
Junction with River Bure to:	
Ludham Bridge	0.9
Irstead Church	4.1
Southern entrance to Barton Broad	4.5
Northern entrance to Barton Broad	5.8
Junction with Stalham Dyke	6.3
Wayford Bridge, Staithes	7.9
Junction with Tyler's Cut, leading to Dilham	8.0
Junction with North Walsham and Dilham Canal	8.3

River Ant Broads and branches
Barton Broad
It is said that Nelson learnt to sail on Barton Broad. It is a widening of the river which is another of the Norfolk Naturalists' Trust nature reserves. Extending to about 170 acres with a depth of 3ft 6ins to 4ft the broad can be shallow in places and channels are marked with red and green marks, here depths are nearer 5ft. Since 1995, a major restoration scheme has been under way to extend the open water available for sailing, dredging to increase the water depth and remove polluted mud to improve water quality.

Sutton Broad
Just over 1¼ miles long, Sutton Broad leads up to the village and staithe.

Stalham Dyke
Sharing an entrance from the River Ant with Sutton Broad, Stalham Dyke is just over 1 mile long with a depth of about 5ft 6ins. The market town of Stalham can be used as a base to explore the northern area of the Broads.

Distance table	*Miles*
Junction with River Ant to:	
Junction with Sutton Dyke (leading to Sutton Staithe Country Club)	0.5
Stalham Staithes	1.1

Old Limekiln Dyke
This dyke is about ½ mile long and 5 to 5ft 6ins deep leading to the staithe at Neatishead village.

River Thurne

Potter Heigham is one of the most famous villages on the Broads, even if its river, the Thurne, is less easily recognised. Leaving the River Bure just east of the River Ant, the Thurne winds northeastward towards the sea. At its eastern extremity the River Thurne becomes Martham Broad and through Candle Dyke leads into Hickling Broad and Horsey Mere. Both of these are quite shallow with slightly brackish water. Horsey Mere branches into Waxham Cut which ends up less than a mile from the coast.

The landscape in this part of the Broads is quite flat giving wonderful vistas, spectacular sunrises and sunsets, and no shelter from biting north and east winds.

Bridges Two fixed bridges, Potter Heigham Old Bridge is very narrow, has only 6ft 8ins headroom and must be treated with respect. All hire craft are required to take a bridge pilot to pass under Potter Heigham Old Bridge.

Towpath There are footpaths along much of the river.

Connections Thurne Dyke, Womack Water, Martham Broad, Candle Dyke, Heigham Sound, Hickling Broad, Horsey Mere and Waxham Cut.

RIVER THURNE Maximum vessel dimensions

From and to	Distance	Length	Beam	Draught	Headroom	Locks
River Bure to Martham Broad	6 miles (9.6km)	60' (18.2m)	7' 6' (2.2m)	5' 6" (1.6m)	6' 8" (2.0m)	None

Distance table   *Miles*
Thurne Mouth, junction with River Bure to:

	Miles
Junction with Thurne Dyke	0.4
Junction with Womack Water	1.2
Repps Staithe	2.0
Potter Heigham Bridge	3.0
Junction with Candle Dyke (leading to Hickling Broad and Horsey Mere)	4.5
Martham Staithe and Ferry	4.8
Junction with Martham Broad	6.0

River Thurne Broads and branches

Thurne Dyke

The dyke leading to Thurne village, has a depth of about 3ft, and is 175yds long. Thurne Dyke Windpump, next to the dyke, is a beautiful example of a white-painted traditional drainage pump.

Womack Water

Womack Water, leading to Ludham, is narrow, winding and quite shallow, with a depth of about 4ft, and is just under a mile long. Ludham was associated with St Benet's Abbey and some old ruins are still visible.

Heigham Sound

Heigham Sound is about 5ft 6ins deep in the navigation channel, elsewhere its about 3ft. The channel is marked and must be kept to as outside the channel it can be very shallow. The rise of tide is as little as 6ins which is unlikely to lift a boat out of the mud.

Hickling Broad

Hickling Broad is a National Nature Reserve. Although there is quite a large surface area of water much of it is shallow and weedy, boats should stay within the marked channel. From the River Thurne, Hickling Broad is reached via Candle Dyke, sometimes known as Kendal Dyke, Heigham Sound and White Slea Mere. Through Hickling Broad to the west is Catfield Dyke and Common where there are moorings.

Distance table   *Miles*
River Thurne to Hickling Broad
Candle Dyke and junction with River Thurne to:

	Miles
Heigham Sound	0.4
Deep Dyke leading to White Slea Mere	1.2
White Slea Mere	1.3
Hickling Broad	1.6

Horsey Mere

Horsey Mere Nature Reserve and Horsey Windpump are owned by the National Trust. There is a staithe at the eastern end of the mere from where it is about ½ mile to Horsey village and 1½ miles to the sea. Its location makes this a popular area for migrating birds and the proximity to the sea means

the water is slightly brackish. From the windpump the views across the countryside are quite breathtaking.

Waxham Cut runs northward out of Horsey Mere for about 1½ miles up to the bridge. It is navigable for boats up to about 30ft in length.

Distance table   *Miles*
River Thurne to Horsey Mere and Waxham Cut
Candle Dyke and junction with River Thurne to:

	Miles
Heigham Sound	0.4
Junction with Meadow Dyke	1.2
Horsey Mere	2.1
Junction with Waxham New Cut	2.8
Waxham Bridge	4.0

Martham Broad

At its eastern end the River Thurne joins Martham Broad and leads to the quiet village of West Somerton where there are moorings. Martham Broad is a nature reserve run by Norfolk Naturalists' Trust.

Distance table   *Miles*
Navigation across Martham Broad to West Somerton
Junction with River Thurne to:

	Miles
Martham Broad	0.1
Junction of Dyke leading to West Somerton	0.5
West Somerton Staithes	0.9

North Walsham and Dilham Canal

Although the original Act of Parliament to canalise the River Ant was promoted in 1812, it wasn't until 1825 that work started. North Walsham was a prosperous wool town and cargoes increased for about 20 years with grain and flour going to the coast, as well as the 'cabbage wherry' which took vegetables from Antingham to Yarmouth market, and coal and building materials were brought inland from Great Yarmouth. Railway competition saw a decline in cargo from the middle of the 19th century until the mid-1880s by which time there was little traffic. The canal was sold to a local miller and wherry owner in 1886. It was sold again in 1906 and then in 1921 when it was bought by millers at Ebridge who formed the North Walsham Canal Company.

The original canal was 8½ miles long with six locks, but the section from Antingham to Swafield Bridge was closed in 1927 and has mostly been returned to farmland. The bottom three locks were in use in 1935 and the public right of navigation still exists to Swafield Bridge although now craft must be portaged past the remaining four locks. Honing Lock is the theoretical head of navigation for small powered craft but reed encroachment and silting

NORTH WALSHAM AND DILHAM CANAL *Maximum vessel dimensions*

From and to	Distance	Length	Beam	Draught	Headroom	Locks
Swafield to Dilham Dyke	7.3 miles (11.7km)	50' (15.2m)	12' 4" (3.7m)	3' (0.9m)	7' (2.1m)	4

mean that few craft, other than canoes, venture above Dilham Dyke. The canal passes through some pretty countryside with woodland, small villages and farmland.

The canal was never taken over when other waterways were nationalised and is still notionally owned by the North Walsham Canal Company. There is no public right of way to walk along the towpath and anyone exploring by foot should use Ordnance Survey maps and be careful not to trespass on private property.

Authority North Walsham Canal Co. Ltd, Ebridge Mills, North Walsham, Norfolk.

Honing Lock to the junction with the River Ant: privately owned.

Bridges 11.

Towpath There is a footpath from Tonnage Bridge to Honing Lock.

Branches East Ruston Branch 0.4 miles. There were also branches to Meeting House Hill and Honing Staithe but now there is little sign of them.

Connections Dilham Dyke leading to Dilham village (Dilham Staithe is available for mooring, it is owned by the East Anglian Waterways Association and leased to the Broads Authority); The River Ant.

Restoration There have been some proposals to restore the canal but there are many interested parties and discussions are underway to arrive at a concensus. It has been agreed that an Ecological Survey should be carried out prior to an Environmental Impact Assessment.

Facilities Some moorings are available in Dilham Dyke.

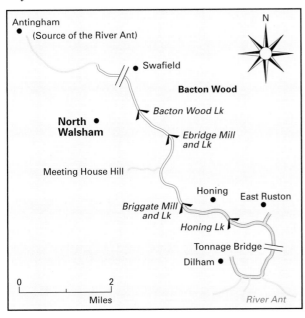

Distance table	Miles
Junction with Dilham Dyke to:	
Tonnage Bridge	0.8
Junction with East Ruston Branch	1.2
Honing Lock No 1	2.1
Honing Bridge	2.4
Briggate Lock No 2	3.3
Ebridge Lock No 3	5.0
Spa Common Bridge (North Walsham 1 mile distant)	5.9
Bacton Wood Lock No 4	6.0
Austin Bridge	6.4
Swafield Bridge	7.3

Bude Canal

The canal was opened in 1823 to transport shell sand inland to try to reduce the acidity of farm land. From the basin by the sea lock, the canal leads up to Marhamchurch from where an extensive tub-boat system served a wide area of north Cornwall and west Devon. The total waterway was over 35 miles with branches towards Holsworthy and Tamar Lake, and up the Tamar Valley it reached Druxton Wharf near Launceston. It was famous for its six inclined planes at Marhamchurch, Hobbacott Down, Venn, Merrifield, Tamerton and Werrington. Tub boats were 20ft long with a beam of 5ft 6ins and a draught of 1ft 8ins carrying 4 tons. Many remains of the tub-boat canal can still be seen.

The system was busy until the 1880s when a combination of railways and artificial fertilisers severely reduced business. The tub-boat section was closed by Act of Parliament in 1891 and the barge canal to Marhamchurch was navigable until 1924. At present, only the sea lock and the basin are in use as a small yacht haven.

Authority North Cornwall District Council, Higher Trenant Road, Wadebridge, Cornwall ☎ 01208 812255.

Controlling Officer The Harbourmaster, The Wharf, Bude, Cornwall ☎ 01288 353111 VHF Ch 12.

Bridge Falcon Bridge only on the navigable section.

Towpath Throughout navigation.

Navigation The approach to Bude from the sea should only be made in quiet weather with offshore winds and as close as possible to slack water. The harbourmaster will lock boats in or out whenever possible, this is usually restricted to 2 hours either side of high water provided 7ft of water is registered on the gauge at the locks. Contact the harbourmaster before attempting to enter and he will advise if locking is possible (his decision is final). The lock is impassable in strong onshore

BUDE CANAL Maximum vessel dimensions

From and to	Distance	Length	Beam	Draught	Headroom	Locks
Bude Sea Lock to Rodd's Bridge	1.3 miles (2.1km)	85' (25.9m)	24' (7.3m)	9' 6" (2.9m)	3' 6" (1.1m)	1

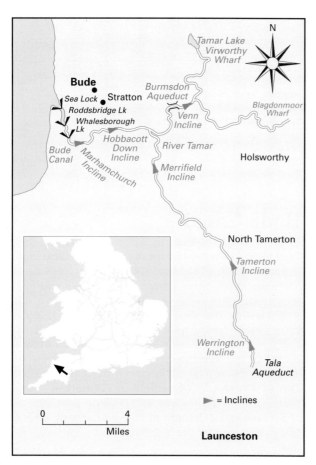

Calder and Hebble Navigation

There is no longer commercial carrying on the Calder and Hebble Navigation but you can still find reminders of its industrial past. Travelling from Wakefield to Sowerby Bridge is a fascinating mixture of traditional Yorkshire industry and beautiful countryside with plenty of warm hospitality along the way. Since the early 1950s, it has not been possible to continue over the Pennines but with active restoration on both the Rochdale Canal and the Huddersfield Narrow Canal through travel is likely to be possible soon after the year 2000.

winds. Fresh water is available on the wharf and the town shops are close by.

Tides High water Bude is 40 minutes before HW Milford Haven, MHWS 7.7m, MHWN 5.8m.

Charts Imray C58, Admiralty 1156.

Restoration Plans to restore the barge canal to Marhamchurch and some of the tub-boat system and inclined planes are being discussed. There is an active restoration society and work camps have been undertaken here by WRG.

Although never quite as profitable as the neighbouring Aire and Calder Navigation, the upper reaches of the River Calder were improved for navigation and opened in 1770. It is still a mix of river and canal and as such can experience rapid changes in water level and volume and flood locks are operated by BW when conditions dictate.

This is an interesting waterway for walkers, anglers and canoeists. For long distance walkers, the towpath connects with the Calderdale Way at Brookfoot near Brighouse.

Authority British Waterways, Lock Lane, Castleford, West Yorkshire WF10 2LH ☎ 01977 554351.

Bridges Numerous.

Towpath Throughout Main Line navigation, mostly good condition.

Branches The Dewsbury Cut runs to moorings at Savile Basin and a museum, the Halifax Arm is now mostly derelict, but the Salterhebble Basin has been restored.

CALDER AND HEBBLE NAVIGATION *Maximum vessel dimensions*

From and to	Distance	Length	Beam	Draught	Headroom	Locks
Fall Ing Lock,Wakefield to Broadcut Top Lock	3.6 miles (5.8km)	120' (36.6m)	17' 6" (5.3m)	6' 6" (2.0m)	11' (3.4m)	5
Broadcut Top Lock to Sowerby Bridge	17.9 miles (28.8km)	57' 6" (17.5m)	14' 2" (4.3m)	5' (1.5m)	9' (2.7m)	33
Dewsbury Old Cut						
Calder and Hebble Navigation to Savile	1 mile (1.6km)	57' 6" (17.5m)	14' 2" (4.3m)	5' (1.5m)	8' (2.4m)	None

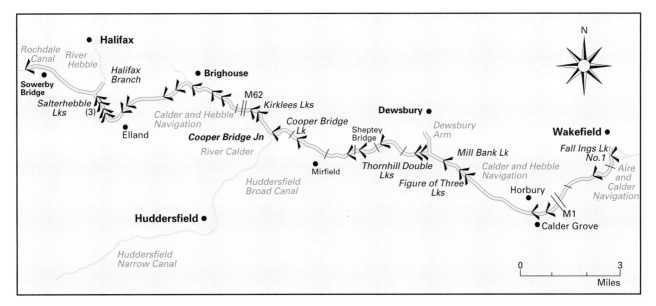

Connections Aire and Calder Navigation at Wakefield, Huddersfield Broad Canal at Kirklees and the Rochdale Canal at Sowerby Bridge.

Navigation The Calder and Hebble has a unique spike for opening gate paddles. These can be obtained from BW or hire companies. Extra care must be taken on this navigation as it is a mixture of river and canal. Water levels and flow can change rapidly and this can affect how a boat handles under bridges, when passing weirs and entering or leaving locks.

River level gauge boards are located at locks which give access to river sections of the navigation. The signing used is as follows:

Green band River level normal, safe to navigate.
Amber band River level above normal. Extra care must be taken. If you want to continue you are advised to go on to the next lock and pass through it.
Red band Flood conditions, unsafe to navigate, lock closed.

Distance table

Fall Ing Lock No 1, junction with the Aire and Calder Navigation Main Line to: Miles

	Miles
Wakefield Flood Lock	0.5
Thornes Lock No 2	1.0
Thornes Flood Lock	2.0
M1 Road Bridge	2.5
Broad Cut Low Lock No 3	2.9
Waller Bridge	3.0
Broad Cut Top Lock No 4	3.3
Horbury Bridge	5.0
Figure of Three Locks Nos 5 and 6	6.0
Mill Bank Lock No 7	6.6
Junction with Dewsbury Arm (Dewsbury Basin 0.8 miles)	7.0
Thornhill Double Locks Nos 8 and 9	7.1
Thornhill Flood Lock	8.0
Greenwood Lock No 10	8.9
Greenwood Flood Lock	9.1
Shepley Bridge	9.5
British Waterways Yard	9.6
Mirfield Boatyard	10.0
Ledgard Flood Lock	10.8
Battye Lock No 12	11.8
Cooper Bridge Lock No 13	12.8
Cooper Bridge Flood Gates	13.0
Junction Huddersfield Broad Canal	13.1
Kirklees Low Lock No 14	13.6
Kirklees Top Lock No 15	13.7
Anchor Pit Flood Lock	14.3
Brighouse Locks Nos 16 and 17	15.1
Brighouse Basin Entrance	15.3
Ganny Lock No 18	15.8
Brookfoot Lock No 19 (flood control point)	16.0
Cromwell Lock No 20	16.4
Park Nook Lock No 21	16.9
Elland Lock No 22	17.1

	Miles
Woodside Mills Lock No 23	18.0
Longleas Lock No 24	18.4
Salterhebble Locks Nos 25 to 27	19.0
Junction with closed Halifax Branch (open for 600 yards)	19.1
Sowerby Bridge Basin	21.5
Town Wharf	

River Cam

The River Cam has a greater impact on its university town than the Thames does in Oxford. The river along the Backs is always full of rowers and punters, the banks have joggers, cyclists and artists and the whole of Cambridge seems imbued with its river.

Although cruisers and rowers have disputes today, this is nothing new and the conservators, who were established by an Act in 1702, have always had the task of balancing demands on the river. In earlier days, it was often a conflict between transport and mill owners, drainage or navigation and today the problems are similar; for example, how to time dredging so it doesn't disrupt training for the Boat Race or the main cruising season. The 13 conservators are local people who hold their meetings in public so they can hear the concerns of user groups.

The conservators are only responsible for the river as far as Bottisham Lock from where the Environment Agency takes over. The lower reaches are wider, flatter and more windswept as they pass Wicken Fen and the Swaffham, Burwell and Reach Lodes.

Authority *From Silver Street, Cambridge to Bottisham Lock* Conservators of the River Cam, The Guildhall, Cambridge CB2 3QJ ☎ 01223 58977.

From Bottisham Lock to junction with the River Ouse Environment Agency, Kingfisher House, Goldhay Way, Orton Goldhay, Peterborough PE2 5ZR ☎ 01733 37181 *Fax* 01733 231840.

Bridges Numerous.

Connections Reach Lode and Burwell Lode can be reached from Upware. Connection is also made with Swaffham Lode and the Great Ouse. Soham Lode is only suitable for light craft as the depth of water is only 1ft 6ins. Bottisham Lode is unnavigable.

Facilities There are plenty of pubs along the river as well as in Cambridge. Many pubs have moorings and there are also public moorings and a boatyard. There is no petrol available along the river. There is a public slip at Upware.

Distance table *Miles*
River Cam
Kings Mill, Cambridge to:

Jesus Green Lock, Cambridge	0.8
Chesterton Ferry	2.5
Fen Ditton	3.5
Baitsbite Lock No 2	4.6
Horningsea	5.3
Clayhythe Bridge (Waterbeach railway station and village 0.5 mile)	6.6
Bottisham Lock No 3	7.6
Mouth of Bottisham Lode (unnavigable)	7.8
Junction with Swaffham Lode	9.0
Upware, junction with Reach and Burwell Lodes	11.3
Popes Corner, junction with River Great Ouse	14.4

Reach Lode and Burwell Lode

Authority Environment Agency, Kingfisher House, Goldhay Way, Orton Goldhay, Peterborough PE2 5ZR ☎ 01733 37181 *Fax* 01733 231840.

Towpath Throughout navigation.

Navigation These navigations were formerly used by fen lighters but are now used only by pleasure craft. At Burwell village there are two arms to the Lode and this gives several good moorings. Wicken Lode is shallow and can only be navigated with care. Except for local inhabitants navigation of Wicken Lode ceases at junction with Monks Lode.

RIVER CAM Maximum vessel dimensions

From and to	Distance	Length	Beam	Draught	Headroom	Locks
River Cam Cambridge to Pope's Corner on River Great Ouse	14.4 miles (23.2km)	100' (30.5m)	14' (4.3m)	4' (1.2m)	9' (2.7m)	3
Reach Lode and Burwell Lode Upware, junction with the River Cam, to Burwell village	3.8 miles (6.1km)	50' (15.2m)	13' 6" (4.1m)	4' (1.2m)	9' (2.7m)	1
Upware to Reach village	3 miles (4.8km)	50' (15.2m)	13' 6" (4.1m)	2' 6" (0.8m)	9' (2.7m)	1
Swaffham Lode Junction with River Cam to Slade Farm	2 miles (3.2km)	96' (29.3m)	15' (4.1m)	2' (0.6m)	9' (2.7m)	1

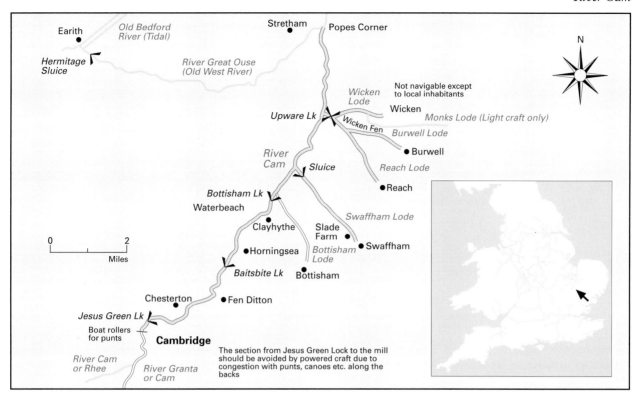

Distance table

Upware, junction with River Cam, to:

	Miles
Reach Lode Sluice (lock)	0.1
Junction with Wicken Lode	0.3
Pout Hall, junction with Reach Lode leading to Reach village, 2.1 miles	0.9
Burwell village	3.8

Wicken Lode (not navigable beyond junction with Monks Lode, except for local residents)

Junction Burwell and Wicken Lodes, to:

New River Drain	1.1
Wicken Fen (National Trust Reserve)	1.5

Swaffham Lode

Authority Environment Agency, Kingfisher House, Goldhay Way, Orton Goldhay, Peterborough PE2 5ZR ☎ 01733 37181 *Fax* 01733 231840.

Towpath Throughout navigation.

Navigation Boats can no longer reach Swaffham, about another 2.3 miles further, because of low bridges and shallow water.

Chelmer and Blackwater Navigation

Opened in 1797, the Chelmer and Blackwater Navigation continued to see timber ships up to Chelmsford until 1972. Approached through the shifting sandbanks of the River Blackwater Estuary, the navigation runs through mostly unspoilt countryside, calm and peaceful rather than exciting, and little known outside its local area. The Chelmer and Blackwater is still an independent navigation under the control of the Company of Proprietors, set up in 1793 at the start of the navigation project.

At the time of the construction of the canal, local mill owners were strongly opposed to it because of the effect on water flow, mostly for flour milling. There are still a number of mills along the canal, built in traditional Essex style, although most of them have now found different uses. Its statutory depth is the lowest of any waterway, being only 2ft.

CHELMER AND BLACKWATER NAVIGATION *Maximum vessel dimensions*

From and to	Distance	Length	Beam	Draught	Headroom	Locks
Heybridge Basin to Chelmsford	13.8 miles (22.1km)	60' (18.3m)	16' (4.9m)	3' (0.9m)	6' 3" (1.9m)	13
Heybridge Basin		107' (32.6m)	26' (7.9m)	12' (3.7m)	Unlimited	

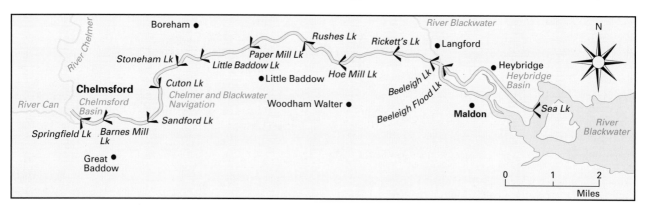

Special shallow draught barges were used to accommodate the lack of water. Visitors can find temporary moorings at Heybridge Basin before proceeding upstream. Moorings are also available at several points on the canal.

Authority The Company of Proprietors of the Chelmer and Blackwater Navigation Limited, Paper Mill Lock, North Hill, Little Baddow, Chelmsford, Essex CM3 4BF ☎ 01245 222025.

Lock-keeper, Heybridge Lock ☎ 01621 853506.

Bridges Several, low headroom at most bridges.

Towpath Throughout navigation.

Navigation The River Blackwater is tidal to Heybridge sea lock. High water is 30 minutes after HW Dover. Tidal range, spring tides 5.1m, neap tides 3.8m.

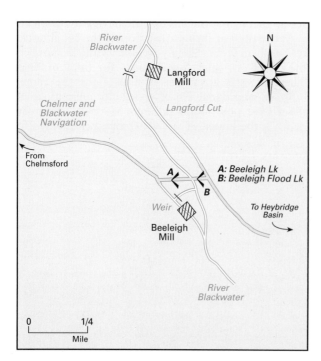

To conserve water in the canal the Heybridge Lock is only worked for 1 hour before HW neaps but longer on spring tides.

Facilities All facilities are available in Chelmsford, and at various small villages along the navigation there are pubs and small shops. At Paper Mill Lock there is water, a sanitary station, refuse disposal and a slipway.

Distance table

Chelmsford Basin to: — Miles

	Miles
Springfield Lock No 1	0.4
Barnes Mill Lock No 2	1.1
Sandford Lock No 3	2.1
Cuton Lock No 4	3.1
Stoneham's Lock No 5	4.0
Little Baddow Lock No 6 and Wharf	4.9
Paper Mill Lock No 7	6.1
Rushes Lock No 8	7.5
Hoe Mill Lock No 9	8.8
Rickett's Lock No 10	10.1
Beeleigh Lock No 11	11.0
Beeleigh Flood Lock No 12	11.5
Heybridge village	12.3
Heybridge Sea Lock No 13	13.0

Chesterfield Canal

The Chesterfield Canal was built to link the towns of Chesterfield, Worksop and Retford with the River Trent and so gain access to more trade. It was one of the earliest canals to be built, being opened on 4th June 1777, and until the early part of this century, it was a commercial success. Part of that success could be put down to coal which was finally its downfall as the effect of mining caused subsidence in the Norwood Tunnel which, after a roof collapse in 1907, severed the upper end of the canal which was then closed.

Under the 1968 Transport Act, the lower part of the canal was classified as a cruiseway and it has been used by pleasure boats ever since. The current head of navigation is Morse Lock, just west of Worksop. Some lengths of canal between the Norwood Tunnel and Chesterfield have been dredged and are now back in water, but many miles were sold off and have been infilled.

The canal passes through pleasant countryside, crossing the River Idle and going into 'The Dukeries', on its way to Chesterfield. The towpath has become a popular walk, the 'Cuckoo Way', and stretches of the canal are used by local angling clubs. For those keen to explore the canal in detail, there is *A Walkers' and Boaters' Guide to the Chesterfield Canal and Cuckoo Way* by Christine Richardson and John Lower which is a good read.

Authority *West Stockwith to Norwood tunnel* British Waterways, Mill Lane, Mill Gate, Newark, Nottinghamshire NG24 4TT ☎ 01636 704481.

Chesterfield to Norwood tunnel many private owners.

Bridges Numerous.

Towpath Towpath throughout navigation, except Drakeholes tunnel.

Tunnels Drakeholes, 154yds, headroom, 10ft; Norwood, 3102yds (closed through subsidence in 1907).

Speed limit 4mph.

Navigation The approach to Stockwith Lock from the River Trent is tidal and due consideration should be given to the wind and tide conditions. The lock works for approximately 2 hours 30 minutes before to approximately 4 hours 30 minutes after high water. The tide is between 2 hours and 2 hours 30 minutes after HW Hull. The lock-keeper requires at least 24-hours notice to book a passage, ☎ 01427 890204. VHF Ch 74.

Restoration Since the early 1990s, restoration has progressed significantly. Tapton Lock No 1 was re-opened in 1990 and further lengths of canal have become navigable. The Chesterfield Canal Society is active in its work and the prospects for full restoration are good.

Facilities For walkers along the Chesterfield to Worksop section there are a number of pubs to choose from. Below Worksop, services for boaters are available at Worksop, Forest Locks, Clayworth and West Stockwith although pump-out is only available at West Stockwith. There is a good choice of pubs along the route. Slipways are available at West Stockwith Basin and Drakeholes Tunnel and, with permission, at Retford and Worksop Boat Club and Retford Mariners Boat Club. There is a link proposed to Rotherham.

Distance table	Miles
Chesterfield to:	
Tapton Lock No 1	0.9
Wheeldon Mill Lock No 2	1.8
Blue Bank Lock No 3	2.4
Dixon Lock No 4	2.9
Hollingwood Lock No 5	3.5
Belk Lane Lock No 6	10.6
Norwood Locks Nos 7–19	11.7
Norwood Tunnel, West End	12.1
Norwood Tunnel, East End	13.9
Thorpe Locks Nos 20–22	16.1
Thorpe Locks Nos 23–34	16.5
Turner Wood Locks Nos 35–41	17.0
Ryton Aqueduct	17.3
Shireoaks Locks Nos 42–44	17.8
Then follows at intervals: Doefield Dunn Lock No 45, Haggonfield Lock No 46, Deep Lock No 47, Stret Lock No 48	
Morse Lock No 49 (present head of navigation)	19.5
Worksop Town Lock No 50	20.0
Bracebridge Lock No 51	20.7
Kilton Low Lock No 52	21.0
Osberton Lock No 53	23.3

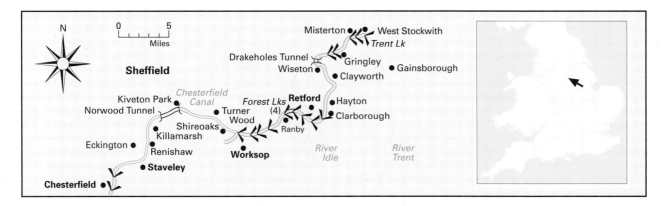

CHESTERFIELD CANAL Maximum vessel dimensions

From and to	Distance	Length	Beam	Draught	Headroom	Locks
River Trent at West Stockwith to Retford	15.5 miles (5.0km)	72' (21.9m)	14' (4.2m)	2' 6" (0.7m)	7' 6" (2.2m)	6
Retford to Chesterfield	30 miles (48.3km)	72' (21.9m)	7' (2.1m)	2' 6" (0.7m)	7' 6" (2.2m)	59

	Miles
Ranby, Chequers Inn	25.2
Forest Top Lock Nos 54–57	26.3
West Retford Lock No 58	29.9
Aqueduct over River Idle	30.1
Retford Town Lock No 59	30.3
Whitsunday Pie Lock No 60	31.8
Clarborough Church Bridge	32.3
Hayton, Boat Inn	34.8
Clayworth Bridge	35.9
Drakeholes Tunnel	39.0
Gringley Top Lock No 61	40.8
Shaw Lock No 62	41.5
Walkeringham Bridge	42.6
Cooper's Bridge	43.8
Misterton Top Lock No 63	44.7
Misterton Low Lock No 64	44.8
Railway Bridge	44.9
Stockwith Bridge	45.4
West Stockwith, Trent Lock No 65, junction with River Trent	45.5

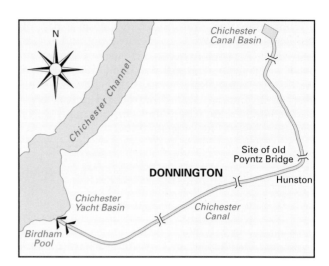

Chichester Canal

The Chichester Canal is the most complete section of a canal which linked London with Portsmouth via the Wey-Arun Junction Canal. One of the principal reasons for its construction was to provide a safe transport route during the Napoleonic wars but these were over long before the canal was completed. What we now call the Chichester Canal was a branch of the Portsmouth and Arundel Canal from Hunston to Chichester, plus the short section from Hunston to Chichester Harbour.

The canal was leased to the Chichester Canal Society in 1984 and considerable restoration work has been carried out by volunteers since then. Currently 2½ miles are navigable and the society has a trip boat on this section. It is also used by rowers, anglers and canoeists, with money from licences being used for further restoration. About ¼ mile is reed bed from Donnington Bridge to Birdham Pool. There are two bridges which cause obstructions to navigation but, if funding can be arranged to raise these, it will be possible to restore the canal to navigation from the town centre to Chichester Harbour.

In the lower reaches, the canal and the sea lock are leased to Premier Marinas. The approaches from seaward to both this marina and Chichester Marina can be tricky as the channels tend to shift.

Authority West Sussex County Council, County Hall, Chichester ☎ 01243 777100.

Bridges Four road bridges, two of these are now major obstructions.

Towpath Throughout navigation.

Connections Formerly to the Portsmouth and Arundel Canal at Hunston.

Restoration A feasibility study has been carried out into the full restoration of the canal, partly for flood prevention measures. Dredging and towpath improvement are on-going, but the major obstruction is two non-navigable road crossings. The Chichester Canal Society co-ordinates the restoration work. For further details contact the membership secretary.

Facilities Trip boat and rowing boats are available from Southgate Basin. There is a café and a pub at the basin and lots of eating places in the town.

Distance table	*Miles*
Chichester Basin to:	
Hunston, junction with the Portsmouth and Arundel Canal	1.4
Donnington	2.1
Birdham Lock	3.3
Salterns Lock (entrance to canal)	4.0
Low Water Channel, Chichester Harbour	4.5

CHICHESTER CANAL *Maximum vessel dimensions*

From and to	Distance	Length	Beam	Draught	Headroom	Locks
Birdham Pool to Chichester Basin	4.5 miles (7.2km)	85' (25.9m)	18' (5.4m)	7' (2.1m)	Unlimited	3

River Colne

The Colne is tidal up to Clochester and is still a busy river with commercial traffic to both Wivenhoe and Colchester, continuing a role which extends back to Roman times. Although navigation Acts were passed throughout the 17th and 18th centuries, there have been few changes to the natural course of the river.

It is a delightful river to cruise with attractive waterfronts and fascinating creeks to explore. Pyefleet Creek is famous for its oysters and fresh shellfish which are often available to buy on summer weekends. Above Wivenhoe, the river effectively dries at low water and the head of navigation is Hythe Bridge which has only 4ft clearance at spring tides.

Authority Colchester Borough Council, Harbourmaster ☎ 01206 827316. VHF Ch 68. Brightlingsea Harbourmaster, ☎ 01206 302200.

Bridges None until Colchester.

Towpath On either bank between Wivenhoe and Colchester.

Navigation High water at Brightlingsea is 55 minutes after HW Dover; HW Colchester approximately 20 minutes later. Spring tides rise 10ft 6ins, neaps rise 7ft 6ins.

Charts Imray Y17, Admiralty 3741.

Facilities Shops, pubs, restaurants and some chandlery are available at Brightlingsea, Wivenhoe and Colchester. There are moorings, a pleasant pub and a slip at Rowhedge but the river dries at low water.

Distance table *Miles*
East Mill, Colchester and East Bridge (tidal limit) to:
Railway Bridge	0.1
Hythe Bridges (effective head of navigation)	0.5
The Hythe (main commercial wharves)	0.8
Haven Quay	1.3
Rowhedge Quay	2.9

	Miles
Junction with Roman River (west bank)	3.2
Cook's Quay (east bank)	3.5
Tidal Barrier	3.6
Fingringhoe Ballast Quay	3.7
Arlesford Creek leading to Thorrington Mill and Quay	5.0
Junction with Geedon Creek (upstream of Rat Island)	6.7
Junction with Pyefleet Channel leading to The Strood, West Mersea	7.7
Westmarsh Point, leading to Brightlingsea and St Osyth Creeks	8.3
Mersea point (west bank) and St Osyth Point (east bank)	8.6
Colne Point, limit of Colchester Borough Council's jurisdiction	11.0

Coventry Canal

From the city centre of Coventry to its junction with the Trent and Mersey Canal at Fradley, the Coventry Canal offers a fascinating mix of urban, industrial and rural landscapes. Between Fazeley and Fradley, the canal was actually built not by the Coventry Canal Company but by the Birmingham and Fazeley Canal and the Trent and Mersey Canal Companies working from opposite ends and meeting at Whittington. This was because shortages of money, and possibly more dubious reasons, delayed the completion of the Coventry Canal and the other companies were keen for the route to be completed to aid through traffic. The 5½ miles from Whittington to Fradley were eventually bought by the Coventry Canal, but the stretch from Fazeley to Whittington is still part of the Birmingham and Fazeley Canal.

This may not be one of the most beautiful canals in the country, but it is an integral part of the Warwick Ring, and the new basin at Coventry has been sympathetically developed and is well worth a visit. Re-opened in 1995 after major redevelopment work the old warehouses and wharves have been converted into offices, craft workshops, restaurants and shops. As you move out of the basin towards Hawkesbury Junction, you pass reminders of past manufacturing. Car production started in Coventry with the old Daimler Power House beside the canal, the only part of the factory to survive the bombing in the Second World War. Further along are Cash's Hundred Houses, three-storey red-brick houses built for weavers with an overhead, steam-driven shaft which linked all the individual looms.

The novelist George Eliot would have seen the construction of the canal as she was born near Nuneaton and some of her novels, in particular *The*

RIVER COLNE Maximum vessel dimensions

From and to	Distance	Length	Beam	Draught	Headroom	Locks
East Mill, Colchester to Colne Point	11 miles (17.7km)	195' (59.4m)	28' (8.5m)	11' (3.3m) springs	Unlimited	None

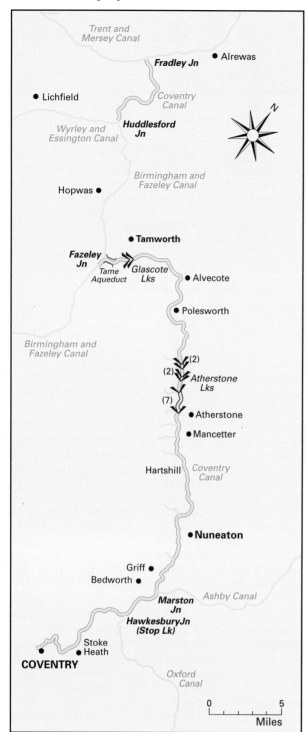

Mill on the Floss, were set in the area. In the early days, the canal's fortunes were a little shaky but once connected to the Trent and Mersey and the Oxford Canal to form a route south, prosperity improved and it was still paying a dividend when the canals were nationalised in 1947.

Authority British Waterways, Fradley Junction, Alrewas, Burton-on-Trent, Staffordshire DE13 7DN ☎ 01283 790236.

Bridges Numerous. One swing bridge and many new bridges for the increased number of roads crossing the canal.

Towpath Throughout navigation. From Coventry to Hawkesbury Junction, it is part of the Coventry to Oxford Waterway Walk. In some places barriers have been erected to deter motorbikes and this may make wheelchair access more difficult.

Branches Griff Colliery Canal, ¾ mile.

Connections The Ashby Canal at Marston, the Wyrley and Essington Canal at Huddlesford, the Trent and Mersey Canal at Fradley, the Oxford Canal at Hawkesbury Junction.

Facilities Coventry Basin can provide all services for boaters with water, refuse disposal and pump-out and it is close to the cathedral and the centre of the city. There are several boatyards along the Coventry Canal and plenty of pubs, restaurants and shops easily accessible.

Distance table	*Miles*
Coventry Basin, to:	
Cash's Hundred Houses	0.7
Navigation Bridge	2.8
New Inn Bridge	4.0
Longford Bridge	4.5
M6	4.8
Hawkesbury Junction, (Sutton Stop), Oxford Canal	5.5
Newdigate Arm (closed)	6.5
Bulkington Bridge	7.3
Marston Junction, Ashby Canal	8.3

COVENTRY CANAL *Maximum vessel dimensions*

From and to	Distance	Length	Beam	Draught	Headroom	Locks
Coventry to Fazeley	27 miles (43.5km)	72' (21.9m)	7' (2.1m)	3' 6" (1.1m)	6' 6" (2.0m)	13
Whittington to Fradley	5.5 miles (8.9km)	72' (21.9m)	7' (2.1m)	3' 6" (1.1m)	6' 6" (2.0m)	None

	Miles
Griff (Griff Arm closed)	9.3
Coton Wharf Bridge	10.0
Boot Bridge	10.3
Wash Lane Bridge	11.1
Nuneaton	11.8
Boon's Wharf	12.8
The Anchor Inn	13.8
Hartshill	14.3
BW Hartshill Yard	14.4
Mancetter Bridge	15.5
Atherstone Top Lock No 1	16.6
Atherstone Bottom Lock No 11	18.3
Railway Bridge	20.3
Polesworth	21.0
Pooley Hall	21.6
M42	22.0
Alvecote Bridge	22.9
Amington Road Bridge	24.8
Glascote Top Lock No 12	25.4
Glascote Bottom Lock No 13	25.6
Fazeley Junction, Birmingham and Fazeley Canal	27.0

Detached Section
Whittington Brook, junction with Birmingham and Fazeley Canal to:

Huddlesford Junction	1.5
Fradley Junction, Trent and Mersey Canal	5.5

Cromford Canal

During the early and middle part of the 19th century the Cromford Canal was a very successful undertaking, transporting coal, stone, textiles and lead products in the Peak Forest area of Derbyshire. Connection with the Erewash Canal in the south opened a route down to London and the High Peak Railway in the north offered a connection right through to the Peak Forest Canal and Manchester. In this area of coal workings subsidence was a problem and in the late 1880s the Butterley Tunnel collapsed, effectively dividing the canal in two. Although repairs were carried out, it collapsed again in 1900 which signalled the end of the canal's working life for all except short distance local transport.

Although the aqueduct across the River Amber at Ambergate has been demolished and the tunnel at Butterley is impassable the Cromford Canal is still fascinating to visit. Along the route of the canal are some fine examples of canal architecture with Butterley Tunnel, Leawood Pumphouse, Wigwell Aqueduct over the River Derwent and, at the southern end, the Grand Northern Basin at Langley Mill. Derbyshire County Council has bought and restored the 5-mile section from Ambergate to Cromford and the Leawood Pumphouse is now restored to working order. The bottom lock has been restored giving access to the Great Northern Basin from the Erewash Canal in Langley which also connected with the Nottingham Canal.

All the locks were in the section between Langley Mill and Butterley Tunnel, much of which has now been filled in and virtually no trace remains of them. The locks were built as broad locks but the tunnels, four in all, were narrow which caused serious hold-ups and bottle-necks. The Butterley Tunnel was 3063yds long and took over 3 hours to leg through.

Authority *Restored section* Ambergate to Cromford: Derbyshire County Council.

Great Northern Basin British Waterways, Trent Lock, Lock Lane, Long Eaton, Nottinghamshire NG24 4TT ☎ 0115 946 1017.

Locks 14 – none now working.

Towpath Along the restored section from Cromford to Ambergate the towpath is good; in other parts there is no public right of way.

Tunnels Butterley, 3063yds; Buckland Hollow, 33yds; Hag, 93yds; and Gregory, 76yds.

Aqueducts Bullbridge over the River Amber; Wigwell over the River Derwent; and a small iron aqueduct over a railway line.

Branches Pinxton Branch, 2.4 miles from Ironville to Pinxton; a private branch of 0.3 miles at Lea Wood.

Connections Erewash Canal and Nottingham Canal at Great Northern Basin; Langley Mill via the Cromford and High Peak tramline to the Peak Forest Canal at Whaley Bridge.

Distance table	Miles
From and to:	
Cromford to Langley Mill	14.5

River Crouch

The River Crouch is a very popular area for yachts, particularly racing boats, as can be seen by anyone who visits during Burnham Week. The river is well buoyed and Battlesbridge can be reached on the tide, but the river becomes increasingly narrow and winding between sandbanks above Stow Creek. Although it is not a very picturesque river with high sea walls, there are plenty of facilities for visiting boats.

RIVER CROUCH Maximum vessel dimensions

From and to	Distance	Length	Beam	Draught	Headroom	Locks
Battlesbridge to River Roach at Holliwell Point	17.5 miles (28.1km)	Unlimited	Unlimited	7' (2.1m)	Unlimited	None

Authority Crouch Harbour Authority, Harbour Office, Belvedere Road, Burnham on Crouch, Essex ☎ 01621 783602.

Bridges None.

Towpath Some stretches of the river have a footpath alongside.

Connections River Roach.

Navigation High water Burnham is 1 hour 10 minutes after HW Dover. Careful pilotage is needed in the approach through the Thames Estuary to the River Crouch.

Charts Imray Y17, Admiralty 3750

Facilities There are full facilities for boats at Burnham Yacht Harbour, although no pump-out, with shops, pubs and restaurants in the town. Further up river, there are local shops in the smaller villages and some moorings will be available.

Distance table

Holliwell Point to:

	Miles
Junction with River Roach	2.6
Burnham-on-Crouch	4.1
Ferry and Timber Yard	6.5
Bridgemarsh Island (eastern end)	7.9
Bridgemarsh Island (western end)	10.4
Ferry (foot passengers) from north to south Fambridges	12.0
Hullbridge Ferry (foot passengers)	15.0
Battlesbridge Mill	17.5

River Dart

A delightful Devon river which winds between steep wooded banks to the medieval town of Totnes with its Norman castle on a mound overlooking the town. It is definitely worth the effort to take a boat up to Totnes Quay. For shallow draught boats or those that sit happily in the mud, the creeks off the main river are great fun to explore. For anyone visiting the West Country's superb rivers, Mark Fishwick's book, *West Country Cruising*, is essential and entertaining reading.

Steam enthusiasts also have the possibility of the Dart Valley Railway from Kingswear to Paignton or Totnes to Buckfastleigh, but there is no connection between the two lines.

Authority Dart Harbour and Navigation Authority, 6 Oxford Street, Dartmouth, Devon TQ6 9AL ☎ 01803 832337.

Bridges None until Totnes.

Towpath None.

Connections Not connected to the inland waterways network. Bow Creek, Old Mill Creek and Dittisham Mill Creek.

Navigation All the creeks dry out at low water so it is advisable to go up near high water and leave about an hour later. It is possible to take the tide up to Totnes where a boat can dry out. Visitor moorings are rather limited but it is a pleasant town and worth a visit.

RIVER DART Maximum vessel dimensions

From and to	Distance	Length	Beam	Draught	Headroom	Locks
Totnes to Kingswear	10.5 miles (16.9km)	Unlimited	Unlimited	Depends on tides	Unlimited	None

The river is canoeable from Buckfastleigh but is a very rocky boulder strewn trip.

High water Dartmouth 5 hours 10 minutes before HW Dover and HW at Totnes is 30 minutes after Dartmouth.

Charts Imray Y47, Admiralty 2253.

Facilities There are three marinas in Dartmouth and drying moorings at Totnes. Dart Marina has a pump-out and slipways. Dartmouth and Totnes have the full range of shops, pubs and restaurants.

Distance table	Miles
Between the Castles to:	
Warfleet Creek	0.4
Dartmouth Yacht Club	0.8
Darthaven Marina, Kingswear	0.9
Dart Marina	1.3
Old Mill Creek	1.6
Noss-on-Dart Marina	2.0
Dittisham	3.6
Galmpton	4.3
Dittisham Mill Creek	4.9
Stoke Gabriel	5.8
Bow Creek	6.4
Totnes Quay	10.4

River Deben

This is a most attractive river and rightly popular with yachtsmen. The reputation of the shingle bar should not put off anyone who wishes to visit the river as local boat owners are always ready to help and there is a pilot on hand. The facilities are plentiful along the river and, from Woodbridge, it is possible to visit the Saxon boat burial at Sutton Hoo which in itself makes the trip worthwhile.

Authority None, an open navigation.

Bridges None.

Towpath None.

Navigation High water Felixstowe Ferry is approximately 30 minutes after HW Dover.

Charts Imray Y15, Admiralty 2693.

Facilities All services and a slipway are available at Woodbridge. A pub, small store and boatyard with a slip are at Waldringfield and a boatyard with a slip and essential stores at Felixstowe Ferry.

Distance table	Miles
Woodbridge Yacht Harbour to:	
Martlesham Creek	1.0
Methersgate Quay	1.9
Waldringfield	3.2
Prettyman's Point	4.9
Ramsholt Quay	5.9
Horse Sand	8.3
Felixstowe Ferry	8.7
River entrance	9.5

River Dee

The estuary of the River Dee is a very old navigation and it is probable that the Romans used the river for transport. The original Acts covering the navigation of the river were dated 1734, 1744 and 1791. The river below Chester is industrial and should only be navigated by sea-worthy craft with crews well versed in tidal waters.

Upstream from Chester, the river is administered by Chester City Council. Although it is tricky to negotiate the weir, the journey, once you are through, is worth the trouble. The countryside is attractive and passes near Eaton Hall with its Iron Bridge carrying the drive. The River Dee is an interesting waterway for trailed boats and, with a draught of not more than 3ft, it is possible to reach Farndon. After a prolonged dry spell, the area around the confluence of the Rivers Dee and Alyn should be viewed with some care.

A licence is required to navigate the river and this can be obtained from the Council at the address below.

Authority *Chester Weir to Point of Air* Environment Agency, North West Region, Richard Fairclough House, Knutsford Road, Warrington WA4 1HG ☎ 01925 653999 *Fax* 01925 415961.

Chester Weir to Almere Ferry Chester City Council, Grosvenor Park, Chester CH1 1QQ ☎ 01244 325681.

British Waterways, Tower Wharf, Chester ☎ 01244 390372.

Bridges Several both above and below the weir.

Towpath A footpath runs along the east bank of the river from Farndon crossing to the west bank at Iron Bridge and back across a footbridge in Chester.

RIVER DEBEN Maximum vessel dimension						
From and to	*Distance*	*Length*	*Beam*	*Draught*	*Headroom*	*Locks*
Woodbridge to the river entrance	9.miles (15.2m)	Unlimited	Unlimited	7' 6" (2.2m) HW	Unlimited	None

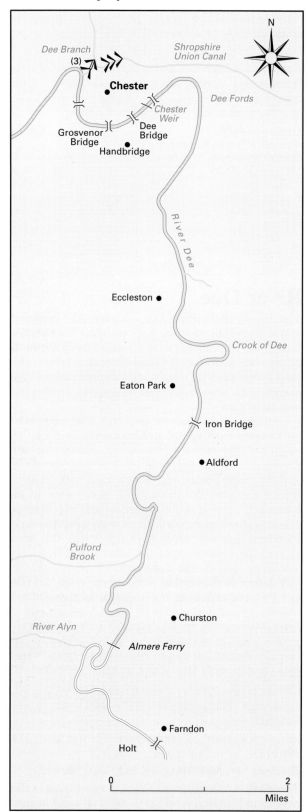

Connections Shropshire Union Canal at Crane Wharf, Chester. Entry to and from the Dee, approximately one hour each side of HW.

Navigation High water at Connah's Quay is at approximately the same time as HW Liverpool. At Crane Wharf, Chester, spring tides rise 9ft. The phenomenon of the bore will be encountered at spring tides between Connah's Quay and Chester. The tidal approaches are very tricky and should only be contemplated by a sea-worthy craft. There is a weir gate operated by the Environment Agency for boats wishing to travel above the weir. It operates on spring tides and must be booked in advance. There is a tight turn after passing under the railway bridge to pass through the water gate in the weir.

Facilities There is a public slip at Chester for trailed boats and a couple of riverside pubs to stop at.

Distance table

	Miles
Farndon Bridge to:	
Almere Ferry	2.0
Pulford Brook	3.5
Ironbridge, Eaton Park and Hall	5.5
Crook of Dee	7.0
Eccleston Ferry	8.0
Chester, Dee Bridge and weir	12.0
Chester, Crane Wharf, junction with the Shropshire Union Canal	14.3
Saltney	14.8
Sandycroft	17.6
Queensferry Bridge	18.9
Railway Bridge	19.6
Connah's Quay	20.8
Point of Air	35.0

RIVER DEE Maximum vessel dimensions

From and to	Distance	Length	Beam	Draught	Headroom	Locks
Farndon to Point of Air	35 miles (56.3km)	Unlimited	Unlimited	3' (0.9m)	9' 6" (2.8m)	None

Derby and Sandiacre Canal

The Derby Canal's engineer was Benjamin Outram. The Act was passed in May 1793 and the branch from Derby to Little Eaton was opened in 1795. The canal was 14½ miles long and ran from the Erewash Canal at Sandiacre to the Trent and Mersey Canal at Swarkestone. It was a broad canal with eight locks which could take craft 72ft long by 14ft wide.

In addition to cargo traffic, passengers travelled from Swarkestone to Derby to the weekly market but by the mid-1850s competition from the railways was affecting traffic and the company cut toll charges. Although the canal company offered the canal to two railway companies neither was interested. The Derby Canal was not nationalised in 1948 and it was abandoned in 1964. The company was wound up in 1974.

The Derby and Sandiacre Canal Company has been formed to restore the canal. In 1993, a restoration report was prepared followed in 1995 by a feasibility study which '...demonstrated that the restoration of the Derby and Sandiacre Canal is feasible in terms of engineering and would bring significant economic and environmental benefits'. The proposal to restore the canal is supported by local authorities but a navigable culvert would be

needed on the Derby Southern Bypass for which the Department of Transport has so far not given approval.

Through the centre of Derby much of the line of the canal has been in-filled and built over but an alternative route has been put forward which would take the canal close to its original route. Where it joins the Trent and Mersey Canal at Swarkestone, a short section of the canal is in water and is used as moorings.

Distance table	Miles
Sandiacre Junction with Erewash Canal to:	
Breaston	1.9
Borrowash Top Lock	4.9
Derby, junction with Little Eaton Branch	8.8
Junction with River Derwent Branch	9.0
White Bear Lock	9.1
Peggs Flood Lock	9.2
Gandy's Wharf	9.3
Osmaston	11.0
Baltimore Bridge, Chellaston	13.5
Swarkestone Junction, Trent and Mersey Canal	14.5

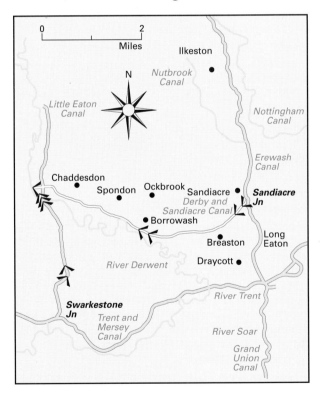

River Derwent

There is a right of navigation to the old tidal limit at Sutton, despite the construction of a tidal barrage at Barmby-on-the-Marsh. Following a long legal battle, the Law Lords ruled that there is no public right of navigation in the Upper River Derwent and in 1993 the Attorney General refused consent for the case to go to the European Court. The Yorkshire Derwent Trust has since been disbanded and so plans to restore the locks and navigation through to Malton, 38 miles from Barmby, have had to be dropped. The Yorkshire Wildlife Trust claim ownership of Sutton Lock and should be contacted at 10 Toft Green, York YO1 1JT, ☎ 01904 659570 by anyone wishing to use the lock.

DERBY AND SANDIACRE CANAL *Maximum vessel dimensions*

From and to	Distance	Length	Beam	Draught	Headroom	Locks
Sandiacre, junction Erewich Canal to Swarkestone, Trent and Mersey Canal	14.5 miles (23.3km)	72' (21.9m	14' (4.2m)	3' (0.9m)	7' (2.1m)	9

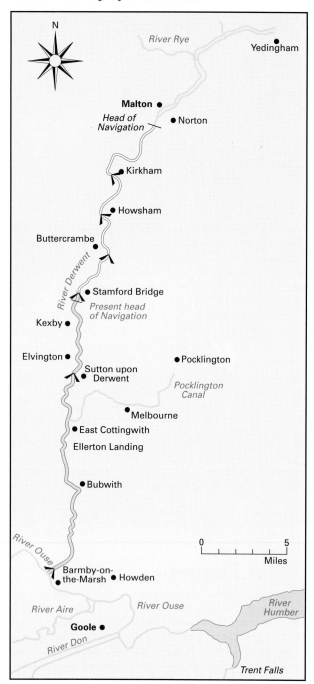

control. Water is extracted from the lower reaches for drinking and any boat owner who wishes to take a boat into the river must have a boat certificate issued by the EA which ensures no fuel or waste can pollute the water course. This is not a navigation licence.

Up as far as the entrance to the Pocklington Canal, the channel is good but above that as far as Sutton Lock, there is a lot of bankside vegetation some of which encroaches well over the channel. Through Sutton Lock, there are still boats up to Stamford Bridge. In the Upper Derwent certain riparian owners allow boat owners to moor along the banks but the boats should not, strictly, venture outside the length in question. The river is an SSSI as far as Stamford Bridge.

Authority There is no navigation authority.

Pollution responsibility Environment Agency, Dales Area, Coverdale House, Amy Johnson Way, York YO3 4UZ ☎ 01904 692296 *Fax* 01904 693748.

Bridges Numerous.

Towpath Unusable along many sections.

Speed limit No vessels to be navigated at such a speed as to do injury to the banks or cause inconvenience, etc.

Connections Pocklington Canal, River Ouse.

Navigation Visitors to the river must contact the Lock Attendant, Barmby Tidal Barrage, Barmby-on-the-Marsh, Goole DN14 7HX ☎ 01757 638579 who can issue a River Derwent boat certificate for a nominal charge. High water Barmby is approximately 1 hour 40 minutes after HW Hull. Navigation above Sutton Lock must only occur with riparian owners permission. Yorkshire Wildlife Trust must be contacted for permission to pass through Sutton Lock.

Facilities There are several pubs and restaurants along the river but very few facilities for boats.

The history of the navigation of the River Derwent is convoluted and for interested readers the explanation in the Ripon Motor Boat Club's *Cruising Guide to the North East Waterways* is highly recommended.

The Environment Agency (EA), and its predecessors, have never opposed navigation on the river but their responsibility is solely for pollution

RIVER DERWENT Maximum vessel dimensions

From and to	Distance	Length	Beam	Draught	Headroom	Locks
Barmby-on-the-Marsh to Stamford Bridge	22 miles (35.4km)	54' 6" (16.6m)	13' 9" (4.1m)	4' (1.2m)	10' 6" (3.2m)	2

Distance table — *Miles*
Barmby-on-the-Marsh Junction with River Ouse to:

	Miles
Barmby-on-the-Marsh village	0.5
Loftsome Bridge	2.1
Wressel	3.0
Breighton	4.9
Menthorpe	5.3
Bubwith, Derwent Bridge	6.9
Ellerton Landing	9.9
Thorganby	10.5
Cottingwith Ferry, junction with Pocklington Canal	11.5
Ings Bridge	13.0
Sutton Lock No 1 (tidal limit)	15.5
Bridge between Elvington and Sutton-on-Derwent	15.6
Kexby Bridge	18.4
Stamford Bridge Lock No 2 (navigation limit)	21.9
Buttercrambe Bridge	24.8
Buttercrambe Lock No 3	25.0
Scrayingham	26.0
Howsham Lock No 4 (site of)	28.5
Kirkham Abbey Lock No 5 (now abolished)	31.3
Cherry Islands	35.4
Malton	38.0

River Don

In its upper section the River Don shadows the Don Navigation and its lower reaches, the 'Dutch River' constructed by Vermuyden in 1625, runs alongside the Aire and Calder Navigation as far as Goole where they both meet the River Ouse. The straight course of the Dutch River experiences very fast tidal currents and the river is usually considered dangerous for pleasure craft unless exceptional care is taken. The river at Fishlake was diverted in 1943 and no longer passes Fishlake Ferry.

Authority Environment Agency, Ridings Area, Olympia House, Gelderd Lane, Gelderd Road, Leeds LS12 6DD ☎ 0113 244 0191 *Fax* 0113 231 2116.

Towpath None.

Navigation High water at Goole is 1 hour after HW Hull. Spring tides rise 13ft, neaps 9ft. The whole river is tidal and conditions can be dangerous when there are exceptionally high tides or a lot of flood water.

Facilities There are really no facilities for pleasure boats.

Distance table — *Miles*
Bramwith Aqueduct to:

	Miles
Fishlake, junction with River Don	3.0
New Bridge, commencement of Dutch River	6.8
Rawcliffe Bridge	8.9
Goole, junction with River Ouse	12.3

Driffield Navigation

The Driffield Navigation was opened in 1770 being an improvement to and extention of the River Hull. In the early 1800s, a new lock was built at Struncheon Hill and the Hull Bridge was raised offering better passage and this improved the profitability of the navigation. The principal cargoes were coal and grain. A passenger service was started in 1817 between Driffield and Hull, but it was not successful. By the 1850s, rail competition was affecting trade but the last keels were using the navigation in 1948.

In 1978 Driffield Navigation Ltd, a registered charity, took over the navigation responsibilities from the Driffield Navigation Commissioners who had effectively disappeared over a number of years. The banks along the River Hull and Driffield Canal are privately owned in places and mooring and landing are not allowed. Any boat wishing to navigate the waterway must be registered with Driffield Navigation Ltd. Only small craft which can be portaged can get past three of the locks, though Town Lock has now been restored.

Authority Driffield Navigation Ltd, 70 Middle Street South, Driffield, East Yorkshire YO25 7QF ☎ 01377 257488.

Bridges There are several bridges which were swing bridges and have now been fixed. At Brigham the swing bridge is in the process of being restored.

Towpath Throughout the Main Line, but there is no towpath on the Frodingham Beck Branch.

Branches Corps Landing 1.8 miles, Frodingham Beck 1.8 miles. This branch is only open to Frodingham Bridge which no longer swings open and restricts navigation. Distance to bridge 1 mile.

Restoration The Driffield Navigation Amenities Association is actively working for the restoration of the waterway. The lock chambers are essentially in

RIVER DON Maximum vessel dimensions

From and to	Distance	Length	Beam	Draught	Headroom	Locks
Bramwith Aqueduct to Goole, River Ouse	12.3 miles (19.8km)	Unlimited	Unlimited	6' 6" (1.9m)	15' (4.5m)	None

DRIFFIELD NAVIGATION *Maximum vessel dimensions*

From and to	Distance	Length	Beam	Draught	Headroom	Locks
Driffield to the River Hull at Aike	11 miles (17.7km)	61' (18.5m)	14' 6"(4.4m)	4' (1.2m)	9' 6" (2.8m)	6

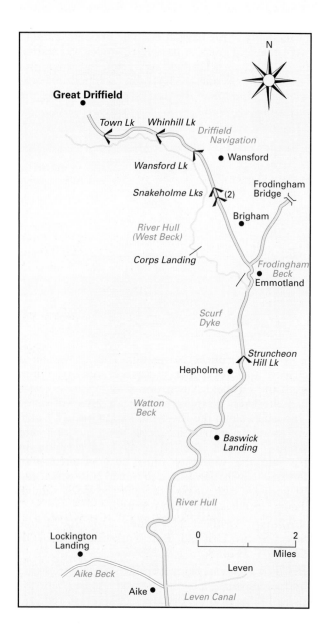

	Miles
Struncheon Hill Locks Nos 6 and 7, junction with River Hull	7.0
Tophill Low Landing	8.3
Baswick Landing	8.5
Aike	11.0

Droitwich Barge Canal and Droitwich Junction Canal

The Droitwich Canal, opened in 1771, was built to transport salt from Droitwich to the Severn. It was constructed as a barge canal so trows or Wich Barges could reach the town. As late as 1854, the Droitwich Junction Canal was opened to connect the Worcester and Birmingham Canal to Droitwich when competition from the railways started. This was built as a narrow canal with the same lock size as the Worcester and Birmingham.

Unfortunately, this was really too late and traffic never returned to a viable level but rescue came in the shape of the Sharpness New Docks Company which took over both the Droitwich and the Worcester and Birmingham canals in 1874. The salt trade gradually declined on the canal and both Droitwich canals were abandoned in 1939.

In 1973, the Droitwich Canals Trust Ltd was established and, with active support from local councils, restoration is well underway. A feasibility study was carried out in 1994 and this shows that it is possible in engineering terms and has economic benefits if the canal is restored. One section of the canal through the town would need to be rerouted and three new locks would need to be built, but with support from the local authorities and considerable volunteer work, not least from the Waterway Recovery Group, great strides have already been made. At present about 3 miles of the Barge Canal are navigable for small trailable craft and the towpath is an attractive walk. To access the River Severn at Hawford, a navigable tunnel under the A449 must be constructed.

Once re-opened the Droitwich canals will offer a short ring, about 22 miles, joining the River Severn at Hawford and returning via the Worcester and Birmingham Canal from Worcester. There is a trip boat on the canal so it is possible to travel along it before it is fully restored.

Authority Droitwich Canals Trust Ltd, 1 Hampton Road, Droitwich, Worcestershire, WR9 9PA. The Trust leases the canal from the Wychavon District Council, Worcester ☎ 01905 774225. Bye-laws are enforced by the Trust.

reasonable repair but some fixed bridges are too low to allow navigation.

Navigation High water at Struncheon Hill Lock is approximately 3 hours after HW Hull. At HWST the rise can be as much as 6 or 7ft in winter and in summer the rise is 3 or 4ft.

Distance table

Driffield Wharves to:	Miles
Driffield Lock No 1	0.4
Whin Hill Lock No 2	1.6
Wansford Lock and village (Lock No 3)	2.5
Snakeholme Locks (Nos 4 and 5, staircase)	3.0
Junction with Frodingham Beck	5.0
Junction with Branch to Corps Landing (unnavigable)	5.8

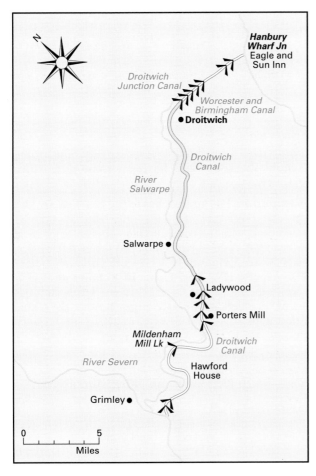

Towpath Throughout the canal.

Restoration It is hoped to complete the restoration by 2000. Volunteer help and financial assistance are welcome. Water supply for a restored canal has been considered in the feasibility study and negotiations have been opened with the Environment Agency and British Waterways to ensure a satisfactory supply would be available.

Distance table	*Miles*
Droitwich, junction with Droitwich Junction Canal to:	
Vines Park, Hampton Road Basin	0.3
Siding Lane Wharf	1.0
Salwarpe Bridge	2.3
Ladywood Locks Nos 1-4	3.0
Porter's Mill Lock No 5	3.5
Mildenham Mill Lock No 6	4.5
Hawford Lock No 7	5.5
Hawford Lock No 8 Junction with River Severn	5.8

Droitwich Junction Canal

Locks Lock No 7, the Barge Lock, regulates the supply of water to the canal from the River Salwarpe and links the Junction Canal to the Droitwich Canal.

Bridges Four.

Towpath There is a short section of towpath at the Hanbury Junction end of the canal.

Distance table	*Miles*
Vines Park, Hampton Road Basin to:	
Hanbury Junction, Worcester and Birmingham Canal	1.5

Exeter Ship Canal

In the 17th and 18th centuries, Exeter was a busy port. Cargoes had to be unloaded at Topsham in the early 1600s owing to the number of weirs on the River Exe and so a canal was proposed to bring ships into the city centre. The canal was opened in 1566 and was the first canal in Britain with pound locks. The canal was extended to Turf Lock, 2 miles downstream, in the late 1820s with 350-ton ships taking goods up to Exeter. By 1844, the railway reached Exeter and the decline of the canal started. It is a pleasant canal and popular for Sunday afternoon walks, but the cost of raising the bridges tends to deter prospective users. In 1997, the last regular user of the canal, the Countess Weir sewage ship, ceased working and Exeter City Council have stopped overnight mooring in the basin which will

Droitwich Barge Canal

Bridges Several, including swing bridges. The first bridge up the canal from Hawford is exactly as built by Brindley and has not been touched since construction.

DROITWICH BARGE & JUNCTION CANAL Maximum vessel dimensions

From and to	Distance	Length	Beam	Draught	Headroom	Locks
Droitwich Barge Canal Droitwich to the River Severn at Hawford	5.8 miles (9.3km)	71' 6" (21.7m)	9' 6" (2.8m)	5' (1.5m)	8' (2.4m)	8
Droitwich Junction Canal Droitwich to Hanbury Junction	1.5 miles (2.4km)	71' 6" (21.7m)	7' 1" (2.1m)	3' (0.9m)	9' 6" (2.8m)	7

EXETER SHIP CANAL *Maximum vessel dimensions*

From and to	Distance	Length	Beam	Draught	Headroom	Locks
Turf Lock, River Exe						
Estuary to Exeter	5.2 miles (8.4km)	122' (37.2m)	26' 3" (8.0m)	9' 10" (3.0m)	32' 10" (10.0m)	2

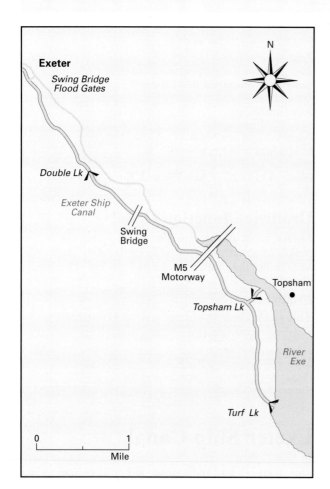

Bridges Four, one swing bridge and one bascule bridge together.

Towpath Throughout navigation, most of the route is in the Riverside Park. There are some cycle paths.

Speed limit 4mph.

Navigation The approaches to the Exe Estuary and up the river are difficult and should not be attempted without considerable experience or local knowledge. A good pilot book should be referred to. High water Exmouth is 4 hours 45 minutes before HW Dover; HW Turf Lock, 15 minutes after HW Exmouth. Tidal range, spring tides 4.1m, neap tides 1.7m. For details of port charges contact the Canal Supervisor.

Charts Imray Y45, Admiralty 2290.

Distance table	*Miles*
Head of Canal Basin, Exeter to:	
Junction with River Exe through Kings Arms Flood Gates	0.2
Double Locks No 1	1.4
Topsham Lock (temporarily closed)	3.8
Turf Lock, No 2 entrance to canal from River Exe Estuary	5.0
Pier head, entrance to Turf Gutway from River Exe Estuary	5.2

River Fal

This is a beautiful estuary and river from St Anthony Head past Falmouth up to Turnaware Point where the River Fal turns eastwards before the Truro River branches off towards the cathedral city of Truro. Coasters still go up to Truro so the channel is well marked. The lower reaches have long been a popular sailing area and there are numerous creeks and bays to be explored.

Authority *From St Anthony Head to Penarrow Point across to Messack Point* Falmouth Harbour Commissioners, Harbour Office, 44 Arwenack Street, Falmouth TR11 3JQ ☎ 01326 312285.

From Penarrow Point across to Messack Point to Truro Carrick District Council, Harbour Office, Town Quay, Truro TR1 2HJ ☎ 01872 72130.

Both Harbour Offices, VHF Ch 12 or 16.

Bridges None.

Towpath None.

Connections Not connected to the inland waterways network. Penryn River, Mylor Creek, Restronguet Creek, Ruan Creek, most of the upper reaches of the creeks dry at low water.

effectively close the canal above the road bridges. The Maritime Museum has closed and the ships that were exhibited have been sold to other collections.

Authority The Corporation of the City of Exeter, Municipal Offices, Exeter.
Canal Supervisor City Basin ☎ 01392 74306.

RIVER FAL Maximum vessel dimensions

From and to	Distance	Length	Beam	Draught	Headroom	Locks
St Anthony Head to Truro	10.7 miles (17.2km)	Unlimited	Unlimited	Depends on tides	Unlimited	None

Navigation High water Falmouth is 6 hours before HW Dover, HW Truro 8 minutes after HW Falmouth. Tidal range, spring tides 4.7m, neap tides 2.3m. Falmouth is a busy ship port and care must be taken when large ships are moving. Past Turnaware Point draught is constrained by tides but large ships have laid up in the Fal for many years so draught is mostly not limiting.

Charts Imray Y58, Admiralty 32.

Facilities All services are available at Falmouth and Truro with pubs, restaurants and small shops at Mylor, Restronguet and St Mawes.

Distance table	Miles
St Anthony Head to:	
St Mawes, east shore	1.3
Penryn River, west shore (2.3 miles)	1.7
Mylor Creek, west shore	3.5
St Just in Roseland, east shore	3.5
Restronguet Creek	4.7
Turnaware Point	5.4
King Harry Ferry	6.3
Lamouth Creek	6.8
Truro River	7.3
Ruan Creek (end of navigation on the Fal)	7.5
Tresillian River	8.7
Malpas	8.8
Truro	10.7
Penryn River	
Entrance to Penryn River to:	
Falmouth Town	0.9
Flushing	1.2
Falmouth Marina	1.6
Penryn	2.3

River Foss

The first Act empowering the Foss Navigation Company to improve the river was passed in 1793. The original intention was for the head of navigation to be Stillington Mill, but lack of capital prevented this and there was no development past Sherrif Hutton. The canal runs for 11½ miles with eight locks from the River Ouse. The navigation was opened in 1805 and was busy for nearly 50 years but, unfortunately, never very profitable.

Today, it is possible to wind the 1.3 miles around the back of the city of York passing Fossgate, one of York's oldest streets, the old Leetham flour mills and under a variety of bridges. The river was used until 1997 for the transport of newsprint to the Yorkshire Evening Press (200 tonnes a week) so care had to be taken to avoid manoeuvring barges.

Authority City Development Officer, City of York, 9 St Leonard's, York YO1 2ET ☎ 01904 613161 Ext 1488.

Bridges Five.

Towpath None.

Distance table	Miles
Monk Bridge to:	
Laverthorpe Bridge	0.3
Foss Bridge	0.8
Castle Mills Bridge and Lock	1.0
Blue Bridge, junction with River Ouse	1.3

RIVER FOSS Maximum vessel dimensions

From and to	Distance	Length	Beam	Draught	Headroom	Locks
Monk Bridge to River Ouse at York	1.3 miles (2.1km)	97' (29.5m)	18' 6" (5.6m)	6' 6" (1.9m)	10' (3.0m)	1

Fossdyke and Witham Navigations

This joint navigation is probably the oldest waterway still in use today. The River Witham from the Wash at Boston was used by the Romans who built the Fossdyke Canal in 120AD, thus providing a through route to the River Trent. Stone to build Lincoln Cathedral was transported along the waterway by the Normans when they started building it at the end of the 11th century. The cathedral on its hill can be seen for miles as you journey along the long straight reaches towards the city.

Throughout the Middle Ages, the navigations became the responsibility of various different owners and groups but little was done to improve navigation. By 1670, Lincoln Corporation took over the Fossdyke but not the Witham until almost 100 years later. By this time, Richard Ellison had taken a 999-year lease on the Fossdyke from the corporation and had started improvements. The Grand Sluice at Boston was constructed in 1763 to exclude the tide and help with flood prevention. Once this was in place, locks were built along the river to improve navigation.

In 1848, the newly formed Great Northern Railway bought the lease to the Fossdyke and Witham Navigations and started seriously to undercut tolls on the waterway. Traffic on the River Witham declined fairly rapidly, but grain was transported to Lincoln on the Fossdyke until 1972. Boston is still an active port in the tidal reach below the sluice.

The navigation passes through fairly flat countryside with long straight stretches and quite high banks, so sometimes there is little to see, but to be able to visit Lincoln and Boston by water offers a new perspective on them. The village of Torksey on the River Trent was a Roman port with a large population for the time, and the main street of Saxilby faces the waterway showing how important it was in the development of the village. South of Lincoln, having passed through the Glory Hole, there are few settlements close to the river demonstrating its importance for drainage. The dual roles of drainage and navigation have frequently come into conflict over the years.

Dogdyke Pumping Station has been restored and the 1855 steam beam-engine can now be seen in action on the first Sunday in the month from May to October. Brayford Pool, on the edge of Lincoln where the Fossdyke and the River Witham meet, is controlled by the Brayford Trust and they offer moorings and other facilities, ☎ 01522 521452. Also in Brayford Pool is the Lincoln Marina ☎ 01522 526896. To visit Boston, the Boston Marina is conveniently placed just upstream of the Grand Sluice Lock, ☎ 01205 364420. The moorings in Boston, including the marina, are closed from 31 October to 31 March so sluicing in the river can occur unimpeded.

Authority British Waterways, Mill Lane, Mill Gate, Newark, Nottinghamshire NG24 4TT ☎ 01636 704481.

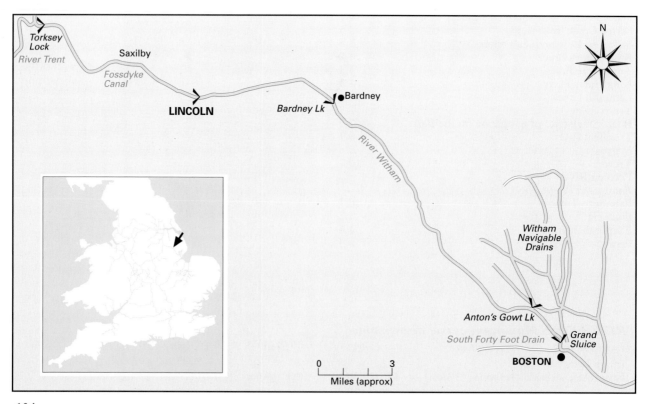

FOSSDYKE AND WITHAM NAVIGATIONS *Maximum vessel dimension*

From and to	Distance	Length	Beam	Draught	Headroom	Locks
Fossdyke Canal River Trent at Torksey to River Witham at High Bridge, Lincoln	11.3 miles (18.1km)	74' 6" (22.7m)	15' 2" (4.6m)	5' (1.5m)	12' (3.6m)	1
River Witham High Bridge Lincoln to outlet of Hobhole Drain	36.5 miles (58.7km)	78' (23.7m)	15' 2" (4.6m)	5' (1.5m)	7' 6" (2.2m)	3

Fossdyke Canal

Bridges Numerous. One lifting bridge before Brayford Pool soon to be replaced by a high level fixed bridge.

Towpath Throughout navigation.

Speed limit 4mph.

Navigation Torksey Lock can be boater operated outside normal working hours. The keeper can be contacted on ☎ 01427 718202 or VHF Ch 74. The lock may be used at most states of the tide.

Facilities Full services at Torksey Yard including pump-out, services at Saxilby and full services at Lincoln. Plenty of pubs and restaurants and things to do in Lincoln.

Distance table	*Miles*
Torksey Lock, junction with River Trent to:	
Torksey Wharf	0.3
Hardwick Ferry	3.1
Drinsey Nook	3.8
Saxilby	5.4
Mill Lane	5.6
Burton Lane	8.1
Skellingthorpe	8.9
Lincoln, west end of Brayford Pool	10.8
Lincoln, junction with upper portion of River Witham	11.1
Lincoln, High Bridge, junction with River Witham Navigation	11.3

River Witham

Bridges 19

Towpath Mostly good, runs along the old railway track on the north bank.

Speed limit 4.5mph between Lincoln and Bardney; 5mph between Bardney and Tattershall and 5.5mph between Tattershall and Boston.

Connections Kyme Eau-Sleaford Canal, Witham Navigable Drains, Horncastle Canal (now disused).

Navigation Water levels in the River Witham can fluctuate significantly and this should be taken into consideration when mooring.

The Grand Sluice at Boston is a sea lock but at high water the sea level is higher than the level of the non-tidal river. The gates close automatically on each high tide. To lock out into the tidal river, boats must pass through 2 hours before or 2 hours after high water. The lock can take boats up to 41ft long

and 12ft beam. The lock-keeper must be notified 24 hours in advance, ☎ 01205 364864 VHF Ch 73.

Below the Grand Sluice, the river effectively dries at low tides. Mooring in the tidal reach is difficult owing to the steepness of the mud bottom. High water at Grand Sluice Boston is 30 minutes after HW Boston Deeps.

Facilities There are services at Bardney Lock, Belle Isle Marina and Boston Marina. Boston has shops, pubs and restaurants and plenty to see.

Distance table	*Miles*
Lincoln, High Bridge, junction with Fossdyke Canal to:	
Lincoln, Stamp End Lock	0.6
Washingborough	2.6
Five Mile Farm House, footbridge	5.4
Bardney Lock	8.5
Junction with Old River Witham navigable to The Tyrwhitt Arms	8.6
Bardney	9.5
Southrey	12.3
Kirkstead Bridge	15.9
Junction with Horncastle Canal (derelict)	19.4
Tattershall Bridge	20.0
Dogdyke Pumping Station	20.9
Chapel Hill, junction with Kyme Eau	21.9
Langrick Bridge	27.3
Anton's Gowt, junction with Witham Navigable Drains	29.4
Boston, Grand Sluice Lock	31.8
Swing Bridge	32.9
Entrance to Boston Dock	33.4
Outlet of Maud Foster Drain (no access)	33.5
Mouth of river and outlet of Hobhole Drain	36.1

River Fowey

Deep in country associated with Daphne du Maurier, Fowey is a popular yachting centre but even in the busy summer season it is a pleasant place to visit. Large ships still come into the jetties above the town to collect the high quality china clay and, as you approach this part of the river, there is often a cloud of white dust in the air. Above Mixtow, the river dries but it is an interesting trip to carry on up to Lostwithiel on the tide.

Authority Fowey Harbour Commissioners, Harbourmaster's Office, Albert Quay, Fowey, Cornwall ☎ 01726 832471.

RIVER FOWEY Maximum vessel dimensions

From and to	Distance	Length	Beam	Draught	Headroom	Locks
St Catherine's Point to Lostwithiel	7 miles (11.3km)	Unlimited	Unlimited	Depends on tide	29' 6" (9m)	None

Bridges None.

Towpath None.

Connections Not connected to the inland waterways network. Pont Pill and Mixtow Pill.

Navigation High water Fowey is 5 hours 50 minutes before HW Dover, HW Lostwithiel is 10 minutes after HW Fowey.

Tidal range, spring tides 4.8m, neap tides 2.3m. Fowey is still a busy commercial harbour and attention must be paid to the movements of large ships by all pleasure boats using the estuary and river.

Charts Imray Y52, Admiralty 31.

Facilities There is no marina at Fowey, only river moorings. Shops, pubs and restaurants are available in the town with some local services at Polruan, across the river.

Distance table

St Catherine's Point to:	Miles
Polruan Town Quay	0.5
Pont Pill, east shore	0.8
Albert Quay, Fowey	0.8
Ferry	1.0
Mixtow Pill	1.5
Penpoll Creek	2.7
St Winnow Point	3.8
Lostwithiel Rail Bridge	6.8

River Frome

From Poole Harbour a fairly shallow draught boat can wind a peaceful 4½ miles up the River Frome to Wareham. This almost seems to be a town that time forgot with its unpretentious high street, some delightful old pubs and a couple of good bistros. Being somewhat off the beaten track to motorised tourists, the town retains a salty atmosphere and welcomes visitors who arrive afloat.

Having left Poole Harbour and its busy yachting activity behind, the river snakes off through reeds and it is with some surprise that you reach the Ridge Wharf Yacht Centre. In a previous existence, this was a wharf to do with clay export but now it offers all types of services to cruising boats. Wareham Quay is about a mile further on, only in high summer does it get really busy.

Authority *River Frome* Environment Agency, South Wessex Area, Rivers House, Sunrise Business Park, Higher Shaftsbury Road, Blandford, Dorset DT11 8ST ☎ 01258 456080 *Fax* 01258 455998.

Poole Harbour Poole Harbour Commissioners, Harbour Office, Town Quay, Poole, Dorset BH15 1HG ☎ 01202 685261 *Fax* 01202 665703. VHF Ch 14.

Towpath Along approximately 2 miles only, commencing at Wareham.

Navigation High water at Wareham is approximately 1 hour after HW Poole. At Wareham there is a bridge which restricts headroom to 8ft at LW springs and 3ft at HW springs.

RIVER FROME Maximum vessel dimensions

From and to	Distance	Length	Beam	Draught	Headroom	Locks
Poole Harbour to Wareham	7.8 miles (12.5km)	Unlimited	Unlimited	5' 6" (1.6m)HW	Unlimited	None

Charts Imray Y23, Admiralty 2611 (these are both of Poole Harbour).

Facilities Marinas in Poole Harbour, slipway and boating services at Ridge Wharf, and shops, pubs and restaurants in Wareham.

River Glen

Flowing through the pleasant countryside of south Lincolnshire, the River Glen passes through some fine bulb growing country. The sluice at the junction with the River Welland was installed in 1824 to control the tide. In the 17th century improvements were intended to aid drainage, but it is likely that navigation on the Bourne Eau would have been possible.

Today, its remoteness from the hurly-burly of cities make it a relaxing river for those who prefer solitude to excitement. The pretty church at Surfleet has a noticeable lean so best to look at it before visiting the pub! Craft over 30ft may find turning difficult especially in the upper reaches above Pinchbeck Bar.

Recently there has been increased silting in the River Welland which may affect the depth of water available for those wishing to visit the Glen.

Authority Environment Agency, Kingfisher House, Goldhay Way, Orton Goldhay, Peterborough PE2 5ZR ☎ 01733 37181 *Fax* 01733 231840.

Bridges 12.

Towpath There is a footpath along the river from Pinchbeck to the junction with the River Welland, see OS Map 131.

Speed limit 7mph. Craft must be navigated at such a speed as not to cause damage or inconvenience.

Navigation High water at the junction with the River Welland is about 15 to 20 minutes after HW Fosdyke Bridge. Passage through Surfleet Sluices should be by prior arrangement with the sluice-keeper.

Facilities Very limited.

Distance table

Junction with River Welland to:	Miles
Entrance Sluices	0.1
A16 Road Bridge at Surfleet	2.4
Crossgate Bridge	3.6
Railway Bridge	4.1
Money Bridge	5.5
Pinchbeck Bars, New Bridge	6.5
Guthram Gowt	8.9
Tongue End (junction with Bourne Eau, not navigable)	11.5

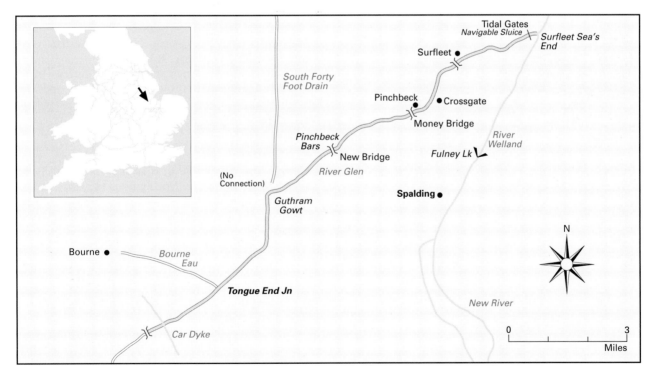

RIVER GLEN Maximum vessel dimensions

From and to	Distance	Length	Beam	Draught	Headroom	Locks
Surfleet Sluice, River Welland to Tongue End	11.5 miles (18.5km)	Unlimited	14' 6" (4.4m)	2' 6" (0.7m)	6' (1.9m)	1

Gloucester and Sharpness Ship Canal

When it was opened in 1826 to by-pass a difficult and tortuous stretch of the River Severn, the Gloucester and Berkeley Ship Canal was the broadest and deepest canal in Britain. Ships of 600 tons could travel to Gloucester. There was a short feeder canal to Cambridge which brought water from the River Cam. At Saul Junction the Stroudwater Canal crossed the Gloucester and Berkeley running from the River Severn at Framilode to Stroud where it joined the Thames and Severn Canal. In the 1870s, the docks at Sharpness were built offering 2000ft of wet dock and the access to the River Severn moved ¾ mile downstream. The canal's name was changed to the Gloucester and Sharpness in the early 1900s. Until the 1980s, the canal was a busy commercial waterway but traffic has declined since the petroleum depot at Quedgeley closed.

There are no locks along its length other than those which give access to the Severn at each end. For a family holiday, it can offer plenty of things to do and see with the National Waterways Museum in Llanthony Warehouse at Gloucester and Slimbridge Wildfowl and Wetlands Trust just a short walk away from the canal at Patch Bridge. From Saul Junction, it is interesting to walk along the Stroudwater Canal and see the progress being made towards restoration.

Authority British Waterways, Llanthony Warehouse, Gloucester Docks, Gloucester GL1 2EJ ☎ 01452 31800 *Fax* 01452 318076.

Gloucester Lock and some bridge-keepers listen on VHF Ch 74.

Sharpness Control, VHF Ch 16.

Sharpness Harbourmaster ☎ 01453 811644.

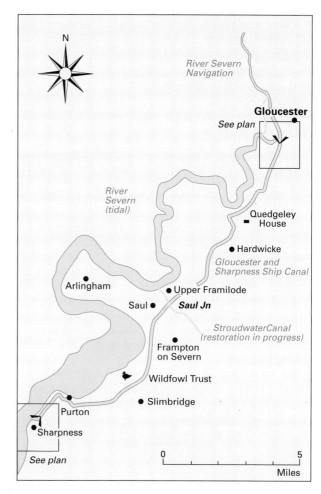

Bridges 17 All bridges are operated by BW staff and controlled by lights. Bridges are operated from 0800 to 1830 in summer time and 0800 to 1615 in winter. Arrangements for out of hours opening should be made in advance with BW at Gloucester.

Towpath From Old Arm to Hempsted Bridge near Gloucester.

Speed limit 6mph.

Navigation High tide at Sharpness about 1 hour after HW Avonmouth. Spring tides rise about 25ft, neap tides rise about 15ft. Bye-laws controlling this canal and the River Severn should be obtained from British Waterways.

Boats wishing to pass through Sharpness Locks into or out of the canal must be at the lock between 2 hours before and 30 minutes after HW. Contact Sharpness Operations on ☎ 01453 511968. To use the lock at the weekend passage must be booked no later than 1530 on Friday.

Large ships still use the canal and their wash can cause a considerable surge, take care when passing or being passed by a ship. Mooring must also allow

GLOUCESTER AND SHARPNESS SHIP CANAL *Maximum vessel dimensions*

From and to	Distance	Length	Beam	Draught	Headroom	Locks
Gloucester to Sharpness, River Severn	16.5 miles (26.5km)	240' (73.1m)	30' (9.1m)	10' (3.0m)	105' (32.0m)	2

for the likely surge so extra lines are recommended. Visitors should use the recognised mooring sites.

Charts Imray C59, Admiralty 1166.

Facilities There are plenty of pubs, restaurants and overnight moorings along the canal. Full facilities, including pump-out, are available at the boatyard at Saul Junction and at Gloucester Docks, other yards are at Sharpness and Hempstead Bridge. All shops and services are available in Gloucester.

Distance table	Miles
Gloucester, entrance lock and junction with River Severn to:	
Gloucester Lock (Bascule Bridge over lock)	
Gloucester Docks (water area 14 acres)	
Llanthony Road Bridge	0.4
Monk Meadow Dock	0.6

	Miles
Monk Meadow Wharf	0.9
Hempstead Bridge	1.5
Sims Bridge	2.3
Rea Bridge	2.8
Sellars Bridge	4.1
Hardwicke Bridge	4.9
Parkend Bridge	6.1
Saul Junction (entrance to Stroudwater Canal)	7.8
Sandfield Bridge	8.1
Fretherne Bridge	8.9
Splatt Bridge	9.8
Cambridge Feeder Branch	11.0
Patch Bridge	
(Slimbridge Wildfowl and Wetlands Trust)	11.9
Purton Upper Bridge	14.3
Purton Lower Bridge	14.4
Sharpness Marine	15.4
High and Low Level Swing Bridges	15.6
Sharpness Docks (water area 20 acres)	
Sharpness Lock	15.9
Tidal Basin Gates	16.3

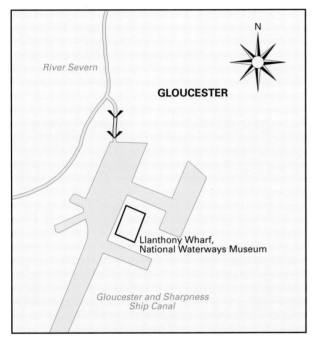

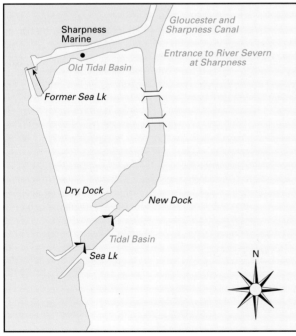

Grantham Canal

Constructed under an Act of 1793, this canal ran from the Trent at Nottingham to Grantham, a distance of over 33 miles and opened in 1797. There were 18 locks, 14ft wide and the main traffic was in coal from the Nottinghamshire coalfields and agricultural produce from the rich farmland of Lincolnshire. A passenger service from Nottingham to Cotgrave started in 1798. After a reluctant takeover by the local railway in 1854, the canal was eventually owned by the London and North Eastern Railway which saw no reason to invest in something which competed with itself. Commercial traffic declined at the start of the 20th century, but recreational boating started and continued until the canal was abandoned in 1936.

As it was used for water supply to agriculture, the canal has mostly been kept in water and is under the jurisdiction of British Waterways. The Grantham Canal Trust, British Waterways and six local authorities have carried out feasibility studies and put forward proposals to restore the canal to cruiseway status. At its junction with the River Trent, the canal would have to find a new route owing to road building which has severed the old

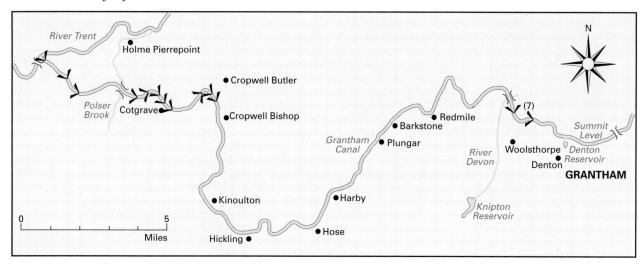

GRANTHAM CANAL Maximum vessel dimensions

From and to	Distance	Length	Beam	Draught	Headroom	Locks
Grantham to River Trent at Nottingham	33 miles (53.1km)	75' (22.8m)	14' (4.2m)	3' (0.9m)	8' (2.4m)	18

route from the river. The proposal is to pass under the A52 along the line of the Polser Brook. At the opposite end, the A1 has severed the canal near Grantham and in the town it has mostly been infilled.

The restoration plans have taken account of the wildlife along the canal, much of which falls into the SSSI category. Economic benefits and the practical engineering aspects have also been thoroughly researched. The canal is mostly rural, passing through the beautiful Vale of Belvoir.

Two sections of the canal are currently navigable by small craft, 4.4 miles near Denton from Woolsthorpe to the A1 near Grantham in Lincolnshire and 2.3 miles from Hickling to Long Clawson in Nottinghamshire, including the canal basin. There is a slipway at Denton and boats can be launched by crane at Hickling. Much of the canal is still in water and boat use of the restored areas is encouraged.

Authority British Waterways, Trent Lock, Lock Lane, Long Eaton, Nottinghamshire NG24 4TT ☎ 0115 946 1017.

Bridges Several, many of which will need to be lifted to allow for navigation.

Towpath The towpath is good throughout the canal with access at each end and most road bridges.

Connections River Trent.

Restoration The Canal Trust is actively restoring the canal and there are proposals under discussion for it to be re-opened by 2000. Three locks of the Woolsthorpe flight have been restored. Once the rest of the flight has been restored, there is a 20-mile lock-free pound which will become navigable.

Distance table
Grantham to: *Miles*

Denton Reservoir	2.6
Woolsthorpe	4.9
River Devon Aqueduct	5.4
Redmile	9.6
Plungar	12.1
Harby	14.6
Hickling	18.6
Long Clawson	20.9
Cropwell Locks	24.1
Fosseway, A46	24.7
Polser Brook Aqueduct	28.0
A52	30.2
River Trent	31.3

You can moor in the heart of Bath just below Pultney Bridge. *Roy Westlake*

Above There is still considerable big ship activity at Ellesmere Port, the western end of the Manchester Ship Canal. *Robin Smithett*

Colourful narrow boats line the Regent's Canal at Little Venice in London. *Jane Cumberlidge*

Below The Standedge Tunnel, on the Huddersfield Narrow Canal, has a parallel railway tunnel. The canal should be open for navigation again by 2000. *Robin Smithett*

The distinctive spire of Abingdon church on the River Thames in Oxfordshire. *Roy Westlake*

A group of working narrow boats at Gas Street Basin in the heart of Birmingham. *Jane Cumberlidge*

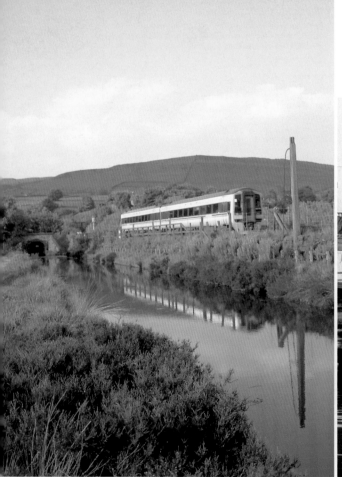

Grand Union Canal

In 1929, in response to increasing competition from the railways, the Grand Junction Canal amalgamated with the Regent's Canal and three Warwickshire canals to form the Grand Union Canal. Other canals involved in the venture were the Old Grand Union Canal, the Leicester Navigation, the Loughborough Navigation, the Erewash Canal and the Hertford Union Canal.

The backbone of this canal system was the Grand Junction Canal which was built under an Act of 1793. The intention was to provide a more direct route to London which avoided the necessity of transhipping at Oxford and travelling by lighter the 100 miles to London. The route of the new canal cut across Northamptonshire and the Chilterns, passing through the mile-long Braunston Tunnel, and joined the Thames at Brentford. The route cut 60 miles off the journey from Birmingham to London.

Many branches were built to link the Grand Junction Canal to towns such as Northampton, Buckingham, Aylesbury, Wendover and Slough. The Leicester Line provided a link to the River Trent and the Humber, while the Northampton Branch linked with the River Nene and the Wash. Through London, a branch was built in the 1820s to Paddington, and then the Regent's Canal through to the Thames at what is now Limehouse Basin.

The majority of the route of the Grand Junction Canal is still through unspoilt rural countryside with wonderful views to admire while you recover your breath between the numerous locks. The Grand Junction was built as a broad canal and attempts were made after the formation of the Grand Union Canal to widen the locks north of Napton through to Birmingham in a modernisation scheme in the 1930s. It was hoped to encourage greater use of the canal for freight carriage, but the plan came too late and the final locks into Birmingham were never widened.

Throughout the Second World War, this was a vital route between London and Birmingham for carrying coal to London and materials for arms manufacture to Birmingham. Many of the boats were run by teams of three young women who were recruited to replace men who had gone to the Front. Commercial carrying on the Grand Union continued into the 1970s, although much reduced by the increase in road transport.

Today, this is a popular cruising route as well as a long distance walk and an opportunity for lots of people to find some peace and quiet close to many centres of population. Whether you want to take a boat out, go for a walk or a bike ride, or have a spot of quiet fishing or bird watching, you are likely to find like-minded people along the Grand Union. It is now the longest single canal in Britain being about 175 miles including the branches and the 5½ miles of the Oxford Canal that are travelled between Napton and Braunston.

There are a variety of publications covering the Grand Union as a whole or in sections. In 1995, GEOprojects issued four new maps covering the Grand Union which include a wealth of information for walkers and boat users.

Authority *Grand Union South* British Waterways, Marsworth Junction, Watery Lane, Marsworth, Tring, Hertfordshire HP23 4LZ ☎ 01442 825938.

Grand Union North British Waterways, Trent Lock, Lock Lane, Long Eaton, Nottinghamshire NG24 4TT ☎ 0115 946 1017.

Bridges Numerous.

Towpath Good throughout navigation except in some tunnels.

Tunnels Blisworth, 3076yds (2812m), no towpath; Braunston, 2049yds (1873m), no towpath; Shrewley, 433yds (396m), separate tunnel for towpath.

Branches Regent's Canal, Hertford Union Canal, Paddington Arm, Slough Arm, Wendover Arm, Aylesbury Arm, Northampton Arm, Welford Arm, Market Harborough Arm, Leicester Line, Erewash Canal, short branches at Warwick and Rickmansworth. There were also the Old Stratford Arm and the Buckingham Arm, but these are now derelict, plus numerous private arms, particularly in the London area, some of the more important ones were:

	Miles
Weeden Military Dock	
(now obstructed by low railway bridge)	0.6
Otter Dock, Yiewsley	1.0
Cowley Hall Dock	0.2
Liddall's	0.2
Cooper's, Yiewsley	0.1
Stockley, Yiewsley	0.1
Pocock's, West Drayton	0.3
Dawley, Yiewsley	0.3
Hanwell Loop, North Hyde	0.3
Victoria Dock, Southall	0.3
Passmore's Dock, Southall	0.3
Maypole Dock, Southall	0.2
Troy Cut, Harefield	0.3

(Some of these have now been filled in. This list has been included for historical interest.)

Speed limit 5mph.

Connections The River Thames at Brentford and Limehouse, and the River Lee through the old Hertford Union Canal, the Oxford Canal between Braunston and Napton, the Stratford-on-Avon Canal at Kingswood Junction, the Birmingham Canal Navigations, the River Trent at Trent Junction, the River Nene at Northampton.

Older canal connections include the Derby and Sandiacre Canal at Sandiacre, the Nutbrook Canal near New Stanton, the Nottingham and the Cromford Canals at Langley Mill.

Navigation Full details of lock times are available from British Waterways.

Tides High water spring tides flow into the canal from the Thames to Brentford Lock, HW Brentford is 1 hour after HW London Bridge.

Facilities All types of facilities are available along the length of the Grand Union Canal. Many detailed guides are published for the whole or sections of the canal and these should be consulted.

Total distances for planning

Main Line

	Miles
Brentford to Birmingham	137.3
Brentford to Langley Mill	167.4
River Thames at Brentford Lock to Braunston Junction	93.5
Braunston Junction to Birmingham	43.5
Norton Junction to Leicester	40.1
Leicester to Langley Mill	37.5
Leicester to Trent Junction	26.1

Distance table

Main Line, Birmingham to Braunston

Locks Rise Salford Junction to Camphill, fall Knowle to Warwick, rise Warwick to Napton.

Salford Bridge to:	*Miles*
Nechells Shallow Lock No 64	0.2
Aston Church Road Bridge No 109	0.7
Saltley Viaduct No 108	1.2
Garrison Bottom Lock No 63	1.4
Duddeston Mill Road Bridge No 106	1.5
Garrison Third Lock No 61	1.8
Landor Street Bridge No 105	1.9
Garrison Top Lock No 59	2.0
Garrison Lane Bridge No 103	2.2
Watery Lane Bridge No 99	2.5
Bordesley Junction to the Digbeth Branch of the BCN	2.6
Camphill Bottom Lock No 57	2.6
Camphill Fifth Lock No 56	2.8
Coventry Road Bridge No 93	2.8
Sandy Lane Bridge No 92	2.9

GRAND UNION CANAL Maximum vessel dimensions

Main Line

From and to	Distance	Length	Beam	Draught	Headroom	Locks
Brentford to Berkhamsted	37.5 miles (60.4km)	72' (21.9m)	14' (4.3m)	3' 6" (1.1m)	7' 6" (2.3m)	48
Berkhamsted to Braunston	61 miles (98.2km)	72' (21.9m)	7' (2.1m)	3' 6" (1.1m)	7' 6" (2.3m)	2
Napton Junction to Camp Hill	35.4 miles (57.0km)	70' (21.3m)	7' (2.1m)	2' 6" (0.8m)	7' (2.1m)	57
Camp Hill to Salford Junction	3.1 miles (5.0km)	70' (21.3m)	7' (2.1m)	2' 6" (0.8m)	6' 6" (2.0m)	6

Main Branches of the Grand Union Canal

	Distance	Length	Beam	Draught	Headroom	Locks
Regent's Canal Limehouse Basin to Warwick Avenue, Paddington Arm	8.6 miles (13.8km)	72' (21.9m)	14' 6" (4.4m)	4' (1.2m)	8' 6" (2.6m)	13
Hertford Union Canal Bethnal Green to Old Ford Junction with River Lee	1.3 miles (2.0km)	78' (23.7m)	14' 6" (4.4m)	4' 6" (1.3m)	8' 6" (2.5m)	3
Paddington Arm Paddington to Bulls Bridge	13.6 miles (21.9km)	72' (21.9m)	14' 6" (4.4m)	4' (1.2m)	8' 6" (2.6m)	None
Slough Arm Cowley Peachey to Slough	4.9 miles (7.9km)	72' (21.9m)	14' (4.3m)	3'6" (1.1m)	7' 6" (2.3m)	None

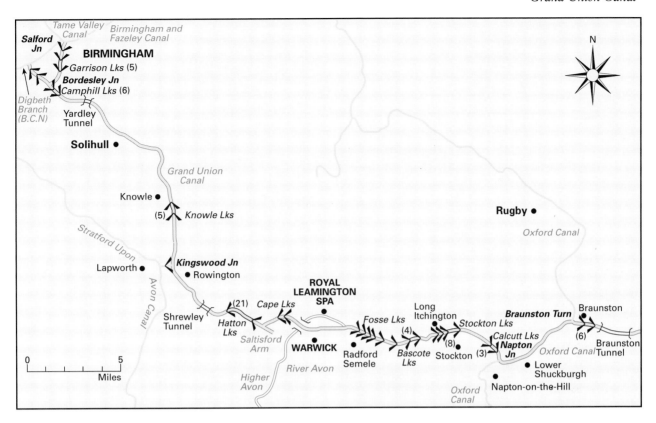

	Miles
Camphill Second Lock No 53	3.0
Camphill Top Lock No 52	3.1
Sampson Road Wharf	3.2
Golden Hillock Bridge No 89	3.9
Tyseley Incinerator	4.7
Tyseley Wharf	5.3
Yardley Road Bridge No 86A	5.8
Lincoln Road Bridge No 85	6.8
Richmond Road Bridge, No 84, Olton	7.2
Dove House Lane Bridge No 82, Ulverley Green	8.0
Rowood Bridge No 80, Solihull	8.7
Elmdon Heath Iron Bridge No 79	9.2
Catherine de Barnes Bridge No 78	10.4
Henwood Bridge No 77	11.1
Barston Lane Bridge No 76, Copt Heath	11.6
Motorway Bridge (M42)	11.7
Copt Heath Bridge No 75	12.0
Waterfield Bridge No 73	12.6
Kixley Bridge No 72	13.0
Kenilworth Road Bridge No 71	13.4
Knowle Top Lock No 51	13.5
Knowle Bottom Lock No 47	13.7
King's Arms Bridge No 70	14.3
Baker's Lane Bridge No 68	14.9
Rising Bridge No 66	16.1
Kingswood Bridge No 65	16.9
Kingswood, junction with the Stratford-on-Avon Canal	17.1
Turner's Green Bridge No 63	17.9
Rowington Hill Bridge No 62	18.5
Northwest end of Shrewley Tunnel (433 yards)	20.2
Hatton Station Bridge No 56	21.1
Hatton Top Lock No 46	22.1
Hatton Hill Bridge No 54	22.3

	Miles
Hatton Middle Lock Bridge No 53	22.8
Ugly Bridge No 52	23.2
Hatton Bottom Lock No 26	24.1
Warwick By-pass Bridge	24.1
Budbrooke, junction with Saltisford Branch (0.3 miles)	24.3
Cape Top Lock No 25, Warwick	24.9
Cape Bottom Lock No 24	25.0
Coventry Road Bridge No 49	25.6
Emscote Bridge No 46	26.2
Avon Aqueduct	26.4
Leam Bridge No 44	26.8
Bishop's Tachbrook Road Bridge No 41, Leamington	27.7
Clemens Street Bridge No 40, Leamington	27.8
Radford Road Bridge No 35	29.1
Radford Bottom Lock No 23	29.8
Fosse Bottom Lock No 22	30.4
Fosse Middle Lock No 21	30.6
Fosse Top Lock No 20	30.9
Wood Lock No 19	31.6
Welsh Road Bridge No 30	32.2
Bascote Bottom Lock No 17	32.2
Bascote Top Lock (staircase pair Nos 15 and 14)	32.8
Cuttle Bridge No 25, Long Itchington	34.3
Stockton Ninth Lock No 12 and junction with Kaye's Arm	34.8
Stockton Bridge No 23	34.9
Stockton Top Lock No 4	35.4
Birdingbury Bridge No 21	35.7
Gibraltar Bridge No 20	36.4
Calcutt Bottom Lock No 3	37.9
Calcutt Top Lock No 1	37.9
Napton, junction with the Oxford Canal	38.5

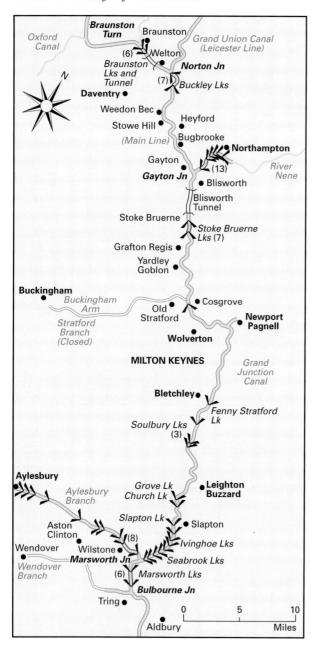

<table>
<tr><td colspan="2"></td></tr>
</table>

Distance table   *Miles*

Braunston Junction to:

Braunston Bottom Lock No 1	0.4
Braunston Top Lock No 6	0.9
Braunston Tunnel, north end	1.2
Braunston Tunnel, south end	2.4
Welton Bridge No 6	2.6
Water Lane Bridge No 9, Norton	3.9
Norton Junction, Leicester Section of the Grand Union	4.2
Buckby Top Lock No 7	4.4
Daventry Road Bridge No 13	4.9
Long Buckby Wharf	5.0
Buckby Bottom Lock No 13	5.7
Muscot Mill Bridge No 18	6.4
Brockhall Bridge No 19	6.8
Watling Street Bridge No 22	7.7
Dodford Road Bridge No 23	8.1
Weedon Station Bridge No 24	8.9
Junction with Weedon Military Dock	9.0
Stow Hill Bridge No 26	9.9
Flore Lane Bridge No 27	10.2
High House Bridge No 29	10.6
Heyford Bridge No 32	11.6
Bugbrooke Bridge No 36	13.0
Bugbrooke Valley Aqueduct	13.3
Banbury Lane Bridge No 43	14.9
Wright's Lane Bridge No 45	15.4
Gayton Junction, junction with the Northampton Branch	16.6
Railway Bridge, Blisworth	17.0
Blisworth Bridge No 51 and Blisworth Mill	17.7
Blisworth Tunnel, north end	18.2
Blisworth Tunnel, south end	19.9
Stoke Bruerne Waterways Museum	20.3
Stoke Bruerne Lock No 18	20.9
Stoke Bruerne Bottom Lock No 20	21.1
Grafton Bridge No 57	22.6
Yardley Bridge No 60	23.9
Thrupp Wharf	25.9
Solomon's Ornamental Bridge No 65	26.6
Cosgrove Junction (Old Stratford and Buckingham Arms)	26.9
Great Ouse Aqueduct	27.4
Galleon Bridge No 68	27.8
Wolverton Bridge No 71 and Wolverton Station	28.8
Bradwell Windmill	29.8
Newport Pagnell Road Bridge No 74	30.2
Wildfowl Centre	30.8
Black Horse Bridge No 76	31.3
Linford Wharf	31.9
Brickyard Bridge No 79	32.8
Little Woolstone Bridge No 83	34.8
Fenny Stratford Lock No 22	38.5
Watling Street Bridge No 96	38.6
Water Eaton Bridge No 98	39.4
Orchard Mill Bridge No 102	40.7
Stoke Hammond Lock No 23	41.4
Soulbury Three Locks Nos 24 to 26	42.5
Old Linslade Bridge No 110	44.1
Leighton Lock No 27	45.4
Leighton Buzzard Bridge No 114	46.2
Grove Lock No 28	47.6
Church Lock No 29	48.1
Slapton Lock No 30	49.8
Slapton Bridge No 120	49.9
Horton Lock No 31	50.4

                    Miles

The through route to London shares the distance between Napton and Braunston with the Oxford Canal from where the bridge numbering starts again.

Fleknoe	41.3
Nethercote	41.5
Wolfhamcote	42.8
Braunston, junction with Oxford Canal, northern section	43.5

Braunston to Brentford

Locks Rise Napton to Braunston Tunnel, fall Norton Junction to Fenny Stratford, rise Fenny Stratford to Bulbourne Junction, fall Cowroast to River Thames.

	Miles
Ivinghoe Bottom Locks Nos 32 and 33	50.5
Ivinghoe Bridge No 123	51.6
Seabrook Bottom Lock No 34	51.8
Seabrook Top Lock No 36	52.3
Cheddington Bridge No 126	52.7
Marsworth Locks Nos 37 and 38	53.4
Marsworth Junction, Aylesbury Branch	54.0
Startopsend Lock No 39	54.3
Marsworth Lock No 40	54.6
Marsworth Top Lock No 45 and Bulbourne Junction (the Wendover Feeder Branch)	55.1
Bulbourne Bridge No 133	55.4
Tring Cutting Bridge No 134	56.0
Bridge No 135, Tring Station	56.8
New Ground Bridge No 136	57.7
Cowroast Lock No 46, Summit Lock	58.2
Dudswell Top Lock No 47	58.6
Dudswell Bottom Lock No 48	58.8
Northchurch Top Lock No 49	59.4
Bushes Lock No 50	59.5
Berkhamstead Top Lock No 53	60.8
Berkhamstead Bottom Lock No 55	61.3
Bourne End Locks Nos 56 to 59	61.8
Bridge No 146	62.9
Bourne End Mill	63.0
Winkwell Locks Nos 60 and 61	63.3
Boxmoor Top Lock No 62	63.9
Fishery Lock No 63	64.4
Boxmoor Bottom Lock No 64	65.0
Two Waters Road Bridge No 151	65.2
Apsley Top Locks Nos 65 to 67	65.6
Nash Mills	66.4
Nash Mills Locks Nos 68 and 69	66.5
Kings Langley Lock No 69A	67.7
Ovaltine Works	67.8
Home Park Mill Lock No 70	68.2
M25	68.4
Home Park Farm Lock No 71	68.7
Hunton Bridge Locks Nos 72 and 73	69.4
M25 Spur	69.9
Lady Capel's Lock No 74, Watford	70.1
Grove Ornamental Bridge No 164	70.4
Grove Mill, Watford	70.5
Cassiobury Park Top Lock No 75	70.9
Cassiobury Park Lock No 76	71.1
Ironbridge Lock No 77	71.5
Cassiobridge Lock No 78	72.3
Cassiobridge No 169	72.4
Croxley Mill	72.8
Common Moor Lock No 79	73.1
Lot Mead Lock No 80	73.9
Batchworth Lock No 81 (junction with the Rickmansworth Branch)	74.6
Stockers Lock No 82	75.4
Springwell Lock No 83	76.1
Copper Mill Lock No 84	77.2
Troy Junction, junction with the Troy Branch (private)	77.5
Black Jack's Lock No 85	77.8
Widewater Lock No 86	78.9
Harefield Marina	79.0
Denham Lock No 87 and Aqueduct over Frays River	80.4
Oxford Road Bridge	80.8
Uxbridge Lock No 88	81.4
Denham Yacht Station	81.6

	Miles
Dolphin Bridge No 186	82.0
Cowley Lock No 89	83.0
Packet Boat Dock	83.9
Cowley Peachey Junction (the Slough Branch)	83.9
Trout Bridge No 191	84.1
West Drayton Station	84.5
Starveal Bridge No 195	85.5
Dawley Bridge No 197	86.1
Woolpack Bridge No 198	86.3
Workhouse Bridge No 199	86.6
Station Road Bridge No 200	86.9
Yeading Brook Aqueduct	87.0
Bulls Bridge Junction (the Paddington Branch)	87.6
Western Road Bridge No 201	87.9
North Hyde Bridge No 202	88.5
Adelaide Marina	88.8
Wolf Bridge No 203	89.0
Maypole Dock	89.5
Norwood Top Lock No 90	89.6

	Miles
Norwood Lock No 91	89.8
Windmill Bridge No 205 (Three Bridges)	90.0
Hanwell Top Lock No 92	90.1
Hanwell Bottom Lock No 97 and	
River Brent	90.5
Osterley Lock No 98	91.4
M4 Motorway Bridge	91.5
Gallows Bridge No 207	91.9
Clitheroe's Lock No 99	92.2
Great West Road Bridge No 208	92.5
Brentford Gauging Lock No 100	92.8
Brentford High Street Bridge	92.9
Thames Locks No 101 and Dock Road	
Bridge	93.3
Junction with the River Thames	93.6

Main Branches of the Grand Union Canal

Regent's Canal

Bridges Numerous.

Tunnels Islington, 960yds (878m), no towpath; Maida Hill, 272yds (249m), no towpath.

Towpath Throughout navigation except the tunnels.

Locks Rise Thames to Camden Town.

Distance table	Miles
Paddington, junction with Paddington Arm to:	
Maida Hill Tunnel	0.4
Finchley Road Bridge	0.9
London Zoo	1.1
Avenue Road Bridge	1.3
Junction with Cumberland Market Branch	1.6

The Regent's Canal is a popular attraction for visitors to London. *Jane Cumberlidge*

	Miles
Hampstead Road Lock No 1, Camden	
Canal Centre	2.3
Hawley Lock No 2	2.4
Kentish Town Lock No 3	2.4
St Pancras Lock No 4	3.1
Maiden Lane Bridge	3.4
London Canal Museum	3.5
Caledonian Road Bridge	3.6
West end of Islington Tunnel	3.8
East end of Islington Tunnel	4.3
City Road Lock No 5	4.3

The entrance lock from the Thames into Limehouse Basin at the start of the Regent's Canal. *Jane Cumberlidge*

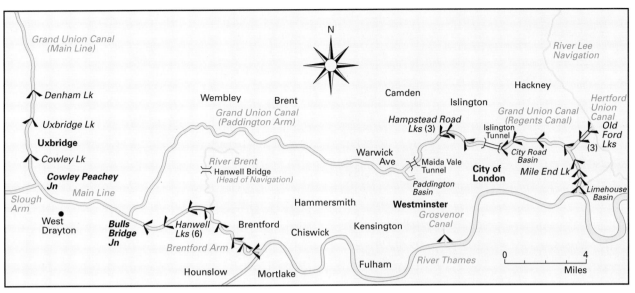

	Miles
Junction with City Road Basin Branch	
(partly filled in)	4.4
Sturts Lock No 6	4.9
Kingsland Road Bridge	5.4
Acton's Lock No 7	5.9
Cambridge Road Bridge	6.3
Old Ford Lock No 8	6.7
Junction with Hertford Union Canal	6.9
Mile End Lock No 9	7.4
Mile End Road Bridge	7.4
Johnson's Lock No 10	7.8
Salmon Lane Lock No 11	8.1
Commercial Road Lock No 12 and entrance to	
Limehouse Basin	8.4
Limehouse Marina and Limehouse Ship	
Lock No 13	
(junction with River Thames)	8.6

Hertford Union Canal

Bridges Seven.

Towpath Throughout the canal.

Distance table

Junction with Main Line to:
Top of Old Ford Three Locks Nos 1–3	0.9
Junction with River Lee (Main Line)	1.2

Paddington Arm

Bridges Six.

Towpath Good throughout navigation. Paddington Basin is private, no towpath.

Tunnels None.

Distance table
Bulls Bridge Junction, junction with the Main Line to:
Hayes Road Bridge No 20	1.2
West End Bridge No 18	2.8
Northold Road Bridge No 17	3.0
Western Avenue Bridge	3.6
Lyons Dock	4.3
Oldfield Lane Bridge No 15	4.7
Greenford Road Bridge	4.9
Ballot Box Bridge No 13	5.8
Piggery Bridge No 12	6.9
Ealing Road Bridge No 11	7.1

	Miles
Aqueduct over River Brent	8.0
Aqueduct over North Circular Road	8.1
Willing's Bridge No 10	8.4
Acton Lane Power Station	9.3
Old Oak Bridge No 7	9.7
Mitre Bridge No 6	10.4
Kensal Green Bridge	11.3
Carlton Bridge No 4	12.0
Harrow Road Bridge No 3	12.4
Ranelagh Road Footbridge	12.7
Westbourne Terrace Bridge, Paddington	12.9
Little Venice, junction with the Regent's	
Canal	12.9
Harrow Road Bridge No 2	12.9
Western Avenue Motorway Extension	13.0
Bishops Road Bridge No 1	13.2
Paddington Basin and Wharves	13.6

Slough Arm

Bridges 12.

Towpath Good throughout navigation.

Distance table
Cowley Peachey Junction, junction with the Main Line to:
Fray's River Aqueduct	0.2
River Colne Aqueduct	0.5
Colne Brook Aqueduct	0.7
M25	1.0
Throney Lane Bridge	1.1
Meeking's Bridge	1.9
Hollow Hill Lane Bridge	2.2
Langley Station Bridge	2.8
Trenches Bridge, Langley	3.2
Langley Schools Bridge	3.4
Middle Green Bridge	3.7
Uxbridge Road Bridge	4.2
Wexham Road Bridge	4.5
Slough Basin and Wharves	4.9

Rickmansworth Branch
Distance table
Batchworth Junction and Lock No 81A to:
Rickmansworth Basin	0.1
Head of Branch by Rickmansworth Gas	
Works (site of)	0.3

The canals are well signposted. *Jane Cumberlidge*

Wendover Arm
Junction with Main Line at Lock 45 to Wendover, currently navigable to Tring Stop Lock.

The branch is 6½ miles (10.4km) but only 1½ miles are navigable at present.

Locks One, the Tring Ford Stop Lock.

Bridges Ten.

Towpath Throughtout distance to Wendover.

Restoration Discussions and proposals are underway for full restoration to Wendover.

Distance table	Miles
Main Line at Bulbourne Junction to:	
Gammel Bridge No 2 and New Mill Wharf	0.6
Tring Ford Pumping Station and Tring Ford Stop Lock	1.5
Buckland Wharf	2.9
Halton Bridge	4.7
Wendover Basin	6.5

Aylesbury Arm
Bridges 19.

Towpath Throughout navigation.

Tunnels None.

Locks Rise Aylesbury to Marsworth Junction.

Distance table	Miles
Marsworth Junction, junction with the Main Line to:	
Marsworth Locks Nos 1 and 2	0.1
Dixon's Gap Bridge No 2	0.5
Wilstone Lock No 9	1.1
Puttenham Locks Nos 10 and 11	1.7
Buckland Bridge No 8	2.5
Buckland Lock No 12	2.6
Red House Lock No 13	2.9
Broughton Lock No 14	4.8
Oakfield Bridge	5.3
Aylesbury Lock No 15	5.5
Walton Mill	5.8
Walton Bridge No 18 Nestlés Works	5.9
Aylesbury Basin	6.2

Old Stratford and Buckingham Arms (derelict)
Originally ran to Buckingham through two locks. A distance of 10¾ miles, these two arms were separate, the Old Stratford being wide and the Buckingham Arm narrow.

Northampton Arm
Bridges 14.

Towpath Throughout navigation.

Tunnels None.

Locks Rise Northampton to Gayton Junction.

Distance table	Miles
Gayton Junction, junction with the Main Line to:	
Gayton Marina	0.1
Milton Road Bridge No 3	0.5
Rothersthorpe Top Lock No 1	0.7
Rothersthorpe Bottom Lock No 13	1.7
Wootton Lock No 14	2.1
Hardingstone Lock No 15	3.0
Duston Mill Bridge No 13 and Hunsbury Hill Industrial Museum	3.3
Northampton Lock No 16	4.1
Cotton End Lock No 17, junction with River Nene	4.8

GRAND UNION CANAL Maximum vessel dimensions – Main Branches of the Grand Union Canal

From and to	Distance	Length	Beam	Draught	Headroom	Locks
Aylesbury Arm						
Marsworth Junction to Aylesbury	6.3 miles (10.1km)	72' (21.9m)	7' (2.1m)	2' 6" (0.8m)	7' (2.1m)	16
Northampton Arm						
Gayton to Northampton	4.8 miles (7.7km)	72' (21.9m)	7' (2.1m)	2' 6" (0.8m)	7' (2.1m)	17
The Leicester Line						
Norton Junction to Foxton Junction	23.1 miles (37.2km)	72' (21.9m)	7' (2.1m)	3' (0.9m)	7' 6" (2.3m)	17
Foxton Junction to Leicester	18.9 miles (30.4km)	70' (21.3m)	7' (2.1m)	2' 6" (0.8m)	6' 9" (2.1m)	24
Leicester to Trent Junction (River Soar)	24.1 miles (38.8km)	72' (21.9m)	10' 6" (3.2m)	3' 6" (1.1m)	7' 6" (2.3m)	18

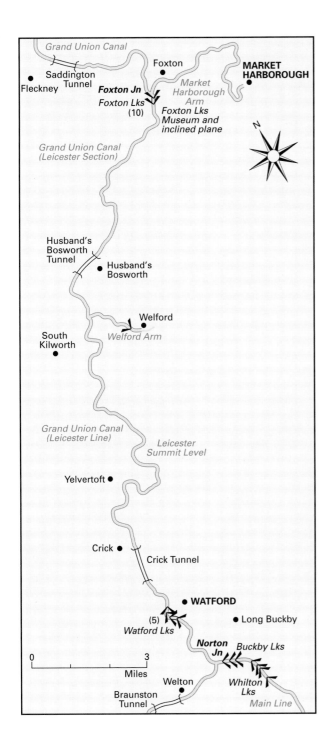

The Leicester Line

Bridges Numerous.

Towpath Throughout the navigation.

Tunnels Crick, 1527½yds (1397m), no towpath; Husbands Bosworth, 1171yds (1071m), no towpath; Saddington, 882yds (807m), no towpath.

Flood Warnings From Leicester onwards much of the navigation is the River Soar. This river is prone to flooding and flood alleviation works are continuing. Flood warning lights operate at many locks in this section and must always be adhered to. Extra care must be taken when passing weirs and be aware that, with high rates of water flow, rubbish can build up at locks and weirs.

Locks Rise Norton Junction to Crick Tunnel, fall Husbands Bosworth Tunnel to Trent Junction. Summit 412ft (126m).

Distance table	Miles
Norton Junction, junction with the Main Line to:	
Watling Street Bridge No 4	1.3
Welton Station Bridge No 5 and Welton	1.8
Watford Locks Nos 1–7	2.2
Motorway Bridge M1	2.4
Crick Tunnel, south end	3.8
Crick Tunnel, north end	4.7
Crick Wharf	4.9
Yelvertoft Bridge No 19	7.2
Haddon Road Bridge No 22	7.9
Darker's Bridge No 23	8.3
Elkington Bridge No 28	10.4
Stokley's Bridge No 31	11.6
South Kilworth Road Bridge No 37	13.7
Aqueduct over River Avon	15.4
Junction with the Welford Branch	15.5
North Kilworth Marina	16.3
Husbands Bosworth Tunnel, south end	17.1
Husbands Bosworth Tunnel, north end	17.8
Morton's Bridge No 56	21.8
Lubenham Wharf Bridge	22.0
Gumley Road Bridge No 60	22.7
Foxton Locks Nos 8 to 17	22.9
Foxton Junction (the Market Harborough Branch)	23.1
Debdale Wharf Bridge No 65	24.4
Smeeton Hills Bridge No 70	25.7
Smeeton Aqueduct	26.4
Saddington Tunnel, south end	26.8
Saddington Tunnel, north end	27.3
Kibworth Top Lock No 18	28.2
Taylor's Lock No 20	28.5
Kibworth Bottom Lock No 21	28.7
Crane's Lock No 22	29.1
Great Glen Station Bridge No 77	29.8

GRAND UNION CANAL Maximum Vessel Dimensions – Main Branches of the Grand Union Canal

From and to	Distance	Length	Beam	Draught	Headroom	Locks
Welford Arm						
Main Canal to Welford Basin	1.6 miles (2.6km)	72' (21.9m)	7' (2.1m)	3' (0.9m)	7' 6" (2.3m)	1
Market Harborough Arm						
Foxton to Market Harborough	5.5 miles (7.7km)	70' (21.3m)	7' (2.1m)	2' 6" (0.8m)	6' 9" (2.0m)	1

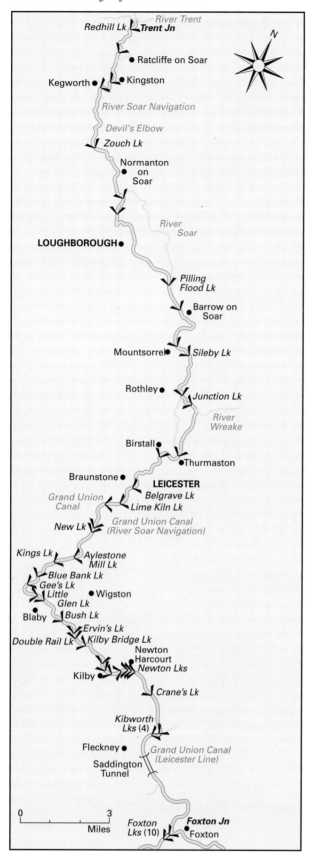

River Trent
Redhill Lk　Trent Jn
● Ratcliffe on Soar
Kegworth ●　● Kingston
River Soar Navigation
Devil's Elbow
Zouch Lk
Normanton
on
Soar
River
Soar
LOUGHBOROUGH ●
Pilling
Flood Lk
● Barrow on
　Soar
Mountsorrel ●　Sileby Lk
Rothley ●　Junction Lk
River
Wreake
Birstall ●
● Thurmaston
Braunstone ●
LEICESTER
Belgrave Lk
Grand Union　*Lime Kiln Lk*
Canal
New Lk
Grand Union Canal
(River Soar Navigation)
Kings Lk　Aylestone
　Mill Lk
Blue Bank Lk
Gee's Lk
Little ●　● Wigston
Glen Lk
Blaby ●　Bush Lk
Ervin's Lk
Double Rail Lk　Kilby Bridge Lk
Newton
Harcourt
Newton Lks
Kilby ●
Crane's Lk
Kibworth
Lks (4)
Fleckney ●　*Grand Union Canal*
Saddington　*(Leicester Line)*
Tunnel
0　　　3
Miles
Foxton　**Foxton Jn**
Lks (10)　● Foxton

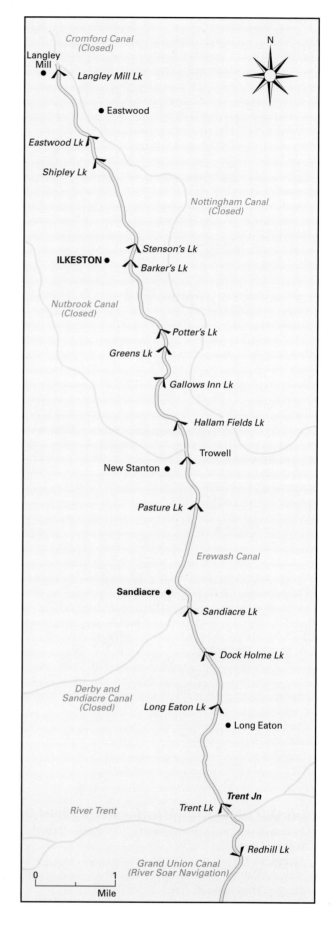

Cromford Canal
(Closed)
Langley
Mill ●　Langley Mill Lk
● Eastwood
Eastwood Lk
Shipley Lk
Nottingham Canal
(Closed)
Stenson's Lk
ILKESTON ●　Barker's Lk
Nutbrook Canal
(Closed)
Potter's Lk
Greens Lk
Gallows Inn Lk
Hallam Fields Lk
Trowell
New Stanton ●
Pasture Lk
Erewash Canal
Sandiacre ●
Sandiacre Lk
Dock Holme Lk
Derby and
Sandiacre Canal
(Closed)　Long Eaton Lk
● Long Eaton
Trent Jn
River Trent　Trent Lk
Redhill Lk
0　　1
Mile
Grand Union Canal
(River Soar Navigation)

	Miles
Newton Church Bridge No 80	30.6
Newton Top Lock No 23	30.8
Spinney Lock No 24	30.9
Wain Bridge No 81, Newton Harcourt	31.0
Top Half Mile Lock No 25	31.2
Bottom Half Mile Lock No 26	31.7
Turnover Lock No 27 and Bridge No 82	31.8
Tythorn Lock No 28	31.9
Bumble Bee Lock No 29	32.2
Kilby Bridge No 87	32.9
Kilby Bridge Lock No 30	33.3
Double Rail Lock No 31	33.7
Ervin's Lock No 32	34.1
Crow Mill Bridge No 92	34.5
Bush Lock No 33	34.9
Little Glen Road Bridge No 94	35.3
Dunn's Lock No 34	35.8
Blaby Bridge No 98	36.0
Whetstone Lane Lock No 35	36.2
Gee's Lock No 36 and Bridge No 101	37.0
Blue Bank Lock No 37	37.4
Kings's Lock No 38	38.3
Canal enters River Soar	38.5
Freestone Bridge No 106	38.6
Aylestone Mill Lock No 39	39.3
St Marys Mill Lock No 40, Gas Museum	39.9
Freeman's Meadow Lock No 41	40.3
Upperton Road Bridge	40.6
Newarke Bridge	40.9
Leicester Castle Ruins	41.0
West Bridge	41.1
Leicester North Lock No 42	42.0
Abbey Park	42.5
Limekiln Lock No 43	42.8
Leicester Waterside Centre	43.2
Belgrave Lock No 44	43.4
Birstall Lock No 45	46.1
Thurmaston Lock No 46	46.1
Barkby Wharf	47.3
Junction Lock No 47	48.3
Cossington Lock No 48	49.0
Sileby Lock No 49	50.4
Mountsorrel Lock No 50	51.4
Granite Wharf	53.0
Barrow Deep Lock No 51	53.4
Pilling's Flood Lock No 52	55.0
Loughborough Wharf	57.0
Loughborough Lock No 53	57.3
Bishops Meadow Lock No 54	58.0
Normanton-on-Soar Ferry	59.4
Zouch Lock No 55	61.1
Kegworth Deep Lock No 56	63.1
Kegworth Shallow Lock No 57	63.6
Ratcliffe-on-Soar Lock No 58	65.0
Redhill Lock No 59	65.8
Junction with River Trent	66.1

This section of the Grand Union Canal joins the River Trent in the Soar Mouth or Red Hill Branch of the Navigation. On leaving the Grand Union Canal (Old Loughborough Navigation Section), all boats must turn upstream to the left until the head of Cranfleet Cut is reached. Downstream leads to Thrumpton Weir only.

Welford Arm

Bridges Three.

Towpath Throughout navigation.

Distance table	*Miles*
Welford Junction, junction with the Leicester Line to:	
Bosworth Mill Bridge No 1	0.3
Gilberts Bridge No 2	0.8
Welford Lock, rise to Welford	1.2
Welford Wharf and Basin	1.6

Market Harborough Arm

Bridges 12.

Towpath Throughout navigation.

Distance table	*Miles*
Foxton Junction, junction with the Leicester Line to:	
Foxton Bridge No 3	0.7
Clarkes Bridge No 5	0.9
Johnson's Bridge No 7	1.3
Gallow's Hill Bridge No 8	2.0
Bowden Hall Bridge No 10	3.4
Uncle Tom's Bridge No 12	4.1
Market Harborough Wharves and Basin	5.5

Erewash Canal

Bridges 32.

Towpath Throughout navigation.

Locks Rise Trent Junction to Langley Mill.

Distance table	*Miles*
Norton Junction, junction with the Grand Union Main Line to:	
Trent Lock No 60 and Toll Office	66.1
Long Eaton Lock No 61	67.9
Dock Holme Lock No 62	68.1
Sandiacre Lock No 63	69.4
Sandiacre Junction, Derby and Sandiacre Canal	69.5
Sandiacre Village	70.4
Junction Lock No 65 and Toll Office	71.6
The White House, junction with Nutbrook Canal (now derelict and abandoned)	71.8
Hallam Fields Lock No 66	72.1
Gallows Inn Lock No 67	72.9
Green's Lock No 68	73.4
Potter's Lock No 69	73.8
Barker's Lock No 70	74.7
Stenson's Lock No 71	75.9
Shipley Lock No 72	76.3
Eastwood Lock No 73	76.6
Langley Mill (junction with Cromford Canal)	77.9

Lock No 14 of the Cromford Canal has been restored and it is now possible to go through this to the Great Northern Basin at the top end of the closed Nottingham Canal.

GRAND UNION CANAL *Maximum Vessel Dimensions – Main Branches of the Grand Union Canal*

From and to	Distance	Length	Beam	Draught	Headroom	Locks
Erewash Canal						
Trent Junction to Langley Mill	11.9 miles (19.2km)	78' (23.8m)	12' 6" (3.8m)	2' 6" (0.8m)	6' (1.8m)	14

Grand Western Canal

There was always an interest in creating a route from the Bristol Channel to the English Channel, and one plan included a canal from Taunton to Tiverton then down to Exeter. An Act was passed in 1796 but work did not begin until 1810. The first section from Lowdwells to Tiverton was open by 1814 but the continuation to Taunton, using vertical lifts and an inclined plane, was not completed until 1838. The whole canal was 24½ miles long.

Today the original length of canal is owned by Devon County Council and it is called the Grand Western Canal Country Park. It is a haven of peace where a gentle walk allows you to appreciate the wildlife all around. No powered craft can use the canal but there are a horse drawn trip boat, electric boats, canoes and rowing boats. It is a popular location for fishermen as there is a wide range of coarse fish in the canal: roach, perch, pike, carp, bream and tench.

Authority Devon County Council, County Hall, Exeter EX2 4QQ ☎ 01392 77977.

Bridges 23.

Towpath Throughout navigation.

Connections This is an isolated canal with no connections.

Navigation Permits must be obtained from Devon County Council to take private craft on the canal.

Restoration Some of the lifts in the abandoned section can still be seen. There is no proposal at present for a major restoration project of the length to Taunton, although there have been discussions between interested parties about the preservation of the remaining canal structures.

Distance table	*Miles*
Lowdwells to:	
Whipcott Wharf	0.9
Burlescombe Wharf	1.8
Ayshford	2.9
Sampford Peverell	5.3
Rock House Wharf	6.5
Halberton	7.1
Road Bridge (A373 road)	8.8
Tiverton	10.8

The canal has become a haven for wildlife and no powered craft are allowed. *Jane Cumberlidge*

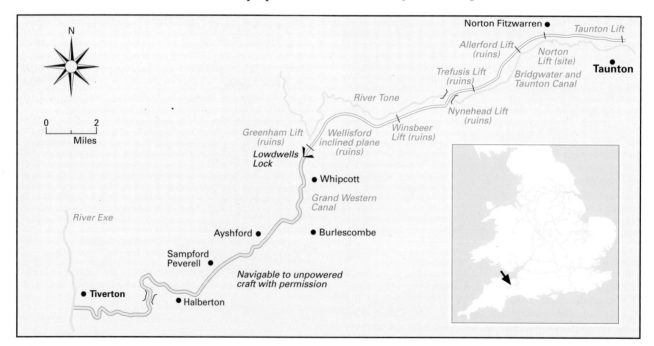

GRAND WESTERN CANAL Maximum Vessel Dimensions

From and to	Distance	Length	Beam	Draught	Headroom	Locks
Lowdwells to Tiverton	10.5 miles (16.9km)	Unlimited	7' (2.1m)	3' 6" (1.1m)	7' 3" (2.2m)	None

GROSVENOR CANAL Maximum vessel dimensions

From and to	Distance	Length	Beam	Draught	Headroom	Locks
Chelsea Bridge to near Ebury Bridge	0.5 miles (0.8km)	90' (27.4m)	18' 6" (5.6m)	7' (2.1m)	8' 6" (2.5m)	1

Grosvenor Canal

Originally built to supply water to Chelsea, this cut was ¾ mile long and ran to a basin now occupied by Victoria Station. It was converted to a navigable canal in 1823. In 1866, it became used for barging away refuse. It was extensively reconstructed in 1929 and at its peak moved more than 8000 tons of refuse every week. The council decided to stop transporting refuse by barge in 1995. The lock was equipped with extra gates to keep out very high tides.

Authority Westminster City Council, City Engineer's Department, Grosvenor Canal Depot, Gatcliff Road, London SW1 ☎ 0171 730 1540.

River Hamble

This is a lovely river but, unfortunately, its very attractions have been its downfall and it is now seriously over-crowded. Even in the 1930s, this was a popular yachting centre and with improved road and rail connections, it is even more popular today with five marinas along its shores. Bursledon Bridge has headroom of 13ft (4m) at MHWS and it is possible to continue for about 2 miles up to Botley. Once the roads are left behind, rural Hampshire reasserts itself and the river is a delight. The River Hamble Harbour Revision Order 1982 applies.

Authority Hampshire County Council, The Castle, Winchester, Hampshire SO23 8UJ ☎ 01962 841841.

Bridges Several.

Towpath None.

Navigation High water 10 minutes before and 1 hour 51 minutes after HW Dover. Range spring tides 3.7m, neap tides 1.9m. As with Southampton Water, there is a double high tide on springs and a 2 hour HW stand on neaps. Draught from Bursledon to Botley is 13ft at HWS, 11ft at HWN.

Charts Imray C15, Admiralty 2022, 1905.

Facilities All facilities for sea-going boats with several pubs and shops handy to the moorings.

Herefordshire and Gloucestershire Canal

This canal was one of the last to be fully opened, with the section to Hereford opening in 1845, but it was also one of the earliest to be closed, in 1889. The first section from Gloucester to Ledbury was open by 1798 with 13 locks and the Oxenhall Tunnel. This had absorbed so much money that the extension of the canal to Hereford seems to have

RIVER HAMBLE Maximum vessel dimensions

From and to	Distance	Length	Beam	Draught	Headroom	Locks
Hamble to Botley	7.5 miles (12km)	Unlimited	Unlimited	Unlimited	13' (4m)	None

HEREFORDSHIRE & GLOUCESTERSHIRE CANAL *Maximum vessel dimensions* (original canal)

From and to	Distance	Length	Beam	Draught	Headroom	Locks
Hereford to Over, Gloucester	34 miles (54.7km)	70' (21.3m)	7' 6" (2.3m)	4' 6" (1.4m)	8' (2.4m)	22

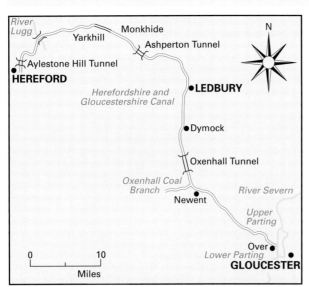

been abandoned until 1827, when Stephen Ballard took over as clerk to the company. After a new Act in 1839 to raise more money, work continued with the Walsopthorne Tunnel, the aqueduct over the River Lugg and the Aylestone Hill Tunnel, until the canal finally reached Hereford. There were 22 locks in all and an 8½ mile summit pound. It was never financially successful and after being leased to the West Midland Railway and GWR the first section was closed in 1881.

The Herefordshire and Gloucestershire Canal Society was formed in 1983 and it became a Trust in 1992, since which time restoration work has accelerated. One major hurdle to full restoration is that there are something in the order of 100 private landowners through whose land the route of the canal runs. About 4 miles, in separate sections, are now in water and a trip boat operates on the Yarkhill to Monkhide section. The Trust Administration Officer is Mrs Lesley Lowe, Chevin, Little Birch, Hereford HR2 8AZ ☎ 01981 540366.

Authority A number of private owners.

Bridges Numerous. Eighteen of the original bridges are still in existence including Skew Bridge at Monkhide which is a listed structure.

Towpath Undergoing restoration. Some short sections are open other parts are in private ownership. Contact the Trust for details.

Tunnels Oxenhall, 2192yds (2004m); Aylestone, 440yds (402m); Ashperton (also called Walsopthorne), 400yds (366m).

Aqueducts Lugg Aqueduct near Hereford was demolished in the 1920s as it caused flooding in the Lugg Valley.

Branches Oxenhall Branch, about 1 mile to two collieries, disused by 1800.

Connections River Severn at Over then via Maisemore Lock to the Upper Parting and Gloucester.

Restoration The Herefordshire and Gloucestershire Canal Trust is working towards a complete restoration of the canal. The five district and two county authorities are supportive of the project in principle, and have undertaken to protect the historic route from development. From the A4103 to Monkhide the canal is in water. Current work centres on the section from the south end of the Oxenhall Tunnel towards Newent and at Yarkhill near Hereford.

Distance table

Gloucester (Over) to:	Miles
Newent	8.5
Oxenhall Coal Branch	9.3
Oxenhall Tunnel, north end	11.0
Dymock	12.5
Ledbury	17.0
Ashperton Tunnel	22.0
Monkhide	25.0
Yarkhill	26.0
River Lugg crossing	31.0
Aylestone Hill Tunnel	33.0
Hereford Basin	34.0

Huddersfield Broad Canal

This waterway was constructed under an Act passed in 1774. It is often known as Sir John Ramsden's Canal, after its promoter. It linked the Huddersfield Narrow Canal to the Calder and Hebble Navigation and, when the project to restore the Huddersfield Narrow is completed, this will offer another trans-Pennine link. Commercial traffic on the canal ceased in 1953 but the canal has been used by cruisers and its cruising potential is being explored. Unlike the adjoining Calder and Hebble Navigation, standard British Waterway windlasses can be used. Aspley Basin at the head of the canal at Huddersfield is now a very useful mooring close to the town centre.

Authority British Waterways, Lock Lane, Castleford, West Yorkshire WF10 2LH ☎ 01977 554351.

Bridges Numerous. The special handcuff key for the Turnbridge Locomotive Lift Bridge can be obtained at Red Doles Lock ☎ 01484 536732.

Towpath Throughout navigation.

Speed limit 3.5mph.

Connections Calder and Hebble Navigation at Cooper Bridge; Huddersfield Narrow Canal at Aspley Basin, Huddersfield.

HUDDERSFIELD BROAD CANAL *Maximum Vessel Dimensions*

From and to	Distance	Length	Beam	Draught	Headroom	Locks
Cooper Bridge on the Calder and Hebble to Aspley Basin, Huddersfield	3.3 miles (5.3km)	57' 6" (17.5m)	14' 2" (4.3m)	3' 6" (1.1m)	9' 4" (2.8m)	9

Facilities All services are available in Huddersfield. Restaurants, pubs and shops and the Aspley Wharf Marina offers moorings, water and a slipway but no pump-out or refuse disposal facilities.

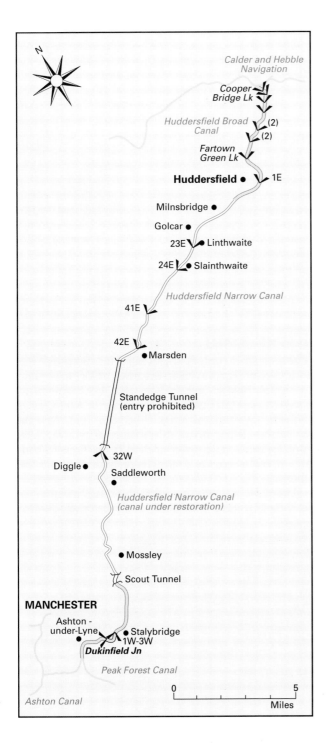

Distance table

Cooper Bridge, Lock No 1 to:	Miles
Lock No 2 Colne Bridge	0.2
Bradley	0.5
Lock No 3 Ladgrave	0.8
Lock No 4 Longlands	1.1
Deighton	1.3
Lock No 5 Turnpike Road	1.6
Lock No 6 Reading	1.8
Lock No 7 Fieldhouse Green	1.9
Lock No 8 Falls	2.1
Fartown Green Lock No 9 (Red Doles)	2.3
Turnbridge Lifting Bridge	3.0
Aspley Basin, Huddersfield	3.3

Huddersfield Narrow Canal

The promoters of the Ashton Canal were to a large extent instrumental in the proposals for the Huddersfield Narrow Canal with their desire for a through route to the waterways of East Yorkshire. In 1794 Acts were passed for both the Huddersfield Narrow Canal and the Rochdale Canal as alternative trans-Pennine routes to the Leeds and Liverpool which had been open in parts since 1773.

Despite the relatively short distance of the canal, just under 20 miles, it was not fully open until 1811, seven years after the Rochdale. It had the longest tunnel in Britain at its summit level of 656ft and with 74 narrow locks and a second tunnel at Scout the canal had numerous engineering problems to overcome and, inevitably, money was short. A transhipment centre was built in Huddersfield as the locks on the Broad Canal, Sir John Ramsden's Canal, were shorter than the standard 70ft, although later shorter narrow boats were built to accommodate this change.

The canal was never highly successful commercially and it was bought by the Huddersfield and Manchester Railway Company in 1845. Gradually less cargo was taken over the summit level, and by the early 20th century there was very little traffic at all. The canal was abandoned in 1944 but fortunately was retained as a water supply channel. In 1948, a group of early IWA activists, including Robert Aickman, took a boat along the abandoned canal and through the 3 miles and 418yds of the Standedge Tunnel. This was to be the last boat to pass through the tunnel.

Since the formation of the Huddersfield Canal Society (☎ 0161 339 1332) in 1974, restoration has been active. Over 15 miles of canal are now navigable in sections varying from 7 miles to ¼ mile. The society runs a trip boat and trailed boats can,

HUDDERSFIELD NARROW CANAL *Maximum vessel dimensions*

From and to	Distance	Length	Beam	Draught	Headroom	Locks
Huddersfield to Ashton-under-Lyne	19.9 miles (32.0km)	70' (21.3m)	7' (2.1m)	3' 6" 1.0m)	7' (2.1m)	74

and hopefully will, use these lengths. Some parts of the canal were sold off and have since been filled in with locks being cascaded. Slaithwaite is one such area but the route of the canal can still be seen and many sections are walkable. Although it cannot be called a pretty canal, much of the countryside it passes through is wild and dramatic and it is very accessible. The Manchester to Huddersfield railway line still runs alongside, and through its own Standedge Tunnel, with plenty of stops so for walking short sections transport is not a problem.

One characteristic of the Huddersfield Narrow Canal is that the locks are numbered from the lowest level to the summit with an E on the east side and a W on the west. From Huddersfield to the summit, they are 1E to 42E and from the summit down to Ashton they are 32W to 1W. The numbering may change slightly once the canal is fully restored as the route may have to be diverted in places.

Authority British Waterways, Top Lock, Church Lane, Marple, Cheshire SK6 6BN ☎ 0161 427 1079.

Bridges Numerous. Some have been culverted.

Towpath Throughout navigation except the Standedge Tunnel, a blockage in Huddersfield and one at Stalybridge.

Tunnels Standedge, 5698yds, no towpath, the longest tunnel in Britain, closed at present (this tunnel also ventilates the adjoining railway tunnel); Scout, 220yds, towpath.

Connections Huddersfield Broad Canal in Huddersfield; Ashton Canal at Ashton-under-Lyne.

Restoration A major restoration programme is underway with support from local authorities. Millennium funding has been secured and the restored canal should be re-opened by the year 2000. A committee has been set up to co-ordinate development work along the canal corridor with the aim of promoting the canal and increasing the number of jobs associated with businesses along the route. A study and report by the Civic Trust recognises the historical legacy and future potential of the canal.

Facilities There are slipways for trailed boats at Huddersfield Polytechnic, Oldham and Slaithwaite. Along the route there are plenty of pubs with shops in the towns.

Distance table *Miles*

Huddersfield, junction with Huddersfield Broad Canal to:

Milnsbridge	2.6
Golcar	3.3
Linthwaite	3.9
Slaithwaite	5.0

	Miles
Head of Lock No 42E, Marsden and northeast end of summit level	7.3
Marsden Railway Station	7.8
Northeast end of Standedge Tunnel	8.3
Southwest end of Standedge Tunnel and Diggle Railway Station	11.4
Head of Lock No 32W, Diggle, and southwest end of summit level	11.5
Saddleworth	13.8
Upper Mill	14.0
Greenfield	14.9
Mossley	16.0
Scout Mill	16.6
Millbrook	17.4
Stalybridge	18.8
Ashton-under Lyne, junction with Ashton Canal	19.9

Navigable sections For the latest information contact the Huddersfield Canal Society ☎ 0161 339 1332.

	Locks
Junction with Ashton Canal to	
Staley Wharf	1W-3W
Stalybridge to Diggle (W end of Standedge Tunnel)	8W-32W
Marsden (E end of Standedge Tunnel) to Slaithwaite	42E-24E
Slaithwaite to Longroyd Bridge	20E-4E
Huddersfield	1E

River Hull

The northern part of the River Hull becomes the Driffield Navigation up to the town of Driffield. The 20 miles below Struncheon Hill Lock down to Kingston-upon-Hull is tidal, but worth exploring if you are cruising the area. The new Hull Marina development has made this a more attractive place to venture to. The lower section is the Port of Hull and there is always plenty of activity around the docks.

There are no recommended moorings in the river in Kingston-upon-Hull itself and visitors should use

RIVER HULL Maximum vessel dimensions

From and to	Distance	Length	Beam	Draught	Headroom	Locks
Struncheon Hill Lock to Grove Hill	9 miles (14.5km)	Unlimited	Unlimited	5' (1.5m)	9' (2.7m)	None
Grove Hill to Hull	11 miles (17.7km)	Unlimited	Unlimited	6' (1.8m)	9' (2.7m)	None
Arram Beck	0.3 miles (0.4km)	Unlimited	Unlimited	3' (0.9m)		None

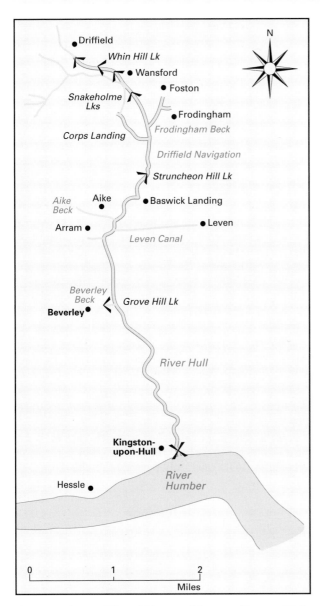

Aike to the city boundary a free navigation.

City boundary to the River Humber Kingston-upon-Hull City Council, Guildhall, Alfred Gelder Street, Hull HU1 2AA ☎ 01482 610610.

For local advice contact Harbourmaster, Associated British Ports, Harbourmaster's Office, PO Box 1, Port House, Northern Gateway, Hull, HU9 5PQ ☎ 01482 327171.

Towpath Throughout navigation, except from mouth of river to Hull Bridge.

Bridges Most of the lifting bridges are manned but Sutton Road Bridge and the new Ennerdale Road Bridge are unmanned and 3 days notice to the Harbourmaster is necessary.

Connections Driffield Navigation, the Leven Canal (no longer navigable and used for fishing only), and Beverley Beck.

Navigation High water at Struncheon Hill 3 hours after HW Hull. The tide flows very strongly at the river mouth and for a considerable distance upstream.

Facilities All services are available in Hull.

Distance table	Miles
Tail of Struncheon Hill Lock and junction with Driffield Navigation to:	
Tophill Low Landing	1.3
Baswick Landing	1.5
Aike, junction with River Hull Navigation	4.0
Junction with Leven Canal (not accessible)	4.5
Junction with Arram Beck	5.6
Tickton, Hull Bridge	7.3
Grove Hill, junction with Beverley Beck	9.0
Wawne Ferry	11.8
Stoneferry	17.5
Hull City Boundary	19.1
Hull, junction with Drypool Basin, leading to Victoria Dock	19.5
Hull, junction with River Humber	20.0

the marina. The Ripon Motor Boat Club publication *Cruising Guide to the North East Waterways* is strongly recommended to anyone visiting this area.

Authority *Struncheon Hill Lock to Aike* Driffield Navigation Ltd, 70 Middle Street South, Driffield, East Yorkshire YO25 7QF ☎ 01377 257488.

River Humber

The River Humber is not an inland waterway but its position linking other inland navigations makes it an important entry in this book. With a thorough knowledge of your craft, your navigation and seamanship skills and a due regard to tide and weather, passage through the Humber should be

RIVER HUMBER Maximum vessel dimensions

From and to	Distance	Length	Beam	Draught	Headroom	Locks
Humber entrance to Trent Falls	36.5 miles (58.7km)	Unlimited	Unlimited	Tidal	Unlimited	None

uneventful. The Harbourmaster's Office at Hull is always willing to offer advice and should be contacted at the planning stage.

The shifting sands in the estuary can make charts out of date by the time the ink is dry so it is important to receive the most recent Notice to Mariners and make any necessary corrections. Pilotage is not a requirement for vessels under 60 metres but contacting Vessel Traffic Services on VHF Ch 12 will alert them to your presence on the river and they can update you on big ship movements.

Always remember that ships of thousands of tons weight cannot stop or manoeuvre in small spaces or at short notice and their range of visibility is distant not close quarters. The Harbourmaster's office produces a *Small Boat Users Guide to the Humber* which is packed with useful information.

Authority Associated British Ports, Harbourmaster's Office, PO Box 1, Port House, Northern Gateway, Hull HU9 5PQ ☎ 01482 327171.

Towpath None.

Connections Rivers Ouse, Trent and Hull are connected with each other by this tidal waterway as well as the River Ancholme and Market Weighton Canal.

Navigation The Associated British Ports publish the Rules and Humber Bye-laws. They also publish annual copies of a chart showing the latest soundings in the Humber between Barton Haven and Spurn Head, and the Upper Reaches; these are regularly updated. Vessel Traffic Services (VTS) broadcast two-hourly traffic and weather reports on VHF Ch 12. It is recommended that all boats keep a listening watch on VHF Ch 12 and report their planned movements to VTS ☎ 01482 212191.

High water at Hull is about 5 hours before HW Dover; HW Ferriby Sluice 18 minutes and HW Trent Falls 30 minutes after HW Hull. Tidal range, spring tides 22ft 4ins, neap tides 15ft 3ins.

Charts Admiralty 109, Imray C25.

Distance table

Left Bank		Right Bank
Miles		*Miles*
Trent Falls junction with River Ouse and River Trent to:		
1.5	Junction with Market Weighton Canal	
2.5	Broomfleet	
	Whitton	2.8
5.5	Brough	
	Winteringham Haven	5.5
	Ferriby Sluice, junction with	
	River Ancholme Drainage and Navigation	8.5
	South Ferriby	9.3
9.0	North Ferriby	
	Chalderness	11.0
	Barton-upon-Humber	12.3
12.0	Hessle	
	New Holland	15.5
17.0	Hull, junction with River Hull	

River Idle

The River Idle runs between deep banks and, although Bawtry is an attractive town, there is little to encourage the cruising boater to visit this waterway. Owing to its use for drainage purposes and the problems of tides from the Trent, access has to be carefully planned and the Environment Agency requires at least 48-hours notice as well as a substantial fee from boats wishing to navigate the waterway.

Authority Environment Agency, Upper Trent Area, Sentinel House, Wellington Crescent, Fradley Park, Lichfield WS13 8RR ☎ 01543 444141 *Fax* 01543 444161.

Towpath The original path is unusable in most places.

Locks There is no lock but a sluice-gate at West Stockwith (sluice-keeper raises gate) which is raised vertically. Boats may only pass on the ebb.

RIVER IDLE Maximum vessel dimensions							
From and to	*Distance*	*Length*		*Beam*	*Draught*	*Headroom*	*Locks*
Bawtry Bridge to Stockwith, River Trent	10.9 miles (17.5km)	Unlimited		18' (5.4m)	2' 6" (0.7m)	9' (2.7m)	None

Connections The River Trent at Stockwith.

Navigation The Rivers Idle and Trent must be at equilibrium for access to be allowed and the pumps at West Stockwith must not be working. High water at West Stockwith is between 2 and 2½ hours after HW Hull. Good directions are available in the *Cruising Guide to the North East Waterways* by the Ripon Motor Boat Club.

Distance table

Bawtry to:	Miles
Newington	2.0
Misson	3.9
Idle Stop	6.9
Misterton Road Bridge	9.0
Misterton Soss	10.0
Stockwith, junction with River Trent	11.0

Ipswich and Stowmarket Navigation

The River Gipping was navigable to Stowmarket in the Middle Ages but few improvements were undertaken until commissioners were appointed under an Act in 1790. After numerous objections from Ipswich Corporation, which feared a loss of business, improvements to the River Gipping went ahead allowing Stowmarket to export woollen products and hops through Ipswich and greatly encouraged the growth of the town. The Navigation Company leased the navigation to the Ipswich and Bury St Edmunds Railway in 1846 and, although it returned to the authority of the company in 1888 when the lease expired, trade never built up again. By 1930, traffic had all but ceased on the waterway and the river was transferred to the East Suffolk Rivers Catchment Board in 1932.

Much of the course of the navigation is still in water and many of the lock chambers are in reasonable repair. As part of its flood control responsibilities the NRA reconstructed several locks

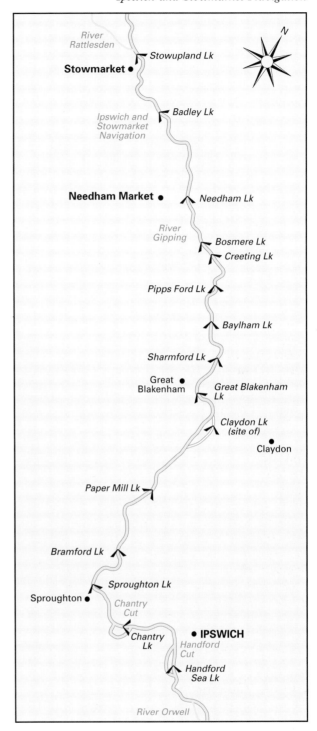

which would now only need gates to make them useable. This is a most attractive waterway with several typical weather-boarded mills along the way and the Museum of East Anglian Life in Stowmarket.

IPSWICH AND STOWMARKET NAVIGATION Maximum Vessel Dimensions

From and to	Distance	Length	Beam	Draught	Headroom	Locks
Stowmarket to Ipswich	15.9 miles (25.5km)	55' (16.7m)	14' (4.2m)	3' (0.9m)	7' (2.1m)	15

Authority Environment Agency, Eastern Area, Cobham Road, Ipswich IP3 9JE ☎ 01473 727712 *Fax* 01473 724205.

Bridges Numerous, several of which have been lowered and obstruct navigation.

Towpath Now a right of way and a delightful walk.

Restoration The Ipswich Branch of the IWA has been the driving force behind the restoration of this navigation. The branch, with the help of WRG, have completed the restoration of Bosmere Lock. There are proposals to run a trip boat from the lock to Needham Market.

Distance table

Stowmarket, Stowupland Bridge, to:

	Miles
Stowupland Lock No 1	0.8
Badley Lock No 2	2.3
Needham Market and Needham Lock No 3	3.9
Barking Lock No 4	4.6
Bosmere Lock No 5	5.4
Pipps Ford Lock No 6	5.8
Baylham and Baylham Lock No 7	6.5
Chamford Lock No 8	7.4
Great Blakenham and Blakenham Lock No 9	8.1
Claydon and Claydon Lock No 10	8.9
Paper Mill Lock No 11	10.4
Bramford and Bramford Lock No 12	11.6
Sproughton and Sproughton Lock No 13	12.8
Chantry Lock No 14	13.8
Ipswich, Tide Lock No 15	15.1
Ipswich, Stoke Bridge	15.9

Kennet and Avon Canal and Navigation

Despite the fact that the Kennet and Avon Canal was one of the first waterways to be identified by the newly formed IWA as being at risk, they were unable to prevent its closure to through navigation in 1951 and it took nearly 40 years of hard work and campaigning to re-open it. The re-opening ceremony was performed by the Queen on 8 August 1990. Originally enabled by an Act in 1794, the canal was opened in 1810 allowing London and Bristol to be connected by water via the Thames, the River Kennet, the Kennet and Avon Canal and finally the River Avon.

Navigation works on the Rivers Kennet and Avon were carried out between 1718 and 1727, much earlier than the construction of the artificial waterway to join them. The improvements on both these rivers were major engineering achievements. The engineer in both cases was John Hore. From Reading to Newbury, 20 locks had to be built to raise the navigation 138ft and many of these locks were turf sided. The Avon was a fast-flowing river in a steep gorge which had to be tamed to allow the passage of cargo vessels from Bristol up to Bath.

John Rennie was the engineer for the canal from Newbury to Bath and he designed a broad canal which sweeps through rolling, fertile countryside. The summit pound is only 2 miles long and passes through the Bruce Tunnel at Savernake, which was a modification proposed by William Jessop. The aqueduct at Dundas is a marvellous example of John Rennies' architecture as the canal crosses the River Avon. Coming into Bath, the canal passes through Sydney Gardens and under Cleveland House, the original headquarters of the canal company.

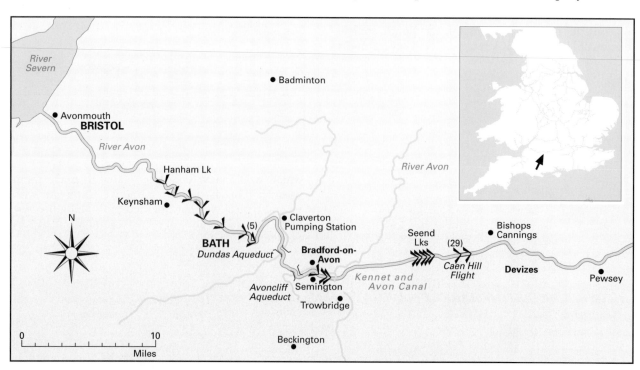

Climbing to over 450ft (137m) above sea level, water supply was always a problem and there are two pumping stations, Crofton, near Great Bedwyn, and Claverton on the outskirts of Bath. Crofton Pumping Station houses one of the oldest working beam engines in the country. The 29 locks near Devizes is the second longest flight in the country and raises the canal by 237ft. The central 16 locks of the Caen Hill Flight have side ponds and are a popular place to picnic and watch others hard at work. In 1996, a back-pumping system was installed to improve the water supply situation and to increase the number of boats which could lock through the flight. This project was jointly funded by the Kennet and Avon Canal Trust, BW and the five local authorities involved in the canal.

The Kennet and Avon is still classed as a remainder waterway which prevents BW from spending money on improvements, but they have ensured that they fully support the work carried out by the trust and the local authorities. Funding has now been secured to carry out the improvements required to bring the canal up to 'cruiseway' standard.

To mark the re-opening of the canal in 1990, GEOprojects published a map which has lots of information for walkers, boat users and cyclists.

Authority British Waterways, The Locks, Bath Road, Devizes, Wiltshire SN10 1EB ☎ 01380 722859.

Bridges Numerous. Some are swing bridges. Aldermaston is an electrically operated lift bridge.

Towpath Throughout navigation, except Savernake Tunnel. Cycling is allowed on the towpath but a permit is required. Information is available from BW in Devizes or the K & A Trust.

Tunnels Savernake, 502yds (459m), no towpath; two short tunnels in Bath.

Aqueducts Rennie's beautiful Dundas Aqueduct near Bathampton built in Bath stone and named after the first chairman of the Kennet and Avon Canal Company; Avoncliff Aqueduct.

Speed limit 4mph.

Restoration To re-establish the Kennet and Avon to cruiseway status considerable work still needs to be done. Problems of leakage occur along the Avon valley section and repair work needs to be carried out on the aqueducts. The Kennet and Avon Trust with BW and local authorities have secured funding through the Heritage Lottery Fund.

Navigation Passage through the Caen Hill Flight is now available seven days a week with two lockings a day, 0900 and 1300, but passage must be booked in advance. At Newbury Parkway, the temporary bridge is the lowest on the canal and at certain water levels clearance can be as little as 6ft 6ins (2.0m); it has been temporary since the Second World War. From Reading to Newbury, parts of the navigation are the River Kennet and the effects of flood water on helmsmanship should not be underestimated, in particular when passing weirs. Similarly, from the junction with the River Avon at Bath, extra care needs to be taken.

KENNET AND AVON CANAL Maximum vessel dimensions

From and to	Distance	Length	Beam	Draught	Headroom	Locks
Reading to Newbury	18 miles (28.9km)	75' (22.8m)	14' (4.2m)	3' (0.9m)	7' 9" (2.3m)	20
Newbury to Bath	57.3 miles (92.2km)	72' (21.9m)	7' (2.1m)	3' (0.9m)	7' (2.1m)	80
or		70' (21.3m)	12' 6" (3.8m)	3' (0.9m)	7' (2.1m)	
River Avon at Bath to						
Hanham Lock	11.2 miles (18.0km)	75' (22.9m)	16' (4.9m)	3' (0.9m)	8' 9" (2.7m)	6

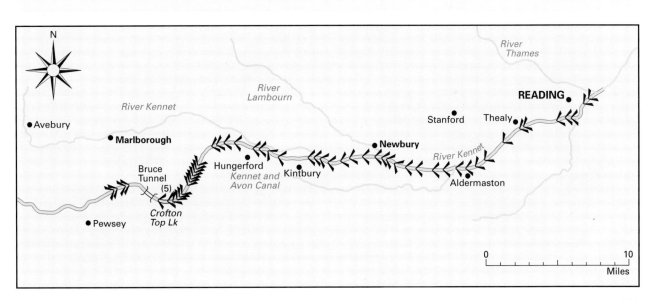

Facilities There are many boatyards, pubs, restaurants and towns and villages along the canal with shops to cater for the needs of the cruising boat. Pump-out facilities are available at Reading, Aldermaston, Newbury, Little Bedwyn (by arrangement), Honey Street, Devizes, Trowbridge, Bradford-on-Avon, Monkton Coombe (by arrangement), Bath and Keynsham. Many of these yards also offer slipway facilities.

Distance table

High Bridge, Reading, River Kennet Section to:

	Miles
County Lock No 106	0.5
Fobney Lock No 105	1.5
Southcote Lock No 104	2.5
Burghfield Bridge	3.6
Burghfield Lock No 103	4.0
M4	5.0
Garston Lock No 102	5.3
Shenfield Lock No 101	6.0
Sulhamstead Lock No 100	6.6
Tile Mill Lock No 99	8.0
Towney Lock No 97	8.4
Padworth Lock No 96	10.0
BW Visitor Centre	10.2
Aldermaston Lock No 95	10.3
Woolhampton Mill and Lock No 94	12.0
Heals Lock No 93	13.3
Midgham Lock No 92	13.8
Colthrop Lock No 91	14.5
Monkey Marsh Lock No 90	15.0
Widmead Lock No 89	16.0
Bulls Lock No 88	16.3
Ham Lock No 87	17.0
Greenham Lock No 86	18.0
Newbury Wharf, start of Kennet and Avon Canal section	
Parkway 'Temporary' Bridge	18.3
Newbury Lock No 85	18.5
Guyers Lock No 84	19.5
Higg's Lock No 83	20.0
Benham Lock No 82	20.6

	Miles
Hamstead Lock No 81	22.0
Copse Lock No 80	22.4
Dreweat's Lock No 79	22.8
Kintbury Lock No 78	24.5
Brunsden Lock No 77	26.1
Wire Lock No 76	26.9
Dunn Mill Lock No 75	27.0
Hungerford Lock No 74	27.5
Hungerford Marsh Lock No 73	28.1
Cobbler's Lock No 72	28.5
Picketfield Lock No 71	29.5
Froxfield Bottom Lock No 70	30.0
Froxfield Middle Lock No 69	30.2
Oakhill Down Lock No 68	30.4
Little Bedwyn Lock No 67	31.3
Potter's Lock No 66	31.6
Burnt Mill Lock No 65	32.1
Bedwyn Church Lock No 64	32.8
Crofton Bottom Lock No 63	33.6
Crofton Pumping Station	34.3
Crofton Top Lock No 55	35.1
Bruce Tunnel, east end	36.0
Burbage Wharf	37.0
Cadley Lock No 54	37.1
Wootton Rivers Bottom Lock No 51	38.0
New Mill Bridge	39.5
Pewsey Wharf	41.5
Wilcot	43.0
Honey Street Wharf	45.5
Horton Bridge	49.5
Kennet and Avon Canal Trust, Devizes	53.3
Devizes Top Lock No 50, Kennet Lock	53.5
Caen Hill Top Lock No 44	54.2
Caen Hill Bottom Lock No 29	54.8
Devizes Bottom Lock No 22	55.5
Seend Top Lock No 21	57.9
Seend Bottom Lock No 17	58.5
Barratt's Lock No 16	60.4
Buckley's Lock No 15, junction with Wilts and Berks Canal	60.5

Boats passing on the Kennet and Avon Canal on a chilly spring day. *Richard Sandland*

Elegant Cleveland House, in Sydney Gardens, Bath, was the headquarters of the Kennet and Avon Canal Company.
Roy Westlake

	Miles
Hilperton Wharf	63.0
Bradford-on-Avon Lock No 14	65.6
Avoncliff Aqueduct	67.4
Limpley Stoke	69.0
Dundas Aqueduct	70.0
Junction with Somerset Coal Canal	70.2
Claverton Pumping Station	71.3
Bathampton Village	73.0
Sydney Gardens Tunnel	74.2
Sydney Wharf Bridge	74.5
Bath, Top Lock No 13	74.6
Bath Deep Lock Nos 8 & 9	75.1
Widcombe Lock No 7, junction with River Avon	75.3
Bath, River Avon section	75.5
Weston Lock No 6	77.8
Railway Bridge	78.3
Railway Bridge	79.5
Kelston Lock No 5	80.8
Saltford Lock No 4	81.5
Swinford Lock No 3	82.3
Port Avon Marina	84.4
Keynsham Lock No 2	84.5
Tail of Hanham Lock No 1, Port of Bristol	86.5

Kyme Eau-Sleaford Canal

The development of the River Slea and the Kyme Eau into the Sleaford Navigation offered an outlet at Boston for traders in Sleaford. The promotion of the navigation included Boston Corporation among the subscribers as it was felt that more trade would come to the port of Boston. There were seven locks in the 12 miles from the River Witham to Sleaford.

During the early part of the 19th century, traffic was active and the venture was profitable. Discussions were started to extend the navigation westward to connect up with the Grantham Canal and so the main inland waterway network, but nothing came of it. By the 1870s, receipts from tolls were falling and in 1881 the navigation was closed.

The waterway remained as a drainage channel and much of it remained navigable for another 50 years. Lower Kyme Lock was replaced by a sluice but, in 1986, this was removed and a lock reinstated. There is an active navigation society and Cobblers Lock has recently been re-opened offering 8 miles of navigable waterway.

The water mill at Cogglesford Lock has been restored by the District Council which is supportive of the restoration of the waterway. The local branch of the IWA and the Sleaford Navigation Society are investigating sources of water, as lack of water and weed growth restrict navigation in the summer. The Society can be contacted through Mr M Chapman, 8 Kirkby Close, Southwell, Nottinghamshire NG25 0DG.

Authority Environment Agency, Harvey Street, Lincoln LN1 1TF ☎ 01522 513100 *Fax* 01522 512927.

Bridges Seven.

Locks Two locks are currently in working order.

Towpath The towpath is not continuous as sections are privately owned. Access is good in places.

KYME EAU-SLEAFORD CANAL *Maximum vessel dimensions*

From and to	Distance	Length	Beam	Draught	Headroom	Locks
Sleaford to Chapel· Hill, River Witham	12.3 miles (19.8km)	70' (21.3m)	14' (4.2m)	3' (0.9m)	6' (1.8m)	7

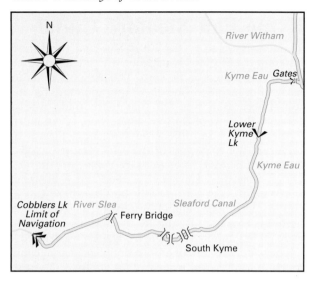

Distance table	Miles
Sleaford (Carre Street Wharf) to:	
Cogglesford Lock and Mill	0.6
Dyers Mill or Bone Mill Lock	1.5
Corn Mill Lock[1]	2.4
Paper Mill Lock	2.6
Haverholme Lock[1] (Haverholme Priory)	3.5
Cobblers Lock (limit of navigation)	4.7
Ewerby Waithe Common	5.8
Halfpenny Hatch	6.4
South Kyme	8.2
Lower Kyme Lock	10.6
Chapel Hill, junction with River Witham	12.3

1. Corn Mill Lock and Haverholme Lock are on private property and permission is needed to visit them.

Lake District

The Lake District has attracted visitors since the early part of the 19th century when taking a tour first became popular. Some of the more famous tourists included the poets Wordsworth and Coleridge whose visits to the area are well documented. Since its creation 100 years ago, the National Trust has been active in the Lake Distict and owns about 25 per cent of the area covered by the National Park. Since 1951, the Lake District National Park Authority has been responsible for the administration of the 885 square miles which we generally refer to as 'the Lakes'. Together, the National Park Authority and the National Trust work to retain the charm and peace of the Lakes, despite the huge number of visitors who now visit every year.

Throughout the area, there are many small tarns and waters in addition to the larger and better known lakes. Many of these are controlled by the National Trust which produces a leaflet outlining where boating and fishing are permitted and who to contact for licences or permits.

For information on launching facilities and permits for boats contact the Lake District National Park Authority which will tell you who to contact if the particular water you are interested in does not come within their jurisdiction. They produce a series of leaflets on the larger lakes and also the bye-laws covering Lake Windermere, which are essential reading for anyone intending to use a boat on the lake.

Authorities Lake District National Park, Murley Moss, Oxenholme Road, Kendal, Cumbria LA9 7RL ☎ 01539 724555 *Fax* 01539 740822.

The National Trust, North West Region, The Hollens, Grasmere, Ambleside, Cumbria LA22 9QZ ☎ 01539 435599.

South Lakeland District Council, Lake Administration Office, Ferry Nab, Bowness-on-Windermere, Cumbria LA23 3JH ☎ 01539 442753.

Principal Lakes

Buttermere (0.9km²)
Owned by the National Trust. A permit is required for canoes, dinghies, windsurfers and rowing boats. No powered craft. For more information contact the National Trust.

Crummock Water (2.6km²)
Owned by the National Trust. A permit is required for canoes, dinghies, windsurfers and rowing boats. No powered craft. No launching facilities.

Thirlmere (3.3km²)
Owned by North West Water. Canoes, dinghies, windsurfers and rowing boats. No powered craft.

Ullswater (8.8km²)
Public Right of Navigation. Blanket 10mph speed limit.

Derwentwater (5.3km²)
Public Right of Navigation. Blanket 10mph speed limit.

Coniston Water (4.7km²)
Public Right of Navigation. Blanket 10mph speed limit.

Bassenthwaite (5.1km²)
Owned by the National Park Authority. Permit required for canoes, windsurfers, fishing and sailing. No powered craft. For more information contact the National Park Authority.

The Grand Union Canal at Stoke Bruerne.
Lester McCarthy -Motor Boat and Yachting

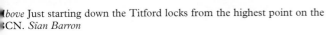

Above Just starting down the Titford locks from the highest point on the BCN. *Sían Barron*

Below The lifting bridge at Talybont-on-Usk on the Monmouthshire and Brecon Canal. *Roy Westlake*

Roses and Castles and the traditional geometric designs which have decorated narrow boats for generations are continued today by many skilled painters. *Jane Cumberlidge*

Wastwater (2.9km²)
Owned by the National Trust. Permit required for rowing boats and canoes only. No powered or sailing craft. For more information contact the National Trust.

Haweswater (3.9km²)
Owned by North West Water as a reservoir. Fishing and sub-aqua permitted but no boating allowed.

Windermere (14.7km²)
Owned by South Lakeland District Council. Public Right of Navigation. All motorised craft must be registered, contact the National Park Authority.

Regulations The lake is controlled by Lake Windermere Collision Rules and National Park Authority Bye-laws. A copy of the regulations is sent on registration. There are lake wardens (South Lakeland District Council), lake rangers (National Park Authority) and police patrols. All their boats are equipped with two-way radio. Lake wardens are based at Ferry Nab ☎ 01539 442753.

Facilities There is a public slip for launching craft over 5hp at Ferry Nab, Bowness. For craft less than 5hp, there are slips at Waterhead and Fell Foot. South Lakeland District Council are responsible for all moorings on the lake and there are a number of public jetties.

Lancaster Canal

The section of the canal which is open today was the first section to be completed in 1797. The 42½ miles are the longest level pound in Britain, crossing the River Lune on Rennies' wonderful stone aqueduct. Unfortunately, plans to cross the River Ribble to join up with the south end to provide a connection with the Leeds and Liverpool Canal did not go smoothly. As a temporary measure, a double tramway was built crossing the Ribble on a trestle bridge to join the two parts and, partly due to problems with finance, this was never replaced with a permanent structure, so the Lancaster Canal has always remained unconnected with the main canal network.

In 1825, the Glasson Dock Branch was completed to give the canal an outlet to the sea via the Lune Estuary. This branch had six locks. The other locks

on the canal are in a ½-mile stretch at Tewitfield, before the final 15-mile level pound which takes the canal into Cumbria and its terminus at Kendal. The Lancaster Canal Company soon saw the potential of passenger traffic and, in 1820, started a daily service between Kendal and Preston, halving the time taken by the stagecoach, to do the journey in 7 hours. The comfort of the boat trip meant that passengers were not lost to the trains when competition started in 1840 and this continued for some time.

This is a delightful and underused canal, winding its way gently between the flat Fylde and the rising hills of the Forest of Bowland with wonderful views across Morecambe Bay towards the Lake District. Preston and Lancaster each have attractions with museums, theatres and restaurants. In Lancaster Maritime Museum you can look at the 1880 plans of the canal which cover 37 sheets.

The opportunity of funding by the Millennium Commission to construct the Ribble Link means the canal is likely to be connected to the rest of the national network in 2000, over 200 years after work first started on the canal. Prospects for restoration of the northern section to Kendal are longer term, with the major obstacle being the M6 which crosses the canal just below the Tewitfield Locks. A full restoration of this canal, with the construction of the Ribble Link, would open up a beautiful cruising area and is to be greatly encouraged.

Authority British Waterways, Main Road, Galgate, Lancaster LA2 0LQ ☎ 01524 751888 *Fax* 01524 75113.

Bridges Numerous. There are some swing bridges.

Towpath Throughout navigation, with a circular walk taking in the Lune Estuary down to Glasson Basin. The northern section of the canal is also good for walking.

Tunnels None in use. Hincaster Tunnel, 377yds long, is on the isolated and closed northern section.

Connections None to the main canal network. River Lune via the Glasson Dock Branch.

Restoration Work continues on the northern section of the canal but a connection across the M6 is the major obstacle. A proposal for a link with the River Ribble has been in the Lancashire Structure Plan for some years and funding by the Millennium Commission has now been agreed. The link will run from the Lancaster Canal to the Ribble Estuary, mostly along the course of the Savick Brook. The link will enable boats from the national canal network to reach the Lancaster Canal via the Tarleton Branch of the Leeds and Liverpool and then the rivers Douglas and Ribble.

Facilities There are several boatyards and mooring sites along the canal with plenty of pubs, restaurants and shops. All services are available in Lancaster and Preston.

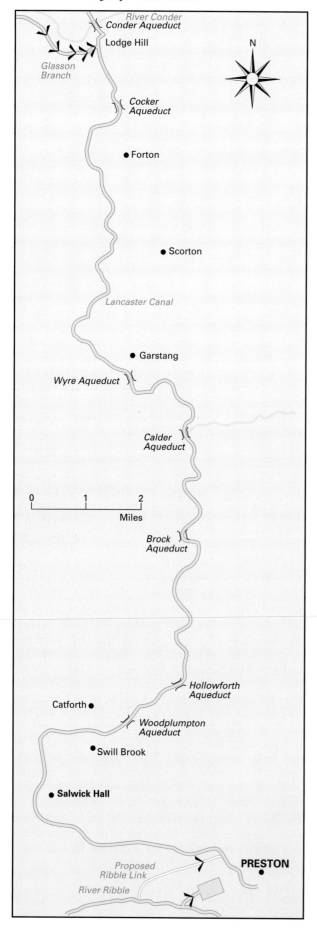

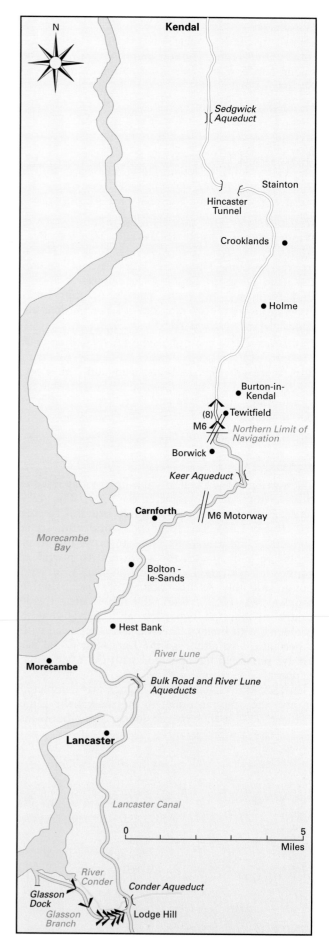

LANCASTER CANAL *Maximum vessel dimensions*

From and to	Distance	Length	Beam	Draught	Headroom	Locks
Preston to Tewitfield	42.5 miles (68.4km)	72' (21.9m)	14' 6" (4.4m)	3' 9" (1.1m)	8' (2.4m)	None
Branch to Glasson	2.9 miles (4.4km)	72' (21.9m)	14' 6" (4.4m)	3' 9" (1.1m)	8' (2.4m)	6
Tewitfield to Kendal	15.5 miles (25.0km)	72' (21.9m)	14' 6" (4.4m)	3' 9" (1.1m)	8' (2.4m)	8

Distance table

Preston (near Old Ashton Basin) to: *Miles*

Bridge 12	0.5
Savick Aqueduct	0.9
Cottam Mill House Bridge	1.5
Salwick Hall Bridge	4.4
Salwick Hall	4.6
Kirkham Bridge	5.0
Swill Brook Basin	7.5
Woodplumpton Aqueduct	7.8
Moons Bridge and Marina	8.8
Hollowforth Aqueduct	9.2
Roebuck Bridge	11.5
Myerscough Hall Bridge	11.8
Brock Aqueduct	12.4
Preston-Lancaster Road Bridge (A6)	12.6
Calder Aqueduct	14.5
Wyre Aqueduct	16.5
Garstang	16.9
Richmond Bridge and Basin	22.8
Cocker Aqueduct	23.3
Lodge Hill, junction with Glasson Dock Branch	24.1
Galgate Basin Wharf	24.3
Conder Aqueduct	24.8
Scotforth Bridge	26.4
British Waterways Depot	29.2
Lancaster Basin	29.5
River Lune Aqueduct	31.9
Hest Bank	34.5
Bolton-le-Sands	35.8
Carnforth	38.3
M6	38.9
Keer Aqueduct	40.5
Disused Quarry Branch	41.0
Borwick Hall Bridge	41.5
Tewitfield, Old Turnpike Bridge	42.0
Tewitfield (bottom of closed locks)	42.3

The canal continues for another 14½ miles to Kendal but is at present not navigable except by small boats which can be carried round obstructions. The Lancaster Canal Trust have a trip boat on part of this section.

Glasson Dock Branch

Lodge Hill, junction with Main Line to:

Lock No 1	0.1
Lock No 2	0.4
Lock No 3	0.5
Lock No 4	1.0
Lock No 5	1.5
Lock No 6 (Thurnham Mill)	1.8
Lancaster-Cockerham Road (A588)	1.9
Entrance to Glasson Dock	2.6
Glasson Basin Lock No 7, junction with Glasson Dock, belonging to Lancaster Port Commissioners	2.9

Lee and Stort Navigation (including the River Lee and the River Stort)

Improvements to the River Lee for navigation purposes are possibly some of the oldest in the country, if you exclude Roman works. From 1190, powers were granted to the Abbot of Waltham to make a cut and, in 1577, the first pound lock with mitred gates was opened at Waltham Abbey. Over the next 200 years further improvements were undertaken but the first Act of the 'canal age' was in 1767 to 'improve the Navigation of the River Lee from the town of Hertford to the River Thames'. Along the 26-mile route, the works encouraged the development of industry but the River Lee was also important to London as a water supply.

In 1653, Izaak Walton wrote *The Compleat Angler* about fishing on the River Lee and it is still a popular anglers' river. The Lee Valley is well known for the wildlife with many migrant birds using it as a stop-over as well as the numerous species which live there all year. The lakes and reservoirs alongside the river are a haven for many other types of wildlife, adding to the attractions of cruising the waterway.

The Lee Valley Regional Park Authority was formally constituted on 1 January 1967 and is responsible for the park which runs for 23 miles from Docklands to Ware. Within the Park are many historical sites, formal sports facilities, lakes for sailing, beautiful woodlands and meadows for walking and quiet enjoyment of the wildlife and surroundings.

Entry to the River Lee can be directly from the Thames through Bow Creek, via Limehouse Basin and the Limehouse Cut or through the Hertford Union Canal, also known as Duckett's Cut, from the Regent's Canal. Bow Creek is tidal and great

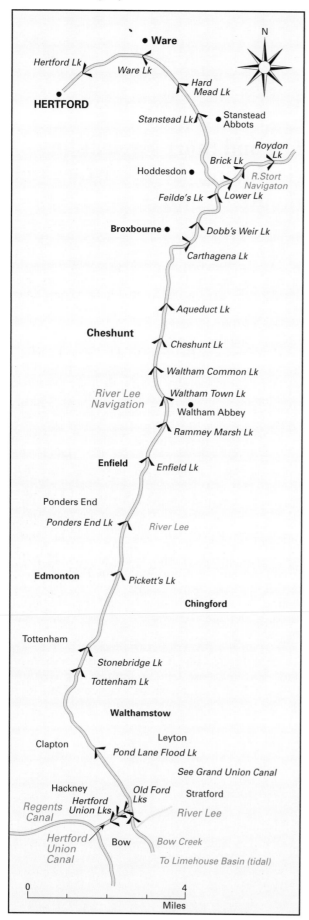

care is needed when navigating this route. Both the rivers Lee and Stort are used for drainage and after heavy rain clearance under bridges can be severely restricted.

Authority British Waterways, The Toll House, Delemeere Terrace, Little Venice, London W2 6ND ☎ 0171 286 6101.

Bridges Numerous. Clearance is affected by river levels and can be greatly reduced after heavy rain.

Towpath Throughout navigation, except Old River Lee Section, St Thomas's Creek, Bow Creek, Abbey Creek and Channelsea River.

Navigation As far as Old Ford Locks, all branches of the river are tidal. Highwater at Limehouse is about 10 minutes before HW London Bridge. Spring tides rise 20ft, neap tides rise 16ft. Bow Locks operate on high tide and passage must be booked with the lock-keeper 24 hours in advance ☎ 0171 987 5661. When the Thames Flood Barrier is in use the working of Bow Locks may be affected.

Facilities There are several boatyards and marinas along the rivers and plenty of pubs, restaurants and shops available.

Distance table	*Miles*
Hertford Town Mill to:	
Dicker Mill Bridge	0.5
Hertford Lock No 1	0.8
New Gauge	1.3
Ware Lock No 2 (EA controlled)	2.3
Ware Bridge	2.9
Hardmead Lock No 3	3.8
Amwell Marsh Bridge	4.3
Stanstead Lock No 4	4.8
Stanstead Bridge	5.1
Rye House Bridge	6.6
Junction with River Stort	7.1
Feilde's Weir Lock No 5	7.3
Dobb's Weir Lock No 6	8.0
Carthagena Lock No 7	8.8
Broxbourne Bridge	9.3
Aqueduct Lock No 8	10.8
Fishers Green Bridge	11.2
Cheshunt Lock No 9	11.8
Waltham Common Lock No 10	12.5
Waltham Town Bridge and Lock No 11	13.3
M25	13.8
Rammey Marsh Lock No 12	14.0
Enfield Lock and BW yard	14.8
Ponder's End Lock No 14	16.8
Pickett's Lock No 15	17.8
Bleak Hall Bridge	18.8
Stonebridge Lock No 16	20.0
Tottenham Lock No 17	20.8
Spring Hill Footbridge	21.9
Lee Bridge	23.0
Middlesex Filter Beds Nature Reserve	23.3
Junction with Hertford Union Canal	24.9
Old Ford Locks No 19 (Semi-tidal)	25.0
Junction with Old River Lee through Old Ford Tide Gates	25.0
Junction with St Thomas's Creek	25.8
Bow Flyover	25.8
Three Mills	26.0
Limehouse Cut	26.2

LEE AND STORT NAVIGATION *Maximum vessel dimensions*

From and to	Distance	Length	Beam	Draught	Headroom	Locks
River Lee						
Hertford to LimehouseBasin,						
River Thames	27.8 miles (44.5km)	85' (25.9m)	16' (4.8m)	4' (1.2m)	6' 9" (2.0m)	21
Bow Back Rivers						
Main Line to Barking						
Road Bridge	1.3 miles (2.0km)	90' (27.4m)	19' 6" (5.9m)	5' (1.5m)	7' 4" (2.2m)	1
Old River Lee,						
City Mills River and						
Waterworks River		88' (26.8m)	19' (5.7m)	5' (1.5m)	7' 4" (2.2m)	None
River Stort						
Bishops Stortford to Hoddesdon,						
River Lee	13.8 miles (22.0km)	86' (26.2m)	13' 3" (4.0m)	3' 7" (1.0m)	6' 3" (1.9m)	15

	Miles
Britannia Bridge Tidal Barrier	27.5
Limehouse Basin	27.6
Limehouse Lock, junction with the River Thames	27.7
Junction with Bow Creek through Bow Tidal Lock	26.3
Bow Creek Tidal Barrier	27.1

Bow Back Rivers

The Bow Back Rivers are a semi-tidal area slightly to the east of the main channel. When a Danish army had sailed up the River Lee to Ware, King Alfred trapped them there for a winter by draining the lower part of the river and the army had to escape by horse. The area, now known as Three Mills, has been an industrial centre for centuries, nine mills were recorded there in the *Domesday Book*. The House Mill is said to be one of the most powerful tide mills ever built and it is in the process of being restored.

Distance table	Miles
Bow Creek	
Head of Bow Creek at tail of Three Mills to:	
Junction with Abbey Creek	0.1
Junction with Main Line of River through	
Bow Tidal Lock	0.3
Barking Road Bridge	1.3
Abbey Creek	
Distance from junction with Bow Creek to	
Abbey Mills, junction with Channelsea River	0.5
Channelsea River	
Abbey Mills, junction with Abbey Creek to	
Phoenix Wharf	0.4

Old River Lee, City Mills River and Waterworks River

It is possible to navigate parts of the Old River Lee at high water but, owing to silting, only small craft would be able to do the full circuit. Navigation of Old River Lee is through Old Ford Tide Gates.

Distance table	Miles
Old Ford Tide Gates, junction with Main Line of river to:	
Junction with Pudding Mill River	0.1
Junction with City Mills River	0.3
Carpenters Road Lock (disused)	0.3
Junction with Waterworks River	0.4

Pudding Mill River is navigable for ½ mile to City Mill. Waterworks River is navigable to West Ham Waterworks also for ½ mile.

River Stort (tributary of the River Lee)

The River Stort joins the River Lee about 7 miles below Hertford and is narrower, more winding and feels more rural than the Lee. Its head of navigation at Bishops Stortford is now rather unprepossessing, but it makes a convenient point to stop and replenish the stores.

Although its history as a navigation is not quite as old as that of the River Lee, the first Act was passed in 1759 and by 1769 there were 15 locks and parts of the river had been canalised to allow for traffic in timber, grain and malting barley. The prime mover in the navigation was George Jackson, who later changed his name to Duckett after he had been made a baronet. His son, also Sir George Duckett, was responsible for the Hertford Union Canal, Duckett's Cut, which linked the Lee and Stort Navigation to the main canal network and avoided the necessity of travelling along the tidal Thames.

Between 1832 and the early 1900s, the navigation passed through a number of hands but, in 1909, after the collapse of Brick Lock at Roydon, the Stort was offered free to the Lee Conservancy Board. Commercial traffic declined dramatically by the end of the Second World War and finished on the Stort in 1972.

As with many waterways, leisure and holiday use gave the river a new lease of life and this is now a popular cruising ground. The attractive mills are a feature of the River Stort and many of them have found new uses. At Roydon Mill, there is a leisure park; Pardon Mill is now a design centre; and Little Hallingbury Mill is a restaurant. The locks on the Stort are 13ft 3ins, narrower than on the Lee which must be remembered by cruisers considering this as a holiday route.

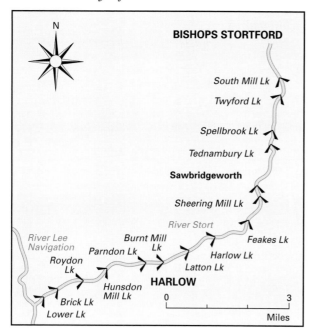

Authority British Waterways, The Toll House, Delemeere Terrace, Little Venice, London W2 6ND ☎ 0171 286 6101.

Bridges Numerous. Clearance is affected by river levels and can be greatly reduced after heavy rain.

Towpath Throughout navigation.

Distance table

Bishop's Stortford to:	Miles
South Mill Lock No 1	1.0
Twyford Lock No 2	1.8
Spellbrook Lock No 3	3.2
Little Hallingbury Mill	3.6
Tednambury Lock No 4	3.8
Sawbridgeworth Lock No 5	5.0
Sheering Mill Lock No 6	5.5
Feakes Lock No 7	6.0
Harlow Lock No 8	7.0
Latton Lock No 9	8.0
Burnt Mill Lock No 10	9.3
Parndon Lock No 11	9.8
Hunsdon Lock No 12	11.0
Roydon Lock No 13	12.1
Roydon Mill	12.4
Roydon Brick Lock No 14	12.8
Roydon Lower Lock No 15	13.4
Junction with River Lee	13.8

Leeds and Liverpool Canal

The longest canal in Britain to have been built by a single company, the Leeds and Liverpool took 40 years to complete and was opened in 1816. Despite financial problems and set-backs, the company stuck to its plan of building a broad canal and it was probably this which ensured its success through the 19th century. It came into full operation later than the other two trans-Pennine routes, the Rochdale and the Huddersfield Narrow Canal, but their more limited carrying capacity led to their early demise, whereas the Leeds and Liverpool has never been seriously threatened with closure.

Water supply to a too short summit level has always caused problems and in dry summers the canal was often closed. It is now one of the most attractive holiday routes for an active and energetic crew. The canal follows the valley of the River Aire from Leeds right up to the summit level past Barnoldswick at the Foulridge Tunnel, 487ft above sea level. There is a famous story of the cow that fell in the canal, it turned in the wrong direction and swam the length of the tunnel, 1640 yards, before it was rescued when, it is said, it was revived with brandy.

There are many wonderful things to see along the Leeds and Liverpool Canal. The Bingley five-rise staircase, Saltaire, near Bradford, built as a work place and new town by Sir Titus Salt in the 1850s; Wigan pier which is now a tourist attraction; and the famous Canal Turn on Aintree Race Course. Although it is still possible to continue to Liverpool and the Mersey, it is not recommended though a redevelopment of Liverpool to encourage tourism to the waterside must be likely in the near future.

The paddles on the Leeds and Liverpool Canal are rather different to most other canals. All locks have ground paddles which must be opened before the gate paddles when filling the locks. There are three unusual types of paddle: box paddles, scissor or jack paddles and lift up paddles. Locally paddles are often called 'cloughs'. The boaters' guide provided by BW should be read to ensure you know how to work these paddles. The guide also includes information on which locks and bridges require handcuff keys before they can be operated.

LEEDS AND LIVERPOOL CANAL *Maximum vessel dimensions*

From and to	Distance	Length	Beam	Draught	Headroom	Locks
Main Line						
Leeds to Liverpool	127 miles (204km)		14' (4.3m)	3' 9" (1.1m)	8' (2.4m)	91
Leeds to Wigan		62' (18.9m)				
Wigan to Liverpool		72' (21.9m)				
Leigh Branch						
Leigh to Wigan	7.5 miles (12.1km)	72' (21.9m)	14' (4.3m)	4' (1.2m)	8' (2.4m)	2
Stanley Dock Branch						
Main Line to Stanley Dock	0.3 miles (0.5km)	72' (21.9m)	14' (4.3m)	4' (1.2m)	8' (2.4m)	4
Rufford Branch						
Main Line at Lathom to Tarleton	7.3 miles (11.8km)	62' (18.9m)	14' (4.3m)	3' 6" (1.1m)	8' (2.4m)	8
Springs Branch						
Main Line to Skipton Rock Staithes	0.5 miles (0.8km)					

Authority East British Waterways Leeds and Liverpool Canal East, Dobson Lock, Apperley Bridge, Bradford BD10 0PY ☎ 01274 611303 Fax 01274 621683.

West British Waterways, Leeds and Liverpool Canal West, Pottery Road, Wigan WN3 5AA ☎ 01942 242239 Fax 01942 821434.

River Ribble and the tidal River Douglas Port of Preston Authority, Dock Offices, Preston, Lancashire ☎ 01772 726711.

Bridges Numerous. Many of these are swing bridges and care must be taken in operating them, particularly the older wooden bridges.

Tunnels Foulridge, near Colne, 1640yds, no towpath; Gannow, near Burnley, 559yds, no towpath.

Branches Rufford Branch to the River Douglas and Ribble Estuary. Leigh Branch from Wigan to the northern end of the Bridgewater Canal. Stanley Dock Branch to Liverpool Docks. Spring Branch, ½ mile at Skipton. Walton Summit Branch is closed and filled in.

Speed limit 4mph.

Connections Aire and Calder Navigation at Leeds, Bridgewater Canal at Leigh.

Navigation River Ribble is navigable to Penwortham Bridge, Preston, but at HWST it is possible to go about 2 miles upstream with a small cruiser.

Facilities There are several boatyards and marinas along the canal and plenty of pubs and restaurants. The route passes through many towns and villages with shops, banks and post offices. Slipways are available at Leeds, Rodley, Bingley, Silsden, Burnley, Adlington, Tarleton and Burscough.

Distance table

Leeds, River Lock No 1 and junction with Aire and Calder Navigation to:

	Miles
Office Lock No 2	0.3
St Ann's Ing Lock No 3	0.5
Oddy 2-rise Locks Nos 4 and 5	0.8
Spring Garden Lock No 6	1.0
Armley Mills (museum)	1.5
Kirkstall Lock No 7	3.5
Forge 3-rise Locks Nos 8–10	4.0
Newlay 3-rise Locks Nos 11–13	4.4
Rodley Wharf	6.3
Dobson 2-rise Locks Nos 14 and 15	9.0
Strangford Swing Bridge	9.9
Field 3-rise Locks Nos 16–18	10.3
Junction with Bradford Canal (abandoned)	12.5
Shipley Warehouses	12.8
Saltaire	13.5
Hirst Lock No 19	14.0
Dowley Gap 2-rise Locks Nos 20 and 21	14.4
Bingley, Dubb Bridge	15.3
Bingley 3 Rise Locks Nos 22–24	15.4
Bingley 5 Rise Lock Nos 25–29	16.5
Granby Bridge, Riddlesden	18.0
Silsden	22.5
Kildwick	24.3
Snaygill Bridge	27.8
Skipton and junction with Springs Branch	29.2
Holme Bridge Lock No 30	33.3
Top Gargrave Lock No 35	35.0
Priest Holme Aqueduct	35.1
Bank Newton Locks Nos 36 to 41	35.5
Cross Keys Inn, East Marton	38.0
Greenberfield Locks Bridge	40.7
Coates Bridge	41.4
Salterforth Bridge	43.5
Foulridge Wharf	45.0
Foulridge Tunnel (controlled by lights)	45.1
Top Lock, Barrowford No 45	46.8
Bottom Lock, Barrowford No 51	47.5
Nelson	48.8
Brierfield	50.3
Burnley Embankment	53.4
Burnley Wharf Visitor Centre	54.5
Weaver's Triangle	54.9
Gannow Tunnel	56.0
Rose Grove Wharf	56.5
Hapton Bridge	58.3
Clayton-le-Moors	62.5
Church Wharf	63.8
Rishton	66.0
Whitebirk Bridge	68.8
Eanam Wharf	70.3
Blackburn Top Lock No 52	71.0

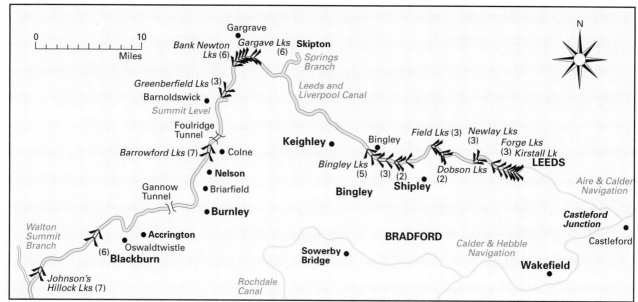

	Miles
Junction with Leigh Branch, between	
Locks Nos 85 and 86	92.0
Wigan Bottom Lock No 87	92.3
Wigan Warehouses	92.5
Pagefield New Lock No 88	93.4
Hell Meadow Lock No 89 (two locks side	
by side)	94.0
M6	95.0
Dean Lock No 90, Gathurst (double lock)	96.0
Appley Bridge	97.5
Appley Lock No 91	98.0
Parbold	99.5
Junction with Rufford Branch	102.5
Burscough Bridge	103.3
New Lane Bridge	104.3
Heaton's Bridge	106.0
Scarisbrick Bridge	107.0
Halsall Bridge	108.5
Downholland Cross Bridge	110.8
Lydiate Hill Bridge	112.8
Lollies Bridge	112.9
Red Lion Bridge	114.3
Maghull Hall Bridge	114.8
Melling	116.8
Blue Anchor Bridge and Aintree Racecourse	118.0
Old Roan Bridge	118.8
Netherton Bridge	119.0
Gorsey Lane Bridge	121.0
Litherland Bridge	122.8
Coffee House Bridge	124.5
Bank Hall	125.5
Sandhills	125.8
Liverpool, junction with Stanley Dock Cut	126.5
Liverpool Docks	127.0

Springs Branch
Junction with Main Line to:

	Miles
Mill Bridge	0.3
Skipton Rock Stone Staithes	0.5

Leigh Branch
Junction with Main Line to:

	Miles
Poolstock Lock No 1 and 2	0.2
Moss Bridge	0.9
Bamfurlong Bridge	3.1
Dover Bridge	4.0

	Miles
Nova Scotia Wharf and Blackburn Bottom	
Lock No 57	71.5
Cherry Tree	73.0
Stanworth Bridge	75.0
Riley Green	76.0
Wheelton	78.8
Johnson's Hillock Locks Nos 58–64	79.3
Junction with Walton Summit Branch	
(now closed)	79.8
Botany Bridge	81.0
Cowling Bridge	82.3
Adlington	85.0
Red House Aqueduct, River Douglas	85.3
Red Rock Bridge	87.5
Wigan Top Lock No 65	90.0
Rose Bridge	91.0

The unusual double bridge at East Marton on the Leeds and Liverpool Canal. *Robin Smithett*

	Miles
Plank Lane Bridge	5.5
Pennington Country Park	6.0
Leigh Warehouses	7.0
Junction with Stretford and Leigh Branch of Bridgewater Canal	7.3
Rufford Branch	
Junction with Main Line to:	
Lathom Locks Nos 1 and 2	0.1
Runnel Brow Lock No 3	0.3
Moss Lock No 4	0.8
German's Lock No 5	1.1
Baldwin's Lock No 6	1.5
Marsh Meadow Swing Bridge	2.5
Rufford Lock No 7	3.0
Rufford Old Hall	3.5
Strand Bridge	5.3
Bank Bridge	6.3
Town End Bridge	6.8
Tarleton Lock No 8, junction with tidal River Douglas	7.3
River Ribble, Estuary and junction with River Douglas	11.3
(entry to navigation controlled by the Port of Preston Authority)	

Louth Navigation

Running from the town of Louth to Tetney Haven on the Humber, the navigation was originally proposed in 1756 but the Act was not passed until 1763. Work started in 1765 and the navigation was finally open to Louth in 1770. It was mostly used to bring coal, timber and general goods into the town and send wool and corn out on the Humber keels and sloops. For some time, the navigation did well

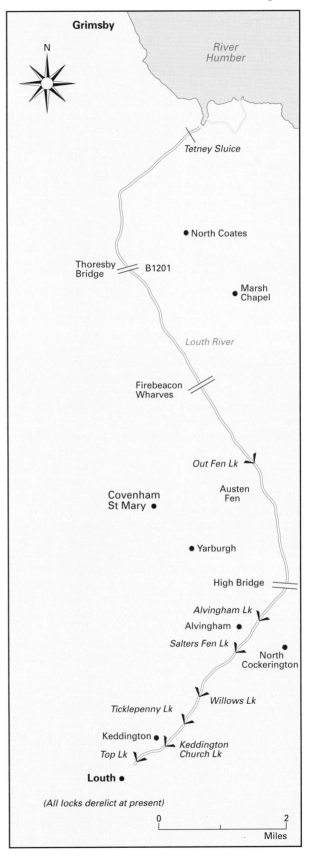

LOUTH NAVIGATION Maximum vessel dimensions (at time of closure)

From and to	Distance	Length	Beam	Draught	Headroom	Locks
Louth to the Humber at Tetney	11.8 miles (18.9km)	72' (21.9m)	15' (4.5m)	5' 6" (1.6m)	Unlimited	8

but, as with so many waterways, the lease was bought by a railway company, in this case the Great Northern in 1847, and was allowed to deteriorate. By the end of the First World War there was little traffic, and serious flooding in 1920 damaged the navigation. The commissoners asked to be relieved of their responsibilities to maintain the waterway and it was legally abandoned in 1924.

In 1986, a group of enthusiasts formed the Louth Navigation Trust. Since then they have been working hard to restore the navigation, much of which is still in water. The local authorities and civic trust support the work and many of the original canalside buildings could be adapted and used for a range of alternative purposes, which would be a great benefit to the environment. Its isolation from the rest of the waterways network has meant it is not as straightforward a proposition to sell to the various funding bodies as some other projects, despite the fact that many of the navigation structures would need relatively little work to restore them to working order.

Authority Environment Agency, Harvey Street, Lincoln LN1 1TF ☎ 01522 513100 *Fax* 01522 512927.

Towpath Throughout waterway.

Distance table	Miles
Louth, River Head to:	
Louth Top Lock No 1	0.3
Keddington Lock No 2	0.6
Ticklepenny Lock No 3	1.0
Willows Lock No 4	1.4
Salter's Fen Lock No 5	2.1
Alvingham Lock No 6	2.5
Out Fen Lock No 7	4.0
Austen Fen	5.0
Beargate Bridge	6.0
Firebeacon	7.0
Thoresby Bridge	8.8
Tetney Lock (site)	10.8
Tetney Warehouse	11.0
Sea Bank, end of canal	11.8

There is a channel from this point to the Humber, a distance of 3½ miles through the sand flats. The channel was marked by beacons.

Lydney Canal and Harbour

The Lydney Canal was proposed because the sill was too shallow for craft to come in to load coal from the Forest of Dean. A proposal to build a tramroad to the Wye at Lydbrook and the canal to Lydney Harbour came under an Act in 1810. The canal was originally connected with Pidcock's Canal, but nothing remains of that.

The outer harbour was built in 1821 and Lydney was a busy railway port for over 100 years. Trade continued into the 1960s until rail access to the harbour ceased. Until the mid-1970s, timber came up to a local mill by barge from Avonmouth. During the mid-1980s, when marina housing developments were popular, the dock was sold for development but so far this has remained as a proposal.

There is an active sailing club based at the dock and members are pleased to help anyone visiting the area by boat.

Authority Environment Agency, Lower Severn Area, Riversmeet House, Newtown Industrial Estate, Northway Lane, Tewkesbury, Gloucestershire GL20 7LG ☎ 01684 850951 *Fax* 01684 293599.

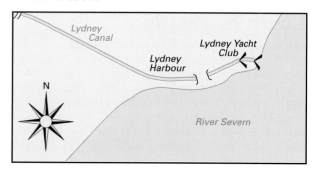

LYDNEY CANAL AND HARBOUR
Lydney Harbour Dimensions

	Normal depth	Length	Width	Entrance	Average depth of water on outer sill MHWS	MHWN
Tidal Basin	24'	270'	75'			
Lower Dock	13.5'	780'	105'	33'	24'	12'
Upper Dock	12'	850'	88'			

Maximum vessel dimensions

From and to	Distance	Length	Beam	Draught	Headroom	Locks
Lydney Station to River Severn	1 mile (1.6km)	100' (30.4m)	24' (7.3m)	12' (3.6m)	Unlimited	1

Towpath Throughout waterway.

Navigation The tides in the River Severn are very strong. Sandbanks outside the harbour are sometimes higher than the level of the sill at the tidal gate. Great care must be taken when approaching or leaving Lydney. Local information can be obtained from the Lydney Yacht Club, The Old Shipyard House, Harbour Road, Lydney, Gloucestershire GL15 4ER ☎ 01594 842573.

Charts Imray C59, Admiralty 1166.

Manchester, Bolton and Bury Canal

This canal was built under an Act of 1791 and both Bolton and Bury were reached within a few weeks of each other in October 1796. The link with the River Irwell at Salford was completed in 1808. Having been partially built as a narrow canal, the locks were enlarged when negotiations were underway for a link with the Leeds and Liverpool Canal, although this never came to fruition.

The canal company turned itself into the Manchester, Bolton and Bury Canal Navigation and Railway Company in 1831, and remained in railway ownership until nationalisation. There was no

through traffic on the canal by 1936, when a disastrous breach severed the Bury Arm from the rest of the canal. During the Second World War, sections of the canal were drained and it was abandoned between 1941 and 1961.

The Manchester, Bolton and Bury Canal Society was formed in 1987 with the aim of restoring the canal and reconnecting it to the national network. The society can be contacted at 36 Trawden Avenue, Smithills, Bolton BL1 6JD.

Authority Where the canal is in water British Waterways, Pottery Road, Wigan, Lancashire WN3 5AA ☎ 01942 242239.

Bridges Numerous.

Towpath From Park House Bridge to Daiseyfield Viaduct and from the junction of the Bolton Branch to the site of Damside Aqueduct, the towpath is walkable.

Tunnels Two at Bury, 66yds and 141yds; two at Salford 34yds and 50yds.

Aqueducts Lumbs Aqueduct; Clifton and Prestolee Aqueducts over the Irwell; on the Bolton Branch, Hall Lane, Foggs and Damside Aqueducts.

Branches Bolton Arm 3 miles. Feeder canal from Burrs Weir to Elton Reservoir 2½ miles (formerly navigable, but never connected for through navigation).

Connections River Irwell and formerly to Fletcher's Canal, a private arm, 1½ miles long.

Restoration The Manchester Bolton and Bury Canal Society are campaigning for a complete restoration of the canal. A 3½-mile section from Ladyshore has been restored and two other sections of about 1½ miles are in water. The society is formulating plans for the restoration with three local authorities and British Waterways. The proposed terminus for the restored canal would be at Daisyfield Viaduct.
(Distance table courtesy of Richard Chester-Browne.)

MANCHESTER, BOLTON AND BURY CANAL Maximum vessel dimensions

From and to	Distance	Length	Beam	Draught	Headroom	Locks
River Irwell to Bury	12.9 miles (20.7km)	68' (20.7m)	14' 2" (4.3m)	3' 6" (1.0m)	9' (2.7m)	17

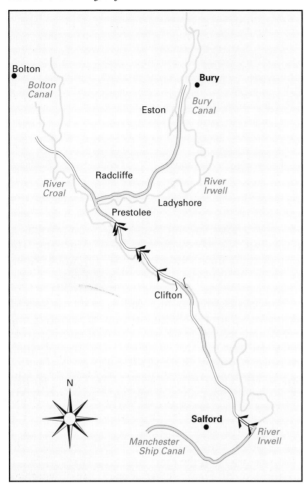

Distance table

Junction with River Irwell, Salford to:	Miles
Top of Salford Locks, No 6	0.4
Park House Bridge	2.6
Lumbs Aqueduct (demolished)	3.6
Junction with Fletcher's Canal and Clifton Aqueduct	4.6
Rhodes Lock No 7	5.5
Giants Seat Locks Nos 8 and 9	6.3
Ringley Locks Nos 10 and 11	7.0
Prestolee Aqueduct	7.8
Prestolee Locks Nos 12–17 (infilled)	7.9
Junction with Bolton Branch	8.0
Site of 1936 Breach	8.1
Ladyshore	8.4
Ladyshore Bridge	8.8
Mount Sion Bridge	9.3
Nickerhole Bridge	9.5
Water Street Bridge	10.3
Whittakers Bridge	10.5
Hampsons Bridge	11.0
Rothwells Bridge	11.3
Bank Top Bridge	11.6
Daisyfield Viaduct	12.4
Canal Terminus, Bury	12.9

Bolton Arm

Junction with Main Line to:	
Hall Lane Aqueduct (site of)	0.9
Damside Aqueduct (site of)	1.9
Canal Terminus, Bolton	3.0

Manchester Ship Canal

The Port of Manchester, which comprises the Manchester Ship Canal, the former great terminal docks at Manchester and other dock systems along the waterway, is controlled by the Manchester Ship Canal Company, which is both proprietor and port authority. The powers of the undertaking are embodied in the Manchester Ship Canal Act 1885, which constitutes it a statutory company. Later Acts, concerned with financial aid afforded by the municipality of Manchester to the Ship Canal Company during the construction of the canal, accorded the corporation an important representation upon the board of directors, and consequently a share in the direction of the undertaking. This combination of municipal and private interests was unique in this country, although not unknown in the case of public utility concerns abroad, and in view of this the following extra historical data has been included for the student by courtesy of the company.

Historical background

For the first 100 years, the composition of the board was almost equally divided between the representatives of the shareholders and those of the corporation: there being ten directors elected by the shareholders and 11 appointed by the corporation, constituting a directorship of 21, of which the chairman was elected by the shareholders' directors, while the deputy chairmanship was held by a corporation director. In the late 1980s, the Manchester City Council sold its controlling interest in the company which is now a subsidiary of Peel Holdings.

Manchester as a port was brought into existence by the construction of the Ship Canal, which was commenced in November 1887 and opened for through traffic on 1 January 1894. The canal, which is 36 miles long, was partly achieved by canalising short stretches of the rivers Irwell and Mersey, but for the greater part of its length was a new cutting unrelated to the course of any previous waterway.

The canal provided Manchester, one of the most closely populated and highly industrialised areas in the country, with a terminal for large ocean-going vessels enjoying the same freight rates as ports on

the seaboard. Such geographical and economic advantages, combined with modern layout and equipment, ensured rapid development and for nearly a century Manchester ranked high amongst the principal ports of the United Kingdom, possessing established shipping connections with the principal ports of 'the world. An important feature of the port's progress has been the development of an industrial zone in the neighbourhood of the docks and along the waterway, a consequence of their enterprise foreseen by the pioneers of the canal, and made possible by the wide powers granted to the company for the acquisition of land along the waterway.

It is difficult today, in view of Manchester's established position in our maritime transport system, to realise the acute controversy which raged round the practicability of the Ship Canal when the scheme was first advanced. In spite of a traditional belief in water transport and the success of the Bridgewater Canal, constructed to link the town with the Mersey Estuary in the mid-18th century, opinion was divided in Manchester on the possible outcome of such a vast enterprise as the Ship Canal. Even the Manchester Chamber of Commerce, which held a special meeting in 1877 to consider reports and plans advanced by two private individuals, George Hicks, a Scotsman, and Hamilton Fulton, a London engineer, approved the scheme with great caution. Outside Manchester, it was for the most part held to be an extravagant dream. The public exhibition of Fulton's model aroused some popular enthusiasm which, however, died down, but was revived in 1881 by encouraging news of improvements being carried out on the Clyde.

It was then that Daniel Adamson assumed leadership of the movement and called together the mayors of Manchester and surrounding towns, commercial magnates and capitalists and leaders in the co-operative and labour movements. Thirteen representatives of Lancashire towns and 55 leading merchants and manufacturers attended, a provisional committee was appointed and engineers briefed. Both Hamilton Fulton and Leader Williams prepared plans and reports, and that of the latter for a canal with several levels maintained by locks was the one laid before Parliament. It underwent many modifications in the several Bills which Parliament considered, but the plans finally passed adhered to the principles he originally laid down.

In July 1882, on the motion of Councillor Bosdin Leech, who became historian of the canal, the Manchester Corporation resolved 'to take up the question of the canal with the vigour and earnestness which its importance demanded', and towards the end of the year a guarantee fund of £25,000 was assured. Many Manchester aldermen and councillors subscribed as individuals, but nothing was contributed from the public purse. When the promoters later turned to the raising of a fund of £100,000 to meet Parliamentary expenses and deposits, the corporation was approached on the grounds that the issue was one of wide local importance. Public opinion was, however, scarcely solid enough to encourage the corporation to respond, although the General Purposes Committee unanimously passed a resolution to the effect that the widening and improving of the rivers Irwell and Mersey and the making of them navigable as a Ship Canal be referred to the parliamentary sub-committee.

The close of the year saw a great deal of enthusiasm. Public meetings were constantly held, at which the aid of Manchester and adjoining corporations was invoked and MPs were called upon to support the Bill. In November, the mayor moved the resolution which had been passed by the General Purposes Committee, that the undertaking and administration of the canal should be vested in a trust for the benefit of the public in general and that Manchester and other local authorities in the neighbourhood of the proposed canal should be authorised to contribute to the cost of, and to take part in, the supervising and the execution of the work and its general management. The press generally held that the council had gone too far, but there was some support for the corporation's contributing towards an undertaking 'which should be of such benefit to the city'. A conference of municipal corporations went to the length of investigating the engineering details and reviewing the economic arguments.

December 1882 saw the first Bill deposited unaided by any official grants. This provided for the creation of a trust on the application to Parliament of local authorities representing a rateable value of £4,000,000. The principles governing a possible transfer to a public trust are embodied in the Act of 1885. On technical grounds, the examiner refused the Bill as it failed to comply with standing orders. Mammoth petitions were presented and an appeal made to a special committee. Standing orders were conditionally suspended. The Bill passed the Commons, but was rejected by the Lords.

Another effort to obtain parliamentary powers demanded more money. Undeterred, the promoters completed their arrangements for depositing a second Bill, which provided for a capital of £8,000,000, and Adamson applied to the corporations of Manchester, Salford and the surrounding boroughs to contribute one penny in the pound on their rateable value in order to strengthen the subscription list and emphasise the reality of their support. When Adamson, with his colleagues, set out for London in January to make arrangements for the parliamentary deposit, he left Manchester acutely divided on the propriety of the municipality acceding to his request, but opinion in favour of municipal aid was apparently stiffening, for in May the corporation decided to contribute £10,000 in the event of the Bill being passed.

Pealing of bells and great jubilation in Manchester and Oldham marked the passage of the second Bill through the Lords, but joy was premature, for the Commons, who had passed the first Bill, rejected the second. The committee met immediately and unanimously resolved to persevere in their efforts to make Manchester a port.

Parliament, as if to make amends, handled the third Bill with great celerity. It passed the Lords' committee in May, the Commons' committee on 3 August, and was referred to the House the same day, obtained its third reading on 5 August and received the royal assent next day, and, according to critical opinion, Manchester was at last fully authorised to start throwing its millions in the 'big ditch'.

The method of raising capital was as acutely debated as the question of finding money for legal expenses. The opinion was advanced, on the one hand, that the workers should not be allowed to risk their savings, and, on the other, that corporations had no right to support private enterprise. Some favoured the local corporations taking shares on the grounds that the canal would be a great highway upon which the prosperity of Lancashire would depend; and that the corporation should obtain influence and voting power in order to prevent the canal becoming a money-making concern or passing into the hands of monopolist railway companies.

The response to the first prospectus was disappointing and the issue was withdrawn and powers sought and obtained for payment of interest out of capital. Adamson, who deserved the gratitude of Manchester better than any man, for his devotion, energy and pluck, resigned, to be succeeded in the chairmanship by Lord Egerton, an appropriate choice, for his kinsman, the Duke of Bridgewater, had by his perseverance secured the success of what was deemed to be one of the foundations of Manchester's prosperity, and in Lord Egerton's words, 'had to beg every shilling for the Bridgewater Canal'. The difficulties of flotation and the consequent misgivings as to the company's prospects brought into being a consultative committee composed of representative citizens (some known critics of the canal were included) which was charged, under the chairmanship of the Mayor of Manchester, to advise on the best methods of raising funds.

In July 1887, a new prospectus was issued and by 4 August the Board of Trade certificate was signed to the effect that the statutory requirements regarding the issue and acceptance of capital had been fulfilled. A list of shareholders published in December 1887, was close upon 39,000. Money difficulties disposed of, the contract was let, and in November Lord Egerton cut the first sod on the site of Eastham Locks. Labour streamed up from all parts of the country and the neighbourhood was dotted with finger-posts directing labourers to the works.

It might be thought that the leaders of this great adventure were now heading along the primrose path with their trials and disappointments behind them, but not so. Landslides occurred, quicksands were encountered and, most costly of all in time and money, unprecedented floods on several occasions broke through the earthworks, submerging large sections of the works and plant and laying thousands of hands idle.

The cumulative effect of such adversities, the growing bill of legal costs and rising labour charges were making demands upon capital which were unprovided for, and by the end of the year, it was found that additional funds, estimated at not less that £1,700,000 would be required. Encouraged by popular opinion, which now strongly favoured municipal aid, the Special Committee of the Council, recommended assistance to the extent of £3,000,000. The general tenor of the report was to the effect that the work could not be postponed without affecting its efficiency and that funds could not be raised by public appeal in a reasonable time. The committee were of the opinion that the company's estimate of the funds required was too low and that even if the obligation to pay interest out of capital was cancelled, it would take approximately £2,500,000 to complete the work, but that it would be prudent that £3,000,000 should be provided.

This eminently practical report was moved by the mayor, Alderman John Mark, and carried unanimously. Manchester approved it but there were mixed views on the decision to cease interest payments out of capital on the existing share capital. Salford Corporation came forward with an offer of £1,000,000 but the Manchester Bill had already been deposited. It was passed in July 1891. The corporation raised the money by issues of 3 per cent debenture stock and elected five directors by ballot to serve on the board of the company. In November there were assurances given that progress was according to plan and funds adequate, but the Special Works Committee, which had recently been set up, was divided and there was some criticism of the estimates, with the result that a representative committee was set up and harmony restored.

Whatever doubts there may have been about the adequacy of the available funds were settled in December by the combined efforts of the Mersey and Irwell, which broke into the Irlam Section and submerged it to a depth of 20ft. During the same flood period, the Bollin broke in, flooding over 2 miles of cutting. The close of 1891 saw the canal opened as far as the Weaver, the new port of Saltport created, and altogether about half the waterway completed.

By the summer of 1892 disquieting rumours were current again, the canal could not be opened till January 1894 (the first reliable prophesy in this direction). About the same time it became apparent that another £1,250,000 was thought necessary to finish the work. In August, the shareholders considered the supplementary estimates and agreed to further borrowing, thereby earning the sympathy and admiration of the whole country. The wary Special Committee recommended £2,000,000 and the city council again carried the report unanimously. Salford again proposed to contribute, but a borough funds meeting, which had supported the proposal before, rejected it on this occasion. A poll, demanded by the mayor, disclosed a large majority in favour. A poll of Oldham ratepayers also favoured a loan.

The Manchester, Salford and Oldham Bills were taken together before a Select Committee of the Lords, which found itself in the unusual position of having to decide between 'various claimants to the honour of lending money'. The Lords decided to confine themselves to the Manchester Corporation Canal Bill and Oldham and Salford withdrew with the credit of having offered to assist the canal undertaking over its difficulties.

The city's representation on the board of the company, which has already been described, was provided for in this Bill of 1892.

The spirit with which the city came to the company's aid was admirably expressed by Alderman Sir John Harwood in seconding the motion to accept the first report of the Special Committee. 'If the council wished to maintain the character of their city,' he said, 'they would never suffer so much money subscribed by so many needy people to lie there as a monument of a want of fidelity to their trust as public servants and of loyalty to the cause, the trade and the interest of a great city.' The spirit and fortitude of the original shareholders is beyond praise. As to the promoters, the canal is their imperishable monument. When capital was first being sought, the view was widely held that the canal would benefit the workers greatly, even were no dividends earned for the investors. Certainly, the benefit of the undertaking to the community from its earliest days is undisputed, although incalculable. Dividends were first paid for the year 1915 and have since been paid without intermission.

With the general fall-off in sea-borne traffic, some parts of the Manchester Docks have gone through a period of dereliction, but in the 1980s and 1990s the interest in waterfront sites all over the country has seen a regeneration of the docks areas. On-going development is improving the Salford Quays area, which used to be Salford Docks 6–9 and the layouts of other docks are being altered with greater emphasis on their use by leisure craft rather than large cargo ships.

Authority The Manchester Ship Canal Company, Quay West, Trafford Wharf Road, Manchester M17 1PL ☎ 0161 872 2411 *Fax* 0161 877 0344.

Locks The entrance from the River Mersey at Eastham has two sets of locks, the large lock is 600ft long by 80ft wide and the medium lock 350ft by 50ft. Similarly at Mode Wheel, Barton, Irlam and Latchford Locks, the locks are 65ft wide and the large locks can accommodate 600ft, 450ft or 150ft, and the small locks 350ft, 250ft or 120ft by using intermediate gates.

Bridges Several. Tide height and flood water may restrict headroom. Advice is available from the Harbourmaster at Eastham. Trafford Road Bridge has now been fixed. With all movable bridges closed, the maximum headroom is 3.1m as far as Woden Street.

Towpath None along the main canal, but paths are being developed as part of the improvements to the Manchester and Salford Quays areas.

Connections *River Mersey at Eastham.*

Shropshire Union Canal at Ellesmere Port For the new access arrangements, see the entry for the Shropshire Union Canal.

River Weaver and Weaver Navigation at Western Point Weston Marsh Lock is 229ft long by 42ft 8ins wide.

River Mersey at Warrington There is still a right of navigation through Walton Lock but it is currently unnavigable. Its closure has been resisted and its future is under consideration.

The former *Salford Docks* can now be accessed by small craft through Welland Lock and Docks 7, 8 and 9 are linked by new canals. There are proposals to develop this area for leisure boating.

River Irwell, Upper Reach Hulme Lock is no longer available for use.

Bridgewater Canal via the new lock in Pomona No 3 Dock.

Branches *Mersey and Irwell Navigation.* Howley and Woolston Locks together with the Woolston Canal (New Cut) are closed. This only leaves a short section east of Warrington Bridge open to the closed Howley Lock.

Runcorn and Latchford Canal (locally known as The Black Bear Canal). Closed by virtue of the Manchester Ship Canal (Black Bear Canal Local Enactment) Order 1976 (SI 1976 No 1084) operative from 6 August 1976. Canal site sold to the Warrington Borough Council in 1977.

Walton Lock Branch 0.4 miles. Connects Mersey and Irwell Navigation near Arpley with Manchester Ship Canal. Walton Lock is now unnavigable in practise but there is still a right of navigation.

MANCHESTER SHIP CANAL Maximum vessel dimensions

From and to	Distance	Length	Beam	Draught	Headroom	Locks
Eastham Locks, River Mersey to Woden Street Footbridge, Manchester	36 miles (57.9km)	600' (182.8m)	65' (19.8m)	28' (8.5m)	70' (21.3m)	5
Woden Street to Hunt's Bank	1.4 miles (2.2km)	Unlimited	25' (7.6m)	4' 6" (1.3m)	15' (4.5m)	None

Pleasure craft on the Ship Canal

Any pleasure craft owners considering including the Ship Canal in an itinerary should contact the company's harbourmaster at Marine Operations, Administration Block, Queen Elizabeth II Dock, Eastham, Wirral L62 0BB. Notes are available from him on the safe use and requirements for small craft on the canal. Narrowboats are no longer considered 'unsuitable' and breasting-up is no longer a requirement. Craft without VHF may pass along the canal provided they keep regular contact with 'shipping control', preferably by mobile phone. Eastham to Old Quay is covered by Shipping Control Eastham ☎ 0151 327 1242 VHF Ch 14, and Old Quay to Woden Street by Latchford ☎ 01925 635249, VHF Ch 14.

The Manchester Ship Canal Company issue a booklet for pleasure craft wishing to use the Upper Reach. This covers Conditions of Use and Cruising Notes and includes a map. This is available from the company's office at the address above.

The Manchester Ship Canal Act 1960

Pleasure Craft

1. Section 52 of the Harbours Clauses Act 1847 as incorporated with the Manchester Ship Canal Acts 1885 to 1960 in its application to the company and the harbourmaster shall notwithstanding the provision of section 33 of the Harbours Clauses Act 1847 as also so incorporated extend so as to empower the harbourmaster unless the following conditions have been or will be complied with:
   a. notice in writing of the date and time on which it is proposed to enter the Harbour and of the intended movement of the pleasure craft in the Harbour has been given to the harbourmaster not less than 48 hours before the time of entry;
   b. on or before the giving of the said notice there has been produced to the harbourmaster:
      i. (a) a passenger steamer's certificate issued by the Ministry of Transport under Part III of the Merchant Shipping Act 1894 or a certificate showing that the pleasure craft is for the time being classed by Lloyds Register of Shipping or some other classification society approved by the company; or (b) a certificate given within the previous 12 months by a surveyor of shipping who is either a member or an associate member of the Institute of Naval Architects or is approved by the company or by a boat builder who is either a member of the Ship and Boat Builders' National Federation or is approved by the company that the pleasure craft is seaworthy and suitable for navigation on the canal; and
      ii. a certificate that the owner is insured in respect of the pleasure craft with an insurer approved by the company against third-party liability in a sum of not less than £50,000;

   c. during such time as the pleasure craft is in the harbour it is:
      i. equipped with the articles specified in the Third Schedule to this Act; and
      ii. in charge of a person over 21 years of age who has such experience of navigation as will enable him to navigate in the Harbour with reasonable competence.
2. Nothwithstanding the provisions of subsection (1) of this section if the harbourmaster is of the opinion that the entry into or movement of the pleasure craft in the Harbour at the date and time specified in a notice given under paragraph (a) of subsection (1) of this section would or would be likely to cause such interference with commercial traffic in the Harbour as to make it necessary for such entry or movement not to take place at the date and time so specified he may postpone such entry or movement for such period as he considers to be necessary to avoid interference with commercial traffic and shall thereupon notify the master of the pleasure craft of a date and time as soon thereafter as is reasonably practicable when the pleasure craft may enter the Harbour or move within it.
3. Subsection (1) of this section shall not apply to a pleasure craft requiring to enter the Harbour from the River Mersey owing to stress of weather or other emergency.

Schedule

1. An adequate anchor and cable.
2. At least two warps each being not less than 50ft in length and of sufficient strength.
3. Such navigation lights and equipment for signalling by sound as will enable the pleasure craft to comply with the International Regulations for Preventing Collisions at Sea and with the company's bye-laws.
4. At least two fire extinguishers of a foam type approved by the Ministry of Transport and maintained in accordance with the Ministry's recommendations.
5. Sufficient life-saving apparatus for as many passengers and crew as the pleasure craft is designed to carry.
6. An Admiralty chart or other chart approved by the company for the harbour and adjacent waters.
7. A copy of the company's bye-laws for the time being in force.
8. A current tidal almanac.

Enquiries should be made to the Manchester Ship Canal Company's Harbourmaster at Marine Operations, Administration Block, Queen Elizabeth II Dock, Eastham, Wirral L62 0BB ☎ 0151 327 1461.

Navigation The Ship Canal may only be used by small craft as a through route. Small craft should not navigate too close to the bank as the slope varies, but, in accordance with the provisions of Bye-law 18, small craft should keep out of the track of ocean-going vessels. Those in charge of small craft should

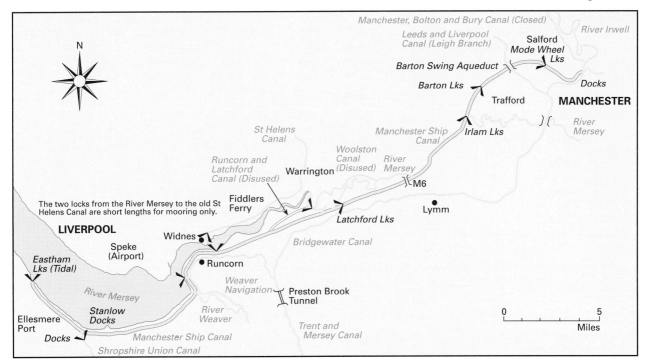

familiarise themselves with the Schedule of Signals and Bye-laws relating to navigation contained in the General Bye-law. The entrance to the Ship Canal at Eastham is 25 miles from the Mersey Bar. The access channel is dredged to a depth of 3.9m below Liverpool Bay Datum.

The levels of the upper sills of the 80ft and 50ft locks at Eastham are 9.7m and 8.8m respectively below statutory level. The outer or lower sill of each lock is 3.9m below Liverpool Bay Datum.

Although deep-sea traffic on the Ship Canal is less frequent than previously, efforts are still made to ensure pleasure craft do not meet large ships when travelling along the canal where possible. In the event of meeting a ship, the person in charge of the pleasure craft should respond in accordance with the company's general bye-laws and the International Regulations for Preventing Collisions at Sea.

- When passing another vessel pleasure craft should avoid getting too close to the canal bank as displacement of water from the passing vessel might cause the pleasure craft to ground.

- Naked lights of any kind must not be produced on deck of any pleasure craft whilst navigating between Stanlow and Ince.

- No pleasure craft should leave any section or berth without first obtaining permission, and information as to traffic movement. It is advisable not to leave until the next section is clear of traffic.

- Pleasure craft should keep a listening watch at all times either on VHF or by mobile phone for instructions from 'shipping control'.

- No pleasure craft shall enter the canal without first contacting the nearest control point and

obtaining final permission to proceed. Such craft must have written permission of the harbourmaster to enter the canal.

- All pleasure-craft owners should be familiar with the company's general bye-laws with special regard to the rules of navigation and signals.

- If there is heavy sluicing at the locks it is not safe for small craft to make a passage.

Permission to use the canal must be made at least 48 hours in advance.

Tides High water on spring tides will flow to Woolston Weir on the weir stream of the River Mersey, just below Woolston Lock (now closed). HW Eastham is about 20 minutes after HW Liverpool, Latchford Locks about 1 hour 15 minutes, Bank Quay, Warrington, about 1 hour 15 minutes, Howley Lock and Walton Lock about 1 hour 20 minutes. Spring tides rise about 2.7m. Heavy rain in the Upper Mersey, coinciding with big spring tides, can significantly increase the expected flow of the tide which can be up to 5.5 knots.

During spring tides the level of high water on the River Mersey is higher than the water level in the canal and tide gates are closed. On occasions of water shortage, high spring tides can be used to raise the water level in the canal.

Tidal levels above Liverpool Bay Datum at Eastham Locks MHWS 8.9m, MHWN 7.0m, MLWN 2.1m, MLWS 0.2m. Highest predicted equinoctial spring tides 9.6m

Charts Imray C52, Admiralty 1951, 3478, 3490.

Facilities This is not really a pleasure craft waterway and as such there are limited facilities for small craft between Weston Point Docks, where the River Weaver joins the canal, and the Pomona Lock and the developing Salford Quays in Manchester.

Distance table

	Side of canal	Dist from Eastham Locks Miles	Dist from Manchester Miles
Eastham Locks	–	0.0	36
Eastham Lay-by	E & W	0.2	35.8
Eastham Crane Berth	W	0.5	35.5
Bankfield Wharf	W	0.6	35.4
Hooton Wharf	W	1.4	34.6
Mount Manisty	E	1.8–2.4	34.2–33.6
Bowaters UK Pulp and Paper Mills	W	2.0	34.0
Pool Hall Wharf	W	2.5	33.5
Ellesmere Port Wharf (entrance to Shropshire Union Canal)	W	2.9	33.1
Ellesmere Port (grain warehouse)	W	3.1	32.2
Stuart Wharf	S	3.5	32.5
Manchester Dry Docks Company Ellesmere Port	S	3.8	32.3
Stanlow Wharf	S	3.9	32.1
Associated Ethyl Wharf	S	4.0	32.0
ICI (Dyestuffs) Wharf	S	4.1	31.9
Esso Petroleum Co Barge Wharf	S	4.4	31.6
Stanlow Oil Docks and Turning Basin	N	4.5	31.5
Stanlow Lay-by	S	4.6	31.4
Ince Coaster Berth	S	5.1	30.9
Ince Oil Berth	S	5.4	30.6
Ince Tying-up Berths	S	5.6	30.4
Ince Wharf	S	6.6	29.4
Holpool Gutter	S	7.7	28.3
Frodsham Pumping Stage	S	8.5	27.5
Weaver Mouth	–	9.9	26.1
Weston Marsh Lock, entrance to Weaver Navigation	E	9.9	26.1
Weaver Sluices	W	10.1	25.9
Weston Mersey Lock (closed)	W	10.9	25.1
Weston Point Docks	E	11.0	25.0
Delamere Dock, entrance to Weaver Navigation	E	11.1	24.9
Weston Point Salt Works (ICI) (tip)	E	11.3	24.7
Runcorn Lay-by	E	11.5	24.5
Bridgewater Lock (closed)	N	11.7	24.3
Runcorn Docks	S	12.3	23.7
Runcorn Railway Bridge	–	12.5	23.5
Widnes Bridge	–	12.6	23.4
Old Quay Lock (closed)	N	13.0	23.0
Old Quay Swing Bridge	–	13.3	22.7
ICI (General Chemicals) Wharf	N	13.5	22.5
ICI (Chem and Met), Astmoor Wharf	N	14.0	22.0
ICI (Chem and Met) Works	–	14.3	21.7
Stone Delph	S	15.1	20.9
Randles Sluices	N	15.4	20.6
Moore Lane Lay by	N	16.4	19.6
Moore Lane Swing Bridge	–	17.1	18.9
Acton Grange Wharf	N	17.5	18.5
Acton Grange Viaduct	–	17.9	18.1
Chester Road Swing Bridge	–	18.7	17.3
Warrington Wharf and Walton Lock	–	19.0	17.0
Northwich Road Swing Bridge and Twenty-Steps Lock (closed)	–	19.4	16.6
Latchford High Level Bridge	–	20.1	15.9
Knutsford Road Swing Bridge	–	20.4	15.6
Latchford Viaduct	–	20.7	15.3
Latchford Locks	–	21.0	15.0
Thelwall Pumping Stage	–	21.5	14.5
Thelwall Ferry	–	21.7	14.3
Statham Pumping Station No 3 (disused)	N	22.5	13.5
Statham Pumping Station No 2	N	22.7	13.3
M6	–	22.8	13.2
Statham Pumping Station No 1	N	23.1	12.9
Rixton Junction	N	24.0	12.0
Warburton High Level Bridge	–	25.1	10.9
Millbank Wharf	S	26.0	10.0
Cadishead Ferry	–	26.6	9.4
Cadishead Viaduct	–	26.9	9.1
Partington Coaling Basin	N & S	27.0-27.4	9.0–8.6
Irlam Wharf (Lancs Steel Corp)	N	27.7	8.3
Mersey Weir	S	28.0	8.0
Irlam Viaduct	–	28.1	7.9
Irlam Wharf (CWS)	N	28.1	7.9
Irlam Locks	–	28.4	7.6
Irlam Ferry	–	28.6	7.4
Hulmes Bridge Ferry	–	29.6	6.4
Barton Locks	–	30.4	5.6
M63	–	30.9	5.1
Barton Road Swing Bridge	–	31.7	4.3
Barton Swing Aqueduct	–	31.7	4.3
Barton Oil Berth	S	31.9	4.1
Irwell Park Lay-by	N	32.1	3.9
Irwell Park Wharf	N	32.3	3.7
Eccles Oil Wharf	N	32.5	3.5
Brown and Polson's Wharf	S	32.7	3.3
Centenary Lift Bridge	–	32.8	3.2
Corn Products Ltd	S	32.9	3.1
Weaste Oil Wharf	N	33.3	2.7
Weaste Lay-by	N	33.5	2.5
Weaste Wharf	–	33.5	2.5
Southern Oil Wharf	–	33.6	2.4
Esso Oil Wharf	S	33.7	2.3
Mode Wheel Locks	–	33.9	2.1

	Side of canal	Dist from Eastham Locks Miles	Dist from Manchester Miles
Manchester Dry Docks Company	S	34.0	2.0
Salford Quay	–	34.0–34.3	2.0–1.7
British Oil and Cake Mills	S	34.3	1.7
No 9 Dock Entrance (closed)	–	34.3	1.7
Trafford Wharf	S	34.4–34.6	1.6-1.4
Turning Basin, Nos 8, 7 and 6 Docks and entrance lock to Salford Quays	–	34.6	1.4
Trafford Road Bridge	–	35.0	1.0
Colgate-Palmolive Company	–	35.3	0.7
Pomona Docks, Nos 3, 2 and 1 and Pomona Lock	S	35.4–35.6	0.6–0.4
Cornbrook Wharf	S	35.7	0.3
Woden Street Footbridge	–	36.0	0.0

River Irwell, Upper Reach

Distance table   *Miles*

Manchester, Woden Street Footbridge, and junction with Manchester Ship Canal to:

Junction with River Medlock and Hulme Locks Branch of the Bridgewater Canal (closed)	0.1
Regent Road Bridge	0.3
Prince's Bridge, junction with Manchester, Bolton and Bury Canal (closed)	0.5
Junction with Manchester and Salford Junction Canal (now only one lock open)	0.6
Irwell Street Bridge	0.8
Albert Bridge	0.9
Blackfriars Bridge	1.1
Victoria Bridge	1.3
Hunt's Bank	1.4

Market Weighton Canal

Originally completed in 1782, the Market Weighton Navigation never actually reached the town but terminated about 2 miles south at Canal Head. It has always had the dual purpose of navigation and drainage and large volumes of water still pour out into the Humber after heavy rain. The canal was active for about 100 years, but the upper section, above Sod House, was abandoned in 1900. Brick traffic in Humber sloops continued into the 1950s.

In 1971, the Weighton Lock and a short section of canal were abandoned but after public pressure the lock was listed as an ancient monument and repairs were put in hand. It is now owned by the

Environment Agency but recent movement has meant another costly refurbishment. It is possible to enter the canal but only by prior arrangement with the Environment Agency at Willerby and payment of the appropriate fee. There is no public right of navigation. The Market Weighton Drainage Board passed its navigation responsibilities to Yorkshire Water but the channel is now overgrown and quite restricted.

Road bridges, in particular the A63 and M62, have severely restricted headroom for navigation, and there is unlikely to be turning room once a craft is past the immediate vicinity of the lock. An additional hazard for anyone contemplating entering this waterway are the regular fishing competitions. The canal is well known as an excellent coarse fishery and local agreements have been drawn up by representatives of the various interested parties so all recreational activities can proceed harmoniously.

Authority Market Weighton Drainage Board, Waterloo Buildings, Pocklington, Yorkshire ☎ 01759 22115.

Lock access Environment Agency, Ridings Area, No 1 Viking Lane, Great Gutter Lane, Willerby, Hull HU10 6DE ☎ 01482 651446.

Towpath On the east side, the towpath and then a public footpath run as far as Market Weighton.

Navigation Only craft capable of tidal cruising should attempt to visit the Market Weighton Canal. Contact must be made with the Willerby office of the Environment Agency well in advance by anyone contemplating visiting the Market Weighton Canal.

Distance table   *Miles*

Weighton Lock, junction with Humber to:

Lantern Lane (public footpath to Broomfleet)	0.6
Broomfleet Landing	1.0
Brickyard Bridge	1.5
Railway Bridge (Main Line to Hull)	1.8
Landing Lane	2.1
Newport, A63 road bridge (lowest bridge)	3.1

MARKET WEIGHTON CANAL Maximum vessel dimensions

From and to	Distance	Length	Beam	Draught	Headroom	Locks
The River Humber to Canal Head	9.5 miles (15.2km)	70' (21.3m)	14' 10" (4.5m)	4' 3" (1.3m)	9' (min) (2.7m)	1

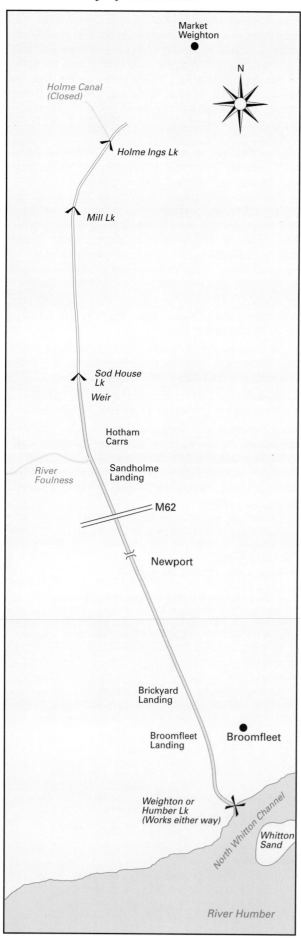

	Miles
M62 Motorway Bridge	3.6
Sandholme Landing Bridge	3.9
River Foulness	4.7
Sod House Lock (effective head of navigation)	5.9
Land of Nod Farm	7.3
Mill Lock	8.0
Holme Ings Lock	8.9
Canal Head	9.5

River Medway

The Medway is said to be the river that divides the Men of Kent from Kentish Men. Rising in Sussex, it flows north and then east and has been navigable and a busy transport route since the 16th century. The lower reaches have a naval history going back to Henry VIII's time and, although there is now no naval presence at Rochester or Chatham, the lower Medway is still busy commercially. The area has many muddy creeks and mudflats favoured by wading birds and navigation should not be taken lightly.

Allington Lock was built after an Act in 1802 making Maidstone and Tonbridge accessible to barges at all states of the tide. The upper river is now managed by the Environment Agency and it is hard to imagine it was once quite an industrial river or that you are so near to London. The countryside is quiet and peaceful with beautiful old stone bridges at Teston, East Farleigh, Yalding, Tonbridge and Aylesford. Oast houses, now mostly converted, remind you of the long history of hop growing and brewing in the area. A trip along the river can become a pilgrimage for fans of Charles Dickens who spent some of his childhood here, set parts of *Great Expectations* and *The Pickwick Papers* in the area and lived at Gadshill in his old age.

In *Slow Boat Through England*, Frederic Doerflinger describes a cruise in a hire boat along the Medway in the 1960s and very little has changed today, except, probably, the prices. The Environment Agency produce a very useful *Guide to the Medway Navigation* and Imray's publish *The River Medway* by Derek Bowskill, both of which are very useful when planning a trip.

Authority *Sheerness to Allington Lock* Medway Ports Authority, The Secretary, Sheerness Docks, Sheerness, Kent ME12 1RX ☎ 01795 561234.

Allington Lock to Tonbridge, Upper Medway Navigation Environment Agency, Guildbourne House, Chatsworth Road, Worthing, West Sussex BN11 1LD ☎ 01903 832000 *Fax* 01903 821832.

Kent Area Office, Millbrook House, Mill Street, East Malling ME19 6BU ☎ 01732 875587 *Fax* 01732 875057.

Navigation Section, Endeavour Park, London Road, Addington, West Malling, Kent ME19 5SH ☎ 01732 838858.

Bridges Numerous. After Tonbridge town quay there are three more bridges with a minimum height of 4ft 6ins to allow navigation for a further 2 miles.

Towpath The Environment Agency and its predecessor the National Rivers Authority have been involved in the Medway River Project to re-establish the public footpaths along the navigation. The footpath passes backwards and forwards across the river.

Speed limit Above Allington Lock, 5 knots.

Connections The Thames Estuary at Strood, the Thames and Medway Canal which is now derelict but a restoration programme is underway.

Navigation The lower reaches of the Medway below Allington Lock are tidal. Passage to and from the river is via the Thames Estuary which should only be attempted in a sea worthy boat with experienced crew. High water at Allington Lock is 50 minutes after HW Sheerness.

Charts Imray Y18, Admiralty 1834, 1835.

Facilities There are several boatyards, marinas and slipways along the river. Maidstone and Tonbridge have all types of shops, and Yalding and Allington have local services.

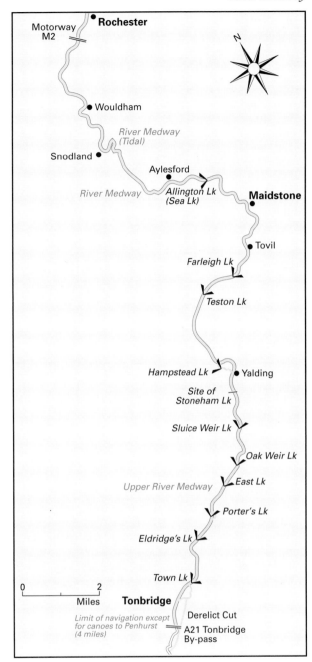

Distance table

Tonbridge Wharf and Bridge to:	*Miles*
Tonbridge Town Lock No 1	0.3
Eldridge's Lock No 2	1.6
Porter's Lock No 3	2.6
East Lock No 4	3.8
Ford Green Bridge	4.3
Oak Weir Lock No 5	4.6
Sluice Weir Lock No 6	6.0
Railway Bridge and Stoneham Old Lock (disused)	7.0

RIVER MEDWAY Maximum vessel dimensions

From and to	Distance	Length	Beam	Draught	Headroom	Locks
Tonbridge Town Quay to Yalding	8.0 miles (12.8km)	80' (24.3m)	18' 6" (5.6m)	4' (1.2m)	8' 4" (2.5m)	7
Yalding to Maidstone	8.0 miles (12.8km)	80' (24.3m)	18' 6" (5.6m)	5' 6" (1.6m)	8' 4" (2.5m)	2
Maidstone to Allington Lock	1.8 miles (2.8km)	175' (53.3m)	21' 6" (6.5m)	6' 6" (1.9m)	8' 4" (2.5m)	1
Allington Lock to Sheerness	25 miles (40.2km)	Unlimited	Unlimited	8' (2.4m) MHW	9' 6" (2.9m)	None

	Miles
Yalding Boatyard	8.0
Hampstead Lock No 7	8.3
Wateringbury Bridge	10.0
Teston Lock No 8	11.1
Teston Bridge	11.5
Barming Bridge	12.8
Farleigh Lock No 9	13.3
Tovil	14.5
Maidstone	15.3
Allington Lock No 10 (tidal lock)	17.8
Forstal	18.8
Preston	19.0
Aylesford	19.3
Mill Hall	20.0
New Hythe	20.8
Hawkwood, Rochester City Stone	22.0
Snodland	22.8
Halling	24.0
Wouldham	24.8
Cuxton	26.5
Rochester Bridge	29.0
Chatham	30.3
Gillingham	33.8
Folly Point, Hoo Island	34.4
Darnett Ness	34.6
Oakhamness Jetty	35.8
Sharp Ness, Burntwick Island	36.4
Port Victoria	40.8
Mouth of Swale and Queenborough Pier	42.0
Sheerness, junction with the estuary of the River Thames	42.8

River Mersey

The River Mersey, and its tributary the Irwell, is one of Britain's large rivers which enabled the area it serves to develop into a major industrial and commercial centre. Without a route to the sea, few of today's principal cities would have developed over the centuries when road transport was slow, difficult and sometimes hazardous. The relatively narrow entrance to the Mersey opens into a wide and sheltered anchorage and, since the Middle Ages, the river has been used for transport and communication.

Today, it cannot be regarded as a significant waterway for leisure use, but its place in the history of Britain's inland waterways should not be overlooked. From the start of the industrial revolution, the river gradually became severely polluted but the Manchester Basin Campaign, backed by the government, is making a significant impact on the problem and water quality is being steadily improved.

The normal tidal limit is Howley Weir but it is navigable for about another 3 miles up to Woolston Weir. Boats can pass Howley Weir on spring tides. Although there is no lock in Woolston Weir, the reach above can be navigated by shallow draught vessels from the Ship Canal.

Authority *Lower Mersey Garston to Liverpool* Mersey Docks and Harbour Company, 39 Gate, Collingwood Dock, Regent Road, Liverpool L3 0AH ☎ 0151 949 6000.

Upper Mersey Bank Quay, Warrington to Garston The Upper Mersey Navigation Commissioners have ceased to exist.

Towpath None.

Connections Weaver Navigation at Weston Point (via the Manchester Ship Canal); Leeds and Liverpool (via Liverpool Docks); Sankey (St Helens) Canal at Widnes and Fiddlers Ferry; Mersey and Irwell Navigation at Warrington (now disused); Manchester Ship Canal at Eastham; (Runcorn Lock to MSC was closed in 1970).

Navigation The Mersey Estuary has fast tides and further upstream shifting sand banks so it is not to be trifled with. Any boat considering approaching the Mersey would be advised to do so on neap tides when the speed of the tide is less. Only well-found sea-going vessels with a crew who are prepared for sea conditions should contemplate navigating the lower reaches. No approach should ever be made in poor visibility.

Liverpool is a commercial port and until recently not suitable for private boats but Liverpool Marina in Brunswick and Coburg Docks offers berthing for visitors.

Tides High water Liverpool is 15 minutes after HW Dover, HW Widnes about 45 minutes after HW Liverpool.

Charts Imray C62, Admiralty 1951, 3490.

RIVER MERSEY *Maximum vessel dimensions*

From and to	Distance	Length	Beam	Draught	Headroom	Locks
Bank Quay, Warrington to Garston	18.8 miles (30.2km)	Unlimited	Unlimited	9' (2.7m)	82' (25m)	None

Distance table

Left Bank Miles	Bank Quay, Warrington to:	Right Bank Miles
	Runcorn, junction with Manchester Ship Canal through Old Quay Lock (closed),	
7.3	Runcorn	
	Runcorn Bridge	
7.5	Widnes, West Bank Dock	7.6
	Runcorn (Bridgewater Lock was closed	
8.5	in 1920)	
9.5	Weston Point	
	Eastham, junction with main entrance	
18.3	to Manchester Ship Canal	
	Garston	18.8
	Dingle Point	21.4
	Birkenhead	
24.0	Liverpool, Prince's Landing Stage	
	Liverpool, Salisbury Dock, giving	24.4
	access through Collingwood and	
	Stanley Docks to the Stanley Dock Cut	
	Branch of the Leeds and	
	Liverpool Canal	25.4
	Low tide access through Langton	
	Dock Lock	
43.1	Mersey Bar Light vessel	43.1

Middle Level Navigation

Between the River Nene and the Great Ouse is a collection of waterways called dykes, drains and rivers constructed to drain the Fens. Collectively they are known as the Middle Level and they have a fascination and beauty all their own. Many of the drains were created under Acts passed between 1750 and 1875, although much of the system was constructed by Vermuyden 100 years earlier. The principal purpose was for drainage but the drains were also used for the transport of agricultural produce. At one time, there were 108 miles of navigable waterways but today it is about 90 miles in total, depending on the draught of your boat.

The drainage of the Fens has caused the peat to shrink and, in many areas, the waterways run above the level of the surroundings within embankments. The enormous level of shrinkage is graphically brought home at Holme Fen where a post which was pushed into the ground in 1851 now stands about 14ft above ground level. In the villages and by the drains, it is common to see buildings tilted at dramatic angles as a result of shrinkage of the ground under them.

The Forty Foot, Twenty Foot and Sixteen Foot are all said to refer to the original width of the waterway when it was constructed under Vermuyden's management. Now it bears no relation to the width of the drain. These straight, man-made cuts contrast strongly with the winding course of the Old River Nene and Well Creek. Wisbech Canal used to join Well Creek near Outwell and Upwell but has long since been filled in; fortunately, the Well Creek was saved from a similar fate. Norfolk County Council had plans to fill in the Well Creek and re-align a road. In 1970, the Well Creek Trust

was incorporated and by 1975 the Creek was again open to navigation. Recent work has enlarged the lock at Marmont Priory to 92ft long. Once Ashline Lock has also been lengthened, a full-length narrow boat will be able to cruise through the Middle Level from the Great Ouse to the Nene and the main canal system.

Throughout the Middle Level there are only seven locks and some may feel the flat countryside is less exciting than canals which cross hills via dozens of locks, but for peace and remoteness the Middle Level takes some beating. The town of March and the villages in this area are delightful and local boat users are always keen to help visitors, while the feeling of openness and freedom engendered by the huge skies offers a different type of escapism.

A detailed *Map of the Middle Level* is produced by Imrays. At present, the Middle Level Commissioners make no charge to boats cruising the waterways, but visiting boats must complete a form and should obtain a copy of the Commissioners' *Navigation Notes* before starting a cruise. Bye-laws for the Middle Level are also available from the Commissioners. Weed growth can be a serious problem and from July onwards weed is cut and weed ropes are used to collect the cut weed. Anyone navigating the Middle Level should untie the weed rope before passing through and ensure that the rope is securely retied behind the boat.

General information about navigation

The navigable drains include:

Bevill's Leam	Black Ham Drain
Forty Foot River	Kings Dyke
New Cut	New Dyke
Old River Nene	Pophams Eau
Ramsey High Lode	Sixteen Foot River
Twenty Foot River	Well Creek
Whittlesey Dyke	

Non-navigable or partly navigable drains include:

Great Raveley Drain	Middle Level Main Drain
Monks Lode	Old Popham's Eau
Pig Water	Yards End Dyke
Yaxley Lode	

The following information is reproduced courtesy of the Middle Level Commissioners. It is updated annually and a copy of the most recent edition of *Navigation of the Middle Level – General Information* should be obtained from the Commissioners by anyone intending to cruise this waterway.

The following notes should be read carefully before navigating the Middle Level.

1. The Middle Level affords a navigable link between the River Great Ouse and the River Nene and a large majority of boat-owners entering the system use it for that purpose. The recommended route is through Stanground Lock, Peterborough, via Kings Dyke,

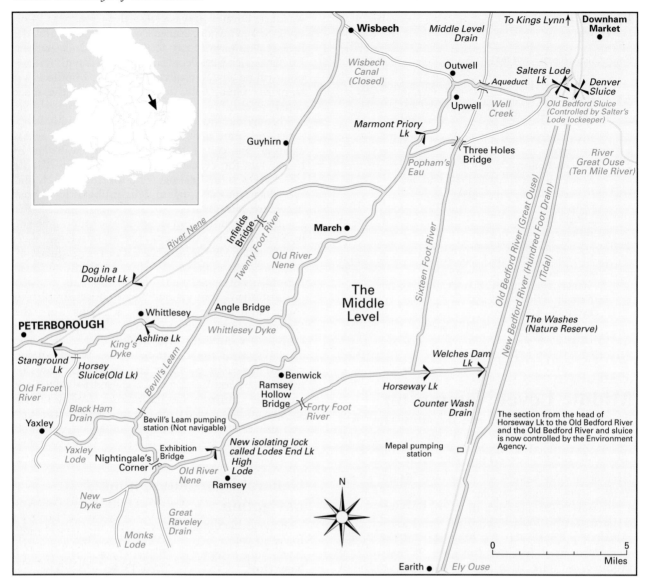

Whittlesey Dyke, the Old River Nene and Well Creek, to the junction with the Great Ouse at Salters Lode Lock.

The waterway's function is the arterial drainage of 267 square miles of highly productive farmland, and the cost of continual channel maintenance is met out of drainage rates, with a contribution from letting of fisheries. No licence fees or toll charges are levied on pleasure boats at present, but the name of each boat should be clearly shown, and visitors will be required to register with lock-keepers at Stanground and Salters Lode when entering the system.

Salters Lode Lock is closed on Christmas Day and Wednesdays during November, December, January, February and the first week of March.

A key which will give access to both March Sanitation Station (see Note 5) and Lodes End Lock Security Compound (see Note 8) can be purchased at Stanground Lock, Salters Lode Lock or the Middle Level Offices in Dartford Road, March (price £2.00).

2. Certain watercourses are subject to erosion of the banks, and elsewhere shallows make navigation difficult. The commissioners therefore request the co-operation of persons navigating between the Great Ouse and the Nene in making passage via the recommended route.

A maximum speed limit of 5mph is operated throughout the system with the exceptions of Whittlesey Dyke (Turningtree Bridge to Ashline Lock), Kings Dyke (Stanground Lock to Ashline Lock) and Well Creek (Marmont Priory Lock to Salters Lode Lock) where the maximum speed limit is 4mph.

Speed must also be reduced for safety reasons and to avoid wash when passing through areas of riverside development, congested areas and/or moored boats.

3. Aquatic weeds occur in most of the system during the summer period and from July onwards weed ropes may be encountered. These ropes must be removed to allow passage and carefully and securely replaced.

4. The Middle Level Bye-laws include the following provisions:
   a. no refuse shall be thrown overboard into the river or deposited on the adjacent banks;
   b. boats shall be properly moored and secured so as not to impede or endanger the passage of other craft (mooring two or more abreast is forbidden);
   c. sunken boats shall be removed forthwith at the owner's expense;
   d. moorings may not be constructed on any Middle Level watercourse without the Commissioners' prior approval and written consent.

   Boat movements during the hours of darkness are prohibited.

5. There are pump-out and chemical toilet emptying facilities at March Sanitation Station which is situated on the site of the old quay adjacent to the Town Bridge. A key is required for access (see Note 1). In the event of malfunction contact Fenland District Council ☎ 01354 654535 (24hr).

   Polluting matter must not be discharged into the waterways from any vessels or from any sanitary appliance thereon.

6. It should be noted that, except where there are public highways, all lands adjoining Middle Level river banks are private property whereon the normal laws of trespass apply. There are public rights of way along some banks.

   The Middle Level waters comprise a valuable coarse fishery, intensively used between mid-June and mid-March. Boat users are requested to afford the usual courtesies to anglers who will be encountered in greatest numbers on Saturdays and Sundays in the season.

During the winter period, ice skating on Well Creek, when conditions allow, is a traditional local sport often attracting thousands of people to the area. Disturbance of the ice while it is forming results in an uneven surface unsuitable for skating. Boat movements under such circumstances are therefore frowned upon locally, and should be avoided.

7. Boat users are advised to avoid the Main Drain (which is navigable only as far as the Well Creek Aqueduct at Mullicourt Priory) and Old Pophams Eau (another dead end) north of Three Holes Bridge as conditions there can be hazardous due to sudden pumping or sluicing operations.

8. The key to March Sanitation Station will also open the padlock on the security fence gate at Lodes End Lock (see Note 1). It is necessary to open this gate to navigate the lock.

   Before leaving the lock please ensure that the penning sluices are fully closed, the security fence gate locked and the chain between the large V-doors in place. The chain must be secured by the large end link to the spring loaded catch in the other door and left loose (not wrapped round the door posts) so that the doors can open the full length of the chain for gravity drainage purposes when conditions allow.

9. Before passing under bridges, please ensure that there is adequate clearance for you and your boat.

   The minimum navigation headrooms referred to in these notes are the approximate minimum clearances which can be encountered at times of maximum water level retention (usually during the summer period) but the information provided is for guidance only. The headrooms may be further reduced for short periods during water transfer (normally in the summer) or at times of excess water/flood (usually during the winter or spring).

   The minimum navigation headrooms at the lowest bridges (at maximum retention level) are as follows:
   Infields Bridge, approximately 5ft 6ins
   Ramsey Hollow Bridge, approximately 5ft 6ins
   Exhibition Bridge, approximately 4ft 6ins

10. Care should also be taken when approaching or travelling close to the river edges where submerged piles and other revetment installed to support and protect the banks could be a hazard.

    A line of old submerged piles supporting the south (park side) bank of the Old River Nene between Marylebone Bridge and the Town Bridge at March has been marked by a series of posts. Please avoid contact/disturbance of the marker posts.

A house affected by shrinkage by the old course of the River Nene in the Middle Level. *Sîan Barron*

11. Please note that an Ouse Key is required to operate Ashline, Marmont Priory (if the lock-keeper is not available), Lodes End and Horseway Locks.

 Ouse Keys can usually be purchased at the following:
 a. Stanground Lock,
 b. Salters Lode Lock,
 c. C.J. Fox, Boat Builders & Hirers, 10 Marina Drive, March (marina off Old River Nene).

Recommended route, Nene-Great Ouse

Total distance, 28½ miles (45.8km).

Stanground Sluice Peterborough[1]
Length 80ft. *Width* 11ft 6ins.
Maximum draught of boats greater than 36ft long not to exceed 2ft 3ins.
Lock-keeper Mr A. Rootham ☎ 01733 66413.
Telephone lock-keeper beforehand and do not enter lock without keeper in attendance.

King's Dyke
8 bridges. Minimum headroom approximately 7ft. Water level may be below navigation level and 24-hours notice to Stanground lock-keeper will avoid possibility of delays while the water level is being adjusted.
Note Restricted length and sharp bend through Briggate, Whittlesey. Width between walls 14ft. Narrow boats up to 70ft long have nevertheless negotiated King's Dyke to Ashline Lock where there is now a landing stage for visitors to Whittlesey and a turning bay.
Whittlesey population 14,000, shops, fuel, leisure centre.

Ashline Lock[2]
Length 58ft. *Width* 11ft 6ins.
Unattended. It is important that boats in the lock are held at least 3ft 3ins clear of the upstream doors to avoid fouling the sill as the water level is lowered. Please ensure that the lock doors and penstocks are properly closed after use. Leakage could rapidly lower the water level in King's Dyke and considerable difficulty could be experienced in restoring a satisfactory navigation level. In the event of problems contact Stanground lock-keeper.

Whittlesey Dyke
7 bridges. Minimum headroom Burnt House Bridge, 7ft approximately.
Main drainage channel.

Old River Nene Floods Ferry to Marmont Priory
3 bridges – ample headroom.
River is wide and deep from Floods Ferry to March and from March to Pophams Eau but the sections through March Town and from Pophams Eau to Marmont Priory Lock are relatively shallow and should be navigated with care.
March population 17,000, Middle Level Offices, Fox's Boatyard, moorings, shops, fuel, sanitation station, leisure centre.

Marmont Priory Lock[2]
Length 92ft. *Width* 12ft.
Lock-keeper Mrs M. Norton ☎ 01945 773959.
Please ensure that the lock doors and penstocks are properly closed after use. Leakage can rapidly lower the water level in Well Creek and it can sometimes take several days to restore a satisfactory navigation level.
Note For navigation headrooms at bridges refer also to Note 9.

Well Creek
15 bridges. Minimum headroom approximately 7ft. Route passes through villages of Upwell, Outwell and Nordelph. Moorings, shops, fuel. Some sections of Well Creek in Upwell and Outwell are narrow and relatively shallow and should be navigated with care.

Salters Lode Lock[1]
Length 62ft. Possible length 80ft on level water (falling tide) or below when tidal conditions allow.
Width 12ft 6ins.
Lock-keeper Mr.P.Grodkiewicz ☎ 01366 382292.
Locking through to tidal river for limited periods each side of high tide. Telephone lock-keeper beforehand and do not enter lock without keeper in attendance. Closed on Wednesdays during the winter period (see Note 1).

Salters Lode to Denver Sluice
(Environment Agency)
½ mile upstream of Salters Lode Lock on the River Great Ouse is Denver Sluice and because this stretch of waterway is tidal it represents a challenge to navigators and restricts the times that craft can enter or leave the Middle Level. There are moorings on both sides of the sluice. The lock-keeper at Denver Sluice must be notified beforehand ☎ 01366 382340. Special care should be taken entering and leaving Salters Lode Lock on the tidal side. Inexperienced navigators should follow the instructions of the lock-keepers.
1. Salters Lode and Stanground Locks have a dual role as sluices as well as navigation locks. Whilst the sluices are open, dangerous undertows may be encountered in

MIDDLE LEVEL NAVIGATION Maximum vessel dimensions

From and to	Distance	Length	Beam	Draught	Headroom	Locks
Main Route	28.5 miles (45.8km)	58' (17.6m)	11' 6" (3.5m)	2' 3" (0.7m)	6' 10" (2.1m)	4
Alternative Route	39.8 miles (64km)	53' (16.2m)	11' 6" (3.5m)	2' 3" (0.7m)	6' (1.8m)	4

the pens and it is for this reason, in particular, that navigators are warned not to enter these locks.

2. Marmont Priory Lock may be negotiated unattended if the lock-keeper is not available but please take special care to ensure that the doors and penstocks are completely closed after use. This lock is similar to Ashline Lock. Please keep clear of upstream sill.

Old Bedford River
Old Bedford Sluice (Environment Agency)
To gain passage into the Old Bedford/Counter Drain system, contact must be made with the Salters Lode Lock-keeper, Mr P Grodkiewicz ☎ 01366 382292.

Welches Dam Lock
(Environment Agency)
Length 47ft. *Width* 11ft.
This lock is to be used (self-operated by users) only at specific weekends made available for navigation. Details upon request from Inland Waterways Association or Environment Agency ☎ 01353 666660.

Horseway Lock
Length 60ft.
This lock is to be used (self operated by users) only at specific weekends in conjunction with Welches Dam Lock.
Note Access through Horseway Lock must only be made during daylight hours on the actual dates specified by the Environment Agency.

Authority The Middle Level Commissioners, Dartford Road, March, Cambridgeshire PE15 8AF ☎ 01354 653232 *Fax* 01354 659619.

Welches Dam Sluice to Horseway Sluice Environment Agency, Kingfisher House, Goldhay Way, Orton Goldhay, Peterborough PE2 5ZR ☎ 01733 371811 *Fax* 01733 231840.

Horseway Sluice is owned by the Middle Level Commissioners.

Bridges Numerous. The lowest bridge in the system is Exhibition Bridge between Mere Mouth and Nightingales Corner where air draught is 4ft 6ins. Air draught on all bridges can be affected by water levels during the summer.

Locks Entering the Middle Level 24-hours notice is required by the lock-keepers, Stanground Lock ☎ 01733 66413 or Salters Lode Lock ☎ 01366 382292. Welches Dam is only opened at certain times, for information contact the Environment Agency ☎ 01733 371811.

Towpath There are public footpaths along many of the drains but all land adjoining the river banks is private property. OS *Landranger* series, Nos 142 and 143, should be refered to for public rights of way. In some cases the path crosses from one bank to the other without a bridge.

Speed limit 4mph.

Navigation Ebb tide on the Great Ouse at Salters Lode runs at 2 knots to 3 knots. Weather conditions can have a considerable effect on the tide and due allowance should be made. High water at Salters Lode is 1 hour 5 minutes after HW King's Lynn.

At the time of going to press, siltation was causing navigation difficulties on the tidal River Ouse between Denver Lock and Salters Lode Lock and through the Old Bedford Sluice. Passage of boats in these areas was very unlikely. Rainfall and tidal effects can change these circumstances and anyone wishing to use these locks should contact the Denver Lock-keeper ☎ 01366 382340 or the Salters Lode Lock-keeper ☎ 01366 382292 for the most up-to-date information.

Facilities There are few established moorings and many banks are privately owned but it is possible to moor where a road runs alongside and usually if there is a footpath. Moorings and a sanitary station are available in March and there are marinas at March and Ramsey.

Distance table   *Miles*
King's Dyke
Head of Stanground Sluice (lock) and junction with Stanground Branch of River Nene, called 'Broadwater', to:
Junction with Pig Water (not navigable)	1.1
Fields End Bridge	2.3
Whittlesey, Ashline Lock	4.3

Whittlesey Dyke
Whittlesey Ashline Lock to:
Angle Corner, junction with Twenty-Foot River and Bevill's Leam	2.8
Floods Ferry, junction with old River Nene	6.1

Bevill's Leam (obstructed by pumping station)
Angle Corner, junction with Whittlesey Dyke and Twenty-Foot River to:
Chapelbridge	1.6
Pondersbridge	3.6
Tebbitts Bridge	4.5
Bevill's Leam Pumping Station (not passable)	4.9

Black Ham Drain
Mere Mouth, junction with Bevill's Leam, and Old River Nene to:
Railway Bridge, ¾ mile southwest of Yaxley village	3.6

Old River Nene
Mere Mouth, junction with Bevill's Leam and Black Ham Drain:
Exhibition Bridge (lowest in system 4ft 6ins)	2.5
Nightingale's Corner, junction with New Dyke (not navigable)	2.8
St Mary's Village and Bridge	3.5
Saunders Bridge, junction with Ramsey High Lode	5.8
Wells Bridge, junction with Forty-Foot River	6.6
Benwick Village and Bridge	10.6
Floods Ferry, junction with Whittlesey Dyke	13.3
Staffurth's Bridge	14.3
March Town Centre	18.3
Reed Fen, junction with Twenty-Foot River	20.4
Low Corner, junction with Popham's Eau	22.4
Marmont Priory Lock	24.1
Upwell Church	25.4
Outwell Basin	26.1

	Miles
New Dyke	
Nightingale's Corner, junction with Old River Nene to:	
Holme Turning Bay	3.3

There are two branches from New Dyke, viz Monks Lode and Great Raveley Drain. The latter is a route to the Woodwalton Fen Nature Reserve which can be visited by appointment.

Ramsey High Lode	
Saunder's Bridge, junction with Old River Nene to:	
Ramsey Mill	1.1

Well Creek	
Outwell Basin to:	
Aqueduct over Middle Level Drain	1.3
Nordelph	3.4
Salter's Lode Lock, junction with River Ouse	5.4

Twenty Foot River	
Angle Corner, junction with Whittlesey Dyke and Bevill's Leam to:	
Poplar Tree Bridge	0.6
Beggars Bridge	1.3
Infields Bridge	4.3
Goosetree Farm	5.8
Hobb's – Lot Bridge	6.8
Reed Fen, junction with Old River Nene	10.4

Popham's Eau	
Low Corner, junction with Old River Nene to:	
Three Holes Bridge, junction with Sixteen Foot River	2.3

Middle Level Drain (navigation not permitted)

Sixteen Foot River	
Three Holes Bridge, junction with Popham's Eau to:	
Cottons Corner	0.8
Bedlam Bridge	4.1
Stonea Railway Station	5.1
Boots Bridge	6.8
Junction with Forty-Foot River (Sixteen Foot Corner)	9.6

Forty Foot River or Vermuyden's Drain	
Wells Bridge, junction with Old River Nene to:	
Forty Foot Bridge	0.5
Puddock Bridge	3.3
Leonard Child's Bridge	5.3
Chatteris Dock (Chatteris distant 1 mile)	6.0
Junction with Sixteen Foot River (Sixteen-Foot Corner)	7.8
Horseway Village	8.9
Horseway Lock	8.1
Welches Dam Lock, and junction with the Old Bedford River and Counterdrain	10.5

(Navigation of this section is under the jurisdiction of the Environment Agency and is restricted to certain weekends)

Condition of the Drains

The following is included for completeness but the Middle Level Commissioners would like all cruising boats to follow their *Navigation Notes* (as reproduced above) and keep to the recommended route.

Note All levels are given to datum 100ft below Ordnance Datum Newlyn, i.e. -100 ODN.

Old Bedford Tidal Sluice
Length 15ft. *Width* 13ft 6ins. *Sill Level* 98.15. *Head* (soffit) 115.0.
Under jurisdiction of Environment Agency. Sluice-keeper ☎ 01366 382292.
Normal water level 103.5. Old Bedford can only be entered at level water in tidal river.

Old Bedford River
No restriction.
Well maintained. Heavy weed growth in summer. Under the jurisdiction of the Environment Agency.

Welches Dam Sluice (lock)
An Environment Agency structure.
Length approx 47ft. *Width* 11ft. *Sill level* 97.0.
Head 6ft 10ins.
Unattended. Two low bridges at this sluice restrict the headroom. If the water level in the channel is high, the headroom is further restricted. Key at Welches Dam Farm.

Forty Foot River, Welches Dam to Horseway
No structural restrictions.
Heavy weed growth. Under jurisdiction of Environment Agency.

Horseway Lock
Length approx 60ft. *Width* 11ft 9 ins. *Sill level* 94.5.
Head unrestricted.
Unattended. Great Ouse windlass required to work lock.

Forty Foot River
All bridges 7ft headroom.
¾ mile to junction with Sixteen Foot River contains shoals, depth not exceeding 2ft 6ins. Remainder of river to Wells Bridge is a drainage channel and well maintained.

Lodes End Lock
Length approx 65ft. *Width* 12ft.
New lock to cater for occasional lower water levels upstream of Bevill's Leam pumping station. Unattended.

River Nene, Lodes End Lock to Flood Ferry
All bridges 7ft headroom.
Drainage channel well maintained. Route passes through village of Benwick.

Whittlesey Dyke
All bridges 7ft headroom.
Drainage channel well maintained

Ashline Lock, Whittlesey
Length 58ft. *Width* 11ft 6ins. *Sill level* 100.9. *Head* unrestricted.
Unattended.

King's Dyke
All bridges 7ft headroom.
Depth of water 3ft 10ins.
Draught not exceeding 2ft 6ins. Water levels are occasionally below navigation level and notice must be given to Stanground lock-keeper 24 hours prior to locking through at Ashline or Stanground, to permit adjustment of water levels if necessary. Restricted length through Briggate, Whittlesey: maximum length of craft which can negotiate sharp bend, 35ft for cruisers and 70ft for narrowboats. Craft should proceed at not more than 1mph to prevent grounding near the bend.

Standground Sluice (lock)
Length 80ft. *Width* 11ft 6ins. *Sill level* 102.34. *Head* 16ft 3ins (with level of 104.34).
Lock attended. Lock-keeper is Mr Rootham to whom 24-hours notice of passage should be given ☎ 01733 66413.

Well Creek Route
Marmont Priory Sluice (Lock)
Length 92ft. *Width* 12ft. 5ft of water over sill.
Officially attended. Owner of sluice cottage keeps key.

Well Creek
6ft headroom at normal water levels.
Several low bridges through the villages of Upwell, Outwell and Nordelph. Sharp turn in Outwell. Proceed with caution.

Salters Lode Sluice (Lock)
Length 63ft. *Width* 12ft 6ins. 6ft 6ins of water over sill. Ample headroom.
Exit to the tidal Ouse at limited periods of the tide. Lock attended, Mr Grodkiewitz ☎ 01366 382292. Apply to him for tidal information and times of exit and entrance. 24-hours notice of passage is required.

River Nene

Rising near Weedon and Yelvertoft, almost as far away from the sea as you can be in England, the River Nene winds its way through beautiful countryside and busy towns and cities to the Wash and the North Sea. For just under 90 miles of this journey, the river is navigable and creates a link between the canals of the Midlands, the Middle Level, the Great Ouse and the sea. The Nene has had an important place in transport history but now recreational use of the river is increasing steadily. Few roads run near to the river enhancing the feeling of peace and remoteness, even at the end of the 20th century.

From its junction with the Grand Union Canal at Northampton, it passes through the 'county of spires and squires' before entering Cambridgeshire where, for miles around, the prospect is dominated by Peterborough Cathedral. Peterborough used to be the tidal limit until the lock and sluice were built at Dog-in-a-Doublet in 1937, a further 5 miles towards the sea.

In its tidal reach, the river passes through Wisbech and the new harbour at Sutton Bridge until it finally comes into the Wash between two towers known as 'the lighthouses'. Tides run swiftly through these 25 miles and you can still meet commercial traffic coming to both Wisbech and Sutton Bridge. As an inland port, Wisbech is most attractive and the waterfront has a distinctly Dutch feel to it.

The countryside and wildlife is varied along the river gradually changing from rolling farmland and stock-rearing country into the wide flat landscapes of the Fens as the river nudges along the edge of Lincolnshire. There is plenty of architectural and historical interest along the way. The remains of Fotheringhay Castle can be seen where Richard II was born and later Mary Queen of Scots was held by her cousin Elizabeth the First until she was executed there. The Nene Valley Steam Railway crosses the river twice near Peterborough, there are fine stone village churches and many of the bridges over the river are old examples of the stone mason's art.

The navigation was promoted by several Acts between 1714 and 1829 but the old River Nene route is now part of the Middle Level. This was a winding and tortuous route and the new cut from Stanground to the Wash made a big difference to the ease of access into the Nene. By the early years of the 20th century, the river was quite derelict in places and difficult to navigate. On the initiative of George Dallas, the river was restored to full navigation by the Catchment Board in the 1920s.

Authority *River mouth to Bevis Hall* The Port Manager, Port Office, Wisbech ☎ 01945 582125.

From Bevis Hall to Northampton Environment Agency, Anglian Region, Kingfisher House, Goldhay Way, Orton Goldhay, Peterborough PE2 5ZR ☎ 01733 371811 *Fax* 01733 231840.

Bridges From the Wash to Dog-in-a-Doublet Lock, three; a swing bridge at Sutton Bridge,

Wisbech Bridge and Guyhirn Bridge, notional headroom is 1.4m and 1.2m respectively but this will vary with the state of the tide. From Dog-in-a-Doublet to Northampton, 66 fixed bridges.

Special care is necessary at a number of bridges, particularly Chester House Bridge, near Wellingborough. The ancient monument bridge at Irthlingborough restricts beam to 13ft although the locks are 14ft wide.

Towpath The Nene Way is a long distance footpath which runs from the Wash Coastal Path to Northampton and beyond the navigable distance of the river. It crosses the river several times and in some places diverts from the riverside through pretty villages along the route. The Ordnance Survey *Landranger* maps show the route of the path.

Locks On the River Nene most of the locks have steel pointing doors upstream and a vertical guillotine gate on the downstream end. Locks should be left with the pointing doors closed and the vertical lift gate raised and locked. A special key is required to operate the vertical gate which can be obtained from the Environment Agency at the address above. Allow two weeks for the application to be processed. Heavy rain can cause rapid changes in water level and warning signs are displayed. In these circumstances, the lock may be 'reversed', the pointing doors chained open and the vertical gate partially lifted, and no attempt should be made to navigate the lock.

Mooring is not permitted within 36m of any locks, sluices or weirs except when navigating through a lock. At Dog-in-a-Doublet, Bedford Road Sluice and Weston Favell mooring is prohibited for 100m either side.

Branches Stanground Branch 0.6 miles from Peterborough to Stanground Lock leading to the Middle Level; West Bridge Branch 0.6 miles at Northampton.

Connections With the Middle Level Navigation (for the River Ouse, etc.) at Peterborough; with the Grand Union Canal (Northampton Branch) at Northampton. The connection to the Thorney River, via two locks (staircase) at Dog-in-a-Doublet has been closed and converted to a fixed sluice. West Bridge Branch is navigable with some difficulty, though not legally abandoned.

Speed limit Within the Environment Agency (EA) jurisdiction 7mph. A copy of the Recreational Bye-laws should be obtained from the EA at the address

above and should be adhered to. Between Peterborough and Dog-in-a-Doublet Lock is a 1 mile stretch which is derestricted and water-skiing is allowed. The start and finish of this length of water are clearly marked.

In the tidal reaches, speed of vessels should be such as not to damage banks or inconvenience other users.

Navigation Wisbech and Sutton Bridge are commercial ports and large cargo vessels can be met in the lower reaches. Up to Dog-in-a-Doublet Lock passage must be timed for the tide to allow both sufficient draught and headroom under Wisbech and Guyhirn bridges. High water Sutton Bridge is about 10 minutes after HW Kings Lynn, HW Wisbech is 50 minutes after HW Kings Lynn, and HW Dog-in-a-Doublet 2 hours 15 minutes after HW Kings Lynn.

Through Wisbech, the banks are lined with steel and concrete piling and there is stone in the river bed. Craft must take great care as tides run strongly, both on the flood and the ebb, wind direction and freshwater coming downstream will also affect the strength of the current and the rise and timing of tides.

Information on mooring in Wisbech and likely large ship movements can be obtained by contacting the Port Manager ☎ 01945 582125.

Anyone taking a craft of near maximum dimensions along the River Nene should contact the EA and the Port Manager at Wisbech.

Facilities Most facilities for boat crews are available at Northampton Lock and the town has all shops and a wide choice of pubs and restaurants. Many of the locks have a toilet block, water supply and rubbish disposal. There are many villages with pubs and a shop and Peterborough offers all types of facilities. Slipways are available at many places along the river.

Distance table *Miles*

Northampton, junction with Northampton Branch of the Grand Union Canal to:

Northampton, South Bridge	0.1
Northampton Lock No 1	0.4
Rush Mills Lock No 2	1.6
Abington Lock No 3	2.0
Weston Favell Lock No 4	2.9
Clifford Hill Lock No 5	3.7
Billing Lock No 6	4.3
Cogenhoe Lock No 7	5.4
Whiston Lock No 8	6.5
White Mills Lock No 9	7.2

RIVER NENE Maximum vessel dimensions

From and to	Distance	Length	Beam	Draught	Headroom	Locks
Northampton to Peterborough	57.3 miles (92.2km)	78' (23.7m)	13' (3.9m)	4' (1.2m)	7' (2.1m)	37
Peterborough to Wisbech	19.3 miles (31.0km)	130' (39.6m)	20' (6.1m)	6-7' (1.9m)	Up to 12' (3.6m)	1
Wisbech to The Wash	11.4 miles (18.4km)	260' (79.2m)	40' (12.2m)	17' (5.1m)	Unlimited	None

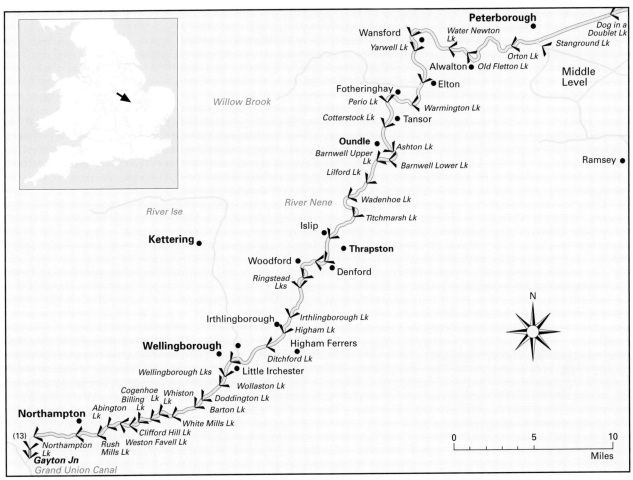

	Miles
Barton Lock No 10	8.1
Doddington Lock No 11	8.8
Wollaston Lock No 12	9.9
Upper Wellingborough Lock No 13	11.2
A45 Bridge	11.3
Lower Wellingborough Lock No 14	12.1
Ditchford Lock No 15	13.9
Higham Lock No 16	15.9
Irthlingborough Bridge	16.3
Irthlingborough Lock No 17	16.8
Upper Ringstead Lock No 18	19.1
Lower Ringstead Lock No 19	19.7
Woodford Lock No 20	21.9
Denford Lock No 21	22.8
A14 Bridge	23.4
Islip Lock No 22	24.2
Titchmarsh Lock No 23	26.3
Wadenhoe Lock No 24	28.7
Lilford Lock No 25	29.7
Upper Barnwell Lock No 26	31.9
Lower Barnwell Lock No 27	32.3
Ashton Lock No 28	34.1
Oundle Bridge	35.0
Cotterstock Lock No 29	36.2
Perio Lock No 30	38.0
Warmington Lock No 31	40.4
Elton Lock No 32	42.0
Yarwell Lock No 33	45.0
Wansford Lock No 34	46.2
A1 Bridge	46.9
Waternewton Lock No 35	49.9

	Miles
Alwalton Lock No 36	51.7
Orton Lock No 37	55.4
Peterborough Bridge	57.3
Peterborough, junction with Branch to Stanground and Middle Level Navigations	57.9
Dog-in-a-Doublet (inn) Lock No 38 (power-operated, with emergency hand operation)	62.5
Popley's Gull	64.2
Guyhirn	70.6
Bevis Hall	74.0
Wisbech Town	76.6
Junction with North Level Main Drain	81.9
Junction with South Holland Main Drain (sluice entrance is only opened at flood times)	83.2
Sutton Bridge	83.9
Guy's Head 'Lighthouses'	86.9
The Wash at Crabs Hole, mouth of river	88.0

New Junction Canal, South Yorkshire

Despite its relatively short length and very straight course, the New Junction Canal is not without charm and interest. Running between the Aire and Calder Navigation and the Sheffield and South Yorkshire Navigation, it crosses two aqueducts, one over the Don the other over the Went, and has two lifting bridges and one swing bridge. Opened in

NEW JUNCTION CANAL Maximum vessel dimensions

From and to	Distance	Length	Beam	Draught	Headroom	Locks
Bramwith Junction to Southfield Junction	5.5 miles (8.9km)	215' (65.5m)	22' 6" (6.9m)	9' (2.7m)	Unlimited	1

1905 to improve transport of coal from Doncaster to Goole in 'Tom Puddings', it still carries commercial traffic but is a pleasant, rural waterway far away from the noise of cars and motorways.

Authority British Waterways, Mill Lane, Mill Gate, Newark, Nottinghamshire NG24 4TT ☎ 01636 704481.

Towpath Throughout navigation.

Speed Limit 6mph.

Distance table   *Miles*
Bramwith, junction with Sheffield and South Yorkshire Navigation to:

Sykehouse Lock	3.5
Southfield Junction	5.5

Nottingham Canal

See River Trent and entry in Miscellaneous Waterways.

River Great Ouse

The Great Ouse and its tributaries comprise the major navigation in East Anglia offering nearly 150 miles of cruising waterways. From the ancient cities of Ely and Cambridge, through remote unspoilt countryside to the tidal reaches and exposed seaway of the Wash, the Great Ouse has a diverse and fascinating character. Throughout its history, the dual roles of navigation and drainage have not always been compatible although they are equally important to the surrounding area.

The course of the river has changed over the ages. Once it flowed via Upware and Wisbech but then in the 13th century its mouth changed to King's Lynn. After this time, the river became important for trade although it was probably not navigable above St Ives. It was not until the 1600s when the government took an interest, and surveys were carried out to see how the navigation could be

improved. Six locks were built above St Ives and then, under an Act of 1655, it was proposed to make the river navigable to Bedford. Despite the Act being passed no work was started on this part of the river until 1687.

It was during this period that Vermuyden was working for the Duke of Bedford and major drainage works were built which ultimately led to the landscape of rich farmland we know today. In the Middle Ages, the Fens would have been extensive marshes and islands with only very small isolated communities, quite wild and hostile country. The draining of the Fens would have had as dramatic an effect on the local population as the Enclosures did in Scotland. Huge lakes and meres, where there were fish and wildfowl, were drained depriving the locals of their principal livelihood. One of the effects of the vast drainage works created by Vermuyden is that the level of the land today is about 15ft below what it was in the 16th century.

The Old Bedford River was cut in 1637 and the Hundred Foot, because it was 100ft wide, was finished by 1651. The sluice at Denver caused considerable siltation and greatly affected the flow of the river. Over the years, there have been many rebuildings and alterations to the navigation works and the fortunes of the navigation have waxed and waned with competition from the railways in the second half of the 19th century and now a rise in the leisure use of the river.

Drainage of the rich agricultural land surrounding the river has always been a priority. Despite the investment in drainage works, there have been a number of devastating floods over the years. Possibly one of the worst was in 1947 after a very severe winter. The successive bodies responsible for the river and drainage of the area had no navigation authority and so they were unable to charge tolls and generate income to reinvest in navigation works. This situation was rectified in 1963 and now the Environment Agency has responsiblity for the Recreational Waterways and licences all craft which use the river. The Great Ouse Boating Association (GOBA) also helps to ensure that navigation rights are upheld and that facilities are available for boat users in the area. For more information the Association can be contacted at GOBA, 84 High Street, Huntingdon, Cambridgeshire PE17 1BS ☎ 01487 830105.

By the early part of the 20th century navigation ceased at St Ives, and then the Great Ouse Catchment Board re-opened navigation first to Godmanchester then to Eaton Socon just before the Second World War. In the 1950s, the Great Ouse Restoration Society was formed to re-open the

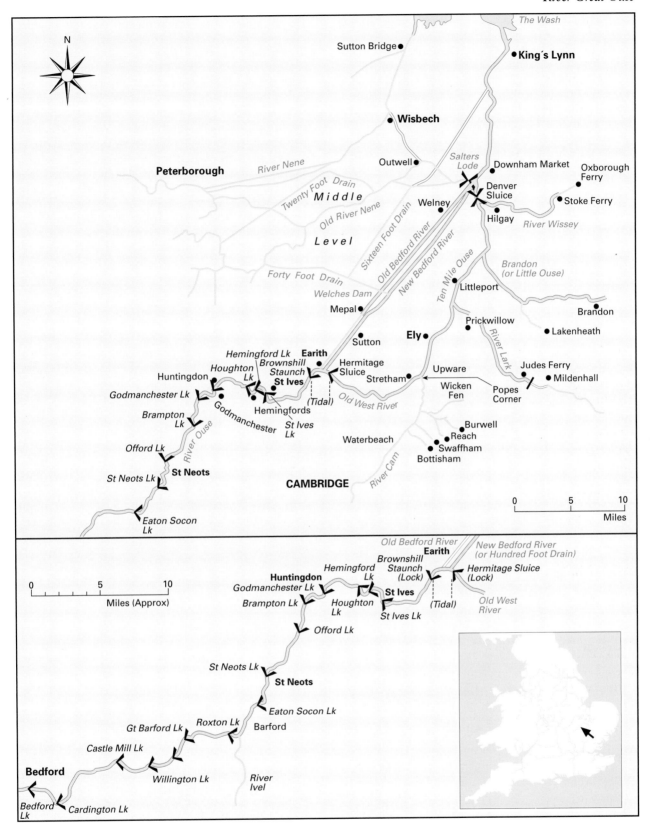

navigation to Bedford and this was achieved by 1978. At the end of the 19th century, there were plans to connect the Great Ouse to the Grand Junction Canal with a canal from Bedford to Soulbury but the Bill to promote it was dropped. This may yet be achieved with a recent proposal to connect the Great Ouse at Bedford to the Grand Union Canal at Milton Keynes.

Cruising the Great Ouse for pleasure, it is best to follow the route of the Old River. Not only does this avoid the straight tidal Hundred Foot or New Bedford River, but it offers the opportunity to divert up the Cam, Lark, Little Ouse or Wissey. With only 16 locks between Bedford and Denver Sluice, the attractions of the river are very different to those of the canals of the Midlands and northern England. The river mostly flows gently through quiet countryside and some beautiful old towns with a wealth of old buildings, museums and historical sites. A 14th-century stone bridge links Huntingdon and Godmanchester and, on the old bridge at St Ives, there is a tiny chapel to St Lawrence. From Brownshill Lock, about 1½ miles upstream from Earith, to Hermitage Lock ½ mile downstream, the river is tidal and it is here that the New Bedford and Old Bedford rivers join the Great Ouse.

Following the Old West River, you only pass fields and farms; there isn't even a sizable village on the river. Not long after Pope's Corner and the junction with the River Cam you come into Ely, dominated by its wonderful cathedral. After Ely, the river is fairly straight and quite wide with the railway running alongside until you reach Littleport, then it bends along the Ten Mile River to Denver. Denver Sluice is one of the largest drainage structures in the country. Once through the lock, you are into tidal waters and have the choice of returning up the New Bedford River to Earith, cutting across to Salters Lode Lock and into the Middle Level or heading down river to King's Lynn and the Wash.

Authority Environment Agency, Anglian Region, Kingfisher House, Goldhay Way, Orton Goldhay, Peterborough PE2 5ZR ☎ 01733 371811 *Fax* 01733 231840.

Dimensions The Environment Agency booklet, *Navigations in the Anglian Region*, gives details of the dimensions of every lock, headroom heights for bridges at HW and LW average spring and neap tides in the tidal reaches and at Normal Water Level in the non-tidal reaches. Draught varies along the river and some patches may be shallower than the minimum draught in the locks. These areas are identified by the EA with distance and location.

Bridges 19 from Bedford to Earith and ten from Earith to the Wash. The two guides to the Great Ouse and the map covering the Middle Level published by Imrays show the headroom of the bridges. In the tidal distance, headroom and draught will be affected by both the state of the tide and the amount of freshwater coming down the river.

Earith to Denver – Headroom under bridges at HW

	Spring Tides	Neap Tides
Earith Bridge	13' 5" (4.1m)	15' 1" (4.6m)
Sutton Gault	9' 6" (2.9m)	13' 2" (4.0m)
Mepal	10' 9" (3.3m)	14' 2" (4.3m)
Railway Bridge	8' 6" (2.6m)	13' 5" (4.1m)
Welney	7' 10" (2.4m)	12' 5" (3.8m)

Denver to The Wash – Headroom under bridges at HW

	Spring Tides	Neap Tides
Downham	8' 6" (2.6m)	11' 11" (3.6m)
Stow	7' 8" (2.3m)	12' 2" (3.7m)
Magdalen	7' 8" (2.3m)	12' 2" (3.7m)
St Germans	8' 2" (2.5m)	12' 9" (3.9m)
Free Bridge	9' 4" (2.8m)	13' 10" (4.2m)

Towpath There are footpaths along most of the river but these are not always on the river bank. The appropriate Ordnance Survey *Landranger* maps should be used to ensure public rights of way are followed.

Connections The River Nene via the Middle Level; The Wash; the Rivers Cam, Lark, Wissey and Little Ouse.

Navigation Boats must carry a current Environment Agency Licence and all boat owners intending to cruise the Great Ouse and its

RIVER GREAT OUSE Maximum vessel dimensions

From and to	Distance	Length	Beam	Draught	Headroom	Locks
Kempston Mill, Bedford to Earith	40.5 miles (65.2km)	85' 4" (26.0m)	10' 4" (3.1m)	3' 3" (1m)	8' 1" (2.5m)	15
Earith to the tail of Denver Sluice (New Bedford River)	20.8 miles (33.5km)	Unlimited	Unlimited	2' (0.6m) (tidal)	7' 10" (2.3m) (min)	None
Denver to The Wash	16 miles (25.7km)	Unlimited	Unlimited	6' (1.8m) (tidal)	7' 8" (2.3m) (min)	None
Old River						
Earith to Denver	31.1 miles (50.0km)	90' (27.4m)	12' 6" (3.8m)	4' (1.2m) (min)	9' 2" (2.8m)	1
Denver Lock		96' 9" (29.5m)	17' 8" (5.4m)	6' 8" (2.0m)	14' 6" (4.5m)	1
Old Bedford River						
Welches Dam to Salters Lode	12.3 miles (19.8km)	Unlimited	15' (4.5m)	3' 6" (1m)	8' (2.4m)	1

Houghton Mill on the Great Ouse. *Sîan Barron*

	Miles
Willington Lock No 4	5.8
Old Mills Lock Site (now abolished)	6.5
Great Barford Lock	7.3
Roxton Lock No 7	9.6
Tempsford Bridge (Anchor Inn)	10.3
Little Barford	12.6
Eaton Socon and Eaton Socon Lock No 8	13.8
St Neots	15.0
St Neots Lock No 9	16.3
Great Paxton	18.0
Offord Lock No 10	20.1
Brampton and Brampton Lock No 11	23.1
Godmanchester Lock No 12	24.4
Huntingdon	25.1
Hartford	26.3
Houghton Lock No 13	27.8
Hemingford Lock No 14	29.4
St Ives Bridge	30.8
St Ives Staunch (lock)	31.1
Holywell	33.5
Brownshill (or Over) Staunch (lock)	36.3
Earith Village (The Crown)	38.0
Earith, commencement of New Bedford River and junction with old course of river (Earith to Denver) and Earith Bridge	38.5
Sutton Bridge	42.1
Mepal Bridge	43.4
Oxlode	47.5
Welney Suspension Bridge	52.8
Termination of Hundred Foot River and junction with old course of river (Earith to Denver) at the tail of Denver Sluice	58.8
Salter's Lode, junction with Old Bedford River and junction with Well Creek	59.1
Downham Bridge (Downham Market distant 1 mile)	60.1
Stow Bridge	62.9
Magdalen Bridge	66.0
Wiggenhall Bridge	68.0
Commencement of Eau Brink Cut	68.4
The Free Bridge and termination of Eau Brink Cut	71.4
King's Lynn, entrance to King's Lynn Docks	72.8
The Wash, mouth of river	74.8

tributaries should acquaint themselves with the Recreational Waterways Bye-laws of the Environment Agency.

The tidal reaches from Denver to King's Lynn and the Wash can be dangerous and only craft suitable for sea-going should consider using the tidal river. High water King's Lynn is 30 minutes after HW Immingham. The range is 19ft (5.8m) on springs and 10ft 6ins (3.2m) on neaps.

In the upper river above Earith, there is generally a minimum depth of 4ft (1.2m) but in several places there are shallows on bends or in the channel when the depth is about 3ft (0.9m).

Facilities There are several boatyards, marinas and quays as well as 48-hour moorings created by the Environment Agency. Pubs and shops are available in most of the small villages and are listed in the maps of the river published by Imrays. The Great Ouse Boating Association also offers moorings at certain locations. There are a number of slipways along the river, the best reference is *Launching on Inland Waterways* by Diana van der Klugt (see bibliography).

Facilities for private boats at King's Lynn are very limited and anyone intending to visit the town or to stop over on passage across the Wash should contact the harbourmaster to arrange a mooring ☎ 01553 773411.

Distance table
(Part of the Upper Great Ouse to Kempston Mill can be navigated 2½ miles above Bedford)

Bedford to:

	Miles
Bedford, Duck Mill Lock (Town Lock)	0.3
Cardington Lock No 2	2.0
Castle Lock (also known as Castle Mills Lock)	3.6

Old River

The Old River is a combination of the Old West River from Earith to the junction with the River Cam, the Ely Ouse from the junction with the Cam to Littleport and the Ten Mile River from Littleport to Denver.

Headrooms under bridges
Old West

Willingham Flat Bridge	9' 4" (2.8m)
Aldreth	10' 6" (3.2m)
Twenty Pence	10' 4" (3.1m)
Stretham Ferry, A10 Bridge	9' 10" (3.0m)
Stretham Ferry, Old Bridge	9' 6" (2.9m)
Stretham Wooden Bridge	9' 10" (3.0m)
A1123 Road Bridge	10' 6" (3.2m)
Wooden Bridge	11' 2" (3.4m)
Railway	11' 2" (3.4m)

Ely Ouse

	Miles
Newmarket Railway	10' 10" (3.3m)
Ely High Bridge	10' 10" (3.3m)
Cutter Railway Bridge	10' 10" (3.3m)
Ely Marina Bridge	10' 6" (3.2m)
Muckhill Railway Bridge	10' 10" (3.3m)
Beet Factory Footbridge	11' 6" (3.5m)
Beet Factory Pipe Line	11' 10" (3.6m)
Adelaide Railway Bridge	11' 10" (3.6m)
Adelaide Road Bridge	11' 10" (3.6m)
Sandhill Bridge	10' 6" (3.2m)

Ten Mile

	Miles
Littleport Bridge	11' 2" (3.4m)
Hilgay Toll Bridge	10' 6" (3.2m)
Railway Bridge	13' 2" (4.0m)
Denver Sluice Foot Bridge	15' 6" (4.7m)
Denver Sluice Road Bridge	15' 2" (4.6m)

Headroom downstream water levels

		Miles
Denver Sluice Foot Bridge	MHWS	7' 7" (2.3m)
	MHWN	11' 7" (3.5m)
Denver Sluice Road Bridge	MHWS	8' 11" (2.7m)
	MHWN	12' 11" (3.9m)

Towpath There is a footpath along most of the river although it gets a little lost around Ely.

Navigation The Old West River between Earith and Popes Corner, the junction with the Cam, is very shallow in places, the depth can be as little as 2ft (0.6m).

Facilities There are full facilities at marinas at Hermitage Lock, Twenty Pence Bridge, Ely and Littleport Boat Haven. The EA and Great Ouse Boating Association offer moorings at several locations along the river and some pubs have moorings for patrons. There is a slipway at Ely.

Distance table
Old Course of River, Earith to Denver (Old West)

Earith, junction with Main Line of river and Hermitage Sluice Lock No 1 to:

	Miles
Aldreth Bridge	3.4
Twenty Pence Ferry	7.1
Stretham Ferry	8.8
Popes Corner, junction with River Cam	11.6
Ely Station Dock (closed)	14.9
Cutter Inn	15.0
Junction with River Lark	18.9
Littleport Bridge	20.9
Brandon Creek, junction with Little Ouse	24.3
Southery Ferry	25.4
Hilgay Bridge	28.0
Junction with River Wissey	30.0
Denver Sluice, and junction with Main Line of river Lock No 2	31.1

Old Bedford River

The Old Bedford River is only navigable as part of the alternative route through the Middle Level from Welches Dam Lock to Old Bedford Sluice, near Salters Lode. This route is only available on certain weekends and is controlled by the Environment Agency. At the time of writing this route was unlikely to be navigable due to siltation. For up-to-date information the Denver lock-keeper ☎ 01366 382340 or the Salters Lode lock-keeper ☎ 01366 382292 should be contacted. The Wildfowl and Wetlands Trust has a centre at Welney near Hundred Foot Bank. The lower part of the river from Earith to Welches Dam is a flood channel and is not navigable.

Navigation The river is tidal and prevailing weather conditions as well as freshwater discharge will affect the flow. Contact should be made with the Environment Agency before visiting the river as access is only available at certain times. See also the entry on the Middle Level Navigation.

Distance table
Old Bedford River

(The Old Bedford from Earith to Welches Dam is unnavigable)

Welches Dam, junction with Forty Foot River and Counter Wash Drain to:

	Miles
Purls Bridge	0.8
Railway Bridge	2.6
Welney Village and Bridge	6.0
Old Bedford Sluice, Salters Lode and junction with River Ouse	12.3

Counter Wash Drain

Welches Dam, junction with Forty Foot River and Old Bedford River to:

Mepal Pumping Engine	3.0

Great Ouse Tributaries

Little Ouse or Brandon River

Originally the Little Ouse was navigable for 22½ miles to Thetford but the navigation weirs in the upper part have long been derelict. The present head of navigation is Brandon Staunch, but in a dinghy it is possible to continue above the village. An aqueduct passes over the Cut-off Channel near Hockwold-cum-Wilton and there is a sluice here for water control in times of flood.

Thetford Corporation were responsible for the river for much of its history. Fison's fertilizer was a major traffic on the river until the start of the First World War with works at Thetford and Two Mile Bottom, trains of lighters were towed by tugs between Thetford and King's Lynn.

Lakenheath Lode was also navigable but now only light craft can explore for a short distance.

Headroom under bridges

Brandon Creek Bridge	10' (3.0m)
St John's Road Bridge	10' 2" (3.1m)
Redmere Bridge	10' (3.0m)

RIVER GREAT OUSE *Maximum vessel dimensions* – Great Ouse Tributaries

From and to	Distance	Length	Beam	Draught	Headroom	Locks
Little Ouse or Brandon River						
Thetford to Brandon Creek, Old River	22.5 miles (36.2km)	Unlimited	Unlimited	4' 4" (1.3m)	8' 10" (2.7m)	None
River Lark						
Branch Bridge to Mildenhall	13 miles (20.9km)	88' (26.8m)	14' 6" (4.4m)	2' 6" (0.7m)	10' 3" (3.1m)	1
River Wissey						
Oxborough Ferry to Great Ouse	10.5 miles (16.9km)	Unlimited	Unlimited	3' 6" (1.0m)	8' 2" (2.5m)	None

Wilton Bridge	10' 10" (3.3m)
Railway bridge	8' 10" (2.7m)

Towpath There are footpaths along most of the navigation including part of Hereward Way long distance path.

Navigation Boats up to 49ft (15m) can turn at the head of navigation, about ¼ mile downstream from Brandon. There is headroom of 10ft as far as the railway bridge about 1 mile downstream from Brandon. There is a depth of about 6ft (1.8m) as far as Wilton Ferry. Care must be taken passing the sluices at Cut-off Channel.

Facilities There are moorings at the mouth of the Little Ouse and moorings and a slipway at Brandon.

Distance table *Miles*
Thetford Town Bridge to:

Thetford New Bridge (A11)	0.1
Thetford Staunch No 1	0.5
Thetford Middle Staunch No 2	1.9
Turfpool Staunch No 3	2.8
Two Mile Bottom	3.4
Croxton Staunch No 4	3.8
Santon Staunch No 5	5.3
Santon Downham Bridge	5.9
Brandon Bridge	8.8
Brandon Staunch No 6 (present head of navigation)	9.1
Railway Bridge (Ely to Norwich line)	10.0
Sheepwash Staunch No 7 (site of)	10.6
Junction with Cut-off Channel	12.5
Cut-off Channel syphon	12.6
Wilton Bridge	13.0
Crosswater Staunch No 8 (site of)	16.5
Junction with Lakenheath Lode, Botany Bay	17.0
Redmere Bridge	18.5
Little Ouse Bridge	20.5
Brandon Creek Bridge and junction with River Great Ouse	22.5

River Lark

From early times the Lark was navigable to Mildenhall and under an Act of 1700 improvements to Bury St Edmunds were put in hand with locks and staunches. The Lark Navigation remained with the Ashley family until 1855 by which time traffic had reduced considerably suffering from competition with the Bury–Ipswich railway.

During the second half of the 19th century, the section above Mildenhall was again improved and a tributary to Tuddenham was made navigable. Unfortunately, the venture failed just as works were completed. The last commercial traffic to Mildenhall was in 1920 but the lock at Isleham is still operational and boats can reach Judes Ferry. There have been suggestions that the river should again be improved to Mildenhall.

Headroom under bridges

Branch Bridge	11' (3.3m)
Prickwillow Railway Bridge	10' 2" (3.1m)
Prickwillow Road Bridge	9' 10" (3.0m)
Judes Ferry Bridge	10' 6" (3.2m)

Towpath There are footpaths from Mildenhall to the Great Ouse, frequently on either side of the river.

Navigation Boats up to 45ft (13.7m) can turn at Judes Ferry Bridge, small craft can reach Mildenhall. As far as Isleham, there is a depth of about 6.6ft (2m).

Facilities Isleham Marina offers all facilities and there are moorings at Prickwillow and Judes Ferry.

Distance table *Miles*
Northgate Dock, Bury St Edmunds (ultimate terminus) to:

Bury St Edmunds Bypass bridge (A45)	0.1
Tollgate Lock No 1	0.6
Tollgate Bridge, Bury St Edmunds (A134 Thetford Road)	0.6
Junction with branch to Fornham Dock (original terminus basin)	0.8
Bury St Edmunds Staunch No 2	0.9
Fornham Staunch No 3	1.7
Fornham Park Lock No 4	1.9
Causeway Bridge, Fornham All Saints	2.0
Ducksluice Farm Lock No 5	2.7
Hengrave Bridge	3.2
Hengrave Lock No 6	3.4
Chimney Mill Lock No 7	3.9
Flempton Lock No 8	4.5
West Stow Staunch with accommodation bridge over (Boyton Staunch No 9)	4.8
Fulling Mill Lock No 10	5.3
Fulling Staunch No 11	5.6
Cherry Ground Lock No 12, Lackford	6.1
Lackford Bridge	6.3
Mill Heath Upper Staunch No 13	6.8
Mill Heath Lower Staunch No 14 Lock	6.9
Farthing Bridge, Icklingham (Cavenham to Icklingham Road)	7.8
Icklingham Lock No 15 and Icklingham Mill Bridge	8.0
Temple Bridge	8.7
Temple Bridge Staunch No 16	8.8
Jack Tree Staunch No 17	9.0

	Miles
Junction with Tuddenham Mill Stream	10.5
Junction with Cut-Off Channel	10.6
Barton Mills New Bridge	10.9
Braton Mill Lock No 18	11.0
Barton Mills Old Bridge	11.0
Barton Hall Staunch No 19	
(Jeffries Halt Staunch)	11.4
Mildenhall Gas Works Lock No 20 (old lock)	12.1
Mildenhall Bridge	12.2
Mildenhall Turf Lock No 21	12.3
Worlington Bridge	13.3
King's Staunch No 24	13.6
Judes Ferry Bridge, West Row	
(limit of navigation)	14.5
Freckenham Gravel Staunch No 25	15.0
Junction with Lee Brook	15.5
Isleham Lock No 26	16.5
Prickwillow Bridge	22.5
Railway Bridge	22.8
Junction with River Great Ouse	24.6

Tuddenham Mill Stream

Junction with the River Lark to:

Tuddenham Mill Stream Staunch No 1	0.8
Tuddenham Mill (terminus of branch)	1.3

River Wissey

The River Wissey joins the Great Ouse about 1 mile from Denver Sluice. It has no locks and is navigable for 10 miles up to Stoke Ferry. A large sugar beet factory was built at Wissington on the side of the river and beet was delivered by barge until the late 1950s.

Headroom under bridges

Hilgay Railway Bridge	8' 8" (2.6m)
Hilgay Road Bridge	8' 2" (2.5m)
Beet Factory Railway Bridge	9' 10" (3.0m)
Beet Factory Pipe	10' 6" (3.2m)
Beet Factory Road Bridge	11' 6" (3.5m)
Wissey Sluice Bridge	7' 11" (2.4m)
Stoke Ferry Bridge	9' 6" (2.9m)

Towpath From Whittington to the Great Ouse there is a footpath, frequently one on each side of the river.

Navigation Small craft can reach Whittington. Care should be taken in times of flood when sluices will be open to divert water into Cut-off Channel. There is a small island in the river opposite Wissington sugar beet factory which should be passed using the south channel. As far as the sugar beet factory, there is a depth of 6ft (1.8m) with some variation due to rainfall.

Facilities There are moorings above the old bridge at Stoke Ferry and at Hilgay where there is also a public slip.

Distance table

Oxborough Ferry to:	Miles
Whittington	1.0
Stoke Ferry Bridge (A134)	1.5
Branch to Cut-Off Channel	2.0
Accommodation Bridge into Stoke Ferry Fen	2.1
Siphon over Cut-Off Channel	2.3
Lode to Northwold Fen	2.6
Methwold Lode (to Methwold village)	3.3
Lode to Stoke Ferry Fen	3.6

	Miles
Lode into Methwold Common	3.9
Wissington New Road Bridge	5.3
Wissington Sugar Beet Factory Wharf	5.4
Wissington Light Railway Bridge	5.6
Hilgay Old Road Bridge	8.4
Hilgay New Road Bridge (A10 Bypass)	8.4
Junction with Great Ouse	10.5

Soham Lode

From River Ouse to Soham Railway Bridge, distance 3½ miles. Only for shallow draught craft up to 1ft 6ins.

Cottenham Lode

Navigable for light craft from the Old West to Cottenham.

River Kym

Navigable for small cruisers for about 1 mile from the main river at St Neots.

River Ouse, Sussex

In the early 1800s, the River Ouse was navigable for 32 miles to Upper Ryelands Bridge. From 1790 to 1814 several Acts were passed to promote the navigation of the river and today it is possible to see remnants of lock chambers, although none are now useable. Until the 1950s, Thames barges used to trade to the cement works at Lewes.

The river passes through some beautiful downland countryside eventually meeting the English Channel at Newhaven. As with other rivers in Sussex, its course and mouth has been changed by storms. Until the 1570s, the mouth of the Ouse was at Seaford, just 2 miles east of Newhaven, but after severe weather an enormous shingle bar was thrown up and the river forced its way out at a village called Meeching. This became a 'New Haven' which gradually grew into a prosperous port, the village lost its name but it grew and developed into what we know today.

It is possible to navigate to Lewes on the tide, and small craft which can be portaged can continue past Hamsey old lock up to the double locks at Barcombe.

RIVER OUSE, SUSSEX Maximum vessel dimensions

From and to	Distance	Length	Beam	Draught	Headroom	Locks
Newhaven Harbour to Lewes	8.2 miles (13.2km)	Unlimited	16' (4.8m)	3' (0.9m)	8' (2.4m)	None
Lewes to Hamsey Lock	1.3 miles (2.1km)	Unlimited	10' (3m)	3' (0.9m)	8' (2.4m)	None

Authority Environment Agency, Southern Region, Guildbourne House, Chatsworth Road, Worthing, Sussex BN11 1LD ☎ 01903 820692 *Fax* 01903 821832. Newhaven Port Authority, Port Office, Beach Road, Newhaven ☎ 01273 514131.

The Upper Ouse Navigation Company set up under the 1814 Act ceased to exist many years ago. The original Acts do not appear to have been subject of any extinguishing Order or Act.

Bridges – Approx depths and headroom at HWST

	Depth	Headroom
Newhaven Swing Bridge	18' (5.4m)	17' (5.1m)
Southease Bridge (swing bridge)	14' (4.2m)	10' (3.0m)
Two railway bridges over Glynde Reach (not over main river)	8' (2.4m)	5' (1.5m)
Southerham Railway Bridge	14' (4.2m)	10' (3.0m)
Lewes Town Bridge to crown of arch	10' (3m)	7' (2.1m)
Lewes Railway Bridge	6' (1.8m)	8' (2.4m)

Towpath Throughout navigation.

Speed limit 5.75mph (5 knots).

Navigation The river is tidal and navigable at highwater to Lewes Bridge for craft drawing up to 6ft, at their own risk.

Above Lewes, it is only possible for small craft to navigate up to the ruins of Hamsey Lock. High water at Lewes is about 1 hour after HW Newhaven. Spring tides rise 9 to 10ft. HW Newhaven is about 2 minutes after HW Dover. At half-tide, the stream near to Southease Bridge runs at about 7 to 8 knots. It should be remembered that Newhaven is a busy port for cross Channel ferries.

Charts Imray C9, Admiralty 2154, 1652.

Facilities Mooring is available at Newhaven Marina on the west shore of the river. There is a public slipway at Lewes by the Town Steps.

Distance table

Ruins of Hamsey Lock to:	Miles
Lewes Corporation Wharf and Phoenix Foundry	1.3
Lewes Bridge	1.5
Lewes Portland Cement and Lime Works	2.0
Southerham Swing Bridge	2.3
Southease Bridge (swing bridge)	5.3
Piddinghoe	6.9
Newhaven Bridge (swing bridge)	8.5
Newhaven Harbour mouth	9.5

River Ouse, Yorkshire

This is a river which has seen commercial navigation since Roman times and the wonderful city of York grew on its strength as a port. The fertile plain around York produced rich agricultural goods which were exported and raw materials were imported to the city. The first Acts of Parliament to improve navigation on the river were passed in the middle of the 17th century with more following for over 100 years. Now the port of Goole takes most of the commercial traffic but the Yorkshire Ouse is still a worthy river to explore for the inland navigator.

The upper reaches from Widdington Ings are probably the most picturesque but there is something on offer for most tastes. Downstream from Linton Lock, you may come across some interesting obstructions called 'clay huts'. These are mounds of clay that slip down from the high banks, mainly in an area between Newton-on-Ouse and Nun Monkton, and you certainly don't want to get too close.

Below Naburn Locks, the river is tidal past the junctions with the River Wharfe, the Selby Canal, the River Derwent and the River Aire. Entry into the Selby Canal brings you back into the main network via the Aire and Calder Navigation. From Goole past the Dutch River, the tides run strongly out into the Humber and both crew and craft must be seaworthy to tackle the lower reaches. There is a small marina in the Aire and Calder Navigation at Goole; do not go into the commercial docks at Goole. Howden Dyke is also a busy wharf with very large ships manoeuvring in the river. Plans are being discussed to increase the traffic of commercial shipping at Selby Docks.

Authority Between Trent Falls and Swale Nab, the river is under the jurisdiction of three authorities:

Trent Falls to Skelton Railway Bridge, Goole Associated British Ports, PO Box 1, Port House, Northern Gateway, Hull HU9 5PQ ☎ 01482 327171.

Skelton Railway Bridge, Goole to Nun Monkton British Waterways, Naburn Lock, Naburn, York YO1 4RU ☎ 01904 728229.

Nun Monkton to Swale Nab Linton Lock Navigation Commissioners, 4 Old Maltongate, Malton, North Yorkshire ☎ 01653 600070.

Draught In the tidal reaches of the river the following draughts can be expected:

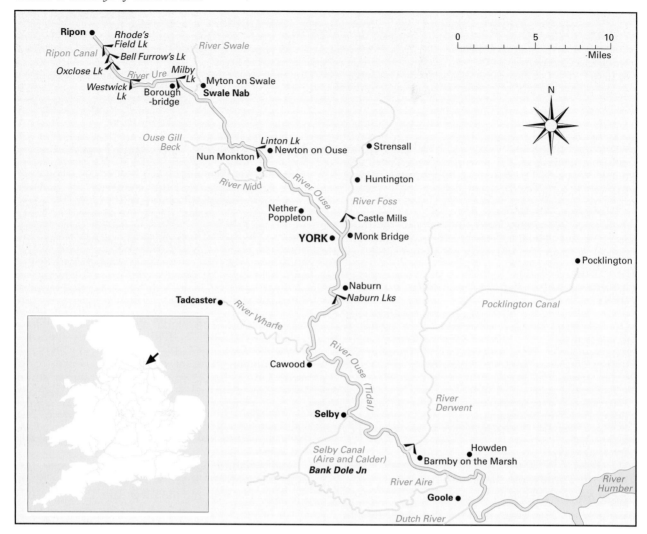

	Springs	*Neaps*
Between Trent Falls and Goole	18' (5.5m)	12' (3.7m)
Between Goole and Selby	13' (4m)	8' (2.4m)
Between Selby and Naburn Locks	8' 6" (2.6m)	6' (1.8m)

Bridges Six swing bridges between Goole and York; three bridges above York. Six short and one long blast is the recognised signal for opening bridges. Maximum headroom 16ft 4ins.

Towpath There is a towpath from Swale Nab to the junction with the River Wharfe, except for a short distance in York.

Connections The river has junctions with Goole Docks and the Aire and Calder Navigation, the River Aire at Asselby Island, the River Derwent at Barmby-on-the-Marsh (17 miles above Trent Falls), Selby Canal at Selby, and River Wharfe at Cawood.

Navigation The Ripon Motor Boat Club publication *Cruising Guide to the North East Waterways* is highly recommended for these waters. Tides refer to HW Hull. High water at Trent Falls is approximately 40 minutes later, Goole 1 hour, Selby 2½ hours, and Naburn Locks 4 hours later. The lower reaches up to Selby carry a large tonnage of heavy shipping and it is advisable to contact the Harbourmaster's Office at Hull for advice before travelling through this section. New Humber and Ouse charts are prepared annually and can be obtained from the harbourmaster. There are port and starboard shore beacons along the Ouse, travelling upstream they are green on the right bank and red on the left bank.

RIVER OUSE, YORKSHIRE Maximum vessel dimensions

From and to	Distance	Length	Beam	Draught	Headroom	Locks
Swale Nab to York	18.0 miles (29.0km)	60' (18.2m)	15' 4" (4.6m)	4' (1.2m)	16' 4" (4.9m)	1
York to Naburn Locks	5.5 miles (8.8km)	150' (45.7m)	25' 6" (7.7m)	8' 6" (2.5m)	25' 6" (7.7m)	1
Naburn Locks to Trent Falls	37.3 miles (60.0km)	Unlimited	Unlimited	Tidal	Unlimited	None

Naburn Locks are manned by British Waterways and open 3 hours before high water to 4½ hours after. During the summer they open on two tides a day between 0600 and 2200 but only the first daylight tide during the winter. It is preferable to book passage through the locks with the lock-keeper ☎ 01904 728229.

Facilities Water, sewage and refuse disposal are available at Linton Lock, and Naburn Marina offers all services including pump-out. Goole Boathouse offers most services for boat crews. York has all types of shops, pubs and restaurants although good moorings in the city are few. Along the river there are many pubs and other places to eat.

Distance table

Swale Nab, junction with River Ure Navigation, and junction with River Swale (unnavigable) to:

	Miles
Aldwark Bridge	4.3
Ouse Gill Beck (unnavigable)	5.6
Linton Lock	7.8
Newton-on-Ouse	8.8
Widdington Ings	9.8
Junction with River Nidd (unnavigable)	10.0
Beningbrough	11.3
Overton	13.3
Nether Poppleton	13.8
Rawcliffe Ings	14.8
Clifton Ings	15.8
York, Lendal Bridge	17.5
York, Ouse Bridge	17.8
York, Skeldergate Bridge	18.0
York, junction with River Foss	18.3
Bishopthorpe	20.8
Naburn Village and Ferry	22.3
Acaster Malbis	22.8
Naburn Locks	23.5
Acaster Selby	26.3
Junction with River Wharfe	28.0
Cawood	29.0
Kelfield	30.3
Riccal Landing	31.5
Barlby	35.3
Selby	36.8
Selby, junction with Selby branch of Aire and Calder Navigation	37.0
Hemingbrough	42.3
Barmby-on-the-Marsh, junction with River Derwent	43.5
Long Drax Railway Bridge	44.1
Asselby Island, junction with River Aire	47.3
Airmyn Ferry	47.8
Howden Dyke, Ferry and Shipyard	50.0
Hook Village (right bank) and Skelton Village (left bank)	50.8
Goole, entrance to docks, and junction with Aire and Calder Navigation Main Line (via Ocean Lock)	52.8
Goole, junction with portion of the River Don known as the Dutch River	52.9
Swinefleet	54.8
Saltmarshe	56.8
Whitgift	57.8
Blacktoft	59.8
Trent Falls, junction with rivers Humber and Trent	60.8

Oxford Canal

This is one of England's most charming canals following a winding route through the valley of the River Cherwell from Oxford to just past Cropredy. From here, it continues to Napton-on-the-Hill before joining the Grand Union Canal to Braunston, then striking off north again to Hawkesbury Junction. One of the attractions of the canal is its bridges, the lifting bridges and the Horseley Iron Work's bridges which carry the towpath over the old loops. Great care must be taken when navigating the lifting bridges, as few rise to the vertical. When cruising a ring route, including the South Oxford and the lower part of the Grand Union, you have a perfect comparison of an early contour canal and a later broad canal designed for faster carrying.

It was really the construction of the Grand Junction Canal from Braunston to Brentford which created the striking difference between the north and south sections of the Oxford Canal. The Oxford was one of the earliest canals to be built with the object of bringing coal from the Coventry coalfields south to Banbury, Oxford and the Thames. The first plans were to make the River Cherwell navigable from Banbury to Oxford and this gives the southern end its rural, sinuous, rather sleepy character. The first of a number of Acts to cover the canal was passed in 1769 and James Brindley was appointed as engineer. Work got underway quickly, but he died in 1772, and the majority of the work passed to his assistant Samuel Simcock. The complete route from the Coventry Canal to the Thames was opened in 1790 but within 15 years it was suffering competition from the Grand Junction Canal which offered a shorter, quicker route to London.

The northern section of the Oxford Canal was shortened by 14 miles in the early 1830s and you can see this now by the occasional missing bridge numbers. Some of the loops of the old canal are still there and are used for moorings. Another modernisation which was put into effect under this scheme was to build a second set of locks at Hillmorton to increase the number of boats that could pass. There are now pairs of narrow locks and each lock acts as a side-pond for its partner.

OXFORD CANAL Maximum vessel dimensions

	Distance	Length	Beam	Draught	Headroom	Locks
Hawkesbury Junction to Braunston Junction	22 miles (25.5km)	7' (21.9m)	7' (2.9m)	2' 9" (0.8m)	6' (1.8m)	4
Napton Junction to Oxford	48 miles (77.2km)	7' (21.9m)	6' 10" (2.0m)	2' 9" (0.8m)	6' 8" (2.0m)	39

Commercial carrying continued on the canal into the 1960s, although trade had declined drastically after the First World War. A dividend was still being paid by the canal company when it was nationalised in 1947. The southern section of the Oxford Canal was the site of one of the earliest campaigns of the IWA when the canal was threatened with closure in the 1950s. Their success meant that the canal was designated a Cruiseway under the 1968 Transport Act. Today, the Oxford Canal is rightly one of the most popular holiday destinations but this can cause some congestion in summer months and also the risk of water shortages.

Authority British Waterways, The Stop House, Braunston, Northamptonshire NN11 7JQ ☎ 01788 890666 *Fax* 01788 890222.

Fradley Junction, Alrewas, Burton-on-Trent, Staffordshire DE13 7DN ☎ 01283 790236 *Fax* 01283 791411.

Bridges Numerous, many lifting.

Towpath Throughout navigation. This is now well developed as a long distance walk. GEOprojects map of the canal is an excellent guide.

Tunnels One at Newbold, 250yds long with a towpath.

Branches Wyken Arm, Stretton Wharf Arm, Fennis Field Arm, Rugby Wharf Arm, Brownsover Arm, Clifton Arm, Old Engine House Arm, Dukes Cut. There are also loops of the old canal but very few of these arms are now navigable.

Speed limit 4mph. It is likely to be less than this, in particular along the summit pound past Wormleighton, owing to the shallowness of the cut.

Connections With the River Thames at Oxford and the Coventry Canal at Hawkesbury Junction. The Oxford Canal shares the same waterway as the Grand Union Canal from Napton Junction to Braunston Junction.

Facilities There are numerous boatyards along the Oxford Canal although not all of them offer pump-out facilities. There is also a wide choice of pubs and restaurants catering for floating customers, many of them have been canal pubs since they were built. Braunston is a famous canal community and offers a range of shops, and many of the villages along the route can provide the essentials. Launching facilities are available at Fenny Compton, Napton and Stretton-under-Fosse.

Distance table Miles

Hawkesbury Junction (Sutton Stop) and Stop Lock No 1, junction with Coventry Canal to:

Tusses Bridge	0.8
Junction with branch to Wyken Old Colliery (Coventry Canal Society moorings)	1.5
M69	3.2
Ansty Bridge	3.5
Hopsford Valley Aqueduct	4.8
M6	5.5
Grime's Bridge	6.3
Stretton Stop Lock and Toll Office, junction with Stretton Wharf Arm	7.0
Junction with Brinklow Wharf Branch	7.5
Easenhall Lane Bridge	7.8
All Oaks Wood	8.0
Hungerfield	8.8
Fennis Field Arm (unnavigable)	9.3
Tuckey's Bridge	10.0
Newbold Tunnel	11.0
Newbold Wharf	11.3
Junction with Rugby Wharf Arm	12.3
Brownsover Arm	12.6
Clifton Arm (unnavigable)	13.7
Hillmorton Locks Nos 2 and 3, 4 and 5 (paired)	15.3
Hillmorton Top Locks Nos 5 and 6 (paired)	15.5
Tarry's Bridge	16.5
Norman's Bridge	17.3
M45	18.2
Barby Wood Bridge	18.3
Willoughby Wharf	20.3
Braunston Turn, junction with Braunston Branch	22.0
Wolfhampcote	22.8
Nethercote	24.0
Flecknoe	24.3
Lower Shuckburgh	25.5
Napton Junction, junction with Birmingham to London Main Line of the Grand Union Canal	27.0
Coventry Road Bridge	27.5
Napton Brickyard	28.3
Napton Bottom Lock No 8	29.0
Then follows Napton Flight Locks Nos 9–14	29.9
Old Engine House Arm	30.1
Napton Locks Nos 15 and 16	30.8
Griffin's Bridge, Wormleighton	36.0
Sherne Hill Bridge	38.0
Fenny Compton	38.3
Claydon Top Lock No 17	41.5
Claydon Flight Locks Nos 18–21	42.0
Elkington's Lock No 22	43.0
Varney's Lock No 23	43.3
Broadmoor Bridge and Lock No 24	43.5
Cropredy Lock No 25	44.5
Slat Mill Lock No 26	45.8
Little Bourton Lock No 27	46.5
M40	47.2

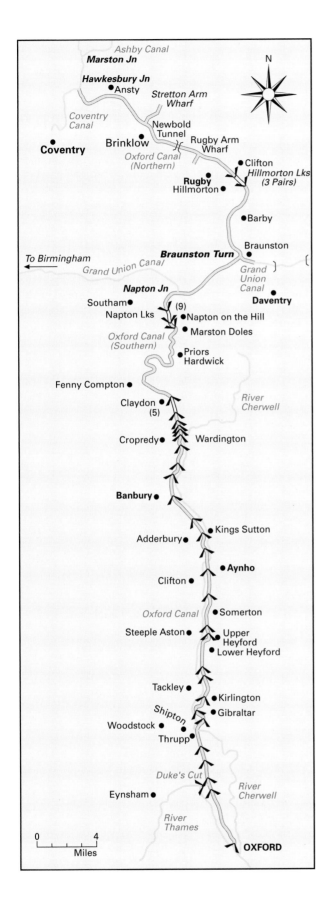

	Miles
Hardwick Lock No 28	47.3
Banbury Lock No 29	49.0
Grant's Lock No 30	51.0
Twyford Wharf	51.8
King's Sutton Lock No 31	52.5
M40	53.3
Nell Bridge and Bridge Lock No 32	54.1
Aynho Weir Lock No 33	54.5
Aynho Wharf	55.5
Souldern Bridge	55.9
Somerton Deep Lock No 34	57.3
Somerton Bridge	57.8
Heyford Common Lock No 35	59.3
Allen's Lock No 36	59.8
Lower Heyford Wharf	60.8
Dashwood's Lock No 37	62.3
Northbrook Lock No 38	62.8
Pigeon's Lock No 39	64.3
Enslow	65.5
Baker's Lock No 40, canal enters River Cherwell	66.0
Shipton Weir Lock No 41, canal leaves River Cherwell	66.8
Thrupp	68.0
Roundham Lock No 42	69.3
Yarnton Lane Bridge	69.8
Kidlington Green Lock No 43	70.3
King's Bridge	71.0
Duke's Lock No 44 and junction with Duke's Cut Branch	71.5
Wolvercote Bridge and Lock No 45	72.3
Walton Well Bridge	74.0
Louse or Isis Lock No 46 and branch to River Thames	74.5
Oxford Hythe Bridge, used for moorings	75.0

Braunston Branch
Junction with Main Line to:

Braunston Toll Office, wharf and junction with Grand Union Canal Main Line	0.5

Duke's Cut Branch

Junction with Main Line and Duke's Cut Lock to junction with River Thames above King's Lock	0.8

This new distance table is thanks to Dr JSA Ashley who has measured it using the latest OS maps. As a result the canal is 2 miles shorter but some discrepancies in previous tables have been resolved.

River Parrett

Improvements to the Parrett were carried out as part of Acts in 1699, 1707 and 1804 to improve the River Tone. There was also an Act in 1795 to improve the navigation from Langport to Ilchester. The Parrett runs through the Somerset Levels which are a unique wildlife landscape. The town of Bridgwater is rich in history. It is not far from Glastonbury and there are said to be associations with King Arthur as well as being deeply involved with the English Civil War. Langport is a delightful village which retains its links with willow cultivation and basket making and is still the best place to visit for unusual basketwork products.

RIVER PARRETT *Maximum vessel dimensions*

From and to	Distance	Length	Beam	Draught	Headroom	Locks
Thorney Mills to Bridgwater Bar	34.3 miles (55.2km)	54' (16.4m)	14' (4.2m)	8' (2.4m)	Unlimited	3

There have been few tourist developments in this area and it retains a quiet charm. In the centre of Bridgwater the redevelopment of the dock area into shops and apartments with a marina has been somewhat constrained by the separation from the river. The marina is on the Bridgwater and Taunton Canal but there is no connection to the river and therefore the sea. Past proposals for a barrage near

Dunball have not, so far, come to anything.

The main purpose of the waterways in the Levels is for drainage during the winter and maintainance of the water table during the summer. The River Parrett is very rarely navigated by private craft although there is a public right of navigation as far as Oath Tidal Lock. Above this the right has been extinguished. The tides are very fierce in the estuary and the time available to a boat to travel up to Bridgwater is extremely limited, added to which there are really no suitable moorings by the town.

Authority *Sea to Bridgwater Bridge* Sedgemoor District Council, The Priory, St Mary Street, Bridgwater, Somerset TA6 3EJ ☎ 01278 4391.

Bridgwater to Thorney Mills Environment Agency, North Wessex Area, Rivers House, East Quay, Bridgwater, Somerset TA6 4YS ☎ 01278 457333 *Fax* 01278 452985.

Locks The locks have been replaced with sluices which are not navigable.

Bridges New bridges in Bridgwater town restrict headroom at high water.

Towpath None below Bridgwater. Above Bridgwater, as far as Thorney Mills.

Connections Rivers Isle and Yeo, also Westport Canal. Tributary River Brue is navigable for 1½ miles to Highbridge. The River Tone is navigable to Newbridge Sluice about 3 miles, from here to Taunton can only be used by light craft that can be portaged.

Navigation The tidal sluice at Oath can be passed during the winter but is closed during the summer to maintain water levels for summer grazing. Langport Lock is now also converted to a sluice. Light craft can ascend the River Isle for about 2 miles but have to be portaged past Midelney Lock, which generally has stop planks fitted in position. The Westport Canal was refurbished in the 1970s by the Wessex Water Authority and is usable by light craft.

Tides are very strong and a bore is common in the lower reaches. High water Bridgwater is about 1 hour 10 minutes after HW Bridgwater Bar. The range on spring tides can be over 30ft (10m).

Distance table

Thorney Mills Bridge Lock (disused) to: *Miles*

Junction with River Isle (leading to Westport Canal)	0.8
Junction with River Yeo	3.0
Langport Bridge	3.8
Langport Lock	3.9
Oath Flood Gates	6.5
Stathe	7.5
Burrow Bridge, junction with River Tone	13.8
Dunwear Brickworks	13.8
Bridgwater, Town Bridge	15.3
Bridgwater, entrance to dock and Bridgwater and Taunton Canal (no access)	15.6
Dunball	18.8
Combwich	23.8
Stert Point	27.9
Junction with River Brue, forming branch to Highbridge	28.4
Burnham-on-Sea	29.3
Bridgwater Bar, mouth of river	34.3

River Brue

Length from junction with River Parrett to Highbridge	1.5

River Yeo

Junction with River Parrett to:

Pibsbury (Weir)	1.0
Little Load Bridge	4.0
Ilchester	8.0

River Isle and Westport Canal

Junction with River Parrett to:

Midelney Lock (out of use)	0.1
Entrance, to Westport Canal	1.0
Westmoor Bridge (lowered)	1.6
Westport Canal Basin and Wharves	3.3

Pocklington Canal

From the River Derwent to within 1 mile of Pocklington, the Pocklington Canal was opened in 1818 for mostly agricultural traffic. Thirty years later the local railway company bought it and through neglect its commercial potential was run down. Despite this, it wasn't until 1932 that trade finally ceased on the canal.

When there was a proposal in 1959 to use the canal course as a dump for sludge from a water treatment works, local interest was aroused and with hard work from many quarters the Pocklington Canal Amenity Society (PCAS) was formed and the canal was saved. So far, 4½ miles are navigable with Walbut Lock and Thornton Lock now fully restored and work progressing well on Coates Lock. PCAS have been helped by the local authority and BW in the restoration projects.

Much of the canal is covered by three Sites of Special Scientific Interest with the west end part of the Wheldrake Ings. This has presented particular problems to the restoration programme but PCAS, WRG NE and other volunteer groups are continuing to restore the locks and reinstate swing bridges, eight of the nine locks being listed buildings and four road bridges are ancient monuments.

This is a wonderfully calm, rural canal winding quietly through farmland below the Yorkshire Wolds.

Authority British Waterways, Naburn Lock, Naburn, York YO1 4RU ☎ 01904 728229.

Bridges Five fixed and seven swing bridges.

Towpath Throughout navigation.

Branches Two short arms to Melbourne village and Bielby village.

Connections With the River Derwent below East Cottingwith.

Navigation The canal is open to boats as far as Melbourne. To reach the canal boats must navigate the tidal River Ouse and the River Derwent. Tide times are based on Hull.

Restoration The full restoration of the canal to navigation is still the aim but further work is dependent on negotiations between BW and English Nature.

Facilities Water supply, rubbish and sewage disposal are available at Melbourne. There are several very pleasant pubs to choose from and an occasional village shop for the essentials.

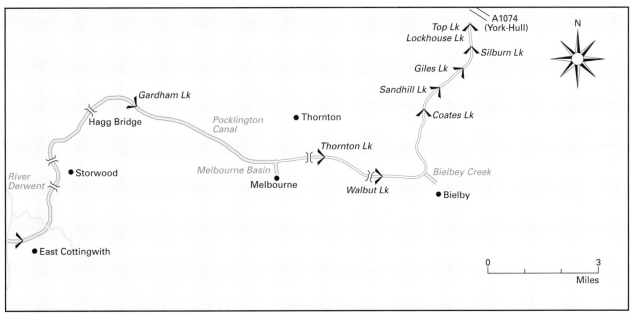

POCKLINGTON CANAL Maximum vessel dimensions

From and to	Distance	Length	Beam	Draught	Headroom	Locks
River Derwent at East Cottingwith to Canal Head, Pocklington	9.5 miles (15.3km)	57' (17.3m)	14' 3" (4.3m)	4' (1.2m)	9' (2.7m)	9

Distance table   *Miles*
Junction with River Derwent to:

East Cottingwith Lock	0.3
East Cottingwith	0.5
Storwood	1.5
Hagg Bridge	2.3
Gardham Lock	3.0
Melbourne	4.9
Junction with arm to Melbourne Basin	4.9
Thornton Lock	5.3
Walbut Lock	6.1
Bielby (junction with Bielby Creek)	7.0
Coates Lock	7.8
Sandhill Lock	8.1
Giles Lock	8.8
Silburn Lock	9.1
Top Lock	9.4
Canal Head (distance 1 mile from Pocklington)	9.5

Ripon Canal

This is the most northerly point of the connected network of waterways and, although only a short canal in itself, the beautiful old town of Ripon is a worthy destination. The canal runs through pleasant countryside from the River Ure into the town. The new basin in the town will provide pleasant facilities once the old warehouse and wharf manager's house have been restored.

The Ripon Motor Boat Club, founded in 1931, have a marina on the west side of the canal about half way between Ripon and the Ure. Visitors' moorings are available but it is best to contact the secretary in advance ☎ 01765 601751. The club also produces a detailed guide to the waterways of the northeast which can be ordered through the secretary.

During the early part of the 19th century, 70-ton cargoes could reach Ripon on Humber keels and there was a regular service to Hull in fly boats.

Authority British Waterways, Naburn Lock, Naburn, York YO1 4RU ☎ 01904 728229 *Fax* 01904 728860.

Bridges Two.

Towpath Good throughout navigation.

Connections To the River Ure.

Restoration Ripon Canal Society have restored the two locks and Harrogate Borough Council have obtained grants to fund the extension to the Bond Gate Green Basin.

Facilities Ripon town has shops and pubs but there are limited facilities for boats.

Distance table   *Miles*
Oxclose Lock and junction with River Ure to:

Ripon Motor Boat Club Marina	1.0
Bell Furrow's Lock	1.3
Rhode's Field Lock	1.5
Bond Gate Green Basin	2.5

RIPON CANAL Maximum vessel dimensions

From and to	Distance	Length	Beam	Draught	Headroom	Locks
Junction with River Ure at Oxclose Lock to Ripon	2.5 miles (4.0km)	58' (17.6m)	14' (4.2m)	3' 6" (1.0m)	8' (2.4m)	3

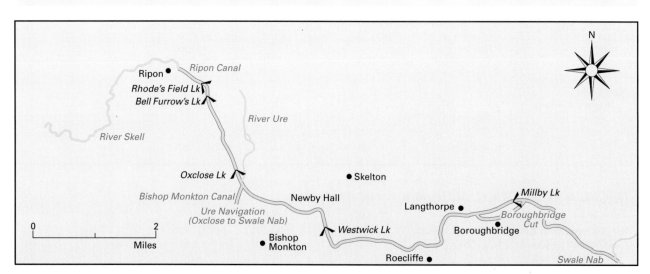

River Roach

This is a charming, winding Essex river, less frequented than its neighbour the Crouch. It is popular with yachtsmen as it offers interesting sailing and there are various creeks to explore off each bank. Havengore Creek leads to Maplin Sands and the Broomway which can be crossed at high water by shallow draught craft.

Firing on the Shoeburyness Gunnery Range is almost continuous on weekdays so anyone intending to use the Havengore route to the Roach should contact the Range Planning Officer ☎ 01702 292271 ext 3211. The bridge-keeper at Havengore Bridge, which has a lifting section, can be contacted during high-water periods on ☎ 01702 292271 ext 3436.

Authority Crouch Harbour Authority, Harbour Office, Belvedere Road, Burnham-on-Crouch, Essex ☎ 01621 783602.

Towpath None.

Branches There is deep water half-way round Potton Island on its west side and light craft can use this channel to enter Havengore Creek and go out to sea near the ancient track called 'the Broomway' at high water. The maximum draught is only 3ft. There is a swing bridge, but navigation is restricted by army artillery practice. Warnings are issued when firing is in progress.

Navigation The approaches to the River Roach are sandy and muddy but, provided good charts and pilot book are used, should present no problem. The lowest reach, Quay Reach, provides good shelter and plenty of water. Through Havengore Creek and across Maplin Sands, there is a 'short cut' to the Thames for shallow draught boats. The tidal limit is about 6 miles up river at Stanbridge Mill.

Charts Imray Y17, Admiralty 3750.

Rochdale Canal

The Rochdale Canal was part of one of three trans-Pennine routes linking Yorkshire with Manchester and the first to be opened. It was promoted by Acts of Parliament at the turn of the 19th century and fully opened in 1804, although carrying had started before that using roads between Manchester and Rochdale. There had been much argument throughout the planning and building stages but, in the end, a broad canal was built.

With over 90 locks on the route, water supply was a serious problem and eventually eight reservoirs were built to supply the canal. All the locks were built with the same rise so that gates were interchangeable and they were big enough to take Mersey flats. Rising to 600ft about 2 miles north of Littleborough, the canal passes through a fine mixture of countryside and urban development and the plans to re-open it as a through-route now look as if they will become a reality.

Through the second half of the 19th century, railway interests were keen to buy the canal and a lease was agreed in 1855. When the lease expired, the canal company was independent again and started another carrying department which was busy until the First World War. The last through-traffic was in 1937 and commercial carrying ceased in 1958. Under an Act of 1952, the canal was closed to navigation except the short distance between the Ashton and Bridgewater canals.

The Rochdale Canal Company was never nationalised and remains the owner of the canal. The Rochdale Canal Trust Ltd was founded in 1984 and includes representatives from the canal company, the metropolitan boroughs of Oldham, Rochdale and Calderdale, the city of Manchester, the IWA, and residual representatives of West Yorkshire and Greater Manchester Councils. The trust now leases the canal and is the navigation

RIVER ROACH Maximum vessel dimensions						
From and to	*Distance*	*Length*	*Beam*	*Draught*	*Headroom*	*Locks*
Wallingsea Ness, River Crouch to Rochford	9.3 miles (14.9km)	Unlimited	Unlimited	6' (1.6m) at HWST	Unlimited	None

authority. They produce a set of *Navigation Notes* which can be obtained by ringing ☎ 01422 844990. In 1996, a wonderful new concert hall, the Bridgewater Hall, was opened at the side of the Bridgewater Basin, an arm of the Rochdale Canal which was formerly part of the Manchester and Salford Junction Canal. Initially, the Rochdale Canal Company is running the moorings for Manchester City Council until a policy for their management is confirmed.

Authority Rochdale Canal Trust Ltd, Chief Executive and Town Clerk, Oldham Metropolitan Borough Council, Civic Centre, West Street, Oldham, Lancashire OL1 1UQ ☎ 0161 911 3000.

Bridges Numerous.

Tunnels Knott Mill, Manchester, 78yds, no towpath; Sowerby Long Bridge, 43yds.

Towpath Good throughout navigation.

Branches There were two branches, Heywood just over 1 mile, which is now mostly filled in, and Rochdale, 0.7 mile, of which a short section remains open and will become part of the new port of Rochdale.

Connections The Calder and Hebble Navigation at Sowerby Bridge; the Bridgewater Canal at Duke's Lock, Manchester; and the Ashton Canal at Ducie Street, Manchester.

Restoration A new lock, Tuel Lane, was opened on 3 May 1996 which reconnected the section from Littleborough to the national network. The lock is 19ft deep and replaces Locks 3 and 4 although all the locks on the canal will not be renumbered. Tuel Lock is operated by a lock-keeper. Funding has now been secured from the Millennium Fund and other sources and a project officer has been appointed to co-ordinate the restoration of the remaining section of the canal to re-establish a trans-Pennine route.

Facilities There are boatyards at Sowerby Bridge and Todmorden which offer all facilities to boaters including pump-out. Water supply, refuse and sewage disposal are available at Hebden Bridge and Littleborough Higher Lock. There are lots of pubs to choose from along the canal with shops in several towns and villages.

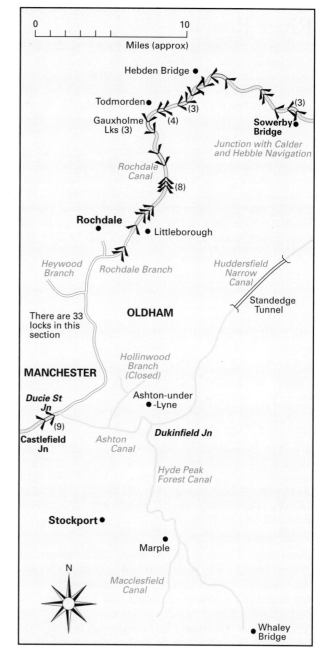

Distance table	Miles
Sowerby Bridge, junction with Calder and Hebble Navigation to:	
First Sowerby Bridge Lock No 1	0.1
Second Sowerby Bridge Lock No 2	0.3
Tuel Lane Locks No 3 and 4	0.4
Brearley Lower Lock No 5	2.9
Brearley Upper Lock No 6	3.1
Broadbottom Lock No 7	4.3
Mayroyd Mill Lock No 8	5.3
Blackpit Lock No 9	5.5
	Miles
Stubbing Lower Lock No 10	5.9
Stubbing Upper Lock No 11	6.0
Rawden Mill Lock No 12	6.8
Callis Lock No 13	7.0
Holmcoat Lock No 14	7.8
Shawplains Lock No 15	8.4
Lob Mill Lock No 16	8.6
Old Royd Lock No 17	9.1
Shop Lock No 18	9.8
Todmorden Lock No 19	9.9
Wadsworth Mill No 20	10.3

ROCHDALE CANAL Maximum vessel dimensions

From and to	Distance	Length	Beam	Draught	Headroom	Locks
Bridgewater Canal to Sowerby Bridge	32 miles (51.5km)	74' (22.6m)	14' 2" (4.3m)	4' (1.2m)	9' (2.7m)	91

	Miles
Shade Lock No 21	10.4
Gauxholme lowest Lock No 22	10.5
Gauxholme Middle Lock No 23	10.6
Gauxholme Highest Lock No 24	10.8
Smithyholm Lock No 25	11.0
Pinnel Lock No 26	11.1
Hollings Lock No 27	11.3
Travis Mill Lock No 28	11.5
Nip Square Lock No 29	11.6
Winterbutlee Lock No 30	11.8
Lightbank Lock No 31	12.0
Sands Lock No 32	12.3
Bottomley Lock No 33	12.4
Warland Lower Lock No 34	12.8
Warland Upper Lock No 35	12.9
Longlees Lock No 36	13.0
West Summit Lock No 37	13.8
First Lock below W Summit Lock No 38	13.9
Second Lock below W Summit Lock No 39	14.0
Punchbowl Lock No 40	14.1
First below Punchbowl	14.2
Second below Punchbowl	14.3
Thickone Lock No 43	14.4
Sladen Lock No 44	14.5
Pike House Lock No 45	14.6
Bent House Lock No 46	15.0
Littleborough Higher Lock No 47	15.3
Littleborough Lower Lock No 48	15.4

This section is not navigable at present

	Miles
Moss Upper Lock No 49	19.0
Moss Lower Lock No 50	19.1
Junction with Rochdale Branch	19.8
Blue Pits Locks Nos 51–53	21.0
Maden Fold, junction with Heywood Branch	21.1
Laneside Flight Locks Nos 54–58	22.2
Laneside Lock No 59	22.6
Boarshaw Lock No 60	23.1
Scowcroft Lock No 61	23.4
Coneygreen Lock No 62	23.5
Walk Mill Lock No 63	23.6
Kay Lane Lock No 64	24.8
Failsworth Lock No 65	26.9
Tannersfield Highest Lock No 66	27.6
Tannersfield Middle Lock No 67	27.8
Tannersfield Lowest Lock No 68	27.9
Newton Heath Lock No 69	28.3
Pinfold Lock No 70	28.5
Shears Lock No 71	28.6
Scotchman's Lock No 72	28.8
Ten Acres Lock No 73	28.9
Drunken Bridge No 74	29.0
Slater's High Lock No 75	29.1
Slater's Lower Lock No 76	29.3
Anthony Lock No 77	29.5
Coalpit Higher Lock No 78	29.8
Coalpit Middle Lock No 79	29.9
Coalpit Lower Lock No 80	30.0
Butler Lane Lock No 81	30.1
Ancoat's Lane Lock No 82	30.6
Brownsfield Lock No 83	30.7

Navigable section

	Miles
Ducie Street, junction with Ashton Canal	30.8
Dale Street Lock No 84	30.9
Piccadilly Lock No 85	31.0
Chorlton Street Lock No 86	31.1
David Street Lock No 87	31.3
Oxford Road Lock No 88	31.4
Tib Lock No 89	31.6
Albion Mills Lock No 90	31.8
Tunnel Lock No 91	31.9
Duke's Lock No 92, junction with Bridgewater Canal	32.0

River Roding

In the Middle Ages, Barking Creek was navigable and was controlled by Barking Abbey. Under an Act of 1737, work was undertaken to improve the navigation to Ilford and trade continued into the early 1800s. Once St Katharine's Dock was completed in 1828, there was regular trade from the City to Ilford.

Barking was also famous for its fishing fleet. The larger boats were out in the North Sea for long periods of time and Barking Smacks brought the catch to the town quay where it was unloaded and taken to Billingsgate Market. The Barking fleet was the first to use ice to pack fish to preserve it and there is still evidence of underground ice-houses near the river. Redevelopment of the area is a long-term plan of the borough council.

From Epping Forest, the River Roding runs through parkland on its way into London. The M11 and North Circular both use the Roding Valley and cross the river several times. The A13 road crosses the creek below Barking restricting headroom to 5.5m at high water springs but craft can still reach the Town Quay and there is a boatyard there with two dry docks and moorings for private boats. The first mile of river from the River Thames contains

RIVER RODING Maximum vessel dimensions						
From and to	Distance	Length	Beam	Draught	Headroom	Locks
Ilford Bridge to Barking Creek	1.8 miles (2.8km)	87' 6" (26.6m)	16' 9" (5.1m)	5' (1.5m)	7' 6" (2.2m)	None

many wharves and is still a busy commercial waterway. The flood barrier at the river mouth is used at the same time as the Thames Barrage and Barking Council have built a new barrage below the Town Quay. This will retain a water level of 6.6ft (2m) in Mill Pool and the Town Quay with access through the barrage available for about 1½ to 2 hours either side of high water. Boats up to 9m beam and 1.5m draught will be able to use the barrage on most tides. Small boats can reach Ilford on the tide, about 4 miles above Barking.

The local authority has improved the Town Quay and Barking Bridge area and is encouraging regeneration and development along the waterway. Discussions are under way about the construction of a marina in the Mill Pool.

Authority *The Thames to Four Gates Bridge, Barking* Port of London Authority, Chief Harbourmaster, London River House, Royal Pier Road, Gravesend, Kent DA12 2BG ☎ 01474 562200.

Above Barking Quay The responsibility for this section is under discussion.

Bridges Numerous.

Towpath None.

Navigation High water at Barking is 25 minutes before HW London Bridge; HW Ilford is the same time as HW London Bridge. There is no lock as such but new tidal doors are being put in place just upstream of Hand Trough Creek.

Distance table	Miles
Ilford Bridge to:	
Barking Bridge	1.5
Town Quay	1.7
Tidal Barrage	2.0
A13 Road Bridge	2.3
Flood Barrier at the River Thames	3.6

River Rother (Eastern)

Although the Environment Agency now acts as the authority for this river, the Rother above Scot's Float Sluice is, in fact, a free right of navigation. The Port of Rye is unique as the Environment Agency is the harbour authority. This is as a result of the importance of the river to agriculture and the Ministry of Agriculture is one of the signatories to the Harbour of Rye Bye-laws.

In Edwardian times, this was a popular river with trips from Scot's Float Sluice, which used to be called Star Lock, to Bodiam Castle. Recently, a trip boat has started between Newenden Bridge and Bodiam. There are now a number of boat moorings in the lower reaches.

In the Middle Ages, the River Rother used to join the sea east of Dungeness but in the hurricane, or Great Storm, of 1287 so much mud and shingle was moved that it nearly buried the Port of Romney and blocked the mouth of the river, so it had to force another course and joined the rivers Brede and Tillingham at Rye.

Rye is one of the Cinque Ports, first chartered in 1155, and still has cobbled streets, inns with low ceilings and a long history of smuggling. It is a delightful town and very popular with visitors. Despite its apparent distance from the sea, Rye is still a busy harbour with the main cargoes being timber, stone and fertilizer.

Authority Environment Agency, Southern Region, Guildbourne House, Chatsworth Road, Worthing, Sussex BN11 1LD ☎ 01903 820692 *Fax* 01903 821832.

Assistant Rivers Operations Controller, Scots Float Depot, Military Road, Playden, Rye, Sussex TN31 7PH ☎ 01797 223256.

Towpath This exists only along parts of the navigation.

Connections River Brede at Rye. This used to be navigable to Brede village and Winchelsea. The entrance lock had double doors opening either way and could admit craft 40ft long by 12ft beam. Craft drawing 3ft could go under the bridge at the entrance with about 8ft of headroom. The navigation rights on the River Brede were abolished by regulation in 1934. The river is still navigable in the winter months. However, during the summer the sluice at Udimore is used to retain water in the upper reaches of the river and therefore this stops the river being navigable there.

The Royal Military Canal used to connect at Iden Lock, but this lock is out of use and much of the canal is weedy.

RIVER ROTHER Maximum Vessel Dimension						
From and to	*Distance*	*Length*	*Beam*	*Draught*	*Headroom*	*Locks*
Rye Harbour to Bodiam	16.4 miles (26.4km)	56' (17.0m)	13' 9" (4.1m)	3' (0.9m)	9' 9" (2.9m)	1

Navigation High water at Rye Bay is about the same as HW Dover. The tidal range is over 19ft (6m) at springs and nearly 11 ft (3.3m) at neaps; the harbour dries at low water. Approaches to Rye should never be made in strong onshore winds and the current in the narrow approach channel can reach over 5 knots (5.75mph) at springs.

Charts Imray C8, Admiralty 536, 1991.

Facilities All moorings below the town of Rye dry out. Strand Quay is a popular mooring and is close to the town. Admiralty Jetty is by the Harbour Office.

Distance table

Bodiam Bridge to:	Miles
Newenden	4.1
Junction with Newmill Channel	6.9
Kitchenham Road Bridge	8.0
Road Bridge	10.0
Junction with Royal Military Canal (Iden Lock closed)	11.5
Scot's Float Sluice	12.5
Railway Bridge	13.8
Rye (junction with River Brede)	14.0
Rye Harbour	15.4
East Pier	16.4

River Brede

Brede Sluice to:	
Langford's Bridge	2.5
Railway Bridge	4.0
Railway Bridge	5.3
Winchelsea (junction with Dimsdale Sewer unnavigable)	5.8
Entrance Lock	7.9

Royal Military Canal

The only canal in England to be built completely by the Government, the Royal Military Canal was started in 1803 in response to the threat of invasion during the Napoleonic wars. Although it only took three years to build, the invasion risk was over by the time the canal was open and its military role was never required. During the Second World War, concrete pill boxes were built when there was the threat of Hitler invading across Romney Marsh, but again it was not put to the test.

The canal has a military road protected by an embankment along the north side. At regular intervals the canal has dogs-leg bends and on these a canon could be set-up to protect the length of canal. Although never tested in the heat of battle, the system would have been effective to contain enemy troops had they landed along the Kent coast as was feared.

The canal fell into disuse during the early part of this century, but recent co-operation between numerous local bodies has seen improvements to the towpath and water quality. Under the management of a project officer based at Kent County Council in Maidstone, the further development of walking and water activities on the canal is now under way. Futher information can be obtained from the Project Co-ordinator, Kent County Council Planning Department, Springfield, Maidstone, Kent ME14 2LX.

Authority Environment Agency, Southern Region, Guildbourne House, Chatsworth Road, Worthing, Sussex BN11 1LD ☎ 01903 820692 *Fax* 01903 821832.

West Hythe Section: Apply to The Treasurer, Civic Centre, Folkestone, Kent ☎ 01303 57388.

ROYAL MILITARY CANAL Maximum vessel dimensions

From and to	Distance	Length	Beam	Draught	Headroom	Locks
West Hythe Sluice to Iden Lock, River Rother	19 miles (30.6km)	Only suitable for canoes and rowing boats				None

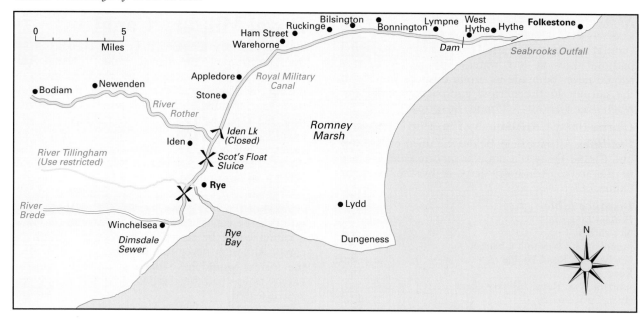

Towpath Throughout the canal. An active programme is underway to develop a 27-mile canal-side path from Pett Level to Seabrook with interpretation sites and way-marked detours to places of interest.

Distance table

	Miles
Iden Lock, junction with River Rother (Iden Lock does not now operate, except for drainage) to:	
Appledore Bridge	3.3
Heigham Farm Bridge	5.5
Railway Bridge	6.3
Ruckinge Bridge	9.0
Bilsington Bridge (Bilsington village distance 1 mile)	10.0
Road Bridge	11.1
Road Bridge	11.9
West Hythe Sluice	19.0
Iden Lock, River Rother	

Sankey (St Helens) Canal

There has always been considerable debate surrounding the claim that the Bridgewater Canal was the first of the new canal age. In 1757, two years before the first Act for the Bridgewater Canal, the Sankey Navigation was open from Sankey Bridges to collieries at Haydock and Parr. In anticipation of opposition from local landowners, the promoters of the Sankey Brook Navigation proposed improving the Sankey Brook as a navigation but there were clauses in the Act of 1755 to allow for navigable cuts. In practise, the Sankey Brook provided water but the course of the brook was not used for the canal. The final line of the canal in the 1830s continued westward from Sankey Lock first to Fiddler's Ferry and finally Widnes.

When the canal company amalgamated with the St Helens and Runcorn Gap Railway in 1845, the name St Helens Canal and Railway Co was adopted with the canal being the more successful partner. Throughout the 19th century the canal was very profitable carrying large tonnages of coal from the number of pits it served in the St Helens coalfield. Earlier this century, traffic changed to chemicals and sugar but, after the First World War, no further traffic went as far as St Helens. Gradually between 1931 and 1963 the whole canal was abandoned.

In 1985, the Sankey Canal Restoration Society was formed with the support of St Helens Groundwork Trust. It has been actively, and practically, finding and restoring the canal although some sections have been infilled and part of the canal is now used for a flood relief scheme. Some lengths of the canal are still in water and at Widnes

SANKEY (ST HELENS) CANAL Maximum vessel dimensions (after restoration)

From and to	Distance	Length	Beam	Draught	Headroom	Locks
Widnes, River Mersey to St Helens	15.2 miles (24.4km)	72' (22m)	13' 10" (4.25m)	5' (1.5m)	6' 6" (2.0m)	11

and Fiddler's Ferry Locks short lengths are used for moorings. For more information, contact the Sankey Canal Restoration Society, c/o The Groundwork Trust, 27 Shaw Street, St Helens WA10 1DN ☎ 01744 739396.

The three local authorities covering the area through which the canal passes fully support the full restoration of the canal and have agreed to protect the route of the canal. Short sections have been restored in each authority's area.

Authority A Trust is being set up between SCARS, and the three local authorities, Halton, Warrington and St Helens.

Bridges The original swing bridges have mostly been replaced with low level road crossings. Headroom will be unlimited from Widnes to Sankey Bridges then 2.4m to Penkford Bridge.

Depth Widnes to Sankey Bridges 2m; Sankey Bridges to St Helens 1.5m.

Towpath Throughout the canal.

Branches Gerard's Bridge, 1½ miles; Blackbrook, 0.6 miles; Boardman's Bridge and Ravenhead Branch filled in; Sutton Branch filled in.

Restoration The society is clearing locks that are accessible and continues to excavate stretches which have been filled in with rubbish and rubble. A full engineering feasibility study has been completed and this confirms the feasibility of a full restoration of the canal. The New Double Locks in St Helens town centre have been restored. It is proposed to

resite Hulme Lock and replace Old Double Locks with two locks on a different alignment. There is a trip boat, St Helen, which is used on the canal.

Distance table	*Miles*
Widnes Lock, River Mersey to:	
Carterhouse Bridge	1.1
Fiddler's Ferry Lock (side lock to River Mersey)	3.4
Sankey Bridges	5.1
Sankey Way (A57)	5.5
Cheshire Lines Railway Bridge	6.1
Bewsey Lock	6.5
Hulme Lock	7.9
Winwick Lock	8.1
Hey Lock	9.4
Bradley Lock	10.2
Earlstown Viaduct	10.5
Newton Common Lock	10.7
Penkford Bridge (A572)	11.0
Engine or Haydock Lock	12.3
Old Double Lock	12.9
Junction with Blackbrook Branch, 0.6 miles, immediately above A58 bridge (proposed new lock)	13.2
Gerard's Bridge Branch, 0.25 miles	14.1
New Double Lock	14.2
Sutton Branch (obliterated, 0.25 miles)	15.0
St Helens town centre	15.2
Ravenhead Branch (obliterated, 0.3 miles)	

River Severn

One of Britain's most majestic rivers, the Severn rises deep in Wales and meanders through beautiful countryside to the Borders where it turns southwards and starts its journey to the Bristol Channel, 220 miles from its source. It has been an active transport route since Roman times and the historic settlements along the river have developed and adapted with the times. At Ironbridge, you can still see the first bridge to be constructed of cast iron which became the building block of the industrial revolution. Today, it is possible to trace the industrial history of the area at the Ironbridge Gorge Museum, but it is difficult to imagine the great smoking furnaces and how hard the life was for the working people of Coalbrookdale.

Until the 1820s, craft could reach Pool Quay, 4½ miles below Welshpool, 128 miles from Gloucester. Passage this far was restricted to the winter when there was sufficient flood water. Traditionally boats were hauled by gangs of men and this practice seemed to continue in some areas even after horse-towing paths had been authorised. Today, the limit of navigation is effectively south of Bewdley only 45 miles upstream from Gloucester, but the river frontages of many towns further up demonstrate the importance of the Severn in their development. Shrewsbury and Bridgnorth were both inland ports and at Bewdley wonderful quays and wharves can still be seen, although a Severn trow hasn't been alongside for many years.

Navigation improvements on the Severn were promoted by Acts of Parliament from 1503 until

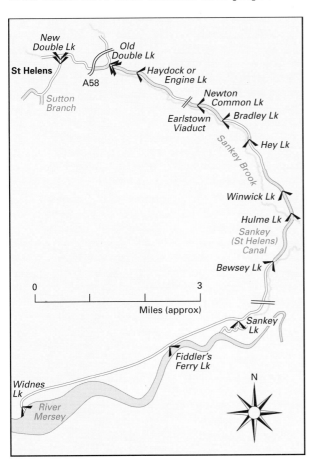

1814 but these were mostly associated with flash locks. There were no pound locks on the river until after the creation of the Severn Commission by an Act of Parliament in 1842, precipitated by the increasing amount of traffic coming to the river through the canal system. The five locks between Gloucester and Stourport were built between 1843 and 1858.

The first canal to join the Severn was the Droitwich Barge Canal in 1771 followed in 1772 by the Staffordshire and Worcestershire Canal. This needed an outlet into the Severn and Stourport was created as an inland port on the site of the small village of Lower Mitton. It is an unassuming town with connections seaward via the river and inland along the canal, impressive basins reflect the importance of the port in years gone by. The riverside at Worcester is dominated by the soaring cathedral, a magnificent building just south of the equally imposing stone bridge. Further downstream, Upton-upon-Severn is a delightful Georgian town followed by Tewkesbury with its Norman abbey and the connection with the River Avon.

At Gloucester, the Severn heads westward through tortuous bends. These became a serious impediment to shipping in the late 1700s and as a result the Gloucester and Sharpness Canal was built. Opened in 1827, the canal greatly eased the problems of taking cargo up the Severn and has been used to bypass a difficult stretch of river ever since. It is still possible to navigate the old course of the river with local knowledge and a suitable craft and the Lydney Yacht Club holds an annual Gloucester Ring Cruise riding the spring tide up to Gloucester Weir and returning to Sharpness via the canal.

It is this narrow, twisting reach of the river which experiences the famous Severn Bore, something over 250 times a year to a greater or lesser degree. The bore is generated by the incoming Atlantic tide and the very rapidly narrowing river, at high springs in the spring and autumn a bore of 9ft can be achieved. Stonebench, near Quedgeley, is said to be one of the best places to watch the bore. Only very experienced surfers and boaters should even consider riding the bore.

Authority British Waterways, Llanthony Warehouse, Gloucester Docks, Gloucester GL1 2EJ ☎ 01452 318000.

Bridges There are several bridges. The main ones are as follows:

	Headroom
Westgate Road, Gloucester	23' 6" (7.2m)
British Railways Bridge, Gloucester	23' 6" (7.2m)
Haw Bridge (take left hand arch)	24' 6" (7.5m)
Mythe Bridge, Tewkesbury	25' 3" (7.7m)
Upton	25' 0" (7.6m)
Worcester	20' 0" (6.1m)

The best channel is through the centre arch, marked by a red light.
Channel on the port side.

Holt Fleet Bridge	28' 7" (8.7m)

A new bridge carries the M50 just south of Upton on Severn.

Towpath There is no towpath as such but various footpaths follow the route of the river. OS *Landranger* maps for the area should be consulted.

Locks All locks on the River Severn are manned.

Speed Limit 8mph for boats heading downstream, 6mph upstream. Bye-laws for the river are published by British Waterways and yachtsmen are recommended to obtain a copy from the authority.

Connections Gloucester and Sharpness Ship Canal; Staffordshire and Worcestershire Canal; the River Avon at Tewkesbury; the Worcestershire and Birmingham Canal at Worcester; and the Droitwich Barge Canal at Hawford Lock (currently not useable but restoration of connection proposed). The Coombe Hill Canal ran for almost 3 miles to take coal to Cheltenham but was abandoned in 1876. The Herefordshire and Gloucestershire Canal ran from Hereford to the Maisemore Channel, opposite Gloucester, and is under restoration.

Navigation From Avonmouth to Sharpness the River Severn can be navigated by any well-found boat in appropriate conditions. The tides run very fast and wind over tide conditions can produce dangerous seas. Any boat owner who wishes to do this trip but has no experience of sea-going should take a pilot from Portishead to Sharpness, or vice versa. Pilots can be arranged through the Sharpness Harbourmaster ☎ 01453 811644 or Amalgamated

RIVER SEVERN Maximum vessel dimensions

From and to	Distance	Length	Beam	Draught	Headroom	Locks
Stourport to Worcester	12.5 miles (20.1km)	90' (27.1m)	19' (5.7m)	6' (1.8m)	20' (6.0m)	3
Worcester to Gloucester	29.5 miles (47.4km)	135' (41.1m)	22' 6.7m)	8' (2.4m)	24' 6" (7.5m)	3

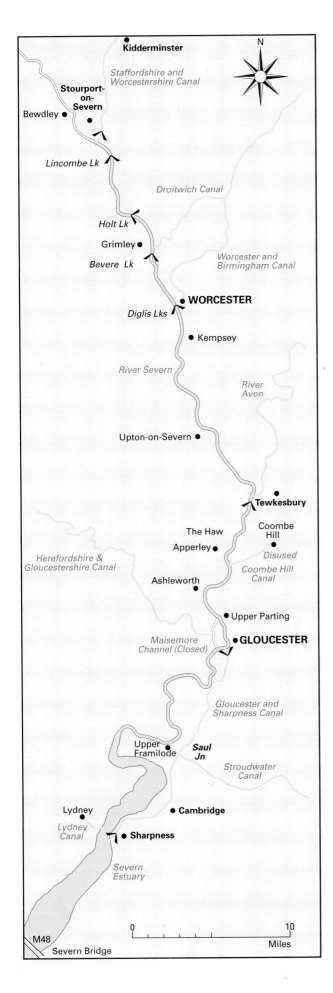

Gloucester Pilots ☎ 01374 226143. The construction of the new Severn Road Bridge (1996) has actually made navigation easier with a well buoyed channel approaching and under the bridge.

A passage through the lower reaches of the River Severn must be carefully planned. Timing is essential and contingencies must be made for adverse weather conditions. Narrow boats are unlikely to have sufficient power to make the passage from Bristol to Sharpness on a single tide and should expect to wait out a tide at Portishead. Mooring facilities are likely to improve at Portishead in the near future. Approaching from Bristol arrival off Sharpness should not be more than 1 hour before high water and no later than HW. All boats intending to make this passage must either have VHF or a mobile phone on board to be able to maintain contact with the office at Sharpness. Prior notification of passage through the lock is required. British Waterways at Sharpness produce a booklet called *Guidance Notes for Small Boat Passage of the Severn Estuary*. A copy of this should be obtained well in advance of any plan to make this passage. It contains information on suitable weather conditions, preparation and equipment, safety equipment, the passage in each direction and useful telephone numbers.

High water Sharpness is about 45 minutes after HW Avonmouth, tidal range is 28ft 6ins (8.7m) at springs and 16ft 9ins (5.1m) at neaps. Large spring tides will run over the weir at Gloucester giving a tidal effect as far as Upper Lode Lock on most springs. The Environment Agency produce a brochure giving times, heights and general information about the Severn Bore which can be obtained from EA, Lower Severn Area, Riversmeet House, Newtown Industrial Estate, Northway Lane, Tewkesbury GL20 7LG ☎ 01684 850951.

Charts Imray C59, Admiralty 1166.

Facilities Between Bristol and Sharpness there are no safe havens although there are plans to develop Portishead Dock into a marina. Above Gloucester, there are relatively few mooring places other than Tewkesbury, Upton-upon-Severn Marina and Worcester and Stourport Marina. Launching isn't easy on the Severn, the slip at Upton Marina goes into shallow water and the access is narrow to the slip at the Lower Lode Hotel, Tewkesbury.

Distance table	*Miles*
Arley Quarry Landing to:	
Upper Arley	1.5
Bewdley Bridge	5.3
Gladder Brook (head of navigation)	8.4
Stourport Bridge	9.0
Stourport, junction with Staffordshire and Worcestershire Canal	9.1
Lincomb Lock No 1	10.4
Hampstall Ferry	11.5
Lenchford Ferry	13.8
Holt Lock No 2	14.6
Holt village	15.5
Grimley	17.0
Hawford, junction with Droitwich Barge Canal	17.6

	Miles
Bevere Lock No 3	18.1
Hallow	19.0
Pope Iron	20.4
Worcester Quay	21.5
Diglis, junction with Worcester and Birmingham Canal	22.0
Diglis Locks No 4 (two locks side by side)	23.4
Teme Junction (River Teme is unnavigable)	23.1
Kempsey	25.1
Pixham	25.6
Clevelode	27.3
Rhydd	28.4
Severn Stoke	29.3
Hanley	31.0
Upton-on-Severn	32.0
Sexton's Lode	33.5
Barley House	34.5
Dowdeswell's Elms	36.5
Tewkesbury Bridge (Bushley distance 1½ miles)	37.6
Tewkesbury, junction with River Avon	38.0
Tewkesbury Lock No 5	38.5
Tewkesbury, Lower Lode and Ferry	39.4
Chaceley (right bank), Deerhurst (left bank)	40.9
Apperley	42.0
Haw Bridge	42.8
Coombe Hill	43.9
Wainlode	44.1
Ashleworth	46.1
Upper Parting, junction with Maisemore Channel from Upper Parting to Lower Parting (now closed)	48.5
Gloucester, Westgate Bridge	50.6
Gloucester, junction with Gloucester and Sharpness Canal	51.0
Gloucester, Llanthony Lock No 6 (closed)	51.4
Gloucester, Upper Parting to Lower Parting (now closed)	52.0

Left Bank Miles		Right Bank Miles
55.4	Stone Bench	
55.8	Elmore	
	Minsterworth	57.0
63.8	Framilode, junction with Stroudwater Canal (closed)	
	Newnham	68.5
	Bullo Pill	69.5
72.3	Fretherne	
78.5	Remains of Severn Railway Bridge	78.5
79.1	Sharpness Point, junction with old entrance to the Gloucester and Sharpness Canal	
79.8	Sharpness Junction, entrance to Sharpness Docks and Gloucester and Sharpness Canal	
	Junction with Lydney Canal and Harbour	81.0
91.0	Severn Bridge, M48	
	Beachley Point and junction with River Wye	92.0
94.5	Severn Bridge, M4	94.5
100.5	Avonmouth, junction with River Avon	

Sheffield and South Yorkshire Navigation

The Sheffield and South Yorkshire Navigation is a combination of canals. In 1751, the River Don was improved to Tinsley with 17 locks between Tinsley and Thorne where packets from Hull used to come and tranship goods for Sheffield. The Stainforth and Keadby Canal connected the River Don with the Trent giving an alternative access to the Humber

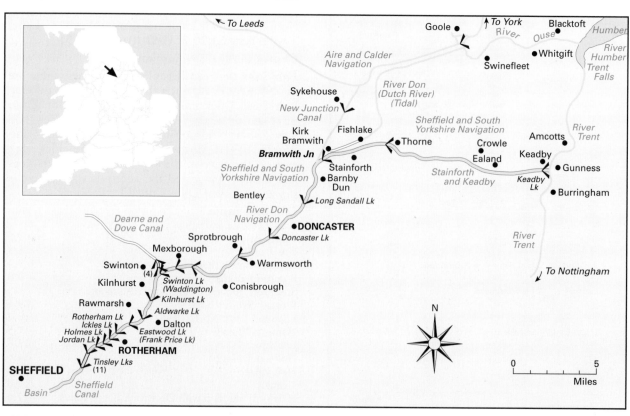

The Hazelhurst Aqueduct which carries the Leek Branch over the Froghall Branch of the Caldon Canal. *Roy Westlake*

Linton Lock, on the Yorkshire Ouse, is another recipient of Millennium funding. *Robin Smithett*

The church at Hemingford Grey on the River Great Ouse. *Sian Barron*

Cowley Cutting on the Shropshire Union Canal. *Robin Smithett*

Carreghofa locks on the Montgomery Canal. *Robin Smithett*

Corpach Basin is at the western end of the Caledonian Canal
Jane Cumberlidge

and the North Sea and was opened in 1802. By 1819, the Cutlers Company of Sheffield had succeeded in getting a canal into the city centre. In 1846, the Dearne and Dove Canal was bought by the Don Navigation. Unlike the Midlands canals, these waterways were built for Yorkshire keels, 61ft long by 15ft wide, they had two masts but when there was no wind they were horse drawn or bow-hauled by the family that worked them.

Throughout the 19th century, the canals and river navigations were successful and formed working arrangements with the developing railway companies in the area. By the 1880s, the railway company had been taken over by the Manchester, Sheffield and Lincolnshire Railway and the interest of the waterways no longer appeared to be as well considered. In 1888, there were further plans for a new route to the sea and the Sheffield and South Yorkshire Canal Company Ltd was formed in 1895. Gradually the plans crystallised into what is now the New Junction Canal which was opened in 1905, the last major canal to be built in England.

During the 20th century, improvements to the Sheffield and South Yorkshire were undertaken to try to modernise them and enable barges and compartment boats to travel easily along the system. The most recent improvements were carried out in the early 1980s enabling 700-tonne craft to reach Mexborough and 400-tonne to Rotherham. The delays in implementing the improvements meant that by the time the enlarged locks were open most of the traffic had fallen away and was carried by road.

As a cruising waterway, the Sheffield and South Yorkshire has a hard marketing job ahead. The residue of heavy industry cannot be transformed over night and there is a degree of prejudice to be overcome. The sympathetic conversion of Victoria Quays in the centre of Sheffield should be an attraction in itself and along the waterway there have been a number of other developments to encourage more use as a leisure waterway. The Don Valley Stadium and Sheffield Arena are close to the canal near the top of the Tinsley Flight and major events are regularly held at both of these venues. Between Mexborough and Conisbrough, two old slag heaps have been converted into the Earth Centre. Of rather older date, Conisbrough Castle is close to the canal along one of the rather more rural stretches, although finding a suitable mooring to visit it isn't all that easy. Despite its industrial history, the wildlife seems to have happily recolonised the waterway and the mixture of urban, industrial and rural surroundings makes the Sheffield and South Yorkshire worth exploring.

Although designated as a Remainder Waterway under the 1968 Act, the Sheffield and Tinsley has now been reclassified as a Cruiseway.

Authority British Waterways, Mill Lane, Mill Gate, Newark, Nottinghamshire NG24 4TT ☎ 01636 704481.

Bridges Numerous with many swing bridges. Built in 1915, the railway swing bridge at Keadby is one of only three in Europe which slides out of the way on winches, worth seeing before someone decides to replace it.

Towpath The towpath is very patchy and along some stretches it is recommended not to try to walk it. Christine Richardson suggests the lengths which are accessible but the OS/Nicholson *Guide No. 7* is rather more conservative. Reference to the relevant OS *Landranger* maps is recommended.

Connections The New Junction Canal; the Dearne and Dove Canal, derelict at present but the subject of an active restoration campaign; the River Trent.

Navigation Keadby Lock is opened on the tide and there are light signals, three red lights mean the lock is not available, a green light will show when there is sufficient water over the sill. The lock-keeper requires 48-hours notice ☎ 01724 782205.

Sections of the navigation are the River Don and river flow, depth and headroom will be affected by rainfall. In times of heavy rain, extra care must be taken when passing weirs. A rise of 2ft above the normal river level is likely to cause difficulty to cruising boats especially when manoeuvring. Gauging sticks are fixed to the top of all locks.

At the Tinsley Flight, it is important to let the lock-keeper know in advance that you want to use the locks as there are several anti-vandal devices ☎ 0114 244 1579 or 1981.

Facilities The facilities for cruising boats throughout the navigation were dramatically improved in the early 1990s. Victoria Quays are an example of how a run-down city dock area can be tastefully developed and regenerated. Along the navigation, there are villages and towns with moorings, shops, pubs and sanitary provision as well as boat clubs, marinas and boatyards. The best guide to the waterway is by Christine Richardson and John Lower (see bibliography). There are two

SHEFFIELD AND SOUTH YORKSHIRE NAVIGATION Maximum vessel dimensions

From and to	Distance	Length	Beam	Draught	Headroom	Locks
Sheffield to Rotherham	6 miles (9.6km)	61' 6" (18.7m)	15' 3" (4.6m)	4' 6" (1.3m)	10' (3.0m)	15
Rotherham to Bramwith	22 miles (35.4km)	229' 8" (70.0m)	20' (6.1m)	8' 2" (2.5m)	10' 6" (3.3m)	9
Bramwith to Keadby, River Trent	14.9 miles (24.0km)	61' 8" (18.8m)	17' (5.2m)	7' 3" (2.2m)	10' 6" (3.3m)	3

slipways in Sheffield for launching trailable craft and two at Thorne on the Stainforth and Keadby Canal.

Distance table

Victoria Quays, Sheffield to: — Miles

Bacon Lane Bridge	1.0
Stainforth Road Bridge	1.3
Shirland Lane Bridge	1.5
Darnall Road Aqueduct	1.7
Sheffield Arena	2.0
Broughton Lane Bridge	2.3
Tinsley Top Lock No 1	2.7
Turnpike Bridge Lock No 8 and M1 Bridge	3.4
Tinsley Low Wharf	3.5
Top Lock of Tinsley Low Locks No 9	3.7
Tinsley Bottom Lock No 11 and River Don Navigation	3.9
Halfpenny Bridge	4.0
Jordan's Lock	4.5
Holmes Lock and Bridge	5.0
Ickles Lock	5.5
Rotherham, junction with River Rother	5.9
Rotherham Lock	6.3
Greaseborough Road Bridge	6.7
Sir Frank Price Lock (formerly Eastwood Lock)	7.6
Aldwarke Lock	8.4
Parkgate Works Bridge	8.8
Thrybergh Bridge	10.0
Kilnhurst Flood Lock	10.4
Hooton Road Bridge	10.9
Burton Ings Bridge	11.6
Swinton Junction (Dearne and Dove Canal) and Waddington Lock	11.9
Swinton Road Bridge	12.1
Mexborough Station and Road Bridge	12.7
Mexborough Top Lock	13.3
Pastures Road Bridge	13.8
Mexborough Low Lock	14.6
River Dearne	15.1
The Earth Centre	15.4
Conisbrough	15.8
Conisbrough Viaduct	16.9
Sprotbrough Flash SSSI	17.7
Sprotbrough Lock	18.2
Don Bridge	18.7
Doncaster Railway Workshops	20.9
Gas House Bight	21.3
Long Sandall Lock	24.9
Sandall Grove	25.9
Barnby Dun Lift Bridge	27.0
Bramwith, junction with New Junction Canal	27.9
Bramwith Lock	28.2
Bramwith Swing Bridge	28.6
Stainforth Bridge	29.9
Dunston Hill Swing Bridge	30.4
M18 Bridge	31.7
Thorne Swing Bridge and Lock	32.6
Wykewell Lift Bridge	33.8
Medge Hall	37.1
Godnow Swing Bridge	38.2
Crowle Wharf	39.5
Keadby Sliding Railway Bridge	42.3
Keadby Lock and junction with River Trent	42.9

Swinton Junction with River Don Navigation to:

Swinton Bottom Lock No 1	0.1
Swinton Top Lock No 4	0.5

Dearne and Dove Canal
Closed from Swinton Top Lock No 4 to Barnsely Junction. (see entry under Barnsley Canal)

Shropshire Union Canal

This was one of the last major canal routes to be built in England and links many traditional market towns with the River Severn. Running from Autherley, near Wolverhampton, to the Manchester Ship Canal at Ellesmere Port, the Shropshire Union, as it is known today, was formed from a group of canal companies which became the Shropshire Union Railways and Canal Company in 1846. The Birmingham and Liverpool Junction Canal, the Chester Canal, the Shropshire Canal, the Shrewsbury Canal, the Ellesmere Canal, both parts of the Montgomery Canal and the Middlewich and Newport Branches all came into the new company. Almost 100 years later, in 1944, much of this fascinating network was abandoned.

Unlike many of the earliest canals which wound around on contours, the main line of the Shropshire Union runs straight across country using cuttings and embankments to provide the shortest possible route. The Shelmore Embankment, near Norbury Junction, proved very costly and took six years to complete because the marl soil kept slipping. The embankment would have been unnecessary had the original route for the canal been followed, but a local landowner, Lord Anson of Norbury Park, refused to allow the canal to be cut through his pheasant covers. Thomas Telford never saw the Birmingham and Liverpool Junction Canal joined to form a through route from Autherley to Nantwich;

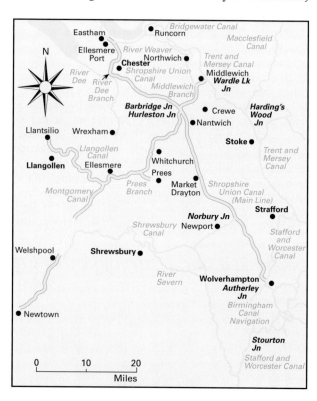

SHROPSHIRE UNION CANAL *Maximum vessel dimensions*

From and to	Distance	Length	Beam	Draught	Headroom	Locks
Autherley Junction to Nantwich (excl)	38 miles (61.1km)	72' (21.9m)	7' (2.1m)	2' 6" (0.7m)	8' (2.4m)	29
Nantwich to Ellesmere Port	28.5 miles (45.8km)	72' (21.9m)	9' (2.7m)	2' 6" (0.7m)	8' (2.4m)	18
Middlewich Branch Barbridge to the junction with the Trent and Mersey Canal at Middlewich	10 miles (16.1km)	70' (21.3m)	7' (2.1m)	3' 4" (1.0m)	8' (2.4m)	4

the first boat passed along it six months after his death, in January 1835.

Today, the Shroppie is a much loved waterway taking you on a gentle journey from the bustle near Wolverhampton, through quiet countryside and sleepy villages to the city of Chester and a cultural tour of the waterways at Ellesmere Port's excellent boat museum. Along the way, it is easy to be diverted along a tempting branch towards Llangollen or Middlewich or to explore the route of the Newport Branch on foot. From Autherley, there are only two locks in the first 25 miles but that doesn't mean the canal is without interest as you pass through deep wooded cuttings alternating with high embankments offering wonderful views across the countryside.

Authority British Waterways, Birch Road, Ellesmere, Shropshire SY12 9AA ☎ 01691 622549.

Whitby Locks, Ellesmere Port: The locks are operated by The Manchester Ship Canal Company, Quay West, Trafford Wharf Road, Manchester M17 1HH ☎ 0161 872 2411 *Fax* 0161 877 0344.

Bridges Numerous including the Double High Bridge at Offley in the Grub Street Cutting.

Towpath Throughout most of the navigation although a few short stretches are poor or not passable. A particularly enjoyable length is that around Chester.

Tunnels Cowley, 81yds.

Aqueducts River Gowy, Moss Hall.

Branches River Dee Branch, 175yds; Middlewich Branch, 10 miles.

Connections The Trent and Mersey Canal via the Middlewich Branch; the River Dee via the River Dee Branch at Chester; and the Llangollen Canal at Hurleston Junction.

Facilities There are many boatyards, marinas, pubs, restaurants and shops close to this very popular cruising route. Slipways are available at Autherley Junction, Brewood, Norbury Junction, Nantwich and Chester.

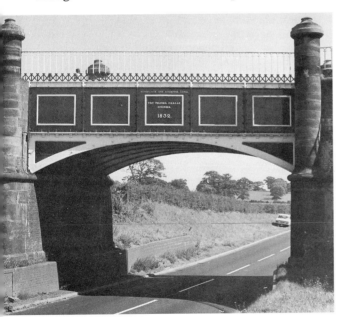

The Stretton Aqueduct over the A5 near Breward was part of Thomas Telford's plan for the Birmingham and Liverpool Canal, which is now part of the Shropshire Union Canal. *Roy Westlake*

Distance table | *Miles*
Autherley Junction, junction with Staffordshire and Worcestershire Canal, Autherley Lock No 1 to:

	Miles
Pendeford Bridge	1.4
Chillington	3.6
Brewood	5.0
Stretton Aqueduct	6.2
Wheaton Aston Lock No 2	7.8
High Onn Wharf	10.8
Cowley Tunnel	12.4
Gnosall Heath	13.0
Norbury Junction (Newport Branch canal course)	15.5
Grub Street Cutting	16.5
Shebdon	19.0
Knighton Factory	20.0
Goldstone Wharf	23.7
Woodseaves Cutting (speed limit 2mph)	24.1
Tyrley Top Lock No 3	25.4

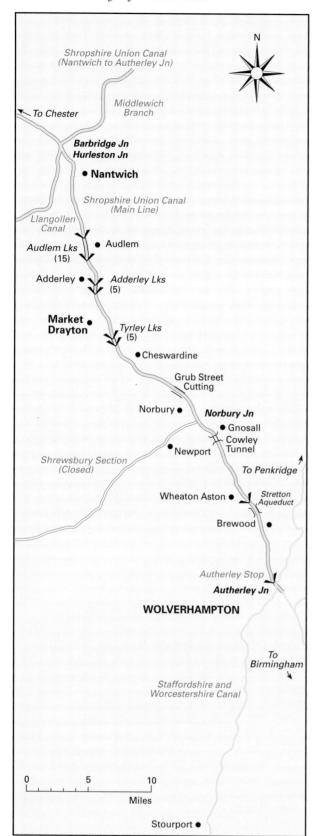

Beeston Stone lock on the Shropshire Union Canal.
Robin Smithett

	Miles
Tyrley Bottom Lock No 7	25.7
Market Drayton Wharf	26.6
Adderley Top Lock No 8	29.9
Adderley Bottom Lock No 12	30.1
Audlem Top Lock No 13	31.5
Audlem Bottom Lock No 27	33.1
Weaver Aqueduct	33.4
Hack Green Lock Nos 28 and 29	36.6
Nantwich Basin	38.8
Hurleston Junction, junction with Llangollen Canal	40.8
Barbridge Junction, junction with Middlewich Branch	42.1
Wardle	43.4
Calveley	43.9
Bunbury Lock Nos 30 and 31 (staircase)	44.9
Tilstone Lock No 32	45.6
Wharton Lock No 35	47.5
Bate's Mill Bridge No 109	47.9
Crows' Nest Bridge No 113	50.3
Egg Bridge, Waverton No 119	53.8
Christleton, Locks Nos 36 and 37	55.4
Tarvin Lock No 38	56.3
Hoole Lane Locks Nos 39 and 40	57.0
Chester Locks Nos 41–43 (staircase)	57.4
Chester, Tower Wharf	57.9
Chester, junction with Branch to River Dee (0.25 mile)	58.0
Mollington	59.9
Backford	61.9
Caughall	62.9
Stoak	63.4
Stanney	64.4
Ellesmere Port Docks, and junction with Manchester Ship Canal, Locks Nos 44–46	66.5

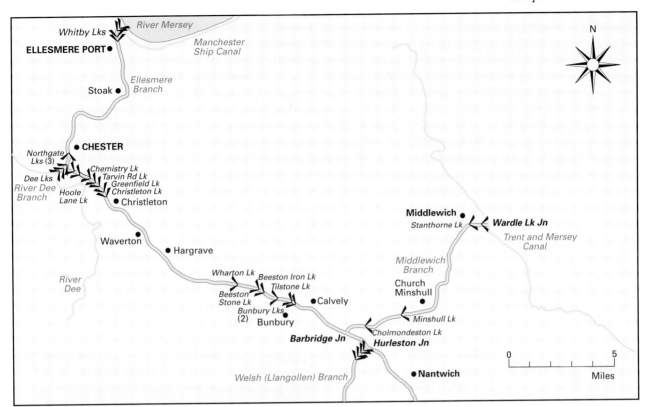

Middlewich Branch

The Middlewich Branch is an important link between two major canal routes, the Trent and Mersey and the Shropshire Union. It is an interesting waterway in its own right as it travels along embankments above the meandering River Weaver. This is salt and cheese country with the fertile Cheshire plain heavily populated with dairy cattle around the historic salt towns of Nantwich, Middlewich and Northwich.

Bridges Numerous.

Tunnels None.

Towpath Mostly in quite good condition.

Distance table	Miles
Barbridge Junction, junction with Main Line, to:	
Cholmondeston Lock No 1	1.4
Minshull Lock No 2	3.0
Weaver Aqueduct	3.8
Church Minshull	4.9
Clive Green	8.0
Stanthorne Lock No 3	9.1
River Wheelock Aqueduct	9.3
Middlewich, Wardle Lock No 4, junction with the Trent and Mersey Canal	10.0

Dee Branch

The branch to the River Dee is ¼ mile from Chester with three locks, called the Dee Locks which fall to the River Dee. The River Dee is accessible 4 hours either side of high water. BW must have 24-hours notice of intention to enter or leave the River Dee via the Dee Branch ☎ 01244 390372.

The old wharf crane at Audlem on the Shropshire Union Canal.
Robin Smithett

Staffordshire and Worcestershire Canal

The engineer for the Staffordshire and Worcestershire Canal was James Brindley and it was the original connection with the Severn of the 'Great Cross' meeting the Trent and Mersey Canal at Great Haywood, east of Stafford. It was opened in 1772 just six years after the Act promoting it was passed. Being an early canal, it is winding, following the land contours mostly through the valleys of the rivers Stour, Penk, Sow and Smestow where it sits happily in its surroundings.

The original proposal was for the canal to join the Severn at Bewdley, but the townspeople were not interested so Brindley chose Lower Mitton, a small village further downstream, which developed into Stourport. The mellow brick wharves and warehouses are still much in evidence with the white clock tower a landmark over one of the basins. At Stourport, there are both wide and narrow locks giving access from the river to the canal although cargo from Severn trows and wide beam boats would have had to be transhipped before travelling up the canal.

The Staffordshire and Worcestershire was an early commercial success and, even after the Birmingham and Liverpool Junction Canal opened, the crucial distance between Autherley and Aldersley Junctions was put to good effect. Until nationalisation in 1948, the canal was owned by the same company, one of the few to resist bids from railway companies, and it paid a dividend to shareholders throughout. Coal from Cannock Chase coal mines was transported by canal to Stourport Power Station until 1949.

Despite the fact that the canal passes the edge of Birmingham, through Wolverhampton and Stafford, it is a peaceful, rural route which has become very popular with many pleasure boats. It forms one part of the Stourport Ring and the northern section is on the Four Counties Ring. The greatest intrusion of the 20th century is when the canal passes under the M6 which makes its presence felt for some time by the noise.

Shortly after Great Haywood Junction, the canal passes through Tixall Wide. This is a broadening out of the canal which some say was for aesthetic reasons to please a local landowner. Other unusual sites along the canal are the circular by-pass weirs, the round lock-keeper's house at Gailey and the octagonal one at Bratch. The summit level is 10 miles long between Gailey and Compton, after the junction with the BCN at Aldersley. Through the more rural southern section, the canal cuts through rich red sandstone and passes close by Kinver Edge.

Authority British Waterways, Norbury Junction, Stafford ST20 0PN ☎ 01785 284253.

Bridges Numerous.

Towpath Throughout navigation.

Tunnels Cookley, 65 yards, towpath; Dunsley, 25 yards, towpath.

Branches Stafford Branch is now a drain and no longer navigable, originally 1 mile. The River Stour Branch was 1.3 miles and is now closed.

Speed limit 3mph.

Connections River Severn at Stourport; Stourbridge Canal at Stourton Junction; Birmingham Canal Navigations Main Line at Aldersley Junction; Shropshire Union Canal at Autherley Junction; Hatherton Branch Canal at Hatherton Junction (now closed); and the Trent and Mersey Canal at Great Haywood.

Facilities There are 15 boatyards and numerous inns by the canal and also facilities nearby as well. Launching slipways are available at Stourport, Kingswinford, Wolverhampton and Penkridge.

Distance table   *Miles*
Stourport, junction with River Severn Main Line and entrance locks (Stourport Lock Nos 1 and 2) to Stourport Basin, to:

York Street Lock No 3	0.1
Gilgal Bridge	0.6
Mitton Chapel Bridge	0.8
Upper Mitton Bridge	1.0
Bullock's Lane Bridge	1.5
Oldington Bridge	2.0
Pratt's Wharf	2.4
Falling Sands Lock No 4	2.8

STAFFORDSHIRE AND WORCESTERSHIRE CANAL Maximum vessel dimensions

From and to	Distance	Length	Beam	Draught	Headroom	Locks
Stourport, River Severn to Autherley Junction	25.1 miles (40.4km)	70' (21.3m)	7' (2.3m)	2' 6" (0.7m)	6' 10" (2.0m)	31
Autherley Junction to Great Haywood Junction	21.0 miles (33.8m)	70' (21.3m)	7' (2.3m)	2' 6" (0.7m)	6' 6" (1.9m)	12

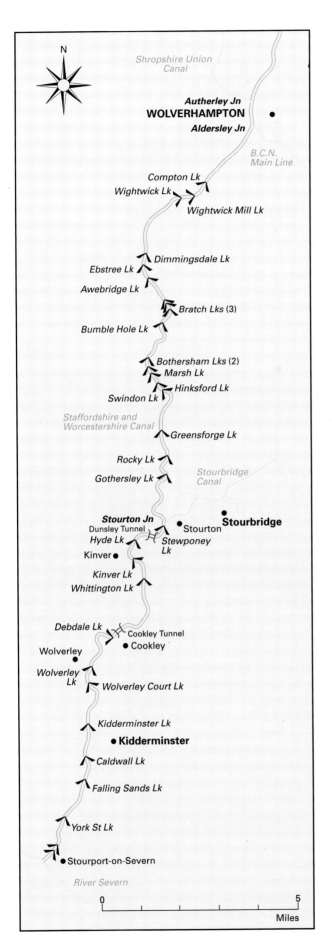

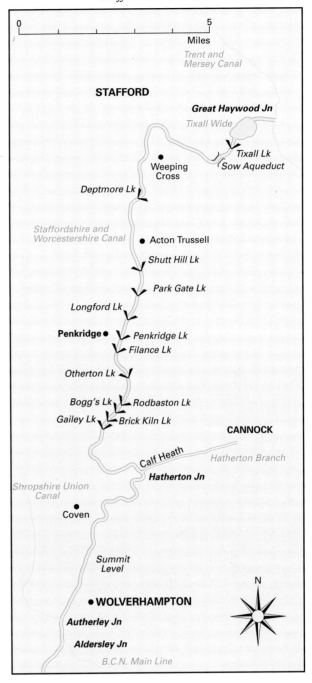

	Miles
Falling Sands Bridge	3.1
Caldwall Lock No 5 and Bridge	3.5
Round Hill Bridge	3.8
Caldwall Mill Bridge	3.8
Kidderminster Lock No 6	4.4
Limekiln Bridge	4.6
Wolverley Court Bridge and Lock No 7	5.6
Wolverley Bridge and Lock No 8	6.1
Wolverley Forge Bridge	6.4
Debdale Bridge and Lock No 9	7.3
Cookley Tunnel	7.5
Austcliffe Bridge	8.0
Clay House Bridge	8.3
Whittington Bridge and Lock No 10	9.5
Whittington Horse Bridge	9.8
Kinver Lock No 11	10.4

	Miles		Miles
Hyde Bridge and Lock No 12	11.0	Radford Bridge	41.3
Dunsley Tunnel	11.6	Baswich Bridge	41.8
Stewponey Lock No 13	12.0	Lodgfield Bridge	42.5
Stourton Junction, junction with		Stoneford Bridge	43.0
Stourbridge Canal	12.3	Milford Bridge	43.8
Gothersley Bridge and Lock No 14	14.0	Tixall Bridge	44.5
Rocky Lock No 15	14.4	Old Hill Bridge and Tixall Lock No 43	44.8
Greensforge Bridge and Lock No 16	15.1	Great Haywood, junction with Trent and	
Hincksford Lock No 17	16.3	Mersey Canal	46.1
Swindon Lock No 18	16.6		
Marsh Lock No 19	16.9		
Botterham Bridge and Locks Nos 20 and 21	17.3		
Wombourn Bridge	17.6		
Bumble Hole Bridge and Lock No 22	18.5		
Bratch Bridge and Locks Nos 23–25	18.9		
Awbridge Lock No 26	19.8		
Ebstree Lock No 27	20.3		
Dimmingsdale Lock No 28 and Reservoir	20.5		
Dimmingsdale Bridge	20.8		
Mops Farm Bridge	21.4		
Castle Croft Bridge	21.8		
Wightwick Bridge	22.3		
Wightwick Lock No 29	22.5		
Wightwick Mill Bridge and Lock No 30	22.6		
Compton Lock No 31 and Bridge	23.3		
Tettenhall Bridge	24.0		
Dunstall Water Bridge	24.6		
Aldersley Junction, Birmingham Canal			
Navigations	25.1		
Autherley Junction, Shropshire Union Canal	25.6		
Marsh Lane Bridge	26.4		
Coven Heath Bridge	27.5		
Cross Green Bridge	28.4		
Slade Heath Bridge	29.0		
Lache's Bridge	29.8		
Moat House Bridge	30.3		
Deepmore Bridge	30.8		
Hatherton, junction with Hatherton			
Branch (closed)	31.0		
Calf Heath Bridge and Wharf	32.1		
Four Ashes	32.1		
Gailey Bridge and Lock No 32	33.4		
Brick-kiln Lock No 33	33.5		
Bogg's Lock No 34	33.8		
Rodbaston Bridge and Lock No 35	34.5		
Otherton Lane Bridge	34.8		
Otherton Lock No 36	35.0		
Lynehill Bridge	35.4		
Filance Lock No 37	35.9		
Penkridge Bridge and Lock No 38	36.1		
Longford Bridge and Lock No 39	36.6		
Teddesley Bridge	37.1		
Park Gate Bridge and Lock No 40	37.5		
Shutt Hill Bridge and Lock No 41	38.3		
Acton Bridge	38.8		
Roseford Bridge	39.6		
Deptmore Lock No 42	40.0		
Hazelestrine Bridge	40.4		

River Stour, Kent

The River Stour flows in a huge loop through east Kent, with tributaries rising not far north of Hythe and joining the sea in Pegwell Bay on the northeast coast. From Pegwell Bay, it was navigable to Canterbury and during Roman times played an important part in both transport and defence of the area. Sandwich, now about 4 miles from the sea, was an important port until the 16th century when severe storms and shifting sands changed the river's course.

Evidence of the Roman occupation can still be seen at Richborough near the mouth of the river, where there are the remains of the Roman fort. It was from here that Watling Street started and the port was the Romans' main connection with the continent.

Now it is only the more intrepid explorers who venture up the River Stour by boat. The approaches from seaward are quite taxing with shifting sand and drying banks. Once into the river the flood runs fast up to the bridge at Sandwich, while you can still meet small coasters at Richborough. Passing Stonar Cut can be difficult as it is used to sluice out the higher river; a signal is raised when the sluices are to be opened and boats should not pass the outfalls at that time.

RIVER STOUR, KENT Maximum vessel dimensions

From and to	Distance	Length	Beam	Draught	Headroom	Locks
Shell Ness, Pegwell Bay to Sandwich	4 miles (6.4km)	Unlimited	Unlimited	11' (3.3m)	Unlimited	None
Sandwich to Fordwich	15 miles (24.2km)	Unlimited	Unlimited	7' (2.1m)	20' (6.1m) (HWS)	None

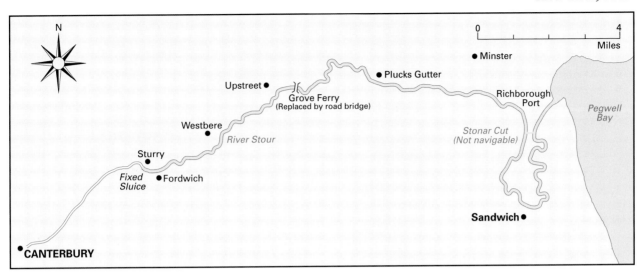

Above Sandwich, passage is only possible for quite small boats as far as Fordwich and above that only for craft which can be portaged. Fordwich is a pleasant Kentish town which was the port for Canterbury for many years. The town is famous for its tiny town hall and its ducking stool.

Authority *From the sea to Poulders Sluice 0.8 mile above Sandwich* Sandwich Port and Haven Commissioners, Clerk's Office, 1 Potter Street, Sandwich, Kent CT14 9DR ☎ 01304 612444. There is no navigation authority for the rest of the river.

Bridges At Sandwich there is the Barbican Bridge which can be opened on application to the toll collector at the bridge house. There are four bridges above this point, the clearance of which is not more than 20ft above high water springs.

Locks None.

Towpath None.

Navigation High water at Sandwich Quay is 1 hour after HW Dover. Spring tides rise 8ft and neap tides rise 7ft at Sandwich. The effect of the wide expanse of Pegwell Bay and the flow in the river is that the tide ebbs for 9 hours and floods for 3 hours with the last hour flooding very rapidly, on springs up to 5 knots. It is possible to moor at the quay in Sandwich, this is accessible 3 hours either side of HW for boats drawing 1m, and there is a small marina.

From the entrance of the river at Pegwell Bay to Richborough, some small coasters can still be encountered. The approaches dry completely at low water and the channel is very steep sided. The tidal range at springs is 10ft 6ins and neaps 7ft 9ins. At Sandwich, deduct about 2ft 6ins.

Charts Imray C8, Admiralty 1827.

Facilities Limited facilities at Sandwich.

Distance table	Miles
Fordwich Mill to:	
Stodmarsh	2.6
Grove Ferry	5.1
Channel to Sarre (old outlet to the sea, not navigable)	8.3
Plucks Gutter	8.4

	Miles
Junction with Little Stour River	8.6
Railway Bridge	11.9
Richborough Castle and Roman Amphitheatre	13.0
Sandwich Bridge	15.3
Richborough, Stonar Cut (unnavigable)	18.4
Shell Ness, Pegwell Bay	19.3

River Stour, Suffolk

John Constable's River Stour now probably represents the quintessential English river. Paintings by Constable, Gainsborough and Nash have preserved the river and the valley on canvas but very much as a working river, not a chocolate box idyll. The river is beautiful, running through a rural landscape with very few towns but delightful unspoilt villages such as Dedham. Constable lived at Flatford, where his father was the miller, and in his paintings the unusual design of the Stour locks can be seen. These have been restored at Dedham and Flatford by the River Stour Trust.

Navigation works on the river were promoted by Acts of Parliament in 1705 and 1781 and there is no record that they have been revoked. Commercial traffic used the river as recently as the 1930s at which time the locks at Stratford St Mary, Dedham, Flatford and Brantham were rebuilt to 95ft long,

RIVER STOUR, SUFFOLK Maximum vessel dimensions

From and to	Distance	Length	Beam	Draught	Headroom	Locks
Sudbury to Cattawade, near Manningtree	23.5 miles (37.8km)	Only small craft can use the river				15

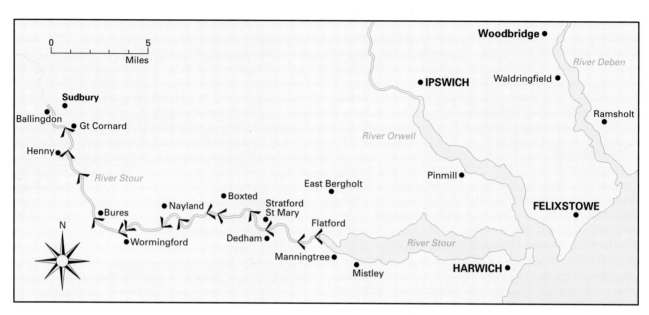

10ft wide and 2ft 9ins draught. Since then the barrage built at Brantham has made the river inaccessible although rollers are in place to allow smaller craft to move between the tidal estuary and the river.

The River Stour Trust was set-up in 1968 and has worked to ensure that future generations will be able to navigate the Stour. Several locks have been rebuilt in the traditional style and it is planned that, in due course, more locks will be brought back into working order. At Sudbury, the basin has been excavated and has water in it again and the old granary is now the headquarters of the Trust with offices, an interpretive centre and a function room overlooking the basin.

Authority Environment Agency, Anglian Region, Eastern Area, Cobham Road, Ipswich, Suffolk ☎ 01473 727712 *Fax* 01473 724205.
The estuary is controlled by the Harwich Harbour Conservancy Board.

Bridges Numerous.

Towpath From Sudbury to Cattawade Barrage.

Restoration The River Stour Trust, formed in 1968, has restored the locks at Flatford and Dedham. An award has been made under the Millennium Lottery Fund towards the restoration of Great Cornard lock which will extend the navigable distance from Sudbury to Henny. Further restoration of the navigation is planned.

Navigation High water at Mistley is about 45 minutes after HW Harwich. The river is tidal from the barrage at Cattawade to Orwell Haven and is used by sea-going vessels. The River Orwell joins the Stour near Orwell Haven and is a tidal

navigation to Ipswich, a distance of 9½ miles. This channel to Ipswich is dredged to 17ft. Due to the currents the tidal portions of the Orwell and Stour should not be attempted without local knowledge.

Powered boats are only allowed on the river between Ballingdon Bridge, Sudbury and Henny Mill, Henny, approximately 2½ miles. Sailing, canoeing and rowing are allowed throughout the length of the river but boats will need to be portaged around fixed structures, many of which have replaced the original locks. The locks at Dedham and Flatford have restricted times of operation as flood defence structures are also in use at these sites.

Facilities There are various launching sites for small craft along the river and for trailed boats at Sudbury. The River Stour Trust runs two trip boats, both electrically powered, and there is an interpretation centre in the Granary, Quay Lane, Sudbury.

Distance table

Sudbury, Ballingdon Bridge, near boathouse to:	Miles
Great Cornard Lock (site of)	1.0
Henny Street Sluices (site of Henny Locks)	2.8
Ruins of Pitmine Lock	3.8
Bures Mill and Sluice (site of Bures Lock)	6.8
Wormingford Mill and Wormingford Lock	9.1
Swan Lock (derelict)	9.4
Wissington Mill and Weir (site of Wissington Lock)	11.4
Nayland Weir (Nayland Lock site)	12.6
Nayland Bridge A134	12.8
Horkesley Lock Site	13.1
Boxted Weir (site of Boxted Lock)	16.1
Langham Weir (site of Langham Lock)	17.1
Langham Bridge	17.5
Higham Hall, junction with River Brett	18.1

	Miles
Stratford St Mary Lock	18.9
Stratford St Mary Bridge	19.6
Dedham Lock	20.5
Dedham Bridge	20.7
Flatford Bridge	22.1
Flatford Lock and Constable's Mill	22.1
Brantham Lock (not in use)	23.6
Cattawade Bridge	24.4
Brantham Barrage and Sluices	24.5
Manningtree	25.1
Mistley	26.1
Parkeston	34.0
Harwich	35.5

Stourbridge Canal

The fact that the Stourbridge Canal and its arm to Stourbridge town is still open is thanks to the hard work and determination of the Staffordshire and Worcestershire Canal Society. Although only a short canal, just over 5 miles from Stourton Junction to the Dudley Canal Line No 1, it is an important link into the Birmingham Canal Navigations and the

heart of Britain's canals. There are two flights of locks, four locks after Stourton Junction, and the famous 'Sixteen', just after the Town Arm, up to the right-hand turn towards the bottom of the Delph Flight on the Dudley Canal.

The canal was completed in 1779, its purpose being to bring coal from the Dudley coal fields to the glass manufacturers around Stourbridge. The old glass furnaces give a special character to the canal and the Stuart Crystal works are still alongside by the 'Sixteen'. At the head of the Town Arm the old bonded warehouse has been restored by the Stourbridge Navigation Trust and is now the Trust's headquarters. The upper part of the canal winds slowly around Brierley Hill and, along this section, there were numerous wharves and factories which used the canal for transport and so contributed to the canal company's income.

All through this area there were rich coal seams and subsidence of canals and collapses into mine workings were always a risk. Mine owners were not supposed to take coal within 12yds of a canal but this was difficult to enforce and in 1903 one such collapse, or 'crowner-in', occured at Wheeley's

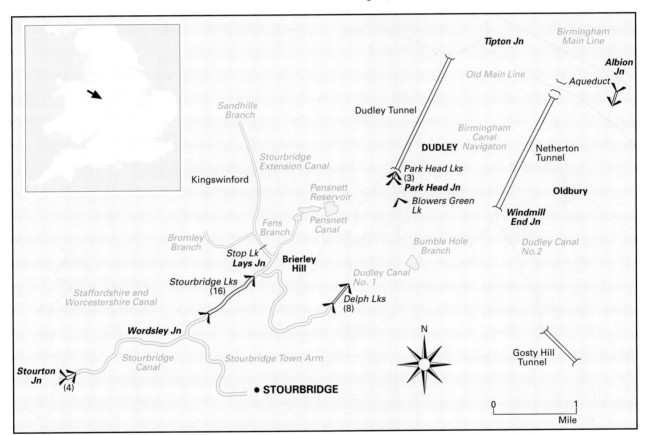

STOURBRIDGE CANAL Maximum vessel dimensions

From and to	Distance	Length	Beam	Draught	Headroom	Locks
Stourton Junction to Black Delph, BCN	5.8 miles (9.3km)	70' (21.3m)	7' (2.1m)	2' 6" (0.7m)	6' (1.8m)	20
Stourbridge Extension Canal						
Brockmoor to Bromley Branch	2 miles (3.2km)	72' (21.9m)	7' (2.1m)	4' (1.2m)	6' 6" (1.9m)	1

Basin. The Stourbridge, as with many other canals, is a fascinating voyage of discovery for anyone interested in Britain's industrial history and a good companion for a walk is Ian Langford's *Towpath Guide No 3, Stourbridge Canal.*

The restoration of the canal in the mid-1960s was a good example of co-operation between the local canal society and British Waterways. It was re-opened in May 1967.

Authority British Waterways, Norbury Junction, Stafford ST20 0PN ☎ 01785 284253.

Bridges Several.

Towpath Throughout navigation. A cycleway has been developed on the Stourbridge Town Arm.

Branches Stourbridge Arm, navigable; Fens Branch; Bromley Branch; and Sandhills Branch, less than 1 mile is currently navigable.

Connections Staffordshire and Worcestershire Canal at Stourton Junction; Dudley No 1 at Black Delph.

Facilities There is one boatyard at Hawne Basin offering full facilities to boaters. This is a very urban canal and there are a few nice pubs close to the canal. Shops can be found at several locations.

Distance table

Stourton Junction, junction with Staffordshire and Worcestershire, Main Line and tail of Stourton Lock No 1 to:	Miles
Head of Stourton Top Lock No 4	0.3
Wordsley Junction, junction with Stourbridge Branch and bottom of the 'Sixteen', Lock No 5	2.0
Buckpool	2.9
Lays Junction, junction with Branch to the Fens on Pensnett Chase, and top of the 'Sixteen', Lock No 20	3.3
Brettell Lane	4.4
Black Delph, junction with Birmingham Canal Navigations, Dudley Canal Line No 1	5.1
Stourbridge Town Arm	
Wordsley Junction, junction with Main Line to:	
Holloway End	0.9
Stourbridge	1.3
Branch to the Fens on Pensnett Chase	
Lays Junction, junction with Main Line, to:	
Brockmoor Junction, junction with Stourbridge Extension Canal	0.3
The Fens, Pensnett Chase	0.8

Stourbridge Extension Canal

This was a much later canal, opened in 1840 when the railways were already active in the area. Many mines and ironworks were already established along its route and so initially it was a very profitable venture. The canal had two branches, the Bromley Branch and the Sandhills Branch and with the main line were all built on one level. The canal was gradually closed from the 1920s and now very little of it remains. The terminal basin is still recognisable but housing and trading estates cover most of the remainder.

The canal is navigable to the stop lock. At Brockmoor Junction, the Fens Branch joins the canal. This is a feeder from the Fens Pools to the Stourbridge Canal main line.

Authority British Waterways, Norbury Junction, Stafford ST20 0PN ☎ 01785 284253.

Towpath Throughout navigation.

Branches Bromley Branch, ¼ mile; Sandhills Branch, ¾ mile.

Distance table

Brockmoor Junction, junction with Stourbridge Canal to:	Miles
Stock Lock, and junction with Bromley Branch	0.2

Stratford-upon-Avon Canal

The Stratford-upon-Avon Canal was promoted by Acts of Parliament in 1793 and 1795 but, by 1796, only 9¾ miles had been cut and all the initial capital had been used up. Building ceased until another Act authorised more money to be raised in 1799 and by 1802 the northern section between the Worcester and Birmingham Canal at King's Norton and the Warwick and Birmingham Canal, now part of the Grand Union, at Kingswood Junction was completed. This enabled the canal company to raise money through tolls and revive flagging interest in the project. Despite this, the southern section was not completed until June 1816.

The canal was initially profitable with the 1830s giving the best dividend to shareholders. Within 20 years the railways were taking traffic from the canal and negotiations started with the Oxford, Worcester and Wolverhampton Railway. These became very protracted and it wasn't until the late 1850s that the railway company finally took over the canal. Later, the railway was taken over by the Great Western Railway and canal traffic declined rapidly, as did maintenance. This particularly affected the southern section and, by the Second World War, the canal was virtually unnavigable.

In 1947, Tom Rolt and *Cressy* made a memorable voyage along the Stratford-upon-Avon Canal requiring GWR to raise Lifford Bridge as it was blocking a statutory right of navigation. Later the route was navigated again by *Beatrice*, Peter Scott's boat, and the bridge was raised. In 1958, Warwickshire County Council announced that it

STRATFORD-UPON-AVON CANAL *Maximum vessel dimensions*

From and to	Distance	Length	Beam	Draught	Headroom	Locks
King's Norton Junction to Stratford-on-Avon	25.5 miles (41.0km)	70' (21.3m)	7' (2.1m)	2' 6" (0.7m)	6' (1.9m)	56

was closing the canal and work would begin on Wilmcote Bridge. They had underestimated the tide of feeling and two members of the recently formed canal society made a passage by canoe and by the production of a dated toll ticket proved that the canal was navigable. Having prevented closure, the mammoth task of restoration had to be addressed. The National Trust took over responsibility for the canal and, under the inspired leadership of David Hutchings, a restoration plan was put into operation. The work was carried out by volunteers, army personnel and prison groups and in 1964 the southern Stratford-upon-Avon Canal was re-opened by HM The Queen Mother.

Since then, the Stratford-upon-Avon Canal has become a very popular cruising route forming one part of the Avon Ring. Its unusual features include the split bridges which allowed a tow rope to pass between so the horse did not have to be unhitched, the barrel roofed lock cottages and the three aqueducts where the towpath is at a lower level than

The barrel roofed lock cottages and split bridges are typical of the Stratford-on-Avon Canal. *Roy Westlake*

the canal giving a 'boat's-eye' view of the surroundings. In 1988, the National Trust handed the canal back to BW and it is now under BW management.

Authority British Waterways, Brome Hall Lane, Lapworth, Solihull, West Midlands B94 5RB ☎ 01564 784634.

Bridges 70. Mostly fixed. Many of these have the distinctive gap in the centre which enabled the tow rope to pass through without unhitching the horse. Three lifting.

Towpath Along most of the navigation, except Brandwood Tunnel. The towpath has been improved over recent years but cycling is not allowed.

Tunnels Brandwood, 352yds, no towpath.

Aqueducts Edstone or Bearley, it crosses a road, railway and water meadows. Two aqueducts over roads, one near Preston Bagot and the other at Wooton Wawen.

Branches Kingswood Branch to the Grand Union Canal.

Connections Grand Union Canal at Kingswood via a short branch; Worcester and Birmingham Canal at King's Norton; River Avon at Stratford.

Facilities Being a very popular cruiseway there are plenty of good eating places and several boatyards offering all facilities for boat crews.

Distance table	*Miles*
King's Norton, junction with Worcester and Birmingham Canal to:	
King's Norton Stop Lock No 1 (guillotine)	0.1
Brandwood Tunnel	1.0
Yardley Wood	3.0
River Cole Aqueduct	3.8
Warrings Green	7.8
M42	8.3
Hockley Heath	9.8
Lifting Bridge No 26	10.0
Lifting Bridge No 28	10.6
Lapworth Top Lock No 2	10.8
Lapworth Lock No 6	11.5
Lapworth Locks Nos 8–14	11.8
Kingswood Junction, branch to Grand Union Canal (lock on branch, No 20)	12.5
Lapworth Lock No 26	13.1
M40	13.2
Lowsonford, Post Office Bridge Lock No 30	14.3
Lowsonford, Fleur de Lys, Lock No 31	14.5
Yarningale Aqueduct	15.5
Preston Bagot Locks Nos 36–38	16.3
Wootton Wawen Aqueduct over A34	18.5
Bearley, Lock No 39	19.6
Bearley Aqueduct Northern End	19.9
Wilmcote Railway Station	21.9

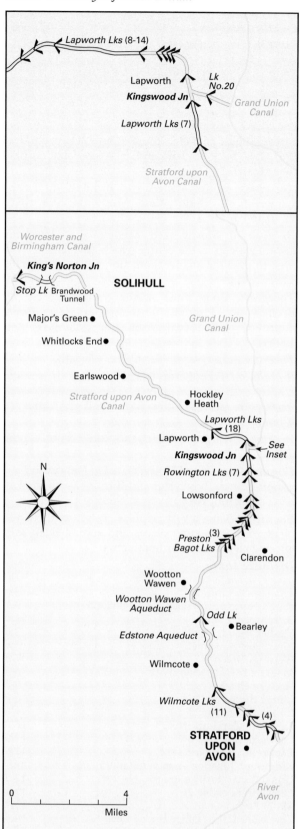

	Miles
Wilmcote Top Lock No 40	22.5
Wilmcote Bottom Lock No 51	23.5
Bishopton and Stratford Locks Nos 52–55	23.8
Stratford-on-Avon Lock No 56, and junction with Upper Avon Navigation	25.5

Kingswood Branch
Kingswood Junction to:

Lock No 20	0.1
Kingswood, junction with Grand Union Canal	0.3

Stroudwater Canal

The Stroudwater Canal was a short waterway which linked the River Severn with the Gloucester and Sharpness Canal and the Thames and Severn Canal. It was one of the earliest canals, originally planned in the 1720s and opened in 1779, and in its heyday was a profitable venture. The canal ran parallel to, but was never a canalisation of, the River Frome. Its restoration is being undertaken by the Cotswold Canals Trust.

Authority The Company of Proprietors of the Stroudwater Navigation, 4/7 Rowcroft, Stroud, Gloucestershire GL5 3BJ. For the Clerk to the Company ☎ 01453 762781.

Bridges Numerous.

Towpath Good throughout.

Connections Gloucester and Sharpness Canal at Saul Junction; Thames and Severn Canal at Wallbridge, originally River Severn at Framilode.

Restoration There are no plans to restore the section between the River Severn and the Gloucester and Sharpness Canal. From Saul, the junction with the Gloucester and Sharpness, to Whitminster Lock has been restored, just over ½ mile, as has about 1¾ miles from Pike Lock to Ryeford Double. Work is in progress from Whitminster to the A38.

Distance table   *Miles*
Wallbridge, Stroud junction with the Thames and Severn Canal to:

	Miles
Dudbridge Foundry Locks No 1 and No 2	0.5
Ryeford Double Locks Nos 3 and 4 (staircase)	1.8
Newtown Lock No 5 (top of five)	3.6
Blunder Lock No 6	4.0
Pike Lock No 7	4.1

STROUDWATER CANAL Maximum vessel dimensions

From and to	Distance	Length	Beam	Draught	Headroom	Locks
Wallbridge, Stroud to Framilode, River Severn	8 miles (12.8km)	70' (21.3m)	15' 6" (4.7m)	5' (1.5m)	11' 6" (3.5m)	13

Dock Lock No 8	4.3
Westfield Lock No 9	4.5
Bristol Road Lock No 10	5.4
Whitminster Lock No 11	6.6
Saul, junction with Gloucester and Sharpness Canal	7.0
Junction Lock No 12	7.1
Tail of Framilode Lock No 13, junction with Severn Estuary	8.0

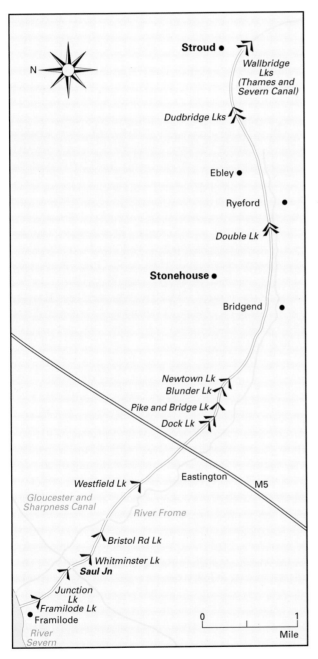

River Tamar

The Tamar River is the boundary between Devon and Cornwall. It rises within 3 miles of the north coast and winds through beautiful countryside, before it is joined by the River Tavy and widens into the Hamoaze and then Plymouth Sound. For centuries a vibrant naval port, Plymouth has developed in the past 30 years into a major centre for sailing.

From Gunnislake, which is effectively the head of navigation, the river passes Morwellham Quay which used to serve as a port for Tavistock. There is now a fascinating canal museum here, well worth a trip by road or water as it demonstrates the importance of canals in the area. It is particularly interesting as it does not readily spring to mind that this area is a great canal centre.

Authority Queen's Harbourmaster, HM Naval Base, Devonport, Devon ☎ 01752 552047.

Bridges The Tamar Bridge at Saltash and one bridge at Calstock. Electricity cables restrict headroom to 40ft on the Tavy and there is a railway bridge near the mouth.

Towpath None.

Connections The Lynher or St Germans River joins the Hamoaze, as the Tamar is called below Saltash Bridge. This is navigable for light craft at high tide to Tideford, a distance of 6½ miles. Maximum draught is 6ft at high water. The River Tavy joins the Tamar 1½ miles above Maristow Quay at high tides, a distance of about 5 miles. Maximum draught to Maristow Quay is 8 to 10ft and 5ft to head of navigation. Both of these rivers are under the same authority as the Tamar.

Navigation High water at Weir Head is 40 minutes after HW Plymouth. Spring tides rise about 5ft, neaps about 1ft.

Charts Imray C14 Admiralty 30, 1967, 1901, 1902.

RIVER TAMAR Maximum Vessel Dimensions

From and to	Distance	Length	Beam	Draught	Headroom	Locks
Weir Head to the Sound	19 miles (30.6km)	Unlimited	Unlimited	5' (1.5m) (HW)	100' (30.4m)	None

Facilities Several marinas in Plymouth plus shops, restaurants, pubs and all other services.

Distance table	*Miles*
Weir Head to:	
Morwellham Quay, Morwell Rocks	1.6
Newy Quay	2.4
Okeltor	3.1
Calstock	4.6
Halton Quay	7.9
Pentillie	8.5
Weirquay	10.5
Cargreen	12.0
Tavy Junction, junction with River Tavy (tidal to Lapwell)	12.1
Saltash Railway Bridge	14.5
Junction with St Germans River	16.0
Devonport	17.5
Plymouth	19.0

River Tees

The construction in 1995 of a tidal barrage below Stockton-on-Tees has completely changed the river for pleasure boats. Above the barrage, there is now 11 miles of freshwater maintained at high water level and, for trailed boats or anyone who can come up the tidal stretch from the North Sea, a very pleasant cruising area has been opened up.

For trailed boats, there are slipways at the barrage lock and at Stockton. The barrage slipway is

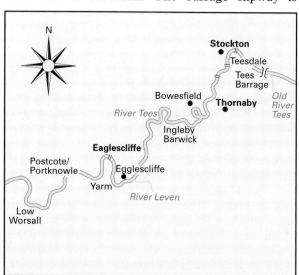

administered by the Tees Barrage Ltd and the Stockton slip is run by Stockton Council which should be contacted at their offices before using the slip.

The passage from the barrage up to Worsall is varied and interesting, with a mixture of industrial and urban areas around Stockton, then through flat meadow land and finally wooded valleys. Along the route are some delightful villages and plans have been proposed to increase the number of mooring places, which are fairly sparse at present. For railway enthusiasts this is, of course, Stephenson country with the impressive viaduct at Yarm as a reminder.

Authority Tees and Hartlepool Port Authority, Queens Square, Middlesbrough ☎ 01642 241121.

Above Tees Barrage: The River Master, Tees Barrage Ltd, Navigation Way, Thornaby, Cleveland TS18 6QA ☎ 01642 633273.

Towpath None.

Navigation The Port of Tees and Hartlepool Authority do not encourage private boats and charge a fee for passage through their jurisdiction. Tees Barrage Ltd are responsible for the lock, the slipway and management above the barrage. It is a requirement that all boats using this waterway must have third-party insurance and boats must be registered with the company. For details of charges contact the River Master (as above).

Distance table	*Miles*
Worsall Weir to:	
Yarm Bridge	3.3
Stockton and Thornaby	10.6
Newport	13.3
Ferry, Middlesbrough to Port Clarence	15.9
Mouth of river at low water	24.0

RIVER TEES Maximum vessel dimensions

From and to	Distance	Length	Beam	Draught	Headroom	Locks
Worsall Weir to Tees Barrage	11 miles (17.7km)	82' (25.0m)	20' (6.0m)	8' 2" (2.5m)	17' 8" (5.4m)	1
Tees Barrage to River Mouth	13 miles (20.9km)	Unlimited	Unlimited	Tidal	Unlimited	None

River Thames

The Thames is probably Britain's best-loved river, as well as its most famous. Rising close to Sapperton Tunnel on the Thames and Severn Canal, the first few miles are a gentle stream flowing through the Cotswolds, only slowly turning into a navigable river. Cricklade is the technical head of navigation but, for all practical purposes, few boats venture above Inglesham and the old junction of the river with the Thames and Severn Canal at the Round House. Hopefully, this connection will be re-established one day to offer the possibility of cruising right across the south of England to the Severn Estuary, via the Thames and Severn, the Stroudwater and then the Gloucester and Sharpness canals.

From Roman times to the present day, the river has played an important role in the economy of Britain and as a transport route and defensive barrier. Castles and old fortifications dating from Roman, Saxon and Norman times can be seen along the length of the river; mills were built to harness the power of the river and weirs to catch the vast number of fish that lived in it. The conflicting demands of navigation with those of mill owners and fishermen have always caused disputes on the river.

Towards the end of the 12th century, Richard I gave the City of London rights over the River Thames at a time when he needed money. The document was rather imprecise and for several hundred years the City was able to exercise its power, despite challenges from all sources, not least from subsequent monarchs. In 1285, the City erected the London Stone at Staines as the extent of its jurisdiction because, at that time, enforcement of a right needed to be by physical means. It was not until 1770, that a body called the Thames Commissioners came into being to attempt to balance the conflicting demands between different river users and riparian owners.

With the coming of the railways, income from barges and cargo went down dramatically and, in 1857, the commissioners were replaced by the Thames Conservancy. The powers of the conservancy were much greater than those of the commissioners, as this new body was backed by government funding and had the powers to control all aspects of the river. This Act of 1857 gave the conservancy jurisdiction from Staines to Yantlet Creek in Kent and a further Act, in 1866, extended this power up river to Cricklade. Considerable work to improve the river structures and the watercourse were carried out by the conservancy and when its powers were transferred to the Thames Water Authority in 1974, the river navigation was in good condition.

London has been a major port as long as it has been a principal city. With the expansion of trade as the New World was being opened up during the 15th, 16th and 17th centuries, wharves and docks developed in London. 'Legal quays' came into being, 20 selected wharves, authorised by the Crown, where foreign goods could be landed between sunrise and sunset. Gradually more wharves had to be included as trade increased, and these were called sufferance wharves, all situated in the Pool of London.

By the end of the 18th century, docking facilities were inadequate and trade with the East and the West Indies was growing rapidly. The West India Merchants and the Corporation of London proposed a Bill to build docks on the Isle of Dogs. This was authorised in 1799, and the West India Docks were opened in August 1802. The success of the docks encouraged other Bills to be proposed, and for the whole of the 19th century Port of London trade was controlled by private dock companies. By the end of the century, there was too much dock space and with larger ships coming in to dock, companies found they did not have the capital available to improve their facilities, as they had been undercutting each other for so long to gain trade.

At the turn of the 20th century, a Royal Commission recommended a new central authority to oversee the Port of London, and in 1908 the Port of London Act transferred the powers for the tidal Thames below Teddington from the conservancy to the Port of London. This transfer came into effect on 31 March 1909 and a stone obelisk, 165yds below Teddington Lock, marks the imaginary line across the Thames where the Thames Conservancy and the Port of London Authority (PLA) meet. The PLA has responsibility for 90 miles of waterway from Teddington to the river mouth.

Although commercial traffic has declined, the tidal Thames is still one of the busiest waterways in the world and the PLA's duties cover all navigational matters on the river: the maintenance of adequate river channels, the regulation of river traffic, the provision and upkeep of a number of public ship and barge moorings, and the licensing of wharves and structures which extend into the river below the high water mark. Other responsibilities include surveying and charting the tideway, the removal of wrecks and obstructions, the prevention of pollution, the registration of certain craft employed exclusively within the limits of the port, and the licensing of lightermen and watermen.

The non-tidal Thames

From its source to Oxford, the upper reaches of the Thames are still very much an angler's river with numerous riverside pubs – at least three are called 'The Trout' and others are The Perch and The Swan. The peace and quiet of this part of the river is partly preserved by the fact that Osney Bridge at Oxford has only 7ft 6ins of headroom, restricting a number of boats from exploring further. Although, practically, only navigable below Inglesham, it is worth exploring the infant Thames by foot if you really want to get to know the river. There are still those who dispute whether the true source is at Thameshead, but this is a good place to start from and, where the Thames joins the Churn, it does appear to be the larger of the two streams.

From Lechlade, the Thames (or Isis) passes through locks and under bridges – Tadpole and Ten Foot are two of the most enchanting names – through Godstow and on to the Duke's Cut where boats can join the Oxford Canal and set off into the miles of narrow canals through the Midlands. Oxford has many attractions with lots to do and see, although the river itself does not run through the heart of the city. Only a little exertion is needed to walk from the river into the centre and all its associated history, culture and bustle; the dreaming spires, the Radcliffe Camera, the Bodleian Library, the Ashmolean Museum and the fascinating Botanic Garden.

Once past Oxford, the Thames starts to take on rather more grandeur and begins to feel its own importance. Through a broad bend past Abingdon, the river travels 9 miles to cover less than 2 miles as the crow flies. Approaching Dorchester and the confluence with the River Thame, the Thames is very attractive before starting out through a rather flatter, fertile agricultural landscape. At Dorchester,

the seventh-century abbey gives an idea of the importance of this town in the Middle Ages.

After passing Benson Lock, you reach Wallingford, which is a very old riverside settlement. Here you will find castle ruins and a bridge with 17 arches, of which only five actually cross the river. From Wallingford down to Cleeve Lock is 6½ miles through a placid stretch of river. Just over half way along, you pass under Moulsford Railway Bridge, one of Brunel's most impressive designs. The railway crosses the river at an angle but, to reduce the effect of the flow on the structure, the piers were built straight in the stream and the arches are wonderfully twisted. The complicated brickwork to produce this fine structure is seen so much better from a boat.

Goring is hardly visible from the river, but the increased activity on the water, with more rowing and sailing boats coming and going, suggests that some larger towns are nearby. At Goring, the Ridgeway Path crosses the Thames, with the Chilterns to the north and the Berkshire Downs to the south. This is Goring Gap, an example of geological activity, where the Thames changed course after the last ice-age; prior to this it would have flowed northeastward to join the Great Ouse and the Rhine. From a certain point on the journey down river, it looks as if there is no way through the surrounding hills. This made the ford at Goring a strategic stronghold in early times.

Past Pangbourne, with its famous college, there is the possibility of seeing Hardwick House before the river enters Mapledurham, where Soames Forsyte had a fine house in *The Forsyte Saga*. There has been a weir here for about 600 years; a lock was constructed in 1777 and this was the first lock on the Thames to be mechanised in 1956. The mill can still be seen just to the north of the river. It was fully

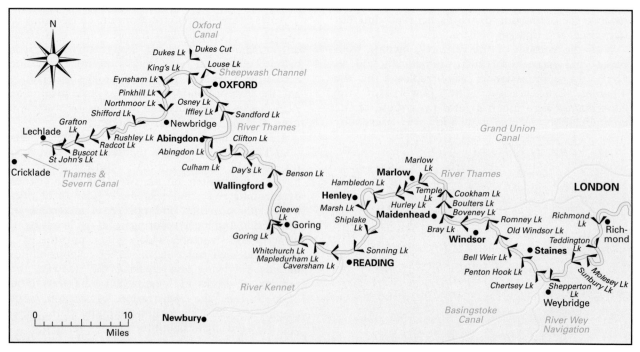

Moorings near the weir at Marlow on the River Thames.
Roy Westlake

restored in the late 1970s and is now the only working flour mill left on the Thames.

Then Reading is reached, bringing with it a more suburban feel to the river, and the course becomes wider with small islands, or eyots, and more boats and activity. The main railway line runs alongside, occasionally veering off through the town centre. Just on the east side of Reading, the River Kennet branches off to the south on its way to the Kennet

Henley-on-Thames. *Roy Westlake*

and Avon Canal and a fascinating cross-country route to Bath and Bristol.

A few miles further downstream, past Sonning and Wargrave, the Thames flows quietly past one of its most famous towns – Henley. Here the river is running almost north-south with the town on the west bank and the regatta course just to the north, downstream of Henley Bridge. The regatta course is 1¼ miles long and the river runs completely straight for this distance. The town's waterfront is attractive and, even without the excitement of the regatta, which takes place the first week of July each year, there is always something happening on the river at Henley. The downstream end of the course is Temple Island, with its famous white temple and surrounding trees. The first Oxford and Cambridge University Boat Race was rowed at Henley in 1829, from Hambleden Lock to Henley Bridge.

Below Henley, the river swings round to the east at Hambleden, where you can walk across the weir bridges to look at the old mill (which no longer grinds corn). Then the Thames slides past Medmenham and Hurley before approaching the white suspension bridge at Marlow. This notable bridge, built in the 1830s, was designed by William Tierney Clark. Marlow now has very good facilities for boaters and lots of interesting shops to part you from your money, as well as that famous hotel – The Compleat Angler.

Now the Thames has to make a wide sweep round Quarry Wood, with many fascinating houses and chalets along the waterside, before reaching Bourne

Clifton Hampden Bridge on the River Thames near Abingdon.
Roy Westlake

End. This is a very popular stretch of the river with lots of activity afloat. After Cookham Bridge, there are several islands and you have to make sure you take the right route to approach the lock. Just after the lock, on the east bank, there is Cliveden House which is owned by the National Trust, with steep hills of beech woods along the Cliveden Reach.

Boulter's Lock, at Taplow, is probably the best known lock on the Thames. In 1995, there was a live reconstruction to celebrate the centenary of the famous painting by Edward J Gregory called *Boulter's Lock, Sunday Afternoon 1895*. The scene was almost identical to that of the picture, with Edwardians out in their punts and launches on the river. Throughout the voyage from Oxford you can almost feel the presence of Jerome K Jerome and Montmorency as the *Three Men in a Boat* made their way from one mishap to the next.

After Maidenhead, you pass under the M4 just below Bray Lock, before reaching Eton and Windsor. Windsor Racecourse is actually on an island and the river approach to Boveney Lock is along the north arm. Throughout this distance the Thames is dominated by Windsor Castle and on the north bank you can see the famous Eton College Boathouse. Having passed under Windsor Bridge and through Romney Lock, the river swings round to the southeast and you pass under two bridges, first the Victoria and then the Albert, as you travel past Windsor Home Park to the east of the castle. Shortly after Old Windsor Lock, Runnymede, site of

the famous battle of 1215, is on the south bank with Magna Carta Island on the north bank; this is where King John signed the Magna Carta, having acceded to his Barons.

From here, the Thames starts to travel through more suburban surroundings – Egham and the M25, Chertsey and Staines, then the River Wey to the south at Weybridge and the last few miles of non-tidal river past Hampton Court and down to Teddington.

The tidal Thames

There is something special about all the great rivers of Europe, penetrating far inland and carrying with them the free spirit of trade, commerce and travel to faraway places.

In Paris, from the city banks of the Seine, you can imagine a whiff of salt air as a westerly breeze raises a chop against the hollow steel sides of the moored barges. The zest of the river somehow brings to mind the quays and docks of Le Havre and the estuary approaches off Honfleur. There is an instant link between the waters of the Channel and the Quai des Tuileries.

In Hamburg, off St Pauli Pier, you sense a teutonic purpose in the fast run of the Elbe. The same river that winds past the elegant town-houses above Mühlenberg and Blankenese carries ocean-going ships for 50 miles through the flat pastures of Holstein and out past treacherous drying sands into the wastes of the German Bight.

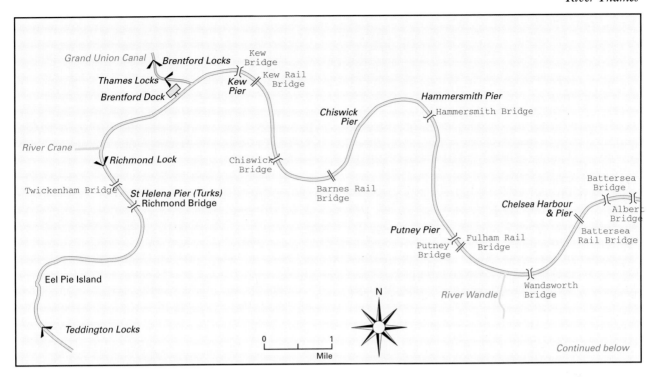

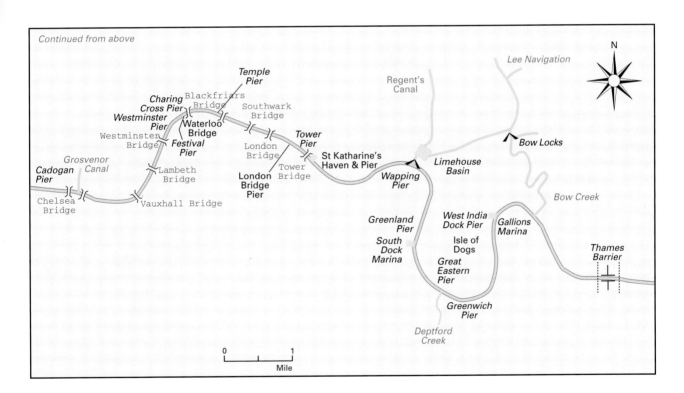

In a similar way, as you pass by boat under Westminster Bridge, you can visualise the long passage of the tidal Thames, from the outer sandbanks off Margate or Walton-on-the-Naze, through the narrowing channel between Sheerness and Southend, and thus into the trail of half-derelict wharves between Tilbury and the India Docks.

Although much of the Thames seems deserted these days, it still has the power to fire the imagination, not least because of those evocative names which have strong links with our maritime past – Gravesend, Woolwich Reach, Greenwich, the Isle of Dogs. There is a certain magic about a grand tidal river that curves majestically through the commercial heart of a capital city. The Thames may carry less commercial traffic now than the Seine or the Elbe, but the ghosts of old trading London, with its colonial wharves and quays and abandoned docks, can still be spirited up even when weary commuters, trudging across Hungerford Bridge towards Waterloo on a raw December night, hear the throb of big marine engines and see a barge towing a string of lighters past the South Bank on the evening tide.

The upstream limit of the tidal Thames is at Teddington Locks, the crossing point between the bustling commercial river and the more placid suburban Thames. From Teddington Locks down to the open estuary at Shivering Sand Tower, you can reckon 78 land miles, or about 68 nautical miles. Teddington is an important transition in a cruise of the Thames, both physically and psychologically. On the south side of the locks are the still reaches of the canalised river, blissfully unaffected by the comings and goings of the tide. On the north side, as you emerge through the gates opposite Toughs Boatyard, you start to come under the influence of the ebbs and flows of the tidal Thames.

Not completely though, because Richmond Lock, another 3 miles downstream, is effectively a half-tide barrage and the last lock on the Thames. From 2 hours before to 2 hours after high water, the patent sluices at Richmond are raised to allow the free passage of craft. This means that the top of each tide rises and falls at Teddington in the normal way, but once the Richmond sluices close again 2 hours after high water, the tide can fall no further at Teddington.

The reach between Teddington and Richmond is therefore like a long tidal basin, in which a minimum depth of 5ft 7ins (1.7m) is retained at all times. When the Richmond sluices are closed, from 2 hours after high water until 2 hours before the next high water, boats can pass through Richmond Lock in the usual way.

After Toughs Boatyard and Swan Island, the river curves east past Twickenham and Eel Pie Island, where you should keep to the Surrey bank to leave the island to the north. Eel Pie Island is a congenial gathering place for boating people, with its boatyards and landing slips, yacht club and rowing club. The Balmy Arms pub stands on the mainland bank just over the bridge, with the Eel Pie pub just behind it in Church Street. The culinary origins of the name of this island are rather obscure. There were said to be plenty of succulent eels around in the good old days, when eels were eels, but neither of these worthy pubs serves eel pie now.

As you head downstream through Horse Reach, Marble Hill Park is over on your port side, a reminder that the London suburbs still have plenty of leafy open spaces. Still keeping to the Surrey side, you leave Glover's Ait to the north and then the river swings north through Richmond, past Richmond Ait and St Helena Pier. Richmond Lock is on the Surrey side and the patent sluices of the tidal barrage are lowered from the three middle spans of Richmond Footbridge.

Once past Richmond Lock, you are out in real tidal water and you should take care when steering through the arches of the famous London bridges, especially as you drop further downstream and the tide gathers weight. Just down from Richmond Lock, past Isleworth Ait (keep to the Surrey side), the river turns east again towards Kew, past Brentford Dock Marina and the Brentford Locks which lead into the Grand Union Canal and the London Ring.

Winding past Kew, Chiswick and Barnes bridges (evocative names that stir memories of countless boat races), the river widens very gradually so that by the time you reach Putney, the Thames seems to gain in status, reaching more imposing proportions opposite Battersea and Chelsea Harbour as it prepares to slide past the famous bridges and embankments of Central London.

Gradually the more scruffy, derelict quays and wharves along this part of the Thames are being tidied up and developed, as the property potential of riverside sites is realised. Of course, it would be a great shame if all the eccentric backwaters were sanitised, since part of the charm of a great capital river lies in all the odd historic quays, workshops, nooks and crannies which you only ever come across by boat. But the tremendous potential which the Thames could make to the atmosphere of London has yet to be fully tapped. This great natural watercourse is still regarded as rather incidental to the daily life of London, glimpsed now and again from a train or a taxi, but not yet captured as part of the living architecture of the capital.

It is always imposing to pass the Houses of Parliament by boat. Westminster Bridge and Pier are striking landmarks. Then the river curves east again under Hungerford Bridge and Waterloo Bridge past the Royal Festival Hall, Queen Elizabeth Hall and the National Theatre. Just opposite the Festival Hall, on the north bank, Cleopatra's Needle remains one of London's most timeless and enigmatic monuments and the Savoy still the most civilised hotel.

Past Blackfriars Bridge and Southwark Bridge, you leave behind the political and administrative centre of London and slip into the financial heartlands. Here, just north of the river, the great dome of St Paul's dominates the City skyline. Not far from the timeless flowing Thames are those great institutions which keep the economic wheels turning – Mansion House, the Bank of England and the Stock Exchange.

Just opposite HMS *Belfast* is the Tower of London and Traitor's Gate, looking exactly as they did when you were first taken there as a child. Tower Bridge is perhaps the most universally recognised emblem of London, but it is still exciting to creep below those splendid Gothic spans conceived by Sir John Barry and Sir Horace Jones in the late 19th century.

Just downstream from Tower Bridge, on the north shore, is the lock gate that leads into St Katharine's Yacht Haven, one of the first dockland developments in London and a fascinating place to moor with your own boat. The lock into St Katharine's is worked from 2 hours before high water to 1½ hours after.

Tower Bridge was once the last bridge on the Thames and it is still the last bridge which provides any restriction to the passage of shipping. Just downstream from Tower Bridge is the historic Pool of London, the point at which trading ships coming upriver would have anchored while their cargoes were unloaded into barges and lighters. C S Forester described the scene during the days of sail, when the Pool would be packed with Naval and coasting ships during the heady days of the Napoleonic Wars:

'. . here was the greatest port in the world; ships at anchor, ships discharging cargo, with only the narrowest channel down the centre. North country collier brigs, Ramsgate trawlers, coasters, grain ships, with the grey Tower looking down on them.'

Not far beyond the Pool, past Wapping Pier and Prospect Pier, you reach the tidal entrance lock into Limehouse Basin, renovated recently by British Waterways. Limehouse Basin is the east entrance to the Regent's Canal, an arm of the Grand Union, and also to Limehouse Cut which leads to the River Lee and, eventually, to Hertford. For a shallow draught boat of the right dimensions, Limehouse

could be the start of a cross-country passage to Birmingham, Liverpool, or even The Wash.

Limehouse Basin is home to a catholic mix of ocean-going yachts, large motor cruisers and brightly painted narrow boats. The blue and red trains of the Docklands Light Railway shuttle past on the skyline every few minutes, making this marina an excellent base for the London sights. Right on the corner of the lock, the smart new headquarters of the Cruising Association offers a warm welcome to anyone arriving by boat.

From Limehouse and Canary Wharf, the Thames winds south and then back north around the main expanse of the old London docklands and the Isle of Dogs, a singular part of the East End surrounded by river on three sides and almost cut off to the north by the old West India Docks. These old docklands, with their long colonial trading associations, are now settling down, after a somewhat shaky start, into a new era as a prosperous commercial and residential quarter of London. It now seems difficult to imagine that, barely 40 years ago, you could see ocean-going ships in the London docks – banana boats, sugar ships and battered freighters carrying general cargo from Yokohama, Singapore and Rangoon.

Right on the south side of the dramatic river sweep that carves out the Isle of Dogs, the old quarter of Greenwich has a waterfront which probably has the most atmosphere of all the waterfronts on the Thames. The *Cutty Sark* and the National Maritime Museum both remain popular tourist attractions and the whole flux of nautical history and naval affairs running through Greenwich cannot help but catch the imagination of all true Englishmen.

To the east of the Isle of Dogs, just beyond the old East India Dock Basin, lies the mouth of Bow Creek, once the river access to an extensive industrial area served by barges and lighters (see the entries for the Rivers Lee and Stort). From here the river curves southeast and then east towards Woolwich and the fantastic space-age structures of the Thames Tidal Barrier.

Well before reaching the barrier, boats equipped with VHF radio should report their estimated time of arrival to Woolwich Radio on VHF Ch 14, asking for instructions. Small private boats are often given clearance to proceed through the barrier using span G, which is the nearest navigable span to the north shore.

Just downstream from the Thames Barrier, you'll probably have to dodge the Woolwich Ferry as it shuttles between two jutting out landing quays, much as it always has done. Not far to the north is the London City Airport, where small commuter planes land and take off between the old King George V and Royal Albert Docks. Then, as the river trends slightly north, you reach the mouth of Barking Creek, which now has its own flood barrier to protect the low valley and hinterland of the River Roding. Much interesting development is taking place further up Barking Creek, above the A13 road

The tidal barrier at the mouth of the River Roding is brought into operation at the same time as the main Thames Barrage. *Jane Cumberlidge*

bridge. A new tidal lock gate now encloses an animated inner harbour area which has added a great deal to the attraction of this corner of outer London.

East of Barking Creek, the river feels much wider and more industrial than hitherto, and you pass some of the famous names of heavy manufacturing. The Ford Motor Works at Dagenham sprawls across vast acres just opposite the Thamesmead sewage works and the power station at Belvedere. Cruising on downstream, the crew of a small boat can start to feel rather insignificant amidst all the grimy factories, but then you pass a tiny boating oasis on the south shore at Erith, where the Erith Yacht Club has provided a haven for like-minded London boatowners since before the war.

Off Dartford, it is strange to imagine the stream of traffic in the tunnel below. The new Dartford Bridge, officially named the Queen Elizabeth II Bridge, is an impressive structure with its generous clearance of 54 metres at MHWS. In St Clement's Reach, the river curves round Broadness towards Tilbury Docks and the busy container terminal on the north shore.

Opposite Tilbury, in Gravesend Reach, the Gravesend Yacht Club have their base in a pleasant locked basin accessible for 1½ hours before high water. This was once the north end of the Gravesend and Rochester Canal, which in the early 19th century connected this part of the Thames with the upper reaches of the Medway.

Downstream from Gravesend, the Thames curves round Coalhouse Point, past the entrance to Mucking Creek and the oil terminal at Shellhaven, to open out into the wide Yantlet Channel. Here you can sniff real sea air, and a brisk wind can raise a respectable chop opposite Canvey Island and the mouth of Holehaven Creek. For small boats unsure about the weather, this is the time to call a halt and tuck into the shelter of Holehaven. Benfleet Creek is another possible bolt-hole, on the northeast side of Canvey Island.

Seaward of Canvey Island, the Thames can be an unforgiving waterway for anyone unprepared. In Sea Reach, the estuary widens considerably. From Shoeburyness across to Garrison Point is about 5 miles and there are mile-wide sandbanks off either shore. On the south side of the estuary, the gap between Garrison Point and the Isle of Grain is the entrance to the River Medway, which curves west towards Gillingham, Chatham and Rochester. On the north side, beyond Shoeburyness and Southend, the low Essex shore trends northeast towards Foulness, with the treacherous shoals of the Maplin Sands extending several miles offshore.

The Shivering Sand Tower, right out in the estuary, is a busy junction from which radiate the numerous buoyed channels of the outer estuary – the Barrow Deep, Knock John Channel, the Knob Channel and Princes Channel.

Seaward of the Shivering Sand Tower lies the extraordinary network of swatchways and drying sands that make the Thames Estuary so challenging and fascinating for small boat navigators. You need to know your business though. The outer Thames Estuary needs treating with respect and is no place for small, shallow-draught inland boats to be pottering about.

Special events on the Thames

Numerous events take place all along the Thames every year and have done throughout history. The great frost fairs of the 17th and 18th centuries went on for long periods of time with stalls, markets and entertainments. At that time, the river was wider and flowed more slowly, and the old London Bridge almost created a dam. During the 19th century, a new bridge and wharves were built which increased the flow of the river, and the tidal river has never frozen completely since.

The first University Boat Race on the Thames was in 1829, and it was held at Henley; Oxford won and at that time Cambridge's colours were pink. The next race was in 1836, with a course between Westminster and Putney. Oxford had dark blue stripes on their white jerseys and Cambridge had pale blue after a supporter fixed a pale blue ribbon to their boat. This time the Cambridge crew won and have kept the pale blue colour ever since. Over the years, the race has undergone several changes; at one stage the course had to be altered owing to the heavy river traffic below Putney, so the race is now rowed each year from Putney to Mortlake. The 1829 Oxford boat still exists and can be seen at the Science Museum in South Kensington. The boats have changed dramatically from stout clinker-built eight-oared wherries to the highly tuned racing machines we know today.

Henley Royal Regatta takes place annually during the first week of July. This is now as much a social event as a rowing event, and Henley remains one of the important London occasions to be seen at.

Numerous yachting events take place on the river from small local dinghy regattas to the races of the old Thames sailing barges. Canoeing is also popular and slaloms have been held at Shepperton and Henley.

Swan-upping is a rather quaint event that has been occurring on the river for hundreds of years. In the reign of Edward IV, no one was permitted to keep swans who did not possess a freehold of at least five marks annual value. Later, by an Act of Henry VII, robbers of swans' eggs were fined 13s 4d for each egg and the penalty for altering the markings of the birds was a year's imprisonment and a fine of £3 6s 8d. As a mark of favour, the King sometimes granted to an individual or a corporation 'a game of swans' and with it the right of a swan mark. Thus, two city companies, whose halls are on the banks of the river, have possessed since the 15th century the privilege of owning and marking the royal birds. These companies are the Vintners' and the Dyers' Guilds, and the reason for the right being granted to

Clockwise from opposite top

The old manager's house and cottages at Dapdune Wharf on the River Wey, now owned by the National Trust. *Jane Cumberlidge*

The Doric columns of the porticos of the bridge keepers houses are unique to the Gloucester and Sharpness Canal. *Jane Cumberlidge*

The 14th century chapel on the bridge at St Ives over the River Great Ouse is one of only four left in Britain. *Jane Cumberlidge*

The Stables restaurant near Kirkintilloch on the Forth and Clyde Canal is the restored canal stables, once in regular use for canal boat horses. *Guthrie Hutton*

The unusual towers of the bridge at Drayton Manor on the Birmingham and Fazeley Canal house the steps for pedestrians to cross the higher level footbridge. *David Morris*

At the bottom of the Bosley locks on the Macclesfield Canal.
Roy Westlake

The peace and tranquillity of a springtime trip on the Warwick Ring. *David Morris*

The Glory Hole in Lincoln, joining the River Witham with the Fossdyke Canal. *Lincolnshire County Council*

RIVER THAMES *Maximum vessel dimensions*

From and to	Distance	Length	Beam	Draught	Headroom	Locks
Lechlade to Osney Lock, Oxford	26.5 miles (42.6km)	109' (33.2m)	14' (4.2m)	3' (0.9m)	7' 6" (2.2m)	12
Oxford to Reading	42.3 miles (68.1km)	120' (36.5m)	17' 3" (5.2m)	4' (1.2m)	11' 8" (3.6m)	11
Reading to Windsor	31.1 miles (50.0km)	130' (39.6m)	17' 6" (5.3m)	4' 6" (1.3m)	12' 6" (3.8m)	13
Windsor to Teddington	24.2 miles (38.9km)	174' (53.0m)	19' 10" (6.0m)	5' 6" (1.6m)	13' 2" (4.0m)	8
Teddington to the Thames Barrier	27 miles (43.4km)	250' (76.2m)	28' 8" (8.1m)	2' 3" (0.7m) (LW)	12' 6" (3.8m)	1

them was probably the Crown's desire to avoid trouble between the Royal Swanherd and the conservancy of the Thames, which was carried out with considerable firmness by the City Corporation.

Swans of a certain age, not marked, were claimed by the Crown and were known as 'clear billed'. The marks were changed in the year 1878, after the Society for the Prevention of Cruelty to Animals had prosecuted (unsuccessfully) the swanherds employed by the Crown and the two city companies.

The marking or 'upping' as it is technically called, is effected by cutting the upper mandible of the bird and stopping the slight bleeding with pitch. The new system of marking, which omits at least half the old number of cuts, consists of two small nicks on either side of the mandible on birds belonging to the Vintners' company, and one nick on the right side of birds belonging to the Dyers. The marking of Royal birds was discontinued about 1910. The two nicks on the Vintners' birds were corrupted to produce the well known tavern sign 'The Swan with Two Necks'.

The process of swan-upping, conducted with much ceremony, takes place in July or August, when the markers of the three owners take count of all swans in the river, and mark the clear-billed birds which have reached maturity. Operations are conducted by officials in six boats and upping is considered good sport from the vigorous resistance offered by the birds. When the boats taking part reach Romney Lock, a short ceremony takes place as this lock is the nearest to the Queen's residence at the Royal Castle of Windsor. The Dyers' and Vintners' boats wait outside the lock so that they may salute the Queen's boats as they pass. The Crown has no desire to increase the number of birds on the river, which is maintained at about 500 grown birds and cygnets – this limits the total to 610, allowing 65 swans to Dyers' and 45 to Vinterns'.

Authority **Teddington to Lechlade** Environment Agency, Thames Region, Kings Meadow House, Kings Meadow Road, Reading RG1 8DQ ☎ 0118 953 5000 *Fax* 0118 950 0388.

Tidal Thames The Port of London Authority, Devon House, 58-60 St Katharine's Way, London E1 9LB ☎ 0171 265 2656 *Fax* 0171 265 2699.

Bridges Numerous, see under each section, tidal and no-tidal.

Towpath The Thames Path is one of 12 designated National Trails funded by the Countryside Commission and maintained by the local authorities through which it passes, in partnership with other bodies. It is 180 miles from end to end and between Teddington and the Thames Barrier it follows both sides of the river. The route is waymarked and detailed guides are now available from bookshops or by contacting the Countryside Commission, John Dower House, Crescent Place, Cheltenham, Gloucestershire GL50 3RA ☎ 01242 521381 *Fax* 01242 584270.

Running from the Thames Barrier to Thames Head in the Cotswolds close to the route of the Thames and Severn Canal, it is possible to walk sections of the path from numerous points of access via public transport. The demise of many of the ancient ferries which used to transport horses across the river, when the towpath changed sides, has meant that the path may not necessarily follow the original route of the towpath. The Thames Path links up with other long-distance paths, such as the Lee Valley Path, the Ridgeway, the Kennet and Avon Canal towpath and various shorter circular walks. At some locations, it is possible to do a round trip by walking one way and taking a boat the other. The GEOprojects Thames map covers the river and the path, and *The River Thames Book* by Chris Cove-Smith has details of the path in each section.

Speed limit 5mph or 4.3 knots above Teddington, 8 knots Teddington to Wandsworth Bridge, the creeks and the inshore area. Below Wandsworth Bridge there is no specific speed limit but speeds should not cause an excessive wash or inconvenience other river users.

Bye-laws Each of the authorities responsible for the River Thames publish user's guides and bye-laws for the area under its control. All those intending to use the river should obtain and study a copy of the relevant guide and bye-laws in advance. Copies can be obtained from the addresses above.

Sound signals The following official signals should be used on the river by powered craft to indicate their intended actions to other vessels:

Signal	Action
1 short blast	I am altering my course to starboard (right).
2 short blasts	I am altering my course to port (left).
3 short blasts	My engines are going astern.
5 or more short blasts	I do not consider you are taking sufficient action to keep clear of me; **or** I do not understand your intentions or actions.
4 short blasts followed by 1 short blast	I am turning round with my bow swinging to starboard (right).
4 short blasts followed by 2 short blasts	I am turning round with my bow swinging to port (left).
1 long blast	I am getting underway.
1 long and 2 short blasts	I am unable to manoeuvre.
2 long blasts followed by 1 short blast	I am about to overtake on your starboard (right) side.
2 long blasts followed by 2 short blasts	I am about to overtake on your port (left) side.

Lights Lights must be shown when navigating between sunset and sunrise or in restricted visibility as follows:

A *bright white light* on the mast or staff at the bow, not less than 4ft (1.2m) above the hull.

A *green light* on the starboard (right) side.

A *red light* on the port (left) side.

A *white light* at the stern.

Unpowered craft should show an all-round white light or two white lights to give the same coverage.

Connections The River Roding, the River Lee, Limehouse Basin and the Regent's Canal, the Grand Union Canal, the River Wey, the River Kennet leading to the Kennet and Avon Canal, the Oxford Canal.

Charts Imray C1 and C2, Admiralty 1183, 1185, 2484.

Facilities Facilities for boat users on the Thames are numerous. The EA provide free 24-hour moorings at several locations. At the locks, there are various facilities such as toilets, drinking water, pump-out and refuse disposal, a list of services is included in the *User's Guide*. There are several marinas along the river offering all facilities to boat users.

For a thorough and comprehensive guide to all the marinas, boatyards, clubs, pubs, restaurants, moorings, launching sites, trip boats and hire companies, as well as information on access by public transport, *The River Thames Book* by Chris Cove-Smith published by Imrays is essential for anyone cruising the river. A lighter weight guide which fits in a pocket is the GEOprojects *River Thames Map* which lists marina and boatyard facilities, boat trip and hire companies, water depths and bridge heights, lock phone numbers and interesting information about the places through which you pass.

Non-tidal River Thames

Environment Agency

Navigation offices Navigation and Recreation Manager, Thames Region, Kings Meadow House, Kings Meadow Road, Reading, Berkshire RG1 8DQ ☎ 0118 953 5525.

Local navigation offices

Cricklade Bridge to tail of Benson Lock Cut Osney Lock, Bridge Street, Oxford OX2 0AX ☎ 01865 721271.

Tail of Benson Lock Cut to tail of Hurley Lower Lock Cut Caversham Lock Island, Kings Meadow Road, Reading RG1 8BP ☎ 0118 953 5533.

Hurley Weir Stream to Penton Hook Lock Boulter's Lock, Raymead Road, Maidenhead SL6 8PE ☎ 01628 22491.

Penton Hook Lower Lock Cut to Teddington Riverside Works, Footbridge Road, Sunbury on Thames TW16 6AP ☎ 01932 781946.

Environment Agency Pollution Hotline ☎ (freephone) 0800 807060.

Out of office hours emergency ☎ 0118 953 5000

Craft registration and weir permits for the Thames: PO Box 214, Reading RG1 8HQ ☎ 0118 953 5650.

Bridges There are 75 bridges on the non-tidal Thames, all are fixed. For the minimum headroom along each section of the river, see the table of dimensions. A full list of bridges with their clearance is given in the EA booklet *A User's Guide to the River Thames* available from the addresses above.

The limiting heights are Osney Bridge, 7ft 6ins; Osney Rail Bridge, 11ft 8ins; Cookham Lock Cut, 12ft 6ins; and Windsor Bridge, 13ft 2ins.

Locks All the locks are manned. Generally staff are available from 0900 to 1900 June, July and August, 0915 to 1600 November to March and 0900 to 1700 or 1800 in the intermediate months. At each lock, the times of staffing are clearly displayed. When staff are not on duty, boat crews may work the locks but do so at their own risk. This does not apply to Teddington Lock which is staffed 24 hours a day. Individual locks may be closed to traffic for cleaning between 0700 and 0900 on weekdays. For information on planned closure times, there is an information line ☎ 0118 953 5520.

Teddington Lock signal lights There is a signal board at the downstream end of Teddington Lock Island. The lights are:
a. central line of red lights indicates that neither the barge lock nor the launch lock are ready for upstream traffic;
b. a flashing red arrow pointing left means the barge lock is not ready for upstream traffic;

c. a flashing white arrow pointing left means the barge lock is available for upstream traffic;

d. a flashing red arrow pointing right means the launch lock is not ready for upstream traffic; and

e. a flashing white arrow pointing right means the launch lock is available.

The skiff lock is not covered by these signals and anyone wishing to use the skiff lock should go to the tail of the lock and await instructions from the lock staff. This lock is not always available and a telephone call in advance is advisable.

Branches Sheepwash Channel to Oxford Canal, River Kennet to the Kennet and Avon Canal at Reading. Minimum headroom is 9ft 8ins under Watlington Bridge but beware of less clearance outside the main channel. Maximum draught of 3ft 3ins. Thames Water jurisdiction extends nearly 1 mile to a limit 70yds eastwards of the High Bridge at Reading. There is one lock (Blakes) which is 122ft 8ins long by 18ft 11ins wide.

Branch to River Wey, at Shepperton, 200ft long linking to the River Wey. This section of river is the remainder of a channel that used to go around an island but is now partly weeded up. St Patrick's stream and part of the River Loddon form a by-pass route round Shiplake Lock. There is a public right of navigation but the route can be dangerous and the current is fast; headroom is limited to 4ft but there is about 10ft beam.

A few side channels and tributaries may be available for navigation but local enquiries are advised. The River Thame is navigable for small cruisers and light craft to Dorchester (Oxon).

Licensing All craft must be registered and licensed with the Environment Agency before they are taken on the river. The licence is not transferable and the licence plate must be fixed to the boat to which it relates where it can easily be seen by lock staff and river patrols. All vessels must be river-worthy. They must conform to The Thames Navigation Licensing and General Bye-laws 1993 and comply with construction and equipment specifications. Since January 1997, a valid Boat Safety Certificate has to be produced when applying for a licence; this requirement is being phased in depending on the age of the craft. The EA must be notified by the owner if there is a change of ownership of a registered boat during the period of registration. The registered name of the vessel should be clearly visible.

Information on licensing and registration of craft can be obtained from Craft Registration and Weir Permits, PO Box 214, Reading RG1 8HQ ☎ 0118 953 5650.

Navigation For full details refer to the Environment Agency's booklet *A User's Guide to the River Thames* and a copy of the Bye-laws.

General Always be aware of other users activities on the river and give them due consideration. Peace and quiet is important and noise carries a long way over water, particularly at night.

Safety NEVER underestimate the power of the river and do not take risks. Weirs are dangerous areas and all warning signs must be adhered to. Always keep children carefully supervised, as the river can be a dangerous place as well as an enjoyable one. Any river activity poses a greater risk when there are strong currents, higher river levels or cold weather conditions. Learn how to help if there is an accident and always contact the nearest lock-keeper or call the emergency services for assistance.

Lifejackets or buoyancy aids should be worn by children and non-swimmers at all times and by everybody on board in adverse weather conditions. Ensure all the crew wear suitable footwear with non-slip soles.

Rules of navigation Always obey the rules of navigation and the bye-laws. Copies are available from Navigation Offices.

Steer on the right hand side when it is safe and practical. Remember, that even when you have the right of way, you have an overriding responsibility to avoid collision.

Avoid turning vessels round near bridges, bends and lock approaches. Do not turn across the bows of an oncoming craft; wait until it is safe.

Keep a sharp lookout ahead and astern and take avoiding action in good time. Keep a sharp lookout for others on or in the water and change speed and direction as necessary to avoid an incident. If in doubt, slow down or stop.

Take extra care when overtaking. Overtaking vessels must keep clear.

In the vicinity of bridges or sharp bends, a vessel going upstream must give way, if necessary, to a vessel coming downstream.

Sound signals Use the appropriate signals as listed above.

Equipment Fire extinguishers must be carried; the number on a boat should be in compliance with the Boat Safety Scheme specifications.

Every vessel must be fitted with a horn or whistle.

Every vessel must carry at least one anchor. Keep the anchor on deck and ready for use at all times.

An efficient bilge pump or baler should be fitted.

Every vessel should carry at least two mooring lines, one at the bow and one at the stern. Each should be at least 23ft (7m) long.

Moorings The Environment Agency has provided free 24-hour moorings at the following sites. Notice boards indicate the extent of the site.

Riverside, Lechlade

Towpath above Pinkhill Lock

Towpath upstream of The Ferryman Inn, Bablock Hythe

Towpath at East Street, Oxford

Towpath above Kennington Railway Bridge, near Iffley

Towpath above Abingdon Lock

Keen Edge Ferry, Shillingford
Towpath below Goring Lock
Towpath above Sonning Lock
Towpath at Lower Lashbrook below Wargrave
Towpath below Marlow Lock
Towpath above Boveney Lock
Towpath below Runnymede Pleasure Ground, Egham
Towpath at Laleham Wharf
Towpath at Dumsey Bend, between Chertsey and Shepperton
Towpath at Weybridge opposite Shepperton Lock
Desborough Island (Old River)
Stevens Eyot below Kingston Bridge

Fishing from the bank at these sites is not allowed between 1 March and 31 October.

Public slipways and launching sites Although you may launch a boat at the following sites, there is not necessarily a right to park a car or a boat trailer, neither are these sites necessarily suitable for large and heavy boats and trailers. If in doubt, please check first with the local Navigation Inspector.

Abingdon Marina
Abingdon, St Helen's Wharf
Aston Ferry, from either bank
Bray Village
Caversham Bridge
Cholsey, Papist Way
Cookham Bridge by Ferry Hotel
Cowey Sale, Walton
East Molesey Drawdock
Henley, Wharf Lane
Kingston Thameside
Marlow, St Peter's Street
Medmenham Ferry
Shepperton Village Wharf
Sunbury, Lower Hampton Road
Teddington Drawdock
Thames Ditton by Swan Hotel

Truss's Island, Chertsey Lane, Staines
Walton Wharf by Anglers Holt
Wargrave, Ferry Lane
West Molesey, Hurst Park
Weybridge, Thames Street

Further sites are listed in *Launching on Inland Waterways* by Diana van der Klugt (see bibliography).

Water, sewage and rubbish disposal Sites for water supply, sewage and rubbish disposal and pump-out facilities at locks are listed in the booklet *A User's Guide to the River Thames*. Private facilities are listed in publications on the Thames (see bibliography).

Marking of obstructions The EA has adopted a system of marking shoals and other obstructions in the river. This is particularly required in the early months of the year before reeds have grown through the surface of shallow water. The shapes of topmarks used are can, triangle, sphere and double sphere. The following illustration with directions for passing them safely, when you proceed upstream, should be studied. Remember, when you navigate downstream, the can and triangle shapes must be passed on your opposite hand. Wrecks or other temporary obstructions in midstream are marked by an isolated danger buoy which may be passed on any side. Where such obstructions must be passed on a particular side, the appropriate can or triangle topmarks will be used. In all cases, craft should pass well clear of a marking buoy. The closure of a navigation arch of a bridge is usually indicated by a large red disk.

It is emphasised that the Environment Agency does not accept responsibility for the marking of obstructions that lie outside the fairway. You must therefore proceed with particular caution when approaching any bank or if you depart from the main navigation route.

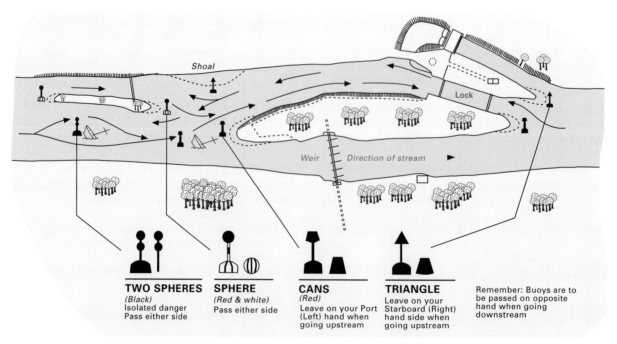

TWO SPHERES *(Black)* Isolated danger Pass either side

SPHERE *(Red & white)* Pass either side

CANS *(Red)* Leave on your Port (Left) hand when going upstream

TRIANGLE Leave on your Starboard (Right) hand side when going upstream

Remember: Buoys are to be passed on opposite hand when going downstream

Tidal River Thames

Port of London Authority

Navigation Offices The Port of London Authority section of the Thames is under the control of The Chief Harbourmaster, Port of London Authority, London River House, Royal Pier Road, Gravesend, Kent DA12 2BG ☎ 01474 562268.

On a day-to-day basis the river is in two sections each controlled by a harbourmaster.

Upper Section, Teddington to Erith Harbourmaster Upper, PLA, Devon House, 58-60 St Katharine's Way, London E1 9LB ☎ 0171 265 2656.

Lower Section, Erith to the sea Harbourmaster Lower, PLA, London House, Royal Pier Road, Gravesend, Kent DA12 2BG ☎ 01474 562212.

For information regarding the Thames Barrier, requests should be made to The Duty Officer, PLA, Thames Barrier Navigation Centre (TBNC), Unit 28, 34 Bowater Road, London SE18 5TF ☎ 0181 855 0315 VHF Ch 14, 16 and 22, call sign *Woolwich Radio*.

All enquiries should be made to the harbourmaster for the appropriate part of the river listed above. Advice can also be obtained from the PLA Harbour Service launches patrolling in all sections.

Bridges Always use the correct navigational arch as shown by the fixed orange light at the crown of the relevant arch. A high intensity isophase (flashing) white light on the main navigational arch both upstream and downstream indicates that one or more large vessels or tugs engaged in towing are about to use that arch. All small vessels must keep out of the way of the arch and its approaches while the light is flashing. Three red discs or red lights in a triangle, point downwards, under an arch mean the arch is closed to all vessels. A bundle of straw or a white light hanging under an arch means the arch has restricted headroom.

The following table gives the generally accepted clearances under the bridges in the tidal Thames at MHWS. 24-hours notice is required if the bascules have to be raised on Tower Bridge, contact the Bridge Master ☎ 0171 403 3761.

Bridge	Clearance below centre span MHWS
Richmond	17' 5" (5.3m)
Richmond Railway	17' 5" (5.3m)
Twickenham	19' 4" (5.9m)
Richmond Footbridge	15' 9" (4.8m)
Kew	17' 5" (5.3m)
Kew Railway	18' 4" (5.6m)
Chiswick	22' 7" (6.9m)
Barnes Railway	17' 8" (5.4m)
Hammersmith	12' 1" (3.7m)
Putney	18' 0" (5.5m)
Wandsworth	19' 0" (5.8m)
Battersea Railway	20' 0" (6.1m)
Battersea	18' 0" (5.5m)
Albert	16' 1" (4.9m)
Chelsea	21' 7" (6.6m)
Victoria Railway	19' 7" (6.0m)
Vauxhall	18' 4" (5.6m)
Lambeth	21' 4" (6.5m)
Westminster	17' 8" (5.4m)
Charing Cross Railway	22' 11" (7.0m)
Waterloo	27' 10" (8.5m)
Blackfriars	23' 3" (7.1m)
Blackfriars Railway	22' 11" (7.0m)
Southwark	24' 3" (7.4m)
Cannon Street Railway	23' 3" (7.1m)
London	29' 2" (8.9m)
Tower (Bascules down)	28' 2" (8.6m)
Tower (Bascules up)	139' 5" (42.5m)
Queen Elizabeth II, Dartford	177' 6" (54.1m)

Locks There is a half tide lock at Richmond which is staffed 24 hours a day. The lock measures 249ft 4ins (76m) long by 26ft 3ins (8m) wide. For 2 hours either side of high water, the sluice gates are raised allowing free passage of craft. When the sluices are down the following signals are displayed:

By night, with sluices down: weir closed, use the lock. A triangle apex down of 3 red lights show at each arch.

By day with sluices down: weir closed, use lock. 3 red discs show. In addition to this, an illuminated sign on the upper end of the lock entrance reads 'Weir closed please use lock'.

By day and night with sluices up: weir open, free navigation. 2 orange lights show at each navigable arch.

The mooring trots along the Deer Park bank are solely for those craft waiting to use the lock. The maintained level of water between Richmond Weir and Teddington locks is 5ft 7ins (1.7m) above ODN. The lock-keeper can be contacted by phone ☎ 0181 940 0634.

Branches The following creeks are under the jurisdiction of the Port of London Authority:

	Miles
Wandsworth Creek	0.3
Bow Creek	1.0
Deptford Creek	0.8
Barking Creek	2.0
Rainham Creek	1.8 (now dammed)

The River Roding is navigable to Ilford, see separate section. The Kensington Canal is now closed. The Grosvenor Canal is owned by Westminster City Council and is not available to the public. The River Crane is navigable for a short distance for small craft through tidal doors to Chertsey Bridge.

Tides At London Bridge tidal range at springs is 21ft 6ins (6.6m) and 15ft (4.6m) at neaps. The river is tidal between Richmond Lock and Teddington Lock for approximately 2 hours either side of HW.

	Times HW London Bridge hrs	*Mean Rise* *Springs* ft	*Neaps* ft
Teddington Lock	0105 after	16	12
Richmond Lock	0105 after	16	12
Brentford (Thames Locks)	0055 after		
Limehouse (Tidal Lock)	0005 before		
Thames Barrier	0020 before		
Bow Locks	Same		

In the upper part of the tideway, the river floods for between 3½ and 5 hours and ebbs for 7 to 8 hours. The stream runs at up to 4 knots (4.6mph). Following heavy rain large volumes of water flowing down river will significantly affect the rate of the stream, the period of flood and ebb and the clearances under bridges. Similarly, when the Thames Barrier is raised the water level above the barrier will be different to those predicted. In these conditions, navigation by small craft is difficult and particularly when close to river structures such as bridges and piers.

Bye-laws Port of London Authority bye-laws can be obtained from The Chief Harbourmaster at the address above. For small boat users the PLA also publish a *Pleasure Users Guide for the Tidal Thames*, a *Leisure Guide* and a *Yachtsman's Guide*, all are available free from the Central Enquiries, PLA, Devon House, 58-60 St Katharine's Way, London E1 9LB ☎ 0171 265 2656.

Navigation For full details refer to the booklets mentioned above.

- *General* All vessels navigating on the tidal Thames must comply with the International Regulations for Preventing Collisions at Sea as modified by the Port of London River Bye-laws 1978 (as amended). They must also comply with the General Directions for Navigation in the Port of London 1991 and the latest Notices to Mariners published by the Port of London Authority.

- Notices at launching and landing sites, slipways and creeks regarding speed restrictions and prohibited activities must be observed.

- Small craft and vessels shall not enter or cross a fairway so as to obstruct another vessel proceeding along the fairway.

- Vessels in doubt that sufficient action is being taken to avoid collision by another vessel, which by the rules you would expect to yield to your vessel, may indicate such doubt by sounding five or more short and rapid blasts on the whistle. See Sound Signals above.

- *Large vessels* Large vessels underway are confined to the deep water part of the channel. They cannot take quick avoiding action and, in narrow channels, may not be able to take any avoiding action at all. Small craft cannot always be seen from a ship's bridge. This may be for up to 1 mile ahead and ½ mile either side of the bow. Always keep clear of large vessels and commercial traffic, especially tugs with barges in tow which will have difficulty manoeuvring.

- Keep to the correct side of the channel, in the shallower water and do not cross ahead of commercial vessels proceeding along the channel. You may be in a blind area under the bow. Because of the confined waters in which commercial vessels must operate power does not necessarily give way to sail (see Rule 9 (b)(c) and Rule 18 (b) of the International Regulations for Preventing Collisions at Sea).

- *Right of way* Any vessel approaching or passing under any bridge or bend in the river when going against the tide should give way to a vessel approaching with the tide.

- *Overtaking* A vessel which is overtaking must keep clear of the slower vessel. Sound signals (see above) to indicate avoiding action should be made in good time.

- *Crossing the river* To cross the river, take the quickest way practicable, keeping a sharp look out for commercial traffic. Any attempt to cross ahead of oncoming traffic in a strong tide could prove very hazardous. A vessel crossing the river has no right of way over a vessel proceeding up or down.

- *Safe Distance from oil tanker jetties* The special fire and security risks attached to oil refinery jetties, and the ships berthed and working there, require additional care to be exercised by river users when navigating in the vicinity of these installations. All vessels should therefore maintain a minimum clearance of 60m from an oil jetty or berthed tanker.

Speed limit See above. Always proceed at a speed appropriate to the local conditions and ensure that there is no damage to persons or property caused by excessive wash. Speed causing damage is an offence, making the owner or master of the craft liable to prosecution. The penalty is a fine of up to £2,500. No person under the age of 16 years is to be in charge of a power boat capable of exceeding 8 knots (or over 10hp). PLA and police launches are equipped with instruments to measure boat speed.

Rowing Rowing boats must, whenever possible, navigate outside the main channel or fairway, but if not shall 'keep as near to the outer limit of the channel or fairway which lies on her starboard side as is safe and practicable'.

Special rules for navigation have been agreed for rowing boats navigating between Richmond Footbridge and Fulham Railway Bridge. Two places have been agreed for crossing the river to enable rowers to work the slack water.

When proceeding with the tide, keep to the starboard side of the fairway.

When proceeding against the tide, navigate as follows:

a. between Richmond Footbridge and Chiswick Bridge Crossing, keep as close as practicable to the Surrey shore;

b. between Chiswick Bridge Crossing and the Chiswick Steps Crossing, keep as close as is practicable to the Middlesex shore;

c. between Chiswick Steps Crossing and Fulham Railway Bridge, keep as close as is practicable to the Surrey shore.

Owners' liability The owner of any craft/vessel should carry third-party insurance to cover the cost of any claim in the case of accident, damage, harbour clearance, towage, etc. Ignorance is no defence in the eyes of the law, consult the river bye-laws.

Radio Vessels of 65ft (20m) or more in length, irrespective of vessel type, must carry a VHF radio telephone capable of communicating with the harbourmaster at Port Control. Each such vessel must maintain a continuous listening watch on the VHF channel appropriate for that part of the Thames in which it is navigating, and must use VHF to make any communications necessary.

Boat owners are reminded that they should hold an appropriate licence to operate VHF radio equipment. Special arrangements on the carriage of VHF radio operates for narrow boats between 65ft (20m) and 82ft (25m) in length which are in transit between the Grand Union Canal and the non-tidal Thames via the Brentford and Teddington Locks. If no VHF is carried, such vessels should telephone the PLA Duty Officer at Woolwich Radio ☎ 0181 855 0315 to report to the duty officer immediately before and again on completion of the transit.

Remember VHF maritime R/T is not CB, please use the correct procedure. The radio is not a telephone and only relevant information should be broadcast. Listen out before transmitting. Do practice at home or in the club.

Do not keep calling. If there is no reply to your call wait 2 or 3 minutes before calling again. Do ensure you have an inter-ship frequency for you and your friends to go to. Do not chatter on Ch 16, nor on the PLA's working frequencies, you are a danger to an emergency user and you are a nuisance to others using their VHF correctly.

If you need assistance, make sure you know where you are. Give a precise location or as near exact as possible. Vague statements are no help to the PLA or to you.

Frequencies Port Control London (Area-Crayfordness to Seaward Limit)
VHF Channels 12[1] Seaward limit to Sea Reach No 4 buoy; 13[1] Sea Reach No 4 buoy to Crayfordness; (14), 16, 18 and 20.
Radar coverage Erith to seaward limit
Tidal information for Walton-on-the-Naze, Margate, Shivering Sands, Southend and Tilbury ☎ 01474 560311.
Woolwich Radio (Area-up river of Crayfordness, including Barrier Control Zone[2])
VHF Channels 14[1], 16 and 22
Radar coverage River Medway and approaches (Medway buoy inwards). Tidal information for Sheerness ☎ 01795 663025.
1. Primary working frequency.
2. Barrier Control Zone. All vessels/craft navigating the river between Margaretness and Blackwall Point are subject to the special navigational requirements concerning passage through the Thames Flood Barrier. Mariners must observe traffic signals displayed on the Flood Barrier Piers to indicate which span(s) are open for navigation. Instructions will also be broadcast by Woolwich Radio on VHF Ch 14.

Radar Fit the biggest and best radar reflector you can afford. If you need radar assistance ask for it, but the PLA can only assist if you can be 'seen' on radar.

Pollution Owners and persons in charge of pleasure craft are reminded that it is an offence, punishable on summary conviction by a fine of up to £2,500, to throw rubbish (tins, bottles, cartons, paper, foodstuffs, etc.) overboard. It is also an offence, punishable on summary conviction by a fine of up to £50,000, to spill, discharge or allow to flow into the tidal Thames any oil, petrol, etc.

While it is not yet an offence to discharge any type of toilet into the tidal Thames, legislation is being formulated to make the act an offence in the near future. In the meantime, owners and persons in charge of pleasure craft should take a socially responsible attitude in this respect. Facilities are available, with 24-hours notice, for owners to pump out holding tanks at Cadogan and Festival Piers.

Noise Noise from internal combustion engines and from entertainment sources (music, loud speakers, etc.) shall be reduced or contained at a reasonable level to avoid annoying other river users or local residents. In the case of combustion engines, noise must be contained by the fitting of efficient silencers, expansion chambers or other contrivances suitable for the purpose.

Anchorages and moorings All anchorages and public moorings within the limits of the Port of London, between Teddington and London Bridge are the property of the authority. Many moorings are held by private firms on licence from the authority. Temporary moorings in the river may be available by contacting the harbourmaster for the relevant section of the river. The PLA produce two brochures for the Tidal Thames, *Leisure Guide* and *Yachtsman's Guide*, which cover the facilities available – yacht, rowing and canoe clubs, marinas, piers, moorings and launching sites.

Piers The following piers may be used for landing by arrangement. The Central Booking Service for the PLA can be contacted on ☎ 0171 265 2666 or by *Fax* 0171 2652699.

Name of pier	Contact
Richmond Landing Stage	PLA
Kew	PLA
Chiswick	0181 742 0057
Hammersmith	0181 748 5405
Putney	PLA
Chelsea Harbour	0171 351 4433
Cadogan	PLA
Lambeth	PLA
Westminster[1]	PLA
Charing Cross[1]	PLA
Festival	PLA
Swan Lane	0171 987 1185 or 730 4812
London Bridge City	PLA
Tower[1]	PLA
St Katharine's	0171 488 0555
Cherry Garden	0171 237 3498/5134
Canary Wharf	0171 418 2000
Scandic	0171 231 1001
West India Dock	0171 987 1185 or 730 4812
Greenland	0171 512 3000
Great Eastern	0171 512 3000
Greenwich	PLA

London City Airport   0171 474 5555
Barrier Garden   0181 854 5555/6
1. Only bookable in off-peak hours

Public slipways and launching sites The following launching sites are likely to be available, but before using them boat owners should contact the harbourmaster for the most recent information on availability, as certain of these may be occupied by commercial craft or otherwise obstructed. There is not necessarily space available at these sites to park cars or trailers. For further details of access, facilities and charges refer to *Launching on Inland Waterways* (see bibliography).

Upper section
Harbourmaster ☎ 0171 265 2656
Teddington Drawdock, Teddington: contact
   ☎ 0181 940 8723
Church Lane, Twickenham
Riverside, Twickenham
Ham Landing, Ham (public car park available)
River Lane, Petersham
Drawdock, Water Lane, Richmond
London Apprentice Inn, Church Street, Isleworth
   (parking available)
Drawdock, Kew Bridge
Grove Park Drawdock, Kew
Ship Drawdock, Mortlake
Small Profits Draw Dock, Barnes
Chiswick Church Drawdock, Church Street, Chiswick
Hammersmith Drawdock, Hammersmith
Putney Drawdock, Putney Bridge
Battersea Drawdock, Battersea

Middle section
Harbourmaster ☎ 0171 265 2656
Newcastle Drawdock and Johnsons Draw Dock, Isle of
   Dogs
Samuda Housing Estate, Isle of Dogs (parking available
   nearby)
Point Drawdock, Greenwich
Bugsby's Hole Causeway, Greenwich

Lower section
Harbourmaster ☎ 01474 562212
Barge House Road, Woolwich
Bell Water Gate, Woolwich
Gravesend Canal Basin, Gravesend: contact
   ☎ 01474 352392 (parking available)

It is strongly recommended that before a visitor uses these facilities he should previously study the warning notice regarding speed and also the general regulations regarding navigation, safety, etc. He should then apply to the harbourmaster, or to any pier-master, for the latest information regarding navigation on the river, when he will be informed of the time and duration of any regattas or boat races that might be in progress during his visit.

Thames Barrier

The Barrier is located at Woolwich Reach 8½ miles below London Bridge. It was completed in 1982 and the design is reminiscent of the Sydney Opera House with the steel fins sweeping up from the river. Each gate weighs 3000 tonnes and it is the largest movable flood barrier in the world.

There are nine piers numbered one to nine from the north shore to the south. The spans are lettered A to K from the south shore to the north. Spans A, H, J and K are permanently closed to navigation.

Woolwich Barrier Control Zone is from Margaretness to Blackwall Point. Communication with the Thames Barrier Navigation Centre is on VHF Ch 14, 22 and 16, and contact should be made as you pass Margaretness or Blackwall Point. For boats without VHF radio, contact should be made prior to approaching the barrier ☎ 0181 855 0315, then pass through between Green Arrows.

Noticeboards are located downstream at Thamesmead and Barking Power Station and upstream at Blackwall Stairs and Blackwall Point. The signals are:
Amber light – proceed with extreme caution
Red light – Navigation within zone prohibited

Lights on the barrier piers indicate:
Red St Andrew's Crosses – Barrier or span in between is closed.
Green Arrows – Span in between is open.

Loud hailers are fitted at certain points to pass instructions. They may also transmit Morse signal K ($-\cdot-$) meaning the barrier is closed.

Depth over sills Gates C, D, E, F 5.8m (Chart Datum) Gates B, G 1.25m (Chart Datum).
It is prohibited to sail through the barrier, engines must be used at all times. Small craft should use the side spans, B or G, wherever possible. The barrier is completely closed for testing one day a month for 1½ hours either side of low water. Individual spans are tested weekly.

Beware When all gates are closed no vessel should navigate within 200 metres of the barrier owing to turbulence. It is extremely dangerous to go through a span marked 'Closed' as the gates may be in a semi-raised position. Small craft must not navigate above Thames Refinery Jetty or below Gulf Oil Island Jetty unless they intend to pass through the barrier.

Distance table   *Miles*
Non-tidal Thames – (Environment Agency)
Teddington boundary obelisk to:

	Miles
Teddington Barge Lock	0.1
Teddington Lock	0.2
Kingston Railway Bridge	1.9
Kingston Bridge	2.1
Raven's Ait (centre)	2.9
Ferry	3.1
Thames Ditton Island	4.1
River Ember, South Bank	4.5
Hampton Court Bridge	4.9
Molesey Lock	5.1

	Miles		*Miles*
Hampton Ferry	5.9	Goring Bridge and Lock	65.8
Platts Eyot	6.6	Cleeve Lock	66.4
Sunbury Lock	8.0	Moulsford Bottom	67.7
Walton Bridge	9.6	Moulsford Railway Bridge	68.4
Desborough Cut, start	9.9	Winterbrook Bridge	70.7
Desborough Cut, end	10.4	Wallingford Bridge	71.7
Shepperton Lock	11.0	Benson Lock	72.9
Chertsey Bridge	12.9	Shillingford Bridge	74.2
Chertsey Lock	13.0	River Thame, North Bank	76.1
M3 Bridge	13.3	Day's Lock	76.9
Laleham	14.2	Clifton Hampden Bridge	79.4
Penton Hook Lock	15.0	Clifton Lock	79.9
Staines Railway Bridge	16.5	Clifton Weir (end of Clifton Cut)	80.5
River Colne, North Bank and Staines Bridge	16.8	Appleford Railway Bridge	81.4
London Stone	17.1	Culham Bridge	82.6
Runnymede Bridge (M25) and Colne Brook	17.7	Culham Lock	82.7
Bell Weir Lock	17.8	River Ock, South Bank	84.5
Magna Carta Island	19.1	Abingdon Bridge	84.8
'The Bells' of Ouzeley	19.9	Abingdon Lock	85.3
Old Windsor Lock	20.8	Nuneham Railway Bridge	86.6
Albert Bridge	21.5	Sandford Lock	89.9
Victoria Bridge	23.0	Kennington Railway Bridge	90.9
Black Pott's Railway Bridge	23.4	Isis Bridge	91.2
Romney Lock	23.8	Iffley Lock	91.5
Windsor Bridge	24.2	Donnington Bridge	92.2
Windsor Railway Viaduct	24.6	River Cherwell, North Bank	92.5
Windsor and Eton By-pass Bridge	24.9	Folly Bridge	93.0
Boveney Lock	26.1	Osney Railway Bridge	93.5
Surly Hall Point	26.7	Osney Lock	93.9
Oakley Court	27.7	Osney Bridge	94.1
Monkey Island	28.8	Sheepwash Channel to Oxford Canal	94.3
Thames Bridge (M4)	29.0	Medley Footbridge	94.5
Bray Lock	29.3	Godstow Lock	96.3
Maidenhead Railway Bridge	30.5	Godstow Bridge	96.4
Maidenhead Bridge	30.7	Thames Bridge	96.5
Boulter's Lock	31.4	King's Lock	97.4
Cookham Lock	33.5	Duke's Cut (entrance to Oxford Canal)	97.5
Cookham Bridge	33.9	River Evenlode, North Bank	98.9
River Wye, North Bank	34.6	Eynsham Lock	100.1
Bourne End Railway Bridge	35.0	Swinford Bridge	100.2
Marlow Lock	37.7	Pinkhill Lock	101.6
Marlow Bridge	37.9	Bablock Hythe Ferry	103.9
Temple Lock	39.4	Northmoor Lock	105.4
Hurley Lock	40.1	Hart's Footbridge	106.4
Medmenham Abbey and Ferry	41.6	New Bridge and River Windrush, North Bank	107.6
Aston	43.2		
Hambleden Lock	43.7	Weir, start of Shifford Cut	110.1
Temple Island	44.6	Shifford Lock	110.2
Henley Bridge	46.0	Weir, end of Shifford Cut	110.7
Marsh Lock	46.9	Tenfoot Bridge	111.9
Hennerton Backwater	47.3	Tadpole Bridge	113.8
Shiplake Railway Bridge	49.3	Rushey Lock	114.5
River Loddon, South Bank	49.4	Old Man's Bridge	116.9
Shiplake Lock	49.5	Radcot Lock	117.1
Sonning Bridge	52.2	Radcot Bridge	117.8
Sonning Lock	52.4	Grafton Lock	119.0
River Kennet, South Bank	54.3	Eaton Weir Footbridge	121.0
Caversham Lock	55.1	Buscot Lock	122.3
Reading Bridge	55.3	River Cole, South bank	123.2
Caversham Bridge	55.8	River Leach, North Bank	123.3
Appletree Eyot	57.7	St John's Lock and Bridge	123.4
Roebuck Ferry	58.6	Ha'penny Bridge, Lechlade (usual head of navigation)	124.1
Mapledurham Lock and Mill	59.5		
Whitchurch Bridge	61.6	River Coln, North Bank, Round House and former entrance to the Thames and Severn Canal	124.8
Whitchurch Lock	61.8		
Child Beale Wildlife Trust	63.1		
Gatehampton Railway Bridge	64.5	St John's Church, Inglesham	125.1

	Miles
Hannington Bridge	128.3
Castle Eaton Bridge	130.9
Water Eaton Footbridge	133.5
River Ray, South Bank	133.6
Eysey Footbridge	134.2
Cricklade Bridge (limit of EA responsibility)	135.2
Thames Head Bridge	140.1

Tidal Thames – (Port of London Authority)
(distance measured along the navigable channel)

Teddington boundary obelisk to:

Eel Pie Island (lower end)	1.1
Ham Landing Stage	1.2
Petersham Drawdock	1.8
Richmond Bridge	2.4
Twickenham Bridge	2.8
Richmond Lock and Footbridge (recording tide gauge)	3.0
West Middlesex Sewage Outfalls	3.6
Church Ferry, Isleworth	3.7
River Brent and Grand Union Canal	4.8
Kew Bridge	5.4
Kew Pier	5.5
Kew Railway Bridge	5.9
Chiswick Bridge	6.7
University Stone, Mortlake	6.8
Barnes Railway Bridge	7.5
Chiswick Ferry Causeway	8.5
Hammersmith Pier (HBC)	9.1
Hammersmith Bridge	9.3
Harrods Quay	9.6
Beverley Brook	10.6
Putney Pier	10.9
University Stone, Putney	11.0
Putney Bridge	11.1
Fulham Railway Bridge	11.3
Wandsworth Creek	11.9
Wandsworth Bridge	12.2
Fulham Generating Station	12.5
Battersea Railway Bridge	13.0
Chelsea Creek and Lots Road Generating Station	13.3
Battersea Road Bridge	13.6
Albert Bridge	13.8
Cadogan Pier	13.9
Chelsea Bridge	14.6
Victoria Railway Bridge	14.7
Battersea Power Station	14.9
Vauxhall Bridge	15.7
Lambeth Bridge	16.2
Westminster Bridge	16.6
Westminster Pier	16.7
Charing Cross Bridge	17.0
Waterloo Bridge	17.2
Blackfriars Road Bridge	17.8
Southwark Bridge	18.2
Cannon Street Railway Bridge	18.3
London Bridge	18.5

Sea miles		*Land miles*
Upper Pool		
0.00	London Bridge	18.5
0.33	Tower Pier (PLA) (recording tide gauge and Tower Bridge Headway Gauge)	18.9
0.49	Tower Bridge	19.1
0.73	St Saviour's Dock	19.4

Sea miles		*Land miles*
Lower Pool		
1.05	Cherry Garden Pier (Tower Bridge Signal Station and Headway Gauge)	19.7
1.26	Wapping Pier	20.0
1.34	Thames Tunnel	20.1
1.62	Rotherhithe Tunnel	20.4
Limehouse Reach		
2.08	Limehouse Basin entrance and Regent's Canal	20.9
2.69	West India Dock Pier	21.6
3.18	Deadman Dock, Deptford	22.2
Greenwich Reach		
3.71	Deptford Generating Station (upper end)	22.8
3.87	Deptford Creek	23.0
4.17	Greenwich Pier and foot tunnel	23.3
4.27	Greenwich Royal Naval College	23.4
Blackwall Reach		
4.99	Victoria Wharf (upper end)	24.3
5.39	India & Millwall Dock (entrance)	24.7
5.55	Blackwall Tunnel (western)	24.9
5.73	Brunswick Wharf generating station (upper end)	25.1
Bugsby's Reach		
6.08	Bow Creek (River Lee)	25.5
6.49	Blackwall Point Generating Station (upper end)	26.0
7.40	Thames Flood Barrier	27.0
7.52	Thames Navigation Sub-Centre	27.2
7.76	Tate and Lyle's Jetty (upper end)	27.5
8.33	Woolwich Ferry and foot tunnel	28.1
Gallions Reach		
8.89	Gallions or Bulls Point	28.8
9.10	King George V Dock (entrance)	29.0
9.23	Thames House, entrance Gallions (Recording tide gauge)	29.2
Barking Reach		
9.87	Margaret Ness Lighthouse	29.9
10.12	Barking Creek (River Roding)	30.2
10.58	Barking Generating Station (upper end)	30.7
Halfway Reach		
11.35	Crossness Point Lighthouse	31.6
11.68	Overhead electric transmission cables	32.0
11.90	Dagenham Dock No 4 Jetty (upper end)	32.2
12.15	Ford's Jetty (upper end, illuminated tide board, ferry)	32.5
12.57	Belvedere Generating Station (upper end)	33.0
Erith Reach		
13.02	Jenningtree Point Lighthouse	33.5
13.88	Rainham Pumping Unit PLA	34.5
14.41	Erith Causeway	35.1
Erith Rands		
14.45	Coldharbour Point Lighthouse	35.2
14.85	Cunis Jetty	35.6
15.34	Rands Light	36.2
15.49	Crayfordness Lighthouse (Petroleum limit for sea-going tankers)	36.4
Long Reach		
15.89	Dartford Creek	36.8
16.29	Harrison's Jetty	37.3
17.22	Littlebrook Generating Station (upper end)	38.4

Sea miles		Land miles
17.65	Dartford Tunnel	38.8
17.98	West Thurrock Oil Terminal (upper end)	39.2
St Clements Reach		
18.75	Stoneness Lighthouse	40.1
19.14	Overhead electric transmission cables	40.9
Northfleet Hope		
20.11	Bradness Lighthouse	41.6
20.85	Tilbury Grain Terminal (upper end)	42.5
21.44	Northfleet Hope Container Terminal (lower end) (Recording tide gauge)	43.2
21.51	Tilbury Dock (entrance)	43.3
21.78	Northfleet Lower Lighthouse	43.6
Gravesend Reach		
22.00	Tilbury Cargo Jetty (upper end)	43.85
22.68	Tilbury Landing Stage (upper end)	44.6
23.13	Thames Navigation Centre, Gravesend	45.1
23.15	Royal Terrace Pier, Trinity House Pilot Station	45.2
23.52	Tilbury Generating Station (upper end)	45.6
25.12	Tilbury Buoy	47.5
Lower Hope		
25.55	Coalhouse Point (petroleum limit) (Night navigation)	47.9
25.78	Ovens Buoy	48.2
26.49	Mucking No 7 Buoy	49.0
27.23	Mucking No 5 Buoy	49.9
Sea Reach		
27.67	Lower Hope Point Beacon	50.4
27.88	Mucking No 3 Buoy	50.6
28.50	Mucking No 1 Buoy	51.3
28.95	West Blyth Buoy	51.9
29.20	Shell Haven Jetties (tanker warning light)	52.1
30.50	Coryton Jetties (recording tide gauge)	53.6
30.79	Mid Blyth Buoy	54.0
31.25	Holehaven Creek (entrance)	54.5
31.85	North Thames Gas Board Jetty (Tanker warning light)	55.2
33.69	Chapman Buoy	57.3
33.82	Sea Reach No 7 Buoy	57.5
34.29	East Blyth Buoy	58.0
35.58	Sea Reach No 6 Buoy	59.9
36.08	Crowstone, London Stone Line	60.1
36.57	Sea Reach No 5 Buoy	60.6
37.57	Southend Pier Head (recording tide gauge)	61.8
38.32	Sea Reach No 4 Buoy	62.7
39.83	Sea Reach No 3 Buoy	64.4
41.85	Sea Reach No 2 Buoy	66.7
43.62	Sea Reach No 1 Buoy (PLA former seaward limit Havengore Creek to Warden Point)	68.8
51.44	Shivering Sand Tower (recording tide gauge) Seaward limit	77.8

Note The above table gives the distances when the various marks are abeam of the normal channel course.

To ascertain tide level above low water datum from Tower Bridge Headway Boards, subtract headway reading from 48ft 6ins (14.8m).

Thames and Medway Canal

This short canal, originally 6½ miles long, connected the Thames at Gravesend to the River Medway at Strood. It was proposed in 1799 by Ralph Dodd as a valuable route in times of war, cutting across country inside the Isle of Grain thus avoiding the Thames Estuary, but by the time it was finally open in 1824, war was no longer a factor. There was a tunnel between Higham and Strood which, when the canal became a railway company in 1844, was shared by barges and trains for a short while but soon the trains took over.

The lower section from Gravesend to Higham remained active until the 1930s, but today only the basin at Gravesend is used for pleasure boats with a lock into the River Thames. The line of the canal has been protected against further development since a local enquiry in 1992.

Authority None.

Bridges One swing bridge and a footbridge in the section to be restored.

Towpath Mostly in good condition, several access points.

Restoration The Thames and Medway Canal Association are proposing to restore 5.5km of canal from Gravesend to Higham. At present the basin at Gravesend is separated from the canal by an industrial estate. Use of the waterway is limited to small craft, rowing boats and canoes, and other restrictions imposed by Railtrack. For information, contact the Secretary, Thames and Medway Canal Association, 60 Sun Lane, Gravesend, Kent DA12 5HL.

THAMES AND MEDWAY CANAL Maximum vessel dimensions

From and to	Distance	Length	Beam	Draught	Headroom	Locks
Gravesend to Strood	6.5 miles (10.4km)	24' 6" (7.5m)	6' 6" (2m)	2' (0.6m)	5' 3" (1.6m)	1

Thames and Severn Canal

This attractive canal winds through the beautiful Cotswold countryside passing through the Golden Valley and close to the source of the River Thames. The proposed full restoration will open up a major cruising ring connecting the Thames, Gloucestershire navigations and the Midlands.

Originally opened in 1789, the canal was built to connect the Stroudwater Navigation to the Thames at Inglesham, upstream from Lechlade, thus making a through route from the River Severn to London. C S Forester's Captain Hornblower travelled this route on a passenger boat from Gloucester to London. On his journey, he discovered how hard it is to leg a boat through Sapperton Tunnel and that helming required rather different skills to those needed for a sailing ship at sea.

The porous Cotswold limestone caused continuing leakage problems at the summit level which, coupled with an inadequate water supply and rapidly developing competition from the railways, undermined the canal's profitability. Around 1900, the canal was bought by the Gloucestershire County Council which did much restoration work to try to stimulate business. By 1927, the decline in trade led to the abandonment of the canal from Whitehall Bridge to Inglesham. In 1933, the remainder of the canal to Wallbridge, including the transhipment port of Brimscombe where cargoes were moved between Severn trows and Thames barges, was also abandoned.

Authority Information is available from: The Cotswold Canals Trust, The Flat Office, CDC Depot, Chesterton Lane, Cirencester, Gloucestershire GL7 1YE ☎ 01285 643440.

Bridges Numerous.

Branches Cirencester, 1½ miles.

Tunnels Sapperton, 3808yds.

Towpath At present about three-quarters of the distance is open to the public and is part of the Thames and Severn Way. Negotiations are underway with landowners to make the whole length accessible.

Summit level 348ft 1in above low water, River Severn, 362ft 6ins above Ordnance datum.

Restoration Coates portal of Sapperton Tunnel was completed in 1976 and the no less magnificent Daneway portal is being restored. Restoration of Wallbridge Lock has taken place and work is underway at South Cerney and elsewhere. Local council support has been encouraging and restoration work is proceeding rapidly. A navigable culvert is being constucted under the new Latton By-pass.

Distance table

Miles

Wallbridge Lower Lock No 1, junction with Stroudwater Navigation to:

Wallbridge Upper Lock (Stroud) No 2	0.3
Bowbridge Lock No 3	0.9
Griffins Lock No 4	1.4
Ham Mill Lock No 5	1.6
Hope Mill Lock No 6	2.0
Gough's Orchard Lock No 7	2.3
Brimscombe Basin (trans-shipment point)	2.5
Bourne Lock No 8	2.8

THAMES AND SEVERN CANAL Maximum vessel dimensions

From and to	Distance	Length	Beam	Draught	Headroom	Locks
Wallbridge on the Stroudwater Navigation to Inglesham on River Thames	28.8 miles (46.3km)	74' (22.5m)	12' 9" (3.8m)	3' 6" (1.0m)	8' 6" (2.5m)	44

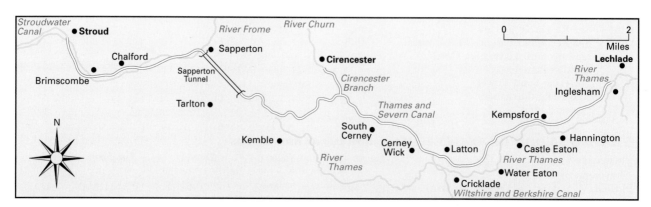

	Miles
Beale's Lock No 9	3.3
St Mary's Lock No 10	3.6
Ile's Lock No 11	3.8
Ballinger's Lock No 12	3.9
Chalford Chapel Lock No 13	4.1
Bell Lock No 14	4.3
Red Lion Lock No 15	4.5
Golden Valley Lock No 16	4.8
Baker's Mill, Lower Lock No 17	5.5
Baker's Mill, Upper Lock No 18	5.6
Puck Mill Lower Lock No 19	5.8
Puck Mill Upper Lock No 20	5.9
Whitehall Lower Lock No 21	6.1
Whitehall Upper Lock No 22	6.6
Bathurst Meadow Lock No 23	6.8
Sikeridge Wood Lower Lock No 24	6.8
Sikeridge Wood Middle Lock No 25	6.9
Sikeridge Wood Upper Lock No 26	7.0
Daneway Basin, Daneway Lower Lock No 27	7.1
Daneway Bridge Daneway Upper Lock No 28	7.1
Sapperton Tunnel (west end)	7.5
Sapperton Tunnel (east end) and Tunnel Inn	9.5
Thames Head Wharf	11.4
Thames Head Pumping Station	11.6
Smerril Aqueduct Stop Gates	12.5
Head of Siddington Upper Lock No 29, junction with the Cirencester Branch	15.3
Siddington Second Lock No 30	15.4
Siddington Third Lock No 31	15.4
Siddington Fourth Lock (low) No 32	15.5
South Cerney Upper Lock No 33	16.7
South Cerney Middle Lock No 34	16.8
South Cerney Low Lock No 35	16.8
Boxwell Spring Lock No 36	17.5
Wilmoorway (upper) Lock No 37	18.0
Wilmoorway Lock No 39	19.4
Latton Junction, junction with Wiltshire and Berkshire Canal, North Wiltshire Branch	20.1
Latton Lock No 40	20.9
Latton Wharf, Cricklade	21.0
Eisey Lock No 41	22.6
Dudgrove Double Locks (2) Nos 42 and 43	28.1
Tail of Inglesham Lock No 44 and junction with River Thames	28.8

River Trent

The Trent is an ancient navigation having been used for transport by the Romans and as an invasion route by the Danes who reached Nottingham. The first Act of Parliament to improve navigation on the Trent was passed in 1699. This started work in a section up to Burton-on-Trent, extending the navigable river by over 18 miles above Wilden Ferry. By 1770, the Trent and Mersey Canal had rather overtaken this navigation, but its arrival benefited the River Trent below Derwent Mouth.

The next improvements were at Newark where a cut was built to ease access to the town. Dredging of the river and construction of a number of weirs and locks continued the improvements and, as a section was completed, tolls were levied gradually working downstream towards Gainsborough. Below Gainsborough, the river was a free navigation. The locks were large enough to pass barges 81ft by 14ft.

In the early part of the 19th century, passenger boats ran frequently between Nottingham and Gainsborough, but by the middle of the century railway competition was affecting profitability. Tolls had to be reduced and improvements were made where possible to regain traffic. In 1906, another Act was passed to authorise further lock construction and Cromwell Lock was enlarged and deepened. In the early 1900s, petroleum transport became an important cargo on the river. Commercial traffic on the Trent continued into the 1960s, although no traffic had been carried above Nottingham for some years. Today, the river below Cromwell Lock is still busy with oil deliveries to power stations and coastal traffic up to Keadby and Gainsborough.

The Trent is a popular river for pleasure craft and there are plenty of things to see along the way. Nottingham itself has a canal museum as well as the famous cricket ground and football team. The landscape around the river changes from urban and industrial to completely rural within very short distances. Just outside Nottingham is Holme Pierpoint, the National Water Sports Centre and Country Park. Between Stoke Hall and Farndon is the site of a Roman villa close to the river which was on the old Fosse Way. At Newark, the seven-arch stone bridge is an ancient monument, and there are several old industrial buildings which are gradually being restored and redeveloped.

Once into the tidal river, the pace quickens slightly and there are few satisfactory moorings. Care has to be taken to avoid the shallow islands in the river and the shelving banks on the inside of bends. The Fossdyke joins the river at Torksey and then you arrive at Gainsborough. This is a nice town to visit, but it isn't made easy if you arrive by boat, as there are virtually no facilities here, which seems unusual in an age of increased use of waterways by pleasure craft.

At West Stockwith, first the Chesterfield Canal and then the River Idle join the river as you travel

The River Trent winds gently below the imposing walls of Newark Castle. *Sian Barron*

into rather flat, but productive, agricultural country. Some old windmills can be seen as reminders of man's continuing fight to wrestle this land from nature. Below Keadby, the land becomes ever flatter as the mouth of the Trent approaches. Waders and other estuary birds appreciate the mudflats around Trent Falls where the river joins the River Ouse and the Humber.

Authority *Derwent Mouth to Gainsborough:* British Waterways, Mill Lane, Mill Gate, Newark, Nottinghamshire NG24 4TT ☎ 01636 704481.

Newark Dyke is owned by the Newark Navigation Commissioners and is leased to British Waterways. *Trent Falls to Gainsborough:* Associated British Ports, Harbourmaster's Office, PO Box 1, Port House, Northern Gateway, Hull, HU9 5PQ ☎ 01482 327171. VHF Ch 16 and 74.

Bridges Numerous bridges, including one fixed railway bridge at Keadby between Trent Falls and Gainsborough.

Towpath Above Derwent Mouth, there is a public footpath. From Derwent Mouth to the A1 at Winthorpe Bridge, the towpath is between the A1 and Cromwell Lock, the right of way along the towpath is currently being disputed in the courts. Below Cromwell Lock, the towpath continues to Gainsborough Bridge. The towpath frequently changes from one bank to the other, often at the site of old ferries which no longer exist, causing some problems in following it. Below Gainsborough, it is necessary to walk along the flood banks to continue the walk along the remainder of the river.

Speed limit 6mph over the ground upstream, and 8mph downstream.

Connections The Grand Union Canal at Trent Junction; Trent and Mersey Canal at Derwent mouth; Beeston Cut and Nottingham Canal; Grantham Canal (under restoration); Fossdyke Canal at Torksey; Chesterfield Canal and River Idle at West Stockwith; and Sheffield and South Yorkshire Navigation at Keadby.

Navigation The tidal section of the River Trent should only be entered by boats equipped with navigation lights, suitable anchor and cable and lifejackets for all members of the crew. The person in charge of the boat must have experience of tidal waters. The eagre, aegir or bore is a tidal wave which reaches between 1ft and 5ft on spring tides between Keadby and Torksey. This is usually only on a tide which is in excess of 25ft at Hull, but can occur on smaller spring tides in certain weather conditions.

The Trent Boating Association produce useful charts on the Trent which can be obtained by telephoning ☎ 01159 262055. The Ripon Motor Boat Club *Cruising Guide to the North East Waterways* includes the Trent; contact the Honorary Secretary, Birchwood, 101 St Wilfred's Road, Harrogate HG2 8LR.

RIVER TRENT Maximum vessel dimensions

From and to	Distance	Length	Beam	Draught	Headroom	Locks
Derwent Mouth to Meadow Lane Lock inc NottinghamCanal	12 miles (19.3km)	81' (24.6m)	14' 6" (4.4m)	3' 3" (1.0m)	8' (2.4m)	6
Meadow Lane Lock to Cromwell Lock	28.8 miles (46.3km)	165' (50.3m)	18' 6" (5.6m)	6' (1.8m)	13' (3.9m)	6
Tidal Trent to Trent Falls	52.6 miles (84.6km)	Unlimited	Unlimited	7' (2.1m)	15' 5" (4.7m)	None

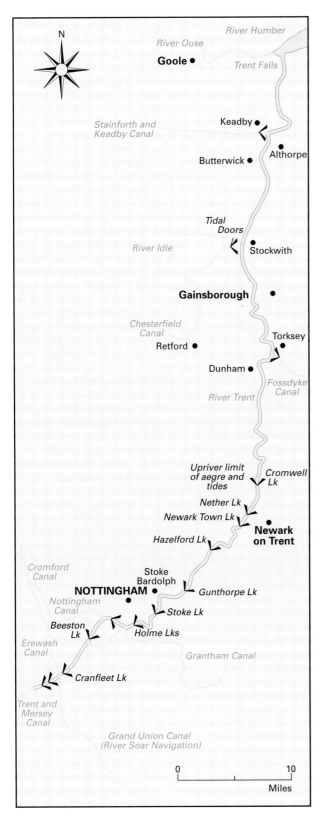

Always give way to large craft which are restricted by their draught. The channel is fairly narrow in parts, particularly where there is shallow water on a bend. At locations with special navigational hazards, warning signs are posted up and downstream to warn boat crews of the danger. Special care must be taken when passing weirs on the River Trent, of

which there are seven, especially in times of heavy rainfall.

Always accept advice from lock-keepers.

The tidal range at Trent Falls is 19ft 4ins (5.9m) at springs and 10ft 6ins (3.2m) at neaps reducing to 4ft 6ins (1.4m) and 3ft 10ins (1.2m) respectively at Torksey. The flood runs for 2¼ hours and the ebb for 9¾ hours in every 12. High water at Trent Falls is 1 hour after HW Immingham, 3 hours after at Gainsborough and 5 hours after at Cromwell Lock.

Facilities There are several marinas and boatyards along the river as well as plenty of moorings, pubs, shops and sanitary stations above Cromwell Lock. In the tidal Trent mooring is more difficult and the rise of tide must be taken into account with mooring lines. BW have provided a mooring pontoon at Dunham.

Distance table

	Miles
Wilden Ferry to:	
British Waterways, Shardlow Depot	0.2
Derwent Mouth, junction with Trent and Mersey Canal	1.4
Sawley Flood Lock No 1	2.1
Sawley Lock No 2 (two locks side by side)	2.5
Head of Cranfleet Cut, junction with Grand Union Canal Erewash Section (left) and junction with River Soar (right)	3.4
Cranfleet Lock No 3	4.1
Thrumpton	4.7
Barton	6.2
Beeston Lock No 4 and commencement of Beeston Cut	8.4
Lenton Chain, termination of Beeston Cut, and junction with Nottingham Canal	11.0
Castle Lock	12.1
Poplar Arms Corner	12.6
Meadow Lane Lock, Nottingham, termination of Nottingham Canal, and junction with Main River	13.4
Nottingham, junction with Grantham Canal (under restoration)	13.6
Colwick Marina	15.4
Holme Lock No 5	15.8
Radcliffe on Trent	18.1
Stoke Bardolph Lock No 6	18.8
Burton Lane End	21.0
East Bridgford	23.5
Gunthorpe Lock No 7	23.6
Hoveringham	25.5
Hazelford Ferry	27.7
Hazelford Lock No 8	28.3
Fiskerton Landing	29.6
East Stoke Wharf	31.4
Farndon Ferry	33.2
Averham Weir, start of Newark Branch	34.4
Farndon Field Maltkiln	35.5
Newark, Mill Bridge	36.4
Newark, Town Lock No 9	36.6
Newark, Town Wharf	36.8
Nether Lock No 10	37.6
Crankley Point, end of Newark Branch	38.3
Muskham	40.5
Cromwell Lock No 11	42.2
Carlton Holme	45.2
Besthorpe Wharf	46.4
South Holme	47.6

	Miles
Girton Gravel Wharf	48.7
Fledborough Viaduct	52.0
Fledborough Beck	52.5
Dunham Bridge	54.2
Laneham Ferry	56.0
Torksey, junction with Fossdyke Canal	58.3
Torksey Viaduct	58.9
Trent Port, Marton	60.5
Littleborough Ferry	61.8
Knaith	63.5
Gainsborough Bridge	68.5
Morton Corner	70.2
Walkerith,	71.9
West Stockwith, junction with Chesterfield Canal	73.0
West Stockwith, junction with River Idle	73.1
Gunthorpe Lincolnshire	75.1
Wildsworth	75.8
Owston Ferry	76.4
Kelfield Corner	78.6
West and East Butterwick	81.8
Burringham	84.3
Althorpe	84.5
Keadby Railway Bridge	85.1
Keadby, junction with Sheffield and South Yorkshire Navigation – Stainforth and Keadby Canal	85.8
Amcotts	88.6
Burton upon Stather	91.8
Trent Falls, junction with River Humber and River Ouse	94.8

Nottingham Canal

Nottingham, Meadow Lane Lock, junction with River Trent to:

Nottingham, Boots Warehouses and junction with Popular Cut to Manvers Street	0.8
Nottingham, British Waterways, Wilford Warehouses	1.1
Castle Lock	1.2
Lenton Chain, junction with Beeston Cut	2.4

Trent and Mersey Canal

The Trent and Mersey Canal was part of James Brindley's idea of a 'Grand Cross' linking the Thames, Severn, Mersey and Humber. The other major player in the proposals to build the canal was Josiah Wedgwood, whose pottery works were in Staffordshire. He was keen to have reliable transport of raw materials in and finished goods out both east and westwards. He eventually built new works on the canal at Etruria and, today, the Wedgwood Visitor Centre is well worth seeing, although the main factory has now moved from its Etruria site.

The first Act of Parliament promoting the canal was passed in 1766 and a further nine Acts were passed over the next 60 years. The canal was originally called the Grand Trunk Canal but it was not completed until five years after Brindley's death. Along its length, there were some outstanding engineering works for the time, not least the 2897 yard Harecastle Tunnel which took 11 years to dig. The tunnel which is in use today is not the original one designed by Brindley, but Telford's later version opened in 1827, which had taken three years to dig and was constructed alongside the original one. It is slightly longer at 2926 yards.

Opened throughout in 1777, the Trent and Mersey canal was an enormous commercial success. The main cargoes, other than pottery, were coal from the Staffordshire coalfields, salt from the salt mines in Cheshire and beer from the breweries around Burton-on-Trent. A £200 share bought in 1784 was worth £2400 in 1824 with share holders receiving as much as 75 per cent dividend in the mid-1800s. Josiah Wedgwood's confidence was well founded and the industrial development of the Potteries was formidable. In the 19th century, this was a very prosperous area and wealthy factory owners had large houses built overlooking the canal, some of which can still be seen today.

The diversity of countryside and interest offered to today's traveller on the Trent and Mersey Canal makes it one of the most varied routes to follow. Some people may feel the Potteries detract from the countryside, but it should never be forgotten that industry and commerce were the driving force for the canal builders and, in the late 1700s and early

TRENT AND MERSEY CANAL *Maximum vessel dimensions*

From and to	Distance	Length	Beam	Draught	Headroom	Locks
Derwent Mouth to Burton-on-Trent	16.5 miles (26.5km)	72' (21.9m)	10' (3.0m)	3' 3" (1.0m)	7' (2.1m)	6
Burton-on-Trent to Harecastle Tunnel	45.3 miles (72.9km)	72' (21.9m)	7' (2.1m)	2' 6" (0.7m)	6' 3" (1.9m)	34
Harecastle Tunnel	1.6 miles (2.5km)	72' (21.9m)	7' (2.1m)	2' 6" (0.7m)	5' 9" (1.7m)	None
Harecastle Tunnel to Croxton Aqueduct	14.2 miles (22.8km)	72' (21.9m)	7' (2.1m)	2' 6" (0.7m)	7' (2.1m)	35
Croxton Aqueduct to Anderton	9.0 miles (14.5km)	72' (21.9m)	9' (2.7m)	2' 3" (0.7m)	6' 3" (1.9m)	None
Anderton to Preston Brook	6.8 miles (10.9km)	72' (21.9m)	9' (2.7m)	3' 4" (1.0m)	6' 6" (2.0m)	1

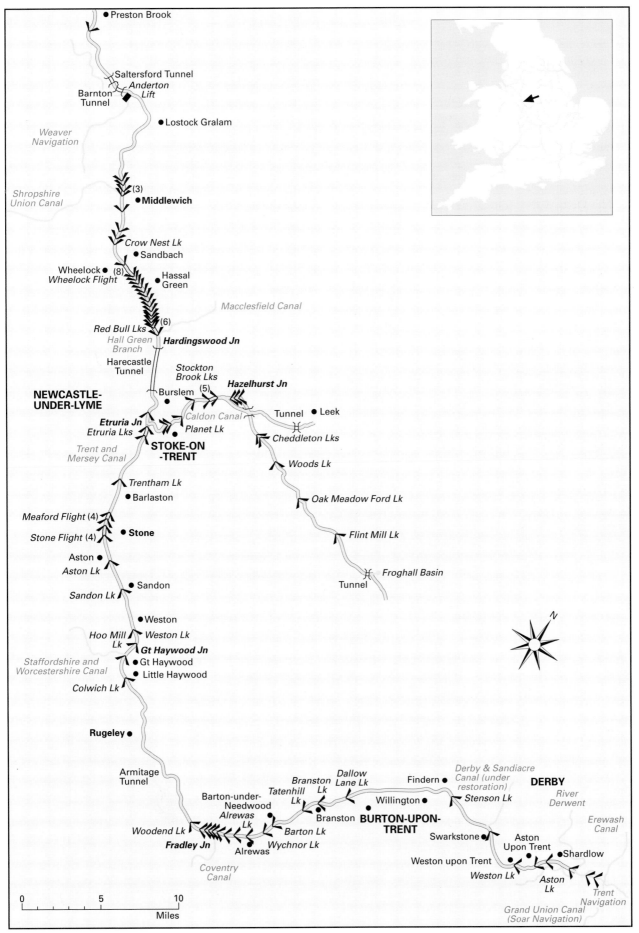

• Preston Brook

Saltersford Tunnel
Anderton
Barnton *Lift*
Tunnel

Weaver
Navigation

• Lostock Gralam

Shropshire
Union Canal

(3)
• **Middlewich**

Crow Nest Lk
• Sandbach

Wheelock • (8)
Wheelock Flight
Hassal
Green

Macclesfield Canal

Red Bull Lks (6)
Hall Green
Branch
Hardingswood Jn

Harecastle
Tunnel

Stockton
Brook Lks
Hazelhurst Jn

NEWCASTLE-
UNDER-LYME
Burslem • (5)
Tunnel • Leek

Etruria Jn
Etruria Lks
Planet Lk
Caldon Canal

Cheddleton Lks

STOKE-ON
-TRENT

Trent and
Mersey Canal
Woods Lk

Trentham Lk
• Barlaston

Oak Meadow Ford Lk

Meaford Flight (4)

Stone Flight (4) • **Stone**
Flint Mill Lk

Aston •
Aston Lk

Froghall Basin
Tunnel
Sandon • Sandon
Sandon Lk

• Weston
Hoo Mill *Weston Lk*
Lk
Gt Haywood Jn
Staffordshire and • Gt Haywood
Worcestershire Canal • Little Haywood

Colwich Lk

Rugeley •

Armitage
Tunnel
Derby & Sandiacre
Canal (under
Branston *Dallow* • Findern *restoration)* **DERBY**
Tatenhill *Lane Lk*
Barton-under- *Lk* • Willington *Stenson Lk* *River*
Needwood *Derwent*
Alrewas Branston **BURTON-UPON-** *Erewash*
Lk **TRENT** *Canal*
Woodend Lk *Barton Lk*
Fradley Jn *Wychnor Lk* Swarkstone • Aston
Alrewas Upon Trent • Shardlow
Coventry Weston upon Trent
Canal *Weston Lk* *Aston*
Lk
Trent
Navigation
Grand Union Canal
(Soar Navigation)

0   5   10
Miles

N

1800s, leisure was unknown to the majority of the population.

From its junction with the River Trent at Derwentmouth, the Trent and Mersey Canal passes first through Shardlow. This was one of the earliest inland ports and should not be missed as, fortunately, the developers of the late 20th century have not ruined it. The old warehouse which spans a section of canal has been converted into a pub and restaurant with the exterior carefully altered to retain its character. There are boatbuilders and repair yards around the village and it retains the flavour of a port.

The Derby Canal joined the Trent and Mersey at Swarkestone Junction from where it ran north to Derby, across the River Derwent in the city and then east to join the Erewash Canal at Sandiacre. An active society is now trying to restore the canal.

The Trent and Mersey Canal follows the valley of the River Trent, running roughly westward until a sharp bend between Stenson and Findern where the canal bears away and heads in a more southerly direction down towards Fradley Junction. This is a fairly rural stretch until you reach Burton-on-Trent, where brewing activities received as much benefit from the canal as the pottery industry did further west. The rather sweet smell of hops greets you long before you reach the town. For ale enthusiasts, a stop at Shobnall Basin, on the site of the old Bond End Canal, affords an opportunity to visit some of the breweries for which Burton-on-Trent has become famous. About a century ago, beer was exported via the Humber to Northern Europe and via Liverpool to India and South America.

As far as Horninglow, in Burton-on-Trent, the canal is wide but after this it becomes a narrow canal as far as, and including, Croxton Aqueduct. From Middlewich to Preston Brook, the canal used to take flats to transport salt but, when work was carried out on the Croxton Aqueduct in the 1930s, it was reduced to the narrower width making Middlewich inaccessible to the wider boats.

Past the Barton Turns, the canal runs alongside the old Roman road, Ryknild Street, before joining the river again for a short distance between Wychnor and Alrewas. Through here the countryside is quite marshy and care must be taken when passing the river weirs, especially after heavy rain. Soon after this, you come to the famous Swan pub at Fradley Junction where the Coventry Canal heads south. This is about the most southerly point of the Trent and Mersey which soon turns northwest again through a right-angle bend just before Woodend Lock.

Armitage is a well-known name in sanitary wear which was taken from the name of the small village where the works are sited. It is usually possible to see large numbers of toilet bowls stacked-up close by the canal. These are now transported by rail or road but they used to be moved by water. Past the village, there was a tunnel but this was opened up in 1971 as subsidence had been causing problems for

many years. The passage is narrow and one-way traffic is necessary to get through. After Rugeley and the power station, the canal has another right-angled bend where it crosses the river. This is called Brindley Bank. The canal now runs along under Cannock Chase until it reaches the junction with the Staffordshire and Worcestershire Canal at Great Haywood.

Aston Lock is the half-way mark between Derwentmouth and Preston Brook. The Trent and Mersey Canal is clearly an early canal as it winds along following the contours of the land and, through Stone and Hem Heath, it is shadowed by the road and the railway line. Reaching Stoke-on-Trent, it has arrived at the summit level. Etruria Junction is where the Caldon Canal branches off and rises by a steep staircase and soon the canal traveller is looking down on the Potteries with the old bottle kilns and flint and bone mills. The original intention was for the Caldon to finish at Uttoxeter, but the last 13 miles were converted to a railway in the mid-1800s.

The Caldon Canal rises to Hazelhurst Junction then falls to Froghall. From Hazelhurst, a branch continues towards Leek, although it does not reach, it, without any locks and still acts as a feeder to the Caldon Canal. The canal was built to bring limestone from the quarries of Caldon Low to the industry in the Potteries. Along much of its route, the Caldon follows the River Churnet. The Denford Aqueduct carries the Leek Branch over the canal, the railway and the river. For many, the Caldon is one of the most delightful canals in the country but part of the attraction is the fact that it is little used, and to encourage greater use would detract from its unhurried, secluded and peaceful character.

Back on the main line, the next notable feature is the Harecastle Tunnel. The one in use today is the 'new' tunnel, built by Telford and opened in 1827. Brindley's original tunnel is alongside and suffered from subsidence, as Telford's is now starting to. There is a height gauge at each end of the tunnel and headroom is now less than 6ft. At the north end of the tunnel, the water is usually dark orange or red, stained by iron.

At Red Bull, the Macclesfield Canal crosses the Trent and Mersey on an aqueduct from Hardings Wood Junction, and then, for just over 6 miles, 25 locks drop the canal into the Cheshire plain. At Middlewich, the canal meets the Shropshire Union along the short Wardle Lock Branch. Winding through the fertile valley of the River Dane, which is crossed at Croxton Aqueduct, the canal reaches Broken Cross and then Anderton with the famous, but currently not working, boat lift.

The Anderton Boat Lift is now a scheduled monument and funding has been secured for a complete restoration. BW, the IWA, the Trent and Mersey Canal Society and the local authorities are all involved and support the plans for the restoration of the lift which is unique in Britain (see the River Weaver entry). Originally, Anderton was a transhipment point between the River Weaver and the Trent and Mersey Canal. In 1875, the first boat lift was opened using a hydraulic piston system to assist in raising one boat in its trough while most of the work was done by the descending trough. In 1908, a new lift was in operation, the one that is still there today, which used a small electric motor to assist the pulleys as again the two tanks were counter-balanced and little additional power was needed to overcome the friction. The lift was closed in 1982 because of structural faults and has not yet re-opened, so there is currently no link between the Weaver and the Trent and Mersey Canal.

From Anderton, it is a relatively short distance to Dutton Stop Lock and the end of the Trent and Mersey Canal, where it joins the Bridgewater Canal just before the Preston Brook Tunnel.

Authority British Waterways, Top Lock, Church Lane, Marple, Cheshire SK6 6BN ☎ 0161 427 1079.

Fradley Junction Alrewas, Burton-on-Trent, Staffordshire DE13 7DN ☎ 01283 790236

Harecastle Tunnel Tunnel-keeper ☎ 01782 837775.

Bridges Numerous.

Towpath Throughout the navigation except in certain tunnels.

Branches Caldon Branch, 17½ miles. Leek Branch, 2¾ miles; this was closed to navigation by Act of 1944. The first 2 miles act as a feeder to the Main Line. Leek Wharves to River Churnet Aqueduct is now filled in. In navigating this branch, it should be noted that a narrow boat can be winded only at the west end of Leek Tunnel. Burslem Branch 700yds, closed. Hall Green Branch 1½ miles. Wardle Lock Branch 100yds.

Tunnels Preston Brook, 1239yds, no towpath; Saltersford, 424yds, no towpath; Barnton, 572yds, no towpath; Harecastle, 2926yds, no towpath; Froghall Caldon Branch, 76yds, maximum air draught 4ft 8ins, no towpath; Leek (Leek Branch), 130yds, no towpath. Armitage Tunnel was opened out in 1971 due to mining subsidence.

Harecastle Tunnel Passage through this tunnel must be booked with the tunnel-keeper at least 48 hours in advance. No more than eight craft are permitted in the tunnel at the same time. The tunnel may only be used when the tunnel keeper is in attendance and their instructions must be followed at all times.

Connections River Trent at Derwent Mouth; Coventry Canal at Fradley; Caldon Branch at Etruria; Staffordshire and Worcestershire at Great Haywood; Burslem Branch at Burslem; Macclesfield Canal at Hardingswood, via Hall Green Branch; River Weaver at Anderton, via Anderton Lift, although this is currently out of commission; and Bridgewater Canal at Preston Brook.

Navigation The canal enters and leaves the River Trent between Alrewas and Wychnor. When passing the weir, boats should navigate with care and close to protective fendering. In times of flood, a passage should not be attempted. On the Caldon Canal near Endon Basin, there is an underwater obstruction in the middle of the canal which must be navigated very carefully.

Facilities This is a busy cruising route and there are numerous boatyards, marinas, pubs, restaurants and shops along the way to cater for all tastes. Slipways are located at several marinas and boatyards.

Distance table

Derwent Mouth and junction with River Trent to:

	Miles
Derwent Mouth Lock No 1	0.3
Shardlow Lock No 2	1.3
Aston Lock No 3	2.8
Weston Lock No 4	4.3
Weston Cliffe	5.0
Cuttle Wharf	6.5
Swarkestone Junction, junction with Derby Canal, and Lock No 5	7.0
Lowes Bridge	7.3
Stenson Lock No 6	10.0
Railway Bridge	10.4
Findern Common	11.0
Railway Bridge	11.7
Willington	12.3
Coach and Horses Bridge	13.3
Stretton	14.7
Horninglow Wharf, Burton-on-Trent	16.5
Dallow Lane Lock No 7	16.9
Shobnall Basin	17.5
Branston Lock No 8	18.5
Tatenhill Lock No 9	21.0
Barton Turn Lock No 10	21.4
Wychnor Lock No 11 Wharf	23.0
Alrewas Lock No 12	24.4
Bagnall Lock No 13	25.0
Common Lock No 14, Fradley Bottom	25.3
Hunt's Lock No 15	25.8
Keeper's Lock No 16	26.1
Fradley Junction Lock No 17 and junction with Coventry Canal	26.3
Fradley Middle Lock No 18	27.0
Shade House Lock No 19	27.1
Wood End Lock No 20	27.3
King's Bromley	28.5
Handsacre	30.5
Armitage	30.8
Armitage Narrows (one-way traffic)	31.8
Spode House	32.1
Brereton	33.8
Rugeley	34.0
Brindley's Bank	35.0
Aqueduct over River Trent	35.1
Colwich Lock No 21	37.6
Haywood Lock No 21	38.9
Haywood Junction, Staffordshire and Worcestershire Canal	39.0
Hoo Mill Lock No 23	39.8
Ingestre and Shirleywich	41.3
Weston Lock No 24	42.5
Sandon Lock No 25	44.5
Aston Lock No 26	46.6
Stone Locks Nos 27–30	48.6
Meaford Locks Nos 31–34	49.8
Meaford Power Station	50.5
Barlaston	52.2
Wedgwood Visitor Centre	53.0

	Miles
Trentham Lock No 35	53.3
Hem Heath	53.8
Sideway Bridge	55.8
Stoke Basin	56.3
Stoke, junction with Newcastle Branch (derelict)	56.8
Stoke Lock No 36	57.0
Cockshute Lock No 37	57.4
Etruria Bottom Lock No 38	57.6
Lock No 39, Shirley's Bone and Flint Mill Museum	57.8
Etruria Summit Lock No 40 and Toll Office	57.9
Etruria, junction with Caldon Branch	58.0
Festival Basin	58.3
Etruria, Wedgwood's Works (site of old works)	58.5
Burslem Junction, junction with Burslem Branch	59.3
Middleport Anderton Boat Co (site of premises)	59.8
Longport	60.0
Tunstall	61.0
Harecastle Tunnel, south end (summit level 365 feet)	61.8
Harecastle Tunnel, north end, Kidsgrove	63.4
Harding's Wood Junction, junction with Hall Green Branch leading to the Macclesfield Canal	63.6
Red Bull Top Lock No 41	63.8
Harding's Wood	63.9
Red Bull Wharf	64.1
Red Bull Bottom Lock No 46	64.6
Lawton Top Lock No 47	65.4
Lawton Bottom Lock No 52	65.9
Snapes Aqueduct	66.1
Thurlwood Locks No 53 and 54	66.8
Chell Aqueduct	67.4
Pierpoint Locks Nos 55 and 56	68.4
Hassall Green Locks Nos 57 and 58	69.0
Malkin's Bank Top Lock No 59	69.5
Malkin's Bank Bottom Lock No 64	70.0
Wheelock Locks Nos 65 and 66	70.3
Wheelock	70.4
Rookery Bridge	72.3
Elton Moss Bridge	72.9
Crow Nest Lock No 67	73.4
Booth Lane Lock Nos 68 and 69	73.8
Rumps Lock No 78	75.5
King's Lock No 71	76.3
Middlewich, junction with Wardle Lock Branch leading to Shropshire Union Canal	76.4
Middlewich Top Lock No 72	76.5
Middlewich Town Centre	76.6
Middlewich Bottom Lock No 74	76.7
Middlewich Big Lock No 75	77.1
Croxton Aqueduct	77.6
Whatcroft Hall	79.4
Broken Cross	82.4
Wincham Wharf	83.3
Wincham	84.4
Marbury Country Park	85.8
Anderton Public Wharf	86.4
Anderton, junction with Anderton Lift Branch of River Weaver Navigation	86.6
Soote Hill Bridge	86.9
Barnton Tunnel, south end	87.4
Saltersford Tunnel, south end	88.1
Little Leigh	89.6
Acton Bridge	90.1
Dutton Wharf	91.4

	Miles
Dutton Stop Lock No 76, south end of Preston Brook	92.5
North end of Preston Brook Tunnel, and junction with Preston Brook Branch of the Bridgewater Canal	93.4

Caldon Branch
Etruria, junction with Main Line to:

	Miles
Bedford Staircase Locks Nos 1 and 2	0.3
Planet Lock No 3	0.7
Hanley	1.6
Ivy House Lift Bridge	2.0
Milton, junction with Foxley Branch Canal (now closed)	4.5
Engine Lock No 4	5.5
Norton Green	5.8
Stockton Brook Locks Nos 5–8	6.8
Stockton Brook Lock No 9	6.9
Endon Basin	7.6
Park Lane Bridge	8.4
Hazelhurst Junction, junction with Leek Branch and Locks Nos 10–12	9.5
Holly Bush Inn, Denford	9.9
Wall Grange Bridge	10.3
Cheddleton Locks Nos 13 and 14	11.3
Wood's Lock No 15	12.0
Canal enters River Churnet, Oak Meadow Ford Lock No 16	13.5
Consall Forge	14.5
Canal leaves River Churnet	14.9
Flint Mill Lock No 17	15.0
Froghall	16.8
Froghall Tunnel (maximum headroom 4.6 feet)	16.9
Froghall Basin	17.5

Leek Branch
Hazelhurst Junction, junction with Caldon Branch to:

	Miles
Leek Tunnel	2.0
Wall Grange Farm Bridge	2.5
River Churnet Aqueduct (canal filled in from this point)	2.8
Leek Wharves	3.3

Burslem Branch (closed)
From Main Line, to:

	Miles
Burslem	0.4

Hall Green Branch
From Harding's Wood Junction to:

	Miles
Hall Green, junction with Macclesfield Canal, halfway between the two stop locks	1.5

Wardle Lock Branch

Extends for 100yds from a junction with the Main Line at the tail of Wardle Lock, Middlewich, to the head of Wardle Lock only, where it joins the Middlewich Branch of the Shropshire Union Canal (one lock, Wardle).

River Tyne

The River Tyne has always been a tidal navigation and surprisingly no statutes were promoted to improve the navigation in early days. The upper reaches are wild, beautiful and well wooded and they are very popular with canoeists. The highly industrialised lower reaches have changed dramatically over the past few years with much of the heavy industry disappearing. The four local authorities which cover the area have various

RIVER TYNE Maximum vessel dimensions

From and to	Distance	Length	Beam	Draught	Headroom	Locks
Hedwin Streams to harbour mouth	19 miles (32.1km)	Unlimited	Unlimited			None
At Newburn				9' (2.7m) LWST	21' (6.4m) HWST	
At harbour entrance				30' (9.1m)		

projects under way to encourage greater use of the river for recreational purposes, but to reach it you need either a sea-going or a trailed boat.

Authority Port of Tyne Authority, Berwick Street, Newcastle-upon-Tyne, NE1 5HS ☎ 0191 232 5541.

Towpath None on river or branches.

Connections Navigable for small craft only at high tide: River Derwent, ¾ mile; River Team, ¾ mile; River Ouseburn, ½ mile; and River Don, ½ mile.

Navigation This is still essentially a working port and the estuary is used mainly by sea-going craft. High tide at Newcastle is 12 minutes after HW Tynemouth; tidal range, spring tides 15ft.

Facilities There are several launching sites between Newburn and Newcastle.

Distance table

Left bank Miles		Right bank Miles
	Boundary Stone at Hedwin Streams to:	
	Ryton	0.5
1.5	Newburn Bridge	
	Stella	2.6
3.8	Junction with Lemington Gut	
4.4	Scotswood Suspension Bridge	4.4
	Junction with River Derwent	4.4
5.6	Opposite Elswick Station	
	Junction with River Team	6.6
7.4	Redheugh Bridge	7.4
7.5	King Edward Bridge	7.5

Left bank Miles		Right bank Miles
	Immediately above the High Level Bridge is a swing bridge Newcastle High Level Bridge,	
7.9	Newcastle	
	Gateshead	7.9
8.8	Junction with Ouseburn	
	Pelaw Main Staithes	11.4
11.8	Walker, River Police Station	
	Hebburn Ferry Landing	12.6
12.8	Wallsend Shipyard	
13.6	Willington Gut	
	Jarrow, Palmer's Dock	14.3
14.4	Howdon authorities yard	
	West end of Jarrow Slake	15.0
15.5	East end of Jarrow Slake (River Don enters Jarrow Slake at the southwest corner)	15.5
	Entrance to Tyne Dock	15.9
16.5	Entrance to Albert Edward Dock	
	South Shields Ferry Landing	17.0
17.1	North Shields Ferry Landing	
18.1	Tynemouth, opposite Black Middens	
18.9	Mouth of harbour	18.9

River Ure

The Yorkshire River Ouse actually changes its name to the Ure at Ouse Gill Beck about 4½ miles south of Swale Nab. This is very attractive cruising country, particularly for those who like to get away

RIVER URE Maximum Vessel Dimensions

From and to	Distance	Length	Beam	Draught	Headroom	Locks
Junction with the River Ouse to junction with the Ripon Canal at Oxclose Lock	8.0 miles (12.8km)	57' (17.3m)	14' 6" (4.4m)	5' (1.5m)	8' 6" (2.6m)	2

from the crowds. Newby Hall is situated above Westwick Lock and there is a pontoon to enable visitors, arriving by boat, to stop off and view the house and gardens.

The navigation was promoted by Acts in 1767 and 1820 as part of quite ambitious plans to improve access in the Swale, the Ouse and by canal to Ripon. The small town of Boroughbridge once boasted no less than 22 coaching inns owing to its strategic position as a crossing point on the Ouse. Later, in the 18th century, Boroughbridge became a port serving Knaresborough with its important linen trade.

Authority British Waterways, Naburn Lock, Naburn, York YO1 4RU ☎ 01904 728229 *Fax* 01904 728860.

Bridges Two.

Towpath Throughout navigation.

Connections River Swale at Swale Nab, navigable to Myton, a distance of about 1 mile; Ripon Canal; and the River Ouse to York.

Distance table	*Miles*
Swale Nab, junction with River Ouse and junction with River Swale to:	
Entrance to Boroughbridge Cut	2.4
Milby Lock No 1	2.5
Boroughbridge Wharf	2.9
Warwick's Brewery	3.0
Langthorpe Landing	3.4
Green's Landing	4.0
Brampton Landing	5.1
Westwick Lock No 2	5.1
Newby Hall Landing	6.5
Sugar Hill Landing	7.5
Junction with Ripon Canal	8.0

River Wansbeck, Northumberland

The River Wansbeck is rarely used for navigation purposes. A saline intrusion barrage was constructed in the early 1980s creating an amenity lake about 2½ miles long. This is mostly used by dinghies and canoeists and there is a riverside park, campsite and picnic area alongside the lake.

The lock can be opened by the park warden but this is a fairly rare occurrence as it is not a simple gate system, as on a canal, and the distance available, once through the lock, is rather restricted. Sea water tops up the lake on a tide of more than 4.7m and this variation in salinity affects the wildlife in and around the lake. A study is now being carried out to review the effectiveness of the barrage.

Authority Wansbeck District Council, Council Offices, Bedlington, Northumberland NE22 5TV ☎ 01670 814444.

For details about use of the lake contact: The Chief Contracts and Leisure Services Officer, Wansbeck District Council, East View, Stakeford, Northumberland NE62 5TR ☎ 01670 819802 *Fax* 01670 520457.

The Wash

The Wash can be said to be an acquired taste. Its reputation for shifting sandbanks, swirling mist and fog, ripping tides and choppy seas are all based on fact, but should not be exaggerated. For many sea-going yachtsmen, these are fascinating waters which will always keep you on your toes, but for the inland boat owner this waterway is essentially a route between rivers. Although never more than a few miles offshore when making a crossing, the proximity of substantial land always seems somewhat tenuous as the coast is so low and flat. The sighting of a church spire or other building, as you approach the next river entrance, is very comforting.

RIVER WANSBECK, NORTHUMBERLAND Maximum vessel dimensions

From and to	Distance	Length	Beam	Draught	Headroom	Locks
Riverside Park to barrage	2.5 miles (4.0km)	30' (9.1m)	8' (2.4m)	5' 3" (1.6m)	8' 6" (2.6m)	1
Barrage to river mouth	0.6 miles (0.9km)					

The Great Ouse, the Nene, the Welland and the Witham flow into the west end of the Wash and are all tidal for some miles from their mouths. From Denver Sluice on the Great Ouse to the Grand Sluice at Boston is 48 nautical miles (55 statute miles) and Wisbech to Boston is 32 nautical miles. These voyages should be carefully planned and not undertaken lightly. At low water, about half of the area of the Wash becomes mud and sand rather than water, and people can be seen walking their dogs or hunting for mussels while waiting for the next tide.

The channels and marks all have wonderfully evocative names. The Roaring Middle Buoy is the principal marker and cross roads near the centre of the Wash, well north of Roaring Middle Sands. Teetotal Channel leads to the Great Ouse leaving Thief Sand to the west and Daseley's Sand to the east. West End and Big Tom buoys guard the entrance to the Nene, and Tab's Head and Dolly Peg mark the dividing point between routes to the Witham and the Welland.

Any boat's crew contemplating crossing the Wash should have either VHF or a mobile phone on board so as to keep in touch with the lock-keepers and harbourmasters. They will inform you of shipping movements and can ensure the lock is ready for a boat's arrival once the tide is making.

Navigation Appropriate charts and pilotage information are essential. Under no circumstances should anyone without sea-going experience consider crossing the Wash without local help or a pilot. The crossing between Boston Grand Sluice and either the Nene or the Great Ouse is over 40 miles and cannot be achieved in a single tide. Quiet weather is absolutely essential, but the area is well marked and in the right conditions a crossing is perfectly practical. Wind over tide will produce a choppy sea even in light winds and such conditions should be avoided.

Tides in the Wash can run very rapidly. The tidal range on spring tides is up to 25ft and 11ft at neaps. High water at King's Lynn, Wisbech and Boston is 4 hours 45 minutes, 4 hours 55 minutes and 5 hours after HW Dover respectively.

Approaching the rivers from the Wash is restricted to 3 hours either side of high water, entering earlier than this runs the risk of the boat grounding and with strong tides serious damage could be caused to a boat.

Pilots There are a number of local people who are prepared to pilot boats across the Wash, some are retired pilots or local fishermen. To arrange a pilot contact the harbourmaster at either Boston ☎ 01205 362328 or King's Lynn ☎ 01553 773411

who will put you in touch with a suitably experienced person.

The East Coast by Derek Bowskill, published by Imrays is an excellent guide to the Wash and the coast as far as Ramsgate. *The Tidal Havens of the Wash and Humber* by Henry Irving is also published by Imrays. There is a series of brochures published by Scantec called *Local Boating on the East Coast* which includes one on the Wash.

Charts Imray Y9, C29, Admiralty 108, 1200.

Authority *River Nene, Wisbech* Wisbech Harbour Authority, Port Manager, Wisbech Harbour, Port Office, Wisbech ☎ 01954 582125.

River Welland Environment Agency, Anglian Region, Sub-Area Office, Spalding, Lincolnshire ☎ 01775 762123.

Downstream of Fosdyke Bridge Port of Fosdyke ☎ 01205 260365.

River Witham, Boston Upstream of Boston Sluice British Waterways, Mill Lane, Mill Gate, Newark, Nottinghamshire NG24 4TT ☎ 01636 704481.

Downstream of Boston Sluice Port Manager, Boston Port Authority ☎ 01205 365571.
Boston Harbourmaster ☎ 01205 362328.

River Great Ouse, Kings Lynn The Kings Lynn Conservancy Board, Harbour Office, Common Staithe, Kings Lynn, Norfolk PE30 1LL ☎ 01553 773411.

River Wear

The River Wear is probably most famous for the wonderful setting of Durham cathedral, high up above a horse-shoe bend in the river. This is, unfortunately, beyond the head of navigation for any form of cruising boat. On a good tide, it is possible to reach Chester-le-Street but the lower reaches are still industrial and very much a working port.

RIVER WEAR Maximum vessel dimensions

From and to	Distance	Length	Beam	Draught	Headroom	Locks
Wearmouth Bridge, Sunderland to Chester-le-Street	0.4 miles (16.7km)	Unlimited	Unlimited	4' 4" (1.3m)	10' (3.0m)	None

Proposals were made and Acts were passed throughout the 18th and early 19th centuries to improve navigation to Chester-le-Street and even Durham. John Smeaton produced a plan for locks and cuts and Ralph Dodd surveyed the line for a canal to Durham in 1796, but no works were ever put in hand.

Authority Port of Sunderland Authority, Barrack Street, Sunderland, Tyne and Wear SR1 2BU ☎ 0191 553 2100.

Navigation Tidal range, spring tides 14ft 9ins, neap tides 7ft 9ins. Chester-le-Street can only be reached on a spring tide.

Facilities There are launching sites at Washington and Sunderland.

Distance table	*Miles*
Chester-le-Street to:	
Biddick Ford	1.3
Lambton Castle	1.5
Fatfield	3.0
Cox Green	4.4
Hylton Boat House	6.9
Sunderland (Wearmouth Bridge)	10.4

River Weaver

This is a 'salt' river and has been used for transporting salt for many centuries. The lower 7 miles to Pickering's Wharf were tidal and pack horses were used to bring salt down to barges to be loaded at high water. In the 17th century, coal was being used to evaporate off the brine and the salt producers wanted improvements up to Winsford to simplify the movement of coal in and salt out. The navigation improvements, promoted under Acts from 1720 to 1829, enabled the salt industry around Northwich, Middlewich and Winsford to prosper and the navigation was successful and profitable throughout the 19th century.

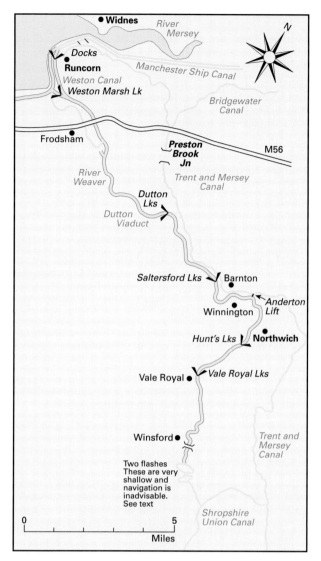

In the early days, Weaver flats were used, bow-hauled by men or sailed as the wind served, and once the Trent and Mersey Canal was opened a system of chutes to load salt from canal barges into the flats was constructed. The salt was taken down the Weaver and then to Liverpool or Manchester from where it was exported around the world. In the early part of the 19th century, the Weston Canal was constructed to avoid the long tidal reach below Frodsham. This was opened in 1810 and greatly eased the use of the river.

In 1856, Edward Leader Williams became the engineer to the navigation and the river was improved to make it suitable for coasters. From 1870 to the end of the century, the navigation was almost completely rebuilt. Probably the most famous development was the boat lift at Anderton

RIVER WEAVER Maximum vessel dimensions

From and to	Distance	Length	Beam	Draught	Headroom	Locks
Winsford Bridge to Northwich	5.5 miles (8.8km)	130' (39.6m)	35' (10.6m)	10' (3.0m)	6' 4" (1.9m)	2
Northwich to Weston Point Docks	14.5 miles (23.3km)	150' (45.7m)	35' (10.6m)	10' (3.0m)	60' (18.2m)	3

opened in 1875. It was thought that this would greatly increase the traffic between the Trent and Mersey Canal and the river, but the salt chutes continued to be used. At the end of the 19th century, about 38,000 tons of salt were tipped down the four chutes annually and 190,000 tons of goods were passing up and down the lift. There was extensive warehousing in Anderton Basin and remains of many industrial buildings and works have been found around the lift site.

The original Anderton Boat Lift worked hydraulically with two counter-balanced boat chambers, as one boat was lowered hydraulic liquid was forced into the piston raising the other chamber the 50ft from the River Weaver to the canal. Although the lift worked very well, chemical contamination of the water started to corrode the pistons and, in 1906, a new boat lift was constructed. To minimise disruption to traffic, it was built over the original lift. It now used counterweights to each boat tank suspended on wire ropes over pulleys. A small electric motor was used to overcome the slight friction on the pulleys. All the rebuilding work was carried out by Weaver Navigation staff supervised by J A Saner, the engineer. Unfortunately, this lift also suffered considerable corrosion as a result of air pollution and it has not been operational since 1983. In 1986, a trust was formed to promote its restoration and in 1994 it was listed as an ancient monument. Funding for the restoration will be in part from the National Heritage Lottery Fund and also from many interested parties. British Waterways, the IWA, Vale Royal Borough Council and Cheshire County Council are committed to its restoration.

Above Winsford, the River Weaver is not under the jurisdiction of BW but shallow draught boats can explore the Winsford flashes. These are shallow lakes, very shallow in places, formed as a result of subsidence of the underground salt workings. In surrounding villages evidence of the salt workings can be seen in crooked lanes and sloping buildings. Many of the buildings are attractive black and white houses and the salt museum in Northwich is well worth a visit.

Authority British Waterways, Canal Office, Birch Road, Ellesmere, Shropshire SY12 9AA ☎ 01696 622549.

Bridges Numerous. The swing bridges are all operated by BW staff but craft needing less than 8ft headroom will not need them to be opened. Prior notice is required if the bridges are to be opened for pleasure craft ☎ 01606 723900.

Towpath There is a footpath alongside the river from Newbridge, below Winsford, to Northwich and then from below the Anderton Boat Lift to Frodsham Marsh, following the Old Navigation from Frodsham Cut. There is no path along the Weston Canal Section.

Branches Anderton Lift Branch, 175yds, length 72ft (21.9m), beam 14ft 6ins (4.4m). The lift is currently inoperable but the renovation of the lift is now underway with support from the IWA, BW, local authorities and financial help from the Lottery. Weston Canal is the lower part of the Weaver Navigation leading to the Manchester Ship Canal. Weston Marsh Lock can be used if BW receive prior notice on ☎ 01606 723900 and clearance has been given by the Manchester Ship Canal Company. Frodsham Cut to Frodsham Lock and the lower river is now closed.

Connections Manchester Ship Canal at Weston Marsh Lock and Weston Point Docks; Trent and Mersey Canal via Anderton Lift Branch (the lift is inoperable at present but a restoration project is in progress).

Navigation The tide flows up to the tail of Frodsham Lock, now closed, via the old line of navigation. High spring tides flow past Frodsham Lock into the main line of the navigation up to Lock No 4 (Dutton) and Weston Point Docks.

The Weaver is still a commercial waterway with ships up to 1000 tonnes sometimes going to Winnington, just below Northwich.

Facilities There are few facilities for pleasure craft. There are some pubs along the river, two boatyards in Northwich and a sanitary station at Town Swing Bridge. The Town Quays in Northwich are suitable for short-stay mooring to see the town. Northwich Marine offers full facilities at Hayhurst Boatyard.

Distance table *Miles*

Winsford Bridge to:

Wharton	0.8
Newbridge Bridge (now fixed)	2.0
Vale Royal Locks No 1	3.3
Hartford Bridge	3.9
Hunt's Locks No 2	5.1
Railway bridge	5.2
Northwich Repair Yard	5.4
Northwich, mouth of River Dane, Hayhurst Swing Bridge	5.5
Town Swing Bridge	5.6
Witton Brook	6.0
Chemical Works	6.8
Junction with Anderton Lift Branch (Trent and Mersey Canal)	7.0
Winnington Chemical Works	7.0
Winnington Swing Bridge	7.3
Saltersford Locks No 3	9.3
Wilbraham's Quay (adjoining main road)	10.3
Acton Swing Bridge	11.1
Dutton Locks No 4	12.4
Pickering's Wharf	13.3
Junction with Old Line of navigation, head of Frodsham Cut to Weston Marsh (now closed)	16.0
Sutton Weir and Sluices	16.5
Sutton Swing Bridge	16.9
Parks Steel Works	17.1
Railway Bridge	17.2
M56 Road Bridge	17.4
Weston Works ICI	18.4
Weston Marsh Side Lock, giving access to Manchester Ship Canal and Old Line of Navigation	19.0

Chemical Works	19.5
Junction with Runcorn and Weston Canal (closed)	19.8
Weston Point Docks, and junction with Manchester Ship Canal (Lock No 5)	20.0

Old Line of Navigation
Head of Frodsham Cut to Weston Marsh Junction with Main Line of Navigation and head of Frodsham Cut to:

Frodsham Lock (now closed to navigation)	0.5
Frodsham Bridge (headway varies with tide)	1.0
Weston Marsh, junction with Manchester Ship Canal, and Main Line of Navigation through Weston Marsh Side Lock	2.3

River Welland

The River Welland flows through England's bulb fields and the historic connections of this area with Holland can be seen in the Dutch style of many of the buildings in Spalding. The river is tidal to Fulney Lock in Spalding, built in 1955-56, then navigable for another 13 miles to Folly River outfall, although this is restricted to quite small craft because of headroom.

The Romans navigated the river between Stamford and Peakirk and remains of a Roman canal can still be seen. These workings are thought to be part of the navigation route the Romans created, including Car Dyke running south to Peterborough. During the 17th century a canal was built with 12 locks to Stamford, a distance of about 34 miles from the Wash. Through the early part of the 19th century the use up to Stamford declined, although plans were still being put forward for canal connections westward to the Grand Union Canal or the Oakham Canal, but nothing was ever started.

The river was straightened and widened after the severe floods of 1947 and, in 1953, the Coronation Channel was constructed to protect Spalding from floods. This joins the river at Cowbit Sluice but is not a navigable channel and includes a nature reserve. Just downstream from Fosdyke is Moulton Marsh Nature Reserve which is managed by the South Lincolnshire Nature Reserves Ltd and Spalding Wildfowlers.

The wharves at Fosdyke are still regularly used for commercial shipping and there is some use by

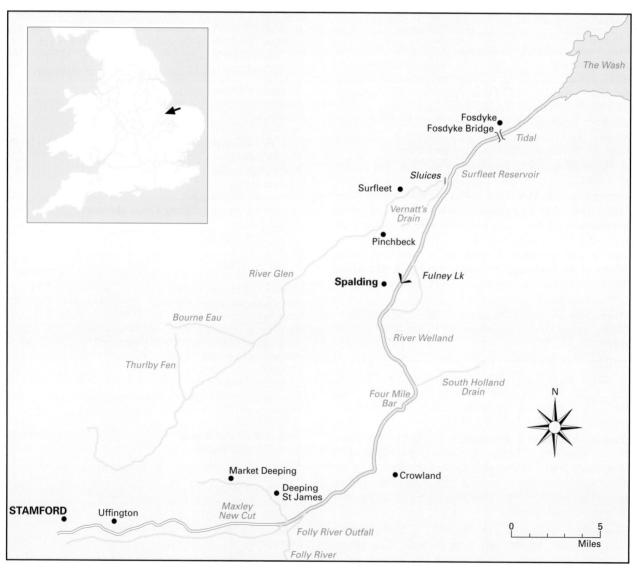

RIVER WELLAND *Maximum vessel dimensions*

From and to	Distance	Length	Beam	Draught	Headroom	Locks
The Wash to Fulney Lock, Spalding	8.9 miles (14.3km)	110' (33.5m)	30' (9.1m)	8' (2.4m) at HW	7' 8" (2.4m) MHWS 13' 9" (4.2m) MHWN	
Fulney Lock at normal summer levels		62' 4" (19.0m)	27' 10" (8.5m)	2' 7" (0.8m)	Unlimited	1
Spalding to Folly River Outfall	13.5 miles (21.7km)	35' (10.6m)	27' 10" (8.5m)	2' 7" (0.8m)	5' 3" (1.6m)	

pleasure craft up to the Folly River outfall. Above this, small craft which can be portaged around obstructions can continue to use the river as far as Stamford.

Authority *Stamford to Fosdyke Bridge* Environment Agency, Anglian Region, Kingfisher House, Goldhay Way, Orton Goldhay, Peterborough PE2 5ZR ☎ 01733 371811 *Fax* 01733 231840.

Fulney Lock Keeper, Spalding ☎ 01775 723350.

Fosdyke Bridge to the Wash Port of Fosdyke Authority ☎ 01205 260365.

Bridges Fosdyke Bridge in the tidal stretch and nine bridges between Spalding and the Folly River Outfall. The headroom under the Fosdyke Bridge varies between 25ft at MLWS and less than 8ft at MHWS, draught will also fluctuate with the tides. Reference should be made to tide tables for the relevant day of an intended passage.

Towpath Fosdyke Bridge to Spalding only.

Connections River Glen, the Wash.

Navigation High water at Spalding is about 1 hour after HW Fosdyke Bridge. Spring tides flow to Spalding, the rise being about 8ft. The river sometimes dries at low tide at Spalding. There is only 2 hours flood tide at Fosdyke, after which the tide runs very hard. Vessels about to navigate the Welland should wait in Clayhole till after half-flood there.

Passage through Fulney Lock is by prior arrangement with the lock-keeper ☎ 01775 723350.

Distance table	Miles
Market Deeping Mill (derelict lock) to:	
Deeping St James (derelict lock)	1.5
Folly River Outfall (commencement of navigation)	3.5
Crowland (1 mile distant)	7.0
St Guthlac's Cross	10.0
Cowbit Sluice, entrance Coronation Channel (not navigable)	15.0
Spalding Bridge	16.0
Fulney Lock	17.0
Junction with River Glen (also called the Reservoir)	20.8
Fosdyke Bridge	23.8
The Wash	25.9

River Wey and Godalming Navigations

The first improvements to the River Wey were carried out by Sir Richard Weston between 1618 and 1620 on his own land, from Stoke Mill to Sutton Green, but in 1651 an Act was passed to improve the navigation from the Thames to Guildford. It was over 100 years before improvements were continued to Godalming by an Act of 1760. For much of the 18th century, the Wey Navigation was run by two families, the Earls of Portmore and the Langtons. Then there were various owners until, in the 1840s, the Stevens family took over the management. In 1912, William Stevens bought the navigation and in 1964 his son, Harry Stevens, gave it to the National Trust.

Although, latterly, the Godalming Navigation was also managed by the Stevens family, it remained as a separate business. It was controlled by commissioners and in 1968 it too was transferred to the National Trust.

Commercial traffic on the navigation included timber, corn, flour, sugar, bark for tanning and gunpowder. Business continued, although in reduced quantities, until the last barge owned by the Stevens family finished in 1969.

The entry to the Wey from the Thames is below Shepperton Lock and, although it is close to London, the river feels remote and peaceful. Its course runs past Wisley, with its small Norman church and the famous gardens run by the Royal Horticultural Society. Throughout the route to

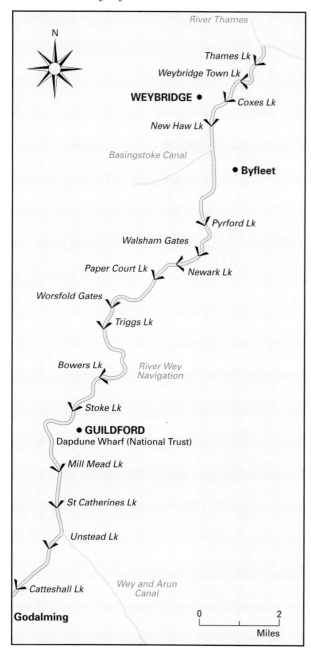

Guildford and Godalming, there are wonderful old houses and gardens to visit. Guildford itself is well worth a visit with its guildhall, cobbled high street, the Tudor Archbishop Abbott's Hospital and the castle remains. Dapdune Wharf is not to be missed as it is the office of the Wey and Godalming Navigation and has an exhibition of barge building and the history of the navigation.

As the canal continues through the hills to Godalming, you pass St Catherine's Chapel where St Catherine's Ferry used to take pilgrims across the river. This has now been replaced with a footbridge to carry the route of the Pilgrim's Way. The Tillingbourne, a tiny stream once canalised for punts to carry gunpowder, enters the Wey near Shalford, a pretty village just off the river. Godalming, at the head of the navigation, is an interesting country town with some fine old buildings dating from Tudor times. There are a number of side streams that can be explored, but in most cases they are very shallow. The whole route feels very rural and is attractive at any time of year.

Authority The National Trust, Dapdune Wharf, Wharf Road, Guildford, Surrey GU1 4RR ☎ 01483 561389.

Bridges 41.

Towpath Throughout navigation, except under Guildford High Street Bridge.

Speed limit 4mph.

Connections Basingstoke Canal, Wey and Arun Junction Canal, River Thames.

Regulations Licences for craft to navigate and/or remain on the River Wey Navigations are granted subject to the bye-laws made under the National Trust Acts of 1907-53. General information, bye-laws and regulations for the navigation can be obtained from the Navigation Officer at the National Trust address given above who will also provide details of charges.

Navigation This is a mixture of canal and river and care must be taken after periods of heavy rain as water flow and levels can alter rapidly. Always check bridge clearances carefully.

Facilities Pyrford Marina and Guildford Boathouse offer full facilities for boats including pump-out. Water supply and refuse disposal is also possible at Godalming. There are slipways at Pyrford Marina, Weybridge Marine and Stoke Lock, Guildford. Guildford can offer all services and there are plenty of pubs to choose from along the river as well as in Godalming or Weybridge.

Distance table   *Miles*
Junction with River Thames to:
Thames Lock No 16 and bridge	0.1
Old Weybridge Bridge and Lock No 15	0.8
Black Boy Bridge	1.1
Coxes Railway Bridge	1.4
Coxes Lock No 14	1.6
New Haw Bridge and Lock No 13 (White Hart Inn)	2.3
Junction with Basingstoke Canal, and towpath bridge	2.9

RIVER WEY AND GOLDAMING NAVIGATION *Maximum vessel dimensions*

From and to	Distance	Length	Beam	Draught	Headroom	Locks
River Thames to Guildford	15.3 miles (24.6km)	72' (21.9m)	13' 10" (4.2m)	3' (0.9m)	7' (2.1m)	12
Guildford to Godalming	4.2 miles (6.8km)	72' (21.9m)	13' 10" (4.2m)	2' 6" (0.8m)	6' (1.8m)	4

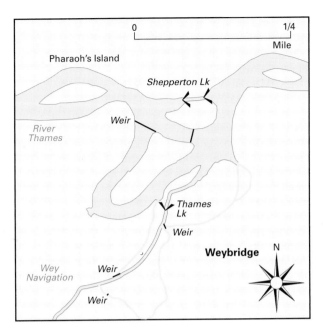

	Miles
High Bridge	8.1
Cart Bridge, Send (New Inn)	8.6
Ashburton Bridge	8.7
Worsfold Gates Lock No 8	8.9
Triggs Lock No 7 and bridge	9.6
Wareham's Bridge	9.8
Send Church Bridge	10.3
Broad Oak Bridge	11.1
Bowers Lock No 6	11.7
Bowers Bridge	11.9
Stoke Lock No 5	12.9
Stoke Bridge (Row Barge Inn)	13.4
Wood Bridge	14.2
Dapdune Railway Bridge and footbridge	14.4
Dapdune Wharf	14.6
Onslow Bridge	15.1
Guildford Wharf and footbridge	15.2
Guildford Bridge	15.3
Mill Mead Lock No 4 and bridge	15.4
Quarry Hill Footbridge	15.6
St Catherine's Footbridge	16.1
St Catherine's Lock No 3 and bridge	16.5
Shalford Railway Bridge	16.8
Broadford Bridge (Parrot Inn)	17.1
Gun's Mouth, Wey and Arun Junction Canal	17.3
Old Railway Bridge	17.5
Unstead Lock No 2	17.7
Unstead Bridge	18.1
Trowers Bridge	18.8
Catteshall Bridge and Lock No 1	19.0
Godalming Wharf	19.5
Godalming Town Bridge	19.6

	Miles
Byfleet Railway Bridge	3.0
Parvis Bridge	3.5
Murray's Bridge	4.0
Dodd's Bridge	4.3
Pyrford Bridge and Lock No 12 (Anchor Inn)	4.8
Pigeon House Bridge	5.4
Walsham Bridge and Gates (Walsham Gates Lock No 11)	5.8
Newark Lock No 10	6.5
Newark Bridge (Seven Stars Inn)	6.8
Paper Court Bridge and Lock No 9	7.3
Tanyard Bridge	7.7

One of the ornate bridges over the River Wey in Guildford.
Richard Sandland

Wey and Arun Junction Canal

'London's Lost Route to the Sea' is the name given to the waterways which connected London to Portsmouth. Opened in 1816, the route left the Thames at Weybridge then followed the River Wey and the Godalming Navigation, before turning

WEY AND ARUN JUNCTION CANAL *Maximum vessel dimensions*

From and to	*Distance*	*Length*	*Beam*	*Draught*	*Headroom*	*Locks*
Stonebridge, River Wey to Newbridge, Arun Navigation	18.5 miles (29.7km)	68' (20.7m)	11' 6" (3.5m)	3' (0.9m)	7' (2.1m)	23

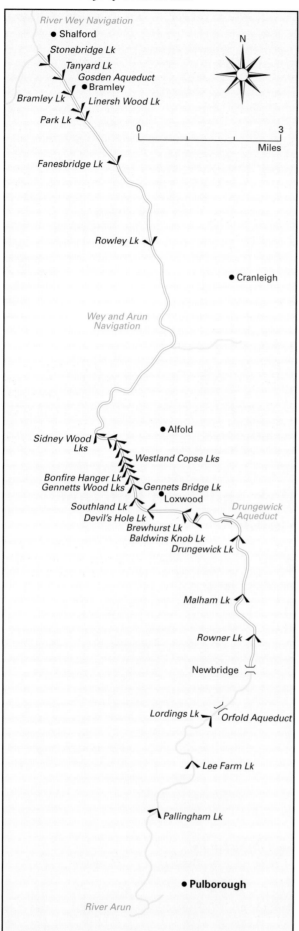

south down the Wey and Arun Junction Canal through the Arun Navigation and the River Arun to Littlehampton, or westward at Ford to Chichester Harbour and Portsmouth.

The Wey and Arun Junction Canal was promoted by the Earl of Egremont in 1810. By the time it was opened, the Napoleonic wars had ended and the traffic that would have benefited from the inland route was again quite safe to travel by sea. For a short time, in the middle of the 18th century, the canal was fairly prosperous but a combination of railway competition, water supply problems and the porous nature of the soil at the summit level saw a rapid reduction in traffic. In 1868, an Act of Abandonment was passed and by the 1870s the canal was closed.

The route of the canal passed into the ownership of numerous people and this is one of the biggest obstacles to a full restoration. Negotiations with owners can be very time-consuming but the Wey and Arun Canal Trust have made enormous progress in restoring the canal. A canal boat operates trips on the section in water near Loxwood, and the Trust organises several activities, as well as the working parties, to restore the canal. A full engineering and feasibility study has been carried out and concluded that a full restoration was feasible and would be of benefit to the local community.

Authority None.

Bridges Numerous. Several have been rebuilt and others will need to be raised or navigable culverts built to allow passage under roads.

Towpath So far 11 miles of the towpath have a public right of way. The rest of the towpath is in private ownership and permission is required to use it. Surrey and West Sussex County Councils are involved with the development of the Wey South Path, a long distance walk from Guildford to near Amberley.

Connections River Wey at Stonebridge, Arun Navigation at Newbridge.

Restoration Wey and Arun Canal Trust Ltd, formed in 1970, aims to fully restore the Wey and Arun Junction Canal and the Arun Navigation to re-establish the route from London to the Channel. To date, three locks have been reconstructed with work well advanced on other lock chambers. Towpath and bankside improvements are also under way at many locations and many bridges have been restored. The Wey and Arun Canal Trust has one of the largest voluntary labour forces working on the canals. For further information contact: Wey and Arun Canal Trust Ltd, 24 Griffiths Avenue, Lancing, West Sussex BN15 0HW ☎ 01903 753099.

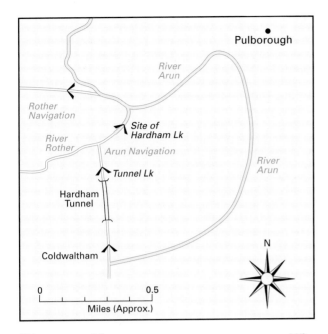

Arun Navigation

This navigation was a short canal cut to connect the River Arun to Newbridge, near Billingshurst, and avoid a large bend in the river near Pulborough and two low bridges. The canal included an aqueduct over the river, a 375-yard tunnel through Hardham Hill, a double staircase lock at Pallingham and three other locks. The last barge went along the section between Pallingham and Newbridge in 1888 and it was abandoned in 1896.

The restoration of this waterway is being carried out by the Wey and Arun Canal Trust as part of the project to re-open the route from London to the sea.

Distance table	Miles
Newbridge Wharf to:	
Orfold Aqueduct	1.3
Lordings Lock (sometimes called Orfold)	1.4
Lee Farm Lock	3.0
Pallingham Quay and Docks	4.4
Pallingham Lock (double)	4.5

Distance table	Miles
Junction with River Wey and Stonebridge to:	
Stonebridge Wharf	0.1
Stonebridge Lock No 23	0.1
Tanyard Lock No 22 and Gosden Aqueduct	0.3
Bramley Lock No 21	0.9
Linersh Wood or Wensby Lock No 20	1.2
Park Lock No 19	1.5
Fanesbridge Lock No 18	1.9
Ruin Common Wharf	3.1
Rowley Lock No 17	4.0
Elm Bridge Wharf (Cranleigh)	5.1
Bridge Wharf Compass Inn	5.9
Tickners Heath and Cobdens Wharves	8.0
Sidney Wood Lock No 16	8.8
Sidney Wood Lock No 15	10.2
Sidney Wood Lock No 14	10.4
Sidney Wood Lock No 13	10.6
Westland Copse Lock No 12	10.7
Westland Copse Lock No 11	10.8
Bonfire Hanger Lock No 10	11.0
Gennets Wood Lock No 9	11.1
Gennets Bridge Lock No 8	11.3
Southland Lock No 7	11.4
Devils Hole Lock No 6	11.8
Loxwood, Onslow Arms Inn	12.2
Brewhurst Lock No 5	12.6
Baldwins Knob Lock No 4	12.9
Drungewick Aqueduct	13.6
Drungewick Lock No 3	14.4
Malham Lock No 2	15.0
Rowner Lock No 1	16.6
Northlands Lifting Bridge	17.8
Newbridge, junction with Arun Navigation	18.5

River Wharfe

Late 19th century plans to improve the navigation of the Wharfe to Tadcaster were short-lived, although carrying continued until 1914. The river rises in the Yorkshire Dales and its upper reaches are popular with canoeists. Tadcaster is a pleasant Yorkshire town but accessibility by boat is greatly affected by the flow of freshwater down the river.

Authority An open navigation.

Bridges Four.

Towpath Throughout the navigation.

Connections River Ouse.

Navigation The river is tidal to Ulleskelf and draught will vary according to springs and neaps. Around Ulleskelf, there are clay huts (shallows) in

RIVER WHARFE Maximum vessel dimensions

From and to	Distance	Length	Beam	Draught	Headroom	Locks
Tadcaster to Ulleskelf	4 miles (6.4km)	Unlimited	Unlimited	3' 6" (1.0m)	8' (2.4m)	None
Ulleskelf to River Ouse	5.3 miles (8.5km)	Unlimited	Unlimited	5' 6" (1.6m)	Unlimited	None

the river which must be negotiated with care. It is recommended that local advice is sought before attempting this river.

Distance table   *Miles*

Tadcaster Bridge to:

Kirkby Wharf	2.5
Ulleskelf	3.9
Ryther	6.6
Nun Appleton Park	7.0
Junction with River Ouse (Yorkshire)	9.3

Wiltshire and Berkshire Canal

The construction of the Wiltshire and Berkshire Canal proceeded slowly. It was originally promoted in 1794 to link the Thames to the newly proposed Kennet and Avon and both canals were opened in 1810. There were further plans to link up with the Grand Junction Canal and the Stratford-upon-Avon Canal, but in 1813 an Act was passed to build the North Wiltshire Canal linking the Wiltshire and Berkshire to the Thames and Severn at Latton.

The canal carried coal from the Somerset coalfield to the Thames and agricultural produce, from the rich farmlands through which it passed, on the return journeys. Some passenger traffic also started but, when the Great Western Railway opened to Bristol in 1841, this traffic soon stopped. Commercial traffic finally ended on the canal in the early 1900s and the two canals were abandoned in 1914.

Support for the restoration of both the Wiltshire and Berkshire Canal and the North Wiltshire Canal has grown since the formation of the Wiltshire and Berkshire Canal Amenity Group in the late 1970s. Local authorities support the work being done by the group and a Trust has now been formed including all interested parties along the line of the canal. This will enable work to progress more quickly and a feasibility study for full restoration has recently been prepared.

Authority None.

Towpath Certain sections are usable but care should be taken to obtain permission where there is no public right of way.

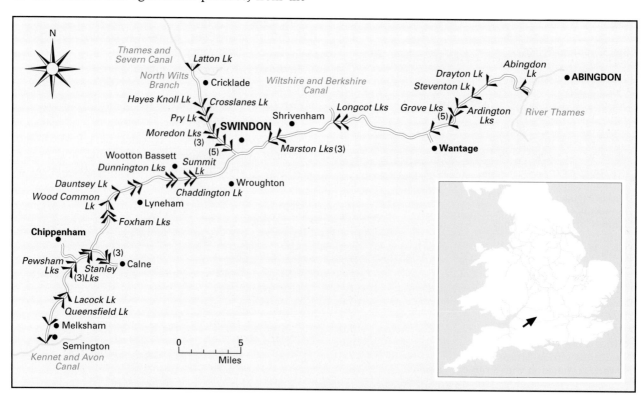

WILTSHIRE AND BERKSHIRE CANAL *Maximum vessel dimensions*

From and to	Distance	Length	Beam	Draught	Headroom	Locks
River Thames at Abingdon to Kennet and Avon Canal at Semington	52.5 miles (84.5km)	74' (22.5m)	7' 6" (2.2m)	3' 6" (1.0m)	8' (2.4m)	42

Branches	Miles	Locks
To Wantage	0.8	
To Longcot Wharf	0.5	
To Calne	3.4	3
To Chippenham	2	
To Latton (North Wiltshire Canal, junction with Thames and Severn Canal)	9	12

Restoration The Wiltshire and Berkshire Canal Amenity Group has been actively restoring accessible parts of the canal with the aim of a complete restoration by about 2020. In 1995, the first boat to cruise on the canal in 94 years was a fitting celebration of the 200th anniversary of the building of the canal. To date, several short sections are back in water and work continues on lock chambers, bridges and clearance of the channel. The group has local branches along the length of the canal and can be contacted at Mountcrest, Downend, Horsley, Stroud, Gloucestershire GL6 0PF.

Distance table

Abingdon Lock, junction with River Thames to:

	Miles
Tythe Barn Lock	0.8
Drayton Lock	2.5
Steventon Lock	4.0
Ardington Marsh Lock	5.4
Ardington Top Lock	5.8
Grove Bottom Lock	7.1
4 more locks to Grove Top Lock	8.3
Challow Wharf	9.3
Uffington Wharf	14.8
Longcot Bottom and Upper Locks	16.5
Marston Bottom Lock	21.3
Two more locks to Marston Top Lock	21.9
Swindon Wharf	24.6
Junction with North Wiltshire Canal	25.1
Summit Lock	30.3
Chaddington Lock	30.6
Dunnington Top and Bottom Locks	31.8
Seven Locks, Lock No 1	34.1
Lock No 7	34.6
Dauntsey Lock	36.4
Wood Common Lock	37.9
Foxham Upper and Lower Locks	39.1
Stanley Top and Bottom Locks	42.9
Pewsham Top, Middle and Bottom Locks	45.1
Laycock Lock	47.6
Queensfield Lock	48.0
Melksham Forest Lock	49.1
Melksham Wharf	50.6
Semington Lock and junction with Kennet and Avon Canal	52.1

Witham Navigable Drains

Witham Navigable Drains is a group of waterways lying to the north of the River Witham and south of a line from Spilsby to Dogdyke. Some are improved streams, but most are man-made cuts dug to drain the fens. In the past, these drains were used to transport agricultural produce and coal but now are only used by pleasure and fishing craft. They are still essentially drainage channels and the depth of water cannot be guaranteed so, on occasion, boats have had extended stays when the water level has dropped unexpectedly. The Lincolnshire Branch of the IWA has an annual cruise around the Drains on the Spring Bank Holiday. Contacting the Drainage Board Foreman on ☎ 01205 310099 is recommended to establish the water level and also he holds the key to the lock at Cowbridge.

Having entered the Drains at Anton's Gowt, you can head north to the Wolds or south back into Boston, but there is no exit into the tidal river at the end of Maud Foster Drain. The Maud Foster Mill, a preserved windmill, can be seen at Willoughby Road, Boston. The mill is used to grind organic flour. St Botolph's Church, familiarly known as Boston Stump, is the largest parish church in England and well worth a visit. From Boston, it is possible to cruise to New York without crossing the Atlantic.

Many of the Drains have names only known to local people but the larger ones, many of which are navigable, include:

Bell Water Drain	Lush's Drain
Castle Dyke	Maud Foster Drain
Cowbridge Drain	Medlam Drain
East Fen Catchwater Drain	New Bolingbroke Drain
Frith Bank Drain	Newham Drain

WITHAM NAVIGABLE DRAINS Maximum vessel dimensions

From and to	Distance	Length	Beam	Draught	Headroom	Locks
Anton's Gowt to Revesby Bridge	10.5 miles (16.9km)	60' (18.2m)	10' (3.0m)	3' (0.9m)	8' (2.4m)	2

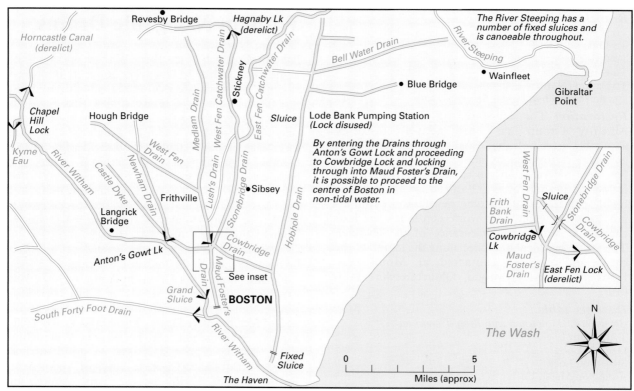

Hobhole Drain

Howbridge Drain

Junction Drain

Stonebridge Drain

West Fen Drain

West Fen Catchwater
Drain

Authority Witham Fourth Internal Drainage Board, 47 Norfolk Street, Boston, Lincolnshire ☎ 01205 310099.

Locks A craft 75ft long by 18ft beam can pass through Anton's Gowt Lock but would be unable to navigate the Drains. East Fen Lock and Hagnaby Lock are now unuseable.

Towpath Only in a few parts of the area.

Branches There are various navigable branches.

Navigation From approximately the end of September to the beginning of April, the level in all drains is lowered and craft may be trapped as this lowering of levels is carried out without warning to boatmen.

Distance table *Miles*

Frith Bank Drain

Anton's Gowt Lock and junction with Newham Drain:

Frith Bank Bridge	0.9
Junction with West Fen Drain	2.1

West Fen Drain

Cowbridge Lock Junction with Frith Bank Drain to:

Junction with Short Drain to aqueduct	0.3
Lush's Bridge and junction with Lush's Drain	0.9
Frithville, junction with Medlam Drain	2.0
Junction with Newham Drain and Howbridge Drain	5.9

Howbridge Drain

Junction with West Fen Drain and Newham Drain to:

Inn, Bunker's Hill	1.1
Hough Bridge	2.4

Miles

Newham Drain

Junction with West Fen Drain and Howbridge Drain to:

Junction with Castle Dyke	0.4
Canister Hall Bridge	1.6
Anton's Gowt, junction with Frith Bank Drain	3.5

Stonebridge Drain

Junction with Maud Foster Drain, Junction Drain and Cowbridge Lock to:

Sibsey Bridge	2.3
Junction with East Fen Catchwater Drain	4.3

West Fen Catchwater Drain

Junction with Stonebridge Drain and East Fen Catchwater Drain to:

Road Bridge, Stickney	2.3
Hagnaby Old Lock (no gates, as there is now no change of level)	4.0
Revesby Bridge (no connection here with Medlam Drain)	6.4

East Fen Catchwater Drain

Junction with West Fen Catchwater Drain and Stonebridge Drain to:

Road Bridge (Main Road, A16)	0.5
Railway Bridge	2.9
Junction with Short Drain (not navigable)	3.4
Road Bridge, Stickford	4.5
Drain continues for another 3 miles but only a small portion of this is navigable	

Cowbridge Drain (or Kelsey Drain)

The aqueduct (Stonebridge Drain passes over Cowbridge Drain) to:

Kelsey Main Road Bridge	0.9
Junction with Hobhole Drain	1.6

Junction Drain
Junction with Maud Foster and Stonebridge Drains and Cowbridge Lock to:
East Fen Lock and Junction with
Cowbridge Drain   0.3

Maud Foster Drain
Junction with Stonebridge Drain, Junction Drain, Cowbridge Lock to:
Rawson's Bridge   0.4
Main Road Bridge   1.6
Sluice Doors (no junction with River Witham)   2.6

Hobhole Drain
Hobhole New Pumping Station (no junction with River Witham) in The Haven to:
Nunn's Road Bridge   1.0
Road Bridge   1.8
Freiston Bridge   2.5
Main Road Bridge   3.1
Junction with Cowbridge Drain   3.6
Bennington Road Bridge   6.5
Old Leake Station   8.3
Lade Bank Old Lock (now a sluice) and
pumping station   9.5
Junction, Drain to Blue Bridge
(navigable for approximately 2 miles)   11.0
Junction with Bell Water Drain, and
Drain 2.25 miles long   11.8
Junction, Drain 1 mile long   12.5
Junction, Drain 1.5 miles long   13.1
Head of Drain   13.8

Bell Water Drain
Junction with Hobhole Drain to:
Hembolme Road Bridge   1.3
Railway Bridge   2.4
Thorpe Culvert, junction with Steeping River
(craft cannot pass sluice into Steeping River)   5.3

Lush's Drain
This is only navigable for approximately 1.5 miles from the junction with West Fen Catchwater Drain at Lush's Bridge

Castle Dyke
This is navigable to Thornton-le-Fen from the junction, with Newham Drain, near Anton's Gowt Lock, a distance of 2.5 miles

New Bolingbroke Drain
Junction with Medlam Drain at Glebe Farm to:
New Bolingbroke Basin   0.5

Medlam Drain
Junction with West Fen Drain to:
Hakerley Bridge   1.5
Medlam Bridge   4.4
Glebe Farm and junction with New Bolingbroke Drain
(long craft should wind here)   5.3
Revesby Bridge (no connection with the West Fen
Catchwater Drain)   6.8

Worcester and Birmingham Canal

The first Act to promote this canal was passed in 1791 and the canal was finally opened throughout in 1815 when the Bar Lock was built in Worcester Bar at Gas Street Basin. Prior to this, the Birmingham Canal Navigation had insisted on a physical barrier to preserve its water, and all cargoes had to be transhipped across the bar. This also meant that the Worcester and Birmingham Canal Company had to provide reservoirs to ensure an adequate water supply to the canal.

This is probably the most heavily locked canal in the country with the longest flight of locks at Tardebigge, 30 locks with a rise of 12ft 6ins in the top lock at about 453ft above sea level. It was by the Top Lock that Tom and Angela Rolt lived in *Cressy* for many years during the War, and the Worcester and Birmingham Canal Society have erected a plaque to commemorate the meeting between the Rolts and Robert and Ray Aickman aboard *Cressy* in August 1945. This meeting led on to another one the following year when the Inland Waterways Association was formed.

From the urban interest of Birmingham and the fascinating Cadbury World at Bournville, the canal enters King's Norton or Wast Hill Tunnel before coming out into rolling Worcestershire countryside. This is the longest of the five tunnels on the canal which were built in an attempt to keep level and not increase the number of locks. Lower Bittel reservoir was built to supply not the canal but mill owners who were not pleased at the prospect of their water supply being managed for the canal. This is now a nature reserve and well worth a visit. At Alvechurch, a new community park has been developed on the section of canal cut off by the route of the M42.

Throughout its winding route down to the cathedral city of Worcester and the River Severn, this is a lovely canal to cruise and, as part of the Avon Ring, is now very popular.

Authority British Waterways, Brome Hall Lane, Lapworth, Solihull, West Midlands B94 6LH ☎ 01564 784634.

Bridges About 88, all fixed.

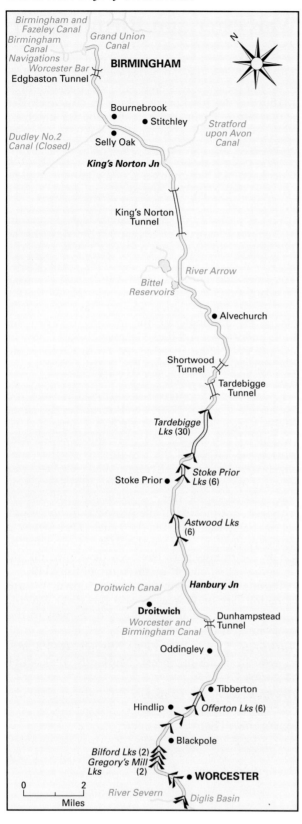

Tunnels There are five tunnels as follows:
Dunhampstead, 236yds (210m), no towpath
Tardebigge, 580yds (530m), no towpath
Shortwood, 613yds (560m), no towpath
King's Norton (Wast Hill), 2726yds (2492m), no towpath
Edgbaston, 105yds (96m), towpath.

Speed limit 4mph.

Towpath Throughout navigation except through the tunnels; good condition and easy access at most bridges.

Branches Bittell Arm, ½ mile, disused.

Connections Dudley No 2 Canal at Selly Oak; Stratford-on-Avon Canal at King's Norton Junction; Droitwich Junction Canal at Hanbury; and River Severn at Diglis Basin.

Facilities Slipways are available at Alvechurch and Droitwich. There are several boatyards and plenty of pubs and restaurants to choose from along the canal. Shops for essential stores are never far away.

Distance table *Miles*

Birmingham, Worcester Bar, junction with Birmingham Canal Navigations, Main Line to:

Birmingham, Granville Street Bridge	0.2
Birmingham, Sturge's and Bloxham's Wharves	0.5
Edgbaston Tunnel	1.1
Stop Gates, Worcester end of Edgbaston Valley	1.8
Prichett's Wharf	2.3
Metchley Park Tip	2.5
Selly Oak Wharves	
Dudley Canal Line No 2 (now closed at this end)	3.0
Birmingham Corporation, Refuse Disposal Department	5.0
Kynoch's Works and Baldwin's Wharf	5.4
King's Norton Junction with Stratford-on-Avon Canal	5.5
King's Norton Wharves	5.8
King's Norton Tunnel (also known as Wast Hill Tunnel)	6.4
Hopwood Wharf	8.8
Junction with Bittell Arm (0.5 miles long, disused)	9.5
Bittell Wharf	9.8
Lane House Wharf	10.0
Cooper's Hill Wharf	10.5
Withybed Green	10.8
Scarfield's Wharf	11.0
Grange Wharf	12.3
Shortwood Tunnel	12.3
Harris' Bridge	12.8
Tardebigge Old Wharf	13.3
Tardebigge Tunnel	13.5
Tardebigge New Wharf	14.0
London Lane, Engine House and Tardebigge Top Lock No 58	14.1
Tardebigge Flight, 30 locks Nos 58–29.	
Round Pond	15.0
Half-way House Bridge	15.3

WORCESTER AND BIRMINGHAM CANAL Maximum vessel dimensions

From and to	Distance	Length	Beam	Draught	Headroom	Locks
Worcester to Worcester Bar, Birmingham	30 miles (48.3km)	71' 6" (21.8m)	7' (2.1m)	3' (0.9m)	8' (2.4m)	58

	Miles
Bate's Wharf (between Locks Nos 29 and 28)	16.3
Then follows in a very short distance Stoke Prior	
Locks Nos 28–23	
Stoke Prior Wharf, Lock No 23	17.3
Astwood Locks Nos 22–17	19.3
Hanbury Wharf and junction with Droitwich	
Junction Canal	20.8
Hadzor Wharf	21.3
Dunhampstead Tunnel	22.3
Dunhampstead Wharf	22.5
Tibberton Wharf	24.3
Offerton Locks Nos 16–11	24.8
Tolladine Lock No 10	25.3
Blackpole Lock No 9	26.0
Blackpole Wharf	26.8
Bilford Bridge, Locks Nos 7 and 8	27.8
Worcester, Gregory's Mill and Locks Nos 6 and 5	28.0
Worcester, Lansdown and Horn Lane Bridge	28.5
Worcester, Lowesmoor Basin	29.0
Worcester, Tallow Hill, Blockhouse, Lock No 4	29.2
Worcester, Sidbury Lock No 3	29.3
Worcester, Diglis Basin, Diglis Canal Locks	
and junction with River Severn, Locks	
Nos 2 and 1	30.0

River Wye

The river rises in mid Wales about 12 miles from Cardigan Bay and flows east and south for 155 miles before joining the Severn, south of Chepstow. It was unique in Britain in that it was a free navigation for 82 miles to Hay-on-Wye, but passage depended on sufficient freshwater to enable craft to pass shoals. In 1995, the NRA and later the Environment Agency took a case to the High Court to apply for the right to impose bye-laws on the Wye and Lugg. At the time of going to press, this was still not resolved and has passed to a Public Enquiry.

This river has always been popular with canoeists from Glasbury-on-Wye to the mouth. The tidal distance is tricky to navigate, but passes through

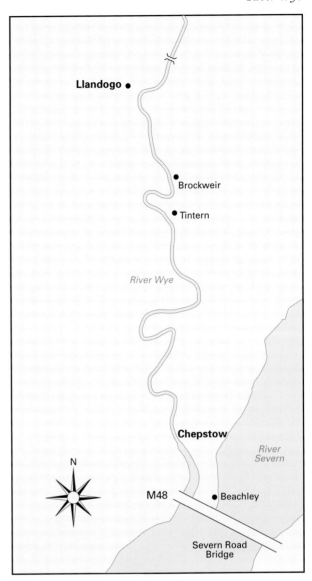

beautiful deep-wooded gorges, past the ruins of Tintern Abbey, as far as Bigsweir. For the inland waterways navigator who seeks all types of challenges, it will reward his perseverance.

Authority An open navigation. Environment Agency have applied to become the navigation authority.

Towpath Although there was a path throughout the River Wye, it is now overgrown and useless.

Navigation High water at Chepstow is 20 minutes after HW Avonmouth, HW Tintern is 40 minutes after HW Avonmouth. To travel upstream, boats should leave Chepstow 2 hours before HW.

RIVER WYE *Maximum vessel dimensions*

From and to	*Distance*	*Length*	*Beam*	*Draught*	*Headroom*	*Locks*
River Severn at Beachley Point to Bigsweir Bridge	15 miles (24.1km)	Unlimited	Unlimited	6' (1.8m)		None

Distance table   Miles

Bigsweir Bridge to:

Llandogo	1.3
Brockweir Ferry	3.1
Tintern Railway Bridge	3.9
Tintern Bridge	4.8
Lancaut Stone Quarries	9.8
Chepstow Bridge	12.0
Beachley Point, junction with River Severn Estuary	15.0

Aqueducts are always crowd pullers. *Jane Cumberlidge*

Inland Waterways of Scotland

The promotion of canals in Scotland was in some ways driven by very different needs to those in England. Trade was always a factor but, during the second half of the 18th century, enclosure of the Highlands, vast sheepwalks causing depopulation, and government concern to prevent further clan rebellions contributed to the desirability to improve access and communications in Scotland. John Knox, a Scot who had lived and prospered in England, was prepared to use his money to improve the prosperity of Scotland and slow down emigration. In the 1780s, he revived the idea of three sea-to-sea routes in Scotland. It was hoped that these would help the fishing industry as well as protect shipping from the hazardous route round Cape Wrath. Canal construction also differed from English canal schemes in that there was a degree of government funding, in some cases, the money coming from the Forfeited Estates Fund.

The Caledonian Canal was surveyed by James Watt, John Rennie and finally by Thomas Telford in 1801 and 1802. This and the Royal Military Canal in Kent were the only fully government-funded canals in Britain. By the time it was completed, the strategic benefit was no longer needed as the Napoleonic wars were over, and it never fulfilled its promise commercially as the advent of steam ships overcame the problems of travelling round the Pentland Firth. The Crinan Canal provides a short cut from the Clyde to the Hebrides, cutting off the Mull of Kintyre. The Forth and Clyde Canal was also built to connect the North Sea with the West Coast of Scotland, it ran through the coalfields of lowland Scotland and became the focal point for Scottish industry. The Union Canal, the Monkland Canal and the Glasgow, Paisley and Johnstone Canal were all barge canals in the Scottish Lowlands.

The restoration of the Forth and Clyde and Union canals and the repair and improvement work being carried out on the Caledonian Canal have secured them into the next century as a valuable recreational resource and important factors in the economy of Scotland.

There are many freshwater lochs in Scotland used for leisure and some excellent rivers for the more experienced canoeist. Before taking any type of craft on a waterway, local enquiries should be made as to right of access and navigation, as there is no automatic public right of access. Many Scottish lakes and rivers are privately owned and others are used for water supply.

Some of the largest lochs used by pleasure boats which are not covered anywhere else in the book are:

Name	Maximum Length Miles (approx)	Maximum Width Miles (approx)
Arkaig	12.0	0.8
Awe	22.8	3.3
Earn	6.5	4.6
Ericht	14.8	1.1
Katrine	8.0	0.8
Lomond	20.8	5.0
Maree	12.0	3.3
Morar	12.0	2.0
Rannoch	9.4	1.1
Shiel	17.5	1.0
Tay	14.5	1.1

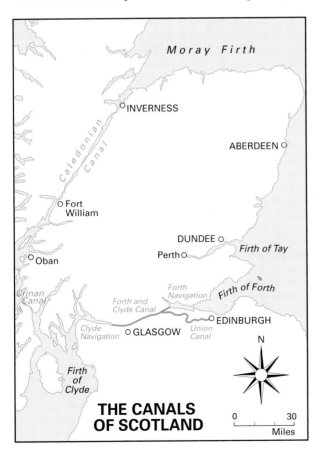

THE CANALS OF SCOTLAND

Caledonian Canal

From the mud and near quagmire at Clachnaharry to the solid granite at Corpach, the engineers and builders of the Caledonian Canal performed an amazing feat of engineering. This must be one of Thomas Telford's greatest achievements in which he was ably assisted by Matthew Davidson, John Telford and Alexander Easton. Of the 60 miles from the Beauly Firth to Loch Linnhe about one third is man-made and two-thirds are natural freshwater lochs lying along the Great Glen.

Although not the first to be asked to survey the route for a canal, Thomas Telford put forward his proposals in 1801 and 1802 and the Acts to raise money were passed in 1803 and 1804. Despite his long experience, his estimates of both the time to complete the work, 9 years, and a cost of £350,000 were far less than was finally needed. At a cost of over £910,000, the canal was opened through its whole length in 1822.

The Napoleonic wars had been a spur to the government to fund the project and it was also intended as a route to ease the passage of sailing ships, which otherwise had to go through the Pentland Firth. By the time the canal was completed, steam ships were finding the Pentland Firth less of a problem and the Napoleonic wars were over but then, as now, cruising the Great Glen for pleasure was a wonderful experience. It may not have served its defensive purpose in the early 1800s, but the canal was to prove vital during the 1914–18 war.

For present day users, the variety of scenery and experiences through the 60 miles would be difficult to repeat anywhere else. At Muirtown Basin, you are within reach of the wonderful city of Inverness, but a walk down to the sea lock at Clachnaharry is essential if you are not in a sea-going vessel. From Tomnahurich Bridge to Loch Dochfour, the canal runs parallel to the River Ness. There is a weir at the east end of Loch Dochfour, where the river leaves, which must be given a wide berth. Sailing across Loch Ness and past Urquhart Castle is to travel through monster territory and all children, young and old, keep a wary eye open, however surreptitiously.

At the southwest end of Loch Ness is Fort Augustus, a charming village with a flight of five locks leading you back into the canal. Loch Oich is the summit level, 106ft above sea level, at the southwest end of which is the Great Glen Water Park. Through the canal along Laggan Avenue takes you down into Loch Lochy from which, passing Gairlochy Locks, you enter the final canalised section before Neptune's Staircase at Banavie and the sea locks at Corpach.

Authority British Waterways, Canal Office, Seaport Marina, Muirtown Wharf, Inverness IV3 5LS ☎ 01463 233140 *Fax* 01463 710942.

Bridges Ten swing bridges, two of which are railway lines, all manned plus Kessock Bridge in the Beauly Firth.

Towpath There are good sections of towpath but it is not a continuous walk for the length of the canal. Reference to large-scale Ordnance Survey maps is recommended.

Speed limit 6mph but less if this causes a breaking wash which can damage canal banks. Always slow down when approaching locks, bridges or passing moored vessels. Minimum passage time is 14 hours but that allows no time to appreciate what you are passing through.

Navigation All locks are mechanised and manned. Do not enter locks until told to do so.

When waiting for a lock, tie up on the pontoons provided as 'hovering' outside can impede boats leaving the lock, and the outflow of water from the lock can be strong making boat handling difficult.

Extra care must be taken navigating Loch Ness which has a depth of 750ft through much of its length. Strong winds and poor visibility can make this a rough piece of open water and it should not be treated lightly. Loch Oich has red and green beacons through its narrowest section as do other navigation hazards through the canal. Red markers are on the northeast side and green on the southwest.

Charts Admiralty Chart 1791 covers the canal.

Information Details are provided by British Waterways in their *Skipper's Guide* which offers hints on using the canal and information on

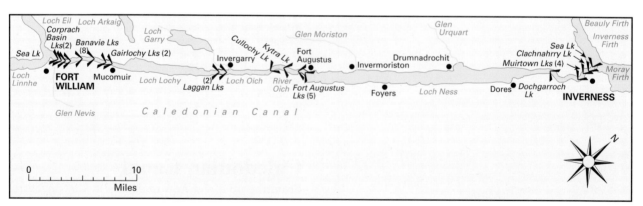

CALEDONIAN CANAL Maximum vessel dimensions

From and to	Distance	Length	Beam	Draught	Headroom	Locks
Clachnaharry to Corpach	60 miles (96.6km)	150' (45.7m)	35' (10.6m)	13' 6" (4.1m)	89' 8" (27.3m)	29

...he Stroudwater Canal at Saul Junction, only this small section has ...oats on at present but restoration is well underway. *Jane Cumberlidge*

...pposite On the Bridgewater Canal, Lymm offers a feeling of rural ...lm, despite its proximity to Manchester. *Robin Smithett*

...he old bridge at Bidford-on-Avon, on the Warwickshire River Avon. ...ian Barron

The basin at Crinan, the western end of the Crinan Canal.
Jane Cumberlidge

The Pontcysyllte aqueduct, on the Llangollen Canal. *Siân Barron*

Rural peace at Pull's Ferry on the River Wensum near Norwich.
Roy Westlake

facilities, working hours and charges. A licence is required even for a single transit of the canal.

Facilities There are three hire companies based on the Caledonian Canal, names and addresses are listed in the section at the beginning of the book. British Waterways have been improving mooring and overnight facilities along the canal and full details can be obtained from the Canal Office. Temple Pier on Loch Ness is a private jetty and should not be used. Slipways are available at Muirtown Wharf, Caley Marina, Tomnahurich Bridge and the Great Glen Water Park, Loch Oich.

The sea lock at Corpach, the western end of the Caledonian Canal. *Jane Cumberlidge*

The delightful split bridge at Moy on the Caledonian Canal. The bridgekeeper has to row across to the far shore to open and close the bridge. *Jane Cumberlidge*

Distance table   *Miles*
From Sea Lock No 1 to:

Clachnaharry Lock No 2	0.2
Muirtown Locks Nos 3–6 (marina)	0.8
Tomnahurich Bridge	1.8
Dochgarroch Lock No 7 (marina)	6.0
Bona Ferry	7.6
Dores Bay	9.7
Urquhart Castle	14.4
Inverfarigaig	18.0
Foyers	19.8
Invermoriston	24.9
Fort Augustus Locks Nos 8–12	31.0
Kytra Lock No 13	33.0
Cullochy Lock No 14	34.8
Invergarry Castle	37.7
Well of Seven Heads Monument	39.1
Great Glen Water Park	39.7
Laggan Swing Bridge	39.8
Laggan Locks Nos 15 and 16 (marina)	41.5
Letterfinlay	46.0
Invergloy	47.8
Achnacarry	49.9
Gairlochy Locks Nos 17 and 18	51.8
Moy Bridge	53.3
Neptune's Staircase, Banavie Locks Nos 19–26	58.4
Corpach Basin Locks Nos 27 and 28	59.6
Corpach (Sea Lock) No 29	60.0

River Clyde

The River Clyde is a very busy commercial port and is not really a pleasure ground for small boats. All small craft wishing to navigate east of Clydeport Container Terminal, a little to the east of Greenock, must obtain a permit from Clyde Port Authority. Dumbarton, on the north side of the river, lies at the mouth of the River Leven with Dumbarton Castle on the east shore. This river tends to silt up and great care must be taken if entering. Fresh water from Loch Lomond is now controlled by a barrage at Balloch.

Redevelopment of Glasgow docks and waterfront may make this an interesting destination in time, particularly once the restoration of the Forth and Clyde Canal is completed.

Authority Clyde Port Operations Ltd, 16 Robertson Street, Glasgow G2 8DS ☎ 0141 221 8733 *Fax* 0141 248 3167.

Bridges Three.

Towpath None.

Navigation Draught from Port of Glasgow to Cambuslang is only 3ft HWS. The range of the tide at Glasgow Docks is 12ft.

Distance table   *Miles*
Cambuslang to:

Rutherglen Bridge	5.5
Glasgow Bridge	7.3
Whiteinch	11.0
Erskine Bridge	18.5
Bowling, junction with Forth and Clyde Canal	19.3
Junction with River Leven (not usually navigable)	21.5
Dumbarton	21.8
Greenock	29.5

Junction with River Clyde to:

Dumbarton Bridge	1.1
Renton (Spring tides usually flow to within ½ mile of Renton)	3.8
Bonhill Bridge	5.8
Jamestown Bridge	6.8
Balloch Bridge	7.3
Balloch Pier	7.8

Crinan Canal

Government interest and private money, led by the Duke of Argyll, saw the plans for the Crinan Canal finally brought into being by 1809. The canal cuts through the neck of the Kintyre peninsula thus avoiding the difficult passage round the Mull of Kintyre and providing access to the Western Isles, reducing the trip by about 80 miles. Its original purpose was to promote economic activity in the islands and the passage of 'Clyde puffers', small cargo ships, was very frequent until earlier this century. It is still possible to see *VIC 32*, well known as the *Vital Spark* from the Para Handy series on television, in the basin at Crinan or on the Caledonian Canal.

A combination of hard whinstone and peat bog caused problems during construction of the canal and, although John Rennie was taken on as engineer, it was eventually completed by Thomas Telford once the canal had been taken into the control of the Commissioners of the Caledonian Canal. The advent of steam engines and larger vessels reduced the dangers associated with the Mull of Kintyre, but the canal still offers a welcome short cut and is much used by yachts and pleasure craft today.

Water supply has always been a problem as the summit pound, 68ft above sea level, is only 4 miles long and is supplied by freshwater lochs and reservoirs in the hills south of the canal. On average, it will require 65,000 gallons of water for a boat to traverse the canal so always lock through with other boats if possible. The views all along the canal are wonderful and particularly breathtaking as you come into Crinan Basin and look out towards the islands.

RIVER CLYDE Maximum Vessel Dimensions

From and to	Distance	Length	Beam	Draught	Headroom	Locks
Cambuslang to Greenock	29.5 miles (47.5km)	Unlimited	Unlimited	21' (6.4m) LWS	Unlimited	None

CRINAN CANAL Maximum vessel dimensions

From and to	Distance	Length	Beam	Draught	Headroom	Locks
Ardrishaig to Crinan	9 miles (14.5km)	88' (26.8m)	20' (6.1m)	9' 6" (2.9m)	95' (28.9m)	15

The sea lock at Crinan. *Jane Cumberlidge*

There are now many long-term moorings for yachts on the canal and a new marina has been developed in Bellanoch Basin. Transit moorings are not available here but many new pontoons have been put in for that purpose. Although less commercial traffic uses the canal now, it can be very busy, especially during the Tobermory and West Highland Yacht Races in July and early August. At all times, care must be taken when navigating the canal as quite strong winds can blow up and there can also be a strong flow of current.

Authority Canal Manager, British Waterways, Canal Office, Pier Square, Ardrishaig, Argyll PA30 8DZ ☎ 01546 603210 *Fax* 01546 603941.

Bridges Six opening bridges. Dunadry Bridge is unusual as it is a rolling bridge.

Towpath This is on the north side of the canal and is very good throughout. It is possible to cycle along it but a BW licence is required.

Speed limit 4mph (the passage can be made in 5 to 6 hours, but it is really too lovely to hurry through).

Information Details are provided by British Waterways in their *Skipper's Guide* which offers hints on using the canal and information on facilities, working hours and charges. A licence is required even for a single transit of the canal.

Navigation Sea-going craft draw about 4ins more in freshwater and this should be borne in mind when using the canal.

Locks Sea locks at Ardrishaig and Crinan and Lock 14 are operated by keepers as are the bridges. All the other locks are operated by boat crews.

Facilities Most facilities for boats are available at Ardrishaig or Crinan. There are a few pubs and small shops along the canal.

Distance table	*Miles*
Ardrishaig Pier and Lock No 2 to:	
Lochgilphead	2.3
Loch No 5	3.8
Lock No 6	3.9
Lock No 7	4.0
Lock No 8 (summit)	4.1
Dunadry Rolling Bridge	5.5
Lock No 13	6.0
Bellanoch Marina	7.3
Crinan, Lock No 14	8.8
Lock No 15 Sea Lock	9.0

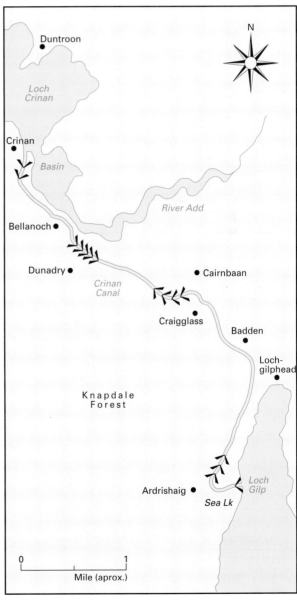

Edinburgh and Glasgow Union Canal

Coal for Edinburgh was the major impetus to the building of the Edinburgh and Glasgow Union Canal and plans were put forward in 1791, but the wars with France delayed the project until 1813 when the route was surveyed again. Coal could be brought from Lanarkshire via the Forth and Clyde Canal as far as Falkirk then onto the Union Canal, opened in 1822, into Port Hopetoun in Edinburgh. This was a wide-beam canal as were some of the other smaller canals in the Scottish Lowlands rather than a ship canal like the Forth and Clyde, Caledonian and Crinan.

The 32 miles of the Union Canal are level with three superb aqueducts to take it over the rivers Almond and Avon and the Water of Leith. Near Falkirk a 696-yard long tunnel was built to avoid the grounds af Callendar House as the owner did not want to see the canal from his house. At the junction with the Forth and Clyde Canal at Falkirk, there was a flight of 11 locks raising boats 112ft. The locks and the area of Port Downie in Falkirk have been filled in, but the plans to restore the canal which have been put to the Millenium Commission include a Ferris Wheel lift to replace the locks.

The canal was abandoned in 1965 but has remained mostly intact and, apart from silting in places, quite a reasonable distance is still accessible to small boats. Some unnavigable culverts have been built to carry new road schemes and there has been infilling and building in Wester Hailes to the west of Edinburgh. It passes through pleasing countryside and offers some delightful towpath walks with many places of interest along the way.

The Linlithgow Union Canal Society's trip boat *Victoria* glides gently past Linlithgow Palace and St Michael's Kirk.
Guthrie Hutton

British Waterways have made considerable efforts to improve access to the canal and there are now four well-developed slipways with parking, though slipping is possible at other sites as well. About 15 miles of canal are now navigable in three sections. For full details contact BW at Glasgow.

The canal is to be fully restored as part of the Millennium Link project which includes the Forth and Clyde Canal. Boats will be able to pass between the two canals on an enormous wheel boat lift which will be at the end of an aqueduct on the canal. This has been called the Antonine Wheel, as it is sited virtually on top of the Antonine Wall, and will be the centre of a business and leisure area around the

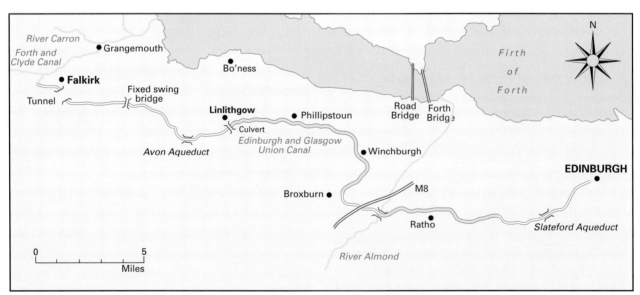

EDINBURGH AND GLASGOW UNION CANAL *Maximum vessel dimensions*

From and to	Distance	Length	Beam	Draught	Headroom	Locks
Edinburgh to Falkirk	31.5 miles (50.7km)	66' (20.1m)	11' 3" (3.4m)	4' (1.2m)	5' (1.5m)	None

canal. A 30ft deep lock and then the 80ft wheel will lower boats from the Union Canal to the Forth and Clyde Canal. This is unlikely to be completed until the spring of 2001 when water-borne traffic will again be able to pass from Edinburgh to Glasgow.

Authority British Waterways, Canal House, Applecross Street, Glasgow G4 9SP ☎ 0141 332 6936.

Bridges Numerous. Lowest bridge, Redhall with 5ft headroom.

Towpath Throughout the navigation with an obstruction at M8.

Tunnels Falkirk, length 696yds, headroom 11ft 9ins with a towpath.

Speed limit 4mph for motor boats.

Restoration Work is being carried out to extend the navigable lengths of canal. The full restoration of this canal is part of a proposal before the Millenium Commisson put forward by a consortium, including British Waterways, Scottish Enterprise, the European Partnership and local authorities, which would re-open the cross-Scotland canal link with the Union canal and the Forth and Clyde Canal.

Distance table	Miles
Port Hopetoun to:	
Slateford Aqueduct	2.3
Ratho	8.0
Lins Mill Aqueduct (over River Almond)	10.3
M8	11.4
Broxburn	12.5
Winchburgh	15.3
Phillipstoun	17.3
Linlithgow	23.5
Avon Aqueduct	23.5
Falkirk Tunnel entrance	29.5
Falkirk Tunnel exit	29.9
Falkirk	30.0
Port Maxwell	32.0

Forth and Clyde Canal

The Forth and Clyde canal was a compromise between a large ship canal promoted by the business interests of Edinburgh who wanted access to the west coast and a small canal which Glasgow businessmen suggested on the grounds of cost and to protect their trade. The final proposal was for a large canal from Grangemouth to Bowling with a branch canal into Glasgow. With many sea-going vessels using the canal, all the bridges were opening to allow masted ships through passage. Much of the central part of the canal follows the Antonine Wall with many sites of historical and archeological interest along the way.

The canal was built from east to west with water being let into the first section to Kirkintilloch in 1773. The first ship to pass through the whole length of the canal was the sloop *Agnes* in August 1790. Although primarily a cargo route, passenger services started in the 1780s taking people from Port Dundas, in Glasgow, to Lock 16 near Falkirk from where they could travel onward by coach. Once the Union Canal was open and connected to the Forth and Clyde Canal in 1822, it was possible for passengers to travel from Port Dundas in Glasgow to Port Hopetoun in Edinburgh by canal.

Timber, coal, sand and clay were major cargoes on the canal, while along the banks industries grew up with shipbuilding, iron works, engineering yards, distilleries and foundries. The advent of steam propulsion brought first paddle steamers and then 'puffers', so called because of the noise they made. These were boats with a steam engine driving a screw for propulsion, but the name long outlived the first design of ship and also the steam engine.

Cargo carrying on the canal came under severe competition from the railways but continued until the First World War, while passenger boats were still busy on parts of the canal until 1939. The canal was abandoned by Act of Parliament on 1 January 1963 and during the 1960s stretches were filled in, while other parts have become unnavigable because of low level and culverted road bridges.

The full restoration of the canal has been agreed with funding from the Millennium Commission, the European Regional Development Fund, Scottish Enterprise, local authorities and private business. The canal will again be linked to the Edinburgh Union Canal with a unique wheel boat lift system which will move the boats from one level to the other, replacing the original 11 locks which have long been filled in. Coast-to-coast traffic is expected to begin in the spring 2000.

Authority British Waterways, Canal House, Applecross Street, Glasgow G4 9SP ☎ 0141 332 6936.

Branch 2½ miles from Stockingfield to Port Dundas (Spiers Wharf).

Summit 156ft above sea level between Wyndford and Stockingfield.

Bridges Numerous, originally many bascule bridges now many fixed bridges.

Aqueducts There are many aqueducts and those over the River Kelvin and the Luggie are scheduled as ancient monuments.

Towpath The towpath offers a cross-Scotland route for walkers and cyclists and includes SSSIs at many locations.

FORTH AND CLYDE CANAL Maximum vessel dimensions

From and to	Distance	Length	Beam	Draught	Headroom	Locks
Bowling to the River Carron	35 miles (56.3km)	66' (20.1m)	19' 8" (6.0m)	6' (1.8m)	10' (3.0m)	39

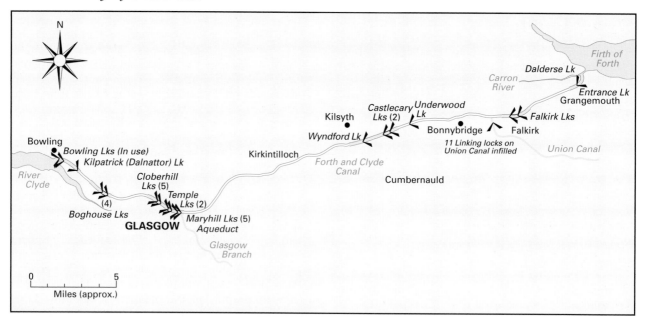

The Kelvin Aqueduct carries the Forth and Clyde Canal over the River Kelvin at Maryhill in Glasgow. *Guthrie Hutton*

Restoration Sections of the canal have been restored to navigation with public slips for launching boats. A proposal for full restoration of the canal to include a boat-lift on the 'ferris-wheel' principle to replace the lock flight filled in at Falkirk was put forward to the Millenium Commission. Details of access and the present situation for navigation can be obtained by contacting BW at the Glasgow office or the Forth and Clyde Canal Society.

Distance table

Bowling Sea Lock No 40 to:	Miles
Old Sea Lock No 39	0.0
Bowling Lock No 38	0.2
Dalnotter Lock No 37	1.2
Dalmuir Culvert	2.8
Kilbowie Road Culvert	3.8
Boghouse Lower Lock No 36 (infilled)	5.1
Garscadden Footbridge Lock No 35	5.3
Boulevard Bridge (infilled)	5.9
Cloberhill Lock No 29	8.5
Temple Lock No 27	7.8
Maryhill Lock No 25	8.7
Stockingfield Junction, Glasgow Branch	9.4
Lambhill Bridge (19)	10.4
Townhead Culvert (13)	16.2
Craigmarloch Bridge (9)	22.4
Wyndford Lock No 20	25.0
Castlecary Lock No 19	26.1
Underwood Lock No 17	27.0
Lock No 16	31.3
Camelon Bridge (infilled)	31.7
Merers Bridge Lock No 8	32.1
Mungalend Lock No 5	32.9
Railway Bridge	33.8
Grangemouth, Old Carron Entrance (infilled)	35.2

River Forth

The Firth of Forth starts at the wide mouth between the Isle of May and Bass Rock. Approaching the two Forth bridges, there are some interesting little islands, Inchkeith, Inchcolm, Inchmickery and Cramond Island, close to the west of Edinburgh. Since its decline as a naval base and a major commercial port, more facilities for pleasure boats have been created with useful facilities for cruising yachts.

A boat can travel upriver towards Stirling, but past Alloa the river becomes very twisting with unmarked shallows so local knowledge must be gained before attempting this.

Authority Forth Ports plc, Tower Place, Leith, Edinburgh EH6 7DB ☎ 0131 554 2703 *Fax* 0131 553 7462.

Bridges Forth Railway Bridge, 142ft; Forth Road Bridge, 145ft; Kincardine Road Bridge, fixed since February 1988, 30ft clearance at MHWS.

Towpath None.

Connections Carron River which leads to the Forth and Clyde Canal at Grangemouth. The entry lock to the canal has now been filled in.

Navigation High water at Stirling 1 hour 45 minutes after HW Leith.

Charts Admiralty Charts 734, 735, 736, 737 and 738 cover the estuary and river to Stirling. Imray Chart C27 covers the area to Grangemouth.

Distance table	Miles
Stirling to:	
Abbey Ford	0.5
Sow Ford	4.8
River Bannock Junction	6.8
Cambus	9.0
Alloa	12.8
River Carron Junction	18.5
(Forth and Clyde Canal runs from 1 mile up the Carron River)	
River Avon Junction	20.5
Port Edgar Marina	29.3
Forth Road Bridge	29.5
South Queensferry	29.7
Forth Railway Bridge	30.1
Granton	37.5
Newhaven	38.6
Portobello	42.6
Isle of May	62.0

River Tay

The River Tay is probably best known as a salmon river and fishing is always a popular activity here. River levels are greatly affected by freshwater flowing from the mountains, and experienced canoeists use the upper reaches for white-water canoeing. At the wide estuary mouth, the Royal Tay Yacht Club, based at Broughty Ferry, has moorings which may be available to visitors. Sailing is a popular sport in the wider stretches of the river. The approach to Perth is narrow and winding with many sand banks and this section has a buoyed channel.

There is an enclosed dock at Dundee. The lock works for 2 hours before high water and the harbour office needs 4-hours notice if a small boat wishes to enter. It is not compulsory for a small boat to take a pilot, but information is available from the Dundee Harbour Office or Port Control on VHF Ch 16 and 12.

Authority *Buddon Ness to Balmerino* The Port of Dundee Ltd, Harbour Chambers, Dock Street, Dundee DD1 3HW ☎ 01382 224121 *Fax* 01382 200834.

Balmerino to Perth Perth Harbour Office, Friarton Road, Perth PH2 8BH ☎ 01738 624056.

Bridges Tay Railway Bridge, 71ft; Tay Road Bridge, 71ft.

Towpath None.

Navigation The entrance to the River Tay is marked by a light buoy and the channel is buoyed with ample width to deal with the largest vessels using the port. The minimum depth of water is 18ft.

Connections River Earn, 2 miles west of Newburgh, navigable for light craft for 6 miles to Bridge of Earn.

RIVER FORTH Maximum vessel dimensions

From and to	Distance	Length	Beam	Draught	Headroom	Locks
Isle of May to Stirling	62 miles (99.8km)	Unlimited	Unlimited	11' (3.3m) HWS	30' (9.1m)	None

RIVER TAY Maximum vessel dimensions

From and to	Distance	Length	Beam	Draught	Headroom	Locks
Buddon Ness to Perth	31 miles (49.9km)	Unlimited	Unlimited	11' (3.3m) HWS	71' (21.6m)	None

Inland Waterways of Wales

Although today there may appear to be few canals and navigable waterways in Wales, during the early part of the 19th century a combination of canals and tramroads flourished through South Wales. Two of our most popular holiday routes are in Wales, the Llangollen and the Monmouthshire and Brecon passing through breathtaking countryside to offer a peaceful break from the rush of the late 20th century.

In South Wales, the Glamorganshire Canal and the Aberdare Canal reached deep into the valleys to serve the many mines, ironworks and lime quarries and it would have been possible to travel from Merthyr Tydfil to Cardiff by water. The canal was open and working before the end of the 18th century, although in the later 1800s it suffered badly from railway competition.

Around the Swansea Valley, many more miles of canal were built which aided the development of industry in this area. There have been interesting proposals to try to restore these waterways and provide a ring route in the area. Further west, more canals were built to link into the Bury Estuary, but little remains of these waterways today.

In the northeast of Wales, the canals were part of the Ellesmere Canal, eventually coming into the Shropshire Union group. Fortunately, because of its

use as a water supply, the Llangollen Canal was not closed when many miles of the Shropshire Union were abandoned in 1944. Now, of course, great progress has been made to restore the Montgomery Canal, offering the prospect of a route into the heart of mid-Wales by the beginning of the 21st century.

Llangollen Canal

The Llangollen Canal probably carries more traffic in the late 1990s than it ever did in its prime as a commercial waterway. The final section of the canal from Pontcysyllte to Llantysilio was built as a feeder for water from the upper reaches of the River Dee, but is the most picturesque section and probably the objective of those who visit the canal. This supplied the whole canal, and much of the main line of the Shropshire Union of which it is a branch, and was the reason it was not abandoned in 1944 when 178 miles of the Shropshire Union network was closed.

The history of the construction of the Ellesmere Canal, as it was originally called, was extremely convoluted but, despite the unpromising potential for trade and the formidable engineering required to construct it, the whole project went ahead in the 1790s with the section to Llantysilio being opened in 1808. William Jessop was the original engineer for

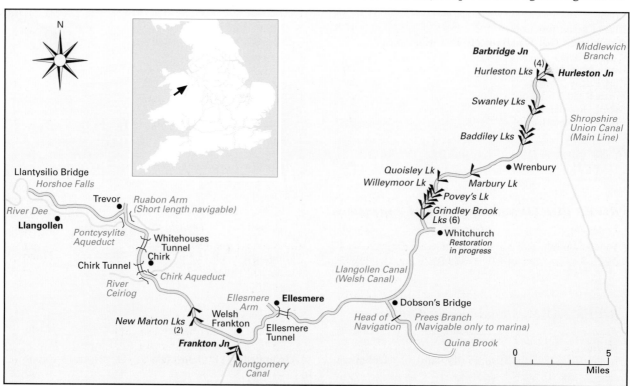

LLANGOLLEN CANAL *Maximum vessel dimensions*

From and to	Distance	Length	Beam	Draught	Headroom	Locks
Hurleston Junction to Llantysilio	46 miles (74km)	70' (21.3m)	6' 10" (2.0m)	2' 3" (0.6m)[1]	7' 6" (2.2m)	21

1. Above Pontcysllte draught is 2'

the canal and later Thomas Telford worked with him and was responsible for the aqueducts at Chirk and Pontcysyllte. Matthew Davidson was the superintendent and the iron master William Hazeldine, nicknamed 'Merlin' Hazeldine by Telford, constructed the massive iron troughs for the aqueducts. The canal also travels through three tunnels; one at Ellesmere, one at Whitehouses and the third at Chirk.

The Llangollen Canal is unusual in that there is a noticeable current on it. The journey from Hurlestone Junction to Horseshoe Falls will take longer than the return as 96 million gallons of water pass down the canal each week. This must be taken into account when navigating the canal as the effect will be more pronounced in narrower and shallower sections such as through the Chirk Tunnel. The Llangollen Canal is also well known for its many lifting bridges. These are very attractive but must be navigated carefully as they do not open to the vertical so it is all too easy to make contact with the cabin roof.

More seasoned canal users tend to visit the Llangollen Canal in spring and autumn, as it can become very congested in the main summer period. If you don't mind chilly weather, the autumn colours on this peaceful canal can be absolutely magical.

Authority British Waterways, Canal Office, Birch Road, Ellesmere, Shropshire SY12 9AA ☎ 01691 622549.

Bridges Numerous, many of them lifting.

Towpath Sections are good but between Bridge 63, near Tetchill, and Bridge 39, below Whixall Moss, there is no access.

Tunnels Ellesmere, 87yds, towpath; Whitehouses, 191yds, towpath; Chirk, 459yds, towpath. No passing in the tunnels.

Aqueducts Pontcysyllte and Chirk. Boats cannot pass on the aqueducts.

Speed limit 4mph but as it is a very shallow canal craft must frequently travel much slower to prevent damage to banks, moored craft and other canal users.

Connections Montgomery Canal at Frankton and the Shropshire Union Canal at Hurleston Junction.

Restoration Work is under way on the Whitchurch Branch from the main canal to Chemistry Bridge with plans to extend to Sherry Mill Hill.

Facilities This is a very popular cruising waterway and is well supplied with pubs, restaurants, shops and boating facilities. Slipways are available at Whixall and Whittington.

Distance table

	Miles
Hurleston Junction with Shropshire Union, to:	
Hurleston Locks Nos 1–4	0.3
Swanley, Locks Nos 5 and 6	2.3
Baddiley, Locks Nos 7–9	4.4
Wrenbury	6.3
Marbury Lock No 10	8.3
Steer Bridge	8.9
Quoisley Lock No 11	9.9
Willeymoor Lock No 12	10.9
Povey's Lock No 13	11.3
Grindley Brook, Lower Lock Nos 14–16	12.3
Grindley Brook, Upper Lock Nos 17–19 (staircase)	12.5
New Mill	13.3
Junction with Whitchurch Branch (restoration in progress)	13.4
Wrexham Road	13.7
Tilstock	16.3
Platt Lane	17.2
Whixall Moss Roving Bridge, junction with Prees Branch	19.0
Bettisfield	20.9
Hampton Bank	21.9
Little Mill	23.6
Junction with Ellesmere Branch 0.25 mile, Ellesmere Depot and Yard	25.8
Tetchill	27.1
Frankton, top of Frankton Locks and junction with Montgomery Canal	29.0
Maestermyn	30.3
Hindford	31.5
New Marton Bottom Lock No 1	32.4
New Marton Top Lock No 2	32.7
St Martin's Moor	33.8
Rhoswiel	35.0
Gledrid	35.3
Chirk Bank	35.8
Chirk Aqueduct	36.1
Chirk, north end of Chirk Tunnel	36.3
Black Park	37.3
Whitehouses Tunnel	37.8
Irish Bridge	38.6
Fron	39.0
Pontcysyllte Aqueduct (southern side)	39.4
Short Arm (remainder of closed Ruabon Branch)	40.0
Plas Isaf	41.6
Trevor	42.6
Llangollen	44.5
Last winding hole (except for very small craft)	44.6
Pentrefelin	45.4
Llantysilio Bridge	46.0
Horseshoe Falls	46.3

Prees Branch

At Quina Brook, there were lime kilns to produce burnt lime for the local farming community but now the unrestored 2½ miles are a nature reserve. The marina is in the old clay pit from which puddle clay was extracted to line the canal.

Locks None.

Distance table   *Miles*
Whixall Moss Roving Bridge, junction with Ellesmere Canal to:
Stark's Lift Bridge   0.5
Whixall Marina (limit of navigation)   1.6
Quina Brook   3.8

Monmouthshire and Brecon Canal

This is really two canals, the Brecon and Abergavenny and the Monmouthshire. The part which is now navigable is mostly the Brecon and Abergavenny and is almost totally within the boundary of the Brecon Beacons National Park. You may not experience the drama of long lock flights or sweeping aqueducts high above a valley as on the other Welsh canal but, for beauty of the countryside and tranquillity, it is unsurpassed.

A new basin next to a theatre has now been built in Brecon which provides a fitting terminus for this lovely waterway. Its water supply comes from the River Usk and, once you have locked down at Brynich, you are into a quiet pound as the canal winds along a contour of the Brecon Beacons looking down into the valley of the Usk. After passing through the Ashford Tunnel, it isn't far before you reach the five locks at Llangynidr and then you are into a winding, 23-mile lock-free stretch down into Monmouthshire. Although it was called the Brecon and Abergavenny Canal, the route is at least a mile from the town of Abergavenny and quite a long pull uphill if you have walked down to the town.

Despite its present calm and rural atmosphere, the canal was built to transport coal, lime, iron and iron ore as well as agricultural products. An extensive network of tramroads was built to supply the canal and their routes can still be discerned today coming down to the wharves at Llanfoist and Llangattock, where you can also see lime kilns.

Authority *Brecon to immediatley south of Solomon's Bridge, Sebastopol, Bridge 47* British Waterways, The Wharf, Govilon, Abergavenny, Monmouthshire NP7 9NY ☎ 01873 830328.

Sebastopol to Newport and Crumlin Branch Local authorities and others.

South of Sebastopol The owners of the canal are obliged to allow passage of water for industrial use in the southern area of the canal. British Waterways still own several bridges south of Sebastopol.

Bridges Numerous. Several lift bridges, one electrically operated using British Waterways toilet key.

Towpath There is a very good towpath throughout the navigable length of the canal but cycling is not permitted. The rest of the canal, after Five Locks in Cwmbran, is accessible in parts. In the Crumlin Arm, there is an information centre and amenity park at the Fourteen Locks but there are no plans to restore these locks or this section of the canal to navigation at present.

Tunnels Ashford, 375yds, height 8ft 4ins, width 10ft 9ins; Cwmbran, 87yds.

Speed limit Notionally 4mph but the canal is very shallow and slower speeds will frequently be needed.

Restoration South of the Five Locks Malpas Lock No 29 and Gwastad Lock No 30 have been put into working order but are isolated at present.

Facilities There are a number of places where trailed boats can be put into the water. The new basin at Brecon offers a delightful terminus, and facilities for boaters are now available at a number of locations along the canal. A new canalside park and visitor centre has recently been opened at Goytre Wharf.

Distance table   *Miles*
Brecon to:
Brynich Bridge   1.5
Brynich Lock No 1   2.1
Aqueduct over River Usk   2.3
Ty-newydd Bridge No 2   3.2
Cambrian Cruisers Marina   3.3
Storehouse Bridge   3.5
Llanfrynach Bridge   3.8
Pencelli Bridge   4.7
Cross Oak Drawbridge   6.0
Talybont   6.8
White Hart Bridge (Talybont-on-Usk)   7.1
Ashford Tunnel   8.0
Llandetty Bridge   8.7
Workhouse Bridge   9.5
Langynidr Lock No 5   9.8
(followed by Locks 4 to 2) Aqueduct   10.2
Llangynidr Lock No 1   10.4
Winding Point   10.8
Dwffrant Bridge   12.5
Llwncelyn Bridge   13.7
Ffawyddog Bridge   15.0
Llangattock Quay (for Crickhowell 1 mile)   15.3
Winding Point   18.4
Gilwern Aqueduct   18.7
Llanwenarth Drawbridge   20.0
Govilon Yard Bridge 97, BW Office   20.8
Llanfoist, Incline Bridge (Abergavenny 1 mile)   21.8
Llanellen Bridge   23.8
Twynglas Bridge   24.3
Winding Point   24.4
Llanover Bridge   25.8

MONMOUTHSHIRE AND BRECON CANAL Maximum vessel dimensions

From and to	Distance	Length	Beam	Draught	Headroom	Locks
Brecon to Cwmbran Tunnel	35 miles (56.3km)	50' (15.2m)	8' 6" (2.5m)	2' 6" (0.7m)	5' 6" (1.6m)	6

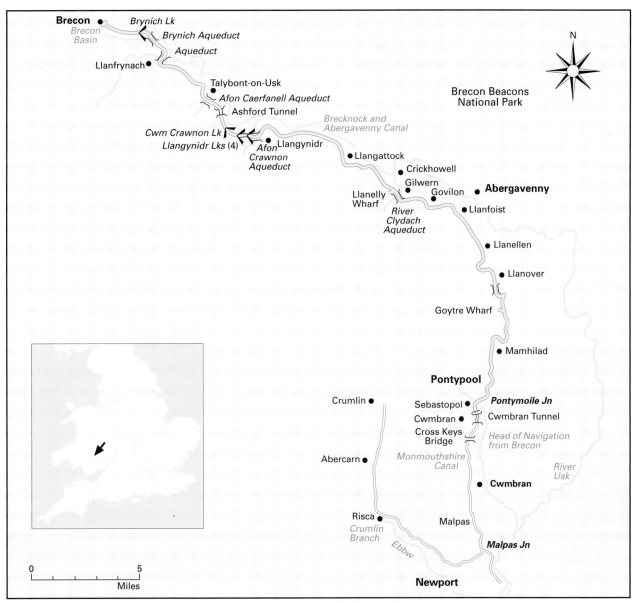

	Miles
Winding Point	27.3
Parc-y-brain Bridge	28.4
Keepers Bridge No 59	31.2
Typoeth Bridge No 56	32.4
Pontymoyle, junction with Monmouthshire Canal	33.3
Crown Bridge	34.3
Pontrhydyyn Wharf	34.5
Cwmbran Tunnel	35.0
Pontnewydd Locks Nos 1–5 (end of navigable section)	35.5
Cwmbran Locks Nos 6–15	36.5
Cwmbran Siding	36.8
Oakfield Locks Nos 16 and 17	37.5
Tycoch Locks Nos 18–27	38.5
Tynyffynon Lock No 28	39.3
Malpas Wharf	40.3
Malpas Lock No 29 (restored)	40.5
Malpas Junction, junction with Crumlin Branch (abandoned)	40.8
Gwastad Lock No 30 (restored)	40.8
Crindau Bridge	41.0
Tunnel Wharf	41.3

	Miles
Newport Corporation Wharf	42.0
Mill Street Lock No 31	42.1
Newport, Llanarth Street	42.4

Montgomery Canal

The waterway we think of today as the Montgomery Canal was built in three sections and was three canals. From Frankton Junction to Llanymynech was a branch of the Ellesmere Canal, the Montgomery Canal Eastern Section ran from Llanymynech to Garthmyl and the final section to Newtown, which wasn't completed until 1821, was the Western Branch. The section from Arddleen to Newtown runs almost parallel to the River Severn, but it never joins it although water from the Severn comes into the Western Branch via the Penarth feeder just east of Newtown.

After a serious breach in 1936, reportedly started by a water vole, the canal was closed and many low

265

level road crossings have made restoration a protracted and expensive problem. Undeterred, the Inland Waterways Association and the Shropshire Union Canal Society started the massive task in the late 1960s and work and campaigning have continued ever since. Sections of the canal are now in water and open to navigation. It is popular with walkers with Offa's Dyke Walk running close by from Garthmyl to Llanymynech where it crosses over to the west side of the canal to head off across country towards the Llangollen Canal which it crosses near Froncysyllte.

Winding from the borders into the heart of mid-Wales, the countryside is beautiful and the canal is a haven for wildlife with many rare and threatened species of insect and plant life, particularly aquatic plants, along its course. About 15 miles of the canal are designated SSSI and the Guilsfield Arm is a nature reserve.

Authority British Waterways, Canal Offices, Birch, Ellesmere, Shropshire SY12 9AA ☎ 01691 622549 *Fax* 01691 623291.

Bridges Numerous. The numbering starts from 71 above Frankton rising to Newtown and from 70 to 1 are on the lower part of the Llangollen Canal. This was because the upper Llangollen canal was originally a water feeder and the Montgomery was the original main line of the Welsh Canal.

Towpath The quality of the towpath is variable but many lengths are good and improvements are underway on other stretches.

Locks Falling to the Wern then rising to Newtown. The last three locks in Newtown have been sold.

Aqueducts Over the River Perry 1¾ miles from Frankton; over the River Vyrnwy just south of Carreghofa Locks; and the Berriew Aqueduct near Garthmyl.

Restoration Work started at Frankton Junction and the four locks, including one dedicated to Graham Palmer, have been restored by the Inland Waterways Association with the first 4 miles now re-opened across the new Perry Aqueduct. The Prince of Wales Section near Welshpool is now 8 miles with a further extension of 3 miles likely to be completed soon. The final section above Freestone Lock has been filled in and restoration is unlikely at present.

By late 1997, the Aston Locks had been completed but the opening of the section to Maesbury had to be postponed. The section from Burgedin to Berriew through Welshpool is open for navigation. It is proposed that Llanymynech to Burgedin should be completed in 1998 and Maesbury to the Welsh Border in 1999.

Facilities Trailed boats can be launched at

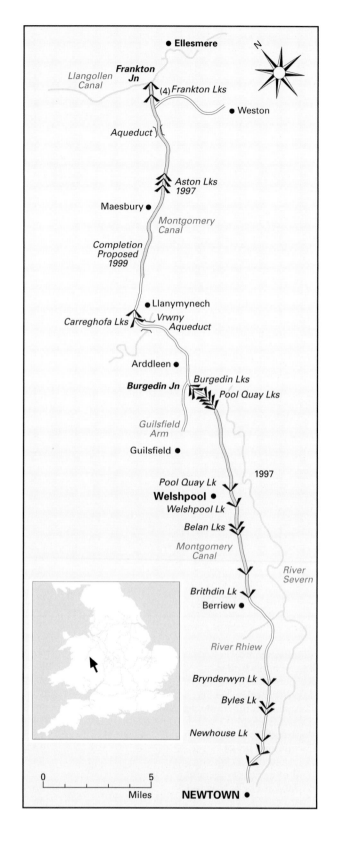

MONTGOMERY CANAL *Maximum vessel dimensions*

From and to	Distance	Length	Beam	Draught	Headroom	Locks
Frankton Junction to Newtown	35 miles (56.3km)	70' (21.3m)	6' 10" (2.1m)	2' 6" (0.8m)	7' 6" (2.3m)	25

Welshpool or Wern. There are several pubs along the canal but so far few facilities for anyone afloat.

Distance table *Miles*
Frankton, junction with Llangollen Canal to:

Frankton Locks Nos 1–4	0.5
Rednal	3.1
Queens Head (inn)	4.1
Aston Locks Nos 5–7	4.9
Maesbury	6.1
Redwith	7.4
Crickheath	8.1
Waen Wen	9.0
Plant	9.4
Llanymynech	10.5
Wall's Bridge, Wharf and Warehouse	10.9
Carreghofa Locks Nos 8 and 9	11.5
Newbridge	12.0
Clopton's Wharf	13.0
Mardu	14.1
Arddleen	15.3
Burgedin, top of Burgedin Locks, and junction with Guilsfield Branch (2 miles, a nature reserve)	15.8
Burgedin Locks Nos 10 and 11	15.8
Gwernfelen	16.3
Bank Lock No 12	17.3
Cabin Lock No 13	17.5
Crowther Lock No 14	17.9
Pool Quay Lock No 15	18.3
Buttington	20.1
Welshpool Lock No 16	21.6
Whitehouse	22.5
Belan Locks 17 and 18	23.0
Brithdair Lock No 19	25.8
Berriew Lock No 20	26.3
Berriew Aqueduct	26.8
Evelvach	26.9
Redgate	27.4
Garthmyl	27.8
Bunker's Hill	29.1
Pennant Dingle	29.9
Brynderwyn Lock No 21	30.8
Byles Lock No 22	31.3
Newhouse Lock No 23	31.8
Aberbechan	32.6
Newton Pumping Station (present head of navigation)	33.0

(The canal to Newtown Basin and the three last locks have been sold)

Swansea Canal

Opened in 1798 the Swansea Canal was originally 16½ miles long, including the Trewyddfa Canal of 1.4 miles, rising from Swansea to Abercraf, over 370ft above sea level with 36 locks for boats 69ft by 7ft 7ins. There were several branches and the canal was connected by tramroads through Brecknockshire serving coal and iron works. Even after it was bought by Great Western Railway, the canal was profitable and saw traffic until 1931. Although abandoned by Acts since 1928, it has continued as a water supply.

Both ends have been filled in but the remaining section from Ynysmeudwy to Clydach is in water and restoration is underway. Only five locks remain and there are two aqueducts. At Coed-Gwilym Park, there is a small canal museum and canoes can be hired. The hopes to create a 35-mile waterway ring in this area of South Wales have not, so far, met approval, as a section would need to pass through the Swansea Docks which is opposed by Associated British Ports.

Authority Lliw Valley Council, County Borough of Swansea and Neath Port Talbot Council.

British Waterways, The Wharf, Govilon, Abergavenny, Gwent NP7 9NY ☎ 01873 830328.

Bridges Several but none which restrict access in the navigable length.

Towpath Good throughout canal.

Connections None.

Restoration Currently 2½ miles in two sections are navigable and the Swansea Canal Society are actively working on the rest of the canal. Negotiations are continuing to develop a waterways ring in the area.

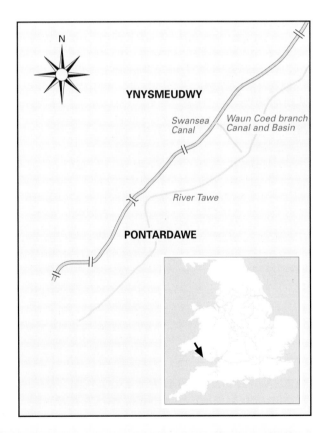

SWANSEA CANAL Maximum vessel dimensions

From and to	Distance	Length	Beam	Draught	Headroom	Locks
Clydach to Ynysmeudwy	5.5 miles (8.9km)	64' (19.5m)	7' 6" (2.3m)	1' 6" (0.5m)	6' (1.8m)	5

Tennant and Neath Canals

Although listed together, these canals were completely separate enterprises and are still privately owned. Together they offer 21 miles of waterway in West Glamorgan and, with the Swansea Canal, are the subject of proposals to create a 35 mile waterway ring in the area. At the time of going to press, these had run into some difficulties with the Associated British Ports as a part of the ring would have to pass through Swansea Docks.

The Neath and Tennant Canals Preservation Society have carried out major work on both canals and are creating a valuable educational and leisure facility for the area. The canals run through a diverse mixture of mountain, woodland and estuary landscape, with a number of historical industrial sites along the way. The canal architecture is also of considerable interest with an 18th century lengthsman's cottage at Resolven and the stables and workshops at Tonna, all restored by the society. There are two aqueducts, one of which is a cast-iron trough made at the Neath Abbey Ironworks.

In the mid-1800s the canals were very prosperous, carrying timber, coal, iron and copper, lime and even cannon balls for the Napoleonic wars. They also served social and recreational purposes as a means of transporting funeral corteges to church or taking the Sunday school outing to the beach at Jersey Marine.

The canals are now used for industrial water supply, but they also serve a valuable purpose as wildlife havens. There are many species of birds and plants, both in and near the water, and fishing is popular on both canals.

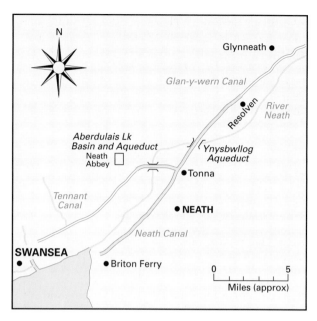

Authority Glyn Neath to Neath and junction with Early of Jersey's Canals: Neath Canal Navigation, Bankside, The Green, Neath, West Glamorgan ☎ 01639 55282.

Port Tennant Navigation Company Ltd, c/o Leeder Property Management, 26 Walters Road, Llansamlet, Swansea SA7 9RW ☎ 01792 55891.

Neath Canal

Opened in 1795, the canal was 10½ miles long with 19 locks from Neath to Glyn-Neath. There were plans to improve the river but, in 1799, this was changed when the canal was extended 2½ miles to Giant's Grave below Neath, where a port developed although there was never any access between the estuary and the canal. The venture was prosperous through the 19th century despite competition from the railway, but by the 1920s traffic had effectively ceased.

Bridges Numerous.

Towpath Throughout navigation but advice should be sought as to access. A linear park is being created with a 3.1 miles (5km) towpath project between Briton Ferry and Neath.

Restoration Considerable improvements have been made with a centre at Resolven, from where a 4-mile section is in water and two small trip boats are run by the preservation society. There has been support for the restoration from the Welsh Office

TENNANT AND NEATH CANALS Maximum vessel dimensions

From and to	Distance	Length	Beam	Draught	Headroom	Locks
Neath Canal Glyn-Neath to Briton Ferry	13 miles (20.9km)	60' (18.2m)	9' (2.7m)	2' 9" (0.8m)	6' (1.8m)	17
Tennant Canal Swansea to Aberdulais	8.4 miles (13.5km)	60' (18.2)	9' (2.7m)	2' 9" (0.8m)	6' (1.8m)	1

and the Prince of Wales Committee and further work is planned. Water pollution from old mine workings has to be resolved before further restoration can be carried out on the canal between Resolven and Tonna.

Distance table	Miles
Glyn Neath, Canal Head to:	
Maesmarchog Lock No 1	0.0
Lamb Lock No 2	1.0
(Locks 1 and 2 are under the A465 trunk road)	
Foxes Lock No 3	
Chain Lock No 4	
Granery Lock No 5	
Bwllfa'r Onn Lock No 6	
Maes-gwyn Lock No 7	2.0
Ynisultor Lock No 8	2.3
Aber-clwyd Lock No 9	2.5
Rheola Lock No 10	3.1
Crugiau Lock No 11	3.6
Resolven Lock No 12	4.3
Farmer's Lock No 13	4.4
Abergarwed Lock No 14	4.8
Ynysarwed Lock No 15	5.3
Gitto Lock No 16	6.0
Witworth Lock No 17	6.9
Lock Machine No 18	7.5
Aberdulais, junction with Tennant Canal	8.6
Lock House Lock No 19	9.1
Neath, Main Road Bridge over canal and junction with Earl of Jersey's Grave and Briton Ferry Canal (½ mile in length and is only used for water supply)	13.0

Tennant Canal

This canal was constructed between 1817 and 1824 by George Tennant. It was a private navigation, 8 miles long with one lock and it joined the Neath Canal at Aberdulais to Swansea Docks. A branch, with one lock, led to Red Jacket Pill but this is now closed to navigation, although canoeable from Aberdulais to Jersey Marine and sections still hold water for water supply. The canal is still owned by the Tennant family.

The canal passes south of Neath Abbey and near here is a section of canal which is a scheduled monument as it has a stone lining to carry the canal through quicksand. The stone was transported to the site by tramroad.

Bridges Numerous.

Towpath The towpath is not a public right of way and advice should be sought by anyone wishing to walk the canal.

Branches Red Jacket Pill to estuary (now closed).

Restoration This is part of a joint project with the Neath Canal.

Distance table	Miles
Aberdulais, junction with Neath Canal to:	
Aberdulais Lock and south end of aqueduct over River Neath	0.1
Neath, Main Road Bridge over canal	1.8
Neath Abbey	3.0
Junction with Red Jacket Pill Branch (now filled)	4.9
Briton Ferry Road, Railway Station	5.8

	Miles
Junction with Glan-y-Wern Canal (closed)	6.4
Junction with Tir-isaf Branch Canal (closed)	7.6
Vale of Neath (inn), Port Tennant	8.0
(Canal from this point to the docks is now infilled and so also are locks)	

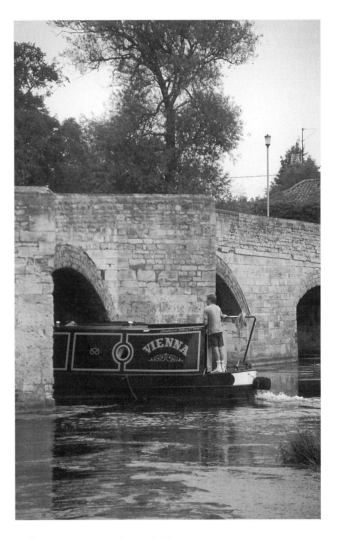

One of the many old stone bridges on the waterways.
Jane Cumberlidge

Appendices

Acts of Parliament

Throughout the second half of the 18th century and the early part of the 19th was the time of the greatest number of Acts of Parliament for the promotion of canals and the development of river navigation in Great Britain. Some of the canals were not completed and a few, mostly the later proposals which were overtaken by the arrival of the railways, were not even started. The peak of 'canal mania' was in 1793 when over 20 new canals were authorised.

Aberdare Canal 1793
Aberdeenshire Canal 1796
River Adur 1807, 1825
Aire and Calder Navigation 1699, 1774, 1820, 1828
River Ancholme 1767, 1802, 1825
Andover Canal 1789
River Arun 1732, 1785, 1793
Ashby-de-la-Zouch Canal 1794
Ashton Canal 1792, 1793, 1798, 1800, 1805
River Avon and Bristol Docks 1700, 1749, 1803, 1806, 1808, 1809
River Avon, Warwickshire 1751, 1793
Upper Avon Navigation 1972
Barnsley Canal 1793
Basingstoke Canal 1778
Beverley Beck 1727, 1744
Birmingham Canal Navigations 1768, 1769, 1783, 1784, 1785, 1794, 1806, 1811, 1815, 1818
Birmingham and Liverpool Junction Canal 1826
Birmingham and Warwick Junction Canal 1840
River Blyth 1757
Bourne Eau 1781
Bradford Canal 1771
Brecknock and Abergavenny Canal 1793
Bridgewater Canal 1759, 1760, 1762, 1766, 1795
Bridgwater and Taunton Canal 1811, 1824
Bude Canal 1774, 1819
Caistor Canal 1793
Calder and Hebble Navigation 1758, 1769, 1825
Caledonian Canal 1803, 1804, 1919
River Cam 1703, 1813, 1857
Carlisle Canal 1721, 1819
Chelmer and Blackwater Navigation 1766, 1793
Chester Canal 1772
Chesterfield Canal 1771
Chichester Canal 1817
River Colne 1623, 1689, 1719, 1740, 1750, 1781
Coombe Hill Canal 1792
Coventry Canal 1768, 1785, 1819
Crinan Canal 1793
Cromford Canal 1789
Croydon Canal 1801
Dartford and Crayford Navigation 1840
Dearne and Dove Canal 1793
River Dee 1734, 1744, 1791
Derby Canal 1793
River Derwent 1701
River Don 1726, 1733, 1821, 1826

Dorset and Somerset Canal 1796
Driffield Navigation 1767, 1801
Droitwich Canal 1768
Dudley Canal 1776, 1785, 1793
Edinburgh and Glasgow Union Canal 1817
Ellesmere Canal 1793
Erewash Canal 1777
Exeter Ship Canal 1539, 1829
Forth and Cart Canal 1836
Forth and Clyde Canal 1768
River Foss 1793, 1801
Glamorganshire Canal 1790
Glasgow, Paisley and Johnstone Canal 1806
Gloucester and Sharpness Ship Canal (Gloucester and Berkeley Canal) 1793, 1797, 1805, 1818, 1822, 1825
Grand Junction Canal 1793, 1794, 1795, 1798, 1801, 1803, 1805, 1812, 1818, 1819
Grand Surrey Canal 1801
Grand Union Canal 1810, 1929, 1932 (see also Regent's Canal, Hertford Union Canal, Grand Junction Canal, Warwick and Napton Canal, Warwick and Birmingham Canal, Birmingham and Warwick Junction Canal, Leicester Navigation, Loughborough Navigation, Erewash Canal, Leicestershire and Northamptonshire Union Canal , Old Grand Union Canal)
Grand Western Canal 1796, 1811, 1812
Grantham Canal 1793
Gresley Canal 1775
Herefordshire and Gloucestershire Canal 1791
Hertford Union Canal (also known as Duckett's Canal) 1824
Huddersfield Broad Canal 1774
Huddersfield Narrow Canal 1794
River Hull 1767, 1801, 1817
River Idle 1720
Ipswich and Stowmarket Navigation 1790
Isle of Dogs Canal 1807
Ivelchester and Langport Canal 1795
Kennet and Avon Navigation 1794, 1796, 1798, 1801, 1805, 1809, 1813
Kensington Canal 1824
Kington and Leominster Canal 1791
Kyme Eau – Sleaford Canal 1794
Lancaster Canal 1792, 1793, 1796, 1800, 1807, 1819
River Lee 1424, 1430, 1561, 1767, 1779, 1805, 1824
Leeds and Liverpool Canal 1770, 1783, 1790, 1794, 1819
Leicester Navigation 1791
Leicestershire and Northamptonshire Union Canal 1793, 1805
Leven Canal 1801
Liskeard and Looe Canal 1825
London and Cambridge Junction Canal 1812
Loughborough Navigation 1766, 1776
Louth Navigation 1763

Tewitfield is the head of navigation on the Lancaster Canal.
Robin Smithett

The Monmouthshire and Brecon Canal is within the Brecon Beacon's National Park for almost its entire length. *Jane Cumberlidge*

The calm of the Ashby Canal near Harborough Magna. *Roy Westlake*

A golden dawn at Hilmorton, on the Northern Oxford Canal. *Sian Barron*

Bank Newton locks on the Leeds and Liverpool Canal. *Stuart Robertson*

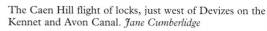

The Caen Hill flight of locks, just west of Devizes on the Kennet and Avon Canal. *Jane Cumberlidge*

Lydney Canal and Harbour 1809, 1810
Macclesfield Canal 1826
Manchester, Bolton and Bury Canal 1791
Manchester Ship Canal 1885
Market Weighton Drainage Navigation 1772
River Medway 1664, 1740, 1792, 1802, 1824
River Mersey 1805
Middle Level Navigation 1753, 1793/4, 1810, 1844, 1848, 1852, 1862, 1874
Middlewich Branch 1827
Monkland Canal 1770, 1790
Monmouthshire Canal 1792, 1793, 1797, 1802, 1804, 1862
Montgomeryshire Canal 1794, 1815
Neath Canal 1791
River Nene 1714, 1725, 1754, 1756, 1794, 1827, 1829
Newcastle-under-Lyme Canal 1795
Newport Pagnell Canal 1814
Norfolk and Suffolk Broads 1670, 1722, 1747, 1772, 1773, 1827, 1866, 1907, 1963
North Walsham and Dilham Canal 1812
North Wiltshire Canal 1813
Nottingham Canal 1792
Nutbrook Canal 1793
Oakham Canal 1793
Old Grand Union Canal 1810
River Great Ouse 1670, 1751, 1795, 1796, 1805, 1810, 1816, 1818, 1819, 1827, 1830
River Ouse (Sussex) 1790, 1791, 1800, 1806, 1814
River Ouse (Yorkshire) 1642, 1657, 1727, 1732, 1767
Oxford Canal 1769, 1775, 1786, 1794, 1799, 1807, 1808, 1829
River Parrett 1699, 1707, 1795, 1804
Peak Forest Canal 1794, 1800, 1805
Pocklington Canal 1815
Portsmouth and Arundel Canal 1817
Regent's Canal and Limehouse Docks 1812, 1813, 1816, 1819 and 1821
Ripon Canal 1767, 1820
Rochdale Canal 1794, 1800, 1804, 1806, 1807
River Roding 1737
River Rother (Eastern) 1826, 1830
Royal Military Canal (Hythe, Kent) 1791, 1807
Sankey (St Helen's) Canal 1755, 1845
Salisbury and Southampton Canal 1795
Selby Canal (Aire and Calder Navigation) 1774
River Severn 1503, 1531, 1532, 1772, 1799, 1803, 1809, 1814
Sheffield and South Yorkshire Navigation 1733, 1815
Shrewsbury Canal 1793
Shropshire (Tub Boat) Canal 1788
Shropshire Union Canal 1772, 1793, 1801, 1804, 1826
Somerset Coal Canal 1794
Staffordshire and Worcestershire Canal 1766, 1790
Stainforth and Keadby Canal 1793, 1798, 1809
River Stort 1759, 1766
River Stour (Kent) 1515, 1825
River Stour (Suffolk) 1705, 1781
Stourbridge Canal 1776
Stourbridge Extension Canal 1837
Stratford-on-Avon Canal 1793, 1795, 1799, 1809, 1815, 1817, 1821
Stroudwater Canal 1730, 1759, 1776
Swansea Canal 1794
Tavistock Canal 1803
Tennant and Neath Canals 1791, 1795, 1798
Thames and Medway Canal 1800
Thames and Severn Canal 1783

River Trent 1699, 1783, 1794, 1906
Trent and Mersey Canal 1766, 1770, 1775, 1776, 1783, 1797 (2 Acts), 1802, 1809, 1827
Ulverston Canal 1793
River Ure 1767, 1820
Warwick and Birmingham Canal 1793, 1796
Warwick and Braunston Canal 1794
Warwick and Napton Canal 1794, 1796, 1809
River Wear 1716, 1726, 1747, 1759 (2 Acts), 1785, 1809, 1819, 1830
River Weaver 1721, 1734, 1760, 1807, 1825, 1829
River Welland 1571, 1774, 1794, 1870
Welsh Canal 1793, 1794, 1796
Wey and Arun Junction Canal 1813
River Wey 1651, 1671, 1683, 1760,
Wiltshire and Berkshire Canal 1795, 1801, 1810, 1813, 1815, 1821
Wisbech Canal 1794
River Witham 1671, 1762, 1808, 1812, 1826, 1829
Worcester and Birmingham Canal 1791, 1798, 1804, 1808, 1815
Wyrley and Essington Canal 1792

Canoeing on inland waterways

Canoeists can often use rivers and other waterways not navigable by powered craft. Many derelict canals, which still hold water, and rivers without named navigation authorities are privately owned and permission to use them must be obtained before setting out. It is strongly recommended that canoeists join a recognised club or the British Canoe Union (BCU). The BCU holds details of canoeable rivers covering rights of navigation and access to waterways. Intending paddlers should be aware that the responsibility rests with the canoeist to check the legal position regarding access and navigation rights before going afloat. The BCU can provide further details and leaflets on relevant topics are available from them at The British Canoe Union, Adbolton Lane, West Bridgford, Nottingham NG2 5AS ☎ 0115 982 1100 *Fax* 0115 982 1797.

The BCU has licensing agreements with British Waterways, the Environment Agency and several other navigation authorities, which enable BCU members to use the waters concerned without purchasing their own individual licence.

British Waterways should be consulted on regulations in force for canoeing on canals and whether tunnels can be used by unpowered craft. For information contact either the local BW office, addresses are in the telephone book, or the head office in Watford (☎ 01923 226422 *Fax* 01923 226081).

This information is also applicable to small dinghies, small rowing boats and other small unpowered craft.

The rights of navigation on rivers and access to rivers can change as a result of changes in the law, local bye-laws or ownership (at the time of going to press the status of the River Wye is the subject of a public enquiry). To avoid the risk of presenting misleading information no list of canoeable rivers has been included in the text.

Small boats on inland waterways

The term 'unpowered' refers to canoes, dinghies, rowing boats, punts and other small unpowered boats. Users of small boats on British Waterways canals and rivers should note the following points:

1. A valid Pleasure Boat Licence should be displayed whilst on any of BW's canals and as with other pleasure boats small boats are subject to the board's licensing conditions and bye-laws.
2. On BW's river navigations all boats should display either a valid Pleasure Boat Licence or a valid River Registration Certificate and are subject to the relevant bye-laws.
3. Unpowered boat users should take extra care near other craft particularly moving craft.
4. As the river navigations have a faster flow than canals, and as some are tidal, unpowered boaters (especially novices) should be sure that they will not be swept away by current. Similarly users of small powered boats should ensure that their engine is capable of navigating against the current.
5. All boats should keep away from weirs and sluices, and BW strongly discourages boaters from 'shooting weirs' on safety grounds.

In addition to the normal licensing conditions, special conditions apply to the use of certain tunnels and lengths of waterways. These are as follows:

1. No unpowered boat shall navigate through the following tunnels except if:
    a. it is safely towed by a powered boat;
    b. it is not manned;
    c. it is fitted with satisfactory tunnel lights.

Canal	Name of tunnel	Yards
Ashby	Snarestone	250
BCN	Dudley	3154
	Gosty Hill	557
	Netherton	3027
Caldon	Froghall	76
	Leek	130
Grand Union	Blisworth	3076
	Braunston	2042
	Crick	1528
	Husbands Bosworth	1166
	Islington	960
	Maida Hill	272
	Saddington	880
	Shrewley	433
Kennet and Avon	Savernake	502
Leeds and Liverpool	Foulridge	1640
	Gannow	559
Llangollen	Chirk	459
	Ellesmere	87
	Whitehouses	191
Mon. and Brecon	Ashford	375

Canal	Name of tunnel	Yards
Peak Forest	Hyde Bank	308
	Woodley (Butterhouse Green)	176
Stratford-upon-Avon	Brandwood	352
Trent and Mersey	Barnton	572
	Harecastle	2926
	Preston Brook	1239
	Saltersford	424
Worcs. and Birmingham	Dunhampstead	236
	Shortwood	613
	Tardebigge	580
	Wast Hill	2726

Boats are not permitted to run their engines in Dudley Tunnel (3172yds) on the Birmingham Canal Navigation, and no boats are allowed into Standedge Tunnel (5698yds) on the Huddersfield Narrow Canal.

2. The following tunnels may be used by unpowered boats provided that:
    a. All boaters are able to swim, wear lifejackets, and have a suitable whistle attached to their bodies, by a substantial lanyard.
    b. All small boats have adequate buoyancy aids and a waterproof torch within them, and are fitted with an adequate white light fixed to the boat and showing ahead.

Canal	Name of tunnel	Yards
BCN	Coseley	360
	Galton	122
	Summit	103
Birmingham and Fazeley	Curdworth	57
Chesterfield	Drakeholes	147
Kennet and Avon	Bath No 1	59
	Bath No 2	55
Oxford	Newbold	250
Shropshire Union	Cowley	81
Staffs. and Worcs.	Cookley	65
	Dunsley	23
Worcs. and Birmingham	Edgbaston	105

3. On the following commercial waterways special conditions may be imposed on the use of small powered and unpowered boats:

Waterway	Length concerned
Aire and Calder Navigation	Leeds Lock to Goole: Fall Ings Lock, Wakefield to Castleford; Selby Canal from Knottingley to Haddesley Lock.
Calder and Hebble Navigation	Wakefield to Greenwood Lock.
Gloucester and Sharpness Canal	Sharpness Dock to Gloucester Lock.
New Junction Canal	Southfield to Bramwith.
Sheffield and South Yorkshire Navigation	Bramwith to bottom of Tinsley Flight at Sheffield.

Details about the nature of the conditions may be obtained from the appropriate area engineer. In general the use of small boats on the Gloucester and Sharpness Canal is discouraged.

Miscellaneous waterways

In addition to the waterways listed in the main section of the book there are many historic waterways around Britain in varying stages of dereliction. Some may be in water and can be used by canoeists and light craft, but it is the responsibility of the user to establish if there is a public right of navigation or obtain permission if it is a private waterway. When portaging round obstructions be sure you are not trespassing on private land.

Derelict canals hold their own fascination and can be of interest to walkers, naturalists and anyone eager to understand more of the history of Britain. For keen canal historians a number of books are listed in the bibliography but three which make good starters are: *The Illustrated History of Canal and River Navigations* by Edward Paget-Tomlinson, *Canals* by Nigel Crowe and Hadfield's *British Canals* revised by Joseph Boughey. For the explorer, M and M Baldwin publish a series of historical canal maps which covers all the waterways authorised by Act of Parliament; care must be taken when hunting for these on the ground as in some cases canals got no further than a plan and others were abandoned after only a short distance had been built. Old towpaths are not necessarily public rights of way and the Ordnance Survey *Landranger* series or the larger scale *Pathfinder* maps for the area should be consulted for footpaths and public rights of way.

ENGLAND

Adelphi Canal A private canal serving a plant near Calow making cannon balls. It was ½ mile long and ran to the nearest road, which linked to the Chesterfield canal. Closed in the middle of the 19th century.

Adur Navigation Closed in 1875. Navigable for canoes from the upper lock near West Grinstead church. There were two locks on the 3.4 miles closed section.

Alike Beck A short river navigation, 1.1 miles through two locks from the River Hull to Lockington landing.

Andover Canal Closed in 1859. Over 14 miles of the 22-mile canal was converted to a railway by the Andover and Redbridge Railway. Portions of the canal are still canoeable and they form part of the River Test, but fishing rights are very keenly preserved and light craft are not permitted the use of the river or old canal cuts.

Avon Navigation, Wiltshire and Hampshire. Navigation works were constructed under an Act of Parliament in 1664, but were all destroyed by a flood soon afterwards. The river is canoeable from Salisbury to Christchurch on the old navigation route and, in good water conditions, from Pewsey. The river is strictly preserved for fishing and light craft are forbidden passage through the various properties though the Act of 1664 does not seem to have been rescinded.

Axe Navigation Navigation above Bleadon ceased over 100 years ago. There was a tide lock at Bleadon, but the only navigable portion for many years has been the tideway up to the railway bridge.

Baybridge Canal Alternative name for canalised section of the Adur.

Bedale Beck An unfinished canal from the junction with the River Swale to Bedale. There were to be two locks but the remains of only one at Leeming can be traced. About 2 miles long.

Bishop Monkton Canal A water ½ mile long that previously ran from south of Oxclose Lock on the River Ure to the canal head on the Westwick to Bishop Monkton Road. Closed mid-1800s.

Black Sluice Drainage and Navigation Constructed under an Act of 1765, it joins the River Witham in Boston about 1 mile below the Grand Sluice. The navigation ran to Guthram Gowt, a distance of 21 miles and it was closed in 1967. A short new cut and a lock would make it possible to connect up with the Rivers Glen and Welland near Spalding.

Blyth Navigation In 1757 this river was made navigable from Halesworth to Blythburgh. Now closed, there were four locks on this section.

Bond End Canal This connected the Trent and Mersey Canal at Shobnall to the River Trent. There was a stop lock and lock on the navigation, which has been disused since about 1875.

Bottisham Lode This has never been closed but is very shallow. It runs from the Cam for 2½ miles to Lode village. The entrance staunch has long been demolished.

Bourne Eau This led from the River Glen in Deeping Fen to Bourne, a distance of 3½ miles. There were two locks, now fixed sluices. The whole route can be used by light craft that can be portaged.

Bradford Canal This canal was 3 miles long and had ten locks. It connected Bradford to the Leeds and Liverpool Canal. It was closed in 1922 by Act of Parliament.

Braunton Canal A short canal made after several grand schemes had come to nothing from Caen River and Knowle Water to Braunton.

Brue Navigation Originally the lower part of the Glastonbury Canal. Only a small part of the tideway is now navigable. There were two short navigations, Brown's and Galton's. These ran from the Brue northwards and were both approximately 1¼ miles long. They ran to North Drain but this does not seem to have been a navigation. There are some remains to be seen.

Bungay Navigation Canalised River Waveney, and three locks now derelict. It was closed 1934 by Order of the Ministry of Agriculture and Fisheries.

This navigation ran from Geldeston to Bungay. The Broads Authority are having discussions about the possible restoration of this waterway.

Caistor Canal This canal was never completed to Caistor in Lincolnshire from the River Ancholme but terminated at Moortown. Originally 4 miles in length with five locks. It was abandoned in 1936.

Calder and Hebble Navigation (Halifax Branch) There were 14 locks on this branch which was 1¾ miles long. Closed by Warrant of the Minister of Transport dated 21 August 1942.

Cam, River, Gloucestershire Used now only as a feeder to the ship canal nearby but previously navigable to Cam Village. Light craft can still use this route just over 1 mile long.

Cann Quarry Canal, Devon A private canal 2 miles long built as a mill channel and a tub-boat canal. Disused about 1836.

Car Dyke An ancient Roman waterway that ran from the Cam near Waterbeach to the River Witham near Lincoln. Modern research does not support previous theories that this was a transport canal except possibly at the northern end.

Carlisle Canal Length 11¼ miles with nine locks. Closed in 1853 and converted into a railway.

Cassington Cut This was built by the Duke of Marlborough and ran from the Thames to the Cassington-Eynsham Road in Oxfordshire. It was ¾ mile long and there was one lock at the entrance.

Chard Canal This canal was opened in 1842. Length 13½ miles, it ran from the Bridgwater and Taunton Canal at Creech St Michael to Chard. None of the old route is usable but the huge embankments and sites of the inclined planes at Thornfalcon, Wrantage, Ilminster and Chard are worth visiting. Closed 1866.

Charnwood Forest Canal This canal was a failure largely due to troubles with the supply reservoir. It was 9¼ miles long and conveyed coal from Charnwood Forest to the Grand Union Canal. Disused 1801. Canal linked to GUC by tramway.

Cinderford Canal A private waterway connecting Mill Pool to an ironworks at Cinderford in the Forest of Dean and was 1¼ miles long.

Cod Beck Junction of the River Swale to Thirsk Though five locks were projected only one was built. Two craft used the waterway in 1770 which was probably the only occasion.

Compstall Navigation A short canal used in connection with the cotton mills at Etherow; used for coal supply.

Coombe Hill Canal Short private canal constructed from the River Severn to the nearby road 3½ miles away. From here goods were taken to Cheltenham by road. It was constructed under an Act in 1792 and closed by an Act in 1876. A start was made on its restoration but the Coombe Hill Canal Trust has since been disbanded.

Croydon Canal Originally ran from Croydon to New Cross where it joined the Grand Surrey Canal. Closed in 1836 and converted into a railway.

Cuckmere, River Navigable at high tide to Alfriston (site of Milton Locks). A bar at the entrance severely limits use of the river. Commercial traffic has used the river to Alfriston.

Cumberland Market Branch Canal A short branch of the Grand Union in London that left the canal in Regent's Park. Filled in during the 1939–45 war, in part. A short length is still open.

Dartford and Crayford Navigation This was a commercial waterway until the 1990s when the North Dartford relief road reduced headroom to less than 6ft close below the wharves. It was promoted by Act of Parliament in 1840. Access is still possible from the Thames and there is a floodgate which is controlled with the Thames Barrier. Authority for the navigation passed to the Port of London Authority from the Commissioners of the Dartford and Crayford Navigation at the time that the road was built. The Minute books and associated documents were then lodged with Maidstone library.

There are footpaths following each bank of the navigation, on the east bank of the River Darent from Dartford to the Thames and on the west bank from Crayford Mill on the Cray to its confluence with the Darent and then to Crayford Ness Light on the Thames.

Derwent, River, Derbyshire This river was made a navigation by an Act of Parliament passed in 1720. From Derby to the Trent at Wilden Ferry, this navigation was later sold to the Derby Canal Company, which superseded this river navigation. The river is canoeable from as high up as Rowsley, though the old navigation section is unattractive.

Dick Brook A very early canalisation from the River Severn to Yarranton Forge (3 miles south of Stourport). It was ¾ mile long with two flash locks.

Dorset and Somerset Canal This canal was intended to connect Bristol with the English Channel, 49 miles, but only 8 miles of a branch were constructed. Owing to lack of finance the canal was abandoned, though it is still remembered for its canal lift constructed at Mells to the design of Mr Fussell. Some structures are still visible and a Dorset and Somerset Canal Study Group has been formed, the coordinator is Mr Derrick Hunt ☎ 01761 434618.

Duke of Sutherland's Tub-boat Canal (Donnington Wood Canal) Commenced at Donnington with a junction with the Old Shropshire Canal and ran by Lilleshall Abbey to Pave Lane. There were two short branches. Total distance about 7 miles. Built by 1769 and closed completely by 1904.

Eardington Underground Canal A canal ½ mile long linking lower and upper Eardington Forges. It was not linked directly to the Severn in the Bridgnorth area.

Eden, River This river was navigable for 10¼ miles, under an Act passed in 1721, but later was disused when the Carlisle Canal was opened. It was tidal throughout, but has silted up so that the tidal limit is 3 miles below Carlisle.

Emmet's Canal Approximately 1 mile long, running to Birkenshaw village, near Bradford. Disused by 1816.

Exeter and Crediton Navigation This canal was promoted by an Act in 1801. Just over ½ mile was excavated but the canal was never completed.

Fleet Canal A canalisation of the River Fleet. This took traffic to Holborn Bridge from the Thames and became derelict in the early 1700s. It has been covered over but is still a water channel.

Fletcher's Canal A private canal once owned by the Clifton and Kersely Coal Co Ltd, and was 1½ miles long. It is now a water feeder to the Manchester, Bolton and Bury Canal. There was one lock only.

Glynne's, Sir John, Canal This is sometimes called the Saltney Canal and was about a mile long. It was a local coal canal serving the Sandycroft colliery.

Glastonbury Canal Joined Glastonbury to the River Brue at Highbridge. Closed in 1853, and sections of the bed were converted to a railway. Many sections are still usable by light craft. It was 14 miles long with two locks.

Grand Surrey Canal An extension of the Surrey Docks now closed. The canal originally ran from Surrey Docks to Camberwell, 2.6 miles with a branch to Peckham ½ mile long. One entrance lock from the Thames.

Greaseborough Canal (Park Gate) Made to serve coal mines near Greaseborough to link with the River Don. It was 1½ miles long with four locks and a ½ mile branch to Newbiggin. A private waterway that was totally disused by 1928.

Gresley's Canal Built to connect the coal mines in Apedale to Newcastle-under-Lyme under an Act of 1775. It is 3 miles long and derelict.

Hackney Canal Constructed by Lord Clifford as a private canal for the export of china clay in 1843. The canal was ½ mile long, and led from its junction with the River Teign estuary at Hackney to the main road nearby. The canal is derelict and the entrance lock has been bricked up. Closed 1955.

Hayle (or Copperhouse) Canal This should not be confused with the Hayle-Camborne project that was never constructed. This was a tidal canal running from the Hayle River to the Tide Mill by Copperhouse Foundry.

Horncastle (or River Bain Navigation) Opened in 1802, this navigation ran from the River Witham, near Tattershall Bridge, to Horncastle. The canal was 11 miles long and there were seven locks. Closed 1865. Most of the old route can be used by canoes.

Isle of Dogs Canal This cut across the Isle of Dogs in the Thames to avoid the large bend in the river. It was little used and was merged into the West Indian Dock in 1829.

Itchen Navigation Bishop Godfrey de Lucy made this river navigable to Alresford in 1200. It fell into disrepair and another navigation was made from Winchester to Southampton by an Act of 1662. An Act of 1710 authorised construction of a completely new navigation 10.4 miles long. There were 15 locks. Most of the route is navigable by light craft but fishing rights are strictly preserved. Closed 1869. Clearance in the Allbrook area by local canal society. Navigation rights have not been abandoned. Four controlling Acts remain.

Ivel River, Bedfordshire This river was made a navigation to Biggleswade in 1759 and to Shefford in 1810. The length was 11 miles of which over 3 miles were called the Shefford Canal. On the first section there were six locks, and from Biggleswade to Shefford there were five locks. Closed 1876. Canoeable throughout.

Ivel River, Somerset (sometimes called River Yeo) The river joins the Parrett 1 mile above Langport Bridge and, under an Act of 1795, attempts were made to make this river a navigation from Langport to Ilchester, but the navigation was a failure. Light craft can still reach Load Bridge which carries the B3165 road.

Ketley Canal Short canal in Shropshire later incorporated into the Shrewsbury Canal. Long derelict, but remembered as it included the first canal inclined plane in England.

Kensington Canal This originally ran from Warwick Road Basin in West London to the Thames. It was 1¾ miles long with one tide lock. Craft using the canal were 8ft by 18ft. Part was converted into a railway when it was acquired by the West London Extension Railway. The bottom section remained in use until 1970 but it has now been disposed of.

Kington, Leominster and Stourport Canal Construction of this canal from Kington to the Severn via Tenbury and Leominster was commenced after the 1791 Act promoting the navigation. Only the section from Leominster to Mamble Wharf was completed. Totally derelict throughout the 18½ miles that were completed.

Lakenheath Lode A drainage channel, once navigable for fen-lighters from Lakenheath Wharf to the Brandon River. There was one navigation weir ¾ mile downstream from Lakenheath. Length 3¼ miles. Usable for light craft only, except the short section 700yds long downstream of the railway bridge which can be used by cruisers for mooring off the Brandon River.

Langford Cut A short private canal from the Chelmer and Blackwater, near Beeleigh, to Langford Mill; about ½ mile long.

Leicester and Melton Mowbray Navigation Opened in 1801 from near Leicester to Melton Mowbray. A river navigation using the Eye and Wreak Rivers. The 11-mile route has long been derelict, but some part is canoeable.

Leven Canal A private canal constructed under Acts of 1801 and 1805. It ran from near Aike on the River Hull to Leven, a distance of 3¼ miles. The entrance lock has been replaced by a fixed sluice and the canal is used for fishing. Closed by Act of Parliament in 1935.

Liskeard and Looe Canal Promoted under an Act of 1825. It ran from Tarras Pill to Moorswater (near Liskeard). Closed after the opening of the railway in 1860. There were 25 locks and the bottom end still retains water.

Little Punchard Gill This was an underground canal to take away mined lead ore from Arkengarthdale in Swaledale.

Lugg Navigation A navigation was constructed in the mid-18th century from Leominster to the River Wye, a distance of 26 miles. Only flash locks appear to have been used. The route is usually canoeable throughout. Navigation was closed after the opening of the Herefordshire and Gloucestershire Canal which crossed the river by a low aqueduct at Wergins Bridge, but this is now demolished.

Manchester and Salford Junction Canal This linked the River Irwell at Water Street, Manchester with the Rochdale Canal. The bottom lock is now a working demonstration outside a new hotel in Manchester, and the Rochdale Canal end is now a basin with the Bridgewater Hall alongside.

Mardyke Purfleet, junction with River Thames, to Bulphan Fen. This was about 5 miles long and some side drains to farms were also used. Used for farm produce and manure distribution. Disused since 1875.

MacMurray's Canal This was a canal just over a ¼ mile long linking the Thames to the Lamb Brewery at Wandsworth. There was an entrance lock and two lifting bridges. There has been recently a scheme to link the nearby Bell Lane Creek to the Wandle to create a navigation to Wandsworth High Street. The canal became disused after the First World War.

Melton Mowbray Navigation Linked to the Grand Union Canal near Syston to Melton Mowbray via 12 broad locks. It was mainly a canalisation of the River Wreak. Closed but sections are canoeable and there are many remains of the old navigation. This is a waterway which could be looked at for restoration, in part at least.

Mersey and Irwell Navigation This was largely taken over by the Manchester Ship Canal works. In recent years the Runcorn and Latchford Canal has closed throughout, including the section known as the Black Bear Canal and also Butchersfield Cut.

Mundon Canal A private waterway running from the River Blackwater to White House Farm, Mundon, near Maldon. It was 1¼ miles long and had an entrance lock.

Nar Navigation Promoted under an Act dated 1751 by which the river was canalised to Westacre. Locks are now fixed sluices. Original distance 15 miles. Closed 1884. Canoeable from Narborough to King's Lynn.

Nent Force Level Nearly 5 miles long, this was a drainage and transport canal for an underground waterway underneath the valley of the River Nent, in Cumbria. A tourist attraction in later years, it is now lost and forgotten as mining has ceased at Alston. The navigable section was no less than 2 miles.

Newcastle-under-Lyme Canal Promoted under Act of 1795. It was 4 miles long, now closed and derelict.

Newdigate Canals A network of canals based on the Arbury Estate near Nuneaton from the junction with the Coventry Canal to Seaswood Lake. There were 5½ miles of canals mainly for coal traffic but also for general goods and recreation. There were 14 locks including one stop lock, but the system was disused by 1820. The coal from the collieries at Griff were conveyed by a separate canal and this coal traffic remained until the early 1960s.

Newport Pagnell Canal Promoted by Act of 1814 to link Newport Pagnell to the Grand Union Canal. Length 1¼ miles with seven locks. Closed in 1864 and partly converted to a railway.

North and South Drove Drains near Spalding, Lincolnshire, still in existence but disused.

North Wiltshire Canal See Wiltshire and Berkshire Canal.

Nottingham Canal Promoted under Act of 1792 the canal ran from the Cromford Canal at Langley Mill to the Trent at Nottingham, a distance of almost 15 miles with 29 locks. There was one short branch in Nottingham. Only the short section of 2½ miles is now used for traffic proceeding to or from the upper Trent. The canal is derelict in sections.

Nutbrook Canal This canal, promoted under an Act of 1793, ran from a junction with the Erewash Canal at the White House to Shipley, a distance of 4½ miles, through thirteen locks. All but the bottom ¼ mile was disused by 1895, and is now derelict.

Oakham Canal Promoted by Acts in 1793 and 1800 and opened in 1802 from Melton Mowbray to Oakham, a distance of 15 miles, through 16 locks. Closed in 1853 and converted in part to a railway. Short sections are still canoeable.

Old Stratford and Buckingham Canals A branch of the Grand Union to Buckingham, 10¾ miles long with two locks. Derelict except for a section at the lower end. The Old Stratford was a wide canal and the Buckingham Canal narrow. They were separate concerns.

Ouse, River, Sussex Constructed under an Act of 1790 and four later Acts, from the sea at Newhaven to Cuckfield, a distance of nearly 30 miles, through

18 locks. Disused to Lindfield since 1861 and to Isfield in 1880. It is usable in the tideway below Hamsey and canoeable from the ruins of Isfield Lock to Hamsey. The original navigation Acts do not appear to have been rescinded.

Par Canal An early canal in Cornwall which ran from Par Harbour to Pontsmill, a distance of nearly 2 miles through one lock. Now closed.

Parrott's Canal This was a short canal that ran from Bedworth to near Hawkesbury junction, a distance of 0.6 mile. Later, this coal canal was taken into the Coventry Canal.

Pensnett Canal This canal was built about 1810 by Lord Ward and was 1¼ miles long. It commences at its junction with the Dudley Canal at the top of Parkhead Locks and leads to Brierley Hill and Pensnett. Now derelict. It was never nationalised with the Birmingham Canal Navigation.

Petworth Canal A branch of the Western Rother Navigation, it ran through two locks to Haslingbourne Bridge near Petworth from near Stopham Bridge.

Pidcock's Canal This ran from Lydney for a distance of 1½ miles. It has long been derelict.

Pillrow Cut The artificial cut linking the Brue and Axe. It does not seem to have been used later than the Middle Ages and drainage works have ruined the Axe and Brue Navigations.

Portsea Canal Part of London's lost route to the sea. This route entered the sea by Chichester Harbour and craft went through the two entrance locks at Milton to Portsea Basins. This was a distance of nearly 2½ miles. To reach Milton Locks craft had a sea route from Chichester Channel around dredged channels via Thorney and Hayling Islands and across Langstone Harbour to Milton Common to enter the canal. Most of this route is now covered with roads and housing, but the entrance lock has been restored.

Portsmouth and Arundel Canal Part of the old London to Portsmouth route. Built under the Act of 1817. The canal left by a lock from the Arun near Ford and through another lock shortly after, it then ran level to the branch to Chichester. From here there were two locks to Chichester Harbour. Barges went round Thorney and Hayling Islands to Portsea Island and into a short canal to Portsmouth. A short section of the Chichester Canal remains open, but the bulk of the canal, apart from Chichester Branch, was closed about 1860. Total length nearly 31 miles.

Romford Canal This canal was proposed from Collier Row Common, Romford to the Thames via Dagenham. There were to be five locks but only one lock was partially constructed and the canal was never completed.

Rother, River (Western) Made navigable in 1793 and linked Midhurst to the River Arun at Stopham. Length 11.1 miles with eight locks. Canoeable from Midhurst. Disused since 1871.

Royal Arsenal Canal (sometimes called the Woolwich Canal) This left the Thames via an entrance lock to Woolwich Arsenal. The top part of the waterway has been filled in but the lower half may be re-opened for amenity purposes.

Runcorn and Weston Canal This ran from the junction with the new line of locks of the Bridgewater Canal to Weston Point, junction with the River Weaver. Distance 1.4 miles and two locks.

Runcorn and Latchford Canal A section of canal holding water about 3 miles long is isolated and disused since construction of the Manchester Ship Canal.

St Columb Canal Promoted by an Act of 1773 from Mawgan Porth in Cornwall to St Columb Porth. Length about 6 miles, it has been derelict for over 150 years.

Salisbury and Southampton Canal This canal ran from Southampton to Redbridge and on to Romsey via the Andover Canal and to Michelmersh where it left the Andover Canal and ran through East Dean to Alderbury Common. It was opened in 1804 but never beyond Alderbury due to financial troubles. By 1808 the canal closed and was never re-opened. There were 11 locks on the section to Alderbury and two sea locks at Southampton and Northam.

Shrewsbury Canal This ran from Shrewsbury to Donnington at first, later it was extended through Newport to Norbury Junction. Total length 25 miles. There were two branches to the Old Shropshire Canal section at Wappenshall, and also to Lubstree Wharf. First section was opened in 1797 and the link to Norbury Junction in 1833. Portions were first constructed as a tub-boat canal and later to a narrow-boat canal. The inclined plane (disused since 1921) raised tub-boats so that they could continue to Donnington, where a junction was made with the Duke of Sutherland's Tub-boat Canal. Closed throughout.

Shropshire Canal A tub-boat canal running from Donnington (junction with Donnington Wood Canal and Old Shropshire Canal section) to Coalport on the River Severn. The canal did not lock into the Severn. There were two branches, one of which was the old Ketley Canal. There were inclined planes in use in several places. Parts were abandoned from 1818 onwards until by 1913 only 1¼ miles were in use at Blist's Hill blast furnaces, but traffic ceased altogether that year.

Somersetshire Coal Canal It was opened in 1802 when an inclined plane was brought into use. This proved unsuccessful and was replaced by 23 locks in 1805. It was 10½ miles long with a 7½ miles long branch from Midford to Radstock. The Radstock arm was never joined by water to the main arm, a tram road connecting the terminus at Twinhoe with Midford (about 1 mile in length). This Radstock arm, which was little used, was converted into a tramway in 1815 and sold to the Somerset and Dorset Railway in 1871. The main line ran from

Dundas (junction with the Kennet and Avon) to Timsbury (Paulton Basin). A short length from the junction with the K & A has been re-opened for moorings.

Speedwell Mine This is an underground canal ½ mile long in Derbyshire. It was used in the past to transport lead ore and it is still open today as a tourist attraction.

Stover Canal A short canal in Devonshire nearly 2 miles long through four locks, it ran from a backwater of the River Teign to Teigngrace. The bottom portion was in use until World War II and closed in 1944. Primitive and unique lock mechanism.

Surrey Canal An extension of the Surrey Docks. This ran through a lock from the docks to Camberwell, a distance of 2½ miles. There was a branch to Peckham ½ mile long. The docks and canal are now closed. Owned by the PLA.

Tavistock Canal Authorised by Act of 1803 the canal was actually built the year before. It was to export copper from Morwellham Quay on the River Tamar and the main line was a 4-mile tub-boat canal to Tavistock on the River Tavy. The 2-mile branch to Mill Hill slate quarries, with an inclined plane, was completed by 1819. There were no locks but a tunnel and two inclined planes. The canal was closed by the Duke of Bedford after he bought it in 1873. In 1933–34 a part was resurrected for use as a hydro-electric generating station. Morwellham Quay is now a fascinating open-air museum.

Tern, River A tributary of the River Severn from the river to Upton Forge, 1½ miles, and other forges. There was an entrance lock from the Severn. Long derelict.

Thorne and Hatfield Moors Peat Canal The Thorne Boating Dyke has been made redundant by the cutting of nearby Stainforth Canal but a new drain, about 2 miles long, was cut at the side of Thorne Waste. This was linked with about 4 miles of other drains for peat extraction until trade died out about 1835. A new waterway system in the area was constructed late in the 19th century to extract the peat moss until this trade also died out in the late 1920s.

Thorney, River This river was navigable from Dog-in-a-Doublet on the River Nene to Thorney Village, about 3 miles, through one lock. Lock now closed but the whole of the route is canoeable. This lock was a double lock, staircase.

Tillingham, River From Rye a portion of the river has in the past been used for navigation.

Tillingbourne, River A short section of the river near Chilworth was canalised to serve the gunpowder mills. Still canoeable.

Tone, River This was the old navigation route to Taunton from Burrow Bridge on the River Parrett. With the opening of the Bridgwater and Taunton Canal this route went out of use. Still navigable on a high tide to Knapp Bridge, a distance of 4.9 miles.

Torrington Canal A private canal about 6 miles long, which had an inclined plane. It linked the Torridge River to Torrington and a short distance above. Closed in 1871. The Rolle aqueduct, named after the family who built the canal, can still be seen across the River Torridge.

Ulverston Canal A short canal, 1½ miles long, promoted under an Act of 1793 linked the town of Ulverston to the sea in the north of Morecambe Bay. It was used by small coasters until it was closed in 1944.

Uttoxeter Canal Constructed about 1805 by the Uttoxeter Canal Company, it left Froghall Basin by a side lock to near Uttoxeter. It was 13 miles long and was closed when the Churnet Valley Railway was built.

Westport Canal A short canal leading to Westport (Somerset). This left the River Isle, a tributary of the Parrett, which was canalised with one lock at Midelney. The canal was closed about 1880 but the Isle is canoeable.

Wisbech Canal Constructed under an Act of 1794, it ran from the River Nene at Wisbech to Outwell where it made a junction with the Middle Level. The length was 5¼ miles and there were two locks, one at either end. The canal is now totally derelict, and was closed by Warrant of the Minister of Transport on 14 June 1926. The canal was filled with water each high tide, as there was no water supply.

Wombridge Canal A private canal linking the coal and ironstone industry at Wombridge with the Shrewsbury Canal at Donnington Wood. Completed in 1789 and shortly after sold to the Shrewsbury Canal. Abandoned in 1931.

Woodeaves Canal A detached canal just over 1¼ miles long built near Ashbourne Derbyshire to serve the cotton mills near Fenny Bentley.

Woolston Canal A section of the Mersey and Irwell Navigation, now closed. There were two locks, one at either end, Paddington and Woolston, and the total distance was 2¼ miles.

Worsley Underground Canals This was a complex system of underground waterways in the coal mines at Worsley totalling 46 miles in length. There were locks, inclined planes and the waterways were on two levels. The system was last used in 1887 and was regularly maintained until 1969. It is now dangerous to enter and has been closed.

SCOTLAND

Aberdeenshire Canal This canal was opened on 31 May 1805. The canal was 18¼ miles long with 17 locks and it ran from Aberdeen to Inverurie. Closed in 1853 and partly converted to a railway.

Bo'ness Canal Built to link Bo'ness and Grangemouth but it was never finished owing to financial problems.

Burnturk Canal Two short canals (near Cupar) linking the lime kilns to Kingskettle, 2 miles and a short length of ½ mile.

Campbeltown Canal This ran from Argyll colliery to Campbeltown, a distance of about three miles. Closed 1855 and its place taken by a light railway, now also closed.

Carlingwark Canal Two short lengths, 1¼ miles and ½ mile from Carlingwark Loch to the Dee.

Dingwall Canal This waterway was tidal and took its water supply from the River Peffrey. It was 2000yds long and is unique in having been constructed under the authority of an Act for building highland roads and bridges. It was completed in 1816. It suffered from silting and later railway competition, and the last meeting of the canal commissioners took place in 1884. The route is still traceable and holds water.

Forth and Cart Junction Canal This was a short canal to improve traffic from the Forth and Clyde Canal to Paisley. It was only ¾ mile long from Whitecrook, on the Forth and Clyde, to the Clyde opposite the River Cart. This was never a success and, having passed to the Caledonian Railway in 1867, it closed in 1893.

Glasgow, Paisley and Johnstone Canal This canal was originally intended to connect Glasgow to Ardrossan, making the latter a port for Glasgow. The first part to be constructed was 11 miles from Johnstone, with no locks but passing through two tunnels in Paisley, to its terminus at Port Eglinton in Glasgow. It opened in 1810 and was successful until competition from railways took the parcel and passenger traffic. It was closed in 1881 and a railway laid in the bed.

Kilbagie Canal This was 1 mile long to take grain from near Alloa to a distillery near Kilbagie. Closed 1862.

Loch Morlich A canal system, mainly on existing river courses in the Cairngorms, closed about 1850. This system high up in the hills was used for floating timber and came into the news in recent years in a case dealing with rights of navigation on the River Spey.

Monkland Canal Coal supplies to Glasgow were the impetus for this canal which ran for 12¼ miles from the Glasgow Branch of the Forth and Clyde Canal to Woodhall. Despite competition from railways the heavy coal traffic kept the canal working until the 1860s. In 1867, along with the Forth and Clyde, the Monkland canal was bought by the Caledonian Railway. The last coal was transported in 1935, but the canal still served as a water feeder to the Forth and Clyde and was not abandoned until 1950. The canal still contains water in several places and some restoration work is underway.

Muirkirk Canal This Ayrshire Canal was built about 1790 for transporting coal and ore.

Perth Town Lode After about 1824 coal was carried to the gas works from the River Tay. It was built to connect the Rivers Almond and Tay.

Stevenston Canal This was 2½ miles long running from Stevenston to Saltcoats. Closed about 1830.

WALES

Aberdare Canal Now closed and converted to a road, after 1900. There were two locks and one stop lock. Length 6¾ miles from Abercynon to Ty-draw.

Ashburnham Canal Built prior to 1800, 1¼ miles long, and this ran from Ffrwd near Pembrey, to the estuary of the Gwendraeth. There was a branch, ¼ mile long to Coed built later. Disused since the early 1800s.

Bowser's Canal A short length of waterway to link a small colliery near Ffrwd to the nearest road.

Burry and Loughor Rivers These rivers were improved under an Act of 1815 and were mainly used for coal traffic which lasted until the coming of railways.

Cyfartha Canal A south Wales tub-boat canal. Closed 1840.

Doctor's Canal (listed sometimes as Dr Thomas's Canal) This canal ran from a junction with the Glamorganshire Canal at Denia to Treforest, a distance of 1 mile. Now derelict. Closed in 1914.

Ffrwd Canal (near Wrexham) A detached part of the Ellesmere Canal that was planned to run from the Dee to Trevor. The route was never built and

Gartsherrie Church reflected in the Gartsherrie Branch of the Monkland Canal at the Summerlee Heritage Park, Coatbridge. *Guthrie Hutton*

this section was about 2 miles long and does not appear ever to have been used.

General Warde's Canal (Yspitty) This Carmarthenshire canal ran from a creek near Yspitty called Townsend's Pill and finally became two branches, one leading to Bynea and the other to Pencrug.

General Warde's Canal (Dafen) A short extension of the Pill at Dafen to inland collieries.

Glamorganshire Canal This canal commenced at Cyfartha and ran via Abercynon Treforest to Cardiff, a distance of 25½ miles through 52 locks. The first half mile was closed in 1865 and the canal was disused above Abercynon after 1898. The Cardiff Corporation closed the canal by Act of Parliament in 1943, except for the bottom pound above the sea lock which was closed in 1950 under Section 27 of the Cardiff Corporation Act, 1943. The section between Tongwynlais and the Melingriffith Works at Whitchurch is maintained for fishing. The rest is virtually extinct.

Giant's Grave and Briton Ferry Canal This canal formed a continuation of the Neath Canal at Giant's Grave. Length ½ mile, no locks. It is now a water feeder to the local factories. One of a group known as 'The Earl of Jersey's Canals'.

Glan-y-Wern Canal This canal joined Red Jacket to Glan-y-Wern, a distance of 3½ miles. Disused since 1910.

Hopkin's Canal A short canal half a mile long and long extinct, leading from Townsend's Pill, Yspitty.

Kidwelly and Llanelly Canal The first section was known as Kymer's Canal and was constructed under an Act dated 1766, this ran from the sea to Pwllyllgod. In 1812 another Act was passed and another 4½ miles added, part of which led to the direction of Llanelly and another part towards Pontyates. Other sections were completed, but only a total of just over 9 miles were built and the canal was never completed. The canal was converted to a railway and part of the canal bed was used for the track.

Kilgetty Canal A short canal in Pembrokeshire that does not ever appear to have been completed.

Llansamlet Canal This ran from Llansamlet, near Swansea, to the River Tawe at Foxhole. Long derelict, 3 miles long.

Llechryd Canal A cut made from the River Teifi to a tinplate works at Castle Malgwyn. The works closed early in the 1800s, but stone material was carried on the River Teifi into the present century.

Morris's Canal This canal in Glamorganshire, built before 1800, was 1 mile long and was incorporated into the Trewyddfa Canal which became part of the Swansea Canal.

Pembrey Canal Opened in 1824 linking the Kidwelly and Llanelly Canal to Pembrey Harbour through one lock. Total distance 2 miles. Closed and partly converted to a railway.

Pen-clawdd Canal Opened in 1814. This canal ran from Pen-clawdd 3.6 miles inland to collieries. There were at least two locks. It was still useable in 1825.

Penrhiwtyn Canal A short canal running from Giant's Grave, 1.4 miles long. Derelict.

Plas Kynaston Canal This Denbighshire canal was only about 1000yds long and was built in 1832 to connect the basins at Trevor on the Ellesmere Canal to works near Cefn-Mawr. Closed during the 1914–18 war.

Rhuddlan Canal A very early canalisation of part of the River Clwyd up to Rhuddlan Castle carried out in the 13th century. This project was one of the earliest recorded canalisation projects bringing the castle within two miles of the sea. The cost was high, in modern terms it would be about £1 million. The engineer is not known, but it is thought likely that James of St George was responsible as he had overall direction of the King's works in North Wales.

Tremadoc Canal A short canal linking the town to the sea.

Wern Canal, Llanelly (also called Pen-y-fan Canal) Short South Wales canal which ran from Copperhouse Dock to Wern Pits, a distance of 1 mile.

Waterways museums

Basingstoke Canal Centre, Mytchett Place Road, Mytchett, Surrey GU16 6DD ☎ 01252 370073 *Fax* 01252 371758.

Batchworth Lock Visitor Centre, 99 Church Street, Rickmansworth, Herts WD3 1JD ☎ 01923 778382.

Birchills Canal Museum, Old Birchills, Walsall WS3 8QD ☎ 01922 645778.

Black Country Museum, Tipton Road, Dudley, West Midlands DY1 4SQ ☎ 01215 579643 *Fax* 01215 574242.

Blakes Lock Museum, Gasworks Road, off Kenavon Drive, Reading RG1 3DH ☎ 0118 901 5145 *Fax* 0118 959 0630.

The Boat Museum, South Pier Road, Ellesmere Port, Cheshire L65 4FW ☎ 0151 355 5017 *Fax* 0151 355 4079.

The Canal Exhibition Centre, Lower Dee Mill, Trevor Road, Llangollen, Clwyd LL20 8RX ☎ 01978 860584 *Fax* 01978 861928.

Canal Museum, Linlithgow Union Canal Society, Manse Road Basin, Linlithgow, West Lothian EH49 6AJ ☎ 01506 842123.

Canal Museum, Canal Street, Nottingham NG1 7ET ☎ 0115 915 6870.

Canal Museum, Stoke Bruerne, Towcester, Northamptonshire NN12 7SE ☎/*Fax* 01604 862229.

Dapdune Wharf (a National Trust museum on the River Wey), Wharf Road, Guildford, Surrey GU1 4RR ☎ 01483 561389 *Fax* 01483 531667.

East Anglia Maritime Museum, 25 Marine Parade, Great Yarmouth NR30 2EN ☎ 01493 842267.

Foxton Canal Museum, Middle Lock, Gumley Road, Foxton, Market Harborough, Leicestershire LE16 7RA ☎ 0116 2792657.

The Gloucester Folk Museum, 99-103 Westgate Street, Gloucester GL1 2PG ☎ 01452 526467 *Fax* 01452 330495.

The Horse Drawn Boat Centre, The Wharf, Wharf Hill, Llangollen, Denbighshire LL20 8TA ☎/*Fax* 01978 860702.

International Sailing Craft Association Maritime Museum, Caldecott Road, Oulton Broad, Lowestoft NR32 2PH ☎ 01502 585606 *Fax* 01502 589014.

Ironbridge Gorge Museum, Ironbridge, Telford, Salop TF8 7AW ☎ 01952 433522 *Fax* 01952 432204.

Kennet and Avon Canal Museum, Canal Centre, Couch Lane, Devizes, Wiltshire SN10 1EB ☎ 01380 721279 *Fax* 01380 727870.

Liverpool Maritime Museum, Albert Dock, Liverpool L3 4AQ ☎ 0151 478 4499 *Fax* 0151 478 4590.

London Canal Museum, Battlebridge Basin, 12/13 New Wharf Road, Kings Cross, London N1 9RT ☎ 0171 713 0836.

The Manchester Museum, Oxford Road, Manchester M13 9PL ☎ 0161 275 2634 *Fax* 0161 275 2676.

Morwellham and Tamar Valley Trust, Morwellham Quay, Tavistock, Devon PL19 8JL ☎ 01822 832766 *Fax* 01822 833808

National Maritime Museum, Greenwich, London SE10 9NF ☎ 0181 858 4422 *Fax* 0181 312 6632.

National Waterways Museum, Llanthony Warehouse, Gloucester Docks, Gloucester GL1 2EH ☎ 01452 318054 *Fax* 01452 318066.

The Science Museum, Exhibition Road, South Kensington, London SW7 2DD ☎ 0171 938 8000 *Fax* 0171 938 8118.

Scottish Maritime Museum Trust, Laird Forge Building, Gotteries Road, Irvine, Ayrshire KA12 8QE ☎ 01294 278283 *Fax* 01294 313211.

Summerlee Heritage Park, Heritage Way, Coatbridge ML5 1QD ☎ 01236 431261 *Fax* 01236 440429.

Town Docks Museum, Queen Victoria Square, Hull HU1 3DX ☎ 01482 613902 *Fax* 01482 613710.

Waterfolk Canal Museum, Old Storehouse, Llanfrynach, Brecon, Powys LD3 7LJ ☎ 01874 665382.

The Waterways Museum, Dutch River Side, Goole, E Yorkshire DN14 5TB ☎ 01405 768730 *Fax* 01405 769868.

The following are some of the engines that are in use at intervals for the benefit of visitors:

Broadland Wind Pumps, Stracey Arms, Horsey (National Trust), Thurne Dyke, How Hill (Tower and How Hill Trestle Windpumps are open for inspection at intervals; Berney Arms is a windmill with associations of Broadland).

Claverton Pumping Station, Ferry Lane, Claverton, Bath, Avon ☎ 01225 515954.

Crofton Pumping Engine, Kennet and Avon Canal, Crofton, Great Bedwyn, Wiltshire.

Dogdyke Pumping Station, River Witham (details from Dogdyke Pumping Station, Preservation Trust, Bridge Farm, Tattershall, Lincoln LN4 4JG ☎ 01526 42583).

Lea Wood Pumping Station, Cromford Canal, near Cromford, Derbyshire ☎ 01629 823204.

Stretham Pumping Engine, Old West River, Fenland (enquiries locally are needed to ascertain visiting times).

There are a number of organisations devoted to preservation of old canal and river craft. These are:

The Dolphin Sailing Barge Museum Trust

The East Coast Sail Trust

The Humber Keel and Sloop Preservation Society

The Maritime Trust

The Narrow Boat Trust

The Norfolk Wherry Trust

Oxford Colleges Barges Preservation Trust

The River Stour Trust

Other craft may have preservation groups formed for their benefit, such as Mersey Flats, Severn Trows etc.

Glossary

Aegir Similar to a bore, encountered on the River Trent and occasionally, though usually not so fierce, on the Yorkshire Ouse.

Balance beam or balance The beam projecting from a lock gate which balances its weight, and by pushing against which the gate is opened or closed.

Barge A term including a variety of vessels, both sailing and non-sailing, in use for canal or river traffic, whose beam is approximately twice that of a narrow boat. The name 'barge' is often applied erroneously to all vessels carrying goods on a canal or river, whether barge, wide boat, narrow boat, lighter or any other vessel.

Bollard Wood or metal posts used for tying up boats at locks and moorings.

Bore A tidal wave, the most famous being on the River Severn.

Bow hauling[1] When a motorboat and butty work through a flight of narrow locks the tow-line is usually detached and the butty bow hauled manually.

Breast or mitre post Of a lock gate, the vertical post of the gate farthest from its hanging; where the gates are in pairs, the two breasts are usually mitred to bed against each other when shut.

Bridge hole The narrow channel beneath an over-bridge.

Butty boat A boat working in company with another boat. The term is generally applied to a boat towed by a motorboat.

Compartment boat Commonly called a 'Tom Pudding', a type of boat which was used on the Aire and Calder Navigation. They were worked in trains with other similar boats.

Cut A boatman's name for a canal, so applied on account of its artificially cut channel, as distinguished from the natural channel of a river.

Doors A Fen term for gates; in the Fens all lock gates are called sluice doors.

Draw To draw a paddle, slacker, slat, weir or staunch is to open it in order to allow the water to escape. The reverse is to 'lower', 'drop' or 'shut in', or in the case of a staunch, to 'set'.

Dydle A Norfolk term meaning to dredge or clean out.

Fender Wood plank or mat to protect boat sides in locks, wharves, etc.

Flash An inland lake caused by subsidence of the ground due to salt-mining. This term is also used for the small inland lakes forming part of the Basingstoke Canal.

Gang Planks[1] Removable planks used to afford a means of passing from one end of a working narrow boat to the other; when in place they run from the top of the cabin aft to the deck cratch forward, being supported in between by upright supports called stands. These stands, which are also removable, fit into mortices in the stretchers and boat's floor and have the gang planks tightly lashed down to them.

Gauging[1] The means of ascertaining by the draught of a vessel the weight of cargo on board for the purpose of taking tolls. The first gauging of canal boats is carried out at a weigh-dock, where particulars of the boat's draught are taken when empty, and when fully loaded, and at intermediate points, such as at every ton of loading. The boat is loaded with weights kept for the purpose, which are lifted in and out by cranes; the result arrived at is then either transferred to graduated scales fixed to the boat's sides, which can be read at any time, or the particulars of each vessel are furnished to each toll office in a book, from which, on gauging the immersion of the boat, the number of tons on board can be at once ascertained. The usual method of gauging a boat for immersion is to take what is called the 'dry inches' – that is, the freeboard, at four points, at one point each side near the bow and at one point each side near the stern. This is done by an instrument consisting of a float in a tube having a bracket projecting from the side of the tube. The bracket is rested on the boat's gunwale and the float indicates the number of inches between that and the level of the water in the canal.

Give way to To concede the right of passage to another boat, for example, empty boats usually give way to loaded boats. The actual passing rule varies on different waterways, keeping to the right being now most general.

Gongoozler An idle and inquisitive person who stands staring for prolonged periods at anything out of the usual. The word is believed to have its origin in the Lake District.

Heel post The vertical post of a lock gate nearest to its hanging and the axis on which the gate turns, being rounded at the back to fit into the hollow quoin in which it partially revolves.

Hollow quoin The recess into which the heel post of a lock gate is fitted and in which it partially revolves when being opened and closed.

Inclined plane A device on wheels which lifts boats from one level to another without using locks.

Invert An inverted arch of brickwork or masonry, used chiefly in canal work to form the bottom of locks and tunnels in cases where lateral or upward pressure has to be sustained.

Keel A type of boat once in extensive use on the Yorkshire rivers and canals.

Land Water A term used to denote the water in a river brought down from up country, in distinction from the water set up by the floodtide from seawards.

Legging[1] A method once used to propel horse-drawn boats through tunnels which have no towing path, the boatman pushing with his feet against the tunnel walls. At one time leggers could be hired at most of the longer tunnels.

Lengthman A canal employee in charge of a particular section or length of waterway.

Let off An appliance for getting rid of some of the water from a canal in rainy weather so that it may not overflow its banks. Originally a trap-door sluice set in the bottom of the canal and worked by a chain, but now resembling the ordinary lock paddle.

Level When two reaches of water, one on each side of a lock or weir, from the flow of the tide or other cause become level, a level is said to be made.

Lighter A term including a variety of vessels in use on the Fens, the Thames, the River Stour (Suffolk) and the Bridgewater Canal. On an average they measure 42ft in length by 10ft beam, but Thames lighters equal barges in size, differing from them in the respect that they have 'swim ends', ie flat, sloping ends like a punt.

Lock, To To work a vessel through a lock.

Narrow boat A craft measuring approximately 70ft long by 7ft beam, extensively used throughout the Midland canal system. Sometimes also referred to as a 'monkey boat' or 'long boat'.

Number ones[1] A traditional canal term for a boat owner who worked for himself as distinct from boats owned by a firm or company.

Paddle A sluice valve, by opening or closing which the water can either be allowed to pass or be retained. Ground paddles are those that admit water to the lock by culverts built in the ground, as distinct from the fly paddles, which are fitted to the gates themselves.

Portage A term for lifting craft round locks and sluices. Light craft can use a derelict waterway even though the locks are out of order.

Pound The stretch of water on a canal between two locks.

Quant Term used in Norfolk meaning a pole or shaft.

Ram's Head The boatman's name for the wooden rudder post of a narrow boat; usually it is bound with a pipe-clayed Turk's-head knot, and occasionally decorated with a horse's tail.

Rimers The posts in the removable portions of weirs on the Upper Thames against which the weir paddles are placed.

Roving Bridge or *Turnover Bridge* A bridge carrying a towing path from one side of a canal to the other.

Scour Bank of silt caused by a flow of water.

Screw A boatman's term for any boat driven by a screw propeller.

Set, To To set a staunch is to close it so that the way may accumulate.

Sill, of a lock Sometimes spelt 'cill'. The bar of masonry below water against which the bottom of the lock gates rest when closed.

Staircase locks Also called risers. A flight or series of locks so arranged that the top gate or gates of each lock, except the highest, form the bottom gate or gates of the lock above. The best example of a staircase in England is the flight of five at Bingley on the Leeds and Liverpool Canal.

Staithe A Midlands and Norfolk term for a wharf.

Stank A temporary water-tight dam constructed of piling from which the water can be pumped to enable below-water repairs to be carried out. The word is also used as a verb, eg 'to stank off'.

Staunch or navigation weir[1] A historical system, no longer seen on the waterways, for overcoming change of level in a navigable river. It consists of a weir provided with a gate through which vessels may pass, and which is equipped with paddles like a lock gate. When proceeding upstream, vessels close the gate behind them and wait until sufficient depth of water has accumulated in the reach above the gate to allow them to proceed. Travelling downstream the procedure is reversed.

Stemmed, Stemmed up The boatman's term for running aground on a mud bank.

Stop A stop or stop lock is generally a gate or lock erected at the junction of one canal with another, to prevent loss of water from one to the other if necessary, normally there being little or no change of level. When the canals were used for commercial use, the canal company would have a toll office at a stop lock where cargoes were declared and gauged and tolls paid.

Stop gates They answer the same purpose as stop grooves and planks, but are made in the form of lock gates, and are always kept open except when required for use. In long canal pounds it is usual for stop gates to be fitted at intervals, so that in the event of a leak or burst the escape of water may be confined to that portion of the pound between two gates.

Stop grooves Vertical grooves, usually provided at the head and tail of a lock and in other situations where underwater repairs may have to be carried out, into which stop planks can be inserted to form a temporary dam or stank.

Stoppage A temporary closing of a waterway for repairs.

Stud The tee-headed pin fitted on bow and stern of a narrow boat to which mooring lines are attached.

Summit level The highest pound of water in a canal, and therefore the pound into which the main supply of water for working the locks has to be delivered. Consequently, in dry weather it is the first to be affected as regards deficiency of navigable depth. The highest summit level in England is that of the Huddersfield Narrow Canal, which is 4½ miles long from Diggle to Marsden, and is 644ft 9ins above Ordnance Datum. For 3¼ miles of this summit level the course of the canal is through Standedge Tunnel.

Swim, To[1] A historical term used by boatmen to describe a boat light in draught and which responded quickly to the helm, such a boat was 'a good swimmer' or was said to 'swim well'.

Tail, of a lock That part immediately below the bottom gates. The equivalent portion above the top gates is called 'the head'.

Tow path The path beside a canal for the use of towing horses, also called in different districts 'haling path' or 'haling way'.

Trow A type of vessel in use on the River Severn; they measure approximately 70ft long by 17ft beam.

Tub boat Small box boat carrying from three to five tons, once used in Shropshire and on the Bude canal in Cornwall.

Turns, Waiting turns or Working turns A system often adopted in dry weather in order to make the utmost use of the water. At any lock a boat must wait for the arrival of another coming in the opposite direction, thus making sure that the maximum of traffic is passed for the water consumed.

Tying point The shallowest point in a navigation. For instance, the bottom sill of Cranfleet Lock, better known to boatmen as Old Sal's Lock, was at one time the tying point on the River Trent between Nottingham and the junction of the Erewash Canal; that is to say, any vessel that could float over this sill could find enough water everywhere else between these places.

Wherry The name given to the sailing vessels which traded over the Rivers Bure, Yare and Waveney and their connecting dykes and broads; they varied considerably from a 12-ton boat about 35ft long by 9ft beam to the *Wonder of Norwich*, 65ft long by 19ft beam.

Wide boat A type of boat in use on canals having wide locks. It is of a size between the narrow boat and the barge, 70ft long by 10 to 11ft beam. Such craft can navigate the Grand Union Canal from London as far north as Berkhamstead.

Wind, To To wind a boat is to turn a boat round.

Winding place, Winding hole, Winning place or Winning hole A wide place in a canal provided for the purpose of turning a boat round.

Windlass Also called in some districts 'a crank', is a handle or key for opening and closing lock paddles, shaped in the form of the letter 'L' and having a square socket at one end to fit on the square of the spindle operating the paddle gear.

Wings[1] In the days before motor boats when men had to leg through tunnels, these were flat pieces of board rigged near the bow of the boat when the tunnel was too wide for the leggers to reach the side walls with their feet from the boat's deck. A fully equipped narrow boat would carry two pairs of wings, a pair of 'narrow-cut wings' for narrow boat canals and a pair of 'broad-cut wings' for the tunnels of barge canals.

1. These are historical terms from the days of working narrow boats, they are unlikely to be in common parlance today.

Bibliography

The bibliography is correct to June 1997.

A number of the books listed below are now out of print but may be found in secondhand bookshops or through a library. Of the numerous bookshops around the country the following have extensive canal sections but that does not mean that others will not have.

M & M Baldwin, 24 High Street, Cleobury Mortimer, Nr Kidderminster, Worcs DY14 8BY ☎ 01299 270110, publishers and booksellers with a series of canal maps.

Patterson Liddle, 10 Margaret's Buildings, Brock Street, Bath BA1 2LP ☎ 01225 426722, many antiquarian books and a good source of Acts of Parliament for the historian.

Shepperton Swan Ltd, The Clock House, Upper Halliford, Shepperton, Middlesex, TW17 8RU ☎ 01932 783319, now only secondhand books on British canals with an extensive collection on European waterways.

General

Aickman, Robert *The River Runs Uphill* 1986
Alborough, Norman *Inland Cruising* Helmsman Books 1995
Atterbury, Paul *English Rivers and Canals* 1984
Atterbury, Paul *Exploring Britain's Canals* Harper Collins 1994
Baldwin, Mark *Canal Books* Baldwin 1985
Baldwin, Mark and Burton, Anthony (eds) *Canals: a new look* Phillimore 1984
Balfe, T. (ed) *The Shannon Book* Irish Shell & Bord Failte
Barrell, Emrhys *The Inland Waterways Manual* Adlard Coles Nautical 1993
Blagrove, David *Waterways of Northamptonshire* Northamptonshire Libraries 1990
Bolton, David *Race Against Time: how Britain's waterways were saved* Methuen 1990
Braithwaite, Lewis *Canals in Towns* A & C Black 1976
Broadhead, Ivan E. *Up the Cut: An Anthology of Inland Waterways* Alan Sutton 1994
Bursche, E. *A Handbook of Water Plants* Frederick Warne 1972
Burton, Anthony *Back Door Britain* André Deutsch 1977
Burton, Anthony *The Waterways of Britain* Collins 1983
Burton, Anthony and Pratt, Derek *Canals in Colour* Blandfords 1974
Burton, Anthony and Pratt, Derek *Canal* David & Charles 1976

Calvert, Roger *Inland Waterways of Britain* J.M. Dent 1976
Chaplin, Peter H. *Waterway Conservation* Whittet Books 1989
Cranfield, John and Bonfiel, Michael, *Waterways Atlas of the British Isles* authors 1966
Darwin, Andrew *Canals and Rivers of Britain* J.M. Dent 1976
Davenport, Sheila *Canal and River Cruising: The IWA Manual* Fernhurst Books 1990
De Maré, Eric *The Canals of England* Alan Sutton 1987
De Salis, Henry Rodolph *Bradshaw's Canals and Navigable Rivers of England and Wales* (1904) David & Charles 1969
Edwards, L.A. *The Inland Waterways of Great Britain* Imray, Laurie, Norie and Wilson 1985
Ellis, E.A. *Wild Flowers of the Waterways & Marshes* Jarrold 1972
Evans, Martin Marix *Canals of England* Weidenfeld & Nicholson 1994
Eyre, Frank and Hadfield, Charles *English Rivers and Canals* Collins 1945
Gagg, John *Canals in Camera* Vols 1 & 2 Ian Allan 1970-1
Gagg, John *The Canaller's Bedside Book* David & Charles 1973
Gagg, John *A Canal and Waterways Armchair Book* David & Charles 1975
Gagg, John *John Gagg's Book of Locks, Canal Tunnels etc* J. Gagg 1975-6
Hadfield, Charles *Canals and Waterways* Raleigh 1966
Hadfield, Charles *Inland Waterways* David & Charles 1977
Hadfield, Charles *The Canal Age* David & Charles 1981
Harris, Robert *Canals and their Architecture* Cave 1980
Holland, Stanley *Canal Coins: inland waterway tokens, medals, badges and buttons* M & M Baldwin 1992
IWA Inland Shipping Group Fact Sheets IWA
Lyons, David C. *The Leeds & Liverpool Canal: a photographic journey* Hendon Pub Co 1977
Mabey, R. *The Unofficial Countryside* Collins 1975
Mackersey, Ian *Tom Rolt and the Cressy Years* M & M Baldwin 1991
McKnight, Hugh *A Source Book of Canals, Locks and Canal Boats* Ward Lock 1974
McKnight, Hugh *The Shell Book of Inland Waterways* David & Charles 1981
McNeill, D.B. *Coastal Passenger Steamers and Inland Navigations in the North of Ireland* Belfast Museum & Art Gallery 1960
McNeill, D.B. *Coastal Passenger Steamers and Inland Navigations in the South of Ireland* Belfast Museum & Art Gallery 1965
Metcalfe, Leon and Vince, John *Discovering Canals* Shire Publications 1975
Paget-Tomlinson, Edward W. *Waterways in the Making* Landscape Press 1996
Pratt, Derek *Discovering London's Canals* Shire 1987
Pratt, Frances *Canal Architecture in Britain* BWB 1976
Ransom, P.J.G. *Waterways Restored* Faber & Faber 1974
Ransom, P.J.G. *The Archaeology of Canals* World's Work 1979
Rolt, L.T.C. *The Inland Waterways of England* Allen & Unwin 1970
Rolt, L.T.C. *Navigable Waterways* Penguin 1985
Roulstone, Michael *Fenland Waterways* Balfour, 1974
Russell, Roland *Discovering Lost Canals* Shire Publications 1980

Seaman, Kenneth *Canal Fishing* Barrie & Jenkins 1971

Sherwood, K.B. *Stoke Bruerne – impact of canal on village* Nene College Northampton 1979

Squires, Roger W. *Canals Revived: The Story of the Waterways Restoration Movement* Moonraker Press 1979

Squires, Roger W. *The New Navvies* Phillimore 1983

Stewart, Sheila *Ramlin Rose* Oxford University Press 1993

Tew, David *Canal Inclines and Lifts* Alan Sutton 1984

Tibbs, Rodney *Fenland River* Terence Dalton 1969

Vince, John *Canals and Canal Architecture* Shire Publications 1976

Ward, J.R. *Finance of Canal Building in 18th Century England* Oxford University Press 1974

Ware, Michael E. *A Canalside Camera 1845-1930* David & Charles 1975

Ware, Michael E. *Britain's Lost Waterways* Moorland Publishing 1989

Westall, George *Inland Cruising on the Rivers and Canals of England and Wales* London Westall 1908

Waterways guides, pilots and maps

Allsop, Niall *The Kennet & Avon Canal: a user's guide* Millstream 1992

Bailey, Eric and Ruth *The Alternative Holiday Guide to the Waterways of Britain and Europe* Ashford 1990

Bowskill, Derek *Northeast Waterways* Imray, Laurie, Norie and Wilson 1986

Bowskill, Derek *The East Coast, A Pilot Guide from the Wash to Ramsgate*, Imray Laurie Norie & Wilson 1992

Bowskill, Derek *The River Medway: a Cruising Guide* Imray, Laurie, Norie & Wilson 1997

Carter, Paul (ed) *Forth & Clyde Canal Guidebook* Strathkelvin District Libraries & Museums 1991

Chelmer and Blackwater Navigation, The IWA Chelmsford Branch 1994

Clarke, Mike *Around and About on the Leeds & Liverpool Canal: a complete tourist guide* Milepost Research 1992

Clew, Kenneth R. *Wessex Waterway: a guide to the Kennet and Avon Canal* Moonraker Press 1978

Coote, Jack E. *East Coast Rivers* Yachting Monthly 1998

Cove-Smith, Chris *London's Waterway Guide* Imray, Laurie, Norie and Wilson 1986

Cove-Smith, Chris *River Thames Book* Imray, Laurie, Norie and Wilson 1996

Coventry's Waterway: a city amenity Coventry Canal Society 1984

Cruising Guide to the North East Waterways Ripon Motor Boat Club

Cunliffe, Tom *The Shell Channel Pilot* Imray, Laurie, Norie and Wilson 1997

Delany, Ruth and Addis, Jeremy *Shannon Guide* Inland Waterways Association of Ireland 1978

Delany, Ruth and Addis, Jeremy *Guide to the Royal Canal of Ireland* Inland Waterways Association of Ireland 1984

Delany, Ruth and Addis, Jeremy *Guide to the Barrow* Inland Waterways Association of Ireland 1991

Delany, Ruth and Addis, Jeremy *Guide to the Grand Canal of Ireland* Inland Waterways Association of Ireland 1992

Denton, John Horsley *A Towpath Guide to the Montgomeryshire Canal and the Llanymynech Branch of the Ellesmere Canal* Lapal 1984

Elwin, Geoff and King, Cathleen *Braunston to Brentford: a guide to the southern Grand Union Canal* Blackhorn 1980

Essex-Lopresti, Michael *Exploring the Regent's Canal* Brewin 1990

Fishwick, Mark *South Coast Cruising* Yachting Monthly 1st edn 1993

Fishwick, Mark *West Country Cruising* Yachting Monthly 3rd edn 1998

Freethy, Ron and Woods, Catherine *Discovering the Leeds to Liverpool Canal* Countryside 1989

GEOprojects Maps
Kennet and Avon Canal 1990
Oxford Canal 1993
River Thames 1994
Grand Union Canal (4 sections) 1995
Basingstoke Canal 2nd Edn 1995
Birmingham Canal Navigations 1996
The Broads 1996
Shropshire Union Canal 1996
Llangollen and Montgomery Canals 1996
Inland Waterways of Great Britain 1997
Caledonian Canal and the Great Glen 1997
Thames Ring, London Ring Atlas 1997

Gilman, H.J. *A Complete Guide to the Macclesfield Canal* M.G. Publications 1992

Hadfield, Charles *Waterway Sights to See* David & Charles 1976

Handford, Michael and Viner, David *Stroudwater and Thames & Severn Canals Towpath Guide* Alan Sutton 1984

Hanna, Peter and Delany, Ruth *Guide to the Barrow, with Navigation Notes for the Nore, Suir and Estuary* Inland Waterways Association of Ireland 1991

Hayward, Graham *Stanford's River Thames* Stanford Maritime 1988

Herbert, Sir A.P. *The Thames* Weidenfeld & Nicholson 1966

Huddersfield Canals: Towpath Guide, The Huddersfield Canal Society 1981

Imray Laurie Norie & Wilson Maps
The Rivers Cam and Lower Great Ouse: Cambridge to Denver Sluice 1993
The Upper River Great Ouse: Bedford to Pope's Corner
The Middle Level
The River Nene: Northampton to Peterborough
The River Wey
Map of the Inland Waterways of Great Britain
The Inland Waterways Directory – Annual IWA

Langford, J. Ian *A Towpath Guide to the Stourbridge Canal* Lapal 1992

Lee and Stort Navigations, A Guide to the ed. Richard Thomas 1994

Livingstone, Helen *Aerofilms Guide: the Thames Path* Ian Allan 1993

Lockmaster Maps

Morris, Jonathan *The Shropshire Union Canal: a towpath guide from Autherley to Nantwich* Management Update 1991

Nicholson Ordnance Survey Guide to the Waterways 1997
 1. London, Grand Union, Oxford & Lee
 2. Severn, Avon & Birmingham
 3. Birmingham & the Heart of England
 4. Four Counties & the Welsh Canals
 5. North West & the Pennines
 6. Nottingham, York & the North East
 7. Thames, Wey, Kennet & Avon

Nicholson Ordnance Survey Inland Waterways Map of Great Britain

Norris, John *The Brecon & Abergavenny Section of the Monmouthshire & Brecon Canal* John Norris 1994

Oliver, Ken, Pribul, Sally and Thomas, Richard *A Guide to the Lee and Stort Navigations* Lee and Stort Planning and Amenities Forum 1994

Parker, Steven and Chester-Browne, Richard *A Towpath Guide to the Manchester, Bolton & Bury Canal* MB&BC Society 1989

Pass, Barbara *Along the Leeds and Liverpool Canal from Adlington to Burnley* Wigan Metropolitan Borough Council 1988

Pearson's Canal Companions
Cheshire Ring
Four Counties Ring and Caldon Canal
Oxford Canal, Grand Union Canal and River Nene
Pennine Waters
Severn and Avon, featuring the Avon Ring
Shropshire Union and Llangollen Canal plus the Montgomery Canal
South Midlands and Warwickshire Ring including the Ashby Canal
Stourport Ring, the Black Country Ring and Birmingham Canal Navigations
East Midlands

Richardson, Christine *Water Ways* Hallamshire Press 1995

Richardson, Christine and Lower, John *A Walkers' and Boaters' Guide to The Chesterfield Canal and Cuckoo Way* Hallamshire Press 1994

Richardson, Christine and Lower, John *The Complete Guide to the Sheffield and South Yorkshire Navigation* Hallamshire Press 1995

Richardson, Christine and Lower, John *The Waterways of Lincoln and Boston* Hallamshire Press 1998

Rowland, Chris and Simpson, John *The Best Waterside Pubs in England & Wales* Alma 1992

Sampson, Carol *The First Mate Guide to the Staffs and Worcs Canal* Carol Sampson 1995

Slater, David *et al* *The Complete Guide to the Lancaster Canal* Lancaster Canal Trust 1989

Van der Klugt, Diana *Launching on Inland Waterways* Opus Book Publishing Ltd 1993

Walford, Bill *Thames Rambler* Bill Walford Publishing 1994

Waterways World Cruising Guides
Coventry, Ashby, Oxford (N) and Birmingham & Fazeley Canals
Grand Union Canal (North) – Birmingham to Stoke Bruerne
Grand Union Canal (South) – Stoke Bruerne to Brentford & Paddington and the Regent's Canal
Llangollen Canal – including Montgomery
Oxford Canal – Hawkesbury Jn to Oxford
Shropshire Union Canal
Staffordshire & Worcestershire Canal
Trent & Mersey Canal – including Caldon
What to do on the Norfolk Broads – Annual Jarrold Publishing

Canal and river craft and carriers

Alsop, Roger and Dodkins, Graham *Working Boats* 1988

Billingham, Nick *Narrow Boats – Care and Mainenance* The Crowood Press 1995

Billingham, Nick *Inland Cruisers – Care and Maintenance* The Crowood Press 1995

Blagrove, David *Bread upon the Waters* Reprint M & M Baldwin 1994

Carr, Frank G.G. *Sailing Barges* Terence Dalton 1989

Chaplin, Tom *Short History of the Narrow Boat* Shepperton Swan 1980

Chaplin, Tom *Narrow Boats* Whittet Books 1989

Conway-Jones, Hugh *Working Life on Severn & Canal* Alan Sutton 1990

Cooper, F.S. and Chancellor, John *A Handbook of Sailing Barges* Adlard Coles Nautical 1989

Cornish, Margaret *Troubled Waters: Memoirs of a Canal Boatwoman* M & M Baldwin 1993

Crabtree, Harold and Clarke, Mike *Railway on the Water: Tom Puddings and the Yorkshire Coal Industry* Sobriety Project 1993

Ellis, Tony *The Sailing Barges of Maritime England* Shepperton Swan 1982

Faulkner, Alan H. *The George & the Mary: a brief history of the Grand Union Canal Carrying Company Ltd* Robert Wilson 1973

Faulkner, Alan H. *F.M.C.: a short history of Fellows Morton and Clayton Limited* Robert Wilson 1975

Faulkner, Alan H. *Claytons of Oldbury* Robert Wilson 1978

Faulkner, Alan H. *Tankers Knottingley* Robert Wilson 1976

Faulkner, Alan H. *Severn & Canal and Cadburys* Robert Wilson 1981

Faulkner, Alan H. *Barlows* Robert Wilson 1986

Faulkner, Alan H. *Willow Wren: the story of the Willow Wren Canal Carrying Co Ltd and Waterways Transport Services Ltd* Waterway Productions 1986

Fletcher, Harry *A Life on the Humber: keeling to shipbuilding* Faber & Faber 1975

Foxon, Tom *Anderton for Orders* J.M. Pearson 1988

Foxon, Tom *Number One!* J.M. Pearson 1991

Frere-Cook, Gervis (ed) *The Decorative Arts of the Mariner* Cassell 1966

Gladwin, D.D. *Passenger Boats on Inland Waterways* Oakwood Press 1979

Hanson, Harry *Canal People* David & Charles 1978

Hanson, Harry *The Canal Boatmen 1760–1914* Alan Sutton 1984

Inland Sailors Museum & Art Gallery Service for Yorkshire & Humberside 1974

Lansdell, Avril *Clothes of the Cut* BWB 1993

Lewery, A.J. *Narrow Boat Painting* David & Charles 1974

Lewery, A.J. *Signwritten Art* 1989

Lewery, A.J. *Popular Art* 1991

Lewery, A.J. *Flowers Afloat* 1996

McDonald, Dan *The Clyde Puffer* Thomas & Lochar 1994

McKnight, Hugh *Canal and River Craft in Pictures* David & Charles 1970

Malster, Robert *Wherries & Waterways* Terence Dalton 1986

Norton, Peter *The End of the Voyage: an account of the last sailing craft of the British coasts* Percival Marshall 1959

O'Connor, J. *Canals, Barges & People* Art & Technics 1950

Paget-Tomlinson, Edward *Mersey and Weaver Flats* Robert Wilson 1974

Paget-Tomlinson, Edward *Britain's Canal and River Craft* Moorland 1979

Pierce, A.J. *Canal People* A & C Black 1978

Schofield, Fred *Humber Keels and Keelmen* Terence Dalton 1988

Smith, D.J. *Canals, Boats and Boaters* Hugh Evelyn 1973

Smith, D.J. *The Horse on the Cut* Patrick Stevens 1982

Smith, D.J. *Discovering the Craft of Inland Waterways* Shire Publications 1987

Smith, Emma *Maiden's Trip* M & M Baldwin 1987

Smith, George *Our Canal Population (1879)* E.P. Publishing 1974

Smith, George *Canal Adventures by Moonlight* Hodder & Stoughton 1881

Smith, Peter L. *A Pictorial History of Canal Craft* Batsford 1979

Smith, Peter L. *Canal Barges & Narrow Boats* Shire Publications 1994

Stammers, Michael *Mersey Flats and Flatmen* Terence Dalton 1993

Sullivan, Dick *Navvyman* Coracle Books 1983

Taylor, Mike *Memories of the Sheffield & South Yorkshire Navigation* Yorkshire Waterway Publications 1988

Ulyatt, Michael E. *Flying Sail – Humber Keels and Sloops* Mr Pye Books 1996

Walker, Anthony J. *Walkers' of Ricky* W.H. Walker & Bros Ltd 1991

Ware, Michael E. *Narrow Boats at Work* Moorland Publishing 1980

Weaver, C.P. and Weaver, C.R. *Steam on Canals* David & Charles 1983

Webb, Mike *Braunston's Boats* Pearson 1983

Webb, Mike *Shroppie Boats* Pearson 1985

Wheat, G. *Leeds & Liverpool Canal Craft* Northern Counties Carriers Ltd 1972

Wilkinson, Tim *Hold on a Minute* M & M Baldwin 1990

Wilson, John K. and Faulkner, Alan H. *Fenland Barge Traffic* Robert Wilson 1972

Wilson, Robert J. *The Number Ones* Robert Wilson 1972

Wilson, Robert J. *Boatyards & Boatbuilding* Robert Wilson 1974

Wilson, Robert J. *Knobsticks: Canal Carrying on the Northern Trent and Mersey* Robert Wilson 1974

Wilson, Robert J. *Life Afloat* Robert Wilson 1976

Wilson, Robert J. *Roses & Castles* Robert Wilson 1976

Woolfit, Susan *Idle Women* M & M Baldwin 1995

Biography

Beckett, Derrick *Telford's Britain* David & Charles 1987

Bode, Harold *James Brindley* Shire Publications 1980

Bracegridle, B. and Miles, P. H. *Great Engineers & Their Works – Thomas Telford* David & Charles 1973

Boucher, Cyril T.G. *John Rennie* Manchester University Press 1963

Boucher, Cyril T.G. *James Brindley, Engineer 1716–1772* Goose & Son 1968

Cruickshank, M. *Thomas Telford* Keele Teaching Unit 1971

Gibb, Sir Alexander *The Story of Telford* Maclehose London 1935

Hadfield, Charles *Thomas Telford's Temptation: Telford and William Jessop's Reputation* M & M Baldwin 1993

Hadfield, Charles and Skempton, A.W. *William Jessop, Engineer* David & Charles 1979

Malet, Hugh *Bridgewater – The Canal Duke 1736-1803* Hendon Publishing 1990

Meynell, Laurence *James Brindley, the pioneer of canals* Laurie 1956

Meteyard, E. *The Life of Josiah Wedgwood 1865*

Pearce, Rhoda M. *Thomas Telford* Shire Publications Ltd 1973

Rolt, L.T.C. *James Watt* Batsford 1962

Rolt, L.T.C. *Newcomen* David & Charles 1964

Rolt, L.T.C. *Thomas Telford* Penguin 1985

Smiles, S. *Lives of the Engineers (1861)* Vol 1 includes J. Brindley, Vol 2 includes J. Rennie and T. Telford David & Charles 1968

Cruises and travelogues

Aubertin, C.J. *A Caravan Afloat* (1916) Reprint 1982

Bird, Vivian *By Lock & Pound* Baldwin 1988

Bolton, David *Journey Without End: a voyage through the English waterways* Methuen 1987

Bonthron, P. *My Holidays on Inland Waterways* Thomas Murby & Co 1916

Bryce, Iris *Canals are My Home* Mason 1979

Bryce, Iris *Canals are My Life* Mason 1982

Bryce, Iris *Canals are My World* Pearson 1986

Colborne, C.L. *Practical Boat Handling on the Thames* David & Charles 1977

Cove-Smith, C. and Chase, R.E. *Pilotage on Inland Waterways* Yachting & Boating 1970

Dashwood, J.B. *The Thames to the Solent by Canal and Sea (1868)* Shepperton Swan 1980

De Maré, Eric *Time on the Thames* Flare Books 1975

Doerflinger, Frederic *Slow Boat through England* W.H. Allen 1986

Doerflinger, Frederic *Slow Boat through Pennine Waters* W.H. Allen 1986

Edwards, L.A. *Holiday Cruising on the Broads and Fens* David & Charles 1972

Emerson, P.H. *On English Lagoons* D. Nutt 1892

Eyles, J. *Cruising Along the Mon & Brec Canal* Starling Press 1972

Farrant, A. *Rowing Holiday by Canal in 1873* Oakwood Press 1977

Forester, C.S. *Hornblower and the Atropos* Penguin 1990

Foster, A.J. *The Ouse* SPCK (c.1891)

Gagg, John *5000 Miles 3000 Locks* Arthur Barker 1973

Gardner, Raymond *Land of Time Enough: a journey through the waterways of Ireland* Hodder & Stoughton 1977

Gayford, Eily *The Amateur Boatwomen: canal boating 1941-1945* Reprint M & M Baldwin 1996

Hankinson, J. *Canal Cruising* Ward Lock & Co 1977

Hassell, J. *A Tour of the Grand Junction Canal in 1819* Cranfield & Bonfiel 1968

Haynes, Ken *Here and There on the Monmouthshire, Brecon & Abergavenny Canal, A Sketch Book* Ken Haynes 1988

Hayward, Richard *Where the Shannon Flows* Dundalgan Press 1978

Kimbrough, Emily *Water, Water, Everywhere* Heinemann 1957

Kimbrough, Emily *A Right Good Crew* Heinemann 1959

Liley, John *Inland Cruising Companion* Stanford Maritime 1977

Liley, John *Journeys of the Swan* Waterways Productions 1983

Link House *The Canals Books* Link House, annually

Llewellyn, Sam *The Worst Journey in the Midlands* Heinemann 1983

Lloyd, Montague and Ann *Through England's Waterways* Imray 1948

Malet, Hugh *In the Wake of the Gods: on the waterways of Ireland* Chatto & Windus 1970

Malet, Hugh *Voyage in a Bowler Hat* Eire & UK M & M Baldwin 1985

Nowlan, David (ed) *Silver River: a celebration of 25 years of the Shannon Boat Rally* Inland Waterways Association of Ireland 1985

O'Sullivan, T.F. *Goodly Barrow* Ward River 1983

Owen, David E. *Water Highways* Phoenix House 1967

Owen, David E. *Water Rallies* J.M. Dent 1969
Owen, David E. *Water Byways* David & Charles 1973
Pilkington, Roger *Thames Waters* Lutterworth Press 1956
Pilkington, Roger *Small Boat on the Thames* Macmillan 1966
Pilkington, Roger *Small Boat Down the Years* Pearson 1987
Poole, John *Narrow Boat Venture* Thornhill Press 1975
Ransom, P.J.G. *Holiday Cruising in Ireland* David & Charles 1971
Rice, H.J. *Thanks for the Memory* Inland Waterways Association of Ireland (Athlone Branch) 1974
Rogers, Mary *Prospect of Erne (NI)* Fermanagh Field Club 1967
Rolt, L.T.C. *Landscape with Canals* Alan Sutton 1984
Rolt, L.T.C. *Green and Silver* Inland Waterways Association of Ireland 1993
Rolt, L.T.C. *Narrow Boat* Alan Sutton 1994
Seymour, John *Sailing through England* Eyre & Spottiswood 1956
Seymour, John *Voyage into England* David & Charles 1966
Smith, Cyril Herbert *Through the Kennet and Avon Canal by Motor Boat in 1928* Shepperton Swan 1990
St Davids, Viscount *The Watney Book of Inland Cruising* Queen Anne Press 1966
Thurston, E. Temple *The Flower of Gloster (1911)* Alan Sutton 1985
Westlake, Roy J. *Britain's Holiday Waterways* Bradford Barton 1975

Canoeing

Blandford, Percy W. *Canoeing Waters* Lutterworth 1966
Bliss, William *Canoeing* Methuen 1947
Guide to the Waterways of the British Isles British Canoe Union (at intervals)
Prothero, F.T.E. and Clark, W.A. *A New Oarsman's Guide* George Philip 1896

Walking

Allsop, Niall and Pearson, Michael *Towpath Trails* J.M. Pearson 1986
Allsop, Niall *The Somersetshire Coal Canal Rediscovered: a walker's guide* Millstream 1988
Bearshaw, Brian *Waterside Walks in Lancashire* Hale 1982
Bearshaw, Brian *Towpaths of England* Hale 1985
Bearshaw, Brian *The Great Towpath Walk from London to York* Hale 1988
Burton, Anthony and Curtis, Neil *The Grand Union Canal Walk* Aurum 1993
Fairfax, Bryan *Walking London's Waterways* David & Charles 1985
Fletcher, John and Margaret *Circular Walks on the Manchester, Bolton & Bury Canal* MB&BC Society 1992
Frost, Roger *Along t'cut: a towpath trail through Burnley* Lancashire County Library 1977
Goodwin, Dave *Waterside Walks in Northamptonshire* Anderson 1978
Groves, Peter and Anthill, Trevor *The Navigation Way: a hundred mile towpath walk* Meridian 1993
Gidman, S.H. *Guide to the Severn Way: East Bank* Gloucestershire County Library 1989
Jebb, Miles *A Guide to the Thames Path* Constable 1988
Merrill, John N. *Canal Walks* (vol 1 Derbyshire and Nottinghamshire; vol 2 Cheshire and Staffordshire; vol 3 Staffordshire; vol 4 Walking the Cheshire Ring; vol 6, Short circular walks on the canals of South Yorkshire) J.N.M. Publications 1986-
Perrott, David *Waterway Walks Around Birmingham* Sigma Leisure 1994
Pierce, Anthony J. *Canalside Walks in the Pennines* Warne 1983
Quinlan, Ray *Canal Walks: Midlands* Alan Sutton 1992
Quinlan, Ray *Canal Walks: South* Alan Sutton 1992
Quinlan, Ray *Canal Walks: North* Alan Sutton 1993
Russell, Roland (ed) *Walking Canals* David and Charles 1984
Swain, Robert *A Walker's Guide to the Lancaster Canal* Cicerone 1990
Vine, Nigel *Pub Walks Along the Kennet and Avon Canal* Countryside Books 1997
Welsh, Mary *Walks from the Leeds–Liverpool Canal* Cicerone Press 1996

Childrens books

Bank, J. and Hume, P. *Fun on the Waterways* Penwork Ltd 1972
Bibby, V. *Saranne* Longmans 1973
Carpenter, H. *The Joshers* Allen & Unwin 1977
De Maré, Eric *York Book of Waterways* Faber & Faber 1965
Dorner, Jane *Canals* Wayland 1973
Farnworth, W. *Canals* Mills & Boon 1973
Gagg, John *Rivers in Britain* Blackwell 1971
Gagg, John *Boats and Boating* Blackwell 1973
Gagg, John *Observers Canals* Claremont Books 1996
Grundy, B. *The Flower of Gloster* Rupert Hart-Davis 1970
Harries, E. *The Narrow Boat* MacMillan 1973
Hutchings, C. *The Story of our Canals* Ladybird Books 1975
Lawrence, B. *Curlew on the Cut* Geoff Dibb 1968
Pearce, R. *History at Source – Canals 1720-1910* Evans Bros Ltd 1972
Pick, C. *Canals and Waterways* Macdonald 1977
Purton, R.W. *Rivers and Canals* Routledge 1972
Ransom, P.J.G. *Your Book of Canals* Faber & Faber 1977
Rice, P. *Narrow Boats* Dinosaur 1976
Ross, A. *Canals in Britain* Blackwell 1971
Samson, D. *Getting to Know Boats* Panda Publications 1972
Smith, P.L. *Canals are Great* P.L. Smith 1977
Tate, S. *The Living River* J.M. Dent 1974
Vialls, Christine *Canals – Industrial Archaeology* A & C Black 1976
Vince, J. *River and Canal Transport* Blandford 1970
Wickson, Roger *Britain's Inland Waterways* Methuen 1968

Historical

Anon *The History of Inland Navigation* 1766
Barker, T.C. *The Sankey Navigation* Sankey Canal Restoration Society 1990
Bick David *The Hereford & Gloucester Canal* Oakwood Press 1994
Biddle, Gordon *Pennine Waterway: a Pictorial History of the Leeds & Liverpool Canal* Dalesman Books 1979
Biddle, Gordon *Lancashire Waterways* Dalesman 1980
Blagrove, David *At the Heart of the Waterways: Braunston: a Canal History* Braunston Boat Shows 1995
Blair, May *Once upon the Lagan: the story of the Lagan Canal* Blackstaff 1981

Body, A.H. *Canals and Waterways (It Happened Around Manchester)* University London Press 1975

Boughey, Joseph *Hadfield's British Canals* Eighth Edition Alan Sutton 1994

Bowyer, Olive *The Peak Forest Canal* New Mills Local History Society 1988

Boyes, John and Russell, Ronald *The Canals of Eastern England* David & Charles 1977

Brake, Roger *The Grand Western Canal* Devon Books 1987

Broadbridge, S.R. *The Birmingham Canal Navigations Vol 1* David & Charles 1974

Buchanan, C.A. *The Bridgwater and Taunton Canal* Somerset Industrial Archaeology Society 1984

Burnby, J.G.L. and Parker, M. *The Navigation of the River Lee (1190–1790)* Edmonton Hundred Historical Society 1978

Burstall, Patricia *The Golden Age of the Thames* David & Charles 1981

Burton, Anthony *The Great Days of the Canals* David & Charles 1989

Burton, Anthony *Canal Mania: 200 years of Britain's waterways* Aurum 1993

Burton, Anthony *The Canal Builders* M & M Baldwin 1993

Cadbury, George and Dobbs S.P. *Canals and Inland Waterways* Pitman 1929

Cameron, A.D. *Getting to know the Crinan Canal* A.D. Cameron 1978

Cameron, A.D. *The Caledonian Canal* Canongate Academic 1994

Chaplin, Peter H. *The Thames from Source to Tideway* Whittet Books 1982

Chell, Bernard W *Nottingham's Lost Canal* Footprint Press 1995

Chester-Browne, Richard *The Other Sixty Miles* Birmingham Canal Navigations Society 1991

Chester-Browne, Richard *The Manchester Bolton & Bury Canal: history in pictures* Fletcher 1995

Childers, J.W. (ed) *Lord Orford's Voyage Round the Fens in 1774* Cambridgeshire Libraries 1987

Clamp, Arthur L. *Let's Explore Old Waterways in Devon* Westway Publications 1970

Clarke, J.N. *The Horncastle and Tattershall Canal* Oakwood Press 1990

Clarke, Mike *The Leeds and Liverpool Canal* Carnegie 1990

Clarke, Mike *Liverpool and its canal* Merseyside Port Folios 1992

Clarke, Peter *The Royal Canal: the Complete Story* Elo Publications 1992

Clew, Kenneth R. *The Dorset & Somerset Canal* David & Charles 1971

Clew, Kenneth R. *The Exeter Canal* Phillimore 1984

Clew, Kenneth R. *The Kennet & Avon Canal* David & Charles 1985

Clew, Kenneth R. *The Somersetshire Coal Canal and Railways* Brans Head 1986

Clew, Kenneth R. *The Dingwall Canal* Dingwall Museum Trust 1988

Clinker. C.R. and Hadfield. Charles *The Ashby-de-la-Zouche Canal and its Railways* AvonAnglia 1978

Compton, Hugh J. *The Oxford Canal* David & Charles 1976

Compton, Hugh and Carr-Gomme, Antony *The Military on English Waterways 1798-1844* Railway and Canal Historical Society 1991

Conway-Jones. Hugh *Gloucester Docks: an illustrated history* Alan Sutton 1984

Corbett, J. *The River Irwell (1907)* E.J. Morten 1974

Corbridge, J.A.A *Pictorial History of the Mersey and Irwell Navigation* E.J. Morten 1979

Course, Edwin *The Itchen Navigation* Southampton University Industrial Archaeology Group 1983

Cove-Smith, Chris *The Grantham Canal Today: a brief history and guide* M.D. Mitchell 1986

Cramphorn, J.F. and Cramphorn A.M. St J. *The story of the Chelmer and Blackwater Navigation through 200 years* Company of Proprietors of the C&BN 1993

Crocker, Glenys *A history of the Basingstoke Canal* Surrey & Hampshire Canal Society 1977

Crowe, Nigel *English Heritage Book of Canals* B.T. Batsford Ltd/English Heritage 1994

Cullimore, David *Shardlow – 18th Century Inland Port* D. Cullimore 1977

Cuss, Edwin and Gardiner, Stanley *The Stroudwater and Thames & Severn Canals in Old Photographs* Alan Sutton 1988

Cuss, Edwin and Gardiner, Stanley *The Stroudwater and Thames & Severn Canals in Old Photographs: a second selection* Alan Sutton 1993

Dalby, L.J. *The Wilts & Berks Canal* Oakwood Press 1986

D'Arcy, Gerard *Portrait of the Grand Canal (Eire)* Transport Research Associates 1969

Davies, Dr Jamie *Shakespeare's Avon: The History of a Navigation* Oakwood Press 1996

Davies, Ken *The Lost Port of Titchfield and its Canal* Lee Press Publications 1995

De Salis, Henry Rodolph *A Chronology of Inland Navigation in Great Britain* Spon 1897

Delany, Ruth *A celebration of 250 years of Ireland's Inland Waterways* Appletree 1986

Delany, Ruth *Ireland's Royal Canal 1789–1992* Lilliput 1992

Delany, Ruth *The Grand Canal of Ireland* The Lilliput Press 1995

Delany, V.T.H. and D.R. *The Canals of the South of Ireland* David & Charles 1966

Denny, Martyn *London's Waterways* Batsford 1977

Denny, Martyn *London & South East England* (historic waterways scenes series) Moorland Publishing Co 1980

Dix, Frank L. *Royal River Highway: a history of the passenger boats and services on the River Thames* David & Charles 1985

Duckham, Baron F. *Navigable Rivers of Yorkshire: their history and traditions* Dalesman Publications 1964

Duckham, Baron F. *The Yorkshire Ouse* David & Charles 1967

Duckham, Baron F. *The Inland Waterways of East Yorkshire 1700–1900* East Yorks Local History Society 1972

Ewans, M.C. *The Haytor Granite Tramway and Stover Canal* David & Charles 1977

Farnie, D.A. *The Manchester Ship Canal and the Rise of the Port of Manchester 1894-1975* Manchester University Press 1980

Faulkner, Alan H. *The Warwick Canals* Railway & Canals Historical Society 1985

Faulkner, Alan H. *The Grand Union Canal in Hertfordshire* Hertfordshire Publications 1987

Faulkner, Alan H. *The Grand Junction Canal* W.H. Walker 1993

Fife, Michael G. and Walls, Peter J. *The River Foss from Yearsley village to York* Sessions 1973

Flanagan, Patrick *The Ballinamore & Ballyconnel Canal* David & Charles 1972

Flanagan, Patrick *The Shannon-Erne Waterway* Wolfhound Press 1994

Forbes, U.A. and Ashford W.H.R. *Our Waterways* John Murray 1906

Fox, Michael and Fox, Peter *Pennine Passage: a history of the Huddersfield Narrow Canal* Huddersfield Canal Society 1988

Foxon, Tom *Anderton for Orders* M & M Baldwin 1997

Freer, Wendy *Women and Children of the Cut* Railway and Canal Historical Society 1995

Gardner, Peter and Foden, Frank *Foxton: Locks and Barge Lift* Leicestershire County Council 1979

Giddings, Geoff *The Aylesbury Arm* The Aylesbury Canal Society 1997

Gladwin, David *Building Britain's Canals* Brewin Books 1988

Gladwin, D.D. *Victorian and Edwardian Canals from Old Photographs* Batsford 1976

Gladwin, D.D. *The Waterways of Britain: a social panorama* Batsford 1976

Gladwin, D.D. *An Illustrated History of British Waterways* Spurbooks 1977

Gladwin, D.D. *A Pictorial History of Canals* Batsford 1977

Gladwin, D.D. *The Canals of Britain* Breedon Books 1994

Gladwin, D.D. and White, J.M. *English Canals (in 3 parts)* Oakwood Press 1967–9

Gladwin, D.D. and White, J.M. *The Canals of the Welsh Valleys and Their Tramroads* Oakwood Press 1991

Goodwin, David *Foxton Locks and the Grand Junction Canal Co.* Leicestershire County Council 1988

Gotch, Christopher *The Gloucester & Sharpness Canal and Robert Mylne* Lantern 1993

Grant, Roderick *The Great Canal: the Manchester Ship Canal* Gordon & Cremonesi 1978

Gray, Ted *A hundred years of the Manchester Ship Canal* Aurora 1993

Griston, Jenny *The North Walsam – Dilham Canal* Cowper Press 1981

Hadfield, Charles *The Canals of South Wales and the Border* David & Charles 1967

Hadfield, Charles *The Canals of South and South East England* David & Charles 1969

Hadfield, Charles *The Canals of the East Midlands (including part of London)* David & Charles 1970

Hadfield, Charles *The Canals of Yorkshire and North East England* Vols 1 and 2 David & Charles 1972–3

Hadfield, Charles *The Canals of the West Midlands* David & Charles 1985

Hadfield, Charles *The Canals of South West England* David & Charles 1985

Hadfield, Charles and Biddle, Gordon *The Canals of North West England* Vols 1 and 2 David & Charles 1970

Hadfield, Charles and Norris, John *Waterways to Stratford* David & Charles 1968

Hadley, Dennis *Waterways' Heraldry* Waterways Museum 1977

Handford, Michael *The Stroudwater Canal* Alan Sutton 1979

Harris, Helen *The Grand Western Canal* David & Charles 1973

Harris, Helen and Ellis, Monica *The Bude Canal* David & Charles 1972

Harris, L.E. *Vermuyden and the Fens* Cleaver-Hume Press 1953

Haskell, Tony *By Waterway to Taunton: a history of the Bridgwater and Taunton Canal and the River Tone Navigation* Somerset Books 1994

Hawthorne, Edward *Electric Boats on the Thames 1889–1914* Alan Sutton 1995

Hayman, Alfred *Mersey and Irwell Navigation to Manchester Ship Canal 1720-1887* Federation of Bridgewater Cruising Clubs 1981

Heneghan, F.D. *The Chichester Canal* Chichester County Council 1958

Household, Humphrey *The Thames & Severn Canal* Alan Sutton 1987

Hughes, Stephen *The Archaeology of the Montgomeryshire Canal* Royal Commission on Ancient and Historical Monuments in Wales 1988

Hutton, Guthrie *A Forth and Clyde Canalbum* Richard Stenlake 1991

Hutton, Guthrie *Caledonian: the Monster Canal* Richard Stenlake 1992

Hutton, Guthrie *Monkland: The Canal that Made Money* Richard Stenlake 1993

Hutton, Guthrie *The Union Canal* Richard Stenlake 1993

Hutton, Guthrie *The Crinan Canal* Richard Stenlake 1994

Jarvis, Adrian *Ellesmere Port: canal town 1795–1921* North Western Museum of Inland Navigation 1977

Jenkins, H.J.K. *Along the Nene, Peterborough's waterway traffic through the centuries* Cambridgeshire Books 1991

Jenks, Alfred E. *The Staffordshire & Worcestershire Canal* Steen 1987

Jeremiah, Josephine *Along the Avon from Stratford to Tewkesbury in Old Photographs* Alan Sutton 1994

Johnson, Guy *Save the Stratford Canal* David & Charles 1983

Keaveney, E. and Brown, D.L. *The Ashton Canal* E. Keaveney and D.L. Brown 1974

Langford, J. Ian *Staffordshire & Worcestershire Canal* Goose & Son 1974

Lead, Peter *The Trent & Mersey Canal* (historic waterways scenes series) Moorland 1980

Lead, Peter *The Caldon Canal and Tramroads including the Uttoxeter and Leek Canals and North Stafford Railway* Oakwood Press 1990

Leech, Sir Bosdin *History of the Manchester Ship Canal 2 Vols* Sherrat & Hughes 1907

Lindsay, Jean *The Canals of Scotland* David & Charles 1968

Lindsay, Jean *The Trent & Mersey Canal* David & Charles 1979

Malster, Robert *East Anglian Coast and Waterways* East Anglian Magazine 1985

Malster, Robert *The Broads* Phillimore 1993

Marriage, John *Barging into Chelmsford: the story of the Chelmer and Blackwater Navigation* Ian Henry 1993

Martin, Don *The Forth & Clyde Canal: a Kirkintilloch view* Strathkelvin District Libraries 1985

Martin, Michael (ed) *Inland Waterways of Ireland Silver Jubilee 1954–79* Inland Waterways of Ireland 1979

May, Robert *The BCN in Pictures* Birmingham Canal Navigations Society 1982

McCutcheon, W.A. *The Canals of the North of Ireland* David & Charles 1965

Miller, M.G. and Fletcher S. *The Melton Mowbray Navigation* Railway & Canal Historical Society 1984

Morris, Richard K. *Canals of Shropshire* Shropshire Books 1991

Mullineux, Frank *The Duke of Bridgewater's Canal* Eccles & District History Society 1988

Ogden, John *Yorkshire's River of Industry – the story of the River Calder* Terence Dalton 1972

Ogden, John *Yorkshire's River Derwent* Terence Dalton 1974

Ogden, John *Yorkshire's River Aire* Terence Dalton 1976

Owen, David *Canals to Manchester* Manchester University Press 1977

Owen, David *Cheshire Waterways* Dalesman 1979

Owen, David *The Manchester Ship Canal* Manchester University Press 1983

Owen, David E. *Staffordshire Waterways* National Waterways Museum 1986

Paget-Tomlinson, E.W. *The Illustrated History of Canal and River Navigations* Sheffield Academic Press 1994

Payne, Robert *The Canal Builders* Macmillan 1959

Pellow, Thomas and Bowen, Paul *The Shroppie* Landscape Press 1985

Pellow, Thomas and Bowen, Paul *Canal to Llangollen* Landscape Press 1988

Phillips, John *A General History of Inland Navigation (1805)* David & Charles 1970

Porteus, J.D. *The Company Town of Goole* University of Hull 1969

Porteous, J. Douglas *Canal Ports: The Urban Achievement of the Canal Age* Academic Press 1978

Pratt, Edwin A. *British Canals – Is their Resuscitation Practicable?* John Murray 1906

Pratt, Edwin A. *Scottish Canals and Waterways* Selwyn & Blount 1922

Pratt, Edwin A. *A History of Inland Transport and Communications (1912)* David & Charles 1970

Priestley, Joseph *Historical Account of the Navigable Rivers and Canals of Great Britain (1831)* David & Charles 1969

Quenby, Ron *Thomas Telford's Aqueducts on the Shropshire Union Canal* Swan Hill Press 1992

Rendell, Joan *The story of the Bude Canal* Stannary 1987

Richardson, Christine *The Waterways Revolution – From the Peaks to the Trent 1768–78* Self Publishing Association 1992

Richardson, Christine *Minutes of the Chesterfield Canal Company 1771–1780* Derbyshire Record Society 1996

Ripley, David *The Peak Forest Tramway including the Peak Forest Canal* Oakwood Press 1989

Ripley, David *The Little Eaton Gangway and the Derby Canal* Oakwood Press 1993

Roffey, James *The Chesterfield Canal* Barracuda 1989

Rolt, Sonia *A Canal Community: The Photographs of Robert Longden* Sutton Publishing 1997

Russell, Ronald *Lost Canals and Waterways of Britain* David & Charles 1982

Russell, Ronald *Country Canal* David & Charles 1991

Shill, Ray *The Industrial Canal – Volume 1 The Coal Trade* Heartland Press 1996

Smith, Peter L. *Yorkshire Waterways* Dalesman 1978

Smith, Peter L. *Canal Architecture* Shire Publications 1986

Smith, Peter L. *The Aire & Calder Navigation* Wakefield Historical Publications 1987

Smith, Peter L. *Discovering Canals in Britain* Shire Publications 1993

Spencer, Herbert *London's Canal* Lund Humphries 1976

Stevens, Philip A. *The Leicester Line* David & Charles 1972

Stevens, Philip A. *The Leicester and Melton Mowbray Navigations* Alan Sutton 1992

Stevens, R.A. Ian *A Towpath Guide to the Brecknock & Abergavenny and Monmouthshire Canals* Goose & Son 1974

Stevenson, Peter *The Nutbrook Canal* David & Charles 1970

Stone, Jean *Voices from the Waterways* Alan Sutton 1997

Summers, Dorothy *The Great Ouse* David & Charles 1973

Swainson, Celia M. *Waterways to Derby* Scarthin 1993

Tew, David *The Melton to Oakham Canal* Sycamore 1984

Tomlinson, V.I. *The Manchester Bolton and Bury Canal* Manchester Bolton and Bury Canal Society 1991

Vine, P.A.L. *The Royal Military Canal* David & Charles 1972

Vine, P.A.L. *West Sussex Waterways* Middleton Press 1985

Vine, P.A.L. *London's Lost Route to the Sea* David & Charles 1986

Vine, P.A.L. *Surrey Waterways* Middleton Press 1987

Vine, P.A.L. *Kent and East Sussex Waterways* Middleton Press 1989

Vine, P.A.L. *Hampshire Waterways* Middleton Press 1990

Vine, P.A.L. *London to Portsmouth Waterway* Middleton Press 1994

Vine, P.A.L. *London's Lost Route to Basingstoke* Alan Sutton 1994

Vine, P.A.L. *London's Lost Route to Midhurst* Alan Sutton 1995

Viner, D.J. *The Thames & Severn Canal* Hendon Press 1975

Ward, J.R. *The Finance of Canal Building in Eighteenth Century England* Oxford University Press 1974

Ware, Michael E. *History in Camera Canals and Waterways* Shire Publications 1987

Warner, Pat *Lock Keeper's Daughter* Shepperton Swan 1986

Welch, Edwin *The Bankrupt Canal: Southampton and Salisbury 1795–1808* City of Southampton 1966

Wheat, G. *On the Duke's Cut* Transport Publishing 1977

Willan, T.S. *The Navigation of the River Weaver in the Eighteenth Century* Chetham Society 1951

Willan, T.S. *Early History of the Don Navigation* Manchester University Press 1962

Willan, T.S. *River Navigation in England 1600–1750* Cass 1964

Wilson, David Gordon *The Making of the Middle Thames* Spurbooks 1977

Wilson, E.A. *The Ellesmere and Llangollen Canal* Phillimore 1975

Wright, Ian L. *Canals in Wales* Bradford Barton 1977

Official publications

British Transport Commission Annual Reports and Accounts 1948–1962 HMSO

British Waterways Six years of Progress BW 1961

British Waterways Board Annual Report and Accounts from 1963

British Waterways Board The Future of the Waterways HMSO 1964

British Waterways Board The Facts about the Waterways BWB 1965

British Waterways Board Leisure and the Waterways BWB 1967

British Waterways Board The Last Ten Years: progress and achievement 1963–72 BWB 1973

British Waterways Board Transport – the water way: the developing role of the waterways in Britain's transport system BWB 1982

Canals and Inland Waterways: report of the Board of Survey (the Rusholme report) British Transport Commission 1955

Committee of Inquiry into Inland Waterways: report (the 'Bowes Report') HMSO 1958

Leisure and Tourism Strategy British Waterways 1994

London Canals Consultative Committee London's Canals GLC 1976

Ministry of Transport British Waterways Recreation and Amenity (Cmnd 3401) HMSO 1967

Report of Royal Commission on the Canals and Inland Navigation of the United Kingdom 12 Volumes HMSO 1907–1909

Index